AF678084

Switzerland and the EU

Studies in EU External Relations

Edited by

Marc Maresceau (*Ghent University*)

Editorial Board

Marise Cremona (*European University Institute*)
Günter Burghardt (*former EU ambassador Washington*)
Alan Dashwood (*University of Cambridge*)
Frank Hoffmeister (*European Commission*)

VOLUME 20

The titles published in this series are listed at *brill.com/seur*

Switzerland and the EU

A Challenging Relationship

Edited by

Marc Maresceau and Christa Tobler

BRILL
NIJHOFF

LEIDEN | BOSTON

The Library of Congress Cataloging-in-Publication Data is available online at https://catalog.loc.gov
LC record available at https://lccn.loc.gov/

Typeface for the Latin, Greek, and Cyrillic scripts: "Brill". See and download: brill.com/brill-typeface.

ISSN 1875-0451
ISBN 978-90-04-50984-9 (hardback)
ISBN 978-90-04-52998-4 (e-book)

Copyright 2023 by Koninklijke Brill NV, Leiden, The Netherlands.
Koninklijke Brill NV incorporates the imprints Brill, Brill Nijhoff, Brill Hotei, Brill Schöningh, Brill Fink, Brill mentis, Vandenhoeck & Ruprecht, Böhlau, V&R unipress and Wageningen Academic.
All rights reserved. No part of this publication may be reproduced, translated, stored in a retrieval system, or transmitted in any form or by any means, electronic, mechanical, photocopying, recording or otherwise, without prior written permission from the publisher. Requests for re-use and/or translations must be addressed to Koninklijke Brill NV via brill.com or copyright.com.

This book is printed on acid-free paper and produced in a sustainable manner.

Printed by Printforce, the Netherlands

Contents

Preface

This important book offers an insightful analysis of the legal and political stakes and challenges underpinning the EU-Switzerland relations, or Switzerland-EU relations if one prefers. Its origins are to be found in a workshop, organised on 19 November 2019 at Ghent University by the Ghent European Law Institute (G.E.L.I.), in close cooperation with the Embassy of Switzerland in Belgium and the Mission of Switzerland to the European Union, on the topic 'Switzerland and the European Union – A Strong Bilateral Partnership with Continental and Global Reach'.[1] The aim was to examine the avenues and challenges of furthering European integration short of EU membership from all angles. It brought together over 200 participants consisting of officials, academic experts and students from Switzerland, the EU, and neighbouring countries, to discuss and reflect on specific issues of the bilateral relationship(s). The keynote speech was delivered by H.E. Roberto Balzaretti, then the Swiss State Secretary for European Affairs.

The Ghent Workshop provided a stimulating forum for deepening understanding and gaining new insights into the complex sectoral or bilateral approach. The focus lay on legal and political aspects including, in particular, the prospects of the conclusion of an institutional agreement between the EU and Switzerland, which was at the time presented 'as an instrument to cement and develop this bilateral approach'. No doubt, it was one of the rare academic events on EU-Switzerland relations organised outside of Switzerland. Its success formed the basis for a broader academic reflection so that in February 2020, the editors of the present volume, Marc Maresceau and Christa Tobler, decided to launch an ambitious research initiative on EU-Switzerland relations leading to the current edited volume for the Brill Series *Studies in EU External Relations* (SEUR) with contributions by a stellar cast of experts.

Almost immediately after the initiation of the book project, the Covid pandemic broke out, so whether to continue or not with the book became an existential practical question. More importantly, as will immediately become clear when reading this book, major difficulties specifically related to the Switzerland-EU relations also emerged rather unexpectedly, which called for a

1 See Press Communiqué of the Swiss Mission to the European Union, Brussels, 19 November 2019, on the Ghent Academic Workshop "Academic Workshop: Switzerland and the European Union – A Strong Bilateral Partnership with Continental and Global Reach", <https://www.eda.admin.ch/missions/mission-eu-brussels/en/home/news/news.html/content/missions/mission-eu-brussels/en/meta/agenda/2019/november/19> (accessed 17 June 2022).

fundamental overhaul in the direction the book would take. Despite this sometimes bumpy – but also very captivating – road towards the publication of this volume, the book has turned out to be an absolute chef d'oeuvre unique in its kind.

Inge Govaere
Director of the Ghent European Law Institute (G.E.L.I.)

Acknowledgements

As editors of this volume, we are very grateful to the authors who have put time and effort into the writing of particularly interesting chapters on what we consider important aspects of the EU-Swiss relationship.

We also wish to thank Ms Mpoi Leuta Hilpert, assistant to Christa Tobler at Basel University, for having carried out the language check on all chapters of this book. It was a lot of work that, at times, had to be done at short notice.

Finally, we are grateful to Brill and in particular to Ingeborg van der Laan, Associate Editor for International Law, for her unwavering support for the publishing of volume 20 in the series *Studies in EU External Relations* (SEUR).

Figures

Abbreviations

AA	Association Agreement
ACER	European Union Agency for Cooperation of Energy Regulators
AEO	Swiss-UK Authorised Economic Operator Mutual Recognition Agreement
AEOI	Automatic Exchange of Information on Financial Accounts in Tax Matters
AFMP	Swiss-EU Agreement on the Free Movement of Persons
AFSJ	Area of Freedom, Security and Justice
AML	Anti-money laundering
AMM	Aceh Monitoring Mission
AEO MRA	Swiss–UK Authorised Economic Operator Mutual Recognition Agreement
AEO-S	AEO safety and security
AS	German *Amtliche Sammlung* (chronological compilation of federal legislation)
ASEM	Asia-Europe Meeting
ATA	Swiss-EU Agreement on Air Transport
BBI	German *Bundesblatt* (Swiss Official Journal)
BEPS	Base Erosion and Profit Shifting
BEREC	European Regulators for Electronic Communications
BSI	British Standards Institution
CapTechs	Capability Technology Groups
CbC MCAA	Multilateral Competent Authority Agreement on the Exchange of Country-by-Country Reports
CbCR	Country-by-country reporting
CC	Swiss Civil Code
CDP	Swiss Christian Democratic Party (now: The Centre)
CEN	European Committee for Standardisation
CENELEC	European Committee for Electrotechnical Standardisation
CETA	Comprehensive Economic and Trade Agreement between Canada and the EU
cf.	Latin: *confer* or *conferatur* (compare)
CFSP	Common Foreign and Security Policy
C-IED	Countering Improvised Explosive Devices
CFR	Code of Federal Regulations (United States)
CFSP	Common Foreign and Security Policy

CHF	Swiss Franc(s)
C-IED	Countering Improvised Explosive Devices
CO	Swiss Code of Obligations
COM	European Commission Document
CRD	EU Citizens' Rights Directive (Directive 2004/38)
CRS	Common Reporting Standard
CSD	United States Central Securities Depository
CSDP	Common Security and Defence Policy
CT	Swiss–Liechtenstein Customs Treaty
DAA	EU-Swiss Dublin Association Agreement
DAC 6	Council Directive (EU) 2018/822 of 25 May 2018 amending Directive 2011/16/EU as regards the mandatory automatic exchange of information in the field of taxation on reportable cross-border arrangements
DCFTA	Deep and Comprehensive Free Trade Area
DFA	Swiss Department of Foreign Affairs
DoJ	United States Department of Justice
DPA	Swiss Federal Data Protection Act
DSM	Dispute Settlement Mechanism
DTA	Treaty for the avoidance of double taxation, double taxation agreement
ECHR	European Convention on Human Rights
EASA	European Aviation Safety Agency
EASO	European Asylum Support Office
EC	European Community
ECHA	European Chemicals Agency
ECHR	European Convention on Human Rights
ECDC	European Centre for Disease Prevention and Control
ECSC	European Coal and Steel Community
ECT	Energy Charter Treaty
EDA	European Defence Agency
EDF	European Defence Fund
EEA	European Economic Area, or: European Environmental Agency
EEAS	European External Action Service
EEC	European Economic Community
EECEA	European Education and Culture Executive Agency
EFTA	European Free Trade Association
e.g.	Latin: *exempli gratia* (for example)
EGNOS	European Geostationary Navigation Overlay Service
EDIDP	European Defence Industrial Development Programme
EIONET	European Environment Information and Observation Network
ELA	European Labour Authority

EMCDDA	European Monitoring Centre for Drugs and Drugs Addiction
EMIR	European Market Infrastructure Regulation
ERA	European Railways Agency
ESA	EFTA Surveillance Authority
ESMAB	Single European Sky Military Aviation Board
ESO	EFTA Statistical Office
etc.	Latin: *et cetera* (and so on)
ETF	European Training Foundation
et seq.	Latin: *et sequitur* (and what follows)
ETSI	European Telecommunications Standards Institute
EU	European Union
EUAM	European Union Advisory Mission
EUFOR	European Union Force
EULEX	European Union Rule of Law Mission
eu-LISA	European Union Agency for the Operational Management of Large-Scale IT Systems in the Area of Freedom, Security and Justice
EUPM	European Union Police Mission in Bosnia and Herzegovina
EUPOL	European Union Police Mission
EUR	Euro(s)
FATCA	Foreign Account Tax Compliance Act
FBAR	Report of Foreign Bank and Financial Accounts
FC	Swiss Federal Constitution
FDPIC	Swiss Federal Data Protection and Information Commissioner
Fed. Gaz.	Swiss Federal Gazette
FF	French *Feuilles fédérale* (Swiss Official Journal)
FinCEN	Financial Crimes Enforcement Network
FINMA	Swiss Financial Market Supervisory Authority
FinMIA	Swiss Financial Market Infrastructure Act
FinIA	Swiss Financial Institutions Act
FinSA	Swiss Financial Services Act
FlaM	Flanking measures
FNIA	Swiss Federal Act on Foreign Nationals and Integration
FRA	Fundamental Rights Agency
Frontex	European Border and Coast Guard Agency
FSC	Swiss Federal Supreme Court
FTA	Free Trade Agreement
G20	Group of Twenty (intergovernmental forum comprising 19 countries and the EU)
GAO	United States Government Accountability Office
GATT	General Agreement on Tariffs and Trade

GATS	General Agreement on Trade in Services
GBP	Pound Sterling
GDP	Gross Domestic Product
GDPR	General Data Protection Regulation
GMP	Good Manufacturing Pratices
GNSS	Global Navigation Satellite System
GPA	Government Procurement Agreement
GSA	European GNSS (Global Navigation Satellite System) Agency
GSP	Generalised System of Preferences
HM	Her Majesty's
HMRC	Her Majesty's Revenue & Customs (UK tax authority)
HS	Harmonized System
ICAO	International Civil Aviation Organization
idem	the same
Ibid.	Latin: *ibidem* (in the same source)
i.a.	Latin: *inter alia* (among others)
i.e.	Latin: *id est* (that is)
IGA	Intergovernmental Agreement
IMI	Internal Market Information System
InstA	Swiss-EU Draft Institutional Agreement
IP	Intellectual Property
IRS	United States Internal Revenue Service
IT	Information technology
JPA	Joint Procurement Agreement
KYC	Know-Your-Customer
LC	Lugano Convention
LGBT	Lesbian, Gay, Bi-sexual, Transsexual
LTA	Swiss-EU Land Transport Agreement
MAWA	Military Airworthiness Authorities
MCAA	Multilateral Competent Authority Agreement
MDR	Medical Devices Regulation
MFN	Most Favoured Nation
MiFID	Markets in Financial Instruments Directive
MiFIR	Markets in Financial Instruments Regulation
MoU	Memorandum of Understanding
MRA	Mutual Recognition Agreement
NCU	Polish National Coordination Unit
NFE	Non-Financial Entity
NFFE	Non-Financial Foreign Entity
NGO	Non-governmental Organisation

No.	number
NPFFI	Non-Participating Foreign Financial Institution
OASI	Swiss Old Age and Survivor's Insurance
OC	Official Compilation of Federal Legislation (*Amtliche Sammlung*)
OECD	Organisation for Economic Co-operation and Development
OJ	Official Journal of the EU
Op. cit.	Latin: *opus citatum* or *opere citato* (in the work already cited)
p.a.	Latin: *per annum* (per year)
ParlA	Swiss Parliament Act
PASEI	Protection of Autonomous Systems Against Enemy Interference
PEM	Pan-Euro-Mediterranean
PESCO	Permanent Structured Cooperation
p.	page
pp.	pages
PPE	Personal Protective Equipment
PWA	Swiss Posted Workers Act
QI	Qualified Intermediary System
RLP	Swiss Radical-Liberal Party
RO	French *Recueil official* (chronological compilation of Swiss federal legislation)
RS	French *Recueil systématique* (Systematic Compilation of Swiss federal legislation)
SAA	EU-Swiss Schengen Association Agreement
SARS-CoV-2	Severe acute respiratory syndrome coronavirus 2
SCM	Subsidies and Countervailing Measures
SDG	Sustainable Development Goals
SEA	Single European Act
SEUFTA	(future) Switzerland- European Union Free Trade Agreement
SEUR	Studies in EU External Relations
SFSC	Swiss Federal Supreme Court
SFTA	Swiss Federal Tax Administration
SH	Canton of Schaffhausen (Switzerland)
SIF	Swiss State Secretary for International Financial Matters
SMA	Swiss-UK Services Mobility Agreement
SP	Swiss Socialist Party
SPP	Swiss People's Party
SPS	Sanitary and phytosanitary measures
SR	Systematic compilation of Swiss federal legislations
SSN	Social Security Number
SSP	Swiss People's Party

TA	Trade Agreement
TBT	Technical Barriers to Trade
TBTA	Swiss Act on Technical Barriers to Trade
TCA	EU-UK Trade and Cooperation Agreement
TERRE	Trans European Replacement Reserves Exchange
TEU	Treaty on European Union
TFEU	Treaty on the Functioning of the European Union
TIN	Taxpayer Identification Number
TPA	Trade and Partnership Agreement, Swiss Therapeutic Products Act
UK	United Kingdom of Great Britain and Northern Ireland
UN	United Nations
UNSC	United Nations Security Council
US/USA	United States of America
USC	Code of Laws of the United States of America
USD	US Dollar(s)
VCLC	Vienna Convention on the Law of Treaties
viz.	Latin: *videlicet* (namely)
WA	Withdrawal Agreement
WTO	World Trade Organization

Notes on Contributors

Georges Baur
is a research fellow with the Liechtenstein-Institut. Previously he served as the Assistant Secretary General of EFTA and as Deputy Head of Mission of the Liechtenstein Mission to the EU, both in Brussels. He obtained his PhD from Zurich University and is a guest lecturer with various European Universities. Georges' main research interests are EU relations with neighbouring (groups of) countries, such as EFTA, UK-EU and Switzerland-EU.

Mattia Brugger
is a graduate student at the University of Oxford. Previously, he was Junior Research Fellow at the Chair of Public Law, European Law and International Economic Law at the University of Zurich.

Merijn Chamon
is Assistant Professor of EU Law at Maastricht University and Visiting Professor at the College of Europe (Bruges). He obtained his PhD at Ghent University. Merijn's research interests encompass EU constitutional law, EU institutional law and the law of EU external relations.

Michael Hahn
is Professor of Law at the University of Bern, Managing Director of its Institute of European and International Economic Law and a Director at its World Trade Institute; he is an Adjunct Professor at the Europa-Institute of Saarland University, where he is also co-editor of the *Zeitschrift für Europarechtliche Studien* (ZEuS) and an Honorary Professor at the University of Waikato School of Law (Hamilton, NZ). He holds degrees from the University of Heidelberg and the University of Michigan Law School. Michael is on the list of arbitrators for CETA, CPTPP, the SADC-EU Economic Partnership Agreement and the TCA and teaches, researches and consults on international trade law, Swiss-EU bilateral relations and EU external relations law.

Christophe Hillion
is Professor of European Law at the University of Oslo; and senior adviser at the Swedish Institute for European Policy Studies (SIEPS) in Stockholm. He has published on the constitutional law and external action of the European Union. He is co-editor of the Common Market Law Review, and a member of the Advisory board of Państwo i Prawo, and Anti-Discrimination Law Review.

Hans-Joachim ("Jochen") Jaeger
is a retired partner of EY and a certified tax advisor and has spent the last 28 years working in tax consulting for banks and financial service providers. He is also a lecturer at the Universities of St. Gallen, Vaduz and the Lucerne University of Applied Sciences and Arts. He studied at the University of St. Gallen, where he also received his doctorate. Jochen was intensively involved in the negotiations of Switzerland and Liechtenstein with the US in the area of FATCA and the implementation of various transparency initiatives (most recently the automatic exchange of information and the DAC6 regulations). He was also a member of various joint working groups of the Swiss Federal Department of Finance.

Christine Kaddous
is Professor of EU law at the University of Geneva, Jean Monnet Chair *ad personam*, Director of the Centre d'études juridiques européennes (CEJE) and of the Master in European and International Governance (MEIG Programme). She is also Visiting Professor at the University Paris II (Panthéon Assas) and has been Visiting Professor at different universities and the College of Europe (Bruges/Natolin). She holds degrees from the Universities of Neuchâtel, Cambridge and Libre de Bruxelles. She practised law in the field of Commercial and trade law. She is on the list of chairpersons for arbitrations and TSD expert panel proceedings for dispute settlement under the trade agreements concluded by the EU with third countries. She teaches, researches and consults on international trade law, internal market law, judicial protection, Swiss-EU bilateral agreements and EU external relations law. She has published extensively. Among her recent publications: *Some Thoughts on the EU New Generation of Free Trade Agreements* (2022); *Die Zusammenarbeit zwischen der EU und der Schweiz* (2022); *Directive 2004/38 on the free movement of citizens* (2020).

Marc Maresceau
(Ghent University) is visiting professor College of Europe, Bruges-Natolin; "Full fellowship", The Johns Hopkins University (Bologna); "Boursier de la Conféderation Suisse"; Leverhulme Fellow, Edinburgh University; British Academy Visiting Fellowship; Belgian Chair, King's College, London; Course Hague Academy of International Law; "professeur invité": Bordeaux, Rennes, Paris II, Nice; professore a contratto : Bologna, Pisa (Scuola Sant' Anna); visiting professor China University of Political Science and Law; Hebrew University, Jerusalem; Roma Tre. Founder and General Editor *Studies in EU External Relations* (SEUR), Brill.

Katharina Manz
is a tax advisor at EY Switzerland, where she provides tax consultancy services to banks and other financial service providers in all areas of Swiss taxation, with a focus on Swiss operational taxes. She is a Swiss-certified tax advisor and holds a Master's degree in Law and Economics from the University of St. Gallen.

Pauline Melin
is Assistant Professor of EU Law at Maastricht University where she obtained her PhD on the external dimension of EU social security coordination in 2018. Prior to her current position, she combined a lectureship at Maastricht University teaching internal market law with a postdoctoral position at KU Leuven. Pauline Melin is also responsible for writing reports on the case-law of the Court of Justice of the European Union for the European Journal of Social Security.

Matthias Oesch
is Professor of Public Law, European Law and International Economic Law at the University of Zurich. Previously, he worked as Attorney-at-Law at Homburger AG, Zurich, as an Assistant Professor at the University of Bern and as Legal Counsel at the State Secretariat for Economic Affairs (Seco) in Bern, Switzerland. He has published extensively in the field of EU Law and Swiss-EU Bilateral Relations, including the following two books: Europarecht, Band I: Grundlagen, Institutionen, Verhältnis Schweiz-EU, 2nd ed. (Stämpfli, 2019); Switzerland – European Union: General Framework, Bilateral Agreements, Autonomous Adaptation (DIKE/Nomos, 2018).

Kurt Pärli
is a Full Professor of Private Social Law at the Law Faculty of the University of Basel since February 2016. His research focuses on discrimination protection law, labour and international labour law, social security law and data protection law. Kurt Pärli is also President of the Swiss Section of the International Association for Labour and Social Security Law (ISLSSL), which was founded in 2017.

Benedikt Pirker
is a Senior Lecturer at the Chair for European Law, International Law and Public Law of the University of Fribourg. He read EU and international law, among others, at the College of Europe and the Graduate Institute Geneva. He taught, among others, at the Universities of Ottawa, St. Gallen and Bern and conducted

research at the European University Institute, Hebrew University Jerusalem, the Max Planck Institute for Comparative Public Law and International Law and the University of Michigan. His broad interest in EU law includes topics of constitutional law, internal market law and external relations.

René Schwok

is a full professor at the Global Studies Institute and the Department of Political Science and International Relations at the University of Geneva. He has been Director of the Global Studies Institute and of the Master in European Studies. He is Director of the Master of Advanced Studies in International Security. He holds a Jean Monnet Chair in Political Science. He specialises in issues related to the external dimension of the European Union, Swiss-European Union relations and security in Europe.

Christa Tobler

is Professor of European Law at the Universities of Basel (Switzerland) and Leiden (the Netherlands). Her publications focus in particular on EU non-discrimination law and EU-Swiss legal relations, seen in the broader context of EU association law; most recently 'Citizenship of the Association': the examples of Turkey and Switzerland', in: Dora Kostakopoulou/Daniel Thym (eds.), *Research Handbook on European Union Citizenship Law and Policy. Navigating Challenges and Crises* (Edward Elgar, 2022), 320-342 (together with Narin Idriz).

Peter Van Elsuwege

is Professor of EU law and Jean Monnet Chair at Ghent University, where he is also co-director of the Ghent European Law Institute (GELI). In addition, he is a visiting professor at the College of Europe (Natolin Campus) and a board member of the Centre for the Law of EU External Relations (CLEER) at the Asser Institute in The Hague. His research activities essentially focus on the law of EU external relations and EU constitutional law.

Introduction

Switzerland and the EU: A Challenging Relationship

Marc Maresceau and Christa Tobler

> De tous les pays de l'Europe, celui qui avait le plus conservé la simplicité et la pauvreté des premiers âges était la Suisse. Si elle n'était pas devenue libre, elle n'aurait point de place dans l'histoire du monde, elle serait confondue avec tant de provinces plus fertiles et plus opulentes, qui suivent les sorts des royaumes où elles sont enclavées : on ne s'attire l'attention que quand on est quelque chose par soi-même.[1]
>
> VOLTAIRE

Notwithstanding the fact that for the European Union (EU), as well as for Switzerland, mutual relations are of crucial importance, there has now for more than a decade been a large degree of institutional and legal uncertainty in that relationship. The main causes of this state of affairs are not always easy to explain, in particular to a non-Swiss readership which is not necessarily familiar with the many "mysteries" of EU-Switzerland relations. Whilst interest in this particular relationship temporarily flared up in the context of the Brexit referendum, the fact remains that few truly know what, in the Brexit context, has been termed the "Swiss model".[2] The present volume covers, in various contributions, different sides of this special relationship.

The initiators of this project are well aware that there is already important literature on EU-Switzerland relations, mostly undertaken by Swiss scholars. This book not only intends to widen somewhat the approach followed so far,

1 *Oeuvres complètes de Voltaire avec des notes et une notice sur la vie de Voltaire. Essai sur les mœurs – Annales de l'Empire* (Paris: Firmin Didot Frères, 1855), Tome troisième, Chapitre LXVI, *De la Suisse, et de sa révolution au commencement du quatorzième siècle*, p. 241.

2 See, for example, the policy paper published by the UK Government, Alternatives to membership: possible models for the United Kingdom outside the European Union, March 2016, <https://assets.publishing.service.gov.uk/government/uploads/system/uploads/attachment_data/file/504661/Alternatives_to_membership_possible_models_for_the_UK_outside_the_EU_Accessible.pdf> (accessed 22 April 2022), p. 45.

© KONINKLIJKE BRILL NV, LEIDEN, 2023 | DOI:10.1163/9789004529984_002

in particular by combining Swiss and EU authorship, but also focuses on some of the topical issues in EU-Switzerland relations which, outside Switzerland, have perhaps not always received the attention they deserve. Consequently, the present publication aims to reach not only the classical Swiss readership but also that in the EU and beyond, in short: anyone interested in the field of EU external relations.

1 Important Relations in a Complex Setting of Non-EU Membership

In this introduction, some aspects of the EU-Swiss relationship are highlighted and, of course, the in-depth chapters of the different contributors to this volume are briefly introduced. It may be useful to start with a short reflection on the importance of EU-Switzerland relations. In the context of economy and trade, the Swiss Government refers to "an essential partnership",[3] and also the European Commission emphasises the importance of the bilateral economic relationship.[4] Indeed, the EU is Switzerland's most important trading partner, whereas Switzerland at the time of writing occupies the fourth most important trading position in EU world trade, after the USA, China and the United Kingdom of Great Britain and Northern Ireland (UK). Taking into consideration Switzerland's very limited geographic size, this is no doubt an impressive record. In addition, there is also a common general background. For example, the Delegation of the European Union to Switzerland and Liechtenstein states on its website, under the keyword "political relations", that Switzerland and the EU "share history, languages, culture, and political values. On the world stage, the EU and Switzerland are like-minded actors, supporting each other in a number of areas".[5]

As will amply be illustrated in this book, the current bilateral relationship operates in a particularly complex political and legal environment.[6] An often-invoked explanation for this situation has to do with what is sometimes seen as the "Swiss specificity" or the "Swiss special case" (a term much employed in

3 See <https://www.eda.admin.ch/missions/mission-eu-brussels/en/home/key-issues/economy-finance.html> (accessed 22 April 2022).

4 See <https://policy.trade.ec.europa.eu/eu-trade-relationships-country-and-region/countries-and-regions/switzerland_en> (accessed 22 April 2022). See also S. Rossi, G. Vallet, 'The economic dimension', in P. Dardanell, O. Mazzoleni (eds.), *Switzerland-EU Relations. Lessons for the UK after Brexit?* (Routledge, 2021), pp. 20–37.

5 See < https://www.eeas.europa.eu/node/410170_tr?s=180> (accessed 22 April 2022).

6 See M. Maresceau, "EU-Switzerland: Quo Vadis?", *Tribute to Gabriel Wilner, Georgia Journal of International and Comparative Law* 39 (2011), 3, pp. 727–755.

the Swiss political debate). This concept is closely intertwined with Swiss history, Swiss neutrality and the Swiss constitutional structure. The latter notably include elements of direct democracy and, more specifically, popular votes. Such votes may be the result either of referenda on federal matters or of initiatives intended to change the Federal Constitution (the latter require a majority of those who vote *and* of the cantons, which are the Swiss federal sub-States; see Articles 138 et seq. of the Swiss Federal Constitution).[7] A considerable number of important domestic issues in Switzerland are decided by means of popular votes and a good number of them are directly or indirectly related to Switzerland's relations with the EU. Their outcome is often (but not always) in favour of European integration.[8]

Obviously, for the purposes of this volume, the most notable feature of Switzerland's specificity is that it is neither part of the European Union (EU) nor of the European Economic Area (EEA) while being fully surrounded by EEA States, namely the EU Member States Austria, France, Germany and Italy and the EEA EFTA State Liechtenstein. The agreement establishing the EEA was signed on 2 May 1992 between, on the one hand, the EU and its Member States and, on the other hand, the States which were then members of the European Free Trade Association (EFTA). The EEA Agreement primarily aims at extending the EU's internal market to the participating EFTA States (the so-called EEA EFTA States). Negotiated with strong Swiss input and signed by the Federal Council (which is the Swiss Federal Government),[9] the EEA was – rather unexpectedly – rejected on 6 December 1992 in a referendum with a narrow majority of 50,3% of the votes of the people and a clear majority of the Swiss cantons. Instead of being an EEA member,[10] and thereby fully integrated into the EU's internal market in the same manner as its fellow EFTA States Iceland, Norway and Liechtenstein, Switzerland is today linked to selected

7 Federal Constitution of the Swiss Confederation of 18 April 1999, SR 101. – SR is the German abbreviation for the systematic compilation of Swiss federal legislation. Note that Switzerland has four national languages and three official languages. The various authors of this volume have consulted different language versions, as reflected in their footnotes. English is neither a national nor an official language of Switzerland. Nevertheless, unofficial English language versions exist for selected pieces of legislation.

8 See P. Sciarini, 'Explaining support for European integration in direct democracy votes', in P. Dardanell, O. Mazzoleni (eds.), *Switzerland-EU Relations. Lessons for the UK after Brexit?* (Routledge, 2021), pp. 104–118.

9 See notably P.G. Nell, *Suisse-Communauté européenne. Au coeur des négotiations sur l'Espace économique européen* (Economica, 2012).

10 See G. Kreis, 'Looking back: 1992 as a critical junction', in P. Dardanell, O. Mazzoleni (eds.), *Switzerland-EU Relations. Lessons for the UK after Brexit?* (Routledge, 2021), pp. 6–19.

parts of the EU's internal market only and a number of additional EU policies through so-called sectoral (typical EU terminology) or bilateral (typical Swiss terminology) agreements.

What is perhaps less well known outside Switzerland is that promptly after the signature of the EEA Agreement, the Swiss Federal Council sent a letter to Brussels requesting talks about Swiss accession to the then European Communities. After the negative EEA referendum, the Swiss application remained inactive for more than two decades. In January 1993, the Federal Council stated that until further notice Switzerland would not start membership negotiations with the European Communities.[11] Afterwards, it also refused, on various occasions, to formally withdraw the Swiss application. It stuck to this even when a popular initiative, that aimed at introducing into the Swiss Federal Constitution a provision stating that Switzerland shall participate in the European integration process and to this end shall seek accession to the European Union, was turned down by a large majority of the people and by all cantons in 2001.[12] Eventually, after increasing domestic political pressure, the Federal Council informed the EU that Switzerland had on 27 July 2016, decided to withdraw the application.[13]

11 See Switzerland's European Policy 1992–1993, <https://www.eda.admin.ch/europa/en/home/europapolitik/chronologie/1992-1993.html> (accessed 22 April 2022).

12 On this initiative, see <https://www.bk.admin.ch/ch/d/pore/vi/vis254.html> (accessed 22 April 2022). – In 2005, the Swiss Federal Council qualified Swiss EU accession as *"une option à terme"* (a longer-term option) and, therefore, refused to withdraw the Swiss application; see *Séance spéciale du Conseil fédéral sur la politique européenne*, 26 October 2005 (<https://www.admin.ch/gov/fr/accueil/documentation/communiques.msg-id-19619.html>, accessed 22 April 2022); also *Europe Report 2006*, 28 June 2006 (for information in English on this report, see <https://www.admin.ch/gov/en/start/documentation/media-releases.msg-id-5883.html>, accessed 22 April 2022). The Federal Council argued that a formal withdrawal was not necessary, given that the changes in the EU over time had made the request of 1992 "irrelevant" or "groundless". The Swiss Federal Parliament disagreed, apparently wishing to bring clarity to the situation; see, e.g., <https://www.parlament.ch/de/ratsbetrieb/suche-curia-vista/geschaeft?AffairId=20143219> (accessed 22 April 2022).

13 See letter of the President of the Swiss Confederation sent to the President of the Council of the EU on 27 July 2016, making clear that, following the rejection of the EEA, *"cette demande est devenue sans objet"* and *"doit être considérée comme retirée"*. The Presidency of the EU, in its answer of 19 October 2016, could not do much more than take good note of the fact "that the Swiss application for EU membership should be considered withdrawn"; for both letters, see <https://www.dfae.admin.ch/missions/mission-eu-brussels/en/home/news/news.html/content/europa/en/meta/news/2016/10/26/EU-Beitrittsgesuch> (accessed 22 April 2022).

Since the rejection of the EEA Agreement, Switzerland has pursued a double strategy with respect to the challenges posed by its European neighbourhood: on the one hand, the "bilateral path" which links Switzerland and the EU through agreements in selected fields, as discussed in various contributions in this volume (see further below). On the other hand, in areas not covered by such agreements, Switzerland has increasingly adapted its internal law to that of the EU.

In the present volume, this alternative or complementary approach, in Switzerland commonly termed "autonomous adaptation", is discussed in the **chapter by Matthias Oesch and Mattia Brugger**. They explain that from the 1980s onwards, the minimisation of economic disadvantages, factual (inter-) dependencies in other areas, and sometimes sheer convenience have led to Swiss law being systematically modelled on EU law. The chapter by Matthias Oesch and Mattia Brugger provides typical examples and it discusses their impact on the law making-techniques in Switzerland. A particular focus is put on data protection law, financial market law and COVID-19-related matters. The chapter also explains why the *Cassis de Dijon* principle, which Switzerland unilaterally introduced in 2010 for products originating in the EEA, goes beyond the classical elements of the policy of autonomous adaptation. The chapter further deals with an ongoing recent project of the Swiss Federal Government following the termination of the negotiations with the EU regarding an Institutional Agreement in spring 2021 (on that latter issue, see further below).

COVID-19-related matters are also the topic of a further **chapter by Christa Tobler**, which focuses on the effect of unilateral measures taken by the EU during the pandemic and their effect on Switzerland, as compared to the EEA EFTA States Iceland, Norway and Liechtenstein. The foundation of the relations of these States with the EU is the EEA Agreement that Switzerland chose to reject. The examples discussed in this chapter relate to the availability of supplies and equipment (more specifically: EU export control measures and joint procurement) and to the movement of persons (more specifically: the EU's traffic light system and the Digital COVID Certificate). There are two guiding questions here: First, is Switzerland treated in the same manner as, or different from, the EEA EFTA States? Second, has the existence, or the lack, of an EU-Swiss agreement, as the case may be, in the field in question been of any relevance? The chapter concludes that, in the time of crisis, Iceland, Liechtenstein and Norway benefitted from a legal framework (namely the EEA Agreement) that is judged by the EU to be of a stabler nature both legally and politically than that resulting from the current Swiss-EU relationship.

2 The Development of the Bilateral Legal Framework over Time

Turning now more specifically to the EU-Swiss agreements, it should be noted that no other country has as many agreements with the EU as Switzerland. At present, far more than 100 agreements are in force, with some 20 of these forming the core.[14] Indeed, a list compiled by the Swiss administration of the EU-Swiss agreements in force fills 30 pages.[15] In terms of their overall quality, in academic writing, the EU-Swiss legal relations are counted among the "privileged partnerships between the EU and its neighbours".[16]

Łazowski[17] has distinguished three phases in the development of legal relations between Switzerland and the EU (or its predecessor institutions, as the case may be):

- The first phase started in the 1950s with the conclusion of a number of agreements on different issues, such as train tariffs, trade in cheese and in watches (this last agreement is still in force).[18]
- A second phase, leading to enhanced bilateralism, began with the conclusion of two Free Trade Agreements (FTAs), one with the then European Coal and Steel Community (ECSC) and another one with the European Economic Community (EEC). This latter agreement is still in force;[19] it is in fact the only one of a group of FTAs concluded by the EEC with the then EFTA States that has survived to this day (if in an amended form). The EEC-Swiss FTA is often seen as the cornerstone of EU-Swiss legal relations. It has proven particularly important not least due to a "development clause" on a

14 See, e.g., M. Oesch, *Switzerland and the European Union. General Framework, Bilateral Agreements, Autonomous Adaptation* (Schulthess, 2018), p. 19.

15 See <https://www.eda.admin.ch/dam/europa/de/documents/publikationen_dea/accords-liste_de.pdf> (accessed 22 April 2022).

16 See notably S. Gstöhl, D. Phinnemore (eds.), *The Proliferation of Privileged Partnerships between the European Union and its Neighbours* (Routledge, 2019).

17 A. Łazowski, 'Chapter 5: Switzerland', in: S. Blockmans, A. Łazowski (eds.), *The European Union and Its Neighbours. A Legal Appraisal of the EU's Policies of Stabilisation, Partnership and Integration* (T.M. Asser Press, 2006), p. 151 et seq. The same approach is followed in C. Tobler, J. Beglinger, *Grundzüge des bilateralen (Wirtschafts-)Rechts. Systematische Darstellung in Text und Tafeln,* 2 volumes: Charts and Text (Dike, 2013), Chart 8.

18 Agreement concerning products of the clock and watch industry between the European Economic Community and its Member States and the Swiss Confederation (for the EU: original agreement of 1967 not published in the OJ, for subsequent changes see OJ 1974, L 118/12 and OJ 1987, C 94/1).

19 Agreement between the European Economic Community and the Swiss Confederation (OJ 1972, L 300/189), as amended.

possible further broadening and deepening of the legal relations between the parties.[20] This Agreement plays an important role in the chapter by Michael Hahn in the present volume (to be introduced in more detail further below). Moreover, still in force from this second phase is the agreement on the establishment of insurance companies.[21]

- A third phase, providing for a widening and deepening of the relationship, followed after the negative vote on the EEA. It saw notably the conclusion of two packages of agreements, in Switzerland commonly referred to as the *Bilaterals I* and the *Bilaterals II*, followed by a number of further agreements.

Given its particular importance, the above-mentioned third phase merits a somewhat more extensive introduction in the following sections. However, before proceeding with this and with an introduction of the book chapters that relate to this phase, it should be added that it is at present open if and how this phase will further develop. As discussed more extensively further below, the Swiss Government decided not to sign an Institutional Agreement (InstA) that it had negotiated with the EU with a view to introducing into five of the existing EU-Swiss Agreements a renewed institutional framework, and with a view to establishing an institutional framework for future agreements. This issue is of relevance for virtually all chapters of the present book.

3 The *Bilaterals I*

3.1 *Negotiations*

Following the EEA referendum of 6 December 1992, the Federal Council decided to continue on the "bilateral path".[22] Already at the beginning of 1993,

---

20 Article 32(1) FTA provides: "Where a Contracting Party considers that it would be useful in the interests of the economies of both Contracting Parties to develop the relations established by the Agreement by extending them to fields not covered thereby, it shall submit a reasoned request to the other Contracting Party. The Contracting Parties may instruct the Joint Committee to examine this request and, where appropriate, to make recommendations to them, particularly with a view to opening negotiations".

21 Agreement between the European Economic Community and the Swiss Confederation on direct insurance other than life assurance (OJ 1991, L 205/3), as amended.

22 For this and the following, see notably: Switzerland's European Policy 1992–1993, <https://www.eda.admin.ch/europa/en/home/europapolitik/chronologie/1992-1993.html> (accessed 18 June 2022), further the accounts of the background to the negotiations by 1) the Federal Council in its Explanatory Memorandum (so-called "dispatch") on the *Bilaterals I*, Botschaft zur Genehmigung der sektoriellen Abkommen zwischen der Schweiz und der EG, BBl 1999 6128, p. 6136 et seq., and 2) the European Commission in the Communication referred to in the following footnote.

it submitted a request to the EU Council to enter into bilateral sectoral negotiations in a wide range of areas, most of which were related to the Free Trade Agreement of 1972. In October 1993, the European Commission published a communication on the future relations with Switzerland,[23] in which it proposed to the Council to open negotiations for a *package* of sectoral agreements. In November 1993, both parties considered progressing exclusively on an agreement-by-agreement basis, the method which had been followed in the past, no longer desirable, as such an approach was enormously time-consuming. The Council declared itself willing to negotiate in seven areas, which covered 10 of the 15 areas that the Swiss Government had originally identified as desirable; at the same time, it went beyond those areas, notably by including free movement of persons, something which the Commission had also already done in the mentioned communication.

In 1994, negotiations between the EU and Switzerland were formally opened. Initially, the views of the parties differed on how to proceed. Whilst the Swiss side wished to approach the seven sectoral areas of negotiation independently of each other and not according to a common timetable, the Council had set the condition that the various agreements had to be negotiated in parallel and signed and brought into force jointly.[24] In fact, grouping different agreements in bilateral negotiations helped to find compromises which would otherwise not easily have been possible. Though a certain degree of "cherry-picking" from either side could not be avoided, at the end of the day, the parties found a compromise and were able to sign in 1999 the *Bilaterals I* package, covering the free movement of persons (essentially: natural persons) and, to some extent, services (here also including the posting of workers, even by legal persons),[25] further air transport,[26] land transport,[27] trade in agricultural products,[28] mutual recognition of conformity assessments (technical barriers to trade),[29] public

23 Communication from the Commission – Future relations with Switzerland, COM(93) 486 final.

24 See Botschaft (n. 21), p. 6138, as well as Federal Council, Bilateral Agreements I, <https://www.eda.admin.ch/europa/en/home/europapolitik/ueberblick/bilaterale-1.html> (accessed 22 April 2022).

25 For the EU, OJ 2002, L 114/6 (as amended); for Switzerland, see the Systematic Compilation of Swiss law (SR), namely SR 0.142.112.681 (consolidated version).

26 For the EU, OJ 2002, L 114/73 (as amended); for Switzerland, SR 0.748.127.192.68 (consolidated version).

27 For the EU, OJ 2002, L 114/91 (as amended); for Switzerland, SR 0.740.72 (consolidated version).

28 For the EU, OJ 2002, L 114/132 (as amended); for Switzerland, SR 0.916.026.81 (consolidated version).

29 For the EU, OJ 2002, L 114/369 (as amended); for Switzerland, SR 0.946.526.81 (consolidated version).

procurement[30] and research.[31] The latter agreement was of limited duration; at the time of writing this introduction, there is no agreement in this field. The present lack of a research agreement is the result of subsequent political developments (including notably the acceptance in Switzerland of the popular initiative on "Mass Immigration" and difficulties in relation to the institutional issues, both of which will also be discussed further below).

3.2 *Competence Issues*

Within the package of the *Bilaterals I*, only the Agreement on the Free Movement of Persons (AFMP) was a mixed agreement that on the EU side, had to be concluded by both the European Community *and* its Member States. Subsequently, the mixed nature of this agreement had as a consequence that Swiss approval was needed for the later EU enlargements of 2004, 2007 and 2013. The extension of the AFMP to the new EU Member States happened through the conclusion of additional protocols. All other agreements of the *Bilaterals I* were automatically extended to the new EU Member States.

On the side of the EU, a somewhat intriguing aspect concerned the legal basis for the conclusion of the *Bilaterals I*. Agreements negotiated by the EU with third States need a substantive and procedural legal basis for their conclusion. The determination of the relevant basis can be complicated both from a legal and a political view. For the conclusion of the *Bilaterals I*, the Commission had initially proposed various substantive legal basis provisions of the (then) EC Treaty.[32] However, the Council completely reviewed this proposal. It followed a more pragmatic approach by deciding that the general provision on association of (then) Article 310 EC (now Article 217 of the Treaty on the Functioning of the European Union, TFEU) ought to be used, together with the general procedural provision for the conclusion of agreements.[33] This may have seemed rather surprising. At the same time, for the EU, the qualification of the *Bilaterals I* as "association agreements" was in line with the case law of

30 For the EU, OJ 2002, L 114/430 (as amended), for Switzerland, SR 0.172.052.68 (consolidated version).

31 For the EU, OJ 2002, L 114/468 (as amended); for Switzerland, see the official, chronological compilation of federal legislation, AS 2002 1998.

32 See COM (1999) 229 final; no less than 12 EC substantive legal basis provisions are referred to in the Commission proposal; for more details see C. Kaddous, 'Les accords sectoriels dans le système des relations extérieurs de l'Union européenne', in D. Felder, C. Kaddous (eds), *Accords bilatéraux Suisse-UE (Commentaires). Bilaterale Abkommen Schweiz-EU (Erste Analysen)* (Helbing & Lichtenhahn-Bruylant, 2001), p. 88 and footnote 40.

33 OJ 2002, L 114/1.

the (then) Court of Justice of the European Communities, according to which an association under what is now Article 217 TFEU creates "special, privileged links with a non-member country which must, at least to a certain extent, take part in the Community [now: Union] system".[34] This is, precisely, the case with the *Bilaterals I*.[35] Since then, consistent case law has confirmed that Article 217 TFEU can be used broadly.[36] Obviously, the choice of the respective internal legal bases for the conclusion of a bilateral agreement is decided by each of the contracting parties themselves. It is not known to the editors of this volume whether there has ever been an official Swiss reaction to the choice of the EU legal basis for the *Bilaterals I*. In any case, from a Swiss perspective, the legal basis chosen by the Council to conclude the *Bilaterals I* could not have any impact on the legal status of these agreements under public international or Swiss domestic law.

3.3 *The "Guillotine Clause"*

An important feature of the package of the *Bilaterals I* is the presence in the seven individual agreements of a termination clause, which in Switzerland is commonly referred to as the "guillotine clause". It stipulates that all agreements shall cease to apply six months after receipt of a notification of termination or of non-renewal of any of the agreements of the *Bilaterals I* package (e.g., Article 25(4) AFMP). Interestingly, the Federal Council in this context uses the term "appropriate parallelism" between the different agreements of the package.[37] As noted by the Federal Council, the "guillotine clause" is the result of

34 CJEU, Case 12/86 *Demirel*, EU:C:1987:400, para. 9. See also C. Tobler, G. Baur, 'Der Binnenmarkt ist (k)ein Schweizer Käse. Zum Assoziationsstatus der Türkei, der EWR/EFTA-Staaten und der Schweiz, insb. mit Bezug auf den EU-Binnenmarkt', in A. Epiney, M. Kern and L. Hehemann (eds), *Schweizerisches Jahrbuch für Europarecht 2014/2015* (Stämpfli and Schulthess, 2015), p. 331.

35 It is in fact the case with many of the *Bilateral Agreements* more generally. In academic writing, the EU-Swiss legal relationship has been qualified as part of a larger policy of exporting EU law through external agreements; see R. Petrov, *Exporting the Acquis Communautaire through European Union External Agreements* (Nomos, 2011), p. 105 et seq.

36 According to that case law, Article 217 TFEU empowers the Union to guarantee commitments towards third countries in *all* the fields covered by the TFEU. Accordingly, it can be used as a legal basis for the conclusion of agreements that cover different areas of law; see most recently CJEU, Case C-479/21 PPU, *SN and SD*, EU:C:2021:929, para. 57. – See generally on the issue of the legal basis of the EU's external relations S. Adam, 'The legal basis of international agreements of the European Union in the post-Lisbon Era', in I. Govaere, E. Lannon, P. Van Elsuwege and S. Adam (eds.), *The European Union in the World. Essays in Honour of Marc Maresceau* (Martinus Nijhoff Publishers, 2014), pp. 65–86.

37 See Botschaft zur Genehmigung der sektoriellen Abkommen zwischen der Schweiz und der EG, BBl 1999 6128, p. 6137. On the concept, see also C. Rapoport, *Les partenariats*

a condition stipulated by the EU for the conclusion of these agreements. By insisting on this clause, the EU wanted to make sure that Switzerland could not subsequently reject the (in certain circles unpopular) AFMP without risking the other agreements of the *Bilaterals I* package.[38] This risk existed notably in view of the fact that the AFMP was initially concluded for a period of seven years only. It was to be renewed indefinitely unless the European Community or Switzerland would notify the other Contracting Party to the contrary before the expiry of the initial period (Article 25(2) AFMP). In Switzerland, the continuation of the AFMP was put to a popular vote together with the extension of the AFMP to Romania and Bulgaria on 8 February 2009. The result of the vote was positive.[39]

Subsequently, the guillotine clause was at least indirectly at issue when the EU's decision to conclude the *Bilaterals I* was challenged before the Court of Justice of the European Union (CJEU), due to the fact that, under the Agricultural Agreement, the wine growers of a Swiss community called "Champagne" were to lose the right to continue to call their product (a non-sparkling white wine) "Champagne" (France had in the negotiations for the *Bilaterals I* imposed exclusivity of this name in favour of its own producers). The action was not successful but was stranded on the strict standing requirements for non-privileged applicants under Article 263 TFEU.[40]

The linking together of the agreements of the *Bilaterals I* also had consequences for political debates and decisions in Switzerland related to the AFMP. When the popular initiative on "Mass Immigration", which aimed at establishing a quota for immigration and national preference in the Swiss labour market was accepted on 8 February 2014,[41] this led to serious disruptions in the relationship with the EU, as this type of measure is – quite obviously – incompatible

entre l'Union européenne et les Etats tiers européens. Etude à la contribution de l'Union européenne à la structure juridique de l'espace européen (Bruylant, 2011), pp. 218–223.

38 Botschaft zur Genehmigung der sektoriellen Abkommen zwischen der Schweiz und der EG, BBl 1999 6128, p. 6156.

39 Volksabstimmung vom 08.02.2009: Bundesbeschluss vom 13.06.2008 über die Genehmigung der Weiterführung des Freizügigkeitsabkommens zwischen der Schweiz und der Europäischen Gemeinschaft und ihren Mitgliedstaaten sowie über die Genehmigung und die Umsetzung des Protokolls über die Ausdehnung des Freizügigkeitsabkommens auf Bulgarien und Rumänien, <https://www.bk.admin.ch/ch/d/pore/va/20090208/index.html> (accessed 8 June 2022).

40 CJEU, Case T-212/02 *Commune de Champagne and Others v Council and Commission*, EU:T:2007:194. See C. Tobler, 'Das Ende des schweizerischen Champagners, Rs. T-212/02 Commune de Champagne et al. gegen Rat und Kommission', *Aktuelle Juristische Praxis* 2008, p. 497.

41 See <https://www.bk.admin.ch/ch/d/pore/vi/vis413.html> (accessed 22 April 2022).

with the AFMP. The vote was subsequently implemented in Swiss federal law in a limited manner in order to avoid a breach of the AFMP.[42] This in turn triggered the launching of a follow-up initiative on limiting the free movement of persons, whose acceptance could have forced the Federal Council to terminate the AFMP. This second initiative was rejected on 27 September 2020.[43]

3.4 *Swiss Decision-Shaping Rights*

On the institutional level, it is worth mentioning a generally little-known declaration[44] related to the *Bilaterals I* in which the Council agrees to far-reaching decision-shaping rights in favour of Switzerland, i.e., participation in EU committees and working parties in view of the adoption of new EU law in the field of the agreements. Previously, broad decision-shaping rights in favour of EU non-Member States were typical for the EEA Agreement only. In the framework of the EU-Swiss bilateral relations, the issue of decision-shaping rights is linked to the *possibility* of the Joint Committees in charge of the agreements to update parts of certain of these agreements in light of new Union law that falls within the subject-matter of a given agreement. Different from EEA law, the *Bilaterals I* in their present shape do not provide for a dynamic system of updating in the light of new EU law on matters covered by these agreements, i.e., a system whereby the parties to the agreement *should* agree to updates, failing which legal consequences are foreseen in the event that such updating does not take place. As will be seen further below, changing the in principle static system of five agreements of the *Bilaterals I* into a dynamic one has been a declared aim of the EU for some time; it is one of the institutional issues that at present complicate the relationship.

3.5 *Particularly Important: The Agreement on the Free Movement of Persons*

Within the group of the *Bilaterals I*, the AFMP is without doubt one of the most important agreements. In the case of this agreement, which the EU was eager to conclude, the association character (in the view of Union law) is made very obvious in the preamble, according to which the parties to the agreement were "resolved to bring about the free movement of persons between them on the basis of the rules applying in the [then] European Community".

42 See P. Uebersax, 'Forum: Ist das vom Parlament beschlossene Ausführungsgesetz zu Art. 121a BV verfassungswidrig?', *Jusletter* 20 March 2017.

43 See <https://www.ejpd.admin.ch/ejpd/de/home/themen/abstimmungen/begrenzungsinitiative.html> (accessed 22 April 2022).

44 E.g., OJ 2002, L 114/429.

Given the eminent importance of this particular agreement, a number of chapters in the present volume relate to matters covered by it, as follows:

The **chapter by Pauline Melin** begins by introducing the unique political and legal framework of the AFMP as a core agreement of the *Bilaterals I* and the EU-Swiss bilateral law as a whole. Thereafter, the chapter focuses on two specific aspects of the updating of the AFMP in view of EU rules on the free movement of persons adopted after the signing of the Agreement, namely, on the one hand, the (almost) complete integration of the EU social security coordination rules into the *acquis* of the AFMP and, on the other hand, the lack of such integration in relation to the EU Citizens' Rights Directive 2004/38 – a matter that has been much debated in the context of the draft Institutional Agreement. In these case studies, the author devotes particular attention to the social security rights of frontier workers and to access to social assistance for job-seekers. Through these case studies, Pauline Melin aims to understand why the AFMP continues to be a very contentious element in the integration process between the EU and Switzerland.

The **chapter by Peter Van Elsuwege** looks into the CJEU case law with a particular focus on the AFMP, as subsequently compared to the case law on the agreements associating Switzerland to the EU's Schengen and Dublin *acquis* (on these, see also further below). In the absence of a framework agreement providing for the homogeneous interpretation of shared legal rules, the CJEU proceeds from the so-called *Polydor* logic, which implies that there is no automatic interpretation by analogy of identically worded provisions included in a bilateral agreement with Switzerland and in the EU Treaties unless there are express provisions to that effect in the agreement itself. The consequences of this approach are illustrated with respect to the CJEU case law regarding the interpretation and application of the AFMP and the agreements associating Switzerland to the EU's Schengen and Dublin *acquis*. The former entails a "static" approach to the incorporation of new EU legislation, implying that there is no obligation to incorporate new EU *acquis*, whereas the latter agreements are "dynamic" in nature, including a procedure for the incorporation of new EU legislation. In comparing both sets of agreements and the relevant case law of the CJEU, this chapter illustrates the law and practice of sectoral bilateralism and the specific challenges of Switzerland's unique model of cooperation with the EU.

The **chapter by Kurt Pärli** deals with the law on the posting of workers and the free movement of services between the EU and Switzerland. After Switzerland had ratified the AFMP, the so-called "social flanking measures" were introduced into Swiss legislation on the posting of workers. They include the Swiss Posted Workers Act and a range of anti-wage dumping measures, such as monitoring, sanctions, the possible introduction of legal standards for minimum wages in specific sectors in case of wage dumping, an obligation to notify the use of posted workers eight days in advance in order to permit controls, facilitation of the general applicability of collective agreements and many more. Kurt Pärli's chapter provides an overview of the relevant legislation and case law, including also the EU legal framework insofar as it is binding on Switzerland through the AFMP. In the past years, some of the Swiss measures were at the centre of a heated debate on their compatibility with the AFMP and also on their relevance for the negotiations on the institutional issues that led to the now-discarded draft Institutional Agreement. Kurt Pärli analyses whether and to what extent the social flanking measures violate the non-discrimination principle under the agreement.

4 The *Bilaterals II* and Beyond

4.1 *Agreements, EU Agencies and Cohesion Payments*

After the signature of the *Bilaterals I* and even before their entry into force, initiatives were launched for a new round of negotiations for a second package of agreements. Formal negotiations for the *Bilaterals II* started in 2001 and in 2004, a political compromise was reached for the different components of the package. While in the negotiations Switzerland pursued a degree of parallelism, this was no longer the case for the entry into force of these agreements. In addition, contrary to what had happened with the *Bilaterals I*, the *Bilaterals II* did not contain a general "guillotine clause" (but instead provisions linking the Schengen and Dublin Association Agreements together, as noted further below).

The *Bilaterals II* cover a broad range of topics which then included Switzerland's association to the EU's Schengen and Dublin systems, the taxation of savings (as it was then called), fighting fraud, trade in processed agricultural products, environment, statistics, the avoidance of double taxation of former EU officials who reside in Switzerland, and media. Further below, two specific issues related to the *Bilaterals II* package will be highlighted, namely the nature of the association of Switzerland to the Schengen and Dublin systems (including the link of the former to the EU's Common and Security Policy), on the one hand, and the taxation of savings income, on the other hand.

At this point, it should be noted that, like the 1999 Research Agreement, the Media Agreement was limited in time and there is at present no agreement in this field. The same is also true for the Agreement on education, vocational training and youth, which was concluded in 2010 for a limited time and which included notably Switzerland's participation in the Union's Erasmus programme; at present, there is no agreement on this field. Other EU-Swiss agreements that were concluded after the package of the *Bilaterals II* cover diverse matters such as customs modalities, satellite navigation, cooperation of the competition authorities, emission trading and the European Asylum Support Office (EASO).

A number of the agreements concluded in this third phase of the development of the EU-Swiss legal relations link Switzerland to EU agencies, as discussed in the present volume in the **chapter by Merijn Chamon**. The author notes that while many EU decentralised agencies are in principle open to third country participation, it remains exceptional that such countries structurally participate in these EU bodies. The exceptions are the EEA EFTA States and Switzerland. Their participation even goes as far as having limited voting rights in some of these bodies. However, the legal set-up through which Switzerland participates in EU agencies is more cumbersome than the mechanism through which the EEA EFTA States' participation in EU agencies is enabled. The chapter takes a closer look at the arrangements concluded between the EU and Switzerland on the modalities of Swiss participation in those agencies. It also reflects on the possible future Swiss participation in further EU agencies in light of the Swiss rejection of the Institutional Agreement.

Furthermore, within the third phase of the development of EU-Swiss legal relations, a Memorandum of Understanding was signed between the parties in 2006. It pertained to financial contributions by Switzerland to projects in the then selected new EU Member States to enhance cohesion within the EU. The **chapter by Benedikt Pirker** provides a comparison between these so-called "Swiss Cohesion Payments", on the one hand, and the EEA and Norway Grants, on the other hand. The chapter compares these payments from a historical and factual perspective, assesses the legal framework underlying the contributions and examines conditionality elements in this context, namely the practice of contributing States to make their payments conditional upon certain facts, be they adherence to common values or the state of relations with the EU. The author finds that cohesion payments are marked by significant political room for action within the legal framework. He also notes that the perspective on the relations with the EU of a contributing State seems to influence the use made of this room for action, with, e.g., Norway treating its contributions more as a part of an overall, durable integration structure, whereas Switzerland seems to perceive cohesion payments predominantly as a political bargaining chip in the relations with the EU. This is visible not least in the present debate within Switzerland on how to proceed after the rejection of the Institutional Agreement.

4.2 *The Nature of the Schengen and Dublin Association Agreements and the Link of the Former to the EU's Common Foreign and Security Policy*

It should be noted that it was Switzerland which requested to be associated with the EU's activities in the fields of Schengen and Dublin. In fact, it had expressed its wish for more intense cooperation in the areas of migration and asylum already when concluding the *Bilaterals I*, in a unilateral declaration.[45] In addition, as noted by the Federal Council in its Explanatory Memorandum on the *Bilaterals II*, the Schengen visa is of great value to the Swiss tourist sector, which is an important part of the national economy and a strong source of employment. With this visa, tourists from, e.g., Asia who need a Schengen visa for their travel to Europe do not have to apply for an additional visa to enter Switzerland.[46]

In light of what has been mentioned above with regard to the EU legal basis for the conclusion of the *Bilaterals I*, it is worthwhile to note that both the Schengen[47] and the Dublin[48] Association Agreements in their titles expressly mention the term "association". But, interestingly enough and different from the *Bilaterals I*, the conclusion of the Schengen Association Agreement (SAA) was not based on the general association provision of the Treaty (then Article 310 EC), but rather on the substantive law provisions of Title IV on "Visas, Asylum, immigration and other policies related to the free movement of persons", the chapter on "Approximation of Laws" and the general procedural provision for the conclusion of agreements.[49] A comparable approach was adopted for the conclusion of the Dublin Association Agreement (DAA).[50]

A particularly noteworthy characteristic of the SAA and the DAA is that they are "dynamic" in nature, meaning that Switzerland *should* regularly agree to new EU law in the fields in question, failing which legal consequences up to

45 Declaration by Switzerland on migration and asylum policy, OJ 2002, L 114/71.

46 See Botschaft zur Genehmigung der bilateralen Abkommen zwischen der Schweiz und der Europäischen Union, einschliesslich der Erlasse zur Umsetzung der Abkommen («Bilaterale II»), BBl 2004 5965, p. 6012.

47 For the EU, OJ 2008, L 53/52 (as amended); for Switzerland, SR 0.362.31 (consolidated version).

48 For the EU, OJ 2008 L 53/5 (as amended); for Switzerland, SR 0.142.392.68 (consolidated version).

49 OJ 2008, L 53/1.

50 OJ 2008, L 53/3.

the automatic termination of the agreements are foreseen (Articles 2(3) and 7 SAA, Articles 1(3) and 4 DAA). This system is thus different from the *Bilaterals I*, whose updating in light of new EU law is merely *possible,* and no legal consequences are foreseen in the event that such updating does not take place. The Schengen and Dublin Association Agreements provide for particularly far-reaching decision-shaping rights of Switzerland, highlighted by the Swiss Federal Administration on a particular website.[51] The dynamic nature of the Schengen and Dublin Association Agreements is further reinforced by the fact that these two agreements are linked to each other: They must be applied simultaneously (Article 15(4) SAA, Article 14(1) DAA) and where one of them is terminated, the other will be considered to have been terminated as well (Article 17(2) SAA; Article 16(2) DAA).

In the present volume, the dynamic nature of the Schengen and Dublin Association Agreements is discussed in more detail in the **chapter by Peter Van Elsuwege** (already mentioned in the context of the AFMP), with an illustrative case study relating to a special "Swiss clause" in the EU's firearms legislation. In Switzerland, the acceptance of the new EU rules as part of the Schengen *acquis* led to a referendum launched by a shooting association. The new rules were accepted in the vote on 19 May 2019.[52] In its information on their implementation, the Swiss Federal Administration underlines the importance of the Swiss decision-shaping rights in this context.[53] In the European Union, the above-mentioned "Swiss clause" led to an action for annulment before the CJEU,[54] as discussed by Peter Van Elsuwege in his chapter. The action was unsuccessful (i.e., the Court upheld the validity of the "Swiss clause").

As stated above, changing the in principle static system of five agreements of the *Bilaterals I* into a dynamic is one of the core institutional issues between the EU and Switzerland. Matthias Oesch[55] noted against the background of the Schengen and Dublin Association Agreements that a dynamic system, while formally respecting the Swiss democratic system, in fact, limits the citizens'

---

51 See <https://www.sem.admin.ch/sem/en/home/international-rueckkehr/kollab-eu-efta/schengen/decision-shaping.html> (accessed 18 June 2022).

52 See <https://www.bk.admin.ch/ch/d/pore/va/20190519/det628.html> (accessed 18 June 2022).

53 See <https://www.ejpd.admin.ch/ejpd/de/home/themen/abstimmungen/waffenrichtlinie.html> (accessed 18 June 2022): "As a member of the Schengen Association, Switzerland was able to cooperate in the amendment of the EU Weapons Directive and prevent more far-reaching regulations." (translation by authors from German).

54 CJEU, Case C-482/17, *Czech Republic v Parliament and Council,* EU:C:2019:1035.

55 M. Oesch, 'Die bilateralen Abkommen Schweiz – EU und die Übernahme von EU-Recht', *Aktuelle Juristische Praxis* 2017, 638–652.

actual freedom of choice in popular votes, since a refusal to update might have legal consequences. A particularly illustrative example of this effect is provided by another Swiss referendum, directed against the incorporation of new EU rules on the European Border and Coast Guard Agency "Frontex" into the EU-Swiss legal relationship. The new Frontex rules included notably a very considerable raise in the agency's budget. Before the vote of 15 May 2022, Federal Councillor Keller-Sutter warned publicly against the rejection of the new Frontex rules.[56] The referendum was defeated with a very high percentage of "no" votes (71,5%).[57] According to Swiss media, the referendum was special for a number of reasons.[58] Notably, it was brought about by migration grassroots organisations in Switzerland whose members are often not Swiss citizens and who collected the necessary number of signatures of Swiss citizens in order to obtain a referendum vote. Further, this led to the first-ever public vote on what the Swiss media have termed "an EU security body", a vote, *nota bene*, held outside the EU. Within the Swiss political parties, the Social Democrats and the Greens supported the referendum. However, they did not oppose Frontex in principle (as the grassroots organisations did in view of the alleged involvement of Frontex in illegal pushbacks of migrants), but they wanted to link the additional funding to an increase in the resettlement quotas. An often-heard argument against the referendum was that denying the increased budget would do nothing to improve the migrants' situation and that Switzerland should use its influence inside Frontex (see Switzerland's influence in EU agencies in the above-mentioned chapter by Merijn Chamon).

The Schengen Association Agreement played an interesting role in the context of the COVID-19 pandemic and, more specifically, in relation to the relevance of the Union's legislation on the EU Digital COVID Certificate for Switzerland. The adoption of that legislation led to the curious situation where only one of the two EU Regulations on the matter is relevant for the purposes of the legal relations between Switzerland and the Union. The EU Digital

56 Bundesrätin Karin Keller-Sutter, '"Wenn wir Frontex ablehnen, hat das Folgen"'. Rede, 2. März 2022: Medienkonferenz zur Abstimmung vom 15. Mai 2022, <https://www.sem.admin.ch/ejpd/de/home/aktuell/reden---interviews/reden/2022/2022-03-02.html> (accessed 7 June 2022).

57 See <https://www.admin.ch/gov/de/start/dokumentation/abstimmungen/20220515/uebernahme-der-eu-verordnung-ueber-die-europaeische-grenz-und-kuestenwache.html> (accessed 8 June 2022).

58 See, e.g., 'Schweiz stimmt der Aufstockung von Frontex zu', *swissinfo* 15 May 2022, <https://www.swissinfo.ch/ger/resultate-abstimmung-frontex_schweiz-stimmt-der-aufstockung-von-frontex-zu/47590748> (accessed 7 June 2022).

COVID Certificate was introduced through Regulation 2021/953,[59] which also provides for an equivalence system for countries outside the EEA, such as Switzerland. The same is true, *vice versa,* for Swiss law vis-à-vis the EU. The interface between the two parties' COVID Certificates has, therefore, not been created on the basis of an EU-Swiss agreement. Rather, on the Swiss side, it is a matter of autonomous adaptation to the EU system, as discussed in the above-mentioned chapter by Matthias Oesch and Mattia Brugger. Conversely, the EU's second Regulation 2021/954[60] on the EU Digital COVID Certificate extends the rules of the main Regulation to third-country nationals legally staying or legally residing in the territories of Member States during the COVID-19 pandemic. Since the territories of Member States for these purposes also include non-Member States that are part of the Schengen area, the second Regulation is part of the EU-Swiss Schengen *acquis*. It has as such been implemented by Switzerland, as discussed in the above-mentioned chapter by Christa Tobler. The example may serve as an illustration of the legal complexities at times involved in the EU-Swiss relations.

In a very different context, the EU-Swiss Schengen Association is also touched upon in the **chapter by Christophe Hillion**, where the author remarks that the Joint Committees in charge of the Schengen Association Agreements concluded by the EFTA States may serve as a forum for dialogue and consultations between these countries and the EU on Schengen-related developments in the fields of the EU Common and Foreign Security Policy (CFSP). Christophe Hillion's chapter discusses the specific cooperation between the EU and the Swiss Confederation in the CFSP terrain. Unlike most European non-Member States – with the noticeable exception of the UK – Switzerland does not as, a matter of principle, *explicitly* align itself with EU foreign policy initiatives. While covering most aspects of EU CFSP, the Swiss cooperation with the Union in that area consists instead of occasional voluntary support, and intermittent association with specific EU CFSP undertakings, through specific sectoral (participation) agreements. Christophe Hillion examines the many areas where the

59 Regulation (EU) 2021/953 of the European Parliament and of the Council of 14 June 2021 on a framework for the issuance, verification and acceptance of interoperable COVID-19 vaccination, test and recovery certificates (EU Digital COVID Certificate) to facilitate free movement during the COVID-19 pandemic (OJ 2021, L 211/1), as amended.

60 Regulation (EU) 2021/954 of the European Parliament and of the Council of 14 June 2021 on a framework for the issuance, verification and acceptance of interoperable COVID-19 vaccination, test and recovery certificates (EU Digital COVID Certificate) with regard to third-country nationals legally staying or residing in the territories of Member States during the COVID-19 pandemic (OJ 2021, L 211/24), as amended.

EU and Switzerland have collaborated even in the absence of agreement, and it gleans some insight into the variety of instruments and specific modalities of this cooperation, as compared to the arrangements the EU has elaborated with the other European States. The chapter also explores (legal) avenues for possible expansion of the CFSP cooperation between the two (difficult) partners, particularly in view of the EU's development of its foreign policy, security and defence policies since the entry into force of the Treaty of Lisbon, and against the backdrop of the Russian invasion of Ukraine.

4.3 *Taxation of Savings*

The present volume contains a **chapter by Hans-Joachim Jaeger and Katharina Manz** that discusses the international background of the evolution of the Agreement on the taxation of savings income, signed in 2004, to an Agreement on the automatic exchange of information in tax matters, as agreed in 2015. As noted in this chapter, few initiatives have changed the tax world and the relationship between financial service providers and their clients more than increasing transparency. Switzerland, still the largest offshore location in the banking and financial services sector, is particularly affected by these developments. The banks are caught between legally anchored bank-client confidentiality ("banking secrecy") and the obligation to provide client data and account movements to foreign tax authorities if such clients are domiciled abroad. Such obligations are regulated by international treaties and directly shape Switzerland's relationship with its foreign partner countries. The chapter traces the development of transparency initiatives internationally and in Switzerland, with a particular focus on the broader international background, starting with the Qualified Intermediary (QI) system in 2001, the EU taxation of savings income and the final withholding tax, and culminating in the automatic exchange of information, the OECD Base Erosion and Profit Shifting (BEPS) initiative and the EU initiatives on mutual administrative assistance. The chapter presents the historical development of these initiatives and provides an overview of how they work.

For the readership of the present volume, it might be useful to also explain in some detail the historical *European* background of the 2004 Agreement, which at the time was, for the EU, by far the most crucial and sensitive agreement of the *Bilaterals II* package. At the 2000 Santa Maria da Feira European Council meeting, the Union Member States in principle agreed on a global package of measures concerning taxation which included *inter alia* automatic exchange of information on savings income. However, trying to obtain unanimity among the Member States was far from easy. Rapidly, it became clear that a transitional period would be necessary to allow Luxembourg, Belgium and Austria to apply a withholding tax on interest income paid in the other Member States.

A serious difficulty in this respect was that this intra-EU arrangement, in order to be workable and efficient, needed also cooperation from neighbouring "key third countries".[61] If any progress on this topic was to be made, the EU would have to conclude bilateral agreements with Switzerland as well as with Liechtenstein, Andorra, San Marino and Monaco.

Needless to say, none of the so-called "key third countries" was particularly eager to move in that direction. Switzerland, for its part, had already come under increasing pressure regarding its banking legislation, in particular, from the USA, while also in the EU and its Member States, pressure had been growing. Rather rapidly, in 2003, within the context of the negotiations for the *Bilaterals II*, a political compromise was reached with the EU and Switzerland for the establishment of "equivalent measures" to the measures applied at the intra-EU level, in the shape of a system of tax retention on EU account holders in Switzerland. The rapidity of this arrangement, which astonished observers from other third countries, was an evident demonstration of a pragmatic and realistic approach from the Swiss authorities, while at the same time still preserving the main ingredients of the almost "holy" principle of Swiss bank-client confidentiality (often termed "banking secrecy").

Within the EU, this crucial political compromise with Switzerland provided the Council with the green light to adopt, on 3 June 2003, its important Directive 2003/48/EC on taxation of savings income in the form of interest payments[62] and to sign, on 26 October 2004, with Switzerland, the "Agreement providing for measures equivalent to those laid down in Council Directive 2003/48/EC on taxation of income in the form of interest payments".[63] In practice, the 2004 Agreement obliged Switzerland to introduce a system of tax retention on EU account holders in Switzerland. Conversely, it did not yet establish the obligation of automatic exchange of information. Indeed, according to Xavier Oberson,[64] Swiss banking secrecy was preserved in its entirety under the bilateral regime of that time.

---

61 Expression used in Presidency conclusions, Santa Maria da Feira European Council, 19 and 20 June 2000, Annex IV, *Report from the ECOFIN Council to the European Council on the tax package*, point 2.c.; for more details, see M. Maresceau, *Bilateral Agreements Concluded by the European Community*, The Hague Academy of International Law, *Recueil des Cours*, vol 309 (2004) (Martinus Nijhoff, 2006), pp. 416–419.

62 OJ 2003, L 157/38 (no longer in force).

63 OJ 2004, L 385/30.

64 X. Oberson, 'Le secret bancaire et l'Accord entre l'Union européenne et la Suisse sur la fiscalité de l'épargne', in C. Kaddous, M. Jametti Greiner (eds.), *Accords bilatéraux II Suisse–EU et autres accords récents* (Helbing & Lichtenhahn/Bruylant, 2006), 557–576, p. 575.

The arrangement with Switzerland, in turn, had a great impact on the four small neighbouring States of the EU already mentioned (Liechtenstein, Andorra, San Marino and Monaco). For all of them, there was indeed no other alternative than negotiating largely similar agreements like the one signed by the EU and Switzerland. Subsequently, the legal tax regime in the EU-Switzerland relations resulting from the entry into force of the "equivalent measures" as agreed in the 2004 Agreement would be fundamentally reviewed in 2015 and be replaced by the principle of automatic exchange of information, as is explained in detail in the chapter by Hans-Joachim Jaeger and Katharina Manz.

5 The Debate around the Institutional Issues

It was in 2010 that one of the editors of this volume (Marc Maresceau) was contacted by Mr Gianluca Grippa, then Head of the European Commission Unit in charge of relations with Switzerland, to participate in a "brainstorming session" on the EU-Switzerland relations. The meeting aimed to address a number of vital issues of this relationship, such as the continuation of the sectoral approach, the possibility of Swiss access to the EU internal market, the EEA relationship, the desirability of Swiss participation in the EU policy fields of the Common Foreign and Security Policy (CFSP) and the European Security and Defence Policy (ESDP). The meeting was organised in Brussels on 22 October 2010, lasted a full day and was, it may be said, unique and original in its kind. It brought together a wide variety of EU officials who, in one way or another, were familiar with one or more aspects of EU-Switzerland relations, and a considerable number of EU Member State representatives involved in EU-Switzerland relations were equally present. In addition, the organiser of the meeting had also invited three academics from EU Member States who had followed EU-Switzerland relations. This was a topic on which Swiss academics had profusely published, but which on the whole and apart from rare exceptions, had been largely ignored by academia outside Switzerland. Similarly, no Swiss officials or Swiss academics were invited to attend the Brussels "brainstorming meeting".

Already before this meeting, signals of growing discontent at the side of the EU over the course of the relations with Switzerland could be discerned. In its 2008 Conclusions on the relations with the EFTA States, the Council observed that Switzerland was not fully applying the 1999 bilateral Agreement on the Free Movement of Persons, while that agreement was one of the pillars of the 1999 *Bilaterals I* package. In particular, the Council was of the opinion that the bilateral law regarding posted workers and the transborder provision of services had not been properly implemented in Switzerland. Furthermore, the Council took the view that certain cantonal tax regimes applied in Switzerland constituted a violation of the State aid provisions of the 1972 FTA (on this dispute, see the chapter by Michael Hahn in this volume, to be introduced in more detail further below). More generally, the Council found that if Switzerland wanted to continue to take part in certain sectors of the EU's internal market, this necessarily implied the setting up of an overarching legal framework guaranteeing a homogeneous and simultaneous application and interpretation of the EU *acquis* relevant for the agreements which had been signed by the parties.[65]

In its December 2010 Conclusions on relations with EFTA Countries, the Council published an important update of its view on the relations with Switzerland,[66] which seemed heavily inspired by the above-mentioned October 2010 "brainstorming operation" held in Brussels. The Council stated that EU-Switzerland bilateral relations were "good, intensive and broad" and it took note of the Swiss Federal Government's comprehensive European Policy Report of 2010.[67] This latter report recalled the various Swiss options for the bilateral relations with the EU, and it reaffirmed the Swiss Government's strong belief in the bilateral or sectoral approach. Indeed, from a Swiss perspective, this model no doubt preserved best its freedom of action, prosperity and values; in other words, it was the most suitable instrument for safeguarding Switzerland's interests in Europe.

The Council, however, while on the one hand acknowledging that this approach had indeed been able to achieve close mutual cooperation between the parties, on the other hand also emphasised that this policy had led to "a highly complex set of multiple agreements". A straightforward critical view on the ongoing relations was expressed in the following terms: "Due to a lack of efficient arrangements for the take-over of new EU *acquis*, including CJEU case law, and for ensuring the supervision and enforcement of the existing agreements, this approach does not ensure the necessary homogeneity in the parts

---

65 See Draft Council conclusions on EU relations with EFTA countries, 5 December 2008, <https://www.llv.li/files/sewr/pdf-llv-sewr-16651_1_08.pdf> (accessed 8 June 2022), para. 27.

66 Council conclusions on EU relations with EFTA countries, 14 December 2010, <https://www.consilium.europa.eu/uedocs/cms_data/docs/pressdata/en/foraff/118458.pdf> (accessed 8 June 2022), as of para. 37.

67 <https://fedlex.data.admin.ch/filestore/fedlex.data.admin.ch/eli/fga/2010/1293/fr/pdf-a/fedlex-data-admin-ch-eli-fga-2010-1293-fr-pdf-a.pdf> (accessed 22 April 2022).

of the internal market and of the EU policies in which Switzerland participates." This situation, it was argued, "resulted in legal uncertainty for authorities, operators and individual citizens" and led to "an incoherent application of certain agreements and the introduction by Switzerland of subsequent legislative measures and practices". The Council's concluding message was outspoken and unambiguous: the bilateral sectoral approach "has become complex and unwieldy to manage and has clearly reached its limits". Consequently, "horizontal issues related to the dynamic adaptation of agreements to the evolving *acquis*, the homogeneous interpretation of the agreements, an independent surveillance and judicial enforcement mechanisms and a dispute settlement mechanism need to be reflected in EU Switzerland agreements". In its Conclusions, the Council did welcome the setting-up of an informal Working Group of the Commission and Swiss authorities.

However, at first, little or no progress was made. In its 2012 Conclusions on relations with the EFTA Countries,[68] the Council stated that, for the EU, progress on institutional matters constituted a *conditio sine qua non* for the conclusion of any negotiation regarding the further participation of Switzerland in the internal market. In order to understand the EU's view on the matter, it is important to note the Council's statement according to which, "by participating in parts of the EU internal market and policies, Switzerland is not only engaging in a bilateral relation but becomes a participant in a multilateral project" – namely in what subsequently would be termed the "extended single (or internal) market", which also includes the EEA EFTA States (in fact, according to the Council's 2010 Conclusions, participation notably in the internal market is "a status normally only granted to members of the EEA"). According to the Council, a renewed institutional framework should present a level of legal certainty and independence equivalent to the mechanisms created under the EEA Agreement. At the time, however, Swiss reluctance brought the Council to conclude that the process of moving towards negotiations on the institutional issues was marked by "a stalemate".

It was only in the second half of 2013 that exploratory talks between the parties on this question evolved in the direction of a possible opening for formal negotiations. On 18 December 2013, the Swiss Federal Government adopted its mandate for such negotiations. In its press release that followed,[69] the Federal

68 See Council conclusions on EU Relations with EFTA Countries, 20 December 2012, <https://www.llv.li/files/sewr/pdf-llv-sewr-5101_13.pdf> (accessed 20 April 2022).

69 'Swiss-EU relations: strengthening the bilateral approach through negotiations on institutional issues', Press release of the Federal Council 18 December 2013, <https://www.admin.ch/gov/en/start/documentation/media-releases.msg-id-51490.html> (accessed 20 April 2022).

Council stated that if "Switzerland wants to protect what it has achieved so far, then a renewal of the bilateral approach is required, on condition that the independence and prosperity of Switzerland are preserved. A new institutional agreement would take into account the close bilateral relations between Switzerland and the EU". At the same time, the Swiss Federal Government also formulated certain limits. Notably, it stated that no future institutional agreement may change either the aims, objectives or the scope of application of the agreements between Switzerland and the EU. In that context, it mentioned specifically the example of the AFMP, where there would "be no adoption of the EU directive on EU citizenship" and where it would be "ensured that Switzerland can maintain the full accompanying measures to the free movement of persons agreement".

Subsequently, the outcome of the vote on the popular initiative on mass immigration in February 2014 created an additional headache in both Switzerland and the EU, as already mentioned. However, notwithstanding this new and serious obstacle in the bilateral relationship, the Council adopted, on 6 May 2014, the mandate for negotiations on an Institutional Agreement.[70] In that decision, the Council could not resist reiterating that the conclusion of "these negotiations and of negotiations on any further agreements on Swiss participation in the EU's internal market was subject to a comprehensive assessment of relations between the EU and Switzerland".

The same message was repeated at the end of 2014 in new Council Conclusions which, tellingly, bore a new name. Rather than addressing the "relations with EFTA Countries", they referred to "a homogeneous extended single market and EU relations with Non-EU Western European countries".[71] In these Conclusions, the Council not only reiterated that without a new institutional framework no further agreements on Swiss participation in the (extended) internal market would be concluded, but it also added that agreements in other areas would be considered carefully, based on an appraisal of the balance of interests on a case-by-case basis. The next Council Conclusions

70 Official French text: *Accord facilitant les relations bilatérales entre l'Union européenne et la Confédération Suisse dans les parties du marché intérieur auxquelles la Suisse participe*, official draft text of November 2028, <https://www.eda.admin.ch/dam/europa/fr/documents/abkommen/Acccord-inst-Projet-de-texte_fr.pdf> (accessed 20 April 2022).

71 Council conclusions on a homogeneous extended single market and EU relations with Non-EU Western European countries, 16 December 2014, <https://www.consilium.europa.eu/uedocs/cms_data/docs/pressdata/en/er/146315.pdf> (accessed 20 April 2022).

of 2017 – now a document specifically on the EU-Swiss relations – again reiterated the already well-known message.[72]

After several years of negotiations, a draft text for the Institutional Agreement (InstA) was published by the Swiss Federal Council in November 2018.[73] It covered five market access agreements of the *Bilaterals I* – namely the AFMP and the agreements on conformity assessments (MRA) and on agricultural products, air and land transport – and it was intended to also set the institutional framework for future market access agreements. It aimed in particular at guaranteeing homogeneity of the bilateral agreements covered by it with the EU law from which they are derived. To this end, it provided for new rules on dynamic updating of the agreements in the light of new EU law, interpretation in line with the CJEU case law and the inclusion in the dispute settlement mechanism of a judicial element (an arbitration tribunal that would turn to the CJEU for questions of interpretation of bilateral law that derives from EU law). In addition, the draft text provided for a modernisation of the State aid regime in the Air Transport Agreement.

However, the text of the draft InstA was not formally initialled by the parties. In international legal practice, it is well known that with the initialling of an agreement (*"parapher l'accord"*) negotiators indicate that they have terminated their work. Instead, the Federal Council in view of the Swiss democratic system (namely the fact that the conclusion of the InstA would require the approval of the Federal Parliament and, most likely through a referendum, also of the people and the cantons), started a domestic process of broad consultations with relevant stakeholders (including, among others, political parties, economic and social organisations etc.), an operation which was perceived by the EU as a mere delaying tactic. In its 2019 Conclusions on the relations with Switzerland,[74] the Council expressed the view that the draft InstA represents a fair and balanced solution to the institutional issues. It strongly regretted that the Swiss Federal Council had not endorsed this outcome in 2018 and it called on the Federal Council to submit the negotiated text for adoption to the Federal Parliament as soon as the above-mentioned consultation would be completed. In addition, the Council emphasised that the conclusion of the

72 Council conclusions on EU relations with the Swiss Confederation, 28 February 2017, <https://www.consilium.europa.eu/en/press/press-releases/2017/02/28/conclusions-eu-swiss-confederation/> (accessed 20 April 2022).

73 See https://www.fdfa.admin.ch/dam/europa/fr/documents/abkommen/Acccord-inst-Projet-de-texte_fr.pdf (accessed 20 April 2022).

74 Council conclusions on EU relations with the Swiss Confederation, 19 February 2019, <https://www.consilium.europa.eu/en/press/press-releases/2019/02/19/council-conclusions-on-eu-relations-with-the-swiss-confederation/> (accessed 20 April 2022).

InstA "on the basis of the present text is a precondition for the EU for the conclusion of future agreements on Swiss participation in the EU's internal market and also an essential element for deciding upon further progress towards mutually beneficial market access", the latter being a reference to the updating of already existing market access agreements.

The Swiss consultations took several months and the results[75] were highlighted in a letter of 7 June 2019 to then Commission President Juncker, signed by the President and the Chancellor of the Swiss Confederation.[76] In this letter, Switzerland stated the need to further clarify certain substantive aspects of the InstA in relation to the application of the EU Citizens' Rights Directive 2004/38, the protection of wages in the context of posted workers and the arrangements regarding State aid. In his reaction of 11 June 2019, President Juncker observed that the requests for clarification, "*ne sont pas sans créer, dans le contexte politique actuel quelques difficultés à l'Union Européenne*" ("are not without creating, in the current political context, some difficulties for the European Union").[77] According to Juncker, the draft InstA together with its annexes and protocols form "*un tout indissociable*". He admitted that perhaps certain clarifications could be provided, but for him, the text and spirit of the InstA could not be renegotiated. In other words, it was evident that on the Swiss request for clarification little was to be expected from the side of the EU.

Eventually, exploratory talks on these issues between Switzerland and the European Commission did not yield the result that the Swiss Government regarded necessary for the signing of the InstA. Convinced that the draft InstA would not pass either in the Federal Parliament or in a referendum, the Federal Council on 26 May 2021 published a report on the negotiations,[78] declared

---

75 See <https://www.eda.admin.ch/europa/en/home/europapolitik/ueberblick/institutionelles-abkommen.html> (accessed 20 April 2022), under "Outcome of the consultations on the draft text of the institutional agreement".

76 See <https://www.eda.admin.ch/dam/europa/en/documents/bericht_konsultationen_insta/20190607_Lettre-CF-President-Commission-europeenne_en.pdf> (accessed 20 April 2022).

77 See <https://www.eda.admin.ch/dam/europa/en/documents/bericht_konsultationen_insta/20190607_Lettre-CF-President-Commission-europeenne_en.pdf> (accessed 20 April 2022).

78 Bericht betreffend die Verhandlungen über ein institutionelles Abkommen zwischen der Schweiz und der EU, 26 May 2021, <https://www.eda.admin.ch/dam/europa/de/documents/abkommen/20210526-bericht_verhandlungen_institutionelles-Abkommen_ch-eu_DE.pdf>(accessed 20 April 2022).

publicly that it would not sign the Agreement[79] and sent a letter to that effect to the European Commission.[80]

In fact, it is not easy to make an assessment of what, after years of negotiations, had been achieved with the draft InstA. One impression is that the draft text manages to find somehow a delicate balance between the various expectations at the negotiation table and that, in itself, is already a real *tour de force*. On the one hand, the EU would have obtained assurances for greater legal certainty, dynamic incorporation of the EU *acquis* and guarantees for homogeneity of the internal market that it considers in line with the requirements of the autonomy of the Union legal order.[81] On the other hand, Switzerland would have been able to consolidate the bilateral approach and its access to the EU market. In addition, it would have managed to a large extent to preserve the principle of respect for sovereignty, as noted by René Schwok in the present volume (see further below), although it must be added that this view is not shared by everybody in Switzerland. For example, as also noted by René Schwok, the largest political party in Switzerland, the Swiss Peoples Party, spoke of surrender of sovereignty and submission, subjugation and colonialism. Others challenge in particular the dispute settlement mechanism foreseen in the InstA and they argue that certain EEA structures could or should rather have been used. Former president of the EFTA Court, Carl Baudenbacher, a staunch critic of the Swiss Government's European policy in general, has gone so far as to call the dispute resolution mechanism provided for in the InstA "amateurish bricolage".[82] Similarly, though in more sober terms, Michael Ambühl, a former Swiss State Secretary and now Professor of Negotiation and Conflict Management at the renowned Swiss Federal Institute of Technology in Zurich, and his collaborator Daniela Scherer have criticised the draft InstA more generally as reflecting an unbalanced outcome of the negotiations.[83]

---

79 No signing of Swiss–EU institutional agreement, Press release of the Federal Council, 21 May 2021, <https://www.eda.admin.ch/eda/en/fdfa/fdfa/aktuell/news.html/content/eda/en/meta/news/2021/5/26/83705.html> (accessed 20 April 2022).

80 See <https://www.eda.admin.ch/dam/europa/en/documents/abkommen/20210526-brief-BR-vdL-InstA_EN.pdf> (accessed 20 April 2022).

81 On this issue, see in particular K. Lenaerts, J.A. Gutiérrez-Fons and S. Adam, 'Exploring the Autonomy of the European Union Legal Order', *Zeitschrift für ausländisches öffentliches Recht und Völkerrecht* 81 (2021) 1, 47–88.

82 See, e.g., C. Baudenbacher, "Britzerland': the problem of dispute resolution post-Brexit', *LSE Blog* 29 October 2018, <https://blogs.lse.ac.uk/brexit/2018/10/29/britzerland-the-problem-of-dispute-resolution-post-brexit/> (accessed 18 June 2022).

83 See, e.g., M. Ambühl, D.S. Scherer, 'Zum Entwurf des Institutionellen AbkommensAuf der Suche nach einem Interessenausgleich', *Jusletter* 4 February 2019.

In the present volume, two contributions deal specifically with the failure of the InstA in Switzerland. The **chapter by René Schwok**, a political scientist, explains the decision by the Federal Council to reject the InstA by reviewing the motivations of the seven Federal Councillors and the pressures to which they were subjected, even from political forces that are not far-right nationalists or traditional Eurosceptics. Further, the chapter highlights the radical nature of the decision to reject the InstA, given that – in the assessment of the author – the agreement had been relatively well negotiated by Switzerland, the EU had made substantial concessions and had not been particularly intransigent, the last remaining obstacles seemed to have been exaggerated and could have been overcome by domestic measures in Switzerland and, finally, the harmful consequences of a rejection of the InstA were well known.

The **chapter by Christine Kaddous** discusses the failure of the InstA from a legal perspective. It compares the current institutional system of the *Bilateral Agreements* and the InstA, focusing on the mechanisms foreseen with regard to the developments in EU law, legal interpretation, surveillance of the application of the agreements, the dispute settlement between the contracting parties as well as the termination clauses. The chapter also explores the consequences of the non-signature of the InstA, including, in particular, the meaning of the "*status quo*" situation and the consequences related to decisions and measures on the side of the EU, such as the refusal to update existing market access agreements and to conclude future access market agreements as well as decisions impacting other fields of the bilateral relationship. The chapter further addresses more generally the deterioration in the relationship between the partners as well as the domestic measures envisaged by Switzerland to partially mitigate these negative effects.

The European Commission has, as a clear demonstration of its dissatisfaction with the course of events, taken various measures that are perceived in Switzerland as unfriendly acts and as expressions of a "pinprick policy". These measures, which are discussed in various chapters in this volume (in particular in those by Christine Kaddous and by Michael Hahn) include, among other issues, the non-extension of the Commission's decision on stock exchange equivalence, the refusal to update the MRA in the light of new EU law on medical devices (despite Switzerland having adapted its internal legislation), the downgrading of Switzerland to a non-associated third country in the EU's research programme Horizon Europe and the refusal to conclude the negotiations on, and to sign, agreements in the fields of health and electricity. It may be added in the latter context that the fact that the Commission excluded Swissgrid, the national electricity grid company, from participation in the European platforms for the exchange of standard products for balancing energy, led Swissgrid to bring an action for annulment against the Commission to the General Court at the CJEU. The case is pending at the time of writing.[84] Featuring 41 international interconnection lines, the Swiss transmission grid is closely linked to the European grid. According to Swissgrid, increasing exclusion from participation in committees and market platforms will have a negative effect on the security of the transmission grid.[85]

6 Perspectives for the Future

On 23 February 2022, the Swiss Federal Council adopted a set of guidelines for a future negotiating package with the EU and informed the public about it in a press release.[86] Regarding the institutional issues, the Federal Council decided on what it terms "a vertical approach", aimed at anchoring provisions on the dynamic updating of Swiss-EU bilateral agreements, dispute settlement, exceptions and safeguard clauses in each market access agreement. The Federal Council added that "[t]he horizontal approach set out in last year's failed institutional agreement is no longer being considered". On a more general level, the Federal Council declared that it will now seek to address the pending issues concerning overall Swiss-EU relations based on a broad packet of measures, which may also include market agreements for electricity and food safety as well as association agreements for research, health and education. Further, the Federal Council is prepared to consider continuing the Swiss cohesion contributions as part of its negotiating package. It would seem that this broader package approach follows the suggestions made in an academic

84 CJEU, Case T-127/21 *Swissgrid v Commission* (pending); also OJ 2021, C 189/18. In the Swiss media, see, e.g. 'Die Schweizer Stromnetzbetreiberin Swissgrid klagt gegen EU-Kommission', *NZZ magazin* 12 June 2021, https://magazin.nzz.ch/schweiz/swissgrid-der-stromnetzbetreiber-klagt-gegen-eu-kommission-ld.1630148> (accessed 18 June 2022). See also: EU General Court to rule on Swissgrid's exclusion from TERRE, EU Law Live 17 May 2021, <https://eulawlive.com/general-court-to-rule-on-swissgrids-exclusion-from-terre/> (accessed 18 June 2022).

85 See <https://www.swissgrid.ch/en/home/newsroom/dossiers/cooperation-europe.html> (accessed 18 June 2022). For academic writing, see B. Hofmann, D. Kolcava and P. Thaler, 'The Role of Switzerland in European Electricity Governance Shaper, Follower, or Outsider?', in P. Hettich, A. Kachi (eds.), *Swiss Energy Governance* (Springer, 2022), pp. 67–92.

86 'EU relations: Federal Council sets out approach for negotiations', Press release of the Federal Council 25 February 2022, <https://www.eda.admin.ch/europa/en/home/aktuell/medienmitteilungen.html/content/eda/en/meta/news/2022/2/25/87349> (accessed 18 June 2022).

opinion commissioned by the Federal External Relations Department from Michael Ambühl and Daniela Scherer.[87]

In the present volume, two chapters deal with the way forward, albeit in different contexts, and these are also the final contributions in this volume.

First, the sectoral approach suggested by the Federal Council in relation to the institutional issues is discussed in the **chapter by Michael Hahn**. The author proposes to start the negotiating process with an ambitious deep and comprehensive Free Trade Agreement (a "Swiss-EU Free Trade Agreement, SEUFTA") which would also provide for the dynamic alignment with EU rules and guarantee market access for Swiss products. The author opines that a successful first package dealing comprehensively with trade in goods, and possibly services, would have a fair chance of success. With regard to dispute settlement, Michael Hahn sees a window for adapting the current EEA law to allow the EFTA Court to be the addressee of referrals for clarifying EU law provisions, as – in the author's eyes – the EFTA Court system has not only a flawless track record of ensuring parallelism with the CJEU's jurisprudence but is also under the ultimate control by the Court of Justice.

Second, the **chapter by Georges Baur** deals with the Switzerland-UK trade relations-post-Brexit. As has been noted in academic writing, the second half of the EU-Swiss negotiations on the InstA were overshadowed by the Brexit negotiations.[88] At the same time, Brexit also meant that the UK fell out of the EU-Swiss bilateral agreements. In view of the fact that the basis for mutual economic relations would cease to exist, Switzerland and the UK had, as a matter of necessity, to develop a new strategy. They decided to continue and expand the existing relations bilaterally. Switzerland developed the so-called "Mind the Gap Strategy" for this purpose. This involved transferring the previous (trade) agreements between Switzerland and the EU into the bilateral Switzerland-UK relationship in a pragmatic manner and by means of a referral technique. In a further step, the two countries are now in the process of expanding the mutual relationship to include new areas, e.g., in the area of financial services. Furthermore, the body of law taken over from the Switzerland-EU relationship is planned to be transferred into a new, modern trade agreement.

---

87 M. Ambühl, D.S. Scherer, *Alternativen im Verhandlungsprozess. Gutachten zuhanden des EDA*, 8 February 2022, <https://www.eda.admin.ch/dam/eda/de/documents/aktuell/news/2021/20211712-gutachten-ambuehl-scherer-alternativen-verhandlungsprozess_DE.pdf> (accessed 18 June 2022). See already M. Ambühl, D. Scherer, 'Schweiz – EU: Wie weiter?', *Jusletter* 2 August 2021.

88 E.g., C. Tobler, 'The EU-Swiss Sectoral Approach Under Pressure: Not Least Because of Brexit', in S. Lorenzmeier, R. Petrov and C. Vedder (eds.), *EU External Relations Law.*

Since the announcement of the Federal Council's new aims in its present policy towards the EU in February 2022, exploratory talks have been conducted between the two parties. In May 2022, it was reported in the Swiss media that the European Commission had sent a letter to the Swiss Government requesting answers to a list of specific questions concerning the institutional issues and that the EU would subsequently decide whether it is ready to start new negotiations based on Switzerland's answers.[89] According to Swiss media reports, the Swiss Secretary of State in her answer stated that Switzerland respects the EU's need to ensure "the homogeneity of the internal market" but that it also reiterated its call for "appropriate exceptions and safeguards".[90]

In June 2022, the Federal Council announced that it intends to step up the exploratory talks with the EU. According to the Federal Council's press release on this issue:

> An interim assessment of the exploratory talks between FDFA State Secretary Livia Leu and Juraj Nociar, Head of Cabinet of EU Commission Vice-President Maroš Šefčovič, concludes that the EU is largely receptive to Switzerland's package proposal. Nevertheless, the EU continues to publicly maintain its well-known positions on the institutional issues, making it difficult to find common ground between Switzerland's and the EU's interests. Their respective positions remain far apart and further clarifications are needed. Furthermore, the exploratory talks have been delayed because of the war in Ukraine; only two rounds of talks have taken place to date. The Federal Council has now decided to step up the exploratory talks with a view to possible future negotiations. If the two sides are to jointly put the bilateral approach on a surer footing for the future, the EU will have to show greater flexibility. The Federal Council will decide on a negotiating mandate once there is a sufficient

---

Shared Competences and Shared Values in Agreements Between the EU and Its Eastern Neighbourhood (Springer, 2021), pp. 107–126.

89 O. Washington, 'Schweiz-EU: Brüssel fordert schriftliche Antworten aus Bern', *radio srf*, Echo der Zeit, <https://www.srf.ch/audio/echo-der-zeit/schweiz-eu-bruessel-fordert-schriftliche-antworten-aus-bern?partId=12189423>. – It may be interesting to note the different reactions in the Swiss media, from 'Liebe Schweiz, willst Du mit mir gehen?' (<https://www.republik.ch/2022/05/17/liebe-schweiz-willst-du-mit-mir-gehen>) to 'Wie antwortet die Schweiz auf den bösen Brief aus Brüssel?' (<https://www.bernerzeitung.ch/wie-antwortet-die-schweiz-auf-den-boesen-brief-aus-bruessel-10-prognosen-180225248235>, all websites accessed 18 June 2022).

90 'Switzerland calls for 'appropriate exceptions and safeguards' in letter to EU', *swissinfo* 2 June 2022, <https://www.swissinfo.ch/eng/switzerland-calls-for--appropriate-exceptions-and-safeguards--in-letter-to-eu/47642900> (accessed 18 June 2022).

> basis for opening negotiations. [...] Switzerland is as keen as ever to find constructive and concrete solutions with the EU in order to consolidate and further develop the bilateral approach in ways that serve the interests of both sides.[91]

Overall, Switzerland at present appears to be situated firmly outside both the EU and the EEA. Though more recently both EU[92] and EEA[93] membership have been put on the table again in the Swiss political debate, the Federal Council at this point clearly wishes to stick to the system of the bilateral agreements. Observers of the recent developments might feel tempted to quote Oscar Wilde's somewhat cynical statement, according to which "the proper basis for marriage is a mutual misunderstanding". In the case of the EU-Swiss relations, there seems to be a good deal of misunderstanding or, at any rate, a lack of understanding. Whilst Switzerland (including also academic voices from the country) complains that the EU and its Member States do not fully understand the country's special needs and the implications of its particular constitutional structure,[94] the EU might feel that Switzerland does not fully understand the logic of the multilateral extended internal market and the consequences that

91 'Federal Council intends to step up exploratory talks with the EU', Press release of the Federal Council 17 June 2022, <https://www.admin.ch/gov/en/start/documentation/media-releases/media-releases-federal-council.msg-id-89322.html> (accessed 18 June 2022).

92 Reconsidering accession to the EU – at least in the longer term – has been urged by the Swiss Democratic Party; see 'SP plant den EU-Beitritt', *watson* 25 February 2022, <https://www.watson.ch/schweiz/sp/459678207-sp-plant-den-eu-beitritt>. In the shorter term, the party has presented a roadmap whose first phase would be a "stabilising agreement" with the EU on matters such as participation to EU programmes; see: Eine europapolitische Roadmap für die blockierte Schweiz, <https://www.sp-ps.ch/de/publikationen/rote-linien/eine-europapolitische-roadmap-fuer-die-blockierte-schweiz>.

93 Reconsidering joining the EEA has been suggested, e.g., by Member of the Federal Parliament, Roland Fischer, through his postulate 21.3678, Integration der Schweiz in den europäischen Binnenmarkt durch einen Beitritt zum EWR, 10 June 2021, <https://www.parlament.ch/fr/ratsbetrieb/suche-curia-vista/geschaeft?AffairId=20213678>; see also 'Nationalrat nimmt Postulat an: Der Bundesrat soll den Beitritt zum EWR erneut prüfen', *Neue Zürcher Zeitung* 8 March 2022. A motion on EEA accession was also tabled by Member of the Federal Parliament, Eric Nussbaumer, namely motion 21.4457, Aufnahme von exploratorischen Gesprächen mit dem EWR-Rat, 15 December 2021, <https://www.parlament.ch/de/ratsbetrieb/suche-curia-vista/geschaeft?AffairId=20214457> (all websites accessed 18 June 2022).

94 See, e.g., the interviews in 'Die EU versteht die Schweiz nicht', *swissinfo* 15 November 2021, <https://www.swissinfo.ch/ger/die-eu-versteht-die-schweiz-nicht/47095906> (accessed 18 June 2022).

it must have on the institutional level. Against this background, it remains to be seen how the exploratory talks between the parties will further develop and whether they will lead to new negotiations, for the mutual benefit of both.

CHAPTER 1

The Policy of Autonomous Adaptation of Swiss Law to EU Law

Matthias Oesch and Mattia Brugger

1 Introduction

Swiss law has always been influenced by foreign legal systems. With respect to EEC/EC/EU law, the following two modes of influence stand at the forefront. First, Switzerland has entered into a variety of treaties with the EEC/EC/EU which oblige it to adjust particular areas of its national law to the law of the EEC/EC/EU.[1] Following the conclusion of the Free Trade Agreement of 1972 between Switzerland and the EEC, no legislative adjustments were required. However, when the *Bilateral Agreements I* of 1999 were concluded, 23 federal laws had to be amended.[2] The implementation of the Schengen and Dublin Association Agreements of 2004 required the amendment of nine federal laws.[3] Since then, countless developments in EU law, and relevant for

1 See, for a general account of the Swiss-EU relations, S. Breitenmoser, 'Sectoral Agreements between the EC and Switzerland: Contents and Contexts', *Common Market Law Review* 40 (2003), pp. 1137–1186; C.H. Church (ed.), *Switzerland and the European Union: a close, contradictory and misunderstood relationship* (Routledge, 2012); T. Cottier, N. Diebold, I. Kölliker, R. Liechti-McKee, M. Oesch, T. Payosova and D. Wüger, *Die Rechtsbeziehungen der Schweiz und der Europäischen Union* (Stämpfli, 2014); S. Lavenex, R. Schwok, 'The Swiss way: The nature of Switzerland's relationship with the EU', in E. Eriksen, J. Fossum (eds.), *The European Union's non-members: independence under hegemony?* (Routledge, 2015), pp. 36–51; M. Maresceau, 'EU-Switzerland: Quo Vadis?', *Georgia Journal of International & Comparative Law* 2011, pp. 727–755; M. Oesch, *Schweiz – Europäische Union: Grundlagen, Bilaterale Abkommen, Autonomer Nachvollzug* (EIZ Publishing, 2020); M. Oesch, *Switzerland and the European Union: General Framework, Bilateral Agreements, Autonomous Adaptation* (Dike, 2018); R. Schwok, *Switzerland – EU: an impossible membership?* (Peter Lang, 2009); C. Tobler, J. Beglinger, *Grundzüge des bilateralen (Wirtschafts-)Rechts Schweiz-EU* (Dike, 2013). – This contribution builds, in part, on the publications written by M. Oesch mentioned *supra*.

2 Dispatch on the Approval of the Sectoral Agreements between Switzerland and the EC (*Bilaterals I*), 23 June 1999, Fed. Gaz. 1999 6128, pp. 6435–6437; T. Cottier, M. Oesch, 'Einleitung', in T. Cottier, M. Oesch (eds.), *Die sektoriellen Abkommen Schweiz-EG* (Stämpfli, 2002), p. 3.

3 Dispatch on the Approval of the Bilateral Agreements between Switzerland and the European Union, including the Acts for the Implementation of the Agreements (*Bilaterals II*), 1 October 2004, Fed. Gaz. 2004 5965, p. 6287.

© KONINKLIJKE BRILL NV, LEIDEN, 2023 | DOI:10.1163/9789004529984_003

Switzerland by virtue of the bilateral agreements, have triggered further legislative adjustments. With regard to the Schengen *acquis* alone, the EU has notified Switzerland of more than 250 developments since 2004.[4] Thus, it is evident that Switzerland has mutated into a rule-taker in the area of applying the bilateral agreements; it routinely adopts new EU legal acts. Although it can participate in the drafting of such acts (*decision-shaping*), it is not involved in the formal decision-making process. Second, Switzerland also regularly adopts EU law where there are no obligations under treaty law to do so. Swiss law is systematically aligned with EU law, in a concept which in Switzerland often is referred to as "autonomous adaptation" or, in a more colloquial manner, "euro-compatibility" or – as also used in this contribution – "EU-compatibility". A very illustrative example is the introduction of "summertime". In spring 1980, the EEC Member States (and other European States) moved the clocks one hour ahead in a concerted action for the first time. This was formalised by Directive 80/737 (Summertime Directive) in 1981, which determined a common date for the beginning of the summertime period. In 1980, however, Switzerland missed out on this joint move of switching to summertime due to a negative vote of the people in a referendum. It became a "time isle" in the middle of Europe and therefore a "special case".[5] Swiss trains started to operate on an emergency schedule to ensure connectivity with public transportation in neighboring countries. Swiss importing and exporting firms adjusted to the working hours of their counterparts in Europe. Those who commuted between Switzerland and a European country had to adapt to having different time zones for work and leisure time. This special regime remained in force for one summer. One year on, in 1981, summertime was also introduced in Switzerland. Since then, the clocks in Switzerland and those in the EU have ticked in parallel.[6] From the 1980s onwards, the minimization of economic disadvantages, factual (inter-)dependencies in other areas, and sometimes sheer convenience have led to Swiss law being systematically modelled on EU law. Hence, the "Brussels effect"[7] is also at work in Switzerland, and this to a very considerable extent.

---

4 See Federal Department of Foreign Affairs, <www.eda.admin.ch/europa/en/home/bilaterale-abkommen/ueberblick/bilaterale-abkommen-2/schengen.html> (accessed 1 February 2022).

5 G. Biaggini, *Kommentar zur Bundesverfassung der Schweizerischen Eidgenossenschaft*, 2nd ed. (Orell Füssli, 2017), para. 5 ad Article 125 (translated by authors from German).

6 Cf. Directive 2000/84/EC; Article 15 of the Federal Act on Metrology, SR 429.1.

7 The apposite term "Brussels effect" was coined by A. Bradford, 'The Brussels Effect', *Northwestern University Law Review* 2012, pp. 1–67; A. Bradford, *The Brussels Effect: How the European Union Rules the World* (OUP, 2020). When analysing the EU's global regulatory power and the externalization of its standards, Bradford uses two pairs of concepts which

This contribution deals with the policy of autonomous adaptation of Swiss law to EU law. It analyses the principle, its concept and purpose, and its relation to the comparative law method (below Section 2). It provides typical examples of this autonomous adadptation in practice and discusses the impact on the law making-techniques in Switzerland (Section 3). It discusses the "EU-compatible" interpretation of Swiss law which is considered indispensable for the practical implementation of autonomous adaptation (Section 4). It examines three special cases in which Switzerland realistically has no other choice than to align Swiss law to EU law, namely the areas of data protection law, financial market law and COVID-19 related matters (Section 5). It explains why the *Cassis de Dijon* principle, which Switzerland unilaterally introduced in 2010 for products originating in the EEA, goes beyond the classical elements of the policy of autonomous adaptation of Swiss law to EU law (Section 6). It discusses the ongoing project of autonomously reviewing Swiss legislation in the ambit of the bilateral agreements; a project initiated by the Swiss Federal Government, the Federal Council, following the termination of the negotiations with the EU regarding an Institutional Agreement in spring 2021 (Section 7). A short epilogue wraps up this paper (Section 8).

2 Policy of Autonomous Adaptation

2.1 *Concept and Purpose*

The evolution of the policy of autonomous adaptation of Swiss law to EEC/EC/EU law as a defining element of legislative activity in Switzerland began in the 1980s. It was triggered by the spectacular revival of the European integration

---

are also relevant to understand the influence EU law has on Swiss law: First, treaty-driven harmonisation vs. market-driven harmonisation; the "Brussels effect" as a form of the latter relies not on agreements but on firms' self-interest in enforcing EU regulations globally (A. Bradford [2020], p. 82 et seq.; cf. also A. Bradford [2012], p. 48). Second, "*de facto* Brussels effect" vs. "*de jure* Brussels effect"; the former describes the incentive multinational corporations have to standardise their production and adhere to a single rule thereby converting the EU's rules into a global rule; subsequently, they tend to lobby their domestic governments to adopt the same standards with the aim of levelling the playing field against their domestic competitors, resulting in the "*de jure* Brussels effect" (A. Bradford [2012], p. 6 and 8). – In Switzerland, alignment is both treaty-driven and market-driven. Switzerland's efforts to systematically align its legislation with that of the EU even where there is no obligation in this respect can be seen as a particular manifestation of the "*de jure* Brussels effect" – the main difference being that Swiss lawmakers are, in principle, aware of these interdependences; there is consensus on the necessity of legal harmonisation, which leaves lobbying with a less important role to play.

process within the framework of the EEC, which took place in the same decade. The Commission's White Paper on Completing the Internal Market of 1985, the Single European Act (SEA) of 1986 and the Cecchini Report on the Cost of Non-Europe of 1988 laid the foundations for the further development of the internal market. Likewise, the plans for the establishment of an economic and monetary union as well as for the creation of a political union became more concrete. Against this background, the Federal Council began actively working to minimise the disadvantages resulting from Switzerland remaining on the side-lines. In 1988, it published its first so-called integration report. It introduced the policy of euro-compatibility as a central pillar of Switzerland's policy towards the EEC: requiring new laws and ordinances, as well as amendments to existing laws and ordinances, to be systematically checked for their compatibility with European law as part of the administration's internal preparatory procedure. It stated that Swiss law should be brought into line with European law even where there is no express treaty obligation to do so:

> Our aim must be to ensure the greatest possible compatibility of our legislation with that of our European partners in areas of cross-border significance (and only there). [...] This striving for parallelism is not about automatically following European law, but rather about preventing the unintentional and unnecessary creation of new legal differences that hinder the generally envisaged mutual recognition of legislation at the European level.[8]

After Switzerland's accession to the EEA was rejected by a referendum in 1992, the Federal Council reaffirmed that it was "in our own interest to continue the systematic examination of the compatibility of current and future Swiss law with European law".[9] The policy of autonomous adaptation was thus elevated to a fundamental legislative maxim and a recurring theme in the Swiss legal order. Of course, deviations from European regulations and directives remain possible; there is no binding obligation to comply with these instruments under Swiss law. The policy of autonomous adaptation only requires that the

8 Report of the Federal Council of 24 August 1988 on Switzerland's Position in the European Integration Process, Fed. Gaz. 1988 III 249, p. 380 (translated by authors from German); see, for a general account of the policy of autonomous adoption, F. Maiani, 'Lost in translation: euro compatibility, legal security, and the autonomous implementation of EU law in Switzerland', *European Law Review* 2013, pp. 29–35.

9 Dispatch on the Follow-up Programme after the Rejection of the EEA Treaty, 24 February 1993, Fed. Gaz. 1993 I 805, p. 821 (translated by authors from German).

compatibility of Swiss legislation with European law be examined. However, regulatory solutions which deviate from those in the EU must be justified by cogent reasoning, and they must only be pursued where a deviation serves Swiss interests and is justifiable from a European policy point of view.[10]

The policy of autonomous adaptation has a twofold purpose:

- Through the consistent alignment of Swiss law to that of the EU, the economic disadvantages resulting from Switzerland's non-membership of the EU or the EEA are minimised, and the competitiveness of the Swiss economy is strengthened.[11]
- Making Swiss law as compatible as possible with European law lays the groundwork for Switzerland to be able to choose between all options of European integration in future, i.e., – as the Federal Council stated in 1993 – for a "possible (later) accession to the EEA or the EC without insurmountable hurdles or, if necessary, an alternative limited to bilateral agreements".[12]

The Federal Council's Explanatory Memoranda ("dispatches") serve as the basis for examining the EU-compatibility of new or amended federal laws. Article 141(1) of the Parliament Act (ParlA)[13] stipulates that the Federal Council shall submit its bills to the Federal Assembly together with an explanatory dispatch. In this dispatch, the Federal Council provides information regarding the objectives pursued by the proposed bill and justifies the method chosen to meet these objectives. Pursuant to Article 141(2)(a) ParlA, the Federal Council also "explains the relationship [of the bill] with European law", focusing on "the use of Switzerland's room for manoeuvre in adopting international law" (Article 141(2)(a^{bis}) ParlA). These explanations can be found in the so-called "Europe

10 M. Oesch, *Schweiz – Europäische Union* (n. 1), para. 333.

11 Similar rationales as those which led Switzerland to systematically align its internal laws to that of the EU also play a role when it comes to the conclusion of free trade agreements with third-party States (although this is usually not dealt with under the heading of the policy of autonomous adaptation). In fact, over the last two decades or so, Switzerland has continuously endeavoured to develop its network of free trade agreements with countries all over the globe ahead of, or at least in parallel to, that of the EU (see M. Oesch, 'Wird die handelspolitische Autonomie der EFTA-Staaten überschätzt?', *Europarecht Beiheft* 1/2020, pp. 329–355). Thus, EU law and policy not only influence Switzerland's domestic law but also the treaties it concludes. A parliamentarian request (Postulate 21.3810 "Adoption of EU law in the area of foreign economic policy", 17 June 2021) calls on the Federal Council to examine whether it would be sensible to align the rules on sustainability in such free trade agreements to those which the EU usually demands to be included in its free trade agreements with third countries.

12 Dispatch Follow-up Programme 1993 (n. 9), p. 810 (translated by authors from German).

13 SR 171.10.

chapter" of the dispatch. The Guide for the Drafting of Dispatches comments on this as follows:

> It must be explained whether the planned acts are compatible with EU law in force or in preparation (which is not binding on Switzerland) and with relevant recommendations in the area of human rights protection (Council of Europe, UN). If a bill adapts Swiss norms to better align with European law, describe the extent and scope of these adaptations. Demonstrate how Switzerland's room for manoeuvre in an autonomous adoption was exploited in the design of the new act [...]. If necessary, explain why the Swiss act differs from the European regulation. Also state whether some synergy or friction can be expected.[14]

In practice, the application of autonomous adaptation is by no means limited to cross-border issues, as was originally intended (and as is still sometimes misleadingly claimed today). It has always exceeded the traditional boundaries of foreign trade law and, in parallel with the continuously expanding EU law, covers an ever-greater number of regulatory areas, thereby causing a "spill-over effect". Nowadays, autonomous adaptation has become the norm in the Federal Government's legislative and regulatory practice. Accordingly, federal law is systematically modelled on European law. In 1998, the Federal Council stated that, with the introduction of the policy of euro-compatibility of Swiss law, a "Europe reflex" (German: "*Europareflex*") was created; new law is "in general euro-compatible, in exceptional cases not".[15] In the Europe Report of 2006, the Federal Council confirmed the policy of autonomous adaptation. At the same time, it recalled that this principle only applies "insofar as it benefits Switzerland's interests".[16]

2.2 *Relation to the Comparative Law Method*

The policy of autonomous adaptation differs from the enactment of foreign-influenced law under the comparative law method. This latter method has

14 Federal Chancellery, Guide for the Drafting of Dispatches (2020), <www.bk.admin.ch/bk/de/home/dokumentation/sprachen/hilfsmittel-textredaktion/leitfaden-fuer-botschaften-des-bundesrates.html> (available in German, French and Italian) (accessed 1 February 2022), p. 25 (translated by authors from German).

15 Response of the Federal Council to the Question 98.1032 "Swisslex II" on 13 May 1998 (translated by the authors).

16 Federal Council, Report on Europe 2006, Fed. Gaz. 2006 6815, p. 6832 (translated by authors from German); cf. also Federal Council, Report on the Evaluation of Switzerland's European Policy 2010, Fed. Gaz. 2010 7239, p. 7288.

been an essential element of the law-making process in Switzerland since the Federation's creation in 1848.[17] For example, the Constitution of 1848 was visibly inspired in part by the US Constitution as well as by the achievements of the French Revolution. The legal situation in other countries – particularly in neighbouring States and, in areas such as economic law and fundamental rights, in the United States – is often dealt with in the dispatches of the Federal Council, which accompany drafts of new acts and revisions of existing acts. Solutions which have been developed to deal with similar issues abroad are compared and critically assessed.

A characteristic feature of the comparative law method is that it does not pursue a pre-defined purpose.[18] No specific legal order is preferred or considered superior to others from the outset, on political or economic grounds, for example. In contrast, the policy of autonomous adaptation is based on a deliberate decision to align Swiss law to EU law and to avoid differences between the two. EU law is not one of several sources which might serve as inspiration for Switzerland: it is the guiding legal order, irrespective of whether or not the European solution is actually the most convincing reference point in a specific case. The process of comparing and critically assessing solutions that other legal systems have developed loses significance. The development and critical assessment of EU law are conducted in Brussels and Strasbourg where the legal orders and traditions of the 27 Member States leave their mark on the legislative process. Switzerland, in contrast, has no access to this process in fields outside the EU-Swiss agreements.

In addition to the policy of autonomous adaptation, EU law has a separate, ongoing influence on Swiss law through the traditional comparative law method. In such cases, the rationale for mitigating the negative consequences of not being a member of the EU or the EEA is irrelevant. Instead, EU law is just one of several sources of inspiration, on equal footing with other relevant bases. Dispatches of the Federal Council which accompany the law-making process frequently refer to EU law (in particular the case law of the CJEU) when fundamental rights are at issue; this is usually in the application of the

17 A. Kley, *Verfassungsgeschichte der Neuzeit*, 4th ed. (Stämpfli, 2020), p. 248; W. Haller, *The Swiss Constitution in a comparative Context*, 2nd ed. (Dike, 2016), paras. 2 and 20–21.

18 P.V. Kunz, 'Instrumente der Rechtsvergleichung in der Schweiz bei der Rechtssetzung und bei der Rechtsanwendung', *Zeitschrift für Vergleichende Rechtswissenschaft* 108 (2009), p. 34; A. Rusch, 'Methoden und Ziele der Rechtsvergleichung', *Jusletter* 13 February 2006, para. 5.

comparative law method.[19] The Swiss Federal Supreme Court also refers to EU law when it is engaged in interpreting fundamental rights.[20]

3 EU-Compatible Legislation

3.1 *Statutory Law*

The first comprehensive adaptation of Swiss law to European law took place within the framework of the so-called Swisslex Bill of 1993. Originally, it was planned that 61 federal laws would have to be adapted, as a consequence of Switzerland's planned accession to the EEA. Two extraordinary sessions of the Parliament were held in 1992 to discuss this bill, which was called Eurolex at the time. After the rejection of the EEA accession by the Swiss voters in a referendum held in December 1992, the planned adjustments to Swiss law were dropped. Nevertheless, some of these reform projects were duly resumed shortly thereafter, renamed the Swisslex Bill. Under this title, 27 legislative revisions, which were essentially intended to adapt Swiss law to EC law, were passed.[21] Since then, a large number of federal acts – designed to be compatible with EC/EU law through the means of autonomous adaptation – have been enacted or amended in various fields.[22] Clearly, autonomous adaptation

19 See, e.g., Dispatch on the Gender Equality Act, 24 February 1993, Fed. Gaz. 1993 I 1248, pp. 1286–1289; Dispatch on the Unification of Criminal Procedure Law, Fed. Gaz. 2006 1085, pp. 1121–1125.

20 See, e.g., Federal Supreme Court, decisions 123 I 152 (19 March 1997); 125 I 21 (7 October 1998) and 139 I 72 (29 June 2012).

21 Dispatch Follow-up Programme (n. 9), p. 805. – Prominent new acts and amendments to existing acts in the Swisslex Bill concerned Articles 40a-g and Article 333 of the Federal Code of Obligations (CO), SR 220; the Federal Product Liability Act, SR 221.112.944; the Federal Package Travel Act, SR 944.3, and the Federal Consumer Credit Act, SR 221.214.1. In addition to the Swisslex package, the Federal Internal Market Act, SR 943.02; the Federal Act on Technical Barriers to Trade, SR 946.51, and the Federal Act on Cartels and other Restraints of Competition, SR 251, were also enacted or, in the latter case, subject to a complete revision in the mid-1990s. These acts are all essentially based on the model rules in the EC/EU.

22 These include, *inter alia*, the Federal Act on the Free Movement of Lawyers, SR 935.61; the Federal Therapeutic Products Act, SR 812.21; the Federal Aviation Act, SR 748.0; the Federal Telecommunications Act, SR 784.11; the Federal National Bank Act, SR 951.11; the Federal Act on Merger, Demerger, Transformation and Transfer of Assets (Merger Act), SR 221.301; the Federal Value Added Tax Act, S 641.20; the Federal Product Safety Act, SR 930.11; the Federal Collective Investment Schemes Act, SR 951.31; further parts of the Federal Gene Technology Act, SR 814.91; the Federal Patent Act, SR 232.14; the Federal Copyright Act, SR 231.1.; the Federal Foodstuffs Act, SR 817.0; the Federal Data Protection Act, SR 235.1.; the

is no longer limited to the traditional area of trade in goods and to regulatory areas with cross-border effect. Nowadays, EU law permeates Swiss law in all its breadth and depth.

There are no official studies considering the extent to which Swiss law is aligned with European law in quantitative terms (i.e., as a percentage of total legislative activity) or in qualitative terms (i.e., with regard to legislation in the "key" areas). The Federal Council has refused to identify federal acts and ordinances that are enacted under the title of autonomous adaptation or to report on the percentage of such enactments in relation to overall legislative activity: "The number of pages of EU legislation that Switzerland has adopted in the last five years is not a relevant quantity. What is more important is the content and scope of the EU law that has been adopted".[23] Academic studies estimate that from 2000 to 2010, between 40% and 60% of (then) new or revised federal acts were influenced by EU law.[24] In some cases, EU law is adopted explicitly and comprehensively; in others, it plays an indirect role in the legislative process. In any case, certainly no insignificant proportion!

3.2 *Subordinate Legislation (Ordinances)*

Autonomous adaptation is not only relevant when the Swiss Federal Parliament enacts new laws and amends existing laws, but also when the Federal Council enacts new ordinances and amends existing ordinances. Insofar as Parliament deliberately legislates in an EU-compatible manner, the delegation of legislative competence contains an implicit requirement that ordinances be EU-compatible. Furthermore, in various areas, the Federal Council is explicitly obliged to take EU law in general (i.e., not necessarily specific EU legal acts) into account when enacting ordinances. This is required, for example, in the formulation of technical standards and regulations that are to be coordinated

---

Federal Financial Market Infrastructure Act, SR 958.1, and – in part – the Federal Financial Services Act, SR 950.1., and the Federal Financial Institutions Act, SR 954.1.

23 Response of the Federal Council to the Interpellation 10.3810 "Flood of laws and loss of sovereignty" on 3 December 2010 (translated by authors from German); see also the response of the Federal Council to the Postulate 06.3839 "Autonomous implementation and labelling of Swiss EU law" on 14 February 2007.

24 Response of the Federal Council to the Interpellation 10.3810 "Flood of laws and loss of sovereignty" on 3 December 2010; with reference to A. Arbia, *The Road not taken: Europeanisation of Laws in Austria and Switzerland (1996–2005)* (Geneva, 2008); E. Kohler, 'Influence du droit européen sur la législation suisse: analyse des années 2004 à 2007', *Jusletter* 31. August 2009; see also R. Gava, P. Sciarini and F. Varone, 'Twenty Years After the EEA Vote: The Europeanization of Swiss Policy-Making', *Swiss Political Science Review* 2014, pp. 197–207; S. Jenni, *Switzerland's Differentiated European Integration* (Palgrave Macmillan, 2016).

with the technical regulations of Switzerland's most important trading partners (Article 4(2) of the Federal Act on Technical Barriers to Trade, TBTA),[25] and for the protection of investors and the guarantee of the transparency and functionality of the market for collective investment schemes (Article 152(2) of the Collective Investment Schemes Act).[26]

In some cases, EU law is expressly declared to be applicable by reference. This typically occurs in ordinances. When EU regulations and directives are directly referred to, they are binding in Switzerland either in their unaltered form or, as the case may be, subject to the explicit adaptations and exceptions provided in the relevant Swiss ordinance. In general, reference is made to the version of the relevant EU legal act in force at the time of the entry into force of the Swiss ordinance (with reference to the source in the Official Journal of the EU). Exceptionally, a dynamic reference to a piece of EU legislation is made; in this case, the currently applicable version of the EU law will apply. An example of such a dynamic reference can be found in Article 133(2) of the Inland Navigation Ordinance, according to which radar equipment may be used on ships if it has a declaration of conformity from the manufacturer in accordance with Directive 2014/90 "as amended in the EU". In the context of the revision of the Federal Therapeutic Products Act (TPA) of 2019,[27] the Parliament even went one step further: Article 82(3) TPA explicitly authorises the Federal Council to refer dynamically to EU law in certain areas; not surprisingly, this provision was the subject of controversial debate in Parliament.[28]

When enacting ordinances, the Federal Council and the public authorities preparing the ordinances are obliged to check their EU compatibility (as is the case for federal acts). The guidelines for the work of the Federal Council (so-called "Red Folder") require that proposals submitted to the Federal Council must contain "a comparison of the envisaged ordinance with foreign law, in particular, that of the EU".[29] It is problematic that such proposals, as well as their justification, are not published in the Federal Gazette (Fed. Gaz.) and are therefore not readily accessible to the public.

25 SR 946.51.

26 SR 951.31.

27 SR 812.21.

28 See Official Bulletin 2019 National Council 83 et seqq.

29 Federal Chancellery, Vergleich mit EU-Recht und Prüfung der Vereinbarkeit mit EU-Recht, <www.bk.admin.ch/bk/de/home/dokumentation/begleitende-rechtssetzung/uebernahme-von-eu-recht-formale-aspekte/vergleich-mit-eu-recht-und-pruefung-der-vereinbarkeit-mit-eu-rec.html> (accessed 1 February 2022). (available in German, French and Italian).

3.3 *Legislative Technique*

When adapting Swiss law to that of the EU, complex questions of legislative technique arise. Is it expedient to assimilate to EU law by means of incorporation – either *verbatim* (i.e., by means of copy and paste) or *mutatis mutandis* (i.e., by means of separate formulation)? Or is it more appropriate to declare an EU regulation or directive applicable by reference? In contrast to the EU Member States, which are obliged by EU law to apply regulations directly and to implement directives, Switzerland is free to decide whether to incorporate regulations into Swiss law and apply directives directly in appropriate cases.[30]

In considering its approach in this context, the Parliament and the Federal Council often face conflicting concerns: they must endeavour to integrate the new acts and ordinances based on EU law into the normative system of Swiss law in the most harmonious manner possible. They must stick to the principle that all important legislative provisions should be enacted in the form of federal law (Article 164 of the Federal Constitution, FC); however, at times the need to flexibly develop Swiss law in step with the rapidly changing EU law may lead to an intuitive preference for ordinances, choosing the form of a federal act only for provisions that are manifestly important (and, if possible, to refrain from incorporation by reference).[31]

In Switzerland, there is a carefully cultivated culture of employing simple and comprehensible legal language in legislation, which should not be abandoned in the adoption of often cumbersomely formulated EU legal acts (regularly characterised by their elaborate and substantively overcharged legal definitions as well as by their lengthy annexes). Ideally, the Parliament and the Federal Council should also have the primary addressees of their laws

---

30 The Federal Chancellery has developed "Rules of Thumb" for the adoption of EU law; in this context, reference is made to the Federal Legislative Guidelines of the Federal Chancellery (<www.bk.admin.ch/apps/gtr/de/index.html>) (accessed 1 February 2022) and the Legislative Guide of the Federal Office of Justice (<www.bj.admin.ch/bj/de/home/staat/legistik/hauptinstrumente.html#>) (accessed 1 February 2022); see also B. Grüter, M. Nussbaumer, 'Redaktionelle Aspekte bei der Übernahme von EU-Recht', in F. Uhlmann, S. Höfler (eds.), *Rechtsetzung im Mehrebenensystem: Gemeinden, Kantone, Bund, EU* (DIKE, 2020), pp. 103–118; on legislative technique in Switzerland in general S. Höfler, M. Nussbaumer and F. Uhlmann, 'Legislation in Switzerland', in U. Karpen, H. Xanthaki (eds.), *Legislation in Europe: A Country by Country Guide* (Hart Publishing, 2020). – The publication of EU legal acts referred to in a Swiss ordinance is specifically regulated: They are included in the Official Compilation only with the title and the reference in the Official Journal of the EU (<www.eur-lex.europa.eu>) (Article 5(2) of the Publications Act; Dispatch Amendment to the Publications Act, 28 August 2013, Fed. Gaz. 2013 7057, p. 7078).

31 B. Grüter, M. Nussbaumer (n. 30), p. 116.

in mind when legislating: the broader and more heterogeneous the circle of addressees, the more likely it is that a different (i.e., simplified) wording will be necessary; the narrower and more specialised the circle, the more likely it will be justified to work by means of reference.[32] Unless the "incorporation by reference" method is chosen, the use of established Swiss legal terminology is generally to be preferred over the terminology used in EU law. In Switzerland, for example, the German expression *"Konzession"* is generally used instead of *"Lizenz"* (licence), *"Bewilligung"* instead of *"Genehmigung"* (authorisation), *"Motorfahrzeug"* instead of *"Kraftfahrzeug"* (motor vehicle).[33] Nevertheless, over the years, terms that were previously not in use in Switzerland have taken root in Swiss legal practice. In the German language, these include, e.g., *"Marktüberwachung"* (market surveillance), *"Inverkehrbringen"* (placing on the market) and *"Verbraucher"* (consumers). All of these terms, coined in Brussels and Strasbourg, have infiltrated Swiss law. At least it can be said that Switzerland is familiar with the pitfalls of multilingualism by virtue of its four national languages, and thus is better suited to cope with the linguistic complexities influenced by the EU's 24 equally binding official languages.

3.4 *Cantonal Level*

The policy of autonomous adaptation applies comprehensively to legislative activity at the federal level, as discussed above. In contrast, within the cantons, there are basically no explicit requirements to systematically adapt cantonal law to EU law. It would appear that an obligation to take EU law into account in the legislative process only exists in the Canton of Fribourg: according to Article 197(2)(f) of the Grand Council Act of 2006, the dispatch on a proposed law, in particular, should include information on "the constitutionality, the conformity with federal law and the EU-compatibility of the draft". In the other cantons, EU law is taken into account on a case-by-case basis if there is an interface in the relevant area, without there being any explicit obligation to do so.

32 *Ibid.*, p. 117.

33 Federal Chancellery, <www.bk.admin.ch/bk/de/home/dokumentation/begleitende-rechtssetzung/uebernahme-von-eu-recht-formale-aspekte/terminologie.html> (accessed 1 February 2022) (available in German, French and Italian). – In French, Swiss law uses *"produit phytosanitaire"* instead of *"produit phytopharmaceutique"*; in Italian, *"omologazione"* instead of *"autorizzazione all'immissione in commercio"* and *"emolumento"* instead of *"tassa"*.

4 EU-Compatible Interpretation

The policy of autonomous adaptation is not limited to legislation. Its purpose – i.e., to mitigate the economic disadvantages that result from Switzerland's non-membership in the EU or the EEA – can only be achieved if those charged with applying the law interpret EU-aligned acts and ordinances in an EU-compatible manner.[34] This is usually done as a matter of routine. Moreover, it is clear that the authorities can only choose an EU-compatible interpretation insofar as the traditional methods of interpretation, i.e., the grammatical, teleological, systematic and historical methods, allow. In a leading case in 2003, the Swiss Federal Supreme Court described the obligation to interpret the law in conformity with European law as follows:

> In case of doubt, Swiss law that has been transposed must be interpreted in conformity with European law. [...] If the Swiss legal system is harmonised with a foreign legal system – in this case the European legal system –, harmonisation must be sought not only in law-making, but also in the interpretation and application of the law, insofar as the methodology to be observed [in Switzerland] permits such harmonisation. [...] The harmonisation of the application of the law must not be based solely on the European legal situation that applied at the time of the adaptation of domestic [i.e., Swiss] law by the legislature. Rather, it must also keep in mind the further development of the law with which harmonisation was sought.[35]

What proves paramount is the Swiss Federal Supreme Court's dictum that an interpretation in conformity with EU law is only possible insofar as the relevant elements of interpretation in Switzerland permit. Should that not be possible, it is up to the Parliament or the Federal Council to revise the norm accordingly.

There are certain instances where an interpretation in conformity with EU law, although appropriate, presents a complex challenge for the administrative authorities and courts. Often, the Parliament or the Federal Council will deliberately endeavour to harmonise certain provisions of a law with that of the

34 See, in general, E. Kohler, *Le rôle du droit de l'Union européenne dans l'interprétation du droit suisse* (Stämpfli, 2015).

35 Swiss Federal Supreme Court, decision 129 III 335 (25 March 2003), cons. 6 (translated by authors from German); rightly, however, autonomously adapted acts and ordinances are not only to be interpreted in conformity with EU law "in case of doubt", but categorically; see also Federal Administrative Court, decision B-3064/2008 (13 September 2010), cons. 3.

EU, and to choose an independent solution for other provisions of the same law, thus implementing an EU legal act à la carte and creating "European law sui generis".[36] In such a case, the requirement of interpretation in conformity with European law naturally only applies to the former areas of such a law. Illustrative examples of such laws – partly modelled on EU legal acts, partly the result of deliberate deviations therefrom – are the Federal Cartel Act and the Federal Value Added Tax Act.[37]

The principle of interpreting Swiss law in conformity with EU law must not lead to a slavish orientation towards the latter, even if it is clear from the interpretation of Swiss law that the Parliament or the Federal Council intended it to be aligned with EU law. The important point remains that it is the Parliament's or Federal Council's decision to follow a European measure in order to compensate for the disadvantages of Switzerland being on Europe's side-lines. However, on occasions, Switzerland's adoption of an EU measure may not properly reflect all of the aims of the EU measure, so that an unreflective adoption of EU law and jurisprudence could lead to unintended results.[38] An example is the Federal Trademark Protection Act of 1992[39] by which Directive 89/104 on the harmonisation of trademark law was autonomously adopted: the Swiss Federal Supreme Court interpreted the provisions on the admissibility of parallel importation as allowing for the international exhaustion of that intellectual property right; by doing so, it came to a conclusion which is not in line with a (later) interpretation of the CJEU, according to which only regional or Community-wide exhaustion applies.[40]

Being able to opt for an EU-compatible interpretation depends on having detailed knowledge of the law and practice of the EU. Such knowledge is

36 E. Kramer, *Juristische Methodenlehre*, 6th ed. (Stämpfli, 2019), p. 354; cf. also T. Cottier et al. (n. 1), para. 214.

37 SR 251 and SR 641.20, respectively. See for the Cartel Act Swiss Federal Supreme Court, decisions 124 III 495 (13 November 1998), cons. 2a; 137 II 199 (11 April 2011), cons. 4.3, and 143 II 297 (28 June 2016). For a full account, see M. Sturny, *Der Einfluss des EU-Rechts auf das schweizerische Kartellrecht: Historische Entwicklung und Analyse* (Stämpfli, 2014); see for the Value Added Tax Act Swiss Federal Supreme Court, decision 124 II 193 (19 March 1998), cons. 6a; for a full account, R. Imstepf, *Der Einfluss des EU-Rechts auf das schweizerische Mehrwertsteuerrecht, unter besonderer Berücksichtigung der Europakompatibilität des Leistungsortes, der ausgenommenen Leistungen und der Steuersätze* (Stämpfli, 2011).

38 T. Cottier, D. Dzamko and E. Evtimov, 'Die europakompatible Auslegung des schweizerischen Rechts', in A. Epiney, S. Theuerkauf and F. Rivière (eds.), *Schweizerisches Jahrbuch für Europarecht* 2003 (Stämpfli/Schulthess, 2004), p. 368.

39 SR 232.11.

40 Swiss Federal Supreme Court, decision 122 III 469 (23 October 1996); CJEU, Case C-355/96, *Silhouette*, EU:C:1998:374.

fundamental considering that it is not possible for Swiss courts to request a preliminary ruling from the CJEU. Remarkably, the Swiss Federal Administrative Court suspended an ongoing case for almost ten months over the course of 2008–2009 in order to wait for a CJEU judgment on a legal question similar to the one before the Swiss court in the relevant case.[41] This demonstrates the typical pragmatism with which Swiss courts often handle EU law issues arising in their daily work. Occasionally, there is no relevant case law of the CJEU or EU Member States' courts available. In such cases, it is up to the Swiss authorities to interpret the relevant provisions in light of the interpretative methods which apply in EU law. In Switzerland, there is considerable variety with respect to the competence of judges and other public authorities to cope with EU law: at times, the authorities carefully deal with EU law and practice, while in some circumstances EU law and practice is entirely ignored. One ruling in which the Swiss Federal Supreme Court dealt with EEC/EC/EU law in an exemplary manner concerned a dispute from 2003 on the interpretation of Article 333 of the Swiss Code of Obligations, which was adapted to EU law as part of the Swisslex package. In the context of the euro-compatible interpretation of this provision, the Swiss Federal Supreme Court meticulously dealt with the interpretation of the relevant Directive 77/187, worked out the implementation and practice in selected EC Member States and analysed the revision of Directive 77/187 by Directive 98/50 and the adoption of Directive 2001/23, which eventually replaced Directive 77/187.[42]

5 Autonomous Adaptation in View of Adequacy and Equivalence Decisions

In certain circumstances, Switzerland realistically has no other choice than to align Swiss law to EU law. It is mainly economic reasons that result in Switzerland being de facto obliged to follow EU law. This is typically the case in data protection law and financial market law. In these fields, the EU grants market access to third countries only insofar as the law of such a third country is equivalent to that of the EU. Similar patterns can also be detected in the process of enacting laws aiming to combat the crisis caused by the COVID-19 pandemic.

41 Federal Administrative Court, decision B-3064/2008 (13 September 2010), referring to CJEU, Case C-482/07, *AHP Manufacturing*, EU:C:2009:501.

42 Swiss Federal Supreme Court, decision 129 III 335 (25 March 2003), cons. 6.

5.1 *Data Protection Law*

According to Article 45 of the General Data Protection Regulation (EU) 2016/679 (GDPR), any transfer of personal data to a third country must ensure that the level of protection for natural persons guaranteed by the regulation and the Charter of Fundamental Rights is not undermined. The European Commission is competent to rule that a third country ensures an adequate level of protection ("adequacy decision", Article 25 GDPR). Data transfers to a country for which such an adequacy decision exists do not require any further authorisation. The European Commission decided in 2000 that Switzerland met the adequacy test under the EU law then in force.[43] This decision was of enormous importance to the Swiss economy. Otherwise, the exchange of data with companies and customers in the EU would have been impeded. Unsurprisingly, there was a basic consensus in Switzerland that the revision of the Federal Data Protection Act of 1992[44] should also conform to EU data protection law – including the EU's balancing of sometimes conflicting fundamental rights, such as the protection of privacy, protection of personal data, freedom of opinion and information as well as economic freedom. Deviations should only be considered insofar as the adequacy of the level of protection is not jeopardised:

> Data traffic [vis-à-vis third countries] is fundamentally subject to the condition that the EU recognises Switzerland's level of data protection as adequate (adequacy decision), which is currently the case. If Switzerland wants to maintain this status, it therefore has every interest in strengthening its data protection regulations and aligning them with EU legislation, even if a literal adaptation to the draft of the EU General Data Protection Regulation is not necessary.[45]

---

43 See for the Commission's adequacy decision C(2000) 2304; see, for a general account, J. Beglinger, C. Tobler, 'Gleichwertigkeit, Angemessenheit, Äquivalenz, Adäquanz: Ein Hotspot in den Beziehungen zwischen der Schweiz und der EU im rechtlichen Kontext', in A. Epiney, P.E. Zlătescu (eds.), *Schweizerisches Jahrbuch für Europarecht* 2019/2020 (Stämpfli/Schulthess, 2020), 547–570.

44 SR 235.1.

45 Federal Office of Justice, Concept for the Revision of the Data Protection Act: Report of the Monitoring Group Revision Data Protection Act, 29 October 2014, pp. 5–6 (translated by authors from German), <www.bj.admin.ch/bj/de/home/staat/gesetzgebung/datenschutzstaerkung/berichte.html> (accessed 1 February 2022) (available in German and French); see also Dispatch Complete Revision Data Protection Act, 15 September 2017, Fed. Gaz. 2017 6941, p. 6965.

Against this background, the CJEU judgments *Schrems I* and *Schrems II* are of particular importance. In the *Schrems I* judgment of 2015, the CJEU invalidated the European Commission's decision that the United States provided an adequate level of protection for transfers of personal data under the Safe Harbor programme.[46] Subsequently, the European Commission and the United States agreed on a new framework for transatlantic data transfers, the EU-US Privacy Shield.[47] In the European Commission's view, the new Privacy Shield eliminated the deficiencies that the CJEU had identified in the Safe Harbor programme in its *Schrems I* judgment. This view was again rejected by the CJEU in the *Schrems II* judgment of 2020, which invalidated the European Commission's decision that the United States provided an adequate level of protection under the Privacy Shield.[48]

Switzerland had also concluded a Safe Harbor Agreement with the United States in 2008.[49] This agreement was largely identical in content to the Safe Harbor programme, which was the basis for the European Commission's adequacy decision of 2000. However, the CJEU *Schrems I* ruling also led to a reconsideration in Switzerland. In the aftermath of the judgment's publication, the Federal Data Protection and Information Commissioner (FDPIC) declared that he no longer considered the Safe Harbor Agreement between Switzerland and the United States to be a sufficient legal basis for the transfer of personal data to the United States, because this agreement was also "problematic from a Swiss perspective in terms of the proportionality of infringements of fundamental rights and constitutional procedural guarantees".[50] Regarding Switzerland's relationship with the EU, the FDPIC came to the following conclusion:

> Even if the invalidation of the Commission's decision on the EU Safe Harbor Framework by the CJEU does not directly affect the Swiss agreement, it will not be possible for Switzerland to take a different stance on the matter and adhere to the US-Swiss Safe Harbor Framework unchanged. In addition to the [...] risks for the fundamental rights of data subjects in Switzerland, such a course of action could also have the consequences of the EU revoking its adequacy decision on the level of

46 CJEU, Case C-362/14, *Schrems I*, EU:C:2015:650.

47 See for the Commission's adequacy decision C(2016) 4176 final.

48 CJEU, Case C-311/18, *Schrems II*, EU:C:2020:559.

49 See SR 0.235.233.6.

50 Federal Data Protection and Information Commissioner, Report and Recommendations to the Federal Council of 14 October 2015 [...] concerning the U.S. Swiss Safe Harbor Framework, p. 3 (translated by authors from German).

> data protection in Switzerland. [...] A revocation of the adequacy decision would have serious consequences for the free exchange of personal data with EU states and could lead to the isolation of Switzerland.[51]

Following negotiations between the EU and the United States, which led to the Privacy Shield being adopted, Switzerland and the United States also declared the Privacy Shield applicable to their relationship.[52] The CJEU had laid the groundwork for this in *Schrems I*, which had a precedent-setting effect radiating far beyond the EU and its Member States. Switzerland benefited from the ruling in that, without it, Switzerland would hardly have been in a position to individually persuade the United States to adopt a Privacy Shield-like solution. Further, such an act of autonomous "pre-enforcement" of rules on the transfer of data would hardly have been advisable, at least from an economic perspective. After the CJEU ruling of 2015, however, Switzerland had no other choice but to make the regulation of data transfers vis-à-vis the United States EU-compatible. In the aftermath of the CJEU *Schrems II* ruling, a similar adjustment can be expected. Compliance with the Swiss-US Privacy Shield would not be sufficient in order to maintain the European Commission's adequacy decision on the level of protection in Switzerland. Not surprisingly, the FDPIC concluded in September 2020 that "despite granting special protection rights to data subjects in Switzerland, the Privacy Shield regime does not provide an adequate level of protection for data disclosure from Switzerland to the US under the Federal Data Protection Act".[53]

The European Commission is obliged to monitor developments in third countries on an ongoing basis and to revoke adequacy decisions if necessary (Article 45(4) and (5) GDPR). According to the generally prevailing view, there is no legal obligation on the part of the European Commission to extend a positive adequacy decision under EU law, even if the third country is convinced that it has an adequate level of protection. The review of the adequacy decision in relation to Switzerland is currently pending; until this point, the EU's previous adequacy decision as regards data protection in Switzerland still stands.

---

51 *Ibid.* (translated by authors from German).

52 See Federal Data Protection and Information Commissioner, Swiss-US Privacy Shield: new framework for data transfers to the US, press release 11 January 2017.

53 Federal Data Protection and Information Commissioner, Privacy Shield CH-USA does not provide an adequate level of data protection in the view of the FDPIC, press release 8 September 2020 (translated by authors from German); see also Federal Data Protection and Information Commissioner, Opinion on the transfer of personal data to the USA and other countries without an adequate level of data protection according to Article 6(1) of the Federal Data Protection Act, 8 September 2020.

5.2 *Financial Market Law*

A similar pattern can be seen in financial market law. The EU legislature enacted several legal acts in recent years to regulate markets for financial instruments and market infrastructure. These include Regulation 648/2012 (EMIR), Regulation 600/2014 (MiFIR) and Directive 2014/65/EU (MiFID II). These legal acts aim to increase transparency, improve investor protection and strengthen competition. They empower the European Commission to adopt equivalence decisions regarding the legal framework in third countries, in order to grant market access to undertakings from these third countries. Some examples of equivalence decisions and their impact on the Swiss financial sector in practice are set out below:[54]

- Investment firms in the EU must ensure that shares are traded on an EU trading venue, with an EU systemic internaliser or on a third-country trading venue deemed equivalent by the European Commission (cf. Article 23 MiFIR, Article 25(4) MiFID II). In the case of a third-country trading venue, the Commission examines whether the rules for the activity of third-country trading venues and their supervision and enforcement are equivalent to the requirements under EU law. The Commission affirmed the equivalence of the legal and supervisory framework applicable to the two exchanges in Switzerland, Six Swiss Exchange Ltd. and bx Swiss Ltd., for 2018.[55] At the end of 2018, the Commission confirmed this decision, and it held that this decision would be valid until 30 June 2019. It announced that a further extension would depend on the progress of negotiations on an Institutional Agreement:

  > This Decision also takes into account the Council conclusions of 28 February 2017, under which a precondition for further developing the sectoral approach with Switzerland remains the establishment of a common institutional framework for existing and future agreements through which Switzerland participates in the Single Market of the Union. When deciding on whether to extend the applicability of this Decision, the Commission has taken the current state of progress towards an agreement establishing that common institutional framework into account. A full draft of the agreement has been agreed by the EU and Swiss negotiators. The Swiss Federal Council has taken note of this agreement and

---

54 See, in general, Communication from the Commission, Equivalence in the area of financial services, COM(2019) 349 final.

55 Implementing Decision (EU) 2017/2441.

has decided to open a phase of domestic consultations that will last until spring 2019.[56]

In June 2019, the Commission decided not to extend its equivalence decision again. Since then, shares of listed companies from the EU can no longer be traded on stock exchanges in Switzerland. Switzerland issued the Ordinance on the Recognition of Foreign Trading Venues for the Trading of Equity Securities of Companies with Registered Office in Switzerland. This act aims to safeguard the functioning of the Swiss stock exchange infrastructure, by requiring that equity securities (e.g., shares) of Swiss companies may only be traded on foreign trading venues where the relevant foreign financial market regulation does not include restrictive provisions that would significantly negatively affect the trading of such equity securities on Swiss trading venues.[57] The wording of the ordinance is neutral, but its aim is to introduce some form of rebalancing and to mitigate the consequences of the EU refusing to recognise the equivalence of Swiss financial market law.[58] This measure may be useful in the short term, in that "the big bang has failed to materialise".[59] In the longer term, however, Switzerland has little interest in artificially dividing and regionalising stock trading between itself and the EU. The same probably applies to the EU.

- The provision of cross-border services to eligible counterparties and professional clients in the EU by third-country firms without an on-the-ground presence is only possible if the European Commission is satisfied that the third country's financial market regulation is equivalent from a prudential perspective (Articles 46–47 MiFIR). Not surprisingly, to minimise the risk of a non-equivalence finding, Switzerland's Federal Financial Market Infrastructure Act (FinMIA) as well as – in part – the Federal Financial Services Act (FinSA) and the Federal Financial Institutions Act (FinIA)[60] are based on the EU's regulation. In the Dispatch on the FinSA and FinIA, the Federal Council made the following comments:

56 Recital 30 Implementing Decision (EU) 2018/2047. – For general accounts of the negotiations on the Institutional Agreement, the contributions by C. Kaddous and R. Schwok in this volume.

57 Federal Department of Finance, Guidance on the Ordinance on the Recognition of Foreign Trading Venues for the Trading of Equity Securities of Companies with Registered Office in Switzerland, 30 November 2018, p. 4, <www.sif.admin.ch/ordinance> (accessed 1 February 2022) (available in English).

58 *Ibid.*, p. 5.

59 *Neue Zürcher Zeitung* 9 August 2019, p. 23 (translated by authors from German).

60 SR 958.1, 950.1 and 954.1, respectively.

> The described deviations of the submitted draft laws from the European standards on financial market regulation can be attributed to a consideration of the special characteristics of the Swiss financial market. However, the proposed regulations do not, in principle, contain any provisions that go beyond the requirements of the European regulations. They do not constitute an obstacle to any equivalence recognition of Switzerland under the MiFIR Regulation.[61]

The Parliament subsequently amended the drafts in several ways and, in doing so, also introduced elements that arguably are not equivalent to the EU requirements.[62] Nevertheless, it is to be hoped that the recognition of equivalence by the European Commission has not been endangered thereby. Market access is simply too significant (even though the permissibility of providing services to retail investors – which are, in fact, economically even more significant – continues to be determined by the law of the Member States, cf. Article 39 MiFID II). Against this background, the adaptation of Swiss law to conform with EU legislation in this area proves to be *de facto* without alternative. A separate, unprejudiced examination of the central legal issues raised by the proposed Swiss legislation takes place only within the parameters set by EU law.

In a similar manner to the approach regarding data protection law, there is a common understanding in the EU that the European Commission is not obliged to initiate the process of assessing the equivalence of the legal framework of a third country, let alone to render a positive equivalence decision.[63] The decision is a unilateral, discretionary act of the EU, both with respect to its adoption and any possible amendment or repeal. As has been the case for the equivalence decision concerning Swiss stock exchanges, political factors can play an important role in the process.

---

61 Dispatch on the FinSA and FinIA, 4 November 2015, Fed. Gaz. 2015 8901, pp. 8939–8940 (translated by authors from German); cf. also Dispatch on the FinIA, 3 September 2014, Fed. Gaz. 2014 7483, pp. 7509–7512.

62 See T. Jutzi, K. Wess and D. Sieradzk, 'Die neue Finanzmarktarchitektur im europäischen Regulierungskontext', *Aktuelle Juristische Praxis* 2020, 572–592; R. Sethe, 'MiFIR/MiFID II – Drittstaatenzugang für die Schweiz und Äquivalenz von FINIG/ FIDLEG', in Gericke (ed.), *Private Equity VI* (Schulthess, 2018), pp. 135–169.

63 It might be argued, however, that the GATS (Articles II and VII, Annex on Financial Services) sets certain limits to the allegedly unlimited discretion to refuse to adopt equivalence decisions. Insofar as the European Commission adopts an equivalence decision to the benefit of one country, others might arguably demand the same treatment if they can demonstrate that they fulfil the necessary requirements.

In 2019, not least against the background of the negotiations on the EU's future relations with the United Kingdom, the European Commission presented a reassessment of its approach to determining the equivalence of regulatory systems in the area of financial services.[64] In this publication, the Commission expressly set out that it considers the "general political context" of a third country when assessing equivalence. The instrument of the equivalence decision has thus mutated into an instrument through which the EU's political interests vis-à-vis third countries can be pursued; interests which bear no or, at the most, only marginal relation to financial services law. The dismal saga of the Commission's stock exchange equivalence refusal decision regarding Switzerland could therefore feasibly be repeated in other areas of financial market law and beyond.

5.3 *COVID-19: Personal Protective Equipment and Digital Certificates*

In early 2020, in the fight against the epidemiological crisis caused by COVID-19, the European Commission made the exportation of certain items of medical protective equipment subject to a specific export authorisation.[65] The affected items were products that were "necessary to prevent the further spreading of the disease, and safeguard the health of medical staff treating infected patients".[66] Exports to the EEA EFTA States, the overseas countries and territories listed in Annex II TFEU, the Faroe Islands, Andorra and San Marino, the Vatican City and Switzerland were exempted from the authorisation requirement, albeit after one week where the restriction did apply to Switzerland and the other abovementioned countries.[67] In return for the granting of this exemption, the European Commission required these countries and territories to impose adequate controls on the export of these items, without specifically setting out any criterion for adequacy:

> The authorities of the excluded countries and territories should offer adequate guarantees that they will control their own exports of the products concerned, so as to avoid undermining the objective pursued by Implementing Regulation (EU) 2020/402. The Commission should closely monitor this aspect.[68]

---

64 Communication from the Commission, Equivalence in the area of financial services, COM(2019) 349 final.

65 Implementing Regulation (EU) 2020/402. – See also the contribution by C. Tobler in this volume.

66 Recital 2 Implementing Regulation (EU) 2020/402.

67 Implementing Regulation (EU) 2020/426.

68 Recital 4 Implementing Regulation (EU) 2020/426.

Subsequently, Switzerland introduced an export licence for the products covered by the EU regulation, with the exception of exports to the EU and the other countries and territories that the EU had exempted from the licensing requirement "insofar as reciprocity is guaranteed" (Article 10d COVID-19 Ordinance 2). The Federal Council pursued a twofold objective in introducing this export licence: first, it was a matter of ensuring that its own medical personnel and other persons in Switzerland continued to have access to such protective equipment. Second, it wanted to ensure that trade in these products between the EU and Switzerland was not jeopardised; in this case – in contrast to data protection law and financial market law – the focus was not on the economy, but on public health and crisis prevention.

In 2021, as vaccines against COVID-19 became increasingly available to the population, a similar pattern of events occurred. In the hope that the measures against the spreading of the virus would soon be relaxed, many European countries developed certificates for vaccinated, recovered or negative-tested people. The EU adopted Regulation (EU) 2021/953 which "sets out a common framework for the issuance, verification and acceptance of interoperable certificates for COVID-19 vaccination, test or recovery certificates to facilitate free movement of EU citizens and their family members during the COVID-19 pandemic".[69] Pursuant to Article 3(10) of this regulation, the Commission can adopt implementing acts establishing that COVID-19 Certificates issued by a third country with which the EU and its Member States concluded an agreement on the free movement of persons (and which does not contain a mechanism of incorporation of EU legal acts) are equivalent to those issued under the Regulation. It is obvious that this provision has been set up with Switzerland in mind.[70] Besides equivalence, reciprocity is a key requirement for approval under Article 3(10) of this regulation. In July 2021, the Commission officially recognised the Swiss COVID-19 Certificate as equivalent.[71] For its part, Switzerland recognised the COVID-19 Certificates issued by EU and EFTA Member States.[72] This laid the necessary foundation for cross-border travel for work and leisure – a welcome and long-awaited outcome.

69 European Commission, Report from the Commission to the European Parliament and the Council pursuant to Article 16(1) of Regulation (EU) 2021/953, COM(2021) 649 final, p. 1.

70 Cf. *ibid.*, p. 5.

71 Commission Implementing Decision (EU) 2021/1126 of 8 July 2021.

72 Federal Office of Public Health, EU recognises Swiss COVID certificate, press release 9 July 2021. – See also the contribution by C. Tobler in this volume.

6 *Cassis de Dijon* Principle

In 2010, the policy of autonomous adaptation of Swiss law to EU law took on a new dimension. Switzerland introduced the *Cassis de Dijon* principle applicable to products originating in the EU/EEA. Importantly, Switzerland took this step unilaterally by amending the Federal Act on Technical Barriers to Trade (Articles 16*a*-16*e* TBTA). By virtue of this amendment, products which are lawfully placed on the market in the EEA – i.e., products which comply with EU/EEA technical regulations and standards (harmonised area) or with the technical regulations and standards of an EU Member State or an EEA EFTA State (non-harmonised area) – can now be marketed and sold in Switzerland. This can be the case even where the relevant Swiss technical regulations and standards are not met. The only further requirement is that products must be labelled in one of the official languages: German, French or Italian. A special regulation applies to foodstuffs: foodstuffs that have been legally placed on the market in the EEA but which do not comply with the provisions of Swiss foodstuffs legislation require a special authorisation for distribution in Switzerland (Article 16c and Article 16d TBTA). This authorisation is granted in the form of a general ruling. For example, ham from Italy (*prosciutto cotto*) with a higher water content than that allowed in Swiss law and cider from Denmark with less fruit juice than that required by Swiss law can be lawfully imported and sold in Switzerland as a general ruling in such products' favour has been granted.[73]

The *Cassis de Dijon* principle, as unilaterally introduced by Switzerland, differs from the classic *Cassis de Dijon* principle well-known in EU common market law. These are systemic deviations resulting from the fact that Switzerland is not institutionally integrated into the EU or the EEA. The main differences, transforming *Cassis de Dijon* to "*Cassis de Berne*",[74] are as follows:

---

73 See, for an overview of the general authorisations granted, <www.blv.admin.ch/blv/en/home/import-und-export/rechts-und-vollzugsgrundlagen/cassis-de-dijon/gesuche.html> (accessed 1 February 2022) (available in English). – A simplification of the authorisation procedure for foodstuffs and the introduction of a notification procedure is being planned (Directorate for European Affairs, Cassis de Dijon principle for foodstuffs will be strengthened, media release 23 July 2019). However, the revision of the food legislation of 2017 and the associated further adaptation of Swiss law to that of the EU in this area led to the importance of the Cassis de Dijon principle under the TBTA diminishing.

74 T. Cottier, D. Herren, 'Das Äquivalenzprinzip im schweizerischen Aussenwirtschaftsrecht: von Cassis de Dijon zu Cassis de Berne', in A. Epiney, N. Gammenthaler (eds.), *Schweizerisches Jahrbuch für Europarecht* 2009/2010 (Stämpfli/Schulthess, 2010), p. 275; cf., for an initial (and positive) assessment of the effects of the Cassis de Dijon principle in Switzerland, State Secretariat for Economic Affairs, Bericht des SECO zu den Auswirkungen der Revision des Bundesgesetzes über die technischen Handelshemmnisse

- Privileged market access is only granted unilaterally, namely to products imported into Switzerland from the EU/EEA. Swiss products do not profit from increased market access upon their exportation to the EU/EEA. In order for Swiss products to profit in this way, the EU would need to introduce the principle unilaterally vis-à-vis Switzerland; this does not seem likely. Alternatively, Switzerland and the EU could negotiate an agreement to this effect, for instance by revising the Free Trade Agreement of 1972 or by introducing the principle into the planned upcoming agreement covering the areas of agriculture, food safety, product safety and public health.[75] However, the status of this future agreement is currently uncertain, as the EU has made its conclusion dependent on the conclusion of an Institutional Agreement.
- The Swiss version of the principle applies to products which conform to EU/EEA regulations and standards (harmonised area) and to products which conform to the regulations and standards of a Member State (non-harmonised area). Conversely, the *Cassis de Dijon* principle in the EU, as a matter of logic, only applies to products which conform to the regulations and standards of a Member State.
- Switzerland unilaterally defines exceptions to the principle. The Parliament and the Federal Council introduced three major exceptions. First, the principle does not apply to products that are subject to an authorisation or notification requirement (e.g., medicinal products). Second, it does not apply to products against which an import ban exists (such as certain munitions and products from a country against which sanctions apply). Third, the Federal Council has defined exceptions in an ordinance, among them being chemical products, alcopops (which do not provide information on the alcohol content) and eggs from hens that live in battery cage, a practice prohibited in Switzerland.[76] The CJEU, which ultimately decides whether such exceptions introduced by EU Member States pursue a legitimate public interest

---

(Einführung des «Cassis de Dijon»-Prinzips in der Schweiz), April 2013, <www.newsd.admin.ch/newsd/message/attachments/30420.pdf> (accessed 1 February 2022) (available in German).

75 The Swiss Federal Supreme Court held that the prohibition of measures having equivalent effect as quantitative restrictions pursuant to Article 13 of the Free Trade Agreement of 1972 does not encompass the principle of mutual recognition of product requirements, i.e., the Cassis de Dijon principle (decision 2A.593/2005 [6 September 2006]). – On a new Swiss-EU FTA, see the contribution by M. Hahn in this volume.

76 See Ordinance on the Placing on the Market of Products Manufactured in Accordance with Foreign Technical Regulations and on their Monitoring on the Market, SR 946.513.8.

and are proportionate (i.e., whether such exceptions are EU-law compliant) has no say as to the legality of exceptions provided for in Switzerland.

The application of the *Cassis de Dijon* principle to products from the EU/EEA in Switzerland may result in reverse discrimination against domestic producers vis-à-vis their European counterparts. To prevent such an effect, a specific provision has been introduced into the Federal Act on Technical Barriers to Trade (Article 16*b* TBTA) allowing domestic producers to tailor their compliance to the regulations and standards of the EU/EEA or their Member States. In essence, producers in Switzerland can choose which regulations and standards – Swiss or European – are to apply with respect to their products.

Regarding the methodology and the content, the unilateral introduction of the *Cassis de Dijon* principle in Switzerland goes beyond the classical elements of the policy of autonomous adaptation of Swiss law to EU law. The principle has a prospective effect. It encompasses future developments in the EU/EEA and their Member States. This surpasses the traditional mode of integration, according to which EU law finds its way into the Swiss legal order statically, i.e., as valid on a specified day. With respect to trade in goods and the removal of non-tariff barriers to trade, the level of integration is now remarkably high.

7 A New Chapter: Stabilex

In 2021, the Federal Council precipitated a new chapter of autonomous adaptation with its abrupt termination of the negotiations on an Institutional Agreement. Since 2008, the EU has been vocal in its criticism that "the present system of bilateral agreements [...] has become complex and unwieldy to manage and has clearly reached its limits".[77] It has asked for Switzerland's cooperation in concluding an Institutional Agreement so as to ensure the necessary homogeneity in the application and further development of the agreements.[78] Switzerland and the EU entered into negotiations in 2014. In 2018, the EU declared the most current draft to be the final text, expecting the Federal Council to sign it and pass it to the Federal Assembly for approval. It reiterated that the conclusion of the Institutional Agreement was a prerequisite for any update to the existing agreements (unless such updates are in the interest of the EU) or the conclusion of new agreements regarding Switzerland's

77 Council of the European Union, Council conclusions on EU relations with EFTA countries, 14 December 2010, para. 48.

78 See for a detailed description of the negotiations and the institutional agreement, M. Oesch, *Schweiz – Europäische Union* (n. 1), para. 101 et seq.

participation in the internal market.[79] However, in spring 2021, the Federal Council concluded that substantial differences remained between Switzerland and the EU in key areas of the draft text. Consequently, it informed the EU of its decision not to sign the text and to terminate negotiations. At the same time, the Federal Council announced three – rather desperate – measures in an attempt to mitigate the negative consequences of terminating negotiations. In summary, Switzerland (i) confirmed its willingness to pursue and further develop the bilateral approach; (ii) set out its intention to establish a political dialogue for a common agenda, including releasing its previously blocked financial contribution to Member States in Eastern Europe (informally called the "cohesion billion");[80] and (iii) confirmed that Swiss legislation implementing the bilateral agreements would be reviewed for potential inconsistencies with EU law, and that such inconsistencies would be eliminated where appropriate, in order to stabilise the bilateral relations.[81]

The last measure – which was initially named "Stabilex", although this was quickly dropped when the Federal Administration realised this was the name of a commercial cleaning product for drinking-water tanks[82] – concerns the EU-compatibility of Swiss law. The Federal Council ordered the administration to analyse any differences between Swiss and EU law in the areas affected by the bilateral agreements and to examine "where autonomous adaptation is possible and sensible in order to reduce areas of friction and thus also contribute to stabilising the relationship with the EU".[83] Thus, the Federal Council's intention is to use autonomous adaptation to limit the scope for criticism from Brussels as well as to prove that it is still willing to continue the bilateral approach by adhering to the EU's internal market rules, even without the envisaged institutional framework, at least where this is "possible and sensible". Without any doubt, such an endeavour is helpful. At the same time, however, Stabilex has arisen at an odd moment. It is remarkable that the Federal Council considers the aftermath of the termination of negotiations as the pertinent moment for comprehensively examining the legislative differences between Switzerland and the EU. One would rather have assumed that such

79 Council of the European Union, Council conclusions on EU relations with the Swiss Confederation, press release 19 February 2019, para. 9.

80 On this issue, see the contribution by B. Pirker in this volume.

81 Federal Council, No signing of Swiss–EU institutional agreement, press release 26 May 2021.

82 *Neue Zürcher Zeitung* 1 July 2021, p. 7.

83 Federal Council, Prüfauftrag zum autonomen Abbau von Regelungsunterschieden zwischen dem Schweizer und dem EU-Recht, Fact Sheet of 26 May 2021 (translated by authors from German); cf. also Federal Council (n. 81).

an analysis had been ongoing throughout negotiations, to allow Switzerland to be properly informed as to the most contentious issues, such as the use of measures to protect wages in Switzerland, the Citizens' Rights Directive and the rules on State aid. Knowledge of the basic differences in interpreting and applying the bilateral agreements would have been fundamental to allow the proper impact-assessment of the rules on dynamic adoption of new EU acts. Such knowledge would also have been key if either party was considering invoking an arbitration panel in order to settle any conflict, as provided for in the draft Institutional Agreement.

Stabilex endeavours to shed light on differences between Swiss law and EU law in areas affected by the bilateral agreements. Systemically, there are two possible reasons for such differences:

- Differences can arise from diverging interpretations of a bilateral agreement by each party. For example, an ongoing prime point of debate has been the "8 days rule", according to which foreign service providers must notify the Swiss authorities of the provision of a service in Switzerland eight days in advance (Article 6(3) of the Posted Workers Act). The EU argues that this period is both unnecessary and discriminatory, and is thus inconsistent with the Agreement on the Free Movement of Persons (AFMP).[84] Switzerland counters that prior notification is necessary in order to organise and ensure on-site monitoring of compliance with the accompanying measures which service providers must meet.[85] Not surprisingly, this was one of the core disagreements between Switzerland and the EU during the negotiations on the Institutional Agreement.[86] Another example is the EU's and Switzerland's probable disagreement over the consistency of a Swiss rule on the medical profession with the AFMP. In Switzerland, in order for a medical practitioner to be authorised to work at the expense of the compulsory health care insurance, he or she must have worked for at least three years at a recognised training institution in Switzerland in the speciality for which health insurance accreditation is requested (Article 37(1) of the Health Insurance Act).[87] The EU might consider this requirement as indirectly discriminatory

84 European Parliament, Resolution of 7 September 2010 on EEA-Switzerland, para. 12; Council of the European Union, Council conclusions of 20 December 2012 on EU relations with EFTA countries, para. 35; see, for a general account, the contribution by K. Pärli in this volume.

85 See for a legal analysis of this argument A. Epiney, L. Hehemann, 'Die Tragweite des Institutionellen Abkommens im Bereich der Arbeitnehmerentsendung', *Jusletter* 8 April 2019, para. 35.

86 Cf. M. Oesch, *Schweiz – Europäische Union* (n. 1), para. 117.

87 See, for the genesis and a preliminary legal analysis of this provision, C. Bissegger, J. Theubet, 'Autorisation du médecin de pratiquer à charge de l'AOS, Examen de la

pursuant to Article 2 AFMP and as inconsistent with Article 55 of Directive 2005/36.[88] Switzerland, however, considers this measure to be necessary to ascertain patient safety and the familiarity of practitioners with the Swiss healthcare system.[89] As a final example, Switzerland and the EU disagree over the interpretation and application of the rules on State aid pursuant to Article 23 of the Free Trade Agreement of 1972 (FTA). The EEC declared in an annex to the FTA that "in the context of the autonomous implementation of Article 23(1) of the Agreement [...], it will assess any practices contrary to that Article on the basis of criteria arising from the application of the rules of Articles 85, 86, 90 and 92 of the Treaty establishing the European Economic Community" (Articles 101, 102, 106 and 107 TFEU). The EU referred to this declaration when it argued that the tax regimes of certain cantons were not compatible with Article 23 FTA; a dispute known as "tax dispute" which was only resolved when Switzerland agreed to revise its laws in accordance with the EU's demands.[90] Aside from this individual and specific dispute, Switzerland has never adopted the EU's reading of interpreting and applying Article 23 FTA based on the rules and practices in the EEC/EC/EU; rather, it has interpreted these rules autonomously, in a less internal market-oriented manner.

- Differences can occur when a new EU legal act that technically falls into the ambit of a bilateral agreement has not yet been included within that very agreement. For example, in the field of the recognition of professional qualifications, the system within the EU has further evolved since the last revision of Directive 2005/36 was duly incorporated into Annex III AFMP.[91] New revisions, brought into force in the EU by Directive 2013/55 and Commission

conformité du futur art. 37 LAMal avec le droit Communautaire', *Jusletter* 8. November 2021. – Until recently, fulfilling a similar requirement (i.e., having worked for at least three years at a recognised training institution in Switzerland) exempted the practitioner from the general obligation of proving a public need for his or her services at the expense of the compulsory health care insurance (former Article 55a(2) of the Federal Health Insurance Act, SR 832.10; see for the interpretation of this provision as being consistent with the AFMP, Federal Administrative Court, decision C-4852/2015 (8 March 2018), cons. 9.6; cf. also Article 37(2) of the Federal Health Insurance Act).

88 See C. Bissegger, J. Theubet (n. 87), para. 10 et seq.; in general, Council of the European Union (n. 79), para. 13.

89 See Official Bulletin 2018 National Council 2161 et seq. – It should be noted that the Federal Council expressed doubts about the conformity of this rule with the AFMP during the parliamentary debates (Official Bulletin 2019 Council of States 250).

90 M. Oesch, *Switzerland and the European Union* (n. 1), para. 224.

91 Cf. for the long and complicated process of introducing this directive into Annex III AFMP, M. Oesch, *Switzerland and the European Union* (n. 1), para. 88.

Implementing Regulation (EU) 2015/983, have not yet made their way into the bilateral *acquis*. Consequently, Switzerland lacks, *inter alia*, access to the Internal Market Information System (IMI) used for digitised administrative cooperation and, notably, the alert mechanism whereby restrictions and prohibitions regarding certain medical and educational professionals are flagged, e.g., after such a person's criminal conviction.[92] Furthermore, both the revision of the Posted Workers Directive 96/71 by Directive 2018/957 and the corresponding Enforcement Directive 2014/67 have not yet been included in the AFMP via the agreement of the parties. The same applies to the incorporation of the Citizens' Rights Directive 2004/38: Switzerland has consistently refused to enter into negotiations on the incorporation of this directive into the bilateral *acquis*. It argues that its adoption would result in additional rights with respect to social security and family reunification which exceed the agreed scope of the AFMP.[93] Lastly, in 2020, the Swiss Parliament instructed the Federal Council to "exclude traditional model airplanes from the adoption of Commission Implementing Regulation 2019/947 and to apply national law" as it deems it unnecessary to set up new rules on the operation of unmanned aircrafts in this field of leisure activity.[94] Remarkably, Switzerland took this position despite having played an active role in the drafting of the Regulation (*decision-shaping*).[95]

Stabilex might well lead to the detection of aspects of Swiss law which are not yet EU-compatible, putting at risk the good functioning of the bilateral *acquis*.[96] However, it is not readily apparent, at least to outsiders, what new insights the Federal Council hopes to gain from this exercise. Those legal differences which have already constituted the most contentious issues between Switzerland and the EU are also likely to be at the top of the list identified through Stabilex. It is also unclear whether Switzerland will be prepared to

92 Cf. Article 56a Directive 2005/36/EC; State Secretariate for Education, Research and Innovation, SBFI NEWS 8/18, <www.sbfi.admin.ch/dam/sbfi/en/dokumente/2019/07/richtlinie-2013-55-eu.pdf.download.pdf/sbfi-news_e.pdf> (accessed 1 February 2022) (in English).

93 Federal Council, Bericht betreffend die Verhandlungen über ein institutionelles Abkommen zwischen der Schweiz und der EU, 26 May 2021, p. 11. – See the contribution by P. Melin in this volume.

94 See Motion 20.3916 "Ausnahme des Modellflugs von der EU-Drohnenregelung", 30 June 2020 (translated by authors from German).

95 Federal Office of Civil Aviation, EU drone regulation in Switzerland, <www.bazl.admin.ch/bazl/en/home/good-to-know/drones-and-aircraft-models/Europaeische_Drohnenregulierung_uebernommen.html> (accessed 1 February 2022) (in English).

96 The Federal Council has announced to present preliminary results in the first half of 2022.

make adjustments to its (EU-inconsistent) internal laws after categorically rejecting the idea of making such amendments during the negotiations on the Institutional Agreement. Of course, it can be argued that it is more attractive for Switzerland to make adjustments autonomously, without a legal commitment to do so vis-à-vis the EU: with this approach, Switzerland would still be in a position to revise any autonomously adapted law again or to introduce specific exceptions at any time, thus renouncing EU-compatibility without breaching bilateral obligations or facing rebalancing measures from the EU. Moreover, every legal difference can be assessed individually under this method, independently from an envisaged package deal with the EU and the latter's red lines. Where the reason for a difference is not political but rather technical, Stabilex also presents a welcome opportunity for the administration to accelerate its efforts to catch up with developments in the EU. However, despite these opportunities, inevitably Stabilex will also clearly reveal the limits of the policy of autonomous adaptation. In many instances, Switzerland depends on the EU's cooperation. A telling example is Switzerland's current lack of participation in the EU's Internal Market Information System (IMI); this system not only tracks persons who are subject to an occupational ban in an EU Member State, but also improves administrative cooperation and mutual assistance in protecting posted workers abroad. To obtain access to the IMI database in future, Switzerland is dependent on the EU deciding to revise the AFMP to include the pertinent directives. Unilateral action by Switzerland alone is simply not an option here.

Overall, it seems doubtful that Stabilex is actually capable of contributing to an improved relationship between the EU and Switzerland – a relationship that has been considerably deteriorating since the termination of the Institutional Agreement negotiations. It is clear that Stabilex is not an effective tool to overcome the limitations inherent in the policy of autonomous adaptation; it is not an *ersatz* for the agreement on a new institutional framework. Therefore, Stabilex is but a new chapter under this title, a concerted one-time effort to systematically assess opportunities for better EU-compatible legislation in Switzerland; not only, as before, in those areas which are unaffected by the bilateral agreements but now also in those areas covered by the bilateral agreements.

8 Epilogue

The policy of autonomous adaptation has led to the systematic alignment of Swiss law to EU law. In 1998, the Federal Council noted that the introduction of this policy had resulted in a "Europe reflex"; new law is "in general euro-compatible, in exceptional cases not".[97] It is standard procedure for the federal offices which prepare new acts and ordinances to inform the Parliament and the Federal Council on the relationship between the draft Swiss law provisions and EU law. The experts in these offices possess profound knowledge of the pertinent EU regulations and directives; it is a walk in the park for them to draft new laws in an EU-compatible way. Thereafter, the Parliament and the Federal Council usually opt for the EU-compatible solution.

Generally speaking, such EU-compatible adjustments do not give rise to controversy. They are made routinely and fly under the radar of the wider public. This is paradigmatically the case with the adoption of technical regulations – the original trigger for the creation of the policy of autonomous adaptation, and its main area of application. The creation of such technical regulations can safely be left to the specialists in the EU, as long as they concern technical details rather than being fundamentally political in some manner. The EU sets the pace; Switzerland follows behind. In this context, the process of autonomously aligning Swiss law to EU law is unproblematic in terms of democratic theory. However, when it comes to politically controversial questions raised by a certain EU measure – questions which the Swiss legislature is best placed to debate and answer itself – it is problematic if there is only a *pro forma* consideration of the merits of a measure, with the alignment with EU law occurring quasi-automatically. The policy of autonomous adaptation must not lead to fundamental political decisions for Switzerland being made in Brussels and Strasbourg. Against this background, it is all the more important that the process of aligning Swiss law to EU law is conducted deliberately and transparently. The authorities should identify the advantages and disadvantages of a certain adaptation and consider alternatives. The Parliament and the Federal Council are responsible for critically reflecting on the preliminary work conducted within the administration. Further, there should be no hesitation to choose an autonomous solution where this is more suitable in the circumstances.

Still, a certain unease remains. The policy of autonomous adaptation results in a substantial part of the law-making process in Switzerland being *de facto* delegated to the EU legislature, whose acts are then also duly implemented in Switzerland. This is problematic. Switzerland has downgraded itself, so to speak, to a passive receptor of EU law, with no opportunity to actively shape the decision-making process in Brussels and Strasbourg. In the end, however,

97 See *supra* section 2.1.

there is arguably no other choice but to accept this state of affairs. It seems to be an inevitable consequence of Switzerland's sectoral integration into the EU legal order as a quasi-Member State: benefitting from the double strategy of having concluded a tight network of *Bilateral Agreements* and of adopting EU law autonomously, whilst remaining unwilling to become a fully-fledged member with all the associated participatory rights and obligations. The associated democratic deficit and the lack of legal certainty (e.g., due to the ambiguity over whether a specific provision is rooted in EU law and is, consequently, to be interpreted accordingly) are just part of the price to be paid for Switzerland's privileged access to the internal market as a third country. Switzerland has chosen this arrangement of its own accord; moreover, it can cancel the same at any time, should it so wish.

Overall, the Federal Council's termination of the negotiations on an Institutional Agreement – from the EU's position, a prerequisite for the continuation and expansion of the tight treaty network with Switzerland – necessarily raises the question as to whether the Swiss model of European integration can still truly be regarded as the "*Königsweg*"[98] (the King's Road). Indeed, the potential result is an erosion of the bilateral legal framework, a prospect neither in the interest of the EU nor in the interest of Switzerland. Since the Swiss approach of cherry-picking seems difficult to maintain and Stabilex is not an effective tool for overcoming the limitations inherent in the policy of autonomous adaptation, the termination of the negotiations on an Institutional Agreement also presents an opportunity to consider potentially more effective methods of safeguarding Switzerland's interests in Europe. Political common sense and foresight – *gouverner, c'est prévoir* – call for all policy options vis-à-vis the EU to be assessed, including the prospect of opting for full EU membership. Even though unlikely in the current political climate, this would entail moving from the policy of simply reproducing developments in EU law, as a rule-taker, towards a more constructive approach and the assumption of (co-) responsibility for policy making on the European level.

98 Cf. D. Freiburghaus, *Königsweg oder Sackgasse? Schweizerische Europapolitik von 1945 bis heute*, 2nd ed. (NZZ Libro, 2015).

CHAPTER 2

The Agreement on the Free Movement of Persons

From the (Almost) Complete Integration of EU acquis *on Social Security Coordination to the Absence of Integration of Directive 2004/38*

*Pauline Melin**

1 Introduction

The Agreement on the free movement of persons[1] (*AFMP*) is a particularly important element in the bits and pieces of legal integration between the EU and Switzerland. It plays a central role in the package of the so-called *Bilaterals I*[2] by providing tailor-made and partial access to the internal market[3] in the field of persons and services. However, the way the AFMP is perceived by the contracting parties is very heterogeneous. On the one hand, the EU considers the free movement of persons to be a fundamental pillar of EU policy and an indivisible part of the internal market.[4] Therefore, the EU insisted on tying the AFMP to the other agreements of the *Bilaterals I* package

* The author would like to express her deep gratitude for the editors' comments and editing work. In addition, the author would like to thank Prof. Andrea Ott for her comments on an earlier draft. All errors or omissions remain the author's responsibility.

1 Agreement between the European Community and its Member States, of the one part, and the Swiss Confederation, of the other, on the free movement of persons (OJ 2002, L 114/6, as amended).

2 The *Bilaterals I* are in fact seven sectoral agreements signed in 1999 on the free movement of persons (AFMP), technical trade barriers, public procurement, agriculture, air transport, land transport (road and rail) and research (though in this last field, there is at present no longer an agreement).

3 Indeed, Switzerland does not participate in the internal market in a manner comparable to the EEA countries for instance; see S. Jenni, *Switzerland's Sectoral Access to the EU's Single Market*, EFTA Studies 8 February 2019, <https://www.liechtenstein-institut.li/application/files/2615/7435/7867/Swiss_EU_Sectoral_Access.pdf> (accessed 1 June 2022). Tobler emphasises the merely *partial* association to the internal market; C. Tobler, 'The EU-Swiss Sectoral Approach Under Pressure: Not Least Because of Brexit', in S. Lorenzmeier, R. Petrov and C. Vedder (eds.), *EU External Relations Law. Shared Competences and Shared Values in Agreements Between the EU and Its Eastern Neighbourhood* (Springer, 2021), p. 108.

4 Council conclusions on a homogeneous extended single market and EU relations with Non-EU Western European countries, Brussels, 16 December 2014, <https://www.consilium.europa.eu/uedocs/cms_data/docs/pressdata/EN/er/146315.pdf> (accessed 1 June 2022), para. 45.

© KONINKLIJKE BRILL NV, LEIDEN, 2023 | DOI:10.1163/9789004529984_004

through the so-called "guillotine clause",[5] in order to ensure that the AFMP in particular could not be too easily rejected by Switzerland, for example in a popular vote.[6] On the other hand, in Switzerland, the free movement of persons regime with the EU Member States remains a contentious issue, stirring up regular political debate and being continuously challenged by almost all Swiss political parties.[7] Considering these differences, it might be argued that the EU-Swiss relationship is based on a grand delusion of a common integration aim and that friction is visible, precisely in the AFMP. That political friction crystallised in the failure of the draft Institutional Agreement (InstA) due to, *inter alia*, the question of the integration of the most important EU *acquis* on the free movement of persons, the EU Citizens' Rights Directive 2004/38.[8]

The purpose of this chapter is to reflect on why the AFMP continues to be an important, yet controversial and politically sensitive piece of integration for the EU-Swiss relations. In Section 2, the political and legal framework of the AFMP will be discussed. The particularities of its institutional structure and content will be highlighted as potential explanations for the constant political frictions around the AFMP. Thereafter, two very different examples of integration of the EU *acquis* in relation to the free movement of persons between Switzerland and the EU after the signature of the AFMP will be provided. In Section 3, the (almost) complete integration of the EU social security coordination rules in the EU-Swiss relations will be discussed. Here, a particular focus will be put on the rules on social security coordination for frontier workers and their access to unemployment benefits. In Section 4, the missing integration in the AFMP of the EU Citizens' Rights Directive will be considered, using as a case study the rights of job-seekers under the AFMP as compared to the Directive.

---

5 Article 25(4) AFMP.

6 M. Oesch, *Switzerland and the European Union. General Framework. Bilateral Agreements. Autonomous Adaptation* (Dike, 2018), p. 21.

7 A. Ott, B. Pirker, 'The EU's norm diffusion to Switzerland – À la carte and in pieces?', in D. Fromage (ed.) *(Re-)defining Membership: Differentiation in and outside the European Union* (OUP, forthcoming 2023).

8 Directive 2004/38/EC of the European Parliament and of the Council of 29 April 2004 on the right of citizens of the Union and their family members to move and reside freely within the territory of the Member States amending Regulation (EEC) No 1612/68 and repealing Directives 64/221/EEC, 68/360/EEC, 72/194/EEC, 73/148/EEC, 75/34/EEC, 75/35/EEC, 90/364/EEC, 90/365/EEC and 93/96/EEC (OJ 2004, L 158/77).

2 The Political and Legal Framework of the AFMP

2.1 *The AFMP's Fragile Political Environment*

The AFMP has to be seen against the backdrop of the Swiss negative referendum in 1992 on participation in the European Economic Area (EEA). Instead of the comprehensive internal market approach and the strong institutional framework provided by the EEA, the EU-Swiss relations are structured around numerous agreements, governed by a large number of Joint Committees and a patchwork of institutional rules.[9] Today, the AFMP sits at the heart of the EU's frustration with the shortcomings of the bilateral cooperation compared to the EEA.

On the Swiss side, there appears to be marked political uneasiness about integrating further with the EU on the issue of the free movement of persons. To some extent, this may be explained by the demographic situation in the country. Switzerland has seen a growth in the population, with two-thirds of this growth being attributed to third-country nationals. According to figures from 2020, 1.4 million EU citizens live in Switzerland and make up 25% of the workforce.[10] More than once, Swiss circles that are critical of immigration launched popular initiatives that threatened the AFMP (and, thereby, also the bilateral process more generally).[11] Most notably, in the vote on the popular initiative of 9 February 2014 on "Mass Immigration", a narrow majority of voters and a clear majority of the Swiss Cantons decided in favour of the introduction into the Swiss Federal Constitution (FC) of new rules that provide, notably, for the reintroduction of quota on migration also with respect to the EU Member States and a national preference when filling job vacancies, and that allow for limitations with respect to social assistance (Article 121a FC).[12] Following the

---

9 See in greater detail: R. Schwok, 'The Bilateral way in a fragilized position', *European Foreign Affairs Review* 2020, pp. 159–176, further M. Maresceau, 'EU-Switzerland: Quo vadis?', *Georgia Journal of International and Comparative Law* 49 (2011), p. 729; A. Lazowski, 'Switzerland', in S. Blockmans, A. Łazowski (eds.), *The European Union and Its Neighbours. A Legal Appraisal of the EU's Policies of Stabilisation, Partnership and Integration* (TCM Asser Press, 2006), pp. 147–184; A. Ott, 'The building blocks and stumbling stones of constructing the European Legal Space', in W.T. Douma, C. Eckes, P. Van Elsuwege, E. Kassoti, A. Ott and R.A. Wessel (eds.), *The Evolving Nature of EU External Relations Law?* (TCM Asser Press, 2021), pp. 205–229.

10 <https://eeas.europa.eu/sites/default/files/str_ifa_eu-switzerlandrelations_factsheet_final.pdf> (accessed 1 June 2022).

11 C. Tobler, 'A Look at the EEA from Switzerland', in EFTA Court (ed.), *The EEA and the EFTA Court. Decentred Integration* (Hart, 2014), p. 542.

12 See also the information in the introduction to this volume.

vote, Switzerland tried to convince the EU to agree to renegotiate the AFMP.[13] However, considering the free movement of persons as a fundamental pillar of EU policy and an indivisible part of the internal market package, the EU rejected the Swiss invitation.[14] Eventually, a clash with the AFMP was avoided through a flexible (in fact: limited) implementation of the new constitutional rules on the level of Swiss federal law. As a result, a further popular initiative aimed at, among others, terminating the AFMP itself was introduced and thereafter rejected on 27 September 2020.[15]

In particular, the outcome of the "Mass Immigration" vote led to a growing mistrust on the EU side, doubting whether Switzerland remained committed to the AFMP. These doubts were amplified when, in spring 2021, the Swiss Federal Government refused to sign the draft Institutional Agreement (InstA).[16] The failure to conclude the InstA was mainly connected to AFMP-related concerns, including the EU Citizens' Rights Directive and wage protection in Switzerland in the context of the posting of workers.[17] As things stand, the political tensions between the EU and Switzerland concerning the failed InstA and, to a certain extent, concerning the future of the AFMP, remain.

2.2 *The AFMP's Unique Legal Framework*

In accordance with Article 1, the objectives of the AFMP are (a) to accord a right of entry, residence, access to work as employed persons, establishment on a self-employed basis and the right to stay in the territory of the Contracting Parties; (b) to facilitate the provision of services in the territory of the

13 According to Article 197(9)(1) FC, international agreements which contravene Article 121a FC were to be renegotiated and amended within three years. However, it has been disputed that this applies to the adaptation of the existing bilateral agreements, see A. Epiney, *Zur rechtlichen Tragweite der Art. 121a, Art. 197 Ziff. 9 BV* (Institut für Europarecht, 2014), <https://www.vd.ch/fileadmin/user_upload/_temp_/avis_de_droit_Epiney_art._121a_g%C3%A9n%C3%A9ral_Deutsch.pdf> (accessed 1 June 2022).

14 See the Council Conclusions on a homogeneous extended single market and EU relations with Non-EU Western European countries of 16 December 2014, <http://www.consilium.europa.eu/uedocs/cms_data/docs/pressdata/en/er/146315.pdf> (accessed 1 June 2022), para. 45.

15 On the initiative, see <https://www.bk.admin.ch/ch/d/pore/vi/vis483.html> (accessed 25 April 2022).

16 On the InstA, see notably the contributions by C. Kaddous and R. Schwok in this volume.

17 See the press release of the Swiss Federal Council explaining why it cannot conclude the IFA. Federal Council, 'Pas de conclusion de l'accord institutionnel Suisse-UE', Press Release, Bern, 26 May 2021, <https://www.admin.ch/gov/fr/accueil/documentation/communiques.msg-id-83705.html> (accessed on 1 June 2022). On wage protection, see the contribution by K. Pärli in this volume.

Contracting Parties, and in particular, to liberalise the provision of services of brief duration; (c) to accord a right of entry into, and residence in, the territory of the Contracting Parties to persons without an economic activity in the host country; (d) to accord the same living, employment and working conditions as those accorded to the parties' own nationals. Article 2 AFMP contains a general provision prohibiting discrimination on the grounds of nationality which has to be applied together with the corresponding non-discrimination provisions of the Annexes to the Agreement. These Annexes – Annex I on the free movement of persons, Annex II on the coordination of the parties' social security systems, and Annex III on the mutual recognition of professional qualifications – aim at providing more detailed rules in their corresponding specific areas. Further, the AFMP includes in Article 13 a standstill clause which commits both sides to not adopt further restrictive measures vis-a-vis each other's nationals.

The legal framework of the AFMP is a unique one, not only in terms of its material scope but also in terms of its institutional structure.

Firstly, if compared to EU (and also to EEA) law, the AFMP is limited in its material scope. According to the Court of Justice of the European Union (CJEU), Switzerland is linked to the EU "by numerous bilateral agreements covering vast fields and prescribing specific rights and obligations, analogous, in some respects, to those laid down by the [TFEU]".[18] The emphasis here is on "*in some respects*". For example, under the AFMP, freedom of establishment is provided only for natural persons, to the exclusion of companies and firms.[19] Further, the provision of services is covered only for a maximum of 90 days per calendar year,[20] and service recipients enjoy travel and residence rights only, to the exclusion of the right to non-discrimination in accessing services.[21]

Secondly, an important particularity of the AFMP, which now belongs to the past, consisted in its asymmetrical transitional rules. They allowed Switzerland to introduce free movement in a phased manner, thereby distinguishing between different groups of EU Member States.[22] They also included safeguard clauses that allowed Switzerland under certain conditions to set,

18 CJEU, Case C-656/11, *UK v Council*, EU:C:2014:97, para. 53.

19 CJEU, Case C-351/08, *Grimme*, EU:C:2009:697, para. 27.

20 Article 5 AFMP; see on this issue also the contribution by K. Pärli in this volume.

21 Article 23 Annex I AFMP; Swiss Federal Supreme Court, decision BGE 133 V 624 (22 October 2007), cons. 4.2 et seq.; CJEU, Case C-70/09, *Hengartner and Gasser*, EU:C:2010:430.

22 This is, in fact, similar to the EU's own internal rules upon the accession of new Member States; see further K. Inglis, 'The Accession Treaty and its Transitional Arrangements: A Twilight Zone for the New Members of the Union' in Ch. Hillion (ed.), *EU Enlargement: A Legal Approach* (Hart Publishing 2004), 77–110; A. Lazowski, 'European Union do not worry,

unilaterally, a limit to the number of new residence permits. In that regard, the "Mass Immigration" vote of 2014 led to difficulties in relation to the inclusion of the EU's most recent Member State, Croatia. Initially, the Swiss Federal Government interpreted Article 121a(4) FC, which prohibits the conclusion of new international agreements contrary to Article 121a FC, as making the signing of the Croatia Protocol impossible. The Swiss Federal Council then decided to apply the Croatia Protocol *de facto* from 1 July 2014, which resulted, in its view, in the same quotas as Croatia would have received if the Protocol had been signed and the above-mentioned transitional rules would have applied.[23] However, the Council of the EU rebutted that these unilateral measures fell short of the provisions of the Protocol and hindered Croatian nationals from relying on the bilateral international agreement between the EU and Switzerland.[24] The Swiss Government eventually agreed to sign the Croatia Protocol, which came into force on 1 January 2017.[25]

Thirdly, the *AFMP* belongs to the large group of EU-Swiss agreements that do not provide for a system of dynamic updating akin to that of the EEA Agreement. Whilst updating is possible, it can be refused by either party without legal consequences being envisaged by the AFMP in such a case. In that sense, the AFMP is said to be static, though, in practice, updates have taken place, namely in the shape of decisions of the AFMP Joint Committee[26] and Protocols extending the Agreement to the new EU Member States. In this regard, an important procedural difference between the AFMP and its Annex I on the free movement of persons, on the one hand, and Annexes II and III

Croatia is behind you: a commentary on the seventh Accession Treaty', *Croatian Yearbook of European Law & Policy* 8 (2012), pp. 1–39.

23 Declaration of the Federal Council pertaining to non-discrimination of Croatian citizens, <http://www.news.admin.ch/NSBSubscriber/message/attachments/34637.pdf> (accessed 1 June 2022). It was argued that this *de facto* application would not violate *de jure* the February 2014 referendum; S. Schürer, 'Eine Sonderlösung für Kroatien', *Berner Zeitung* 24 February 2014, <http://www.bernerzeitung.ch/schweiz/standard/Eine-Sonderloesung-fuer-Kroatien/story/31097079> (accessed 1 June 2022).

24 Council Conclusions on a homogeneous extended single market and EU relations with non-EU Western European countries of 16 December 2014, para. 47.

25 Protocol to the Agreement between the European Community and its Member States, of the one part, and the Swiss Confederation, of the other, on the free movement of persons, regarding the participation of the Republic of Croatia as a Contracting Party, following its accession the European Union (OJ 2017, L 31/3). Today, no transitional rules apply to Croatia anymore; see <https://www.admin.ch/gov/de/start/dokumentation/medienmitteilungen.msg-id-86240.html> (accessed 1 June 2022).

26 See <https://www.fedlex.admin.ch/de/sector-specific-agreements/joint-committees-decisions-register/7> (accessed 1 June 2022).

on social security and professional qualifications, on the other hand, needs to be noted. Under Article 18 AFMP, the Contracting Parties may submit proposals for amendments to the EU-Swiss Joint Committee. However, only amendments relating to Annexes II or III may enter into force based on a mere decision of the Joint Committee for which a simplified procedure applies. For amendments relating to Annex I, as well as to the main body of the AFMP, the ordinary revision procedure has to be followed. Even with the simplified procedure for amendments related to Annexes II and III, integration of EU *acquis* relevant for the EU-Swiss bilateral relation does not go without political hiccups as further discussed in the context of social security coordination in Section 3.1 of this chapter.

Fourthly and finally, there may be differences in the interpretation of the AFMP's rules as compared to EU law.[27] On the general level of the EU-Swiss legal relations, the CJEU has stressed that – similar to the EU-Turkey association[28] – "the objective of these agreements, including the EC-Switzerland Agreement on the Free Movement of Persons, is to strengthen the economic ties between the European Union and the Swiss Confederation".[29] Accordingly, the EU-Swiss agreements cannot profit from an automatic integration-friendly reading of its provisions. Rather, "the interpretation given to the provisions of Union law concerning that market cannot be automatically applied by analogy to the interpretation of the Agreement, unless there are express provisions to that effect laid down by the Agreement itself".[30] In the context of the AFMP, this applies even though Article 16(2) AFMP contains a homogeneity clause with respect to its interpretation. That clause distinguishes between CJEU case law rendered before and after the signature of the AFMP. While case law from before the signature needs to be taken into account, later case law will be brought to the attention of Switzerland and the Joint Committee will determine its implications. In practice, however, the Swiss Federal Supreme Court takes "younger" CJEU case law into account in the interest of a parallel interpretation and it will deviate from CJEU case law only if compelling reasons

27 See also the contribution by P. Van Elsuwege in this volume.

28 See CJEU, Case C-371/08, *Ziebell*, EU:C:2011:809, para. 64: "the EEC-Turkey Association pursues a solely economic purpose". See further on this case M. Maresceau, 'A reflection on the *Ziebell* judgment', in V. Kronenberger, M.T. D'Alessio and V. Placco (eds.), *De Rome à Lisbonne: les juridictions de l'Union européenne à la croisée des chemins* (Bruylant, 2013), pp. 85–103.

29 CJEU, Case C-656/11, *UK v Council*, EU:C:2014:97, para. 53, also Case C-506/10, *Graf and Engel*, EU:C:2011:643, para. 33.

30 See, e.g., CJEU, Case C-541/08, *Fokus Invest*, EU:C:2010:74, para. 28.

speak against parallel interpretation.[31] Furthermore, if there is a dispute about the interpretation and application of the agreement, Article 19 AFMP stipulates that the Joint Committee will try to resolve it.[32]

The legal framework briefly sketched above has resulted in friction between the parties on the interpretation and evolution of the AFMP. The EU starts from the understanding that if EU rules are extended to third States, allowing them to profit from the advantages of the EU system, then a level-playing field needs to be secured by rules that guarantee homogeneity through a dynamic adaptation to the EU's relevant *acquis* and an efficient system of dispute settlement.[33] Indeed, the EU's wish for renewed institutional rules for key market access agreements – including, notably, the AFMP – has to be seen against the background of the fact that discrepancies between EU law and EU-Swiss sectoral law have widened.

In the remainder of this chapter, a closer look will be taken at the adaptation of the AFMP in two of its sub-fields, namely firstly, the coordination of the social security systems under Annex II AFMP with its (almost) complete integration of the relevant EU law and, secondly, the still missing and much-contested integration of the EU Citizens' Rights Directive under Annex I AFMP. In relation to the mutual recognition of professional qualifications under Annex III AFMP, reference can be made to the recent work by Günthardt.[34]

---

31 For instance, Swiss Federal Supreme Court, decision 140 II 112 (31 January 2014), cons. 3.2.; A. Ott and B. Pirker, 'The EU's norm diffusion to Switzerland – À la carte and in pieces?', in D. Fromage (ed.) *(Re-)defining Membership: Differentiation in and outside the European Union*, (OUP, forthcoming 2023); M. Maresceau, 'Les accords d'intégration dans les relations de proximité de l'Union Européenne', in C. Blumann (ed.), *Les frontières de l'Union européenne* (Bruylant, 2013), pp. 177–178; M. Maresceau, 'On the external dimension of Directive 2004/38/EC', in I. Govaere, D. Hanf (eds.) *Scrutinizing Internal and External Dimensions of European Law. Liber Amicorum Paul Demaret, Vol. II* (College of Europe Studies No.17, 2013), pp. 774–775.

32 The practical implications of the parallel (potentially different) interpretation and the lack of a judicial cooperation mechanism will be further elaborated upon in section 3.1.2 of this chapter, in the context of social security coordination between the contracting parties.

33 See further C. Baudenbacher, 'The Judicial Dimension of the European Neighbourhood Policy', *EU Diplomacy Papers* 8 (2013), <http://aei.pitt.edu/47407/1/edp-8-2013_baudenbacher_(1).pdf> (accessed 1 June 2022), p. 22, with further references to the rejected Swiss proposal of a Swiss pillar with a Swiss surveillance authority overseen by the Swiss Federal Supreme Court. See also Council, Negotiating mandate for an EU-Switzerland institutional framework agreement, 6 May 2014, 9525/14, <https://www.consilium.europa.eu/uedocs/cms_data/docs/pressdata/en/er/142503.pdf> (accessed 1 June 2022).

34 J. Günthardt, *Switzerland and the European Union: The implications of the institutional framework and the right of free movement for the mutual recognition of professional qualifications* (Nomos/Dike, 2021), as well as J. Günthardt, 'Die Nichtaufdatierung der bilateralen

3 Social Security Coordination between the EU and Switzerland: An (Almost) Complete Integration

With regard to the rules on social security coordination, the level of integration that the EU has achieved with Switzerland can largely be compared with that achieved with the EEA EFTA States. However, there is one big difference: the underdeveloped institutional framework with Switzerland is the element that makes the integration of social security coordination merely *almost* complete. Below, the institutional framework will be discussed in Section 3.1, followed by a selection of important substantive rules of the current institutional framework for the social security coordination for frontier workers in Section 3.2.

3.1 *The Institutional Framework Relevant for Social Security Coordination*

3.1.1 The Special Status of Switzerland for the Application of the EU Social Security Coordination Rules

Given the high mobility of workers across the Swiss-EU borders, the EU and Switzerland agreed in Article 8 AFMP to coordinate their social security systems. That coordination has been achieved through Annex II AFMP. Article 1(1) Annex II specifies that "the contracting parties agree, with regard to the coordination of social security schemes, to apply among themselves the Community acts to which reference is made, as in force at the date of signature of the Agreement and as amended by section A of the Annex, or rules equivalent to such acts". Currently, Regulation 883/2004[35] and its implementing Regulation 987/2009[36] are listed in Section A of Annex II.[37]

The social security coordination between the EU and Switzerland is one of the most integrated[38] between the EU and a third

Abkommen Schweiz–EU am Beispiel der Diplomanerkennung', *Schweizerische Juristen-Zeitung* 118 (2022), pp. 159–171.

35 Regulation (EC) No 883/2004 of the European Parliament and of the Council of 29 April 2004 on the coordination of social security systems (OJ 2004, L 166/1).

36 Regulation (EC) No 987/2009 of the European Parliament and of the Council of 16 September 2009 laying down the procedure for implementing Regulation (EC) No 883/2004 (OJ 2009, L 284/1).

37 It should be noted that when the EU adopts amendments to those Regulations, such amendments also have to be added to Section A of the Annex II if the parties to the AFMP agree to the update.

38 Together with the coordination with the EEA EFTA States where similar case law has been rendered. See for instance, CJEU, Case C-431/11, *UK v Council*, EU:C:2013:589. See further N. Rennuy & P. Van Elsuwege, 'Integration without membership and the dynamic

country.[39] Indeed, for the purpose of social security coordination, Switzerland is not considered as a third country but is instead equated to a Member State, as stated by the CJEU first in *Schwemmer*,[40] and afterwards repeated in *Xhymshiti*[41] and *UK v Council*.[42]

The *Schwemmer* case concerned the overlapping of family benefits from Germany and Switzerland in the context of Article 76 of Regulation 1408/71[43] and Article 10 of Regulation 574/72.[44] [45] The CJEU clarified that Regulations 1408/71 and 574/72 could be applied to the dispute in the main proceedings since the Swiss Confederation ought to be included in the expression "Member States" found in those Regulations.[46]

In *Xhymshiti*, a similar question arose, albeit this time in the context of Regulation 859/2003,[47] which had not been labelled as a text relevant for Switzerland (or for the EEA).[48] The referring court then asked the CJEU whether third-country nationals living in a Member State of the EU and working in Switzerland could rely on Regulation 859/2003.[49] The CJEU ruled that although Switzerland was to be equated with a Member State of the European Union for the purpose of the application of EU social security coordination regulations,

development of EU law: United Kingdom v. Council (EEA)' 51 *Common Law Market Review* (2014), pp. 935–954.

39 For an overview of the different type of integration the EU has with third countries on social security coordination, see P. Melin, *The External Dimension of EU Social Security Coordination: Towards a Common EU Approach*, SEUR (Brill, 2019).

40 CJEU, Case C-16/09, *Schwemmer*, EU:C:2010:605, para.31.

41 CJEU, Case C-247/09, *Xhymshiti*, EU:C:2010:698, para. 31.

42 CJEU, Case C-656/11, *UK v Council*, EU:C:2014:97, para. 65.

43 Council Regulation (EEC) No 1408/71 of 14 June 1971 on the application of social security schemes to employed persons, to self-employed persons and to members of their families moving within the Community, consolidated version (OJ English Special Edition 1971(II), p. 416).

44 Regulation (EEC) No 574/72 of the Council of 21 March 1972 fixing the procedure for implementing Regulation (EEC) No 1408/71 on the application of social security schemes to employed persons and their families moving within the Community (OJ 1972, L 74/1).

45 CJEU, Case C-16/09, *Schwemmer*, EU:C:2010:605, paras. 28–29. This case is discussed in more details in P. Melin, *The External Dimension of EU Social Security Coordination: Towards a Common EU Approach*, SEUR vol. 15 (Brill, 2019), p. 83.

46 CJEU, Case C-16/09, *Schwemmer*, EU:C:2010:605, para. 31.

47 Regulation (EC) No 859/2003 of 14 May 2003 extending the provisions of Regulation (EEC) No 1408/71 and Regulation (EEC) No 574/72 to nationals of third countries who are not already covered by those provisions solely on the ground of their nationality (OJ 2003, L 124/1).

48 This case is discussed in more details in P. Melin (n. 45), pp. 83–84.

49 CJEU, Case C-247/09, *Xhymshiti*, EU:C:2010:698.

Regulation 859/2003 was not part of the AFMP *acquis*.[50] Consequently, Regulation 859/2003 could not be applied to third-country nationals involved in a cross-border situation between an EU Member State and Switzerland.

In *UK v Council*, the UK asked the CJEU to annul the EU Council Decision on the position of the EU to be taken in the EU-Swiss Joint Committee which concerned the amendment of Annex II with references to the new Regulation 883/2004 and Regulation 987/2009. The UK contested the use of Article 48 TFEU as the legal basis for the Council Decision. The UK argued that Article 48 TFEU is a provision reserved for the free movement of workers between the EU Member States, whereas Article 79(2)(b) TFEU concerns third-country nationals and therefore should be used when dealing with third countries.[51] However, the CJEU confirmed that the EU could use Article 48 TFEU since Switzerland had already been equated with a Member State of the EU for the purposes of applying the EU social security coordination rules.[52]

3.1.2 The Impact of the Institutional Framework on Social Security Coordination

The current institutional framework has an impact on the social security coordination rules between the EU Member States and Switzerland. In this section, two aspects of this framework will be discussed: the need for regular updates of the AFMP to match the revisions of the EU social security coordination rules and the lack of a judicial cooperation mechanism.

As explained above, Annex II makes direct references to EU Regulations on social security coordination. When the EU adopts new rules or revises old ones, the question can be raised as to whether the new or revised rules are to be included in the Annex II AFMP through a Decision of the Joint Committee.[53] This updating process has been politically difficult not only at the level of the Joint Committee but also at the EU level itself.

At the time of the adoption of Annex II, the EU rules on social security coordination were enshrined in Regulation 1408/71 and its implementing Regulation 574/72. When the EU updated its legislation by replacing Regulation

50 *Ibid.*, para. 35.

51 CJEU, Case C-656/11, *UK v Council*, EU:C:2014:97, para. 28.

52 *Ibid.*, para. 65. See on this case P. Melin, 'The Search of EU Competence(s) for the Externalization of Social Security Coordination: Where There's a Will, There's a Way. Case C-81/13 *United Kingdom v. Council* (Turkish Case)', 22 *Maastricht Journal of European and Comparative Law* (2015), pp. 440–453. See also the contribution by P. Van Elsuwege in this volume.

53 The procedure for amendment of the Annex II is described above in section 2.1. of this chapter.

1408/71 with Regulation 883/2004 and Regulation 574/72 with Regulation 987/2009, the references to the new EU rules were equally updated in Annex II AFMP.[54] However, as discussed above, on the EU's side, this update did not happen as smoothly as expected. The Council Decision on the EU's position was challenged before the CJEU through an annulment procedure triggered by the UK on grounds of incorrect legal basis.[55] While the CJEU ultimately rejected the arguments of the UK, this legal challenge slowed down the process of updating Annex II AFMP.

Furthermore, Regulations 883/2004 and 987/2009 have been regularly amended by the EU since their adoption. Those amendments have been incorporated into Annex II AFMP up until 2013.[56] Hence, the social security coordination rules applicable between the EU Member States and Switzerland only concern the rules contained in Regulations 883/2004 and 987/2009 as amended up until 2013. There is, therefore, at present a gap in this respect. Additionally, Regulations 883/2004 and 987/2009 are currently being revised by the EU.[57] If adopted at the EU level, this would mean that the references to the EU Regulations would have to be updated as well in Section A of Annex II. If not, then the social security coordination between the contracting parties will continue to erode further.

Another element of the current institutional framework between the EU and Switzerland that is problematic for social security coordination is the absence of a judicial cooperation mechanism. Currently, national courts of the EU Member States and Swiss courts are both competent to interpret the social security coordination rules contained in the AFMP. However, only the courts from the EU Member States can send a preliminary ruling question to the CJEU for interpretation of the Regulations. Conversely, there is no such possibility for the Swiss courts (and no such procedure was foreseen in the draft InstA). From an EU law point of view, this situation not only implies a lack of oversight

---

54 Decision No 1/2012 of the Joint Committee established under the Agreement between the European Community and its Member States, of the one part, and the Swiss Confederation, of the other, on the free movement of persons of 31 March 2012, replacing Annex II to that Agreement on the coordination of social security schemes (2012/195/EU) (OJ 2012, L 103/51).

55 CJEU, Case C-656/11, *UK v Council*, EU:C:2014:97.

56 The latest amendment of Regulation 883/2004 that is included in Section A of Annex II AFMP is Regulation 517/2013 of 13 May 2013.

57 Proposal for a Regulation of the European Parliament and of the Council amending Regulation (EC) No 883/2004 on the coordination of social security systems and regulation (EC) No 987/2009 laying down the procedure for implementing Regulation (EC) No 883/2004, COM(2016) 815 final.

on uniform interpretation, but it is also a missed opportunity of ending disputes through an authoritative interpretation by the CJEU.

An important judgment of the Swiss Federal Supreme Court of 13 July 2020[58] may serve to illustrate the fact that this situation has direct consequences for individuals in Switzerland. Ms A, a Portuguese national, lived in Germany before moving to Switzerland in 2014. She received an old-age pension from Germany and she continued to be covered by a German (private) healthcare insurance. When her application to join the Swiss healthcare system was turned down, she appealed that decision. The Swiss Federal Supreme Court, applying Annex II AFMP and noting that Germany was the competent State for her pension, found that Ms A should be insured and pay contributions in Germany.[59]

The case has to be seen against the background of Article 24 of Regulation 883/2004, on residence in a Member State other than the competent Member State, read in conjunction with the procedure set out in Article 24 of Regulation 987/2009. According to these provisions, benefits in kind are provided to insured persons and their family members who receive a pension in the State of residence (here Switzerland) at the cost of the State competent for the pension (here Germany). To benefit from that system, the persons in question must register with the responsible institution in the State of residence. Their right to benefits in kind in the Member State of residence is certified by a document issued by the competent institution upon request of the insured person or upon request of the institution of the place of residence. The problem in the case of A was that her private insurer was unable to produce the required document, due to the fact that the German authorities consider that private insurance schemes are not coordinated by Regulations 883/2004 and 987/2009.[60] In other words, A was meant to be insured in Germany pursuant to the conflict rules of Regulation 883/2004,[61] but could not benefit from receiving the benefits in kind in Switzerland under Article 17 of Regulation 883/2004 due to the fact that she was privately insured.[62]

The Federal Supreme Court considered that the interpretation by the German authorities in respect of private insurers was contrary to the objectives

58 Swiss Federal Supreme Court, decision BGE 9C_557/2019 (13 July 2020).

59 *Ibid.*, cons. 3.3.2.

60 *Ibid.*, cons. 6.2.1. and 6.2.2.

61 See also cons. 6.3.2.2. where the Swiss Federal Supreme Court refers to another case (decision 144 V 127) where the same conclusion was held when it comes to the application of the conflict rules.

62 *Ibid.*, cons. 6.3.2.

of the coordination system created by the EU Regulations[63] and that it led to an unsatisfactory situation for A.[64] However, it also pointed out that, in the absence of a mechanism of judicial cooperation between Switzerland and the EU, such as the possibility for Swiss courts to request from the CJEU a preliminary ruling that would be binding (also) on the courts in the EU Members States, any interpretation of the Federal Supreme Court would be unable to change A's situation in Germany.[65] In that regard, the Federal Supreme Court indicated that the only practical solution for A was to ask again the German authorities to issue a decision on her right to benefit in kind under Article 24(1) of Regulation 833/2004. She might then appeal that decision before German courts which could and should, in the last instance, refer the question to the CJEU.[66]

Overall, the current institutional framework between the EU and Switzerland has an impact on the social security coordination between the contracting parties. On one hand, the difficulties in regularly updating the amendments of the EU Regulations on social security coordination led to the situation where the existing (almost) complete integration is slowly eroding. On the other hand, the absence of a judicial cooperation mechanism is not offering a guarantee of uniform interpretation and legal certainty for individuals involved in cross-border cases. While the first issue can be solved rather easily by continuing to integrate the amendments of the EU Regulations that are relevant for Switzerland into the Annex II AFMP, the second issue requires a change of the institutional framework.

3.2 *The Social Security Coordination Rules for Frontier Workers*

Cross-border mobility of workers between the EU Member States and Switzerland has increased since the adoption of the AFMP and its Annex II on social security coordination. In the last 25 years, the population of frontier workers in Switzerland has doubled. For the first quarter of 2022, the Swiss Federal Statistical Office reports that there are 365'437 frontier workers in Switzerland, and the great majority of those workers come from France (203'689), followed by Italy (86'322) and Germany (63'547).[67] It is interesting to note that the flux of

63 *Ibid.,* cons. 6.3.2.1.

64 For all the specific reasons related to A's situation, see cons. 6.3.3.

65 *Ibid.*, cons. 6.3.4.

66 *Ibid.*, cons. 6.3.4.

67 Federal Statistical Office, Cross-border commuters, data from the 1st quarter 2022, <https://www.bfs.admin.ch/bfs/en/home/statistics/work-income/employment-working-hours/economically-active-population/cross-border-commuters.html> (accessed on 1 June 2022).

frontier workers from the EU Member States to Switzerland is higher than any flux of frontier workers between the EU Member States. Indeed, as reported by Eurostat, the biggest flux of frontier workers between the EU Member States is between Poland and Germany with 121'502 workers.[68] This flux is lower than the sole flux of workers coming from France to work in Switzerland. These data show how important the situation of frontier workers is for the EU and Switzerland. It is therefore not astonishing that with the large number of workers crossing Swiss borders every day, questions concerning their social security contributions and rights are also increasing.

The next section will turn to the most relevant and (politically) controversial rules for frontier workers. But before doing that, the concept of "frontier worker" needs to be defined. Pursuant to Article 7(1) of Annex I AFMP, a frontier worker is an employed person who "is a national of a Contracting Party who has his residence in the territory of a Contracting Party and who pursues an activity as an employed person in the territory of the other Contracting Party, returning to his place of residence, as a rule, every day, or at least once a week". This definition essentially corresponds to that in Article 1(f) of Regulation 883/2004.

3.2.1 Conflict Rules Determining the Competent State and the Issue of Qualification of Social Security Benefits

Under Article 11 of Regulation 883/2004, the general rule is that a person should be subject to the social security legislation of one Member State only. This is commonly referred to as "the single State principle".[69] A frontier worker who resides in one Member State and works in another Member State shall be subject to the social security legislation of the State where he/she pursues his/her activity as an employed or self-employed person.[70]

The rule determining the applicable legislation is of course only relevant for the social security benefits listed under its material scope.[71] Sometimes, issues concerning the qualification of social security benefits arise and lead to a situation where it is not clear which State's legislation should be applied.

68 Eurostat data on people crossing borders, <https://ec.europa.eu/eurostat/cache/digpub/eumove/bloc-2c.html?lang=en> (accessed on 1 June 2022).

69 For more details on how the rules on determining the applicable legislation work, please see the reference books by M. Fuchs, R. Cornelissen, *EU Social Security Law: A Commentary on EU Regulations 883/2004 and 987/2009* (C.H. Beck, Hart, 2015), and by F. Pennings, *European Social Security Law*, 7th edition (Intersentia, 2021).

70 Article 11(3)(a) of Regulation 883/2004.

71 Article 3(3) of Regulation 883/2004.

The *Dreyer* judgment rendered by the CJEU on 14 March 2019 is a perfect illustration of this.[72] It concerned the question of whether certain French benefits could be classified as social security benefits within the meaning of Article 3(3) of Regulation 883/2004 in order to determine which State was competent for levying contributions. Mr and Mrs Dreyer, French nationals residing in France, were insured under the Swiss social security scheme given the fact that Mr Dreyer had worked his entire career in Switzerland. By a tax adjustment notice, the French tax authorities announced that they should pay contributions in France. The couple argued that the contributions in question were social security contributions which fell under the single State principle.

The CJEU recalled that for a benefit to be regarded as a "social security benefit" under Article 3 of Regulation 883/2004, it must relate to one of the risks listed in Article 3(1) and it must be granted to recipients without any individual and discretionary assessment of personal needs, on the basis of "a legally defined position".[73] In that respect, the CJEU emphasised that the entitlement to the benefits as such is based on objective, legally defined criteria (such as age or loss of independence) and does not require an individual assessment.[74] An individual assessment is required only for the method of calculation and for the exact amount to be granted to the recipients.[75] The CJEU concluded that benefits of the type in question in the *Dreyer* case should be classified as "social security benefits" for the purpose of Article 3 of Regulation 883/2004. This meant that the Dreyer couple was not subject to the French social security legislation, as they were already subject to the Swiss legislation.

3.2.2 Equal Treatment and the Waiving of the Residence Criteria

Next to the single State principle and the rule for determining the competent State, Regulation 883/2004 provides for equality of treatment of frontier workers under Article 4.[76]

Of particular relevance for frontier workers is Article 7 on the waiving of residence criteria. Under this provision, a Member State cannot reduce, amend, suspend or withdraw benefits on the ground that the beneficiary resides in

72 CJEU, Case C-372/18, *Dreyer*, EU:C:2019:206. This case is examined in more detail in A.-P. van der Mei, P. Melin, 'Overview of recent cases before the Court of Justice of the European Union (February 2019-June 2019)', *European Journal of Social Security* Vol. 21(3) (2019), pp. 272–273.

73 *Ibid.*, para.32.

74 *Ibid.*, paras. 34, 37–39.

75 *Ibid.*, paras. 36–37.

76 Article 9 of Annex I AFMP provides for equal treatment of working conditions, tax concessions, education in vocational training, *welfare benefits*, etc. (emphasis added).

another Member State. This rule is very important for EU frontier workers since, in Switzerland, the general rule is that family benefits are paid only for children who are resident in Switzerland.[77] As a result of Article 7 of Regulation 883/2004, EU frontier workers can receive family benefits for their family members even if they do not reside in Switzerland.

Furthermore, it may be that a cross-border worker is entitled to family benefits in the State of residence in addition to the State where this person works. Article 68(1)(a) of Regulation 883/2004 provides that rights available based on an activity as an employed or self-employed person take priority over rights obtained on the basis of residence. In case of overlapping entitlements to family benefits, Article 68(2) requires those benefits to be provided in accordance with the legislation that has priority. For other benefits granted by virtue of other legislation, Article 68(2) requires them to be suspended up to the amount provided by the legislation that has priority and then if relevant, a differential supplement is to be paid for the sum exceeding that amount. The objective of that rule against overlapping benefits is to ensure that a person entitled to benefits in several States receives a total amount of benefits corresponding to the amount of the most favourable benefit under the legislation of one of those States.[78]

Since Switzerland and its neighbours do not have the same currency, there are sometimes problems in calculating the differential supplement to which a cross-border worker might be entitled. In *GP*,[79] the CJEU clarified that the rules for the calculation of the supplementary family benefits[80] are not affected by the fact that the allowance is paid in Swiss Francs by a Swiss institution.[81] Furthermore, the CJEU held that the rate of conversion for the calculation of

77 Article 4 of the Federal Act on Family Allowances, Loi fédérale sur les allocations familiales et les aides financières allouées aux organisations familiales du 24 mars 2006 (Loi sur les allocations familiales, LAFam), SR 836.2. For those children living in a non-EU/EEA country but whose parent works in Switzerland, there might be a possibility to get family benefits from Switzerland if Switzerland has a bilateral agreement on that point with the non-EU/EEA country concerned.

78 CJEU, Case C-250/13, *Wagener*, EU:C:2014:278, para. 45.

79 CJEU, Case C-473/18, *GP*, EU:C:2019:662. This case concerned a dispute regarding the date that needed to be taken into account for determining the exchange rate for the calculation of supplementary family benefits to be paid by Germany to a cross-border worker working in Switzerland but residing in Germany.

80 Article 68(2) of Regulation 883/2004, Article 90 of Regulation 987/2009 and Decision No H3 of 15 October 2009 concerning the date to be taken into consideration for determining the rates of conversion referred to in Article 90 of Regulation (EC) No 987/2009 of the European Parliament and of the Council (OJ 2009, C 106/56).

81 CJEU, Case C-473/18, *GP*, EU:C:2019:662, paras. 22–28.

the difference of benefits for the purpose of receiving a supplement[82] should be that of the day on which the competent institution of the State of employment makes payment of the family benefit in question.[83]

3.2.3 Access to Unemployment Benefits

Article 65 of Regulation 883/2004 provides for unemployment benefits for frontier workers. It distinguishes the situation of partially unemployed frontier workers, on the one hand,[84] and wholly unemployed frontier workers, on the other hand.[85]

A partially unemployed frontier worker is a person who retains a link with the State of employment according to the *De Laat* case law.[86] Unemployment benefits will be provided to a partially unemployed frontier worker by and in accordance with the legislation of the State of last employment in return for which he or she needs to make himself/herself available to his/her employer or to the employment services of that State.[87] For example, an Italian citizen resides in Italy and works full-time in Switzerland. If this person's employer reduces the working hours to part-time employment, the frontier worker will be considered partially unemployed and can claim unemployment benefits from Switzerland.

By contrast, a wholly unemployed frontier worker will have to claim unemployment benefits in the State of residence.[88] Furthermore, wholly unemployed frontier workers will have to make themselves available to the employment services of the State of residence with the possibility, as a supplementary step, to make themselves available to the employment services of the State of last employment.[89] The payment of the unemployment benefits will be at the expense of the State of residence, except for the first three

82 Paragraph 2 of Decision No H3 of 15 October 2009 refers to "the day when the operation is performed by the institution".

83 CJEU, Case C-473/18, *GP*, EU:C:2019:662, paras. 29–52.

84 Article 65(1) of Regulation 883/2004.

85 Article 65(2) of Regulation 883/2004. There is also a more specific rule for wholly unemployed self-employed frontier workers where no unemployment benefits system for self-employed persons exists in the State of residence (Article 65a of Regulation 883/2204).

86 CJEU, Case C-444/98, *De Laat*, EU:C:2001:165. This criterion has been interpreted by the Administrative Commission (Commission responsible for interpreting and solving disputes on EU social security coordination) as "whether or not there is any contractual link between the parties". See Decision No 205 of 17 October 2005 on the scope of the notion of "partial unemployment" with regard to frontier workers (OJ 2005, L 130/37).

87 Article 65(1) of Regulation 883/2004.

88 Article 65(5)(a) of Regulation 883/2004.

89 Article 65(2) of Regulation 883/2004.

months[90] where the State of last employment will reimburse the State of residence up to the amount the worker would have been entitled to in that State of last employment.[91] For example, a German citizen residing in Germany but working in Switzerland should claim unemployment benefits from Germany when becoming wholly unemployed. Switzerland will then have to reimburse Germany up to the amount of unemployment benefits the German worker would have been entitled to in Switzerland. The German worker could however register with the Swiss unemployment services to remain available for employment in Switzerland.

In order to calculate the amount of unemployment benefits, periods of insurance completed under the legislation of any other State should be taken into account by the competent institution.[92] One of the few cases from the CJEU on the issue of unemployment benefits in a cross-border situation with Switzerland deals with the method of calculation of the amount of unemployment benefits.[93] Article 62(1) of Regulation 883/2004 provides that, when a Member State chooses to calculate unemployment benefits on the basis of the amount of the previous salary, the calculation must be based on the salary with respect to the last activity as an employed person. In Germany, unemployment benefits are calculated on the basis of the amount of the previous salary only when the person has completed 150 days of contributions. In the case of *ZP*, the German authorities only considered the contributions paid in Germany, failing to take into account the periods of contributions completed in Switzerland. The CJEU reminded the German authorities that Article 62(1) of Regulation 883/2004 leaves them a choice to base the calculation of the benefits on the amount of the previous salary but once that choice is made, there is no derogation allowed.[94] Furthermore, the Court recalled that under Article 62(2), a Member State can fix a reference period for the purpose of determining the salary. However, the Court ruled that periods of contributions completed under the legislation of another Member State must be taken into account otherwise workers who have exercised their right to free movement

90 Three months can be extended to five months when the unemployed frontier worker has, during the preceding 24 months, completed periods of employment or self-employment of at least 12 months in the State of employment (Article 65(7) Regulation 883/2004).

91 Article 65(6) of Regulation 883/2004.

92 Article 61(1) of Regulation 883/2004.

93 CJEU, Case C-29/19, *ZP*, EU:C:2020:36. This case is discussed in more detail in P. Melin, 'Overview of recent cases before the Court of Justice of the European Union (October 2019-January 2020)', *European Journal of Social Security* Vol. 22 (1) (2020), pp. 68–69.

94 *Ibid.*, paras. 27 and 28.

would be treated less favourably compared to those workers who spent their entire career in one Member State.[95]

Finally a brief note on the situation of EU job-seekers' entitlement to unemployment benefits in Switzerland: According to the rules of Regulation 883/2004, job-seekers can obtain unemployment benefits from the State of last activity and export those unemployment benefits to another Member State (Switzerland included) for a maximum of three months,[96] which can be extended to six months.[97] For example, a French citizen working and residing in France who becomes unemployed can go to Switzerland for three months while keeping unemployment benefits paid by France. The InstA would not have changed these rules, which means that the fear that that agreement would have increased job-seekers' rights is unfounded as far as social security entitlements under Regulations 883/2004 and 987/2009 are concerned. This question must, however, be distinguished from the right to social assistance under the EU Citizen's Directive.

4 The EU Citizens' Rights Directive: Not Part of the EU-Swiss *acquis*

Whilst the level of integration between the EU and Switzerland in respect of the coordination of the social security systems can largely be compared to that achieved with the EEA EFTA States, the same is not true with respect to the free movement rules enshrined in the EU Citizens' Rights Directive 2004/38. Below, the general nature of this Directive and the attitude of Switzerland towards it are discussed in Section 4.1. This is followed in Section 4.2. by a brief case study on the legal position of job-seekers under the AFMP and Directive 2004/38.

4.1 *Swiss Reluctance vis-à-vis Directive 2004/38*

The EU Citizens' Rights Directive consolidates the free movement rights of EU citizens and their family members in one piece of legislation, replacing the previous sectoral approach with specific Directives on workers, self-employed persons, or students.[98] As some of the core rights of the Directive lie in the

95 *Ibid.*, paras. 30 and 37.

96 Article 64(3) of Regulation 883/2004.

97 *Ibid.*

98 For a discussion related to EU Citizens' Rights Directive in the EU-Swiss relations, see M. Maresceau, 'On the external dimension of Directive 2004/38/EC' (n. 32), pp. 773–775. For a detailed overview on Directive 2004/38, see E. Guild, S. Peers and J. Tomkin, *The EU Citizenship Directive: A Commentary*, 2nd edition (Oxford University Press, 2019).

concept of Union citizenship,[99] it might seem counter-intuitive to apply it to non-EU nationals. Nonetheless, Directive 2004/38 also applies to EEA nationals to whom Union citizenship has not been extended. Indeed, in a logic of being part of the internal market, the EEA EFTA States have agreed to include the EU Citizens' Rights Directive into the *acquis* of the EEA Agreement after a long and complicated debate resulting in a reservation with respect to future CJEU case law on the Union citizenship.[100]

Contrary to the incorporation of the EU Citizens' Rights Directive into the EEA Agreement, the Swiss Confederation has repeatedly refused to include that EU *acquis* into its bilateral relationship with the EU and, more specifically, the AFMP. Its latest instance can be witnessed in the failure to adopt the InstA where the inclusion of Directive 2004/38 into the EU-Swiss bilateral relationship was a crucial point for the EU. On the Swiss side, reservations exist notably in relation to the right to permanent residence under Article 16 et seq. of the Directive, the right to equal treatment with regard to, *inter alia*, social assistance under Article 24 and protection against expulsion under Article 28 of Directive 2004/38.[101] The debate on these issues is also reflected in Swiss academic writing.[102]

Under the present rules, the mobility of EU citizens and Swiss nationals is regulated in detail by the rules in Annex I AFMP, which are a combination of original provisions from the Annex I itself and of provisions from some (old) EU measures that have been incorporated into the AFMP.[103] These rules do

99 Article 20 TFEU for the concept of Union citizenship and Article 21 TFEU for the right to move and reside freely within the Union; see P. Craig, G. de Búrca, *EU law. Text, Cases, and Materials*, 7th edition (Oxford University Press, 2020), p. 894.

100 See further M. Maresceau, 'On the external dimension of Directive 2004/38/EC' (n. 32), p. 772; C. Tobler, 'Free movement of Persons in the EU v. in the EEA: of Effect-Related Homogeneity and a Reversed *Polydor* Principle', in N. Cambien, D. Kochenov and E. Muir (eds.), *European Citizenship under Stress*, Nijhoff Studies in European Union Law, Vol. 16 (Brill, 2020), 482–507.

101 See the press release of the Swiss Federal Council explaining why it cannot conclude the InstA. Federal Council, "Pas de conclusion de l'accord institutionnel Suisse-UE", Press Release, Bern, 26 May 2021, <https://www.admin.ch/gov/fr/accueil/documentation/communiques.msg-id-83705.html> (accessed on 1 June 2022). See also Federal Council, Rapport relatif aux négociations sur un accord-cadre institutionnel entre la Suisse et l'UE, 26 May 2021, <https://www.newsd.admin.ch/newsd/message/attachments/66827.pdf> (accessed 1 June 2022), p. 33.

102 See, e.g., A. Epiney, 'Das Institutionelle Abkommen und die Unionsbürgerrichtlinie', *Jusletter* 11 March 2019, which puts a particular focus on the link of certain new provisions in the Directive as compared to previous legislation with Union citizenship.

103 For example, Regulation (EEC) No 1251/70 of the Commission of 29 June 1970 on the right of workers to remain in the territory of a Member State after having been employed in that State (OJ 1970, L 142/24) or Council Directive 75/34/EEC of 17 December 1974 concerning

not include the issues mentioned in the preceding paragraph. In Switzerland, the provisions of the Annex I AFMP have been implemented by an Ordinance from the Federal Council.[104]

There are substantial differences between the rules under Directive 2004/38 and the current rules on the free movement of persons between the EU and Switzerland under the AFMP. For example, contrary to previous Union law, the EU Citizens' Rights Directive provides for the right of residence without the need for a permit. At the most, the Member States may require EU citizens to register.[105] In contrast, residence under the AFMP remains conditioned on the possession of a permit that is valid for a determined period of time only.[106] Under the applicable Swiss rules, there are different categories of such permits, including in particular permits for 5 years (so-called "B EU/EFTA permits"), short-stay permits (L EU/EFTA permits) and working permits for cross-border commuters (G EU/EFTA permits).[107]

It is not the aim of this contribution to provide a comprehensive comparison between the rights under the EU Citizens' Rights Directive and the rights under Annex I AFMP.[108] Instead, specific attention will be paid in the next section to the position of job-seekers as a brief case study as to why there might be reluctance from the Swiss side to agree to incorporate the rules of Directive 2004/38 into the AFMP. The reason for choosing this focus is that access to social assistance for, among others, foreign job-seekers is one of the sensitive issues in Switzerland. In 2014, the "Mass Immigration" vote resulted in the adoption of several limiting provisions on residence rights of foreign job-seekers and their access to social assistance, as discussed further below (see Section 4.3). In the same vein, the incorporation of the EU Citizens' Rights Directive into the AFMP is often considered in the Swiss political and public discourse as

---

the right of nationals of a Member State to remain in the territory of another Member State after having pursued therein an activity in a self-employed capacity (OJ 1974, L 14/10).

104 Ordinance on the Free Movement of Persons of 22 May 2002 adopted by the Swiss Federal Council, SR 142.203, available in French at <https://www.fedlex.admin.ch/eli/cc/2002/261/fr> (accessed on 1 June 2022).

105 Namely in the case of residence longer than three months; see Article 8(1) to (3) of Directive 2004/38.

106 See, e.g., Article 2(1) of Annex I AFMP.

107 Article 4(1) of the Ordinance on free movement of persons. See <https://www.sem.admin.ch/sem/en/home/themen/aufenthalt/eu_efta.html> (accessed 15 June 2022).

108 For a comparison between the provisions of Directive 2004/38 and the provisions of Annex I AFMP, see M. Jay, 'Homogeneity, the Free Movement of Persons and Integration without Membership: Mission Impossible?' *Croatian Yearbook of European Law & Policy* 8 (2012), pp. 104–111.

opening the doors for more rights for persons who are not economically active in Switzerland. In its press release on the decision not to sign the InstA,[109] the Swiss Federal Council stated that for Switzerland to incorporate the Directive into the AMFP, explicit exemptions would need to be granted: "Without these exceptions, there is a risk that the rights enjoyed by persons accorded freedom of movement would be extended. The impact of this could include higher social security costs. Adopting the [Directive] in its entirety would effectively constitute a paradigm shift in Switzerland's migration policy – a policy which enjoys wide support among the Swiss population and cantons". The Federal Council added that it intends to defend Switzerland's "vital interests" in this respect.

4.2 *Job-Seekers: Residence Rights*

Turning now specifically to job-seekers under Directive 2004/38, one needs to distinguish between two categories of job-seekers. On the one hand, a person can be considered a "first-time job-seeker" due to the fact that he or she has never worked before in the country where he or she is seeking work. For example, fresh graduates who have never worked would fit in that category. On the other hand, a person can be considered a job-seeker after having completed a period of employment or self-employment in the country where he or she is now again seeking work.

First-time job-seekers are entitled to visit the "Contracting States" pursuant to Article 2(1) second paragraph of Annex I AFMP. Furthermore, under the same provision, they are granted the right to reside for a reasonable amount of time, i.e., up to six months, in order to search for a job. In Switzerland, the Ordinance on the free movement of persons indicates that EU nationals do not need a residence permit if they stay for less than three months to seek work. This corresponds to Article 10 of the Swiss Foreign Nationals and Integration Act[110] which grants a right to stay without gainful employment for up to three months without the need to apply for a residence permit. After three months, EU citizens are entitled to a "short-stay permit" for three months per year as

109 Federal Council, "Pas de conclusion de l'accord institutionnel Suisse-UE", Press Release, Bern, 26 May 2021, <https://www.admin.ch/gov/fr/accueil/documentation/communiqu es.msg-id-83705.html> (accessed 1 June 2022).

110 Federal Act on Foreign Nationals and Integration of 16 December 2005 (Foreign Nationals and Integration Act, FNIA), SR 142.20. An unofficial English translation is available at <https://fedlex.data.admin.ch/filestore/fedlex.data.admin.ch/eli/cc/2007/758/20200401/en/pdf-a/fedlex-data-admin-ch-eli-cc-2007-758-20200401-en-pdf-a.pdf> (accessed 14 June 2022).

long as they can show that they have sufficient means to support themselves and comprehensive sickness insurance.[111] That period can be extended to a full year as long as the EU citizen can demonstrate efforts in finding employment and that there are real chances of being employed.[112]

Under the EU Citizens' Rights Directive, any person falling within the scope of the Directive can move to another State for the first three months without any other condition than being in possession of a valid identity card or passport.[113] After three months, Directive 2004/38 distinguishes between economically active and economically inactive persons. "First time job-seekers" fall under the category of economically inactive persons and will have to prove that they have comprehensive sickness insurance coverage and that they possess sufficient financial resources in order not to become a burden on the social security system of the host State.[114] Furthermore, Article 14(4)(b) of Directive 2004/38 provides that the Member States should not expel persons who have entered their territory to seek employment if such persons can provide evidence that they are continuing to seek employment and that they have a genuine chance of finding employment.

As a result, the incorporation of the EU Citizens' Rights Directive into the *acquis* of the AFMP would not change anything to the current residence rights of EU "first time job-seekers" in Switzerland. During the first three months, they are treated in the same manner under the Directive and Annex I in conjunction with the Ordinance: no specific condition is attached to the right of residence. After three months, the same rationale as that found in Directive 2004/38 is followed in Switzerland: job-seekers will have to show that they have sufficient resources. The only notable difference is that the duration of stay for the purpose of finding a job in Switzerland is limited from three to twelve months whereas no such limit exists under the EU Citizens' Rights Directive.

Turning now to the second category of job-seekers, their residence rights depend on their previous status as employed (Article 6 of Annex I AFMP) or self-employed persons (Article 12 of Annex I AFMP). Article 6(1) of Annex I AFMP provides that a worker who is employed for one year or more should receive a residence permit for at least five years. This permit is automatically renewed for at least another five years. That automatic renewal can, however, be limited to a shorter duration of at least one year in case the worker has

111 Article 24 (1) of the Annex I AFMP in conjunction with Article 18(2) of the Ordinance on free movement of persons.

112 Article 18(3) of the Swiss Ordinance on free movement of persons.

113 Article 6 of Directive 2004/38.

114 Article 7(1)(b) of Directive 2004/38.

become unemployed for more than twelve consecutive months.[115] On the other hand, Article 6(6) states that a valid residence permit may not be withdrawn from employed persons merely on the grounds that these persons are no longer working because they are involuntarily unemployed or unable to work due to an accident or illness.[116] Article 2(1) second paragraph also mentions that a person shall have the right to remain after employment for a period of up to one year[117] in order to seek employment.

In the Swiss Foreign Nationals and Integration Act, Article 61a concerns specifically the expiry of the right of residence of EU and EFTA nationals. According to this provision, the right of residence of EU citizens shall expire six months after the involuntary termination of their employment: when they have a short-stay permit;[118] when they have any other permit if employment ends within the first twelve months of residence;[119] or when they have a residence permit[120] if the involuntary unemployment arises following the first twelve months of residence.[121] However, this does not apply in the case of termination of employment due to temporary incapacity to work as a result of illness, accident or disability, or to persons who may invoke a right to remain under the AFMP or the EFTA Convention.

With respect to potential differences under the EU Citizens' Rights Directive, it should be noted that involuntarily unemployed job-seekers retain their status as workers or self-employed persons for the purposes of residence if certain conditions are fulfilled.[122] Apart from specific cases,[123] Directive 2004/38 makes a distinction between job-seekers who have been employed for more than one year before being unemployed and the others. The same condition will apply to both categories: they need to be registered as job-seekers with the relevant employment office.[124] However, in the case of job-seekers who have not been employed for more than one year before unemployment, the

115 Article 6(1) of Annex I.
116 Article 12(6) of Annex I AFMP provides the same for self-employed persons.
117 Residence to up to one year will then be on a "short stay permit" pursuant to Article 32 of the Federal Act on Foreign Nationals and Integration.
118 Article 61a(1) of the Federal Act on Foreign Nationals and Integration.
119 *Ibid.*
120 I.e., for longer than one year pursuant to Article 33 of the Federal Act on Foreign Nationals and Integration.
121 Article 61a(4) of the Federal Act on Foreign Nationals and Integration.
122 Article 7(3) *juncto* Article 7(1)(a) of Directive 2004/38.
123 Covering job-seekers who are unable to work due to illness or accident or those who embark on vocational training (Article 7(3)(a) and (d) of Directive 2004/38).
124 Article 7(3)(b) and (c) *juncto* Article 7(1)(a) of Directive 2004/38.

retention of the right of residence is limited to six months.[125] In this respect, therefore, the EU Citizens' Rights Directive is less advantageous than Annex I AFMP, which provides for one-year retention.[126] Based on this quick comparison, the Swiss Foreign Nationals and Integration Act seems to be more in line with Directive 2004/38 than with Annex I AFMP. Therefore, the refusal of the Swiss Government to incorporate the Directive into the AFMP cannot be explained when it comes to the right of residence of job-seekers alone.

4.3 *Job-Seekers: Access to Social Assistance*

However, matters may be different with respect to access to social assistance for job-seekers in Switzerland. Whilst Article 2(1) Annex I AFMP grants job-seekers the same assistance from employment agencies as nationals receive, it also states that job-seekers may be excluded from social assistance for the duration of their residence.[127] Switzerland in the wake of the "Mass Immigration" vote introduced new federal provisions on this issue. For first-time job-seekers, Article 29a of the Foreign Nationals and Integration Act[128] states that foreign nationals residing in Switzerland solely to seek employment, and their family members, are not entitled to social assistance. For other job-seekers, Article 61a(3) of the same Act stipulates that there is no right to social assistance in the period from the termination of employment until the expiry of the right of residence in accordance with paragraphs 1 and 2.

Regarding social assistance, the EU Citizens' Rights Directive is more generous than the current rules under Annex I and Swiss law. First of all, the term "social assistance" under the Directive has been defined in *Brey* as referring to "all assistance schemes established by the public authorities, whether at national, regional or local level, to which recourse may be had by an individual who does not have resources sufficient to meet his own basic needs and those of his family and who by reason of that fact may, during his period of residence, become a burden on the public finances of the host Member State which could have consequences for the overall level of assistance which may be granted by that State".[129]

---

125 Article 7(3)(c) *juncto* Article 7(1)(a) of Directive 2004/38.

126 Article 2(1) second paragraph of Annex I AFMP.

127 Note that the German, French and Italian language versions of the provision mention "social assistance". Confusingly, the English language version as published in the Official Journal of the EU refers to "social security schemes".

128 B. Kahil-Wolff Hummer, 'Chapter 20: Access to Social Protection by Immigrants, Emigrants and Resident Nationals in Switzerland', in J.-M. Lafleur, D. Vintila (eds.), *Migration and Social Protection in Europe and Beyond Vol 3* (Springer, 2020), p. 339.

129 CJEU, Case C-140/12, *Brey*, EU:C:2013:565, para. 61.

Next, Article 24(1) of the EU Citizens' Rights Directive provides for equal treatment with regard to, *inter alia,* access to social assistance. There are, however, limits to that equal treatment in the second paragraph of Article 24. The host Member State is not obliged to confer entitlement to social assistance on nationals of another Member State or their family members during the first three months of residency. [130] Additionally, while a first-time job-seeker cannot be expelled after three months under the conditions of Article 14(4)(b) of Directive 2004/38, Member States are not obliged to grant that job-seeker social assistance. In a constant jurisprudence since *Dano*,[131] the CJEU has held that in order to benefit from the equal treatment provision regarding access to social assistance, a person must comply with the conditions of residency set out in Article 7(1) of Directive 2004/38.[132] Job-seekers, since they are economically inactive persons, should have sufficient resources for themselves and their family members in order to have a right of residence under Article 7(1)(b) of the EU Citizens' Rights Directive and to benefit from equal treatment with regard to social assistance. Still, in *Dano*, the CJEU considered that the condition of having sufficient resources was meant "to prevent economically inactive Union citizens from using the host Member State's welfare system to fund their means of subsistence".[133]

Overall, if Switzerland were to agree to the incorporation of the EU Citizens' Rights Directive into the AFMP, it would have to grant access to social assistance for EU job-seekers having a right of residence in Switzerland under the same conditions as Swiss nationals who have access to social assistance. This indicates that the Swiss difficulties with respect to Directive 2004/38 and job-seekers are not related to their residence status but rather to the potential right(s) that might be derived from their residence, such as access to social benefits. As indicated above (see Section 4.1), the Swiss Government is opposed to what it perceives as a change of paradigm in the Swiss legal system.

130 It should be noted that in its latest judgment, the CJEU ruled that the right to equal treatment with regard to access to social security benefits can be relied upon from the moment the EU citizen has a right of residence in the host Member State (that includes residence based on Article 6(1) of Directive 2004/38). See CJEU, Case C-411/20 *S v Familienkasse Niedersachsen-Bremen*, ECLI:EU:C:2022:602. For more details, see P. Melin, S. Sivonen, 'Overview of recent cases before the Court of Justice of the European Union (March 2022-September 2022)', *European Journal of Social Security* (forthcoming, 2023).

131 See CJEU, Case C-333/13, *Dano*, EU:C:2014:2358; Case C-67/14, *Alimanovic*, EU :C :2015 :597 ; Case C-299/14, *Garcia Nieto*, EU :C :2016 :114 ; Case C-181/19, *Jobcenter Krefeld*, EU:C:2020:794; Case C-709/20, *CG*, EU:C:2021:602.

132 CJEU, Case C-333/13, *Dano*, EU:C:2014:2358, para. 71.

133 *Ibid.*, para. 76.

5 Conclusion

Due to the Swiss geographical position surrounded by EU / EEA EFTA Member States, the mobility of persons between the EU and Switzerland is an important matter with many practical and political implications. As discussed in this chapter, the AFMP has been the subject of political friction between the contracting parties with diverging opinions on how the free movement of persons needs to evolve. Overall, the integration of EU *acquis* related to the free movement of persons has been a complex process ranging from the (almost) complete integration of the EU social security coordination rules in Annex II AFMP to the absence of integration of the EU's most important *acquis* on the free movement of persons, the EU Citizens' Rights Directive.

As highlighted in Section 2 of this chapter, four institutional aspects of the bilateral relations could explain the difficulties experienced in the AFMP. Firstly, the AFMP is a tailor-made agreement providing partial access to the internal market in the area of free movement of services and persons. Hence, its material scope is different from other agreements, such as the EEA. While differentiation is not necessarily a negative characteristic, the missing important piece of the EU *acquis* on the free movement of persons, the EU Citizens' Rights Directive, remains a stumbling block/rock in the EU-Swiss bilateral integration process. Secondly, the transitional rules that have been in place in the past regarding certain Member States such as Croatia have intensified the political friction between the contracting parties. Thirdly, the lack of dynamic updating of the *Bilaterals*, the AFMP included, in light of revised relevant EU *acquis* has created a slow erosion of the integration. The current EU "pinprick" policy used as a way to force the Swiss side to come to a conclusion on institutional matters has only accelerated that erosion. Fourthly and finally, the absence of a judicial cooperation mechanism does not secure a uniform interpretation of the AFMP. As it was demonstrated in Section 3.1.2, even in the (almost) complete integration of the EU *acquis* on social security coordination, the absence of dynamic updating and judicial cooperation mechanism remains problematic.

Considering the important number of frontier workers between the EU Member States and Switzerland, Section 3 discussed the social security coordination rules for frontier workers. By considering some controversial issues such as the access to unemployment benefits for frontier workers and jobseekers, Section 3 revealed that the current rules on social security coordination between the EU and Switzerland are rather working well but will require a constant update in line with the relevant revisions at the EU level. Finally, the fear voiced by Switzerland that the draft InstA would have had a financial impact on its social security system could not be explained based on the rules on social security coordination between the two contracting parties.

A more plausible explanation of that fear can be found in the potential incorporation of the EU Citizens' Rights Directive, an issue unresolved by the draft InstA. In Section 4, the current rules of Annex I AFMP and of the EU Citizens' Rights Directive concerning residence rights and access to social assistance for job-seekers were compared. On the right of residence, this comparison in fact highlighted that the Swiss law was more in line with the EU Citizen's Rights Directive than with the rules of the Annex I AFMP. However, if Switzerland would agree to the incorporation of the EU Citizens' Rights Directive into the AFMP, it would have to grant access to social assistance for EU job-seekers having a right of residence in Switzerland on the basis of Directive 2004/38 under the same conditions as Swiss nationals have access to social assistance. In that sense, the fear from the Swiss side is not related *per se* to the residence rights of job-seekers but rather to the potential derived right(s) from their residence status, such as access to social benefits.

Overall, this contribution has demonstrated that the free movement of persons is a controversial yet essential piece of the integration process. From the (almost) complete integration of the social security coordination rules to the absence of integration of the EU Citizens' Rights Directive, there are valid reasons for both the EU and Switzerland to stand by their positions. However, the current political dead-end has already consequences for the free movement of persons with the slow erosion between the rules of the AFMP and the EU *acquis*. What solution might be favoured, only the future will tell us but the necessity to find one is undeniable for the sake of people moving across the Swiss-EU borders.

CHAPTER 3

Sectoral Bilateralism

Lessons from the Case Law of the Court of Justice of the European Union

Peter Van Elsuwege

1 Introduction

The negative outcome of a popular vote on the signature of the Agreement on the European Economic Area (EEA) in 1992 has been a defining moment in the evolution of the relationship between Switzerland and the EU.[1] As a consequence, the initial ambitions of association and even potential membership made place for an approach which can be described as *sectoral bilateralism*. The key feature of this model is the gradual development of close bilateral relations in response to specific needs but without a general framework agreement. On several occasions, the EU emphasised the limits of this approach. In particular, the complexity and incompleteness of the system of bilateral agreements with the resulting legal uncertainty for citizens and businesses brought the EU to insist on a new institutional arrangement.[2]

Leaving aside the difficulties surrounding the conclusion of an EU-Switzerland Institutional Agreement (InstA) and its implications,[3] this contribution focuses on the relevant case law of the Court of Justice of the European Union (CJEU). In particular, the aim of this chapter is to assess the key features of the existing approach of sectoral bilateralism from the perspective of EU external relations law. Specific attention is devoted to the interpretation and application of the Agreement on Free Movement of Persons (AFMP)[4] and the agreements associating Switzerland to the EU's Schengen and Dublin *acquis*.[5]

1 Agreement on the European Economic Area (EEA) (OJ 1994, L 1).

2 Council of the EU, 'Conclusions on EU Relations with the Swiss Confederation', doc. 6767/17, Brussels, 28 February 2017.

3 See the contributions by C. Kaddous and R. Schwok to this volume.

4 Agreement between the European Community and its Member States, of the one part, and the Swiss Confederation, of the other, on the free movement of persons (OJ 2002, L 114/6).

5 Agreement between the European Community and the Swiss Confederation concerning the criteria and mechanisms for establishing the State responsible for examining a request for asylum lodged in a Member State or in Switzerland, OJ (2008) L 53/5 (hereafter "Dublin Association Agreement"); Agreement between the European Union, the European

© KONINKLIJKE BRILL NV, LEIDEN, 2023 | DOI:10.1163/9789004529984_005

The former entails a "static" approach to the incorporation of new EU legislation, implying that there is no obligation to incorporate new EU *acquis*, whereas the latter agreements are "dynamic" in nature, including a procedure for the continuous incorporation of new EU legislation.[6] In comparing both sets of agreements and the relevant case law of the CJEU, this chapter illustrates the law and practice of sectoral bilateralism and the specific challenges of Switzerland's unique model of cooperation with the EU.

2 Switzerland and the EU Internal Market: Differentiated Integration

As upheld by the Court of Justice on several occasions, the rejection of the EEA Agreement implies that Switzerland "did not subscribe to the project of an economically integrated entity with a single market, based on common rules between its member states."[7] Alternatively, the objective of the EU-Switzerland bilateral agreements is to enhance deep sectoral cooperation and to strengthen the economic ties. Whereas certain agreements have an explicit integration-oriented dimension,[8] implying a commitment to apply selected EU legislation, the absence of a comprehensive integration objective into the internal market has significant implications. In particular, as determined in the case law of the Court of Justice, the interpretation of specific commitments under the EU's international agreements largely depends upon their integration objectives in relation to the EU internal market. As can be derived from the classic *Polydor* case, a textual parallelism between certain provisions of an international agreement and those of the EU Treaties is insufficient to ensure an

---

Community and the Swiss Confederation on the Swiss Confederation's association with the implementation, application and development of the Schengen *acquis* (OJ 2008, L 53/52) (hereafter "Schengen Association Agreement").

6 On the difference between "static" and "dynamic" models for the adoption of the legislative frameworks, see also A. Lazowski, 'Enhanced Multilateralism and Enhanced Bilateralism: Integration without Membership in the European Union', *Common Market Law Review* 45 (2008), p. 1444.

7 CJEU, Case C-351/08, *Grimme*, EU:C:2009:697, para. 27; Case C-541/08, *Fokus Invest*, EU:C:2010:74, para. 28; see also Case C-70/09, *Hengartner and Gasser*, EU:C:2010:430, para. 41; Case C-355/16, *Picart*, EU:C:2018:184, para. 29.

8 Reference can be made to the Agreement on Free Movement of Persons, the Agreement on Air Transport and the Agreements on the association of Switzerland to the Schengen and Dublin *acquis*, see M. Maresceau, 'Les accords d'intégration dans les relations de proximité de l'Union européenne', in C. Blumann (ed.), *Les frontières de l'Union européenne* (Bruylant, 2013), p. 176; also M. Maresceau, 'EU-Switzerland: *Quo Vadis ?*', *Georgia Journal of International and Comparative Law*, 39 (2011), pp. 727–755.

identical interpretation. The legal consequences attributed to the respective provisions depend upon the aim and context of the agreement in comparison to the aim and context of the EU Treaties.[9] The latter constitute the constitutional framework of a separate legal order providing for the establishment of a Single Market having the characteristics of a domestic market. This specific and far-reaching objective implies that the Court's case law regarding the interpretation of the internal market rules cannot automatically be transposed in relation to third countries.[10]

The implications of this basic principle have been clearly illustrated in the CJEU's case law regarding the EU's relations with Switzerland. On several occasions, the Court of Justice proceeded from the observation that the interpretation given to provisions of EU law concerning the internal market does not automatically apply under the EU-Swiss bilateral agreements unless there are express provisions to that effect in the agreements themselves.[11] Accordingly, Swiss nationals may face restrictions that would be unacceptable in the EU internal market and, *vice versa*, EU nationals may be confronted with similar issues in Switzerland.

A typical example is the dispute regarding the unilateral decision of the German authorities to limit the use of certain flight routes to the airport of Zurich. The Swiss Government contested the compatibility of those measures with the freedom to provide services based upon the EU-Swiss bilateral agreement on air transport.[12] After the Commission had rejected a Swiss complaint,[13] the issue was brought before the Court of Justice. In this respect, it is

---

9 CJEU, Case 270/80, *Polydor*, EU:C:1982:43, para. 15–16; see also Case C-312/91, *Metalsa*, EU:C:1993:279, para. 11.

10 On the implications of the *Polydor* principle, see also C. Tobler, 'Context-related Interpretation of Association Agreements. The *Polydor* Principle in a Comparative Perspective: EEA Law, Ankara Association Law and Market Access Agreements between Switzerland and the EU', in D. Thym, M. Zoeteweij-Turhan (eds.), *Rights of Third-Country Nationals under EU Association Agreements. Degrees of Free Movement and Citizenship* (Brill, 2015), pp. 101–126.

11 See, e.g., CJEU, Case C-351/08, *Grimme*, EU:C:2009:697, para. 27; C-541/08, *Fokus Invest*, EU:C:2010:74, para. 28; Case C-70/09, *Hengartner and Gasser*, EU:C:2010:430, para. 42; Case C-547/10P, *Switzerland v Commission*, EU:C:2013:139, para. 81; Case C-355/16, *Picart*, EU:C:2018:184, para. 29.

12 Agreement between the European Community and the Swiss Confederation on Air Transport (OJ 2002, L 114/73).

13 Commission Decision 2004/12 of 5 December 2003 on a procedure relating to the application of Article 18(2), first sentence, of the Agreement between the European Community and the Swiss Confederation on air transport and Council Regulation (EEC) No 2408/92 (OJ 2004, L 4/13).

noteworthy that Article 20 of the Air Transport Agreement provides that all questions concerning the validity of decisions of the EU institutions adopted in the framework of this agreement fall within "the exclusive competence of the Court of Justice of the European Communities."[14] In its order of 14 July 2015, the Court of Justice interpreted this expression as including also the Court of First Instance (now the "General Court").[15] Accordingly, it decided that Switzerland's action for annulment had to be brought before the latter Court first. Arguably, this interpretation ignored the intentions of Switzerland in accepting the inclusion of Article 20 of the Air Transport Agreement.[16] Apart from this procedural question, the dispute also clarified the limits of a reasoning based upon parallelism with EU internal market rules. Both the General Court and, upon appeal, the Court of Justice rejected the complaint of Switzerland taking into account that the EU-Swiss air transport agreement "does not contain any specific provision such as to enable the air carriers concerned to benefit from the provisions of European Union law on the freedom to provide services. The interpretation given to those provisions cannot, therefore, be transposed to that agreement."[17]

As a corollary of the *Polydor* principle, it may be concluded that from an EU law perspective the extension of the internal market beyond the EU's borders should go hand in hand with legal instruments guaranteeing the homogeneous interpretation and application of the shared legal rules.[18] This basic rule can be derived from a comparative analysis of three largely comparable cases initiated by the UK against the Council regarding the choice of a legal basis for the adoption of an EU position needed for the enactment of new EU rules on social security coordination in relation to the EEA countries, Switzerland and

14 Article 20 of the Agreement between the European Community and the Swiss Confederation on Air Transport (OJ 2002, L 114/73).

15 CJEU, Case C-70/04, *Switzerland v Commission*, EU:C:2005:468, para. 18.

16 See M. Maresceau, *Quo Vadis* (n. 8), pp. 749–750.

17 CJEU, Case C-547/10P, *Confédération Suisse v European Commission*, EU:C:2013:139, para. 81. On this approach, see L.M. Baudenbacher, 'EuGH überträgt die Polydor-Rechtsprechung auch auf das Luftverkehrsabkommen', *European Law Reporter* 2013, pp. 173–182, and C. Tobler, 'Luftverkehrsrecht: Auslegung des Luftverkehrsabkommens EU-Schweiz – Keine Anwendbarkeit der Dienstleistungsfreiheit', *Europäische Zeitschrift für Wirtschaftsrecht* 2013, pp. 432–434.

18 P. Van Elsuwege, 'Exporting the internal market beyond the EU's borders: between political ambition and legal reality', in F. Amtenbrink, G. Davies, D. Kochenov and J. Lindeboom (eds.), *The Internal Market and the Future of European Integration. Essays in Honour of Laurence W. Gormley* (Cambridge University Press, 2019), p. 645.

Turkey respectively.[19] In all three cases, the UK argued that this decision could not be legally adopted on the basis of Article 48 TFEU dealing with the social security dimension of the free movement of workers within the EU internal market. Rather, it took the view that Article 79(2)(b) TFEU, which refers to the rights of third-country nationals residing legally in the Union and belonging to the Treaty rules on the Area of Freedom, Security and Justice (AFSJ), constituted the correct legal basis.

What may seem at first sight to be a rather technical discussion about the choice of legal basis has in fact far-reaching constitutional implications. In particular, the cases concern the question to what extent competences attributed in the EU Treaties with regard to the internal EU legal order can be used to make EU law applicable outside the territory of the Union. The UK argued that Article 48 TFEU only concerns the free movement of EU nationals within the Union implying that it cannot be used as a legal basis in relation to third-country nationals and beyond the EU's borders. The CJEU, however, rejected this approach in light of the international commitments undertaken by the EU and its Member States. It observed that the EEA Agreement essentially extends the territorial and personal scope of the EU internal market rules to the participating EFTA States and their nationals to conclude that Article 48 TFEU is the appropriate legal basis.[20] Even though the established legal framework with Switzerland has less far-reaching ambitions regarding the internal market, a specific provision in the bilateral Agreement on Free Movement of Persons implies that at least for the issue of social security coordination Switzerland is to be treated as if it is a Member State of the EU.[21] In this context, Article 48 TFEU could also be used as the sole legal basis. To the contrary, the association law with Turkey does not include such far-reaching objectives implying that Turkey cannot be placed on the same footing as the EU Member States as far as the application of the internal market legislation, in this case, the regulation on the coordination of social security systems, is concerned. *Mutatis mutandis,*

---

19 CJEU, Case C-431/11, *UK v Council* (*EEA*), EU:C:2013:589; Case C-656/11, *UK v Council* (*Switzerland*), EU:C:2014:97; Case C-81/13, *UK v Council* (*Turkey*), EU:C:2014:2449. On social security coordination and on the Switzerland case, see also the contribution by P. Melin in this volume.

20 CJEU, Case C-431/11, *UK v Council* (*EEA*), EU:C:2013:589, paras. 58–61.

21 Article 8 of the EU-Switzerland Agreement on Free Movement of Persons reproduces the provisions currently in Article 48(a) and (b) TFEU. Moreover, Articles 1 and 2 and Section A of Annex II to this Agreement provide that the term "Member States" contained in specific EU regulations on the coordination of social security schemes is deemed to include also the Swiss Confederation. See CJEU, Case C-656/11, *UK v Council* (*Switzerland*), EU:C:2014:97, paras. 56–58.

Article 48 TFEU cannot be the sole legal basis for adopting the EU's position in the EU-Turkey Association Council.[22]

The combined reading of the three *UK v Council* cases reveals that the use of EU internal market competences as a legal basis for exporting the Union's internal legislation abroad presupposes the existence of integration-oriented agreements providing for the homogeneous interpretation and application of the shared legal rules.[23] The EEA Agreement is the only agreement concluded by the EU which contains an explicit reference to the homogeneity principle and an institutional structure designed for this purpose. As a result, the participating EFTA countries (Norway, Iceland, Liechtenstein) have become "virtual" EU Member States which apply the entire internal market legislation by analogy.[24] With respect to Switzerland, the situation is more complicated. In the absence of an overarching institutional framework, the homogeneous application of the exported EU *acquis* is limited to areas where this is explicitly foreseen under the sectoral agreements. This is, for instance, the case with respect to questions of social security coordination for migrant workers. In accordance with Article 1 of Annex II to the AFMP, the term "Member State(s)" contained in EU legal acts referred to in this annex shall be understood to also include Switzerland. One of those legal acts is Regulation 833/2004 on the coordination of social security systems.[25] It follows that for the interpretation and application of this Regulation, it does not matter that a national of an EU Member State went to Switzerland instead of another EU Member State.[26] The situation is different with respect to areas of the EU *acquis* where (the annexes to) the EU-Swiss agreements do not include such express provisions. This is, for instance, the case with respect to the right to freedom of establishment, where there are significant differences between the personal and material scope of this right within the EU legal order and in the framework of EU-Swiss bilateral relations (see *infra*).[27]

As a consequence, the specific interpretation of the shared legal rules varies depending upon the specific commitments under the respective agreements.

22 CJEU, Case C-81/13, *UK v Council (Turkey)*, EU:C:2014:2449, para. 59.

23 N. Rennuy, P. Van Elsuwege, 'Integration without membership and the dynamic development of EU law: *United Kingdom v Council (EEA)*', *Common Market Law Review* 51 (2014), p. 946.

24 See, in this respect, also CJEU, Case C-476/10, *projekart Errichtungsgesellschaft et. al.*, EU:C:2011:422, para. 37.

25 Regulation (EC) No 883/2004 of the European Parliament and of the Council of 29 April 2004 on the coordination of social security systems (OJ 2004, L 166/1).

26 CJEU, Case C-551/16, *Klein Schiphorst*, EU:C:2018:200, paras. 27–29.

27 See, e.g., CJEU, Case C-355/16, *Picart*, EU:C:2018:184, paras. 29–32.

The result is a *sui generis* form of differentiated integration, to be distinguished from the EEA model of comprehensive integration into the internal market and other agreements strengthening the economic ties between the EU and its neighbours.[28]

3 Switzerland and the Agreement on Free Movement of Persons: Illustrating the Limits of Sectoral Bilateralism

The limitations of the model of sectoral bilateralism can be illustrated with the case law of the Court of Justice regarding the Agreement on Free Movement of Persons (AFMP). The latter was concluded in 1999 as part of the so-called *Bilaterals I* package.[29] It is an agreement with a clear integration dimension. This can already be derived from the preamble, which provides that the Contracting Parties are determined "to bring about the free movement of persons between them on the basis of the rules applying in the European [Union]."[30] Moreover, Article 16 AFMP includes an obligation for the Contracting Parties to take "all measures necessary to ensure that those rights and obligations equivalent to those contained in the legal acts of the European [Union] to which reference is made are applied in relations between them." Insofar as the agreement involves concepts of EU law, "account shall be taken of relevant case-law of the Court of Justice of the European [Union] prior to the date of its signature."[31] With respect to subsequent judicial developments at EU level, the agreement only foresees that this case law "shall be brought to Switzerland's attention",

---

28 S. Breitenmoser, 'Sectoral Agreements between the EC and Switzerland: Context and Content', *Common Market Law Review* 40 (2003), p. 1185; M.-L. Oberg, *The Boundaries of the EU Internal Market. Participation without Membership* (Cambridge University Press, 2020), p. 24.

29 "*Bilaterals I*" refers to a package of seven bilateral agreements signed in 1999, covering free movement of persons, overland transport, air transport, agriculture, research, technical barriers to trade and public procurement. They are all published in OJ 2002, L 114/1, and tied together on the basis of a so-called "guillotine clause" implying that the seven agreements enter into force at the same time and can only be terminated together. For comments, see C. Kaddous, 'The Relations between the EU and Switzerland', in A. Dashwood and M. Maresceau (eds.), *Law and Practice of EU External Relations. Salient Features of a Changing Landscape* (Cambridge University Press, 2008), pp. 231–243.

30 Agreement between the European Community and its Member States, of the one part, and the Swiss Confederation, of the other, on the free movement of persons (OJ 2002, L 114/6). For comments, see A. Borghi, *La libre circulation des personnes entre la Suisse et l'UE. Commentaire article par article de l'accord du 21 juin 1999* (Edis, 2010).

31 *Ibid.*, Article 16(2) AFMP.

with a role for the Joint Committee to determine its implications in order to ensure that the Agreement works properly.[32] This rather soft approach, which is also reflected in the procedure to deal with legislative developments[33] and the settlement of disputes,[34] may be regarded as one of the weaknesses of the established legal framework.[35] Arguably, it is one of the key elements preventing a homogeneous interpretation of the shared legal rules.

In the absence of more explicit legal provisions regarding the dynamic integration of Switzerland in the EU internal market, the Court of Justice indicated the limitations of the AFMP on several occasions. For instance, in *Grimme*, the Court dismissed the applicant's claim that the scope of the AFMP provisions on the right to freedom of establishment covered both natural and legal persons as guaranteed under the *acquis communautaire*. Proceeding from the *Polydor* logic that the interpretation of the EU's internal market legislation cannot be automatically applied by analogy to the interpretation of the AFMP, the Court of Justice found that the latter agreement was essentially confined to the granting of rights to natural persons.[36] The Court refused to go beyond the mere wording of the agreement, implying that the material scope of the right of establishment under the AFMP does not include legal persons. Consequently, the equal treatment between companies and natural persons for the purpose of the right of establishment as laid down in Article 54 TFEU does not apply in the context of the EU-Swiss AFMP.[37]

In *Hengartner and Gasser*, the Court of Justice explicitly provided that "the [EU] Treaty provisions on freedom of establishment cannot apply to a national of a non-member country such as the Swiss Federation."[38] It also excluded an interpretation by analogy as it applies in the framework of the EEA Agreement. Although the AFMP also covers many areas of EU law, this is not sufficient to justify a dynamic, teleological interpretation leading to a homogeneous application of the various provisions. As observed by Advocate General Jääskinen in this case, the coverage of the AFMP "is limited by the specific nature of its provisions and because it contains provisions designed to limit or to clarify its material or temporal scope."[39] These limitations "are foreign to European

32 *Ibid.*
33 Article 17 AFMP.
34 Article 19 AFMP.
35 M. Maresceau, *Quo Vadis* (n. 8), p. 743.
36 CJEU, Case C-351/08, *Grimme*, EU:C:2009:697, paras. 31–39.
37 CJEU, Case C-541/08, *Fokus Invest*, EU:C:2010:74, para. 34.
38 CJEU, Case C-70/09, *Hengartner and Gasser*, EU:C:2010:430, para. 26.
39 Opinion of Advocate General Jääskinen in Case C-70/09, *Hengartner and Gasser*, EU:C:2010:289, para. 46.

Union law."[40] Hence, the AFMP is interpreted as a standard international agreement, in line with the Vienna Convention on the Law of Treaties. This implies an interpretation "in good faith in accordance with the ordinary meaning to be given to its terms in their context and in light of its object and purpose."[41]

Applied to the specific issue at stake, i.e., the application of differential tax regimes between Swiss and EU nationals for the use of services such as the lease of a right to hunt, the Court concluded that the AFMP did not preclude such differentiation even though this would be prohibited in the context of the EU internal market. In this respect, it is noteworthy that the case concerned the so-called "passive" freedom of services involving the rights of service recipients. Hence, the key question was whether the Court's case law about the scope of the right to services in EU law as interpreted in *Luisi and Carbone* could also be transposed to the AFMP. In this landmark judgment, the Court of Justice clarified that the freedom of services within the EU internal market includes the right of service recipients to go to another Member State in order to receive a service there without facing any restrictions.[42] In *Hengartner and Gasser*, the Court of Justice did not follow this line of reasoning and simply observed that the AFMP and its annexes "do not contain any specific rule intended to allow recipients of services to benefit from the principle of non-discrimination."[43] Together with the classic rule that provisions of EU law concerning the internal market cannot be automatically applied by analogy in the absence of specific provisions to that effect, the Court rejected the inclusion of similar rights for service recipients in the framework of EU-Swiss relations.[44] Arguably, the Court's reliance on the *Polydor* principle was perhaps unnecessary in this particular case. Taking into account that the AFMP remains silent on market access rights of service recipients, it may have simply observed that such situations fall outside the scope of this agreement.[45]

In subsequent case law, the Court of Justice further clarified the different scope of the right to freedom of establishment under the AFMP in comparison to this right under Article 49 TFEU. In *Picart*, the Court stressed the more limited scope of the notion of "self-employed persons" within the meaning of

---

40 *Ibid.*

41 CJEU, Case C-70/09, *Hengartner and Gasser*, EU:C:2010:430, para. 36.

42 CJEU, Joint cases 286/82 and 26/83, *Luisi and Carbone*, EU:C:1984:35, para. 16.

43 CJEU, Case C-70/09, *Hengartner and Gasser*, EU:C:2010:430, para. 40.

44 It is noteworthy that the Court of Justice also rejected an interpretation by analogy to the reasoning in *Luisi and Carbone* in the framework of EU-Turkey relations. See CJEU, Case C-221/11, *Demirkan*, EU:C:2013:583, para. 62.

45 C. Tobler (n. 10), p. 110.

the AFMP. Proceeding from a textual interpretation of Article 12(1) of Annex I to the AFMP, it found that the right of establishment under this agreement is restricted to "natural persons who are nationals of a Contracting Party and wish to become established in the territory of another Contracting Party *in order to pursue a self-employed activity in that territory*."[46] Article 13 of the same Annex deals with the specific situation of self-employed frontier workers, who in principle return to their place of residence every day or at least once a week. Accordingly, a French national who had moved his residence to Switzerland while maintaining his economic activity in France but did not fall within the definition of a self-employed frontier worker, could not benefit from the right to free movement of establishment under the AFMP in a dispute with the French tax authorities concerning the re-assessment of the unrealised gain on the shares which he had declared when he transferred his tax residence from France to Switzerland (case *Picart*). Significantly, a comparable situation within the EU internal market would fall within the scope of application of the right to freedom of establishment as defined under Article 49 TFEU.[47] However, such a comparison was not deemed relevant in this case since "neither the wording nor the scope of [Article 49 TFEU] can be treated as analogous to those of the relevant provisions of the AFMP."[48]

Despite this narrow interpretation of the scope of the AFMP in cases such as *Grimme, Hengarter and Gasser* or *Picart*, the Court proceeds from an interpretation based on general principles of EU law for the material interpretation of rules falling within the scope of application of the AFMP. In *Graf and Engel*, for instance, the Court interpreted the principle of equal treatment with regard to access to a self-employed activity under the AFMP with a reference to the interpretation of this principle in the EU legal order.[49] In this respect, the Court relied on the more general context of relations between the EU and Switzerland for the interpretation of the relevant provisions. After observing that Switzerland opted not to participate in the EEA or the internal market, it was emphasised that Switzerland is "nevertheless linked to the Union by numerous agreements covering a wide range of areas and prescribing rights and specific obligations, analogous, in some respects to those laid down by the Treaty. The general objective of these agreements [...] is to strengthen the economic ties between the European Union and the Swiss Confederation."

46 CJEU, Case C-355/16, *Picart*, EU:C:2018:184, para. 22 (emphasis added).

47 CJEU, Case C-470/04, *N*, EU:C:2006:525.

48 CJEU, Case C-355/16, *Picart*, EU:C:2018:184, para. 31.

49 CJEU, Case C-506/10, *Graf and Engel*, EU:C:2011:643, para. 26.

Accordingly, it was concluded that derogations from fundamental rules such as the principle of equal treatment must be interpreted strictly.[50]

A similar approach was followed in *Wächtler*. The latter case concerned a dispute between a German national and the German tax authorities following the transfer of his residence from Germany to Switzerland and concerning the taxation of unrealised capital gains with respect to the shares held by him in a company established in Switzerland of which he was the managing director. Deferral of the payment of the tax would have been possible if the transfer of the residence had been to an EU or to an EEA EFTA State. Contrary to the situation at stake in *Picart* (cf. *supra*), the activity pursued by Mr Wächtler in Switzerland was not that of a shareholding-management activity. He was a self-employed entrepreneur providing IT consultancy services through a company, rather than being an investor or a mere silent shareholder.[51] Hence, the situation of Mr Wächtler fell within the personal scope of the AFMP, raising subsequent questions about the substantive interpretation of the principle of equal treatment as laid down in Article 15(2) of Annex I to the AFMP. In this respect, the Court of Justice observed that the principle of equal treatment is a concept of EU law which already existed at the date of signature of the AFMP.[52]

As far as the post-signature case law is concerned, it was held that this also has to be taken into account even when the Joint Committee has not determined its implications in so far as it does nothing more than clarify or confirm the principles established before.[53] Proceeding from those considerations, the Court of Justice observed that "the right of establishment, within the meaning of EU law, has the aim not only of ensuring that foreign nationals are treated in the host Member State in the same way as nationals of that State, but also of preventing restrictions on that right issuing from the Member State of origin of the national concerned."[54] Accordingly, it found that "in certain circumstances and in the light of the applicable provisions, nationals of a Contracting Party of the AFMP may claim rights under that agreement not only against the State to which they exercise freedom of movement but also against their State of origin."[55] In other words, Mr Wächtler – as a German national and self-employed person falling within the scope of the AFMP – could rely on the principle of equal treatment against Germany.

50 *Ibid.*, para. 33.
51 Opinion of AG Wathelet in Case C-581/17, *Wächtler*, EU:C:2018:779, para. 43.
52 CJEU, Case C-581/17, *Wächtler*, EU:C:2019:138, para. 55.
53 *Ibid.*, para. 39.
54 *Ibid.*, para. 51.
55 *Ibid.*, para. 52.

With respect to the substantive interpretation of the principle of equal treatment, the Court pointed at the difference in fiscal treatment of Mr Wächtler as compared to other German nationals who also pursued a self-employed activity by means of a company in which they own shares but who maintained their domicile in Germany. Hence, the fiscal disadvantage for Mr Wächtler as a result of the transfer of his domicile to Switzerland may impede his right of establishment as guaranteed under the AFMP.[56] In the absence of any justifications based on overriding reasons of general interest, the tax regime as applied to persons in the situation of Mr Wächtler constitutes "an unjustified restriction on the right to establishment provided for by the AFMP."[57] However, the judgment does not explicitly clarify whether the principle of equality under the AFMP also includes a prohibition of non-discriminatory restrictions.[58]

In any event, the CJEU appears to avoid a hard distinction between "pre-signature" and "post-signature" case law for situations falling with the scope of the AFMP, at least as far as the interpretation of well-established concepts of EU law is concerned. Arguably, any other solution would be utterly artificial and contradict the objective to realize free movement among the parties "on the basis of the rules applying in the European [Union]."[59] Interestingly enough, such an approach is also reflected in the case law of the Swiss Federal Supreme Court (FSC). The latter developed the general principle that post-signature case law of the CJEU will be taken into account in light of the objective of the AFMP to establish parallel legal rules.[60] At the same time, the FSC also emphasised its own interpretative autonomy since the CJEU has no competence to decide on the interpretation of the AFMP for Switzerland. Accordingly, the FSC is not precluded from following a different approach "when there are serious grounds for this."[61]

Even though the FSC has been rather consistent in applying a so-called doctrine of "EU-compatible interpretation",[62] the fact remains that Switzerland

56 *Ibid.*, paras. 56–57.

57 *Ibid.*, para. 67.

58 See B. Pirker, L. Matter, 'Recent Practice: Europarecht: Schweiz–Europäische Union', *Swiss Review of International and European Law* 30 (2020), p. 88.

59 See the preamble to the AFMP (n. 30).

60 F. Maiani, 'CJEU Citations in the Case Law of the Swiss Federal Supreme Court. A Quantitative/Qualitative Analysis', in A. Reich, H.-W. Micklitz (eds.), *The Impact of the European Court of Justice on Neighbouring Countries* (Oxford University Press, 2020), pp. 99–100.

61 *Ibid.*, p. 100.

62 This doctrine implies that Swiss legislation that has been autonomously adapted to EU law must be interpreted in light of the subsequent development of the latter; see F. Maiani

retains a large degree of autonomy in deciding on the incorporation of EU law developments in the bilateral *acquis*. This dependence on the "goodwill" of the Swiss authorities, including the Swiss courts, is difficult to reconcile with the EU's increased insistence on the creation of homogeneous market conditions and a level playing field within the bilateral relationship.[63] It is also the main reason behind the EU's position that the conclusion of a new institutional arrangement including guarantees for the homogeneous interpretation of shared legal rules is a precondition for the further development of the bilateral relationship with Switzerland.

The key challenge is the possible divergence between the rules applicable within the EU and those applicable to Switzerland's participation in the internal market. Whereas Switzerland mostly agrees to regularly update the bilateral agreements in light of the evolutions in EU law,[64] this is not always an easy exercise. This is particularly obvious in relation to the free movement of persons, where the EU *acquis* significantly developed since the signature of the AFMP in 1999. A crucial evolution is the growing EU *acquis* regarding the rights connected to EU citizenship and the adoption of the EU Citizens' Rights Directive 2004/38.[65] The latter replaced the previous piecemeal approach to the right of free movement and residence for EU citizens and their family members. Switzerland, however, consistently refused to incorporate this new Directive within the framework of the AFMP. The main reason is that a full update would involve additional entitlements in relation to social welfare rights for economically inactive persons, students and family members. In addition, a more principled argument concerns the observation that the concept of Union citizenship cannot apply with respect to a third country such as Switzerland.[66]

(n. 60), p. 102. On autonomous adaptation, see also the contribution by M. Oesch and M. Brugger in this volume.

63 M. Maresceau, *Quo Vadis* (n. 8), p. 745.

64 See, for instance, Decision No 1/2020 of the Joint European Union/Switzerland Air Transport Committee set up under the Agreement between the European Community and the Swiss Confederation on Air Transport of 15 June 2020 replacing the Annex to the Agreement between the European Community and the Swiss Confederation on Air Transport (OJ 2020, L 194/17).

65 Directive 2004/38/EC of the European Parliament and of the Council of 29 April 2004 on the right of citizens of the Union and their family members to move and reside freely within the territory of the Member States (OJ 2004, L 158/77).

66 It is noteworthy, in this respect, that the incorporation of Directive 2004/38 in the EEA also raised similar concerns. This has been pragmatically solved through the adoption of a Joint Declaration added to the relevant Joint Committee Decision. However, this solution is not uncontroversial in the sense that it left a wide margin of appreciation to the

A direct consequence of the Swiss refusal to incorporate Directive 2004/38 in the framework of the AFMP is the emergence of a gap between the law applicable in the EU and that applicable in EU-Swiss relations.[67] The latter is still based on references to old directives, which have all been repealed and replaced in the EU legal order. As a result, the administrative authorities and courts in the EU and Switzerland are confronted with the challenging task to avoid, as far as possible, the emergence of contradictory interpretations. Such an approach obviously raises questions in terms of legal certainty, transparency and efficiency.[68] Without entering into the discussion about the possible options for the further development of EU-Swiss relations in general and the incorporation of Directive 2004/38 in the AFMP in particular, it suffices to observe that the "static" nature of the current arrangement does not allow for the full and consistent participation of Switzerland in the EU internal market. The result is a rather fragmented approach, ranging from the in principle full application of certain EU legal acts – notably with respect to the social security coordination of migrant workers – to a more limited integration in relation to the freedom of establishment and services.[69]

4 Integration without Membership: Association to the Schengen and the Dublin *acquis*

Finally, it is noteworthy that the EU and Switzerland also concluded more dynamic integration agreements. Of particular significance are the bilateral agreements providing for the association of Switzerland to the Schengen and the Dublin *acquis*.[70] Both agreements proceed from an explicit integration logic. They include a list of relevant EU legislation, which is to be implemented and applied by Switzerland. Moreover, the agreements include an incorporation procedure to cope with the development of the relevant EU *acquis*. In essence, this implies an obligation for the Council of the EU to immediately notify Switzerland of new legal acts falling within the scope of the agreements.

---

courts. See C. Tobler, 'Free Movement of Persons in the EU v. in the EEA: Of Effect-Related Homogeneity and A Reversed *Polydor* Principle', *European Papers* 3 (2018), pp. 1429–1451.

67 M. Oesch, 'Switzerland-EU Bilateral Agreements. The Incorporation of EU Law and The Continuous Erosion of Democratic Rights', *Yearbook of European Law* 39 (2020), pp. 609–610. See also the contribution by P. Melin in this volume.

68 *Ibid.*, p. 612.

69 For this difference, see again the contribution by P. Melin in this volume.

70 Dublin Association Agreement and Schengen Association Agreement (n. 5).

Switzerland then has to decide about the acceptance of this new legislation and its implementation in its internal legal order. This decision is to be notified to the Council and the Commission within 30 days after the adoption of the acts or measures concerned.[71] Significantly, the procedure takes into account the implications of the Swiss constitutional system of direct democracy in the sense that there is a two-year time period to notify the EU about the definitive approval of the new rules when a referendum is to be organised. In the meantime, Switzerland is expected to implement the act or measure in question on a provisional basis. When such a provisional application is not possible and if it causes difficulties for the smooth operation of the Schengen cooperation, the situation shall be examined by the Mixed Committee and the EU may take appropriate and proportionate measures against Switzerland.[72] When Switzerland does not approve the incorporation of a legal act within the envisaged time limit and the Mixed Committee subsequently fails to reach a mutually agreeable solution within 90 days, the agreement in question is deemed to be terminated.[73] Due to the inherent link between the Schengen and Dublin Association Agreements, the non-implementation of one agreement also leads to the non-application of the other agreement.[74]

This dynamic procedure is closely connected to the subject-matter of the agreements. The areas covered by the Schengen and Dublin system require the uniform application of mutually shared legal rules. Without the prompt incorporation of new developments, the proper functioning of the entire system would be jeopardised.[75] This far-reaching form of "integration without membership" goes hand in hand with some form of "participation without membership." This implies a role in the decision-shaping process of relevant EU legislation[76] as well as a right to submit observations to the Court of Justice in cases where

71 Article 7 (2) (a) of the Schengen Association Agreement and Article 4(2) of the Dublin Association Agreement.

72 Article 7 (2) (b) of the Schengen Association Agreement and Article 4(3) and (4) of the Dublin Association Agreement.

73 Article 7 (4) of the Schengen Association Agreement. With respect to the Dublin *acquis*, the agreement will first be suspended and, in the absence of a solution after 90 days, terminated. See Article 4(6) and (7) of the Dublin Association Agreement.

74 Article 15 (4) of the Schengen Association Agreement and Article 14(2) of the Dublin Association Agreement.

75 Oesch (n. 67), p. 613.

76 For the drafting of new legislation in a field covered by the agreements, the Commission shall informally seek the advice of Swiss experts in the same way as it seeks the advice from experts of the Member States. See Article 6 of the Schengen Association Agreement and Article 2(6) of the Dublin Association Agreement.

a court in a Member State has submitted a request for a preliminary ruling concerning the interpretation of the relevant *acquis*.[77]

The implications of the Swiss participation in the Schengen and Dublin system can be illustrated with the incorporation of a new EU Directive on the control of the acquisition and possession of weapons (also known as the Firearms Directive).[78] The latter was adopted in the wake of the terrorist attacks in Paris in 2015 and provided, amongst others, for stricter rules on the private possession of firearms. Taking into account that the Directive forms part of the Schengen *acquis*, it also affected Switzerland. In this respect, it is noteworthy that Switzerland actively contributed to the shaping of this new legislation. In light of the Swiss long-standing tradition that former military conscripts can keep their weapons once their military duties have been fulfilled, a specific provision was included in Article 6(6) of the EU Firearms Directive. This provision allowed "Member States applying a military system based on general conscription and having in place over the last 50 years a system of transfer of military firearms to persons leaving the army after fulfilling their military duties [...] an authorization to keep one firearm used during the mandatory military period."[79]

Whereas the exception is drafted in neutral terms, it was obviously tailored to the specific situation of Switzerland. This was also explicitly recognised by Advocate General Sharpston and the Court of Justice in an action for annulment initiated by the Czech Republic.[80] One of the arguments concerned precisely the granting of this specific derogation which constituted, in the view of the Czech Republic, a breach of the principle of non-discrimination.[81] Since no other Member State can benefit from the derogation, it was deemed to introduce an unjustified difference in treatment. Moreover, the required period of 50 years for the existence of the system of conservation of firearms after the end of military duties was considered to be "arbitrary and disproportionate."[82]

77 Article 8(2) of the Schengen Association Agreement and Article 5(2) of the Dublin Association Agreement.

78 Directive (EU) 2017/853 of the European Parliament and of the Council of 17 May 2017 amending Council Directive 91/477/EEC on control of the acquisition and possession of weapons (OJ 2017, L 137/22).

79 *Ibid.*

80 Advocate General Sharpston even referred to the second subparagraph of Article 6 (6) of the Directive as "the Swiss exception." CJEU, Case C-482/17, *Czech Republic v Parliament and Council*, EU:C:2019:321, para. 138.

81 CJEU, Case C-482/17, *Czech Republic v Parliament and Council*, EU:C:2019:1035, paras. 159–162.

82 *Ibid.*, para. 161.

Hungary, which intervened in support of the Czech Republic, further pointed at the different conditions applicable to former conscripts and target shooters who do not come from military service. The Court of Justice dismissed all those arguments on the ground that the situation of Switzerland is not comparable to that of the other Member States, implying that the derogation does not violate the principle of equality.[83] In particular, the Court found that the derogation "takes into account both the culture and traditions of the Swiss Confederation and the fact that, owing to those traditions, that State has the proven experience and ability to trace and monitor the persons and weapons concerned, which gives reason to assume that the public security and safety objectives pursued by the contested directive will, despite that derogation, be achieved."[84] States without a similar tradition and the proven experience and ability to trace and monitor the persons and weapons concerned are in a completely different situation and, therefore, do not face any discriminatory treatment.[85]

Significantly, the recognition of the Swiss exception is not related to its status as a third country but follows from the application of a general principle of EU law. Moreover, it is part and parcel of the EU legal act and not the result of (a protocol to) an international agreement or a decision of a joint committee under such an agreement. This example illustrates how the association of Switzerland with the Schengen *acquis* and the dynamic adaptation and participation mechanisms foreseen under this arrangement allow for a far-reaching form of integration without membership. This stands in stark contrast to the static approach under other bilateral agreements, most notably the AFMP (cf. *supra*). As argued above, the latter almost unavoidably leads to divergences in the scope and interpretation of the shared legal rules. Of course, the dynamic model of the Schengen and Dublin association also has certain drawbacks from the perspective of a non-Member State. The opportunity cost of a refusal to incorporate new EU acts is very high, implying the potential termination of the agreement.[86] Accordingly, the actual autonomy of Switzerland to disagree with

83 The principle of equality, as a general principle of EU law, implies that "comparable situations must not be treated differently and different situations must not be treated in the same way unless such treatment is objectively justified." *Ibid.*, paras. 164 and 161.

84 *Ibid.*, para. 166.

85 *Ibid.*, para. 167.

86 It is noteworthy that a referendum on the incorporation of the new Firearms Directive was organized in Switzerland on 19 May 2019. A majority of 66,4% of the voters supported the incorporation. Accordingly, a potential crisis regarding Switzerland's participation in the Schengen area could be avoided. See Arrêté fédéral portant approbation et mise en œuvre de l'échange de notes entre la Suisse et l'UE concernant la reprise de la directive

legal evolutions in the Schengen and Dublin system is very limited. Whereas this is partly compensated with the possibility to take part in the decision-shaping process of the new EU legislation, the actual influence of a country such as Switzerland largely depends upon the goodwill of the EU institutions and its Member States. The example of the Firearms Directive illustrates that this may have a concrete impact but the formal legal foundations for third-country participation remain rather limited.[87]

5 Conclusion

The unique model of sectoral bilateralism for the development of EU-Swiss legal relations is not the result of a pre-determined blueprint but rather the consequence of a gradual evolution following the Swiss rejection of the EEA Agreement in 1992. The latter remains an important point of reference, also in the case law of the Court of Justice. It has become a standard practice to proceed from the observation that Switzerland did not join the EEA and, as a corollary, it is not a full participant in the EU internal market which has the objective to remove all obstacles to create an area of free movement analogous to that provided by a national market.[88] Alternatively, the bilateral agreements between the EU and Switzerland cover a wide range of areas involving specific rights and obligations which are, in some respects, analogous to those included in the EU Treaties. Hence, the non-participation of Switzerland in the entire internal market *acquis* along the lines of the EEA Agreement cannot conceal the existence of a "partial participation"[89] in the extended internal market.[90]

(UE) 2017/853 modifiant la directive de l'UE sur les armes (Développement de l'acquis de Schengen), RO (2019) 2415.

87 M. Oesch (n. 67), p. 620.

88 See, e.g., CJEU, Case C-70/09, *Hengartner and Gasser*, EU:C:2010:430, para. 41.

89 Significantly, the modalities of a partial participation in the EU internal market also largely influenced the discussions about Brexit and the future EU-UK relations. One of the core elements concerned the 'indivisibility' of the four freedoms as a principle of EU law and politics. See, in this respect: Editorial Comments, 'Is the "indivisibility" of the four freedoms a principle of EU law?', *Common Market Law Review* 56 (2019), pp. 1189–1200, and C. Tobler, 'Finally Brexit – Alternative Modelle der EU-Integration: von Modellen und Bausteinen', in J. Sild (ed.), *Potentiale und Grenzen europäischer Integration. Tagungsband des 20. Österreichischen Europarechtstages 2021 in Liechtenstein* (Jan Sramek Verlag, 2022), pp. 135-158.

90 On the different modes of participation in the EU internal market, see C. Tobler, J. Hardenbol and B. Mellar, *Internal Market Beyond the EU: EEA and Switzerland*, Briefing Paper for the European Parliament, PE 429.993, January 2010,

In the absence of an institutional agreement providing for the homogeneous interpretation of the shared legal rules, the Court of Justice proceeds from the so-called *Polydor* logic, which implies that there is no automatic interpretation by analogy of identically worded provisions included in a bilateral agreement with Switzerland and in the EU Treaties unless there are express provisions to that effect in the agreement itself. Such specific provisions can, for instance, be found in Annex II to the AFMP as far as the coordination of social security mechanisms is concerned and where it is explicitly mentioned that for the application of relevant EU legislation Switzerland is deemed to be treated as if it is a Member State. In general, however, there are significant differences in the scope and interpretation of the shared legal rules.

A key point of reference is the case law regarding the freedom of establishment. The latter has a narrower personal scope under the AFMP and is limited to the situation of natural persons pursuing self-employed economic activities in the territory of another contracting party. However, as far as the interpretation of rules falling within the scope of the AFMP is concerned, the Court of Justice also proceeds from an interpretation based on general principles of EU law when such principles are already well-established in the pre-signature case law of the Court. Significantly, also post-signature case law can be taken into account – even without the intervention of the Joint Committee – when it only clarifies or confirms the principles established before the signature of the AFMP.

The result is a case-by-case analysis where the CJEU, on the one hand, highlights the different scope of the AFMP in comparison to the right to free movement within the EU internal market and, on the other hand, takes into account the objective of the AFMP to develop a relationship based on shared legal rules and principles. The Court's case law appears to meander between both parameters, complicating the understanding of the EU-Swiss relationship in practice.[91] The "static" nature of the agreement creates additional challenges, with the evolution of the EU's domestic rules regarding EU citizenship under Directive 2004/38 as a case in point.

<https://www.europarl.europa.eu/RegData/etudes/note/join/2010/429993/IPOL-IMCO_NT(2010)429993_EN.pdf> (accessed 5 March 2022).

91 The term "meandering" is borrowed from Benedikt Pirker who argued that "there is a certain meandering in the reasoning of the Court on the AFMP." See B. Pirker, 'Case C-355/16 Picart: The narrow interpretation of the Swiss-EU Agreement on the Free Movement of Persons as a lesson for Brexit?', *European Law Blog*, 22 March 2018, <https://europeanlawblog.eu/2018/03/22/case-c-355-16-picart-the-narrow-interpretation-of-the-swiss-eu-agreement-on-the-free-movement-of-persons-as-a-lesson-for-brexit/> (accessed 5 March 2022).

Finally, the "static" approach of the AFMP stands in contrast to the "dynamic" model of the agreements associating Switzerland to the Schengen and Dublin *acquis*. The example of the Firearms Directive illustrates how this goes hand in hand with decision-shaping possibilities. In this context, Switzerland is *de facto* treated as an EU Member State as far as the interpretation of the applicable legislation is concerned. Of course, this dynamic model of integration without membership also comes at a cost. Even though the agreements take into account the particular Swiss system of direct democracy, allowing for the organisation of a referendum before the incorporation of new EU legal acts, the cost of non-compliance is very high.

Taken together, the case law of the Court of Justice is a reflection of the complex legal framework of EU-Switzerland relations. The combined approach of "static" and "dynamic" integration agreements in the absence of an overarching governance structure clearly illustrates the challenges of the Swiss model of sectoral bilateralism. In the absence of a more developed legal framework to deal with evolutions of EU law, surveillance and dispute settlement, the general objective of "equivalence of legislation" is difficult to achieve.[92] Given the difficulties surrounding the conclusion of a new Institutional Agreement, the question of how the bilateral relations can further develop in the future remains.

---

92 C. Kaddous, 'Switzerland and the EU. Current Issues and New Challenges under the Draft Institutional Framework Agreement', in S. Gstöhl, D. Phinnemore (eds.), *The Proliferation of Privileged Partnerships between the European Union and its Neighbours* (Routledge, 2019), p. 73.

CHAPTER 4

The Swiss Posted Workers Act and Free Movement of Services

Kurt Pärli

1 Introduction

The EU–Swiss Agreement on the Free Movement of Persons (AFMP) states the right to provide cross-border services during a maximum of 90 days per calendar year (Article 5(2) AFMP, read in connection with Article 18 of Annex I AFMP).[1] For the case where the service provider uses its own personnel by posting them in the territory of another contracting State, Article 22(2) Annex I AFMP reserves the applicability of national laws, regulations and administrative provisions on working and employment conditions and in this context makes reference to the EU Posted Workers Directive 96/71 (in the form as it existed at the time of signing the AFMP).[2] This Directive is, therefore, part of EU-Swiss legal *acquis* and must be complied with by the parties to the Agreement.

The AFMP, concluded in 1999, entered into force in 2002 after a Swiss referendum held in 2000. Consent for the agreement was very high with 67% of those voting in its favour.[3] However, before the referendum, there were concerns that high wages and good working conditions in Switzerland could come under pressure due to the liberalisation of services foreseen in the AFMP. Fearing social dumping in view of its comparatively high level of salaries, Switzerland adopted so-called "flanking measures", notably through the Swiss Posted Workers Act (PWA),[4] which has since been amended on several

1 Agreement between the European Community and its Member States, of the one part, and the Swiss Confederation, of the other, on the free movement of persons (OJ 2002, L 114/6), as amended.

2 Directive 96/71/EC of the European Parliament and of the Council of 16 December 1996 concerning the posting of workers in the framework of the provision of services (OJ 1997, L 18/1).

3 On the vote, which was for the package of the so-called *Bilaterals I*, see https://www.bk.admin.ch/ch/d/pore/va/20000521/det464.html (accessed 1 June 2022).

4 Where there is no English version of Swiss legislation, the information given will be in the German language: Bundesgesetz vom 8. Oktober 1999 über die flankierenden Massnahmen bei entsandten Arbeitnehmerinnen und Arbeitnehmern und über die Kontrolle der in Normalarbeitsverträgen vorgesehenen Mindestlöhne (Entsendegesetz, EntsG), SR 823.20.

© KONINKLIJKE BRILL NV, LEIDEN, 2023 | DOI:10.1163/9789004529984_006

occasions. The European Union takes the view that certain flanking measures are contrary to the obligations of Switzerland under the AFMP.[5] The parties have so far not been able to resolve this dispute, neither in the Joint Committee that is in charge of the AFMP nor through the conclusion of an Institutional Agreement (InstA),[6] which would have obliged Switzerland to agree to the incorporation of more recent EU law that includes, among others, the posting of workers into the EU-Swiss legal *acquis*, whilst providing for certain specific rules in this respect. In May 2021, the Swiss Federal Government rejected the InstA, not least because, in the event of its adoption, the PWA would have had to be amended.

Against this background, the present chapter will first give an overview of the Swiss flanking measures (below Section 2). It will then turn to EU and EU-Swiss law on posting (Section 3) and to Swiss resistance to EU law on the posting of workers (Section 4). Thereafter, the chapter will discuss selected Swiss flanking measures and their compatibility with the AFMP as it is now in force (Section 5). In this respect, the author will argue that, contrary to the view of the European Union and of certain academic writers, these measures are in line with the AFMP.

2 Overview of the Swiss Posted Workers Act

2.1 *Development of the Swiss Flanking Measures*

The original flanking measures of 2004 ("Flanking Measures I") essentially consisted of three elements: firstly, the PWA was enacted. Its aim is to subject employees temporarily posted to Switzerland by a foreign employer in the context of providing a cross-border service to the minimum wage and other working conditions applicable in Switzerland. Secondly, the hurdles for declaring collective employment agreements generally binding were lowered. In the event of repeated abusive undercutting of minimum wages, the provisions on minimum wages and working hours contained in collective agreements could now more easily be declared generally binding. Thirdly, a path was opened for quasi-statutory binding minimum wages. For sectors without a

5 See, e.g., Council conclusions on EU relations with the Swiss Confederation of 19 February 2019, <https://www.consilium.europa.eu/en/press/press-releases/2019/02/19/council-conclusions-on-eu-relations-with-the-swiss-confederation/> (accessed 1 June 2022), para. 13.

6 On the Institutional Agreement, see the contributions by C. Kaddous and by R. Schwok in this volume.

collective labour agreement (or without a collective labour agreement that can be declared universally binding), the Confederation and the cantons can introduce binding minimum wages in a fixed-term standard employment contract in the event of repeated abuse.

In view of the extension of the free movement of persons to the ten new Member States that joined the EU in 2004, improvements to the flanking measures were adopted in 2006 ("Flanking Measures II"). For example, the notification requirements under the PWA were made more specific and deposit obligations and stricter penalties against posting companies responsible for misconduct were introduced. In addition, a new provision was included into the Swiss Code of Obligations, following EU law requiring posting companies to provide written information on essential elements of the employment contract within four weeks of the start of an employment relationship.[7]

In 2012, strong measures against bogus self-employment were enshrined and the provisions on liability for subcontractors and the employers' notification obligations regarding the gross wages of posted workers were amended ("Flanking Measures III").

The most recent amendments were adopted in 2016 ("Flanking Measures IV"). They concern notably the liability of the first entrepreneur and a further tightening of sanctions.

In addition, a further amendment to the PWA is in the pipeline. It concerns cantonal minimum wages, which in future must also be complied with by posting companies.[8] Overall, the development of the PWA since 2004 has been characterised, on the one hand, by a tightening of subcontractor liability, control obligations and sanctions against companies which are responsible for misconduct and, on the other hand, by an extension of the scope of the regulations. Importantly, the PWA now also regulates the control of domestic employers and sanctions against such employers if they violate provisions on the minimum wage. The strict liability rules for first-time entrepreneurs also

7 Council Directive 91/533/EC of 14 October 1991 on an employer's obligation to inform employees of the conditions applicable to the contract or employment relationship (OJ 1991, L 277/32). This directive will be repealed by 1 August 2022 and replaced by Directive (EU) 2019/1152 of the European Parliament and of the Council of 20 June 2019 on transparent and predictable working conditions in the European Union (OJ 2019, L 186/105). See M. Maul-Sartori, 'Richtlinienvorschlag transparente und verlässliche Arbeitsbedingungen – mehr als eine Überarbeitung der Nachweisrichtlinie', *Zeitschrift für europäisches Sozial- und Arbeitsrecht* 9/2018, p. 369.

8 'Federal Council adopts dispatch on amendment of the Posted Workers Act', <https://www.admin.ch/gov/de/start/dokumentation/medienmitteilungen.msg-id-83284.html> (accessed 1 June 2022).

apply to both domestic and foreign employers. This extension of the scope of the PWA led to a change in the title of the Act, which is now called "Federal Act on Accompanying Measures for Posted Workers and on the Control of Minimum Wages Provided for in Normal Employment Contracts" (though the official short form of the title continues to be "Posted Workers Act", PWA).

2.2 *Overview of the scope and Content of the Swiss Posting of Workers Act*

At the heart of the Swiss law on the posting of workers is the obligation of the foreign employer, stated in Article 2(1) PWA, to grant employees posted to Switzerland the Swiss minimum working and wage conditions stipulated in federal laws, in ordinances of the Federal Council, in generally binding collective agreements or in standard employment contracts. The minimum wage includes all kind of bonuses such as paid overtime or Sunday work. The calculation of the minimum wage must also recognise qualifications and work experience obtained abroad. The Swiss Federal Supreme Court has qualified the failure to take into account a foreign professional's experience in a collective employment agreement as indirect discrimination on grounds of nationality prohibited under Articles 2 and 7 AFMP in conjunction with Article 9 Annex I AFMP.[9] The minimum working conditions to be respected by foreign employers include working time and rest periods, minimum annual paid holiday, occupational health and safety, protection of pregnant women, women who have recently given birth, children and young people and equal treatment of men and women.

Article 6 PWA imposes a notification obligation on foreign employers (and only on them, to the exclusion of domestic employers). Under para. 3 of this provision, work may not start until at least eight days after notification of the planned deployment in Switzerland (so-called "8 days rule"). A declaration that the minimum wage and working conditions in accordance with the law on the posting of workers have been observed must be submitted with the notification to the relevant canton, which then forwards it to the joint and tripartite commissions which are responsible for on-site monitoring of the posting.

The PWA makes provision for the joint and several liability of the main contractor.[10] If work is carried out by subcontractors, the main contractor is also liable under civil law for the subcontractors' non-compliance with the net minimum wages and the working conditions. The main contractor is jointly

9 Swiss Federal Supreme Court, decision A_593/2009 (5 March 2009).

10 Article 5 PWA. For further information see M. Favre, E. Ramel, 'La sous-traitance, Questions choisies', *Journées du droit de la construction* 2015, p. 119.

and severally liable for all subcontractors who come after them in the order chain. However, the main contractors can exempt themselves from liability if they can show that, each time work is passed on, they have taken all necessary care required by the circumstances with regard to the observation of the wage and working conditions. It was and still is necessary to prevent abusive undercutting of minimum wages and minimum working conditions in the context of postings by also tightening subcontractor liability. The legislator has decided to apply the stricter liability also to domestic situations. This means that – different from the 8 days rule – Switzerland is spared the possible accusation of discrimination against foreign service providers in breach of the AFMP.

Finally, the PWA regulates the control and sanctioning of failing employers and lays down responsibilities.[11] Depending on the type of non-compliance, various authorities at federal or cantonal level or social partnership institutions may be involved. There is a wide range of sanctions, some of them quite heavy. The PWA imposes administrative sanctions with fines up to 30'000 Swiss Francs, criminal sanctions with fines up to one Million Swiss Francs and a ban from the Swiss market from one up to five years. Furthermore, the costs of the inspection can be imposed on the offending employer. Sanctioned companies are put on a public list that can be consulted to determine whether a service provider has committed a major breach of the PWA in the past. Finally, the PWA lays down the right of Unions or employer-organisations to bring action seeking an investigation of possible violations of the PWA.[12]

3 EU Law and EU-Swiss Law on the Posting of Workers

The Swiss legislation on posting outlined above must be seen in the context of the EU-Swiss AFMP, which in turn incorporates certain EU law on this matter into the EU-Swiss legal *acquis*.

3.1 *EU Law and Case Law on Posting*

Secondary EU (then EC) law on the posting of workers has existed since the adoption of Directive 96/71. In judgments on cases that arose before the

11 Sanctions are regulated in Article 9 and 12 PWA, control and responsibilities in Articles 7, 7a, 8, and 14 PWA, see K. Pärli, *Entsendegesetz*, 2nd ed., (Stämpfli, 2021), p. 193 et seq., and further S. Progin-Theuerkauf, S. Ousmane, 'Kommentar zu Article 5 FZA', in C. Amarelle, M. Nguyen (eds.), *Code annoté de droit des migrations, Volume III: Accord sur la libre circulation des personnes (ALCP)* (Stämpfli, 2014), p. 55.

12 Article 11 PWA.

applicability of the Directive, the Court of Justice of the European Union (CJEU) recognised the right of the Member States to extend their legislation or collective labour agreements relating to minimum wages, to any person employed, even temporarily, within their territory, no matter in which country the employer was established, and to enforce those rules by appropriate means.[13] Directive 96/71 introduced specific rules on the terms and conditions of employment (though not on enforcement) that, whilst focusing on the protection of posted workers, in fact, limited the Member States' room for action in this respect. The EU strengthened worker protection through Directive 2014/67 on the enforcement of Directive 96/71[14] and by amending the latter Directive through Directive 2018/957.[15] Actions for annulment brought by Hungary and by Poland were unsuccessful. Among other arguments, these States claimed that the Directive creates restrictions on freedom to provide services that are contrary to Article 56 TFEU. The Court noted that the Directive 2018/957 seeks, in particular "to ensure that greater account is taken of the protection of posted workers, though always in a way that is consistent with the objective of ensuring that the freedom to provide services in the host Member State can be exercised fairly".[16] Most recently, the EU adopted Directive 2020/1057 providing for specific rules for the posting of drivers in the road transport sector,[17] which apply in addition to Directives 97/61 and 2014/

---

13 CJEU, Case C-113/89, *Rush Portuguesa*, EU:C:1990:142, para. 18; Case C-43/93, *Vander Elst*, EU:C:1994:310, para. 23.

14 Directive 2014/67/EU of the European Parliament and of the Council of 15 May 2014 on the enforcement of Directive 96/71/EC concerning the posting of workers in the framework of the provision of services and amending Regulation (EU) No 1024/2012 on administrative cooperation using the Internal Market Information System ('IMI Regulation') (OJ 2014, L 159/11).

15 Directive (EU) 2018/957 of the European Parliament and of the Council of 28 June 2018 amending Directive 96/71/EC concerning the posting of workers in the framework of the provision of services (OJ 2018, L 173/16). For a comprehensive overview about the revision of the Posting Directive see B. Furåker, B. Larsson, 'Revision of the EU Posting of Workers Directive, Social Dumping and Trade Unions' Position', in B. Furåker, B. Larrson (eds.), *Trade Union Cooperation in Europe, Patterns, Conditions, Issues*, (Palgrave Pivot, 2020), p. 109; T. Klein, A. Schneider, 'Die Änderung der Entsenderichtlinie', *Soziales Recht* 9(1) (2019), p. 21. An interesting look into the development of the revision can be found in R. Zahn, 'Revision of the Posted Workers Directive: A Europeanisation Perspective', *Cambridge Yearbook of European Legal Studies* 19 (2017), p. 187.

16 CJEU, Case C-620/18, *Hungary v Parliament and Council*, ECLI:EU:C:2020:1001, para. 53, and Case C-626/18, *Poland v Parliament and Council*, EU:C:2020:1000, para. 58.

17 Directive (EU) 2020/1057 of the European Parliament and of the Council of 15 July 2020 laying down specific rules with respect to Directive 96/71/EC and Directive 2014/67/EU for posting drivers in the road transport sector and amending Directive 2006/22/EC as regards enforcement requirements and Regulation (EU) No 1024/2012 (OJ 2020, L 249/49).

67.[18] Directive 2020/1057 establishes sector-specific rules reflecting the particularities of the highly mobile workforce in the road transport sector and providing a balance between the social protection of drivers and the freedom of operators to provide cross-border services. So far, most of the CJEU case law on the Union's secondary law on posting relates to Directive 96/71 in its original form.

The secondary law on posting employs different regulation techniques. For example, with respect to certain terms and conditions of employment (including minimum wages among others) Article 3(1) of Directive 96/71 contains specific coordinating EU rules. For other matters, Article 3(10) reserves the application of national law, on the basis of equal treatment and in compliance with the Treaties. In this latter case, the Treaty rules apply via the Directive. Conversely, matters relating to the enforcement of national rules on terms and conditions of employment in the event of posting are not covered by Directive 96/71. Before the time of the applicability of the Enforcement Directive 2014/67, they fell directly under the Treaty rules on freedom to provide services.[19] This latter approach remains relevant in the context of the AFMP, as that Agreement at present does not include Directive 2014/67 in its *acquis*.

Under the Treaty rules on the freedom to provide services (Article 56 TFEU et seq.), direct and indirect discrimination on grounds of nationality as well as non-discriminatory restrictions are prohibited. In the context of expressly different treatment of domestic and foreign service providers, it may be possible for the Member State in question to argue that their situation is not comparable but rather displays objective differences. If so, different treatment in accordance with the difference (i.e., treatment proportionate to the difference in the situation of domestic and foreign service providers) will prevent a finding of discrimination.[20]

At the time of writing, a number of actions for annulment of parts of this Directive are pending at the Court of Justice, e.g., CJEU, Case C-555/20 *Poland v Parliament and Council* (pending).

18 The CJEU decided in Case C-815/18, *Nederlandse Vakbeweging*, ECLI:EU:C:2020:976, that the general Posting Directive 96/71 does not seek to introduce a common transport policy for the purposes of Article 91 TFEU and that it is, therefore, applicable to the transnational provision of services in the road transport sector, with the exception of services involving merchant navy seagoing personnel as provided for by the Directive (paras. 8 and 35–41).

19 See e.g., CJEU, Case C-33/17, *Čepelnik v Vavti*, EU:C:2018:896; Case C-577/10 *Commission v Belgium*, EU:C:2012:814.

20 CJEU, Case C-577/10, *Commission v Belgium*, EU:C:2012:814, paras. 48 and 49; CJEU, Joined cases C-49/98, C-50/98, C-52/98 to C-54/98 and C-68/98 to C-71/98, *Finalarte*, EU:C:2001:564, paras. 63, 64 and 74.

The prohibitions of discrimination and of restrictions are subject to justification on grounds of public policy, public security and public health (Article 52(1) read in connection with Article 62 TFEU). In the context of posting, the need for enforcement and control measures can be subsumed under the justification ground of public policy in the light of CJEU case law.[21] Effective control measures of posting law regulations further serve to maintain social peace, which is also to be counted as public order.[22] The CJEU has so far refused to allow justifications for direct discrimination other than those listed in Article 52 TFEU.[23]

In the cases of indirect discrimination and restrictions, CJEU case law in addition has recognized broader possibilities of objective justification. Already early in its case law on posting, the Court recognised the protection of workers as overriding requirement in the public interest (i.e., as a legitimate aim) that can be relied on in order to avoid a finding of a restriction of the posting company's freedom to provide services.[24] More recently, the Court also accepted protection against social dumping[25] as a ground for objective justification. The CJEU has not yet specified what exactly is meant by "social dumping".[26]

All justification must comply with the requirements of proportionality, i.e., the measure chosen must be suitable and requisite (necessary).[27] Furthermore, it must be analysed whether the desired protection of workers

21 CJEU, Case C-319/06, *Commission v Luxembourg*, EU:C:2008:350; see *inter alia* para. 50; Case C-490/04, *Commission v Germany*, EU:C:2007:430, para. 86.

22 CJEU, Case C-490/04, *Commission v Germany*, EU:C:2007:430, para. 86; CJEU, Case C-319/06, *Commission v Luxembourg*, ECLI:EU:C:2008:350, para. 50 et seq. See also A. Epiney, 'Zur Tragweite des Freizügigkeitsabkommens im Bereich der Arbeitnehmerentsendung', in A. Epiney, B. Metz and R. Mosters (eds.), *Das Personenfreizügigkeitsabkommen Schweiz/EU* (Schulthess, 2011), p. 100.

23 See CJEU, Case C-136/00, *Danner*, EU:C:2002:558, para. 56; the Court did not follow a different suggestion by Advocate General Jacobs in his Opinion in Case C-136/00, *Danner*, EU:C:2002:198, para. 40.

24 CJEU, Joined cases C-369/96 and C-376/96, *Arblade*, EU:C:2001:564, para. 33; Case C-165/98, *Mazzoleni and ISA*, EU:C:2001:162, para. 27; Case C-164/99, *Portugaia Construções*, EU:C:2002:40, para. 20. See J. Heuschmid, F. Schierle, 'Dienstleistungsfreiheit und Arbeitnehmerentsendung', in U. Preis, A. Sagan (eds.), *EU-Arbeitsrecht* (Dr. Otto Schmidt, 2015), para. 22.

25 CJEU, Case C-341/05, *Laval*, EU:C:2007:809, para. 103; further Case C-255/04, *Commission v France*, EU:C:2006:401, paras. 46 and 52; Case C-60/03, *Wolff and Müller*, EU:C:2004:610, paras. 35 and 41; Case C-577/10, *Commission v Belgium*, EU:C:2012:814, para. 45.

26 See however the Opinion of Advocate General Szpunar in CJEU, Case C-16/18, *Dobersberger*, ECLI:EU:C:2019:638, paras. 29 and 29, who is arguing, that "what is 'social dumping' for some is, quite simply, 'employment' for others".

27 See CJEU, Case C-99/16, *Lahorgue*, EU:C:2017:391, para. 31, and the case law cited therein.

outweighs the burden for the employer.[28] In the context of the proportionality test, the national measures must also be assessed against the standards of the EU Charter of Fundamental Rights, notably under Article 47 (right to an effective remedy and to a fair trial) and Article 48 (presumption of innocence and right of defence).[29]

The CJEU regularly examines proportionality strictly, especially with regard to necessity.[30] In the context of posting, two aspects are of particular importance. Unclear and not easily accessible regulations that lead to a great deal of effort for the employer are not proportionate.[31] CJEU rulings on the Union's coordinating social security law are further relevant in this context: according to this, A1 certificates on the existence of the social security status in the posting State are in principle valid and if there is a suspicion of abuse, a time-consuming procedure must be contested.[32] Consequently, the CJEU ruled that a Belgian law which had authorised the competent national authorities to declare the issuing of A1 certificates by posted workers to be an abuse of rights in certain cases was in breach of Union law.[33]

Overall, the Court's case law on posting has been the subject of much criticism. Decisions such as *Laval*[34] and *Viking*,[35] but also *Rüffert*,[36] *Commission v Luxembourg*[37] and *Bundesdruckerei*[38] are used as evidence for the primacy

28 J. Heuschmid, F. Schierle, 'Dienstleistungsfreiheit und Arbeitnehmerentsendung', in U. Preis, A. Sagan (eds.), *EU-Arbeitsrecht* (Dr. Otto Schmidt, 2015), para. 26.

29 See CJEU, Opinion of Advocate General Wahl in Case C-33/17, *Čepelnik v Vavti*, EU:C:2018:311, para. 93 et seq.

30 CJEU, Case C-244/04, *Commission v Germany*, EU:C:2006:49, para. 41; CJEU, Case C-577/10, *Commission v Belgium*, EU:C:2012:814, paras. 55, 56.

31 CJEU, Case C-319/06, *Commission v Luxembourg*, EU:C:2008:350, paras. 80–82; CJEU, Joined Cases C-369/96 and C-376/96, EU:C:1999:575, para. 61.

32 A1 certificates are not only binding on the competent social security institutions, but in principle also on the courts of the Member States and can therefore not be disregarded, see CJEU, Case C-2/05, *Herbosch Kiere*, EU:C:2006:68, para. 32, and Case C-620/15, *A-Rosa Flussschiff*, EU:C:2017:309, para. 51, confirmed in Case C-527/16, *Alpenrind*, EU:C:2018:669. However, in Case C-359/16, *Altun and others*, EU:C:2018:63, the CJEU recognised that a national authority may withdraw the effect of a fraudulently obtained A-101 certificate if certain conditions are met.

33 CJEU, Case C-356/15, *Commission v Belgium*, EU:C:2018:555. On social security under the EFMP, see the contribution by P. Melin in this volume.

34 CJEU, Case C-341/05, *Laval*, EU:C:2007:809.

35 CJEU, Case C-438/05, *Viking*, EU:C:2007:772.

36 CJEU, Case C-346/06, *Rüffert*, EU:C:2008:189.

37 CJEU, Case C-319/06, *Commission v Luxembourg*, EU:C:2008:350.

38 CJEU, Case C-549/13, *Bundesdruckerei*, EU:C:2014:2235.

of the freedom to provide services over worker protection.[39] Specifically with regard to the acceptability of measures by EU Member States to combat wage and social dumping in the case of posting, the *Čepelnik*[40] decision is cited as a (further) example of the business-friendly course of the CJEU.[41] The CJEU also went very far in the *Dobersberger*[42] case on highly mobile workers (in this case: staff in on-board bistros on trains travelling between Hungary and Austria). According to the CJEU, Directive 96/71 is not applicable in such a situation.[43] In the broader context of EU law, fears about the (overly) business-friendly positions of the CJEU have been voiced in relation to decisions on discrimination on grounds of age[44] and religion,[45] the transfer of

39 See e.g., N. Absenger, D. Seikel, 'Die Auswirkungen der EuGH-Rechtsprechung auf das Tarifvertragssystem in Deutschland', *Industrielle Beziehungen. Zeitschrift für Arbeit, Organisation und Management* 22(1) (2015), p. 51; T. Blanke, 'Die Entscheidung des EuGH in den Fällen Viking, Laval und Rüffert – Domestizierung des Streikrechts und europaweite Nivellierung der industriellen Beziehungen', *Oldenburger Studien zur Europäisierung und zur transnationalen Regulierung* 18/2008, p. 1; H. Wissmann, 'Arbeitnehmergrundrechte und Europäische Marktfreiheiten: Zwischenruf: Viking und Laval: EG-Grundfreiheiten über alles?', *Arbeit und Recht* 5 (2009), p. 149; N. Hös, 'The principle of Proportionality in the Viking and Laval Cases: An appropriate standard of judicial review?', *European University Institute Working paper* 6/2009, p. 28 et seq.

40 CJEU, Case C-33/17, *Čepelnik*, EU:C:2018:896, and Case C-64/18, *Maksimovic*, EU:C:2019:723.

41 C. Wiesinger, 'Dienstleistungsfreiheit und Lohn- und Sozialdumping – Die Sicherheitsleistung nach dem LSD-BG im Lichte des EuGH-Urteils Čepelnik', *Arbeits- und SozialrechtsKartei* 2019, p. 12; J. Schitter, 'Grenzüberschreitender Dienstleistungsverkehr: Zahlungsstopp und Sicherheitsleistung für LSD-BG-Strafen unionsrechtswidrig', *Zeitschrift für Arbeits- und Sozialrecht* 3/2019, p. 177; W. Gagawczuk, 'Zahlung einer Sicherheitsleistung durch den Dienstleistungsempfänger nach dem AVRAG', *Das Recht der Arbeit* 3/2019, p. 227. In particular, the CJEU is criticised for a lack of understanding of domestic (specifically: Austrian) law.

42 CJEU, Case C-16/18, *Dobersberger*, EU:C:2019:1110.

43 See J. Heindl, M. Lenglinger, 'The Problem with Highly Mobile Workers in the EU: A Critical Analysis of the Court of Justice of the European Union Judgement in *Dobersberger* Regarding the Posting of Workers', *Austria Comparative Labor Law & Policy Journal* Dispatch no. 28 (2020), <https://cllpj.law.illinois.edu/content/dispatches/2020/October-Dispatch-2020.pdf> (accessed 1 June 2022).

44 See in particular CJEU, Case C-447/09, *Prigge*, EU:C:2011:573, on this J. Schubert, K. Jerchel, 'Die Entwicklung des europäischen Arbeitsrechts 2011/2012', *Europäische Zeitschrift für Wirtschaftsrecht* 24 (2012), p. 96, who criticise that the CJEU did not deal with the relationship between Article 21 Charter of Fundamental Rights (protection against discrimination) and Article 28 Charter of Fundamental Rights (freedom of association).

45 See notably CJEU, Case C-157/15, *Achbita*, EU:C:2017:203. The Court's reference to freedom of enterprise is criticised in part of the labour law doctrine; see e.g., U. Preis, K. Morgenbrodt, 'Religiöse Symbole am Arbeitsplatz zwischen Gleichbehandlung und unternehmerischer Freiheit, Das Kopftuch in Luxemburg', *Zeitschrift für europäisches*

undertakings[46] and with regard to the relationship of competition law and labour law.[47]

However, a view according to which economic freedoms generally take precedence over labour and social protection in EU law does not stand up to closer scrutiny. This is shown, for example, by the CJEU rulings on the importance of annual leave as a fundamental right enshrined in Article 31(2) of the EU Charter of Fundamental Rights and the obligation of employers to record the actual working hours of employees on a daily basis also strengthens workers' rights.[48] This is also important in the context of posting, as it forces companies that post employees to comply with the working time regulations applicable in the host country and in particular to record daily working time.[49] Advocate General Tanchev described the right to paid annual leave as the most fundamental employee right in the EU Charter.[50] The Charter of Fundamental Rights also states other labour-related rights, including in particular the right to protection against dismissal (Article 30) and the right to safe and healthy working conditions (Article 31) with considerable, if not yet fully developed, effect. Overall, the Court's case law on the Charter has considerably strengthened labour rights.

However, protective labour law standards may be in tension with fundamental economic freedoms both at EU level and in the Member States. Which way the pendulum swings depends on the legal, economic and political context, as can be seen in the CJEU rulings on posting. For example, the *Regio Post*[51] and *Sähköalojen* rulings[52] show a greater willingness on the part of the

Sozial- und Arbeitsrecht 8/2017, p. 309. More recently, see CJEU, Joined Cases C-804/18 and C-341/19, *Wabe and Müller*, EU:C:2021:594.

46 CJEU, Case C-426/11, *Alemo-Herron*, EU:C:2013:521. Critical J. Heuschmid, 'Dynamische Bezugsnahmeklausel beim Betriebsübergang: Anmerkung zum Urteil des EuGH vom 18. Juli 2013 C-426/11', *Arbeit und Recht* 1/2013, p. 498.

47 CJEU, Case C-413/13, *Kunsten*, EU:C:2014:2411. Critical M. Fuchs, 'Tarifverträge Selbstständiger und europäisches Wettbewerbsrecht', *Zeitschrift für europäisches Sozial- und Arbeitsrecht* 8/2016, p. 297.

48 CJEU, Case C-55/18, *CCOO*, EU:C:2019:402; see K. Lörcher, 'Vorwärts – Zurück zu den ‚basics': Die Mitgliedstaaten müssen die Arbeitgeber verpflichten, ein verlässliches System zur Erfassung der täglichen Arbeitszeit einzurichten – Anmerkung zum EuGH (Grosse Kammer) vom 14.5.2019 – C-55/18 – Comisiones Obreras (CCOO)', *HSI-Newsletter* 2019, p. 4 et seq.

49 S. Stefanova-Behlert, 'Posting of employees within Europe: News from Brussels', *Expertenforum Arbeitsrecht*, 14 May 2019, <https://efarbeitsrecht.net/entsendung-von-mitarbeitern/> (accessed 1 June 2022).

50 Opinion of Advocate General Tanchev in Case C-214/16, *King v Dollar*, EU:C:2017:439, para. 36.

51 CJEU, Case C-115/14, *RegioPost*, EU:C:2015:760.

52 CJEU, Case C-396/13, *Sähköalojen ammattiliittory*, EU:C:2015:86.

CJEU to take worker protection seriously even within the framework of the original Directive 96/71. It should also be noted that initially, the protection of workers under EU secondary law was limited. For example, under Article 3(1) of Directive 96/71, in its original form, Member States were entitled to insist on terms and conditions of employment such as minimum wages only where these existed based on law, regulation or administrative provision or based on collective agreements or arbitration awards that had been declared universally applicable. Where that was not the case, the Member States could not insist on domestic wages.[53] Notably with Directive 2018/957, the EU legislator has taken up the criticism of an unduly broad freedom to provide services and widened the protection against social dumping.[54] In particular, the principle that pay must be in accordance to the State of posting has been strengthened.[55] The implementation period for Directive 2018/957 ended on 30 July 2020.[56]

53 See, e.g., CJEU, Case C-341/05, *Laval*, EU:C:2007:809, paras. 54 et seq.

54 See A. Epiney, L. Hehemann, 'Die Tragweite des institutionellen Abkommens im Bereich der Arbeitnehmerentsendung', *Jusletter* 8 April 2019, para. 17: "Thus, the emphasis of the Union's posting regulations has probably shifted from the realisation of the free movement of services to the guarantee of a coherent protection of workers. [...] Overall, the new Posting of Workers Directive is characterised by a stricter approach to wage and social dumping [...]." See furthermore: M. Höpner, C. Haas, 'Dürfen europäische Gesetze Grundfreiheiten einschränken?', *MPIfG Discussion Paper* No. 21/2 (2021), Max Planck Institute for the Study of Societies, <http://hdl.handle.net/21.11116/0000-0008-34BC-A> (accessed 1 June 2022). – The revision of the posting-Directive also leads to the question if and how fare the Union legislature is bound by the fundamental freedoms. Some scholars are arguing the binding is loose and its contours were yet unclear, see V. Bogoeski, The Revision of the Posted Workers Directive as a Polanyian Response to Commodification of Labor in Europe, *Global Perspectives* 2 (1) (2021), p. 1 (online journal: <https://doi.org/10.1525/gp.2021.18740>, accessed 1 June 2022).

55 R. Santagata De Castro, 'EU Law on Posting of Workers and the Attempt to Revitalize Equal Treatment', *Italian Labour Law E-Journal* 12 (2), p. 149.

56 There are so far no decisions yet about the Posting Directive in its new version. However, there are cases about the Enforcement Directive 2014/67; see CJEU, Case C-645/18, *Bezirkshauptmannschaft Hartberg-Fürstenfeld*, ECLI:EU:C:2019:1108; Case C-140/19, *Bezirkshauptmannschaft Hartberg-Fürstenfeld i*, ECLI:EU:C:2019:1103 and Opinion of Advocate General Bobek on Case C-205/20, *Bezirkshauptmannschaft Hartberg-Fürstenfeld*, ECLI:EU:C:2021:759. The General Advocate came to the conclusion that the requirement of proportionality of penalties laid down in Article 20 of Directive 2014/67/EU is directly effective. National courts and administrative authorities must take all appropriate measures to ensure the implementation of that provision, disapply any national provision in so far as its application would lead to a result contrary to EU law.

3.2 *The EU-Swiss AFMP, Services and Posting*

The Court of Justice's case law on posting – whether on Treaty rules or on secondary legislation – is important in Switzerland due to Article 16(2) AFMP. According to this provision, insofar as the application of the Agreement involves concepts of Union law, account shall be taken of the relevant CJEU case-law prior to the date of the signature of the Agreement (i.e., 21 June 1999). The Swiss Federal Supreme Court has decided that it will also take into account subsequent CJEU case law as long as there are no convincing reasons that mitigate against this.[57]

The AFMP provides for a *limited freedom* to provide services.[58] For example, Article 22(3) Annex I AFMP reserves the national rules on the activities of temporary and interim employment agencies prevailing in all contracting parties at the time of the Agreement's entry into force.[59] Further, Article 5 AFMP limits their provision to 90 days per calendar year. This limit applies per service provider. It does not matter how many workers a service provider posts cross-border per day – only one day will be subtracted from the 90 days quota.[60] A service provider who wishes to offer his services in Switzerland for more than 90 days per calendar year needs a permit under the Swiss Foreign Nationals and Integration Act.[61]

---

57 Specifically with regard to the PWA, see Swiss Federal Supreme Court, decision 2C_150/2016 (22 May 2017), cons. C.2.2: "Insofar as terms of the model developed at European level – Directive 96/71/EC [...] – are used, the case law under Union law as it existed prior to the signing of the Agreement on the Free Movement of Persons is also taken into account [...]; more recent rulings of the ECJ are taken into account by the Federal Supreme Court in the interest of a parallel legal situation, unless there are good reasons to the contrary [...]." See also Swiss Federal Supreme Court, decision 140 II 447 (11 August 2014), cons. C.4.3. On the interpretation of the EU-Swiss law, see the contribution by P. Van Elsuwege in this volume.

58 Efforts to reach an agreement on a comprehensive services agreement have not been successful, see T. Cottier, N. Diebold, I. Kölliker, R. Liechti-McKee, M. Oesch, T. Payosova and D. Wüger, *Die Rechtsbeziehungen der Schweiz und der Europäischen Union* (Stämpfli, 2014), paras. 542 et seq.; M. Oesch, *Europarecht, Band I: Grundlagen, Institutionen, Verhältnis Schweiz-EU*, 2nd ed. (Stämpfli, 2019), para. 904.

59 I. Theurillat Langenegger, 'Personalverleih aus dem Ausland', *Mitteilungen des Instituts für Schweizerisches Arbeitsrecht* (2008), p. 109 et seq., p. 113.

60 K. Pärli (n. 11), para. 18 on Article 1 PWA.

61 Staatsekretariat für Migration, SEM. Anhänge zu den Weisungen VFP, Weisungen und Erläuterungen zur Verordnung über den freien Personenverkehr, VFP01/2021 (not available in English), <https://www.sem.admin.ch/sem/de/home/publiservice/weisungen-kreisschreiben/fza.html> (accessed 1 June 2022).

The AFMP's regulation on service providers goes also for other reasons less far than the freedom to provide services within the EU.[62] This applies in particular to the passive freedom to provide services under Article 5(3) AFMP, which only exists in accordance with Article 23 Annex I AFMP.[63] Therefore, a person covered by the Swiss social security system cannot invoke the case law of the CJEU to claim reimbursement of the costs of outpatient treatment received in another EU country.[64] The interpretation that the AFMP does not cover the passive freedom to provide services is not accepted by all scholars. It is argued that the scope of protection and the scope of the freedom to provide services in the AFMP on the one hand and in Union law on the other hand are basically parallel and would in particular include not only the active freedom to provide services but also the passive freedom to provide services and correspondence services.[65]

The (limited) right to provide services is specified in more detail in Article 17 seq. of Annex I AFMP, including in particular a prohibition of discrimination on grounds of nationality. As under EU law, discrimination can be direct or indirect. Conversely, to date, there is no CJEU case law on the applicability of a prohibition of restrictions in the context of services under the AFMP, and it is debated in academic writing whether or not such a prohibition applies.[66] This presents a particular challenge in the current context since the Court of Justice, in the context of the Treaty rules on the freedom to provide services, often relies on the prohibition of restrictions (e.g., the obligation to appoint a representative domiciled in the country,[67] the obligation to comply with collectively

62 See also the case law of the CJEU, Case C-70/09, *Hengartner und Gasser*, ECLI:EU:C:2010:430, para. 40 et seq., and Case C-547/10, *Switzerland v Commission*, ECLI:EU:C:2013:139, para. 78 et seq., further H. Seiler, 'Einfluss des europäischen Rechts und der europäischen Rechtsprechung auf die schweizerische Rechtspflege', *Zeitschrift des Bernischen Juristenvereins* 150/2014, p. 265 et seq.

63 H. Seiler (n. 62), p. 265 et seq.

64 Leading decision of the Swiss Federal Supreme Court, decision 133 V 624 (22 October 2007), cons. 4.3.

65 A. Epiney, B. Metz and B. Pirker, *Zur Parallelität der Rechtsentwicklung in der EU und in der Schweiz, Ein Beitrag zur rechtlichen Tragweite der "Bilateralen Abkommen"*, Forum Europarecht 24 (Schulthess, 2012), p. 216.

66 See e.g., A. Epiney, P. Zbinden, 'Arbeitnehmerentsendung und Freizügigkeitsabkommen Schweiz – EG. Zur Tragweite und Auslegung der Dienstleistungsfreiheit im Freizügigkeitsabkommen Schweiz – EG', *Cahiers fribourgeois de droit européen* no 8 (University of Fribourg, 2009), p. 17.

67 CJEU, Case C-319/06, *Commission v Luxembourg*, EU:C:2008:350. The Court sometimes also refers to restrictions when interpreting Directive 96/71/EC in the light of the Treaty provisions on the provision of services; e.g., in Case C-346/06, *Rüffert*, EU:C:2008:189.

agreed wages in the performance of public contracts[68] and the requirement of a work permit for posted workers who are third-country nationals).[69] Similar to EU law, both direct and indirect discrimination can be justified on grounds of public order, public security or public health (Article 5 AFMP), and for indirect discrimination there is also the broader possibility of objective justification. In addition, these general rules on services apply in the context of posting where Directive 96/71 refers back to the Treaty as well as in cases outside the scope of the Directive (e.g., rules on enforcement and control).

Article 22(2) Annex I AFMP reserves national laws, regulations and administrative provisions "providing for the application of working and employment conditions to employed persons posted for the purposes of providing a service", and in this context makes reference to Article 16 AFMP and to Directive 96/71. In this framework, service providers must comply with the labour law in the country of destination if and to the extent that this is provided for in the domestic legal system and is compatible with the relevant provisions of the AFMP, including also Directive 96/71. In its Explanatory Memoranda to the Swiss legislator on amendment of the PWA, the Swiss Federal Council (Federal Government) regularly draws attention to the compatibility of proposed amendments with the Directive 96/71.[70] However, Switzerland is not obliged to follow the subsequent legislative development of the EU Directives on the posting of workers.[71] So far, neither Directive 2014/67 nor Directive 2018/957 have been incorporated into the AFMP *acquis*.[72] This would have changed with the InstA, as discussed in the next section.

4 Swiss Resistance to EU Law on the Posting of Workers

In the debate on the InstA, trade unions, in particular, expressed the fear that the protection of wages and working conditions under the PWA would be weakened in Switzerland.[73] Other stakeholders, namely the Swiss trade

68 CJEU, Case C-346/06, *Rüffert*, EU:C:2008:189.

69 CJEU, Case C-445/03, *Commission v Luxemburg*, EU:C:2004:655. See also Case C-18/17, *Danieli & C. Officine Meccaniche and Others*, EU:C:2018:904.

70 Botschaft des Bundesrates zur Änderung des Entsendegesetzes vom 1. Juli 2015, BBI 2015 5845, p. 5859.

71 K. Pärli, Einleitung (n. 11), para. 42.

72 *Ibid.*, para. 9.

73 The position of the Swiss Federation of Trade Unions (SGB) can be found here: https://www.eda.admin.ch/dam/europa/fr/documents/abkommen/20210526-bericht_verhandlungen_institutionelles-Abkommen_ch-eu_FR.pdf (accessed 1 June 2022); see also

association and the Swiss employers' association as well as the parliamentary commission for Economic Affairs and Taxations, also expressed concern.[74] On a fundamental level, there was opposition to the obligation, provided for under the InstA, to incorporate new EU law dynamically into the AFMP and to follow relevant CJEU case law even if handed down after the date of the signature of the AFMP.[75]

With respect to specific issues under the Swiss legislation on posting, criticism related mainly to the following changes to the Swiss flanking measures envisaged by the draft InstA:

- Only four (working) days for advance notification of posting, rather than eight days as under current Swiss legislation, and moreover only in certain sectors on the basis of a so-called "objective risk analysis", with periodical review.[76] This would have required an amendment to Article 6 PWA;
- A deposit requirement for service providers only in the case of prior breach of obligations and limited to sectors determined on the basis of an objective risk assessment.[77] This would have required changes to Article 2(2)ter PWA;
- Rather than the right to demand documents from self-employed workers in order to combat bogus self-employment, only subsequent checks and also restriction to certain documents.[78] This would have required an amendment to Article 1a and probably also to Article 1b PWA.

In May 2021, the Swiss Federal Government rejected the draft InstA, not least in view of these issues.[79] Consequently, in this situation, the AFMP in its present,

---

the report of the Federal Council on the consultations on the institutional agreement between Switzerland and the European Union of 7 June 2019, p. 9 et seq., <https://www.eda.admin.ch/dam/dea/de/documents/bericht_konsultationen_insta/BR-Bericht-Konsulationen-InstA-190607_de.pdf> (accessed 1 June 2022).

74 Schweizerischer Gewerbeverband, Positionspapier Institutionelles Abkommen Schweiz – EU (InstA), p. 1; Kommission für Wirtschaft und Abgaben (WAK-S), Kommissionsmotion „Zusatzverhandlungen zum institutionellen Abkommen mit der EU", WAK-S 19.3416 vom 09. April 2019; Schweizerischer Arbeitgeberverband, Stellungnahme zum institutionellen Rahmenabkommen vom 17. April 2019, p. 2.

75 Article 4 InstA (uniform interpretation), Article 5 InstA (integration of legal acts), Article 18 InstA (implementation of measures), Protocol 1, No. 1, obligation to incorporate Directives 2014/67/EU and 2018/957/EU into the AFMP. See on these issues also S. Breitenmoser, 'Gründe für das Scheitern des Institutionellen Rahmenabkommens', *Aktuelle Juristische Praxis* (2021), p. 1489 et seq.

76 InstA, Protocol 1 on the applicable rules to take account of the specific features of the Swiss labour market, point 2, first indent.

77 *Ibid.*, point 2, second indent.

78 *Ibid.*, point 2, third indent.

79 *Ibid.*, point 2, third indent.

unaltered form – which notably does not include the Enforcement Directive 2014/67 – remains the sole framework for assessing the compatibility of the Swiss flanking measures with this agreement.

5 Specific Problems of the PWA in the Context of the AFMP

The following part of this chapter will focus on the three specific issues listed in the previous part and their compatibility with the AFMP. They all relate to control and enforcement in the context of posting. As such, they do not fall under Directive 96/71 but rather under the Agreement's provisions on the freedom to provide services, as seen against the background of the legitimate aim of worker protection.

5.1 *Fighting False Self-Employment*

Since the entry into force of the AFMP, self-employed service providers have the right to offer their services in Switzerland for a maximum of 90 days per calendar year without having to obtain a permit under foreign law (Article 5 AFMP and Article 17 et seq. Annex I AFMP). The PWA is generally not applicable to self-employed persons. According to Article 1 PWA, the law only regulates the minimum working and wage conditions for employees. Self-employed service providers are not bound by these conditions. The term "employee" is defined by Swiss law.[80]

The different treatment with regard to the compensation to be paid for work performed and with regard to applicable health and safety regulations for posted employees on the one hand and for self-employed service providers, on the other hand, creates incentives for so-called false self-employment.[81]

It is more cost-effective for a non-resident service provider to send its employees outside an employment relationship to provide the service in Switzerland. It is obvious that false self-employment runs counter to the objectives of the law on the posting of workers as an important component of the accompanying measures.[82] The PWA therefore states that self-employed service providers must report to the competent cantonal authority before commencing

80 Article 1a(1) PWA, see also the decision of the Swiss Federal Supreme Court, decision 2C_1126/2018 (9 August 2019), cons. 3.1.

81 Botschaft des Bundesrates zum Bundesgesetz über die Anpassung der flankierenden Massnahmen zur Personenfreizügigkeit vom 02. März 2012, BBI 2012 3397, p. 3405 (reference according to footnote 4).

82 K. Pärli (n. 11), para. 7 on Article 1a PWA.

their activities in Switzerland.[83] In addition, the law demands various documentation obligations from the self-employed foreign service provider.[84] If the person fails to comply with these obligations, the supervisory body has the power to order the interruption of work.[85] In the event of non-fulfilment or incomplete fulfilment of the documentation obligation, sanction proceedings are also carried out.[86] If the competent authorities have clarified the status of a person working temporarily in Switzerland and come to the conclusion that the person is not self-employed, it must be clarified who is the employer of the person concerned.[87]

If it turns out that a Swiss company is to be designated as the employer, then there is no posting within the meaning of Article 1 PWA. If a foreign company is found to be the employer of the false self-employed person, there is a breach of the reporting obligation under Article 6 PWA and the competent authorities may impose the sanctions provided for in Article 9(2)(a) PWA. The possibility of sanctioning the documentation obligation, which has existed since 2012, is actively applied in practice. According to official information, a fine was imposed in 729 cases in 2016 and in 610 cases in 2019. In 2020, a fine was also imposed in 403 cases due to violations of the documentation obligation.[88]

The question arises as to whether the obligations for self-employed service providers are compatible with the freedom to provide services under the AFMP. In particular, the prohibition of discrimination on the basis of nationality is at the forefront. For the Swiss legislator and the Federal Government those measures did not violate the AFMP.[89] There is no judgment of the Federal Supreme Court so far.[90] However, it is remarkable that at the European level the CJEU

83 Article 1a (2a) PWA and Article 9 (1bis) of the Ordinance on the introduction of the AFMP (Verordnung über den freien Personenverkehr, VFP).

84 Article 1a (2a-c) PWA.

85 Article 1b PWA.

86 Article 9 (2a) PWA.

87 K. Pärli (n. 11), para. 20 on Article 1a PWA.

88 SECO, Report on the flanking measures 2016, p. 24; SECO, Report on the flanking measures 2019, p. 48; SECO Report on the flanking measures 2020, p. 46, <https://www.seco.admin.ch/seco/de/home/Publikationen_Dienstleistungen/Publikationen_und_Formulare/Arbeit/Personenfreizuegigkeit_und_Arbeitsbeziehungen/berichte-des-seco-ueber-den-vollzug-der-flankierenden-massnahmen.html> (accessed 1 June 2022).

89 Botschaft des Bundesrates zum Bundesgesetz über die Anpassung der flankierenden Massnahmen zur Personenfreizügigkeit vom 02. März 2012, BBI 2012 3397, p. 3428.

90 There is a decision of the Federal Supreme Court of 2010 (before Article 1a PWA entered in to force), see Swiss Federal Supreme Court, decision 2_C.714/2010 (14 December 2010). The court decided in favor of the foreign company. For more details see K. Pärli (n. 11), para. 6 on Article 1a.

also held that foreign self-employed service providers who temporarily enter the territory of another Member State are in a situation objectively different from that in which self-employed service providers established in that Member State find themselves with regard to the necessary controls.[91]

5.2 *The 8 Days Rule*

The notification must be made no later than eight days before the start of the deployment (Article 6(1) in conjunction with Article 6(3) PWA). The day of notification is not counted in the calculation of the time limit. Work may not commence before the expiry of these eight days, unless an exception is expressly provided for in the law.[92] If, for example, a foreign enterprise notifies the posting of employees only three days before the planned start of the work, it may commence work five days after the intended start date because only then will the eight-day waiting period have been observed.

The waiting period for the beginning of work is not an end in itself. It serves to enable the competent control bodies to carry out the controls provided for by law.[93] Some Swiss (European law) scholars argue that the eight-day notification period is problematic in light of the AFMP and relevant decisions of the CJEU.[94] In particular, the complaint is that the rules are not proportionate. The objectives envisaged by the law on the posting of workers would also be achieved by a milder measure, e.g., by a mere obligation to register without a

---

91 CJEU, Case C-577/10, *Commission v Belgium*, EU:C:2012:814, para. 47.

92 Article 6(5)(b) PWA in conjunction with Article 6(3) of the Ordinance on workers posted to Switzerland, SR 823.201.

93 A. Heine, 'Die flankierenden Massnahmen im Spannungsverhältnis zwischen Vollzug des Entsendegesetzes und der Vertragsfreiheit im Arbeitsrecht', *Aktuelle Juristische Praxis* (2006), p. 471 et seq.; Staatssekretariat für Wirtschaft SECO, Kommentar Flankierende Massnahmen zur Personenfreizügigkeit, 2008 (reference according to footnote 4); R. Wyler, 'Les conditions de travail, la libre circulation et le detachement des travailleurs – Les legislations et les questions qu'elles posent', in H. Stöckli, J. Zufferey (eds.), *Aktuelles Vergaberecht 2008 / Marchés Publics 2008, BR – Beiträge aus dem Institut für schweizerisches und internationales Baurecht*, Universität Freiburg Band/Nr. 17, (2008), S. 256; Aargau Appeal Court, 11 June 2010, E. 4.1 (Administrative and judicial decisions of the canton of Aargau (AGVE) 2010, p. 364).

94 See C. Tobler, 'Die flankierenden Massnahmen der Schweiz in einem erneuerten System des bilateralen Rechts', *Jusletter* 30 September 2013, para. 61; A. Epiney, 'Zur Tragweite des Freizügigkeitsabkommens im Bereich der Arbeitnehmerentsendung', in A. Epiney, B. Metz and R. Mosters (eds.), *Das Personenfreizügigkeitsabkommen Schweiz/EU* (Schulthess, 2011), p. 81 et seq., see as well B. Lauterburg, P. Zurkinden, *Institutionelles Abkommen – Rechtsgutachten zuhanden der WAK-N: Auswirkungen auf die flankierenden Massnahmen* (Bern, 2019), para. 43.

waiting period for taking up work.[95] It is further said that the necessary controls would also be possible after the start of work.[96] Experience to date, by contrast, has shown, that the prior notification requirement together with the control and sanction measures have proven their worth.[97] The Federal Council rightly pointed out and regularly draws attention to the fact that public confidence in the accompanying measures and thus in the functioning of the PWA as a bulwark against wage dumping ultimately forms the basis for opening up the labour market through the AFMP.[98] It should be added that the introduction of the work ban before the end of the eight-day period by referendum in connection with the extension of the free movement of persons to the new EU Member States is to a large extent democratically legitimised.[99]

Switzerland would have had to reduce the notification period from eight to four days if the InstA had been concluded. Protocol 1 to the InstA allowed a prior notification requirement of four days only for certain sectors, which would have to be determined on the basis of an objective risk analysis. This makes it clear that the regulation envisaged in Protocol 1 to the InstA would have resulted in a fundamental adaptation of Article 6 PWA.[100]

Neither in Protocol 1 nor elsewhere in the InstA were there any indications as to what is to be understood by an "objective risk analysis". However, indications can be found in the Enforcement Directive. Article 10 of Directive 2014/67 provides that checks on compliance with working conditions and wages should not be standardised. Checks on the basis of a risk assessment and supplementary random checks are permissible. It is noteworthy that Protocol 1 to the InstA uses the term "objective risk analysis", whereas the Enforcement Directive only refers to a "risk analysis". This raises the question of whether Protocol 1 deliberately sets the hurdle for the permitted performance of such a risk assessment very high. Article 10(1) of Directive 2014/67 specifies which criteria may be taken into account in such a risk assessment. Among other things, areas in which many workers are posted, the execution of large infrastructure projects, long subcontracting chains, special problems and needs in certain areas, violations of the regulations in the past and the risk to certain groups of workers are mentioned. The list of criteria is not exhaustive, i.e., Member States may also use other criteria to carry out the risk assessment.

95 C. Tobler (n. 94), para. 61.
96 A. Epiney, P. Zbinden (n. 66), p. 31.
97 Report of the state secretary for Economy (SECO), Report 2016 (FlaM-Berichte), p. 28.
98 K. Pärli (n. 11), para. 22 on Article 6 PWA (with further sources).
99 K. Pärli (n. 11), para. 22 and Footnote 41 on Article 6 PWA.
100 B. Lauterburg, P. Zurkinden (n. 94), p. 18 et seq.

Since Protocol 1 refers to Directive 2014/67, it can be assumed that the terms "in certain sectors on the basis of an objective risk analysis" must be understood in the sense of the regulation in Article 10(1) Directive 2014/67, whereby it must be taken into account that with the addition of the adjective "objective" the examination must be particularly strict. There are good reasons to call the current approach of the Swiss authorities to the enforcement of the PWA a "risk-based approach".[101]

5.3 *Sanctions*

In 2016 the supervisory authorities audited Swiss working conditions and wages in around 42'000 companies and of approximately 164'000 persons. In the same year, 2'453 fines and 741 interdictions prohibiting work in Switzerland were pronounced. The execution organs made an effort to execute controls in a targeted way considering the risks to the employment market. The efficiency of the flanking measures has been monitored over the last few years, for example in regards to the extension of the AFMP to new Member States.

Decision 140 II 447 of 11 August 2014 of the Swiss Federal Supreme Court represents a milestone in the jurisdiction of the law on the posting of workers. This case concerns the admissibility of a service ban for a period of two years and six months against an Italian company due to repeated disregard of occupational safety regulations during work on construction sites in the canton of Ticino. In view of the documented multiple violations; there was no doubt that this was a serious case. In particular, the company complained before the Federal Supreme Court that the ban on services contravened the principle of non-discrimination on the grounds of nationality enshrined in Article 2 AFMP. An employer based in Switzerland would only be charged higher accident insurance premiums for the same offence. The Federal Supreme Court did not follow this reasoning. On the one hand, it pointed out that, in addition to the increase in accident insurance rates, fines or exclusion from submission procedures could also be imposed on Swiss employers for violations of safety and protection regulations.[102] The fact that the service block could only be imposed on a foreign company was objectively justified and did not violate the AFMP, not even in the light of the case law of the CJEU being taken into account.

In a further case, the Federal Supreme Court had to decide whether the first and one-off violation of the working time regulations could be qualified as a 'not minor violation' of Article 2 PWA and whether a service ban could be

101 K. Pärli (n. 11), para. 49 on Article 6 PWA.

102 Swiss Federal Supreme Court, decision 140 II 447 (11 August 2014), cons. C.5.3.

imposed accordingly.[103] The complainant asserted that this sanction constituted an inadmissible interference with economic freedom (Article 27 of the Swiss Federal Constitution, FC) and was not proportionate. In particular, the complainant observed that the interpretation of the indefinite legal concept of a "minor infringement" had not been based on a former leading case.[104] In that earlier case, a repeated and gross violation of Article 2 PWA led to a two-and-a-half-year suspension of services. In the complainant's more recent case, only a single violation of the maximum working hours was at issue. The Federal Supreme Court did not follow this reasoning. There was no minor violation within the meaning of Article 2 PWA (in the version relevant for the case assessment), because the company had at least accepted a disregard of the working time regulations when planning the assignment. The Federal Supreme Court recalled that the working time provisions of the Labour Code ultimately also serve the purpose of occupational safety and that in this respect an equally strong sanctioning is justified. Furthermore, for the Federal Supreme Court, the sanction imposed was proportionate, especially in view of the fact that the freedom to provide services for providers is limited in time within the scope of application of the AFMP. If the violation of the working time regulations could only be sanctioned with a fine, this could simply be taken into account in the pricing and the employee protection envisaged by the law on the posting of workers would prove to be illusory.

Service restrictions represent a massive encroachment on economic freedom and must also be assessed in light of the AFMP. However, the initial situation is that regulations governing foreigners limit access to the Swiss services market. Therefore, an appeal to constitutional economic freedom presupposes an entitlement under Swiss Aliens Law to take action in Switzerland. Within the scope of application of the AFMP, the freedom to provide services is limited to 90 days per calendar year. However, this freedom is not unrestricted either, but can be limited by provisions for the protection of employees. The obligation to comply with occupational safety, working time and rest period regulations does not constitute an inadmissible interference with the (restricted) freedom to provide services under the AFMP.

More specifically, in the earlier case the Federal Supreme Court stated that a sanction imposing a ban on the provision of services to foreign service providers for a certain time does not constitute a violation of the prohibition of discrimination under the AFMP.[105] Since such a ban is not imposed on domestic

103 Swiss Federal Supreme Court, decision 2C_246/2016 (12 October 2016).

104 Namely Swiss Federal Supreme Court, decision 140 II 447 (11 August 2014).

105 *Ibid.*, cons. 5.4. et seq.

companies in the event of the same misconduct, the foreign company is in a worse position. However, the court held that the situation of a domestic company carrying out a service contract in Switzerland with its employees and the situation of a foreign company posting employees to Switzerland to carry out a contract under the limited freedom to provide services are objectively different things. Referring to CJEU case law,[106] the Federal Supreme Court concluded that a ban on the provision of services is, therefore, in principle permissible.

Overall, the sanctions provided for in the Swiss PWA take account of the principle of proportionality. Sanctions are also imposed against Swiss employers who violate minimum wages and minimum working conditions.[107] Only the ban on services is directed solely against foreign employers. According to the convincing remarks of the Swiss Federal Supreme Court, however, this does not constitute a violation of the prohibition of discrimination under the AFMP because the situation of a domestic company that executes a service contract in Switzerland with its employees and a foreign company that sends employees to Switzerland to execute a contract within the framework of the limited freedom to provide services is objectively different.

6 Summary and Conclusions

Part of the freedom to provide services in the AFMP – which is limited to 90 days per calendar year – is the right of the service provider to post employees to the state of destination in order to fulfill a service contract. The conditions of posting of workers and in particular the obligation to comply with the minimum wage and minimum working conditions applicable in Switzerland are laid down in the PWA.

The liberalisation of the Swiss labour and services market within the framework of the AFMP triggered fears that wages in Switzerland would come under pressure. An effective law on posting of workers was, and still is, the key to the acceptance of the AFMP among the population. It is therefore obvious that questions about the compatibility of Swiss regulations on the posting of workers with the AFMP and with EU law are the subject of controversial debate. There are also different assessments from the perspective of legal studies, in particular European law, on the one hand, and legal but also political assessments and concerns in the labour law sphere on the other hand.

---

106 CJEU, Case C-577/10, *Commission v Belgium*, EU:C:2012:814, paras. 47–49.

107 Article 9 (2c-d) and Article 5 (3) PWA. See for further sources and an overview of case law K. Pärli (n. 11), para. 107 on Article 9 PWA.

Trade union stakeholders in particular have seen (certain) rulings of the CJEU and statements of the European Commission as proof of the primacy of basic economic freedoms over workers' and social protection. Against this background, it is not surprising that the proposed reduction of the delay from 8 to 4 days in the InstA provoked strong opposition and, together with other reasons, caused the InstA to fail.

However, it would be wrong to make a general assumption that Swiss labour and social law as a whole is superior to EU law in terms of the level of protection. In fact, the Swiss legislature (so-called autonomously) adopted EU labour law standards in various areas in connection with the planned (but failed) accession to the EEA. This applies in particular to Swiss legislation on sex equality in employment,[108] certain provisions on working time,[109] data protection under labour law,[110] protection in the event of mass dismissal and transfer of undertakings,[111] information on certain aspects of the employment relationship[112] and worker participation.[113] Indeed, EU labour law in many areas has served as a model for improving the level of protection in Switzerland.

Similarly, it would be short-sighted to assume that the case law of the Swiss Federal Supreme Court on questions of interpretation in connection with the AFMP is more employee-friendly than the corresponding case law of the CJEU. This is exemplified by the cases relating to adjustments to the wages of cross-border workers (wages in euros instead of Swiss Francs), which were carried out as cost-saving measures. In contrast to the CJEU, which accepted the horizontal direct effect of Article 45 TFEU,[114] the Swiss Federal Supreme Court left open the question of the horizontal direct effect of the prohibition of discrimination on grounds of nationality under Articles 2 and 7 AFMP in conjunction

108 A. Epiney, M. Duttwiler, 'Das Recht der Gleichstellung von Mann und Frau im europäischen Gemeinschaftsrecht und schweizerischen Recht – Konvergenzen und Divergenzen', *Schweizerisches Zentralblatt für Staats- und Verwaltungsrecht* 2004, p. 37.

109 See comprehensively, W. Uebe, 'Gestaltung des Arbeitsverhältnisses', in K. Pärli, T. Baumgartner, E. Demir, C. Junghanss, S. Licci and W. Uebe (eds.), *Arbeitsrecht im internationalen Kontext* (Dike, 2016), p. 588 et seq.

110 See S. Licci, 'Arbeitnehmerschutz bei Betriebsübergang und Massenentlassungen', in Pärli et al. (n. 109), p. 769 et seq.

111 *Ibid.*, p. 769 et seq.

112 Article 330b CO.

113 See in detail K. Pärli, 'Mitwirkungsrechte der Arbeitnehmenden im schweizerischen Arbeitsrecht – Einfluss des Arbeitsvölkerrechts und des EU-Arbeitsrechts', *Global Europe Basel Papers on Europe in a Global Perspective* No. 117, 2019, p. 18 et seq.

114 CJEU, Case C-281/98, *Angonese*, EU:C:2000:296, para. 45; Case C-94/07, *Raccanelli*, EU:C:2008:425, para. 43; Case C-172/11, *Erny*, EU:C:2014:157, para. 36.

with Article 9 Annex I AFMP.[115] This is problematic. Indeed, if the Federal Supreme Court, in disregard of the AFMP's prohibition of discrimination, allows wage cuts for cross-border commuters on the basis of their cross-border commuter status, this puts pressure on the wages of domestic employees.

For the further development of the relationship between Switzerland and the EU, the law on the posting of workers holds a key position. This is not necessarily due to legal or economic reasons, but rather to the political sensitivities described above. It therefore makes sense, on the one hand, for the defenders of Swiss wage labour conditions to keep a differentiated view of the level of social protection in the EU. On the other hand, European law scholars are also called upon to consider the context of the AFMP and the accompanying measures – especially the PWA. It must be recognised that the current rules have a high level of democratic legitimacy, are supported by the social partners and have proven their worth in practice. This is shown not least by the fact that the Swiss services market is still very attractive for foreign service providers, even with reporting deadlines and high sanctions for violations of the regulations.

---

115 Swiss Federal Supreme Court, decisions 4A_215/2017 and 4A_230/2018 (15 January 2019), discussed by K. Pärli, 'Eurolohn: Berufung auf das Diskriminierungsverbot ist rechtmissbräuchlich', *Jusletter* 20 May 2019.

CHAPTER 5

COVID-19, Switzerland and the EU

Pandemic-Related EU Action and Its Legal Effect on Switzerland as Compared to the EEA EFTA States

Christa Tobler

1 Introduction

After the first COVID-19 or coronavirus disease cases were reported in China on 31 December 2019,[1] the coronavirus quickly spread to other countries. In Europe, the first case was reported in France on 24 January 2020[2] and the first Swiss case followed on 25 February 2020.[3] In the face of an increasingly global pandemic, a response going beyond national action was needed. On 2 April 2020, almost all UN Member States – including Switzerland – signed a UN Resolution to strengthen global solidarity and cooperation in dealing with the pandemic.[4] However, it has been argued that this and other resolutions have been limited to exhortations of the need for global solidarity and a pledge by the States to cooperate in order to address COVID-19. Real action in response to COVID-19 within the UN system remained the responsibility of the UN Member States,[5] and the actual response by the States left much to be desired.

1 World Health Organization, Timeline: WHO's COVID-19 response, <https://www.who.int/emergencies/diseases/novel-coronavirus-2019/interactive-timeline?gclid=EAIaIQobChMIpaC-xODQ8gIVz-J3ChoowADwEAAYASAAEgL1ifD_BwE#!> (accessed 31 March 2022).

2 European Commission, Time line of EU action, <https://ec.europa.eu/info/live-work-travel-eu/coronavirus-response/timeline-eu-action_en> (accessed 31 March 2022).

3 Swiss Federal Government, Media Release of 25 February 2020, New Coronavirus 2019-nCoV: First Confirmed Case in Switzerland, <https://www.bag.admin.ch/bag/en/home/das-bag/aktuell/medienmitteilungen.msg-id-78233.html> (accessed 31 March 2022).

4 UN General Assembly, Resolution: Global solidarity to fight the coronavirus disease (COVID-19), 2 April 2020, UN Document A/RES/74/270.

5 N. Syam, *The UN General Assembly Resolutions on COVID-19: Solemn Assurances for Access to Health Technologies without an Action Plan*, South Center Policy Brief Nr. 81, July 2020, <https://www.southcentre.int/wp-content/uploads/2020/07/PB-81.pdf> (accessed 31 March 2022), pp. 7 and 2, respectively.

© KONINKLIJKE BRILL NV, LEIDEN, 2023 | DOI:10.1163/9789004529984_007

For example, given the uneven distribution of vaccines, some commentators have gone so far as to refer to "corona vaccine apartheid".[6]

In Europe, the EU's competences in the field of public health have increased over time[7] but they remain limited, notably under Article 168 TFEU. At the same time, health also plays a role in areas where the Union's competences do include the creation of harmonising Union law, such as the free movement of goods and persons.[8] The EU has tried to play a meaningful role in dealing with the COVID-19 pandemic through common action in a number of fields.[9] Such action has to be seen against the background of the Union's aim to build a European Health Union in order to protect the health of Europeans and to collectively respond to cross-border health crises.[10]

For the Union's neighbours, common Union action may present challenges. Will they be included or left out? This question is particularly relevant for Switzerland, which is fully surrounded by States that are members of the European Economic Area (EEA),[11] namely the EU Member States Austria, France, Germany and Italy,[12] and the EEA EFTA State Liechtenstein. With Liechtenstein, Switzerland has particularly close ties, not least through the European Free Trade Association, EFTA (which also includes Iceland and

6 J. Dugard, J. Handmaker and B. Porter, 'Mobilising human rights to address coronavirus vaccine apartheid', *Opinio Juris* 18 February 2021, <http://opiniojuris.org/2021/02/18/mobilising-human-rights-to-address-coronavirus-vaccine-apartheid/> (accessed 31 March 2022).

7 See A. Ruijter, *EU Health Law & Policy: Expansion of EU Power in Public Health and Health Care* (Oxford University Press, 2019).

8 Generally on EU health law see T.K. Hervey, C.A. Young and L.E. Bishop, *Research Handbook on EU Health Law and Policy* (Edward Elgar, 2017).

9 On the EU COVID-19 response in general, see <https://ec.europa.eu/info/live-work-travel-eu/coronavirus-response_en#euactions> (accessed 31 March 2022). More generally on the EU and the COVID-19 pandemic, see L. van Middelaar, *Pandemonium. Saving Europe* (agenda publishing, 2021).

10 European Commission, European Health Union, <https://ec.europa.eu/info/strategy/priorities-2019-2024/promoting-our-european-way-life/european-health-union_en> (accessed 31 March 2022). See further Communication from the Commission to the European Parliament, the Council, the European Economic and Social Committee and the Committee of the Regions: Building a European Health Union: Reinforcing the EU's resilience for cross-border health threats, COM(2020) 724 final.

11 European Economic Area Agreement (OJ 1994, L 1/3), as amended.

12 Generally on the Swiss-EU relations in the English language, see M. Oesch, *Switzerland and the European Union. General Framework, Bilateral Agreements, Autonomous Adaptation* (Schulthess, 2018). Published in 2018, this work does not yet address the COVID-19 situation in the Swiss-EU relations; in this respect, a subsequent version in the German language will be used in this contribution.

Norway).[13] Switzerland and Liechtenstein have cooperated particularly closely on COVID-19 matters. But what about cooperation with the EU?

The present contribution discusses examples of common EU action in the context of COVID-19 with a view to their legal effects in relation to Switzerland. The examples chosen relate to the availability of supplies and equipment, more specifically: EU export control measures and joint procurement (below Section 2.), and to the movement of persons, more specifically: the EU's traffic light system and the Digital COVID Certificate (Section 3.). In examining these cases, there are two guiding questions: First, is Switzerland treated in the same manner as, or different from, its fellow EFTA members, who, different from Switzerland, are also members of the EEA (hence: "EEA EFTA States")? Second, has the existence, or the lack, of a Swiss-EU agreement, as the case may be, in the field in question been of relevance?

As a general background to these questions, it should be noted that neither under public international law nor under EU law is there a general rule to the effect that all third countries must be treated equally.[14] Accordingly, any right to equal treatment as well as any right to a specific type of treatment will depend on the existence of a multilateral agreement (e.g., WTO law or EEA law) or a bilateral agreement between the State in question and the EU (e.g., a bilateral agreement between the EU and Switzerland).

2 Availability of Supplies and Equipment

Among the generally shared concerns in any pandemic is the availability of vital supplies such as personal protective equipment (PPE) and vaccines. In this respect, EU common action included, among others, export control measures (below Section 2.1) and the joint procurement of vaccines (Section 2.2).

---

13 Convention establishing the European Free Trade Association (EFTA), signed in 1960 ("Stockholm Convention"; as amended notably by the "Vaduz Convention"), see <https://www.efta.int/Legal-Text/EFTA-Convention-1152> (accessed 31 March 2022). Generally on the EFTA, see G. Baur, *The European Free Trade Association: An Intergovernmental Platform for Trade Relations* (Intersentia, 2020).

14 See, e.g., CJEU, Case C-272/15 *Swiss International Air Lines AG v The Secretary of State for Energy and Climate Change and Environment Agency*, EU:C:2016:993, paras. 25 and 26. In the EU, this is sometimes called the "Balkan-Import Export principle", in reference to the Court of Justice's judgment in Case 55–75 *Balkan-Import Export GmbH v Hauptzollamt Berlin-Packhof*, EU:C:1976:8, para. 14. More recently, the Court stated in Opinion 1/17 (*CETA*), EU:C:2019:341, para. 173, that Article 20 of the Charter does not oblige the Union to accord, in its external relations, equal treatment to different non-Member States.

2.1 *EU Export Control Measures in Relation to Goods*

Under EU law, unilateral export measures can be taken in the framework of the Union's strong competence in the field of the external trade in goods under Articles 206 TFEU et seq. and, more particularly, under Regulation 2015/479 on common rules for exports.[15] Such measures may, in addition, be covered by agreements concluded by the Union with a non-member State. For example, the Swiss-EU Free Trade Agreement (FTA)[16] applies, among others, to the cross-border trade in industrial goods (Article 2 FTA). Article 13A FTA in principle prohibits quantitative restrictions on exports and of measures having equivalent effect. However, this is subject to the derogations listed in Article 20 FTA, which largely corresponds to Article 36 TFEU and which also includes the derogation ground of the protection of public health. In this framework, proportionate restrictive measures that do not amount to an arbitrary discrimination or a disguised restriction are lawful also as a matter of the Agreement.

However, export control measures make the cross-border trade in goods more complicated and costly and are, therefore, in principle not desirable.[17] During the COVID-19 pandemic, the EU introduced a number of export restrictions. Fearing a shortage of PPE, such as medical face masks, the Commission in mid-March 2020 introduced a temporary authorisation requirement for the export of PPE out of the EU. At first, the requirement applied to all non-Member States alike based on Implementing Regulation 2020/402.[18] However, shortly thereafter, the Commission exempted a number of countries and territories through Implementing Regulation 2020/426.[19] For an explanation of this change in approach, the preamble refers to close factual market integration:

> The single market for medical and personal protective equipment is closely integrated beyond the boundaries of the Union, and so are its

15 Regulation (EU) 2015/479 of the European Parliament and of the Council of 11 March 2015 on common rules for exports (OJ 2015, L 83/34).

16 Agreement between the European Economic Community and the Swiss Confederation (OJ English Special Edition Series I Chapter 1972, L300/191), as amended.

17 Compare: B.M. Hoekman, M. Fiorini and A. Yildirim, *Export restrictions: a negative-sum policy response to the COVID-19 crisis*, EUI Working Paper RSCAS 2020/23 (European University Institute, 2020), see also: 'Vaccine exports. To have and to hold', *The Economist* March 27th 2021, p. 18.

18 Commission Implementing Regulation (EU) 2020/402 of 14 March 2020 making the exportation of certain products subject to the production of an export authorization (OJ 2020, L 77I/1), no longer in effect.

19 Commission Implementing Regulation (EU) 2020/426 of 19 March 2020 amending Implementing Regulation (EU) 2020/402 making the exportation of certain products subject to the production of an export authorization (OJ 2020, L 84I/1), no longer in effect.

> production value chains and distribution networks. This is particularly the case of the four member States of the European Free Trade Association. Consequently, subjecting exports of certain personal protection equipment to these countries to an export authorisation would be counterproductive, given the close integration of the production value chains and distribution networks, when such equipment is an essential product necessary to prevent the further spreading of the disease and safeguard the health of medical staff treating infected patients. It is therefore appropriate to exclude such countries from the scope of application of Implementing Regulation (EU) 2020/402.

In line with the reference to the four EFTA States in the preamble, the exemptions introduced through Article 1(3) of Implementing Regulation 2020/426 related to Norway, Iceland, Liechtenstein and Switzerland,[20] further to the overseas countries and territories listed in Annex II of the Treaty and to the Faeroe Islands, Andorra, San Marino and the Vatican City – though not to the EU Candidate States in the Western Balkans, a fact that was noted critically in that region at the time.[21] As this writer noted elsewhere,[22] the exemption in favour of the EFTA States followed diplomatic steps taken vis-à-vis the EU by the Governments of Switzerland, on the one hand, and of the EEA EFTA States, on the other hand, pointing to the special legal relationship of these countries with the EU. The result was that all four EFTA States were treated equally for the better, i.e., under the amended rules all of them enjoyed an exemption from the requirement for an export authorisation in relation to PPE.

---

20 Switzerland also introduced an export authorisation requirement, exempting the same countries as does the EU, under the condition of reciprocity (Article 10d of the then COVID-19 Ordinance 2, amendment of 25 March 2020). The relevant provision was subsequently deleted; Amendment of 1 April 2020 to the Ordinance on Measures to Combat the Coronavirus (COVID-19) (COVID-19 Ordinance 2), AS 2020 1131.

21 See: B. Gecić, *COVID-19: EU Amends Regulation on Medical Equipment Export Controls: EFTA out, Western Balkans still in?*, 20 March 2020, <https://www.coronavirus.geciclaw.com/covid-19-eu-amends-guidelines-on-medical-equipment-export-controls-efta-out-western-balkans-still-in/> (accessed 31 March 2022).

22 C. Tobler, 'EU corona emergency law: Restrictions on the export of protective equipment, notably from the EU into third countries like Switzerland (Regulation 2020/402)', *Analysis.efta-studies.org* 30 March 2020, <https://www.efta-studies.org/eu-corona-emergency-law> (accessed 31 March 2022). See also EFTA, Exports of equipment to fight COVID-19 authorised from the EU to the EFTA States, 3 March 2020, <https://www.efta.int/EEA/news/Exports-equipment-fight-COVID-19-authorised-EU-EFTA-States-517331> (accessed 31 March 2022).

The same applied at first with respect to the EU's temporary rules on export authorisations for vaccines. Again, the preamble of Implementing Regulation 2021/111, adopted at the end of January 2021,[23] mentioned the close integration of the market for medical products and the need for exemptions. However, this time it referred more broadly to "the member States of the European Free Trade Area, and the Western Balkans which are engaged in a process of deep integration with the Union". In this original version of the EU rules, the list of exemptions in Article 1(5) "based on the principle of solidarity" was quite long and included exports to Albania, Andorra, Bosnia and Herzegovina, the Faeroe Islands, Iceland, Kosovo, Liechtenstein, Montenegro, Norway, Macedonia, San Marino, Serbia, Switzerland, the Vatican City, the overseas countries and territories listed in Annex II of the TFEU, Büsingen, Helgoland, Livigno, Ceuta and Melilla, Algeria, Egypt, Jordan, Lebanon, Libya, Morocco, Palestine, Syria, Tunisia, Armenia, Azerbaijan, Belarus, Georgia, Israel, Moldova and Ukraine. Implementing Regulation 2021/111 applied for six weeks; it was succeeded by Implementing Regulation (EU) 2021/442,[24] which was also of temporary application and which in Article 1(9) contained the same list of exemptions.

Academic writing from the perspective of WTO law raised the question of whether "by serving one sauce to the goose (Switzerland) and another to the gander (Brazil)", the requirement of non-discrimination under Article XI.1 GATT was met.[25] In the Swiss media, the exemption in favour of Switzerland, i.e., the fact of being "the goose", was noted with satisfaction.[26] However, it did not last long, and Switzerland turned from a goose into a gander. In March 2021, the Commission, prompted by suspicions of circumvention of export restrictions via the route of exempted countries and territories and by the concern on uneven levels of vaccination, decided to temporarily suspend some of

23 Commission Implementing Regulation (EU) 2021/111 of 29 January 2021 making the exportation of certain products subject to the production of an export authorization (OJ 2021, L 31I/1), no longer in effect.

24 Commission Implementing Regulation (EU) 2021/442 of 11 March 2021 making the exportation of certain products subject to the production of an export authorization (OJ 2021, L 85/190), no longer in effect.

25 Guest Post by H. Horn, P. Mavroidis, *What's Sauce for the Goose is not Sauce for the Gander? On Discriminatory Export Quotas for Vaccines,* February 2021, <https://ielp.worldtradelaw.net/2021/02/guest-post-whats-sauce-for-the-goose-is-not-sauce-for-the-gander-on-discriminatory-export-quotas-for.html> (accessed 31 March 2022).

26 'Swiss exempt from EU vaccine export controls', *swissinfo* 29 January 2021, <https://www.swissinfo.ch/eng/swiss-exempt-from-eu-vaccine-export-controls/46329832> (accessed 31 March 2022).

the above-mentioned exemptions through new rules set up in Implementing Regulation 2021/521,[27] in order "to gain a full picture of vaccine trade".[28]

The suspension concerned 17 countries, among them also all four EFTA States, which at that stage were still treated identically, though now for the worse. According to media reports,[29] the Swiss Federal Administration, citing the integration of the markets as well as the common interests of the EU and Switzerland in fighting the pandemic, demanded the reinstatement of the exemption in favour of Switzerland, but to no avail. Again, the Swiss media commented on the change in the rules. The Swiss daily *Neue Zürcher Zeitung* noted that due to the excellent cooperation between Switzerland and the EU with respect to vaccines, the new EU rules were not expected to have negative consequences for Switzerland in practice.[30] However, in academic writing originating from Switzerland, concern was voiced in view of the potential economic consequences, including the spreading of this type of trade measure.[31]

The situation changed again when the Commission amended the export rules for vaccines through Implementing Regulation 2021/734 of May 2021.[32] Among other issues, it changed the list of exemptions. In the new version, the list again included the EEA EFTA States but continued to exclude Switzerland. The validity of the new EU rules was subsequently extended twice, through Regulation 2021/1071[33] and through Regulation 2021/

27 Commission Implementing Regulation (EU) 2021/521 of 24 March 2021 making specific arrangements to the mechanism making the exportation of certain products subject to the production of an export authorization (OJ 2021, L 104/52), no longer in effect.

28 European Commission, Press release, 24 March 2021: Commission strengthens transparency and authorisation mechanism for exports of COVID-19 vaccines, <https://ec.europa.eu/commission/presscorner/detail/en/ip_21_1352> (accessed 31 March 2022).

29 E.g., 'Coronavirus-Update: Corona – Schweiz will Ausnahme von EU-Exportbewilligungspflicht zurück', *cash* 4 April 2021; 'EU stuft Schweiz bei Impfstoff-Importen ab – Bund fordert Änderung', *Telebasel* 4 April 2021; 'Impfstoff-Diplomatie: EU-Regeln befeuern die Diskussion um staatliche Investitionen bei Lonza', *Neue Zürcher Zeitung* 6 April 2021.

30 EU-Kommission verschärft Kontrollen für die Ausfuhr von Corona-Impfstoffen und nimmt auch die Schweiz ins Visier, *Neue Zürcher Zeitung* 24 March 2021.

31 S. Evenett, 'Export Controls on COVID-19 Vaccines: Has the EU Opened Pandora's Box?', *Journal of World Trade* 55(3) (2021), p. 397; also voxEU CEPR of 21 February 2021, <https://voxeu.org/content/export-controls-covid-19-vaccines-has-eu-opened-pandora-s-box> (accessed 31 March 2022).

32 Commission Implementing Regulation (EU) 2021/734 of 5 May 2021 amending Implementing Regulation (EU) 2021/521 making specific arrangements to the mechanism making certain products subject to the production of an export authorization (OJ 2021, L 158/13), no longer in effect.

33 Commission Implementing Regulation (EU) 2021/1071 of 29 June 2021 amending Implementing Regulation (EU) 2021/442 and Implementing Regulation (EU) 2021/521

1728,[34] until the end of 2021. Since then, Regulation 2021/2071 has been providing for an export surveillance mechanism for a period of two years.[35]

With respect to the exemption in favour of the EEA EFTA States, the preamble to Implementing Regulation 2021/734 explained:

> Iceland, Liechtenstein and Norway (the EEA EFTA States) participate in the Union's internal market in accordance with the Agreement on the European Economic Area. Most exports to the EEA EFTA States consist of vaccine procured by a Member State pursuant to an Advance Purchasing Agreement concluded by the Union and resold to those countries. On the basis of the information gathered through the application of Implementing Regulation (EU) 2021/521, there is no indication that exports are being channelled through the EEA EFTA States to other countries not exempted from the export authorization mechanism pursuant to Article 1(9) of Implementing Regulation (EU) 2021/442. Therefore, it is not necessary to continue the suspension of the exemption from that mechanism with regard to exports to the EEA EFTA States.

The Commission, rather than emphasising commonalities, now relied on differentiating factors that do not apply to Switzerland: namely the EEA EFTA States' (in principle full) participation in the Union's internal market as well as the joint procurement of vaccines (on the latter, see the following part of this contribution). According to the Commission (as reported by the Swiss media), the basis for the different treatment was of an objective nature. However, the Swiss media,[36] observing that there was now expressly different treatment of Switzerland as compared to the EEA EFTA States, suggested that there might also have been political reasons related to the difficulties with the draft

related to the mechanism making certain products subject to the production of an export authorization (OJ 2021, L 230/28), no longer in effect.

34 Commission Implementing Regulation (EU) 2021/1728 of 29 September 2021 amending Implementing Regulation (EU) 2021/442 and Implementing Regulation (EU) 2021/521 related to the mechanism making certain products subject to the production of an export authorization (OJ 2021, L 345/34), no longer in effect.

35 Commission Implementing Regulation (EU) 2021/2071 of 25 November 2021 subjecting certain vaccines and active substances used for the manufacture of such vaccines to export surveillance (OJ 2021, L 421/52).

36 See, e.g., 'Ungleichbehandlung – Impfstoffe: EU hebt Exportkontrollen für Liechtenstein auf – nicht aber für die Schweiz', *St. Galler Tagblatt* 6 May 2021; 'Bewilligung für Corona-Impfstoff: Brüssel behandelt die Schweiz schlechter als Liechtenstein', *Berner Zeitung* 5 May 2021.

Swiss-EU Institutional Agreement (InstA).[37] The media also suggested that the difference in treatment might have been part of an attempt on the side of the Union to put pressure on Switzerland to sign the InstA (which the Swiss Federal Government subsequently decided not to do).[38] As is noted elsewhere in this volume, the InstA was intended to amend a number of existing Swiss-EU economic agreements – which do not include the Swiss-EU Free Trade Agreement –, notably in terms of the rules on their functioning (interpretation, amendment, dispute settlement).[39]

It submitted that it is difficult to judge whether the differences relied on by the Commission in order to explain the difference in treatment of the EEA EFTA States, on the one hand, and of Switzerland, on the other hand, were relevant in the present context or whether the EU indeed simply created a political link with the InstA. If the latter, it might be argued that the different treatment of Switzerland amounted to arbitrary discrimination in contradiction to Article 20 FTA. However, if such a breach were indeed argued, there would be very limited possibilities to address the matter, namely merely through consultations in the Joint Committee as provided in Article 29(2) FTA. In contrast, the Agreement does not provide for a judicial element for dispute resolution.

2.2 *The EU's Joint Procurement Agreement Initiative*

Against the background of the H1N1 influenza pandemic of 2009, the Council asked the Commission to develop a mechanism to jointly procure medical countermeasures that would support fair and equitable access to, and distribution of, vaccines for the future.[40] This led to the Joint Procurement Agreement

37 There is no publicly available English language version. In the original French: *Accord facilitant les relations bilatérales entre l'Union Européenne et la Confédération Suisse dans les parties du marché intérieur auxquelles la Suisse participe,* 23 novembre 2018, <https://www.eda.admin.ch/dam/europa/fr/documents/abkommen/Acccord-inst-Projet-de-texte_fr.pdf> (accessed 31 March 2022).

38 Swiss Federal Government, Media Release of 26 May 2021, No signing of Swiss–EU institutional agreement, <https://www.admin.ch/gov/en/start/documentation/media-releases.msg-id-83705.html> (accessed 31 March 2022).

39 On the Institutional Agreement, see the chapters by C. Kaddous and by R. Schwok in this volume.

40 Thus <https://ec.europa.eu/health/security/preparedness_response_en> (accessed 31 March 2022), under the heading "Joint Procurement of medical countermeasures: ensuring proper preparedness". – The World Health Organization has published a policy brief on joint procurement: J. Espín, J. Rovira, A. Calleja, N. Azzopardi-Muscat, E. Richardson, W. Palm and D. Panteli, *How can voluntary cross-border collaboration in public procurement improve access to health technologies in Europe?*, WHO Policy Brief 21 (WHO Regional Office for Europe, 2016), <https://www.euro.who.int/__data/assets/pdf_file/0009/331992/PB21.pdf> (accessed 31 March 2022).

(JPA),[41] in which the EU has a coordinating role only; the actual purchase of vaccines is carried out by the participating States. Participation in the JPA by the States is voluntary.

The joint procurement mechanism, hailed as an innovative form of EU public health action,[42] has been used in the COVID-19 pandemic in order to purchase vaccines beyond EU membership. According to Article 5(1) of Decision 1082/2013,[43] which forms the legal basis for the JPA, the EU institutions and any Member States which so desire may engage in a joint procurement procedure. However, the circle of potential participants is wider under the EU's financial law, according to which joint procurement "may be conducted with EFTA States and Union candidate countries if that possibility has been specifically provided for in a bilateral or multilateral treaty" (Article 165(2) of Regulation 2018/1046).[44] Conversely, Article 12(2)(a) of a proposal for a new Regulation on serious cross-border threats to health mentions "Members States, European Free Trade Association (EFTA) States and Union candidate countries", without reference to bilateral or multilateral treaties.[45]

Under the rules in force at the time of writing, however, the existence of such a treaty is decisive. Based on the EEA Agreement, Decision 1082/2013 has been integrated into the EEA legal *acquis*,[46] allowing Iceland, Liechtenstein

41 The text of the JPA can be found in the annex to Commission Decision of 10.4.2014 on approval of the Joint Procurement Agreement to procure medical countermeasures pursuant to Decision 1082/2013/EU, C(2014) 2258 final, <https://ec.europa.eu/health/sites/health/files/docs/key-document/c2014_2258_en.pdf> (accessed 31 March 2022). There is an Explanatory note: <https://ec.europa.eu/health/sites/health/files/preparedness_response/docs/jpa_explanatory_en.pdf> (accessed 31 March 2022).

42 E.g., N. Azzopardi-Muscat, P. Schroder-Bäck and H. Brand, 'The European Union Joint Procurement Agreement for cross-border health threats: what is the potential for this new mechanism of health system collaboration?', *Health Economics, Policy and Law* 12(1) 2017, 43–59.

43 Decision No 1082/2013/EU of the European Parliament and of the Council of 22 October 2013 on serious cross-border threats to health and repealing Decision No 2119/98/EC (OJ 2013, L 293/1).

44 Regulation (EU, Euratom) 2018/1046 of the European Parliament and of the Council of 18 July 2018 on the financial rules applicable to the general budget of the Union, amending Regulations (EU) No 1296/2013, (EU) No 1301/2013, (EU) No 1303/2013, (EU) No 1304/2013, (EU) No 1309/2013, (EU) No 1316/2013, (EU) No 223/2014, (EU) No 283/2014, and Decision No 541/2014/EU and repealing Regulation (EU, Euratom) No 966/2012 (OJ 2018, L 193/1).

45 Proposal for a Regulation of the European Parliament and the Council on serious cross-border threats to health and repealing Decision No 1082/2013/EU, COM(2020) 727 final.

46 Decision of the EEA Joint Committee 73/2015 of 20 March 2015 amending Protocol 31 to the EEA Agreement, on cooperation in specific fields outside the four freedoms (OJ 2016, L 129/87).

and Norway to become part of the JPA.[47] Conversely, in the case of Switzerland, such a treaty is as of yet missing. According to information by the Swiss Federal Government, the EU and Switzerland have already finalised a draft agreement in the field of public health in 2015. This draft provides for Switzerland to participate in mechanisms to address serious cross-border health threats (also including the possibility to participate in joint procurement), the European Centre for Disease Prevention and Control (ECDC) and the EU Health Action Programme.[48] Whilst the Swiss Federal Government appears to see the draft agreement strictly as a cooperation agreement, the EU in addition conceives of it as a market access agreement, which it has said to be willing to sign only once a new institutional framework for a number of already existing agreements as well as for future market access agreements will be in place.[49] According to information received by this author from the Swiss administration, the draft agreement does not include cross-border patient mobility which, in the EU, is internal market law.[50] It does, however, include data-related issues, which the EU in the framework of its Digital Single Market Strategy[51] and now also in the framework of the plans for a European Health Data Space[52] qualifies as internal market law.

Overall, the EU's Joint Procurement Agreement Initiative for COVID-19 vaccines provides an example of a field where a Swiss-EU Agreement is lacking due to the unwillingness of the EU to sign such an agreement, which in turn leads to different treatment of Switzerland as compared to the EEA EFTA States. As the next part of this contribution will show, the same is true for the EU corona traffic light system.

47 See <https://ec.europa.eu/health/preparedness_response/joint_procurement/jpa_signature_de> (accessed 31 March 2022).

48 For official Swiss information see <https://www.bag.admin.ch/bag/en/home/strategie-und-politik/internationale-beziehungen/zusammenarbeit-mit-der-europaeischen-union.html> (accessed 31 March 2022); in academic writing M. Oesch, *Schweiz – Europäische Union. Grundlagen, Bilaterale Abkommen, Autonomer Nachvollzug* (EIZ Publishing, 2020), p. 26.

49 See the information given by the Swiss Government in its response to a parliamentary question on this issue, <https://www.parlament.ch/de/ratsbetrieb/suche-curia-vista/geschaeft?AffairId=20181079> (accessed 31 March 2022).

50 Directive 2011/24/EU of the European Parliament and of the Council of 9 March 2011 on the application of patients' rights in cross-border healthcare (OJ 2011, L 88/45), as amended.

51 See <https://eufordigital.eu/discover-eu/eu-digital-single-market/> (accessed 31 March 2022).

52 Proposal for a Regulation of the European Parliament and of the Council on the European Health Data Space, COM(2022) 197 final.

3 Movement of Persons

The concern for containing the spreading of the corona virus led to measures that affected the movement of people, both inside individual countries and in cross-border situations. Whilst agreements between Switzerland and the EU grant movement and residence rights under certain conditions and further include Switzerland in the Schengen system, they also contain derogations in the interest of the protection of public health (e.g., Article 5 of Annex I to the Agreement on the Free Movement of Persons, AFMP,[53] and Article 8(2) of the Schengen Borders Code,[54] which applies to Switzerland in the context of the Schengen Association Agreement).[55] Similar to the situation in relation to the free movement of goods, these derogations allow for proportionate measures that restrict the movement of people. Both Switzerland and the EU have adopted restrictive measures. However, different from the field of the free movement of goods, the EU only used its competences in this field to a modest extent. Instead, both the Commission and the Council urged voluntary cooperation among the EU Member States.[56] In the following, two initiatives of the Union are discussed, namely the EU "traffic light system" (below Section 3.1) and the Digital COVID Certificate (Section 3.2).

3.1 *The EU's Traffic Light System*

In October 2020, the Council adopted Recommendation 2020/1475 on a coordinated approach to the restriction of free movement in response to the COVID-19 pandemic.[57] The key points of this so-called "traffic light system" are a mapping of the risk of COVID-19 transmission and a coordinated approach

---

53 Agreement between the European Community and its Member States, of the one part, and the Swiss Confederation, of the other, on the free movement of persons (OJ 2002, L 114/6), as amended.

54 Regulation (EU) 2016/399 of the European Parliament and of the Council of 9 March 2016 on a Union Code on the rules governing the movement of persons across borders (Schengen Borders Code) (OJ 2016, L 7 7/1), as amended.

55 Agreement between the European Union, the European Community and the Swiss Confederation on the Swiss Confederation's association with the implementation, application and development of the Schengen *acquis* (OJ 2008, L 53/52), as amended.

56 For the Commission, see <https://ec.europa.eu/info/live-work-travel-eu/coronavirus-response/overview-commissions-response_en#borders-and-mobility> (accessed 31 March 2022), under the keyword "borders and mobility", and for the Council, Council Conclusions on COVID-19 (OJ 2020, C 57/4).

57 Council Recommendation (EU) 2020/1475 of 13 October 2020 on a coordinated approach to the restriction of free movement in response to the COVID-19 pandemic (OJ 2020, L 337/3).

as to the measures which may appropriately be applied by the Member States to persons moving between areas, depending on the level of risk of transmission in those areas. Under the traffic light system, the Member States share epidemiological data with the European Centre for Disease Control (ECDC) which then publishes a map of Europe, updated weekly, using a variety of colours depending on the risk in a given region. The original idea of the system was that whilst there should be no restrictions if people travel from a "green" region, in the case of travelling from an "orange" or a "red" region, national Governments may ask for tests or impose quarantine.[58] Subsequently, the colour dark red was added: Travellers arriving from areas marked in this manner should be subject to reinforced public health measures. The Recommendation also emphasised that so-called essential travellers and cross-border commuters should in principle be exempted from travel restrictions linked to COVID-19. In January 2022, Recommendation 2020/1475 was replaced by Recommendation 2022/107,[59] with the aim of further adapting the common approach set out in the previous Recommendation.

Being non-binding according to Article 288 TFEU, such Recommendations do not oblige the Member States to precisely follow their approach. For example, the Netherlands has used its own colour code coupled with its own travel advice, a code that it applies differently from the EU map.[60]

The European Union's map with weekly updates on the EU corona situation can be found on the ECDC website.[61] It shows no information for Switzerland. In contrast, the EEA EFTA countries are included. Whilst the Commission's proposal for the original Recommendation mentioned the EEA EFTA States only,[62] Recommendation 2020/1475, as eventually adopted, stated that the map "should also include data from Iceland, Liechtenstein, Norway and, as soon

58 See for general information <https://ec.europa.eu/info/sites/default/files/factsheet_-_coronavirus_-_a_coordinated_approach_to_measures_restricting_free_movement_in_the_eu.pdf> (accessed 31 March 2022), under "Borders and mobility".

59 Council Recommendation (EU) 2022/107 of 25 January 2022 on a coordinated approach to facilitate safe free movement during the COVID-19 pandemic and replacing Recommendation (EU) 2020/147 (OJ 2022, L 18/110).

60 Namely green: "The security risks are comparable to the situation in the Netherlands"; yellow: "Careful, there are security risks"; orange: "Serious security risks"; red: "Very serious security risks"; see <https://www.nederlandwereldwijd.nl/documenten/vragen-en-antwoorden/wat-betekenen-de-kleurcodes-bij-reisadviezenA (accessed 31 March 2022).

61 Maps in support of the Council Recommendation on a coordinated approach to travel measures in the EU, <https://www.ecdc.europa.eu/en/covid-19/situation-updates/weekly-maps-coordinated-restriction-free-movement> (accessed 31 March 2022).

62 Proposal for a Council Recommendation on a coordinated approach to the restriction of free movement in response to the COVID-19 pandemic, COM(2020) 499 final, point 12.

as conditions allow, the Swiss Confederation" (point 10). A footnote regarding Switzerland explained that this is

> [s]ubject to an agreement concluded between the EU and the Swiss Confederation on the cooperation on public health, including on the participation of the Swiss Confederation to the European Centre for Disease Prevention and Control according to Regulation (EC) No 851/2004 of the European Parliament and of the Council of 21 April 2004 establishing a European Centre for disease prevention and control (OJ L 142, 30.4.2004, p. 1).[63]

The same now appears in the new Recommendation 2022/107.

In other words, according to the EU, the decisive issue for present purposes is not the existence of an agreement on the free movement of persons (which does exist between Switzerland and the EU) but rather the existence of common rules on health that regulate certain matters (which is missing between Switzerland and the EU). According to Oesch,[64] the EU's reasoning in this respect is "formalistic". Similar to the joint procurement of vaccines, therefore, the EEA Agreement allows for the EEA EFTA States to be included in the EU's corona traffic light system whilst for Switzerland, a treaty basis for such inclusion is as of yet missing.

3.2 *The Digital COVID Certificate*

In March 2021, the Commission, based on Article 21(2) TFEU, proposed a Regulation on what was then termed the "Digital Green Certificate",[65] as well as a further Regulation based on Article 77(2)(c) TFEU with respect to third-country nationals legally staying or legally residing in the territories of Member

63 It may be interesting to note the legal basis for this action: The Commission had proposed Articles 21(2), 46, 52(2), 168(6) and 292 TFEU, thus also including the free movement for workers and freedom of establishment. These were, however, removed by the Council which, with respect to free movement, left only Articles. 21(2) TFEU (in addition to Articles 168(6) and 292 TFEU). EEA law does not contain a provision akin to Article 21(2) TFEU. Even so, the Recommendation is labelled as a "text with EEA relevance". The same is true for Regulation 2021/953 on the Digital COVID Certificate, discussed in the next section.

64 M. Oesch, 'Schweiz und Europa', in F. Ruhli, A. Thier (eds.), *Weissbuch Corona. Die Schweiz nach der Pandemie, Befunde – Erkenntnisse – Perspektiven* (NZZ Libro, 2021), p. 121.

65 Proposal for a Regulation of the European Parliament and of the Council on a framework for the issuance, verification and acceptance of interoperable certificates on vaccination, testing and recovery to facilitate free movement during the COVID-19 pandemic (Digital Green Certificate), COM(2021) 130 final.

States during the COVID-19 pandemic.[66] In its Explanatory Memorandum on the former, the Commission recalled the right of EU citizens to move and reside freely within the European Union, which "is one of the EU's most cherished achievements, and an important driver of its economy". It then noted that, in the context of the restrictions adopted by the Member States in order to limit the spread of COVID-19, travellers were asked to provide various types of documentary evidence, such as medical certificates, test results or declarations, without there being standardised and secured formats. According to the Commission, this led to problems, in spite of the existence of Guidelines on proof of vaccination for medical purposes published by the eHealth Network, a voluntary network connecting national authorities responsible for eHealth.[67] In order to facilitate free movement, the Commission, therefore, proposed a binding, uniform EU-wide framework for the issuance, verification and acceptance of vaccination, test and recovery certificates. At the same time, the Commission's proposal did not aim at harmonising travel restrictions as such, which were meant to remain a matter for the Member States to decide upon.

On 14 June 2021, the two Regulations – following a very fast ordinary legislative procedure – were adopted, now referring to the "EU Digital COVID Certificate" (Regulations 2021/953[68] and 2021/954).[69] Early academic assessments considered the certificate from different angles, such as data protection[70]

66 Proposal for a Regulation of the European Parliament and of the Council on a framework for the issuance, verification and acceptance of interoperable certificates on vaccination, testing and recovery to third-country nationals legally staying or legally residing in the territories of Member States during the COVID-19 pandemic (Digital Green Certificate), COM(2021) 140 final.

67 eHealth Network, Guidelines on verifiable vaccination certificates - basic interoperability elements, Release 2 of 12 March 2021, <https://ec.europa.eu/health/sites/health/files/ehealth/docs/vaccination-proof_interoperability-guidelines_en.pdf> (accessed 31 March 2022).

68 Regulation (EU) 2021/953 of the European Parliament and of the Council of 14 June 2021 on a framework for the issuance, verification and acceptance of interoperable COVID-19 vaccination, test and recovery certificates (EU Digital COVID Certificate) to facilitate free movement during the COVID-19 pandemic (OJ 2021, L 211/1), as amended. – An action for annulment has been declared inadmissible by the Court; CJEU, Case T-527/21, *Stefania Abenante v Parliament and Council*, EU:T:2022:278.

69 Regulation (EU) 2021/954 of the European Parliament and of the Council of 14 June 2021 on a framework for the issuance, verification and acceptance of interoperable COVID-19 vaccination, test and recovery certificates (EU Digital COVID Certificate) with regard to third-country nationals legally staying or residing in the territories of Member States during the COVID-19 pandemic (OJ 2021, L 211/24), as amended.

70 O.J. Gstrein, A. Alemanno and L. Bialasiewicz, 'The EU Digital COVID Certificate: A Preliminary Data Protection Impact Assessment', *European Journal of Risk Regulation* 12 (2021), p. 370.

and the free movement of persons. In the latter context, it has been argued that, given the vaccination campaign in the EU States, the EU Digital COVID Certificate is a significant step forward in the recovery of the free movement of persons.[71] At the same time, it has been pointed out that the Digital COVID Certificate in fact limits free movement and concern has been raised in relation to the requirement of proportionality (and in particular of choosing the least restrictive option) when restricting free movement due to public health reasons.[72] In a broader context, it has been argued that the system leads to discrimination against certain groups of non-Europeans.[73]

The basic Regulation 2021/953 notably contains rules on the certificates as such (Article 3 et seq.), on a "trust framework for the Digital COVID Certificate" (Article 4), on COVID-19 certificates and other documentation issued by a third country (Article 8) and on data protection (Article 10). With respect to restrictions of free movement, Article 11 confirms the Member States' competence to impose restrictions on grounds of public health. It adds, however, that "where Member States accept vaccination certificates, test certificates indicating a negative result or certificates of recovery, they shall refrain from imposing additional restrictions to free movement, such as additional travel-related testing for SARS-CoV-2 infection or travel-related quarantine or self-isolation, unless they are necessary and proportionate for the purpose of safeguarding public health in response to the COVID-19 pandemic, also taking into account available scientific evidence, including epidemiological data published by the ECDC on the basis of Recommendation (EU) 2020/1475". The Member States imposing such measures must inform the Commission as well as the other Member States. In this respect, therefore, the Regulation goes somewhat further than the Commission's proposal. Even so, it leaves considerable room for action for the Member States. Indeed, the obligation as quoted above is

71 L.H. Sancho, *Algunas claves para entender el certificado COVID digital de la Unión Europea*, Càtedra Jean Monnet Working Paper 4/2021 (European University Institute, 2021), p. 14.

72 I. Goldner Lang, 'EU COVID-19 Certificates: A Critical Analysis', *European Journal of Risk Regulation* 12 (2021), Special Issue 2: Symposium on COVID-19 Certificates and Special Issue on the Global Governance of Alcohol, p. 298, p. 300 et seq. Previously from the same author and along the same lines: Iris Goldner Lang, *Are COVID Certificates the Answer to Safe EU Travel During the Pandemic?*, Bill of Health 26 April 2021, <https://blog.petrieflom.law.harvard.edu/2021/04/26/are-covid-certificates-the-answer-to-safe-eu-travel-during-the-pandemic/> (accessed 31 March 2022).

73 A. Binagwaho, G. Carlsson, 'Why are EU vaccine passes discriminating against Africans? The EU's digital travel certificate paves the way for a two-tier vaccine system', *Politico* 8 July 2021, <https://www.politico.eu/article/africa-europe-travel-digital-green-certificate-coronavirus-restrictions-vaccine-covishield-oxford-astrazeneca/> (accessed 31 March 2022).

"without prejudice to the Member States' competence to impose restrictions on grounds of public health".

With respect to non-EU Member States, different situations have to be distinguished. First, Regulation 2021/953 is labelled "text with EEA relevance". On 30 June 2021, the EEA Joint Committee decided to incorporate the Regulation into EEA law.[74] Second, with respect to certificates issued in a non-Member State outside the EEA, Regulation 2021/953 provides for the possibility of equivalence decisions by the Commission. Third, Regulation 2021/954 contains rules relating to certificates with regard to third-country nationals legally staying or legally residing in the territories of Member States during the COVID-19 pandemic (which, as will be noted below, for these purposes also include non-Member States that are part of the Schengen area). For Switzerland, the latter two approaches are relevant.

The preamble to Regulation 2021/954 states that this Regulation constitutes a development of the provisions of the Schengen *acquis* and it explicitly mentions, among others, Switzerland in this context.[75] The Schengen framework of the Regulation is confirmed by its legal basis, which is Article 77(2)(c) TFEU, concerning the conditions under which nationals of third countries shall have the freedom to travel within the Union for a short period. In contrast, Regulation 2021/953 is based on Article 21 TFEU, which concerns the right of Union citizens to move and reside freely within the territory of the Member States. As noted by the Swiss Federal Administration, the fact that only Regulation 2021/954 is Schengen-relevant created a rather special situation for Switzerland, given that this Regulation does not itself regulate the COVID-19 certificate but merely extends the provisions of the main Regulation 2021/953 to additional persons. As a result of the nexus between the two Regulations in terms of content, Switzerland in fact enjoyed Schengen-related decisions shaping rights in relation to both Regulations. The Swiss Federal Administration states that Switzerland "adopted and implemented" not only Regulation 2021/954 (the Third-Country Regulation), but also "the main Regulation [i.e., Regulation

---

74 Decision of the EEA Joint Committee No 187/2021 of 30 June 2021 amending Annex V (Free movement of workers) and Annex VIII (Right of establishment) to the EEA Agreement, <https://www.efta.int/sites/default/files/documents/legal-texts/eea/other-legal-documents/adopted-joint-committee-decisions/2021%20-%20English/187-2021.pdf> (accessed 31 March 2022) (not yet published in the OJ at the time of writing).

75 The preamble contains specific considerations with respect to the various non-EU Schengen States; for Switzerland, see cons. 18; for Norway and Iceland, cons. 17, and for Liechtenstein, cons. 19.

2021/953] to the extent necessary for the adoption and implementation of the Third Country Regulation".[76]

At the same time, an equivalence decision under the main Regulation 2021/943 was required. Articles 3(10) and 8(2) of this Regulation clearly provide for two distinct equivalence regimes. Both are formulated in a general manner and do not mention specific countries. However, as noted by the Commission, Article 3(10) currently covers only Switzerland.[77] It is, therefore, a special "Swiss equivalence clause". Article 3(10) provides:

> The Commission may adopt implementing acts establishing that COVID-19 certificates issued by a third country with which the Union and the Member States have concluded an agreement on the free movement of persons allowing the contracting parties to restrict such free movement on grounds of public health in a non-discriminatory manner and which does not contain a mechanism of incorporation of Union legal acts are equivalent to those issued in accordance with this Regulation. Where the Commission adopts such implementing acts, the certificates concerned shall be accepted under the conditions referred to in Article 5(5), Article 6(5) and Article 7(8). Before adopting such implementing acts, the Commission shall assess whether such a third country issues certificates equivalent to those issued in accordance with this Regulation and has provided formal assurances that it will accept certificates issued by the Member States. The implementing acts referred to in the first subparagraph of this paragraph shall be adopted in accordance with the examination procedure referred to in Article 14(2).

In the first half of 2021, Switzerland developed its own COVID Certificate which was introduced on 7 June 2021.[78] During the phase of development

76 Bundesamt für Gesundheit, Erläuterungen zur Verordnung über Zertifikate zum Nachweis einer Covid-19-Impfung, einer Covid-19-Genesung oder eines Covid-19-Testergebnisses (Covid-19-Verordnung Zertifikate), Version vom 7. April 2022, <https://www.bag.admin.ch/dam/bag/de/dokumente/mt/k-und-i/aktuelle-ausbrueche-pandemien/2019-nCoV/erlaeuterungen-covid-zertifikat.pdf.download.pdf/Erl%C3%A4uterungen%20oder%20Covid-19-Verordnung%20Zertifikate.pdf> (accessed 30 April 2022; translation by author from German), p. 2.

77 Report from the Commission to the European Parliament and the Council pursuant to Article 16(1) of Regulation (EU) 2021/953, COM(2021) 649 final, p. 5. See also the contribution by M. Oesch and M. Brugger in this volume.

78 Swiss Federal Government, Media Release of 4 June 2022, COVID-19: Federal Council adopts ordinance on COVID-19 certificates, <https://www.admin.ch/gov/en/start/documentation/media-releases.msg-id-83837.html> (accessed 31 March 2022).

of their respective certificates, the Swiss and EU authorities were in touch with each other in view of the eventual recognition of each other's certificates. Switzerland already on 4 June 2021 adopted a COVID-19 Regulation "Certificates"[79] that includes a part on certificates issued in other countries. Article 22 specifically deals with the recognition of certificates issued by a Member State of the EU or the EFTA.[80] The relevant States were subsequently added in the annex to the Regulation.[81]

The EU Digital COVID Certificate was introduced on 1 July 2021.[82] On 8 July 2021, the Commission adopted an equivalence decision in relation to Switzerland.[83] In the preamble, the Commission notes that Union citizens and Swiss nationals enjoy reciprocal rights of entry and residence based on the Swiss-EU AFMP, an agreement that provides for the possibility to restrict free movement for public health reasons and that does not contain a mechanism of incorporation of Union acts. In order to explain this latter element, it should be noted that whilst amendments of the Agreement in the light of new EU law are possible under Article 18 AFMP (namely either in a simplified procedure through the Joint Committee that is in charge of the Agreement, for matters relating to the coordination of the social security systems and relating to the mutual recognition of professional qualifications, or through ordinary Treaty revision for other issues), this is voluntary. Distinct from the EEA Agreement,

79 Ordinance on Certificates to Prove Covid-19 Vaccination, Covid-19 Recovery or a Covid-19-Test Result (Covid-19 Certificates Ordinance) of 4 June 2021, SR 818.102.2.

80 Article 22 provides: "1 The recognised vaccination, recovery and test certificates issued by a member state of the European Union (EU) or a state of the European Free Trade Association (EFTA) are listed in Annex 5. 2 The Federal Department of Finance (FDF) shall update Annex 5 continuously in consultation with the Federal Department of Home Affairs (FDHA) and the Federal Department of Foreign Affairs (FDFA). 3 It shall include in the Annex certificates that were issued in accordance with the provisions applicable in the EU and whose states of origin grant reciprocal rights. However, it may decide not to include certificates for vaccines that are not authorised for the EU by the European Medicines Agency in accordance with Regulation (EC) No. 726/2004".

81 Amendment of the Regulation of 7 July 2021, in force since 9 July 2021 (AS 2021 428).

82 See generally: European Council/Council of the European Union, EU digital COVID certificate: how it works, <https://www.consilium.europa.eu/en/policies/coronavirus/eu-digital-covid-certificate/> (accessed 31 March 2022).

83 Commission Implementing Decision (EU) 2021/1126 of 8 July 2021 establishing the equivalence of COVID-19 certificates issued by Switzerland to the certificates issued in accordance with Regulation (EU) 2021/953 of the European Parliament and of the Council (OJ 2021 L 243/49). See also the media release of 9 July 2021 of the Swiss Federal Government: EU recognises Swiss COVID certificate, <https://www.admin.ch/gov/en/start/documentation/media-releases.msg-id-84383.html> (accessed 31 March 2022).

the Swiss-EU AFMP does not provide for legal consequences in the case of a refusal of an update on the side of one of the parties.[84]

With regard to COVID-19 certificates, therefore, the finding is that all four EFTA States apply a system which is based on the same rationale and which follows the same model as that of the EU. In so far and on the practical level, there is ultimately equal treatment. However, whilst the EEA EFTA States on the basis of EEA law directly participate in the EU system, Switzerland is legally not part of that system but has instead developed its own system that follows the EU model.[85] Subsequently, the EU and Switzerland each unilaterally decided to recognise the other's certificate.

It is obvious that unilateral equivalence decisions provide for a less secure and less stable legal position than would an agreement (as exemplified, in the Swiss-EU relations in the context of stock exchange equivalence).[86] Although Article 3(10) of Regulation 2021/953 does not make it explicit, one can draw the conclusion that, from the point of view of the EU, an equivalence mechanism for Switzerland was necessary due to the lack of a *dynamic* system of updating in the AFMP. In this context, it may be interesting to note that the Swiss Federal Administration, in explaining the approach taken, refers to "the absence of a possibility for rapid adoption of the Regulation by a decision of the Joint Committee within the framework of the AFMP".[87] This seems to imply the view that the problem in relation to Switzerland, rather than the lack of the dynamic nature of the AFMP, was the *lack of time* for a solution in the framework of the AFMP.

---

84 Commonly agreed updates have happened on several occasions. Conversely, the Swiss Federal Government has refused changes to the AFMP in the light of Directive 2004/38 (Directive 2004/38/EC of the European Parliament and of the Council of 29 April 2004 on the right of citizens of the Union and their family members to move and reside freely within the territory of the Member States amending Regulation (EEC) No 1612/68 and repealing Directives 64/221/EEC, 68/360/EEC, 72/194/EEC, 73/148/EEC, 75/34/EEC, 75/35/EEC, 90/364/EEC, 90/365/EEC and 93/96/EEC (OJ 2004, L 158/77), as amended). This was also one of the contentious issues in the negotiations on the Institutional Agreement. Conversely, the Directive is part of EEA law; see C. Tobler, 'Free Movement of Persons in the EU v. in the EEA: Of Effect-Related Homogeneity and a Reversed *Polydor* Principle', in N. Cambien/D. Kochenov/E. Muir (eds.), *European Citizenship under Stress. Social Justice, Brexit and Other Challenges* (Brill Nijhoff, 2020), p. 482.

85 On the Swiss COVID certificate, see S. Schlauri, 'Der digitale COVID-Impfausweis', *Jusletter IT* 27 May 2021.

86 On this and more generally on the issue of equivalence in the Swiss-EU relations see J. Beglinger/C. Tobler, 'Gleichwertigkeit, Angemessenheit, Äquivalenz, Adäquanz', in A. Epiney, P.E. Zlătescu (eds.), *Schweizerisches Jahrbuch für Europarecht = Annuaire suisse de droit européen 2019/2020* (Schulthess, 2020), p. 547, with further references.

87 See Bundesamt für Gesundheit (n. 76), p. 2.

As it is, Switzerland's COVID Certificate in relation to Swiss nationals and persons benefitting from the AFMP is an example of autonomous adaptation, as noted by Oesch and Brugger elsewhere in this volume and as also recognised by the Federal Administration.[88] At the same time in relation to third-country-nationals, the COVID certificate is an example of dynamic alignment due to the qualification of Regulation 2021/954 as part of the Schengen *acquis*.

4 Findings and Conclusion

In Swiss academic writing, Oesch[89] noted in 2020 that whilst not everything was easy, the good understanding between the EU and Switzerland and the recognition of the importance of close and constructive cooperation to address the challenges posed by COVID-19 were impressively manifested in combating the pandemic during spring of 2020.

The present contribution showed that, in certain respects, things turned out less positive thereafter. The contribution focused in particular on the treatment of Switzerland with respect to certain COVID-related common EU actions, as compared to the treatment of the EEA EFTA States Iceland, Liechtenstein and Norway. It was found that whilst Switzerland was treated equally beneficially as its fellow EFTA States in the context of EU export restrictions for personal protective equipment in 2020, the same was not true in relation to export restrictions for vaccines in 2021. In the first case, the EU (through the Commission) put the emphasis on factual commonalities in order to justify the same treatment of all four EFTA States. In the second case, at some point, the Commission shifted towards (alleged) legal and factual differences in order to justify different treatment, against which Switzerland protested to no avail. Suspicions were uttered in the Swiss media that the real reason for the EU's attitude might be the Swiss reluctance to sign the Institutional Agreement. It was noted that it is difficult to judge whether, in the circumstances, it could be argued that the EU's action amounts to arbitrary discrimination contrary to Article 20 FTA.

It was also noted that there are limited possibilities to address perceived problems, namely through consultations in the Joint Committee that is in charge of the FTA. In fact, an example of the limits of this approach is provided by the Swiss steps taken against the EU steel sanctions vis-à-vis the

88 See the contribution by M. Oesch and M. Brugger in this volume. See also Bundesamt für Gesundheit (n.76), p. 3.

89 M. Oesch (n. 48), p. 229 et seq.

USA, for which – again – an exemption applies to the EEA EFTA States but not to Switzerland.[90] Here, the Commission based the exemption in favour of Norway, Iceland and Liechtenstein on the close integration of markets with EEA members, the overall figures of imports from these countries, and the low risk of trade diversion.[91] No such factors are relied upon in relation to Switzerland, on the contrary: according to the Commission, the application of the safeguard measures to Switzerland is justified under Article 26 FTA (consideration 196 in the preamble to Commission Implementing Regulation 2019/159). Disagreeing with this interpretation, Switzerland raised the matter repeatedly in the Joint Committee, arguing that the EU must fully respect its obligations under the FTA.[92] The consultations have so far not led to a satisfactory solution for Switzerland.

Different treatment of Switzerland was also found in respect of the joint procurement of vaccines, the corona traffic light system and – on the legal, though ultimately not the factual level – the Digital COVID Certificate. In the last of these cases, the reason for the legally different treatment appears to be the lack of a system of dynamic updating in the AFMP. In the other two cases, the reason cited by the EU for not allowing the inclusion of Switzerland in the relevant EU systems is the lack of a bilateral health agreement. For Switzerland, the lack of this agreement is particularly unsatisfactory as the stumbling block on the way to the signature is the Union, which has created a political tie of this issue with the acceptance by Switzerland of new institutional rules for certain other, already existing agreements. Here, the political motives on the side of the EU are obvious, but then there is no basis for a legal obligation whose breach by the EU could be argued.

Overall and hardly surprising, the discussion has shown the relevance of political motives, notably on the side of the EU, in dealing with the various COVID-19-related matters in its relations with Switzerland. In comparison,

---

90 In 2018, the EU adopted provisional safeguard measures which became definitive through Commission Implementing Regulation (EU) 2019/159 of 31 January 2019 imposing definitive safeguard measures against imports of certain steel products (OJ 2019, L 31/27), and whose temporal application was subsequently extended.

91 Thus consideration 196 in the preamble to Commission Implementing Regulation (EU) 2021/1029 of 24 June 2021 amending Commission Implementing Regulation (EU) 2019/159 to prolong the safeguard measure on imports of certain steel products (OJ 2021, L 225I/1).

92 See the information provided by the Swiss State Secretariat for Economic Affairs SECO, Safeguard measures on steel imports, <https://www.seco.admin.ch/seco/en/home/Aussenwirtschaftspolitik_Wirtschaftliche_Zusammenarbeit/Wirtschaftsbeziehungen/Warenverkehr/handelsschutzmassnahmen/EU_schutzmassnahmen_stahl.html> (accessed 31 March 2022).

Switzerland's fellow EFTA States Iceland, Liechtenstein and Norway benefit from a legal framework (namely the EEA Agreement) that is judged by the EU to be stabler both legally and politically.

CHAPTER 6

Switzerland's Structural Participation in EU Agencies

Merijn Chamon

1 Introduction

A little studied aspect of the relationship between the EU and Switzerland is the extent to which the latter is structurally integrated into institutional arrangements set up by the EU legislator. While there is a plethora of EU bodies, offices, committees, working groups, etc., to which Swiss representatives may be invited, the present chapter will focus specifically on the most advanced bodies set up by the EU legislator: the EU decentralised agencies. These bodies are permanent bodies under EU public law, established by the EU institutions through secondary legislation and endowed with their own legal personality.[1] This excludes "autonomous" bodies or entities such as the European External Action Service, Eurostat, the executive agencies established pursuant to Regulation 58/2003,[2] etc.

Of course, the exclusion of these other "autonomous" bodies, and especially the executive agencies, from the scope of this chapter is not because Switzerland cannot have any relations with these bodies that merit further study. Indeed, the executive agencies' typical function is to manage the many ambitious programmes of the EU which are often open to third country participation. The European Education and Culture Executive Agency (EECEA),[3] for instance, manages the Erasmus+ programme which is open to third countries. Currently, however, Switzerland is not an associated country to the Erasmus+

1 M. Chamon, *EU Agencies: Legal and Political Limits to the Transformation of the EU Administration* (Oxford University Press, 2016), p. 10.

2 Council Regulation 58/2003/EC of 19 December 2002 laying down the statute for executive agencies to be entrusted with certain tasks in the management of Community programmes (OJ 2003, L 11/1).

3 See Commission Implementing Decision 2021/173/EU establishing the European Climate, Infrastructure and Environment Executive Agency, the European Health and Digital Executive Agency, the European Research Executive Agency, the European Innovation Council and SMEs Executive Agency, the European Research Council Executive Agency, and the European Education and Culture Executive Agency (OJ 2021, L 50/9).

© KONINKLIJKE BRILL NV, LEIDEN, 2023 | DOI:10.1163/9789004529984_008

programme anymore[4] and Swiss institutions will only be able to participate *ad hoc* as legal entities associated with a partner country,[5] like institutions from the UK and the Faroe Islands. Yet, even if Switzerland becomes associated (again) to Erasmus+, it will not *structurally* participate in the EECEA, since third country participation is not foreseen in executive agencies. That is different for the decentralised agencies on which this chapter focuses.

Before looking into the extent of Switzerland's participation in the EU agencies, this chapter will first sketch the internal EU context in which the phenomenon of EU agencification should be placed (Section 2). This will reveal that EU agencification is essentially an internally focused development of the EU's institutional framework, begging the question of what the external dimension to this internal phenomenon is. Having explored that issue in Section 3, the chapter moves on to the specific question as to why a third country would be interested in participating in an (internal) EU body (Section 4.1) and how this is legally realised in practice (Section 4.2). Having set the scene, the chapter will then proceed to identify the agencies in which Switzerland participates and how this participation is legally made possible, revealing a range of legal techniques relied upon by the EU and Switzerland (Section 5). Looking to the future, Section 6 briefly discusses ongoing negotiations on Swiss participation in additional EU agencies, further revealing how the legal techniques relied upon to allow for such participation are policy area-dependent and subject to continuous development. Finally, and although its fate is highly uncertain given the Swiss Government's decision of 26 May 2021 not to sign the Institutional Agreement with the EU, the relevance of that agreement for the question of Swiss participation in EU agencies is also further explored (Section 7).

2 A Primer on EU Agencification

One defining trend in the EU's institutional development over the past decades is the phenomenon of agencification, or the establishment and empowerment of EU agencies.[6] In a nutshell, commentators originally explained the surge of

4 This following the negative result of the referendum held in 2014 on free movement; see also the introduction to this volume.

5 See Article 20 of Regulation 2021/817/EU of the European Parliament and of the Council establishing Erasmus+: the Union Programme for education and training, youth and sport (OJ 2021, L 189/1).

6 M. Chamon (n. 1), p. 10.

EU agencies since the 1990s by reference to functional arguments, i.e., invoking the typical functional reasons why independent agencies have sprung in different legal systems.[7] In doing so, the same reasons relied upon to explain national agencification were recycled, disregarding the fact that agencification is always the result of a polity's specific constitutional and inter-institutional dynamics.[8] More recently, it is being recognised that under a new institutionalist reading of EU agencification, EU agencies may be conceived as constituting a form of administrative integration (i.e., centralisation), which became necessary in the era following the Single European Act to realise the EU's ambitious internal market agenda. Rational Choice New Institutionalism thereby explains why the EU institutions and Member States have struck a grand compromise on the hybrid structures, which EU agencies are, as the organisational means to realise this administrative integration, while Historical New Institutionalism helps in explaining how establishing agencies or further empowering existing ones has by now become entrenched as the default response to policy needs or crises at EU level.[9]

If EU agencies are exponents and facilitators of administrative integration, the question arises what Switzerland's position vis-à-vis these agencies is. Having taken the principled position to stay outside of the political integration project, and at the same time feeling the irresistible gravitational pull of the EU's internal market, means Switzerland could find itself anywhere between the extremes of staying outside all EU agencies or participating in all the agencies of those sectors in which it has set up cooperation with the EU.

7 See D. Kelemen, A. Tarrant, 'The political foundations of the Eurocracy', *West European Politics* 34 (2011), p. 923.

8 D. Halberstam, 'The promise of comparative administrative law: a constitutional perspective on independent agencies', in S. Rose-Ackerman, P. Lindseth (eds.), *Comparative administrative law* (Edward Elgar, 2010), pp. 193–200.

9 M. Chamon (n. 1), p. 111–115. A recent illustration of this is the project of a European Health Union launched by the Commission in the wake of the COVID19-pandemic. The three proposals tabled in November 2020 foresee in the strengthening of the mandates of the European Medicines Agency and the European Centre for Disease Prevention and Control (two EU agencies) and of that of the Health Security Committee (without transforming the latter into a proper agency). See European Commission, COM(2020) 725 final. In addition, at the end of March 2021, the Commission also launched a public consultation on a to be established body, the Health Emergency Preparedness and Response Authority, which might become a new agency of the EU.

3 EU Agencies and the External Dimension

Virtually every act establishing an EU agency recognises the international context in which that agency will operate, and most establishing acts also task the agency concerned to be actively involved in the international sphere. However, the types of external action in which the establishing acts foresee do vary. As Ott, Vos and Coman-Kund point out, three main types of external action may be discerned: EU agencies can (i) be a forum open to third countries or even international organisations, (ii) assist the EU institutions in their external policy and (iii) engage in relations with third countries or international organisations in their own right.[10] In what follows, this chapter will focus on the first type of external action and will thereby evidently focus on Switzerland's (possible) participation in EU agencies. It should immediately be clarified here that the issue of a third country's participation in an EU agency is not binary. Instead, as Lavenex notes, participation ranges "from full membership to association without voting rights, observer status [to] punctual participation in particular functions and fora."[11] Looking at the highest form of participation, the present chapter will focus on the structural and permanent participation of Switzerland in EU agencies. That type of participation thus goes beyond "lower" forms of participation which may consist of (occasionally) sending experts to attend technical meetings held in the agency or even sending an observer to the Management Board of an agency.[12]

---

10 A. Ott, E. Vos and F. Coman-Kund, 'EU agencies and their international mandate: A new category of global actors?', CLEER *Working Papers* 7(2013), p. 8.

11 S. Lavenex, 'The external face of differentiated integration: third country participation in EU sectoral bodies', *Journal of European Public Policy* 22 (2015), p. 838.

12 The European Labour Authority (ELA), for instance is an agency in which Switzerland has an observer status on the Management Board. However, only countries which fully participate in the agency are represented by a member on the Management Board and as the Rules of Procedure of the ELA Management Board make clear, there is a clear difference between non-voting members (representing non-EU countries that structurally participate in the ELA) and observers. See ELA Management Board, Decision 1/2019 of 17 October 2019 laying down the Rules of Procedure, <https://www.ela.europa.eu/sites/default/files/2020-12/2019-10-17_Rules-of-Procedure-Management-Board.pdf> (accessed 15 June 2022).

4 The Rationale and Legal Framework for Third Countries' Structural Participation in EU Agencies

Before looking into the legal techniques that have been worked out to allow third countries to participate in EU agencies, it is useful to delve deeper into the question of what drives non-EU States to be involved in those EU bodies, especially if the countries concerned have no ambition to become EU Member States, as is the case for Switzerland.

4.1 *Why Do Third Countries Participate in EU Agencies?*

In EU studies, two hypotheses have been advanced in this respect: under the first, foreign policy hypothesis, the integration of third countries in EU agencies serves the EU's general foreign policy. From this perspective, "[o]rganizational inclusion [in an EU agency] aims to prepare for EU accession, familiarize with the *acquis communautaire* or, from a more symbolic perspective, express a privileged relation with the Union."[13] In contrast, under the second, functional interdependence hypothesis, third countries will (only) integrate into those agencies that have been made responsible for managing, or facilitating the management of, economic sectors where the externalities of non-cooperation are high.[14] In the case of Switzerland, this would mean that under the first hypothesis, Switzerland's participation in EU agencies should be relatively consistent across all EU agencies and be at a relatively low level, given Switzerland's policy of not politically associating itself to the EU. Conversely, under the second hypothesis, Switzerland's participation in EU agencies will be uneven across agencies and may be significant for those agencies operating in sectors in which the EU and Switzerland have set up cooperation to manage interdependencies. At least in relation to the countries in the EU's European Neighbourhood Programme, of which Switzerland is not part, Rimkutė and Shyrokykh have found that the functional interdependencies hypothesis has greater explanatory value. As will be shown below, the same hypothesis also appears to be validated when Switzerland's participation in EU agencies is analysed.[15] One particular recent event provides ample illustration of an externality which may convince a third country like Switzerland

13 S. Lavenex (n. 1), p. 837.

14 D. Rimkutė, K. Shyrokykh, 'Transferring the acquis through EU agencies: The case of the European neighbourhood policy countries', in H. Hofmann, E. Vos and M. Chamon (eds.), *The External Dimension of EU Agencies and Bodies. Law and Policy* (Edward Elgar, 2019), p. 191.

15 *Ibid.*

to seek participation in EU agencies: when a global pandemic hits, a country's response to a large extent depends on the quality of the data that it has access to. Given Switzerland's geographic location, that means it is of paramount importance to have access to the data compiled by the European Centre for Disease Prevention and Control (ECDC). To have full and continued access to the ECDC, structural participation in the agency then becomes crucial.[16]

4.2 *The General Legal Framework for Third Countries' Participation in EU Agencies*

Although it cannot be *a priori* excluded that third countries might participate in an EU agency in absence of an explicit provision to this end in the establishing act of the agency, those acts will typically set out the basic requirements for third countries to be able to participate on a structural basis in an EU agency.[17] The first such provision was introduced in the European Environment Agency Regulation in 1990, Article 19 of which originally read:

> The Agency is open to countries which are not members of the European Communities but which share the concern of the Communities and the Member States for the objectives of the Agency under agreements concluded between them and the Community following the procedure in Article 228 of the Treaty.[18]

Following the recast of the agency's Regulation in 2009, this provision remained unaltered apart from the reference to Article 228 of the EEC Treaty (now Article 218 TFEU). Following the European Environment Agency Regulation, an identical provision was included in the European Monitoring Centre for

---

16 See also Conseil fédéral suisse, Rapport sur la politique extérieure 2020, FF 2021 230, pp. 43–44.

17 It should be noted that already in the 1991 Intergovernmental Conference (IGC), the Commission proposed amendments to the current Article 218 TFEU (then Article 228 of the EEC Treaty) *inter alia* to the effect that international agreements making "*provision for participation by non-member countries or international organizations in bodies set up by Community law*" be concluded by the Council using QMV with the Parliament's assent. See European Commission, 'Initial Contribution by the Commission to the IGC on Political Union', SEC (91) 500, p. 21.

18 Council Regulation 1210/90/EEC on the establishment of the European Environment Agency and the European Environment Information and Observation Network (OJ 1990, L 120/1). This Regulation has been repealed and replaced by Regulation 401/2009/EC of the European Parliament and of the Council on the European Environment Agency and the European Environment Information and Observation Network (OJ 2009, L 126/13).

Drugs and Drugs Addiction (EMCDDA) Regulation.[19] In the European Training Foundation (ETF) Regulation, this provision was elaborated, and it was added that the "agreements shall inter alia specify the nature and extent of and the detailed rules for the participation of these countries in the work of the Foundation, including provisions on financial contributions and staff."[20] This has by now become the standard clause relied on by the EU legislator.

In further establishing acts,[21] the following three fundamental elements may then be identified if a provision on the structural participation of third countries is foreseen. In order for such participation to be possible, (i) the EU needs to have concluded an agreement with the third country in question, (ii) the third country needs to apply relevant EU legislation in the field,[22] (iii) the agreement must lay down the specific rules for the third country's participation in the agency.[23] As a result, despite the EU agencies' independence, it

19 See Article 13 of Council Regulation 302/93/EEC on the establishment of a European Monitoring Centre for Drugs and Drug Addiction (OJ 1993, L 36/1). This Regulation has been repealed and replaced by Regulation 1920/2006/EC of the European Parliament and of the Council on the European Monitoring Centre for Drugs and Drug Addiction (OJ 2006, L 376/1).

20 See Article 16 of Council Regulation 1360/90/EEC establishing a European Training Foundation (OJ 1990, L 131/1). This Regulation has been repealed and replaced by Regulation 1339/2008/EC of the European Parliament and of the Council of 16 December 2008 establishing a European Training Foundation (OJ 2008, L 354/82).

21 See Article 43 of Regulation 2019/942/EU establishing a European Union Agency for the Cooperation of Energy Regulators (OJ 2019, L 158/22); Article 129 of Regulation 2018/1139/EU on common rules in the field of civil aviation and establishing a European Union Aviation Safety Agency, (OJ 2018, L 212/1); Article 30 of Regulation 851/2004/EC establishing a European Centre for disease prevention and control, (OJ 2004, L 142/1); Article 49 of Regulation 178/2002/EC laying down the general principles and requirements of food law, establishing the European Food Safety Authority and laying down procedures in matters of food safety, (OJ 2002, L 31/1); Article 19 of Regulation 1922/2006/EC on establishing a European Institute for Gender Equality, (OJ 2006, L 403/9); Article 17 of Regulation 1406/2002/EC establishing a European Maritime Safety Agency (OJ 2002, L 208/1); Article 42 of Regulation 2019/881/EU on ENISA (the European Union Agency for Cybersecurity) and on information and communications technology cybersecurity certification (OJ 2019, L 151/15); Article 44 of Regulation 2016/796/EU on the European Union Agency for Railways (OJ 2016, L 138/1); Articles 75 of the Regulations setting up the European Supervisory Authorities (OJ 2010, L 331/12) (OJ 2010, L 331/48) (OJ 2010, L 331/84).

22 Rapoport notes that this is in fact a formidable requirement which de facto excludes participation in an agency for a lot of third countries. See C. Rapoport, *Les partenariats entre l'Union européenne et les états tiers européens: étude de la contribution de l'Union européenne à la structuration juridique de l'espace européen* (Bruylant, 2011), pp. 503–507.

23 An important aspect here is the financial contribution which third countries are required to make in order to cover the costs of their participation. In more detail, see C. Rapoport (n. 22), pp. 543–550.

merits underlining that it will be the political institutions deciding whether and which third countries may participate structurally in an agency and that this is never left to the agency itself to decide. This is so also for the exceptional cases where a specific agreement is not required for a third country to participate.

A first such example is the Fundamental Rights Agency (FRA) since Article 28 of the FRA Regulation provides that countries which have concluded a stabilisation and association agreement can participate in the FRA as observers, pursuant to a decision of the Association Council setting out the practical arrangements which are otherwise found in the specific bilateral agreements.[24]

A second special case is provided by the European Economic Area (EEA) Agreement. Norway, Iceland and Liechtenstein structurally participate in many EU agencies through the Agreement.[25] This is made possible through the decisions of the Joint Committee amending the Annexes or Protocols to the Agreement whenever the EU adopts new relevant legal acts. The decisions typically provide that Norway, Iceland and Liechtenstein shall participate fully in the Board of the agency concerned and that they shall have the same rights and obligations within that Board as the EU Member States, apart from the right to vote. Similar provisions may then also be found as regards the agencies' expert bodies, where relevant. This allows Norway, Iceland and Liechtenstein to participate in those agencies without having to conclude a specific agreement to this end with the EU. Despite this advantage over other non-Member States, the Commission in the past has still expressed its discontent about the "lengthy negotiations between the EU and the EEA EFTA States [...] before incorporating new legal acts, whenever the status or level of participation of these States in EU agencies needs to be addressed."[26] As an alternative, even for the EEA States, the Commission suggested a horizontal agreement specifically aimed at Norway, Iceland, and Liechtenstein's participation in EU agencies.[27] However, while the EEA States responded positively to the suggestion, it does not seem to have been pursued since.[28]

---

24 See, e.g., Decision 1/2018 of the EU-Serbia Stabilisation and Association Council on the participation of Serbia as an observer in the European Union Agency for Fundamental Rights' work and the respective modalities thereof (OJ 2018, L 229/9).

25 See the list at <http://www.efta.int/eea/eu-agencies> (accessed 15 June 2022).

26 European Commission, A review of the functioning of the European Economic Area, SWD(2012) 425 final, p. 10.

27 *Ibid.*

28 As the Commission itself noted in 2012, any agreement would have to be in line with the principle of institutional autonomy. As a 2019 legal note of the EFTA Secretariat makes clear, however, the EEA's two-pillar approach is very difficult to square with the full

As will be shown below, while the three fundamental elements have not been deviated from in the EU's relations with Switzerland, the way in which they are concretely given effect has proven to be very malleable, resulting in three distinct techniques to enable Switzerland's structural participation in EU agencies: the default option, the "EASA option" and the "ERA option" (see Section 5).

4.3 *Participation in EU Agencies from the Swiss' Perspective*

Given that third countries can only participate in EU agencies after having concluded an international agreement with the EU, it is important to clarify the internal Swiss legal framework for the conclusion of treaties. According to Article 54(1) of the Swiss Federal Constitution (FC), foreign relations are the responsibility of the Confederation. Negotiations are the responsibility of the Federal Council, i.e., the Government of the Swiss Confederation. Article 166(2) FC provides that international agreements are approved by the Federal Assembly, with the exception of those that are concluded by the Federal Council under a statutory provision or an international treaty. Article 7a of the Law on the organisation of the government and administration[29] adds that the Federal Council is competent for minor agreements and provides examples of what is to be considered as minor (e.g., agreements that do not create new obligations or agreements executing obligations already entered into) and what is not considered minor (e.g., agreements involving significant financial obligations). Article 7a thereby clarifies that agreements which come within the scope of Article 141 FC are never to be considered minor. Article 141 FC defines the issues on which popular referenda may be organised (as opposed to Article 140 of the Constitution which identifies the issues on which a popular referendum is mandatory).

Under this legal framework, the agreements which Switzerland must conclude before it can structurally participate in EU agencies will typically be subject to the approval of Federal Assembly and cannot be concluded by the Federal Council on its own, unless a power is delegated to the Federal Council by the Federal Assembly.[30] Since these agreements will typically come within

participation of EEA EFTA States in EU agencies and requires multiple EEA-specific adaptations. See Legal Notes by the EFTA Secretariat on the EEA Agreement, EFTA Bulletin, June 2019, pp. 20–25. The scope for a horizontal agreement then seems limited. In addition, while the EEA EFTA States might be convinced, if a horizontal agreement would also mean that by default they have voting rights in EU agencies (unlike now), that would require a paradigm shift on the EU side.

29 Loi sur l'organisation du gouvernement et de l'administration, RO 1997 2022.

30 See for instance Switzerland's participation in EASA, Frontex and eu-LISA.

the scope of Article 141(1)(d)(3) FC, they may also form the subject of a popular referendum.[31] In so far as the agreements need to be transposed into legislation, they will (also) come under Article 141(1)(a) FC.

Next to the question of the internal steps that Switzerland has to take to conclude and ratify its agreements with the EU, there is the question of how subsequent developments in the EU *acquis* may be incorporated into the Swiss legal order. The internal Swiss legal framework on this point is characterised by the same logic which applies to the conclusion of international agreements.[32] Broadly, three *modi operandi* may apply. A first model applies to EU acts which are either not binding, not intended for Switzerland or only concern it indirectly. In such cases, Switzerland takes note of the act in question and informs the EU by means of a diplomatic note. This decision rests with the Federal Council. A second model applies to binding acts falling within the sole competence of the Federal Council and whose implementation does not require legislative changes (and which do not come within the exclusive domain of the legislature as defined in Article 164 of the Constitution). The exchanges of notes under this model qualify as international treaties which the Federal Council can conclude on its own. Under the last model, the approval of the Parliament is required, either because they come under the competence of the Federal Assembly or because they require legislative adaptations. The exchange of notes under this third model qualifies as international treaties which the Federal Council cannot, therefore, conclude on its own and a facultative referendum will typically be possible.[33] Specifically for the Schengen and Dublin *acquis*, Switzerland is bound by a deadline of two years before which it needs to have ensured the proper incorporation of any developments of the *acquis*.[34] While this deadline used to be malleable, it emerges from the

31 Citing the example of Switzerland's participation in the European Environment Agency, see Minh Son Nguyen, 'La Gestion des Dechets en Droit Administratif International', *Swiss Review of International and European Law* 24 (2014), pp. 56–57.

32 See Rapport du Conseil fédéral en exécution du postulat Hans Fehr 10.3857 du 1er octobre 2010, 7 June 2013, FF 2013 5685, pp. 5701–5702.

33 This framework thus requires every development in the EU *acquis* to be properly qualified in order to know which of the three models will apply. For the development of the Schengen *acquis*, see <https://www.bj.admin.ch/dam/bj/de/data/sicherheit/schengen-dublin/uebersichten/weiterentwicklungen-schengen-d.pdf> (accessed 15 June 2022).

34 See Article 7(2)(b) of the Agreement between the European Union, the European Community and the Swiss Confederation on the Swiss Confederation's association with the implementation, application and development of the Schengen *acquis* (OJ 2008, L 53/52), and Article 4(3) of the Agreement between the European Community and the Swiss Confederation concerning the criteria and mechanisms for establishing the State

practice that the EU has become more strict: delaying the transposition of the substantive *acquis* in order to make sure that it coincides with the entry into force of the agreement that allows for Switzerland's participation in the relevant agency does not seem to be tolerated anymore by the EU side.[35]

This distinction between the development of the EU *acquis* and the conclusion of agreements is important since the full participation of Switzerland in an EU agency will typically require Switzerland to incorporate the substantive *acquis* through one internal procedure and the conclusion of an agreement with the EU enabling the participation in the agency through a second procedure. Because both procedures ultimately have the same aim, Swiss internal practice sees the Federal Assembly typically delegating the power to the Federal Council to conclude the second agreement.

Taking a step back from the legal framework which governs Switzerland's participation in the EU's agencies, it is clear that, politically, Switzerland is confronted with the same dual challenge as the EFTA States that participate in the European Economic Area,[36] and it is not uncommon (especially regarding developments in the Schengen *acquis*) that Switzerland negotiates together with the other EFTA States on their participation in EU agencies. This allows these non-Member States to form a coalition against the European Commission during the negotiations, maximising their (limited) leverage over the EU.[37] First, these non-Member States insist on pretending (both to their citizens and to the EU) that they are sovereign States. This claim of sovereignty is buttressed by the internal legal framework (*in casu* of Switzerland) noted above. Second, accepting that they are in fact not sovereign at all when it comes to their relations with the EU, these countries also aim to maximise their influence over the development of the EU *acquis*. The achievement of this aim is constrained and limited by EU law and more concretely, the degree to which EU law leaves scope for non-Member States to be involved in decision-making. Within these constraints, the aims for a State like Switzerland in the negotiations with

---

responsible for examining a request for asylum lodged in a Member State or in Switzerland (OJ 2008, L 51/5).

35 See Message relatif à l'approbation de l'arrangement entre la Suisse, la Norvège, l'Islande et le Liechtenstein, d'une part, et l'Union européenne, d'autre part, concernant la participation de ces États à l'agence européenne pour la gestion opérationnelle des systèmes d'information à grande échelle (eu-LISA), 23 February 2019, FF 2019 2099, pp. 2103–2104.

36 On this see A. Müller, 'Unionsrechtliche Grenzen der Beteiligung von Drittstaaten an Entscheidungen der Europäischen Union', *Europarecht* Beiheft 1 (2020), pp. 33–49.

37 Expressly noting as such, see Message portant approbation de l'arrangement entre la Suisse et l'Union européenne sur les modalités de la participation de la Suisse au Bureau européen d'appui en matière d'asile (EASO), 3 September 2014, FF 2014 6653, pp. 6661–6662.

the EU are limited, although they are not simply a unilateral affair of the EU imposing its will. For instance, since for some EU agencies, there is a limited right to vote for non-Member States in the Management Board, negotiations will then typically focus (from a Swiss perspective) on maximising this right to vote. Another negotiable issue is the exact financial contribution key which will determine how much Switzerland has to pay to the EU for the privilege of participating in its agencies. The positions taken internally in Switzerland on the Institutional Agreement perfectly reflect the dual tension described above and the same tension is visible in the discussion on Swiss participation in EU agencies.[38]

5 Switzerland's Structural Participation in EU Agencies

Like all other third countries other than the three EEA EFTA States, Switzerland's participation in EU agencies is determined *ad hoc*. A paper from 2010 from the Swiss Federal Government lists the EU agencies with which Switzerland has formal ties and those with which such ties could be established in the future.[39] However, there are important differences between the agencies lumped together under the first "formal ties" category as defined by that paper: the conclusion of agreements or arrangements between the EU agency concerned and its Swiss counterpart[40] or even Switzerland itself[41] may result in a formalised tie but does not necessarily equate to a *structural* and *permanent* participation, the type of participation on which this chapter focuses.

5.1 *The Notion of Structural Participation*

As noted above, while EU agencies may sometimes be qualified as independent bodies, their independence does not encompass the authority to decide for themselves who their members are. A formalised tie between Switzerland

38 See the discussion in B. Pirker, L. Matter, 'Europarecht: Schweiz-Europäische Union', *Swiss Review of International and European Law* 31 (2021), pp. 124–128.

39 Bericht des Bundesrates zum Verhältnis der Schweiz zu den europäischen Agenturen, September 2010, <http://www.news.admin.ch/NSBSubscriber/message/attachments/20546.pdf> (accessed 15 June 2022), pp. 9–13.

40 See the 2012 Administrative Arrangement between the European Defence Agency (EDA) and the Swiss Federal Department of Defence, Civil Protection and Sports of the Swiss Confederation, as well as the 2006 Cooperation Agreement between the Swiss Police Institute and CEPOL.

41 See the 2008 Agreement between Eurojust and Switzerland (FF 2010 41); the 2005 Agreement between Europol and Switzerland (FF 2005 931).

and an EU agency can then not result in structural participation, since only the EU institutions can allow such participation of third countries. The (non-binding) Common Approach on EU Decentralised Agencies of 2012, an inter-institutional agreement between the Parliament, Council and Commission, indeed explicitly clarifies that whatever external action the EU Agencies engage in, they cannot bind the EU or the Member States.[42] The Common Approach leaves open the question of whether the EU agencies might conclude international agreements in their own name, but an analysis of the agencies' establishing acts and their practice reveals that EU agencies do not have international legal personality and that it is not envisaged that they should conclude international agreements (even in their own name).[43] The agreements which Switzerland concluded with Europol and Eurojust,[44] and which the Swiss Government paper of 2010 lists as examples of formalised ties, are cases in point since they do not foresee structural participation. Under the pre-Lisbon legal framework, both third-pillar agencies could conclude formal agreements on their own behalf with third countries.[45] When these agencies' establishing acts were recast following the entry into force of the Lisbon Treaty, the EU institutions aligned Europol and Eurojust with the other EU agencies, prescribing that they may only conclude *arrangements* with international counterparts.[46] Generally, such arrangements may be used to formalise ties and set up structured cooperation but that does not equate with the full and structural cooperation in an EU agency. All this also translates into the internal Swiss decision-making on those "formal ties". Some arrangements between Switzerland and EU agencies may be concluded by the Federal Council on its own, but the issue of Switzerland's structural participation in an EU agency will depend on the approval of the Federal Assembly (possibly delegated to the Federal Council) (see Section 4.3).

That the question of structural participation is far from clear, is further illustrated by Bekkedal's study devoted to the EEA EFTA States' participation

42 See point 25 of the Common Approach on EU Decentralised Agencies, Council Doc. 11450/12.

43 See M. Chamon, 'A constitutional twilight zone: EU decentralized agencies' external relations', *Common Market Law Review* 56 (2019), pp. 1509–1548.

44 See supra n. 40.

45 See Article 26(3) of the original Europol Convention (OJ 1995, C 316/1); Article 27(3) of Council Decision 2002/187/EC setting up Eurojust with a view to reinforcing the fight against serious crime (OJ 2002, L 63/1).

46 See Article 23(3) of Regulation 2016/794/EU on the European Union Agency for Law Enforcement Cooperation (OJ 2016, L 135/53); Article 52(2) of Regulation 2018/1727/EU on the European Union Agency for Criminal Justice Cooperation (OJ 2018, L 295/138).

in EU agencies. Differently from the 2010 Swiss Federal Government's paper, Bekkedal notes that "Switzerland participates in 6 EU agencies: the European Environment Agency, EASA [European Aviation Safety Agency] and ECHA [European Chemicals Agency] (internal market), Frontex [European Border and Coast Guard Agency], EASO [European Asylum Support Office], and eu-LISA [European Union Agency for the Operational Management of Large-Scale IT Systems in the Area of Freedom, Security and Justice] (Schengen)."[47] Just like the Swiss Federal Government's 2010 study, Bekkedal also lumps together legally different situations. Only in five of these agencies does Switzerland *fully* participate. Indeed, this is not the case for Switzerland's participation in ECHA. Switzerland's *partial* involvement in ECHA is the result of the extension of mutual recognition between the EU and Switzerland of the regulation of biocides.[48] The 2002 Agreement between the European Community and the Swiss Confederation on mutual recognition in relation to conformity assessment[49] was concluded as part of the *Bilaterals I*. The Joint Committee on mutual recognition set up by the agreement may amend the annexes of the agreement. In 2015, the Joint Committee added the product sector of biocidal products to Annex I.[50] This followed the adoption in 2012 of the EU Biocidal Products Regulation.[51] Since this mutual recognition essentially means that the ECHA provides services to the Swiss authorities, the 2015 Decision also provides that Switzerland must pay a contribution relative to its Gross Domestic Product (GDP) to the ECHA. And while a Commission Declaration annexed to the Decision provides that Swiss experts will be invited to expert group and committee meetings, the Decision does not provide that Swiss authorities will be structurally participating in ECHA and will, for instance, have no membership in the Management Board. Any *ad hoc* participation is then limited to the

47 T. Bekkedal, 'Third State participation in EU agencies: Exploring the EEA precedent', *Common Market Law Review* 56 (2019), p. 384.

48 See C. Kaddous, C. Tobler, 'Droit Européen: Suisse-Union Européenne / Europarecht: Schweiz-Europäische Union', *Swiss Review of International and European Law* 25 (2015), p. 597.

49 Agreement between the European Community and the Swiss Confederation on mutual recognition in relation to conformity assessment (OJ 2002, L 114/369).

50 Decision No 1/2015 of the Committee established under the Agreement between the European Community and the Swiss Confederation on mutual recognition in relation to conformity assessment of 14 April 2015 on the amendment of Chapter 16 on construction products, Chapter 18 on biocidal products and the update of legal references listed in Annex 1 (OJ 2015, L 171/25).

51 See Regulation 528/2012/EU concerning the making available on the market and use of biocidal products (OJ 2012, L 167/1).

issues dealt with by ECHA pursuant to the Biocidal Products Regulation (and not the other EU legislative acts entrusting tasks to ECHA).

Turning to the five agencies in which Switzerland does structurally and fully participate, it must be noted that the technique relied upon to realise this participation may differ from one agency to the next. In any event, for each separate agency, a different instrument is required. Unlike the EEA EFTA States, there is no single overarching agreement based on which specific instruments are adopted. For Switzerland, the instrument allowing it to participate is in a sense a stand-alone instrument, but it is evidently embedded in a (pre-)existing web of formalised relations. As will be shown below, roughly three techniques have been or will be, relied upon: (i) the conclusion of a dedicated agreement under Article 218 TFEU (the default option), (ii) the adoption of a decision by a body established under an existing agreement pursuant to Article 218(9) TFEU (the "EASA option"), and (iii) the adoption of an arrangement between the agency itself and Switzerland (the "ERA option").

Since a lot of the provisions of the instruments allowing for Switzerland's participation in EU agencies are identical from one instrument to the next, the following section will not describe each single instrument exhaustively.[52] To avoid repetition, first, the common denominator of these instruments will be presented, following which the context in which these instruments have been

52 The instruments themselves are all published in the EU's Official Journal (OJ). See Decision 1/2019 of the Joint European Union/Switzerland Air Transport Committee set up under the Agreement between the European Community and the Swiss Confederation on Air Transport of 22 August 2019 replacing the Annex to the Agreement between the European Community and the Swiss Confederation on Air Transport (OJ 2019, L 226/1) (hereafter the EASA Annex); See the Agreement between the European Community and the Swiss Confederation concerning the participation of Switzerland in the European Environment Agency and the European Environment Information and Observation Network (OJ 2006, L 90/3) (hereafter: European Environment Agency Agreement); Arrangement between the European Community, of the one part, and the Swiss Confederation and the Principality of Liechtenstein, of the other part, on the modalities of the participation by those States in the European Agency for the Management of Operational Cooperation at the External Borders of the Member States of the European Union (OJ 2010, L 243/4) (hereafter: Frontex arrangement); Arrangement between the European Union and the Swiss Confederation on the modalities of its participation in the European Asylum Support Office (OJ 2016, L 65/22) (hereafter: EASO arrangement); Arrangement between the European Union, of the one part, and the Kingdom of Norway, the Republic of Iceland, the Swiss Confederation and the Principality of Liechtenstein, of the other part, on the participation by those states in the European Agency for the operational management of large-scale IT systems in the area of freedom, security and justice (OJ 2019, L 138/11) (hereafter: eu-LISA arrangement).

agreed to will be discussed and their notable features (deviating or adding to the common denominator) will be flagged.

5.2 *Common Denominator of the Instruments Providing for Switzerland's Participation in EU Agencies*

Since the purpose of all the instruments involved is the same (namely allowing a third country to participate structurally in an EU body), it is unsurprising to see that most of these instruments' provisions are identical regardless of the agencies to which they apply.

The instruments will always prescribe that Switzerland can send a representative to the Management Board of the agency concerned and it will explicitly clarify that that representative will not have the right to vote.[53] Still, two exceptions to the lack of a right to vote are provided in relation to the agencies involved in the Schengen *acquis* (cf. *infra*). In this regard, the European Commission is apparently stricter in its approach to deny third countries the right to vote than is the EU legislator.[54] A further privilege afforded to Switzerland is that the instruments enable the agencies to hire Swiss nationals as part of their contract staff,[55] although some instruments explicitly exclude Swiss nationals from filling the post of Executive Director.[56]

Just like all the regulations setting up EU agencies provide for these agencies' legal personality and require the Member States to ensure that they enjoy the most extensive legal capacity available to legal persons in their national legal order, the same requirement is imposed on Switzerland.[57] A further requirement typically imposed on Switzerland is that it must apply the EU's

53 See Article 2 EASO arrangement, Article 3 European Environment Agency agreement, point (d) of the EASA Annex, Article 2 of the eu-LISA arrangement, Article 1 of the Frontex arrangement.

54 See C. Tobler, 'Zur Beteiligung der Schweiz an der Europäischen IT-Agentur', *Jusletter* 1.10.2012, pp. 13–15.

55 See Article 1 EASO arrangement, Article 13 European Environment Agency agreement, point (b) of the EASA Annex, Article 9 of the eu-LISA arrangement, Article 8 of the Frontex arrangement.

56 See Article 8(4) EASO arrangement, Article 9(4) of the eu-LISA arrangement, Article 8(3) of the Frontex arrangement. The Frontex arrangement also excludes Swiss nationals from the post of Chair (or Deputy Chair) of the Management Board, even though these are not staff members of the agency as such.

57 See Article 5 EASO arrangement, Article 11 European Environment Agency agreement, Article 5 of the eu-LISA arrangement, Article 4 of the Frontex arrangement. For the EASA, this results from the horizontal provision to read references to "Member States" in EU legislation as including Switzerland for these purposes.

Protocol on Privileges and Immunities to the agency,[58] mirroring the relevant provisions in the agencies' establishing regulations. Similarly, apart from the Frontex arrangement, the instruments foresee Switzerland accepting that the EU's financial control mechanisms are applied in and to Switzerland in so far as it participates in the agency.[59] A further very relevant requirement concerns the financial obligations imposed on Switzerland. All instruments require Switzerland to contribute financially to the relevant agency's functioning but the precise method of calculating the contribution varies (cf. *infra*). In terms of general provisions, the instruments are typically concluded for an unlimited period and may be denounced by notification, following which they will cease to apply after six months.[60]

Having set out this "common denominator", the following subsections zoom in on the particularities of the specific instruments in place.

5.3 *European Aviation Safety Agency* (EASA)

Switzerland's participation in the EASA is enabled through the 1999 Agreement between the European Community and the Swiss Confederation on Air Transport[61] which is part of the *Bilaterals I*.[62] In 2006, the Joint Committee established under that agreement amended the agreement's annex with the necessary provisions providing for Switzerland's participation.[63] In an annex to

58 See Article 9 EASO arrangement, Article 12 European Environment Agency agreement, point (c) of the EASA Annex, Article 8 of the eu-LISA arrangement, Article 7 of the Frontex arrangement.

59 See Article 11 EASO arrangement, Article 16 European Environment Agency agreement, point (f) of the EASA Annex, Article 11 of the eu-LISA arrangement, Article 1 of the Frontex arrangement.

60 See Article 14 EASO arrangement, Article 19 European Environment Agency agreement, Article 15 of the eu-LISA arrangement, Article 15 of the Frontex arrangement. For Frontex, denouncing the arrangement is only possible as a result of the termination of the agreement involving Switzerland in the Schengen *acquis*. Given the technique employed to allow for Switzerland's participation in the EASA, the issues of duration and termination do not pose themselves.

61 Agreement between the European Community and the Swiss Confederation on Air Transport (OJ 2002, L 114/73).

62 From the Swiss perspective, see notably Message sur la participation de la Suisse à l'Agence européenne de la sécurité aérienne AESA, 25 May 2005, FF 2005 3651.

63 See Decision 3/2006 of the Community/Switzerland Air Transport Committee amending the Annex to the Agreement between the European Community and the Swiss Confederation on Air Transport (OJ 2006, L 318/31). From an internal Swiss perspective, it may be noted that in 2009, after Switzerland had already joined the EASA, the Federal Council proposed that the Assembly would grant it a power to conclude minor international agreements, so that future revisions of the EASA Regulation (and decisions by the mixed committee) would not each time require the approval of the Federal Assembly

the Decision, the Joint Committee de facto amends EU legislation by prescribing how certain provisions are to be read to include Switzerland in their scope. Formally however, the EU legislation is not amended, it is merely taken up into the *acquis* of the agreement. The current provisions allowing for Switzerland's participation were laid down in 2019.[64] This technique is therefore different from the technique relied upon to allow for Switzerland's participation in other agencies, which involves the conclusion of a separate agreement that does not *de facto* amend the agencies' establishing regulations. The substantive provisions adopted by the Joint Committee do not as such deviate from the common denominator identified above. Two features of the method of calculating Switzerland's contribution to the EASA's budget are notable however. First, the contribution is calculated on the basis of the EASA's budget that is not covered by the fees and charges received by EASA (the agency being partially self-financed). Second, the contribution is calculated taking into account Switzerland's contribution to the International Civil Aviation Organization (ICAO) relative to the EU Member States' contribution to the ICAO.[65]

5.4 *European Environmental Agency* (EEA)

Switzerland's participation in the EEA is enabled through a dedicated international agreement concluded in 2006.[66] Since the agreement is not embedded in a broader framework of formalised relations, it is more elaborate than the other instruments. Apart from some provisions that are very specific to the European Environment Information and Observation Network (EIONET) (for which Switzerland has to identify competent national bodies and to which it needs to send data), the agreement allowing for Switzerland's participation in the EEA adds a specific institutional framework in addition to the common denominator of provisions identified above. The Joint Committee's function

---

before they would be binding on Switzerland. This resulted in the current Article 3a of the civil aviation law as introduced by the amendment of 1 December 2010, RO 2011 1119.

64 See Decision 1/2019 of the Joint European Union/Switzerland Air Transport Committee set up under the Agreement between the European Community and the Swiss Confederation on Air Transport of 22 August 2019 replacing the Annex to the Agreement between the European Community and the Swiss Confederation on Air Transport (OJ 2019, L 226/1).

65 See point (e) of the EASA Annex.

66 See the Agreement between the European Community and the Swiss Confederation concerning the participation of Switzerland in the European Environment Agency and the European Environment Information and Observation Network (2006, L90/37). Arrêté fédéral portant approbation de l'accord bilatéral entre la Suisse et la Communauté européenne sur la participation de la Suisse à l'Agence européenne pour l'environnement et au réseau EIONET, 17 December 2004, FF 2004 6703.

is to allow an exchange of views between the parties but it is also empowered to amend the annexes to the agreement.[67] These annexes *inter alia* list the relevant EU secondary legislation for which Switzerland will be treated as an EU Member State and the calculation of Switzerland's contribution to the EEA budget. Remarkably, that contribution is calculated based on the subsidy from the EU budget which the EEA receives divided by the total number of States participating in the EEA. Unlike the formulas applicable to other agencies, Switzerland, therefore, does not contribute based on its economic strength.

5.5 *Frontex*

Switzerland's participation in Frontex is realised through an arrangement between the EU and Switzerland. While there is a 2004 international agreement between the EC, EU and Switzerland associating the latter with the Schengen *acquis*,[68] that agreement simply ensures that Switzerland implements and applies the Schengen *acquis*. While the Frontex Regulation evidently forms part of the Schengen *acquis*, it only prescribes the participation of Schengen-associated third countries in the agency, but it does not lay down the modalities for this itself. Instead, it foresees that "arrangements developed under the relevant provisions of their association agreements that specify the nature and extent of, and the detailed rules for, the participation by those countries in the work of the Agency, including provisions on financial contributions and staff, shall apply."[69] The relevant arrangement was subsequently concluded in 2010. On the EU side, this was done pursuant to Article 218 TFEU, i.e., as a proper international agreement.[70] On the Swiss side, this

67 See Article 12 of the agreement concerning Switzerland's participation in the European Environment Agency.

68 Agreement between the European Union, the European Community and the Swiss Confederation on the Swiss Confederation's association with the implementation, application and development of the Schengen *acquis* (OJ 2008, L 53/52).

69 See Article 101(3) of Regulation 2019/1896/EU of the European Parliament and of the Council of 13 November 2019 on the European Border and Coast Guard (OJ 2019, L 295/1). This provision dates back to the original Frontex Regulation where the relevant provision was only slightly different. See Article 21(3) of Council Regulation 2007/2004/EC of 26 October 2004 establishing a European Agency for the Management of Operational Cooperation at the External Borders of the Member States of the European Union (OJ 2004, L 349/1).

70 See Council Decision 2010/490/EU of 26 July 2010 on the conclusion, on behalf of the Union, of the Arrangement between the European Community, of the one part, and the Swiss Confederation and the Principality of Liechtenstein, of the other part, on the modalities of the participation by those States in the European Agency for the Management of Operational Cooperation at the External Borders of the Member States of the European Union (OJ 2010, L 243/2).

was concluded by the Federal Council which had received a mandate to that end from the Federal Assembly.[71]

The technique on the EU side is therefore the same as with the European Environment Agency albeit that the instrument is not qualified as an agreement and that the arrangement forms part of a much denser normative framework. On the Swiss side, also the technique is different, since it is simplified compared to the ordinary treaty making procedure. The arrangement itself provides that Switzerland will pay a contribution to the Frontex budget in accordance with its gross domestic product.[72] Differently from the common denominator, it provides that Switzerland can wield limited voting rights in the Management Board.[73] That these voting rights (and those of Liechtenstein, Norway and Iceland) are exceptional, is reflected in a Joint Declaration annexed to the arrangement which provides that the voting rights "may therefore not be regarded as a legal or political precedent for any other field of cooperation between the parties to the Arrangement or for the participation of other third countries in other agencies of the Union. In no circumstances may these voting rights be exercised in respect of decisions of a regulatory or legislative nature."[74] The Frontex arrangement further contains additional rules on Protection and confidentiality of data,[75] and the role of the Court of Justice of the European Union to rule on the agency's non-contractual liability (and its contractual liability if an arbitration clause so provides).[76]

5.6 *European Asylum Support Office* (EASO)

Simultaneously with its participation in Schengen, Switzerland also participates in the EU's Dublin system on the basis of a (separate) international agreement since 2008.[77] Differently from Frontex, EASO was only established after Switzerland's formal participation in the Dublin system. Mindful of this, the

---

71 See Arrêté fédéral portant approbation et mise en œuvre des échanges de notes entre la Suisse et la Communauté européenne concernant la reprise du règlement FRONTEX et du règlement RABIT (Développements de l'acquis de Schengen), 3 October 2008, FF 2008 7597.

72 See Article 2 of the arrangement *iuncto* Article 11 of the agreement association Switzerland with the Schengen *acquis*.

73 See Article 1 Frontex arrangement.

74 See the Joint Declaration annexed to the Frontex arrangement.

75 See Article 3 Frontex arrangement.

76 See Articles 5 and 6 Frontex arrangement.

77 Agreement between the European Community and the Swiss Confederation concerning the criteria and mechanisms for establishing the State responsible for examining a request for asylum lodged in a Member State or in Switzerland (OJ 2008, L 51/5).

EASO Regulation, in its recitals, foresees that "to fulfil its purpose, the Support Office should be open to participation by countries which have concluded agreements with the Union by virtue of which they have adopted and apply law of the Union in the fields covered by this Regulation, in particular Iceland, Liechtenstein, Norway and Switzerland."[78] Just like in the case of Frontex, Switzerland's participation was not made possible through the basic agreement (i.e., the association of Switzerland to the Dublin system), but through a separate agreement, in line with Article 49(1) of the EASO Regulation which prescribes that separate arrangements with all of the Dublin-associated States should be concluded to allow for their participation in EASO.[79] For EASO, just like for Frontex, Switzerland contributes based on its GDP. In contrast to the common denominator identified above, and similar to the Frontex arrangement, the EASO arrangement contains provisions on data protection,[80] and the role of the Court of Justice of the European Union to rule on the agency's non-contractual liability (and its contractual liability if an arbitration clause so provides).[81] Although Switzerland tried to acquire voting rights in the Management Board,[82] like in the case of Frontex, this was denied by the EU. Unlike both the common denominator and the Frontex arrangement, the EASO arrangement also sets up a committee to monitor the proper implementation of the arrangement.[83]

5.7 *European Union Agency for the Operational Management of Large-Scale IT Systems in the Area of Freedom, Security and Justice (eu-LISA)*

Since the eu-LISA manages several databases used in the management of the Schengen and Dublin systems, Switzerland not only participates in Frontex and EASO, but also in eu-LISA since 2020.[84] Article 37 of the eu-LISA Regulation provides that "[u]nder the relevant provisions of their association agreements,

78 See Recital 24 of the Preamble to Regulation 439/2010/EU establishing a European Asylum Support Office (OJ 2010, L 132/11).

79 On the Swiss side, the agreement was approved by the Federal Assembly in March 2015, allowing the Federal Council to ratify it. The period for holding a facultative referendum lapsed in July 2015 without a referendum being called. See Arrêté fédéral, 20 March 2015, RO 2015 2555.

80 See Article 4 EASO arrangement.

81 See Articles 6 and 7 EASO arrangement.

82 See Message portant approbation de l'arrangement entre la Suisse et l'Union européenne sur les modalités de la participation de la Suisse au Bureau européen d'appui en matière d'asile (EASO), 3 September 2014, FF 2014 6653, p. 6661.

83 See Article 11 EASO arrangement.

84 On the Swiss side, the agreement was approved by the Federal Assembly in September 2019, allowing the Federal Council to ratify it. The period for holding a facultative

arrangements shall be made in order to specify, inter alia, the nature and extent of, and the detailed rules for, the participation by countries associated with the implementation, application and development of the Schengen *acquis* and Eurodac-related measures in the work of the Agency, including provisions on financial contributions, staff and voting rights." Just like the Frontex arrangement, the eu-LISA arrangement foresees that Switzerland will have limited voting rights in the agency's Management Board and advisory groups.[85] However, the actual list of decisions on which Switzerland will have the right to vote is considerable rather than 'limited'.[86] For the participation in eu-LISA, Switzerland contributes relative to its GDP. Differently from the common denominator identified above, and similar to the Frontex and EASO arrangements, the eu-LISA arrangement contains provisions on the role of the Court of Justice of the European Union to rule on the agency's non-contractual liability (and its contractual liability if an arbitration clause so provides).[87] Unlike the other arrangements, there is no provision on data protection but there is an explicit provision on dispute settlement, providing for a role of the Mixed Committee set up by the Agreements associating Switzerland to the Schengen and Dublin systems.[88]

6 Future of Switzerland's Participation in EU Agencies

The above sections devoted to the specific instruments show that institutional learning is happening in terms of the substance of these instruments. It may therefore be expected that the common denominator identified in Section 5.1 will be progressively enriched and codified when new instruments allowing for Switzerland's structural participation are adopted or when existing instruments are revised. At the time this chapter was finalised, the Commission was negotiating agreements allowing Switzerland to structurally participate in two further EU agencies. The Council has thus authorised the Commission to negotiate agreements on Switzerland's participation in the European Railways Agency (ERA)[89] and in the European GNSS (Global Navigation Satellite System)

referendum lapsed in January 2020 without a referendum being called. See Arrêté fédéral, 27 September 2019, RO 2020 737.

85 See Articles 2 and 3 eu-LISA arrangement.

86 See Article 2 eu-LISA arrangement.

87 See Articles 6 and 7 eu-LISA arrangement.

88 See Article 12 eu-LISA agreement.

89 See Council Document 15695/2017.

Agency (GSA).[90] How these negotiations will be affected by Switzerland's decision not to sign the Institutional Agreement (InstA) (cf. *infra*) remains unclear.

Switzerland already participates in the GNSS programmes by virtue of the GNSS Cooperation Agreement.[91] That agreement provides that the EU and Switzerland are to conclude a further agreement to also allow Switzerland to participate fully in the European GNSS Agency.[92] The negotiations on this agreement have already been concluded, but the European Commission has refused to initial the negotiated text in light of the problems with the InstA.[93] The legal constellation itself, however, is very similar to that of Switzerland's participation in Frontex and EASO: after having concluded substantive agreements, integrating Switzerland in a certain area of the EU *acquis*, the logical next step is a further agreement allowing for Switzerland's participation in the internal EU institutional mechanism set up to ensure the proper implementation of that substantive *acquis*.

In contrast, Switzerland's future participation in ERA would be enabled in a completely novel manner: as part of the *Bilaterals I*, Switzerland and the EU have concluded a Land Transport Agreement.[94] Following the EU's adoption of successive "railway packages" (the last one being the fourth railway package of 2016), the Joint Committee set up pursuant to the agreement has continuously updated the annex of the agreement. However, contrary to how Switzerland's participation in EASA was realised, the Joint Committee under the Land Transport Agreement is not empowered to amend the agreement to allow Switzerland to participate in the ERA.[95] While the Air Transport Agreement contains a chapter dedicated to enforcement, one of its provisions foreseeing that "the Community institutions shall enjoy the powers granted to them under the provisions of the regulations and directives whose application is explicitly confirmed in the Annex",[96] no such provision is included in the Land Transport Agreement. In the Land Transport Agreement, Switzerland has therefore not accepted the principle that the EU institutions and bodies may exercise the

90 See Council Document 6673/2018.

91 Cooperation Agreement between the European Union and its Member States, of the one part, and the Swiss Confederation, of the other, on the European Satellite Navigation Programmes (OJ 2014, L 15/3).

92 *Ibid.*, Article 16.

93 Conseil fédéral suisse, Rapport sur la politique extérieure 2020, FF 2021 230, p. 44.

94 Agreement between the European Community and the Swiss Confederation on the Carriage of Goods and Passengers by Rail and Road (OJ 2002, L 114/91).

95 See Recital 6 of Decision 2/2019 of the Community/Switzerland Inland Transport Committee (OJ 2019, L 13/43). European Commission, COM(2017) 644 final, p. 3.

96 See Article 18(2) of the Air Transport Agreement.

powers they have under EU legislation with regard to Switzerland. To ensure participation, the Agreement would therefore first need to be amended.[97]

Whether, from an EU perspective, this is legally absolutely necessary may be doubted, however. Article 52(6) *iuncto* Article 49 of the Land Transport Agreement could already be read as implicitly allowing the Joint Committee to take the necessary measures to allow Switzerland's participation in the ERA. The Joint Committee would then adopt a decision analogously to the decision adopted by the Joint Committee under the Air Transport Agreement for the EASA. Legally speaking, the need to amend the Agreement, from an EU perspective, itself might just as much be the consequence of a new type of provision in the ERA Regulation which was recast in 2016. Unlike all the other mechanisms discussed above, the ERA Regulation prescribes that it will be ERA itself (together with Switzerland) that defines the further modalities of participation on issues such as personnel and finances.[98] Even if the relevant provision prescribes that the ERA can only conclude that arrangement with Switzerland following the agreement of the Commission, this mechanism is still markedly different from those relied upon in the context of the other agencies, since the modalities will not be contained in an agreement in the sense of Article 218 TFEU or a decision in the sense of Article 218(9) TFEU. Under the ERA Regulation then, the solution adopted for the EASA is not a possibility anymore. While the "ERA-option" constitutes a novel technique, it should be stressed that it is still in line with the fundamental elements identified above in Section 4.2: while the ERA, together with Switzerland, will set the modalities of participation, the principle decision which allows Switzerland to structurally participate in the ERA is still taken by the Council (which will need to agree to revise the Agreement) and the ERA cannot conclude the arrangement without the Commission's consent.

Finally, the developments related to the Body of European Regulators for Electronic Communications (BEREC), which is not strictly an agency, may be indicative of a stricter approach at the EU side of Swiss participation in EU agencies. Under the original BEREC Regulation, third countries could act as observers within BEREC. However, that possibility was removed when the BEREC Regulation was reviewed and third countries can now only participate structurally (not as observers). For this, however, a dedicated agreement between the EU and the third country is needed, something for which there

97 European Commission, COM(2017) 644 final, p. 3.

98 See Article 75(2) of Regulation 2016/796/EU on the European Union Agency for Railways (OJ 2016, L 138/1).

does not seem to be much appetite on the EU side given the Swiss refusal to conclude the Institutional Agreement.[99]

7 The Institutional Agreement

The Institutional Agreement (InstA) which the EU and Switzerland had been negotiating since 2014 was not directly relevant to the question of Switzerland's participation in EU agencies.[100] The agreement's "framework"-nature mostly related to the creation of a horizontal dispute settlement mechanism and common provisions for future sectoral agreements and did not extend to the specific question of participation in EU agencies.[101] As such, there was no provision in the draft InstA that prescribed or enabled Switzerland's future participation in EU agencies. The future agreements to which the InstA would have applied, pursuant to Article 2(1), would therefore still have had to prescribe or enable Switzerland's participation in the relevant EU agency. Likewise, the horizontal provisions in Article 13 of the draft InstA did not explicitly foresee the possibility for the sectoral committees to decide on Swiss participation when integrating the relevant EU legal acts in the sectoral agreement at issue. Whether the "EASA option" would be followed thus depended on the terms of the sectoral agreement in question. Still, the InstA could have potentially ensured greater coherence as regards the modalities for Swiss participation in EU agencies in the future by virtue of its mixed horizontal committee foreseen in Article 15. If the "EASA option" would be relied on to a greater extent in the future, the horizontal committee could have assisted in further developing the common denominator identified in Section 5.2, since it would have supervised and coordinated the work of the different sectoral committees.[102]

While no immediate direct link between the InstA and the question of Swiss participation in EU agencies can be identified, there still is an important indirect connection between both. In addition to the future participation discussed in section 6, it should be noted here that the EU and Switzerland have been negotiating an electricity cooperation agreement already since 2007.

99 See L. Mäder, 'Schweiz wegen des fehlenden Rahmenabkommens aus der europäischen Telekom-Behörde ausgeschlossen', *Neue Zürcher Zeitung* 21 February 2019.

100 For the text of the agreement, see the version of 23 November 2018 available at <https://www.eda.admin.ch/dam/europa/fr/documents/abkommen/Acccord-inst-Projet-de-texte_fr.pdf> (accessed 15 June 2022).

101 See the contributions by C. Kaddous and R. Schwok in this volume.

102 See Article 15(1) of the draft InstA.

Given the developments in the EU *acquis* on the internal market for electricity, it is to be expected that any future agreement will contain a clause related to Switzerland's participation in the EU's Agency for Cooperation of Energy Regulators (ACER). Article 43 of the current ACER Regulation indeed allows for the participation of third countries and makes this subject to a cooperation agreement. It is reported, however, that the EU is making the conclusion of that cooperation agreement conditional upon Switzerland concluding the InstA.[103] Now that Switzerland has decided not to sign the InstA, which might only have a limited impact on its current structural participation in EU agencies, its future participation in other EU agencies might have become less certain. If the EU insists, Switzerland's participation in ACER will therefore ultimately depend on the entry into force of the InstA or on an alternative solution to the InstA. From a political perspective, the EU could also tie the ongoing negotiations on Swiss participation in the GSA, ERA and BEREC to the fate of the InstA, putting maximum pressure on Switzerland to compromise on its red line.

8 Conclusion

This chapter presented an illustration of the peculiar position which Switzerland takes up in European cooperation and how its choice not to be part of the EEA, but to opt for a bilateral approach, is not merely a question of form. Unlike the EEA EFTA States, Switzerland does not structurally participate in the majority of EU agencies. Switzerland's insistence on its individual sovereignty thus results in a less integrated position in the structures and bodies set up under EU law. The content of the instruments through which Switzerland participates in EU agencies clearly reflects a common philosophy and is gradually developed and refined.

However, the present chapter has also illustrated how Switzerland's insistence on its individual sovereignty comes at a price of cumbersome procedures and decision-making and at reduced shared sovereignty: Switzerland is a decision-taker, it typically does not acquire voting rights in EU agencies, and it depends on the good will of the EU institutions to continue its privileged position as a close partner. From a more pragmatic perspective, it seems obvious that it is in the interest of Switzerland to nominally give up individual

103 P. Thaler, *Energy Cooperation between the EU and Switzerland*, Govtran Policy Brief 2020/01, p. 1, <https://www.govtran.eu/wp-content/uploads/2020/01/Policy-Brief-GOVTRAN.pdf> (accessed 15 June 2022); C. Kaddous, C. Tobler (n. 48), p. 594.

sovereignty and be associated more broadly and deeply in EU agencies. Indeed, if a third country's involvement in EU agencies is determined by functional interdependencies, Switzerland should participate more intensively in EU agencies than an EEA country like Iceland (which, due to its economic and geographic position is functionally less interdependent with the EU).

Overall, then, both the EU and Switzerland are losing parties in their cooperation since their bilateral cooperation seems stuck at a suboptimal level and because the bilateral approach results in excessively costly and cumbersome procedures (for both Switzerland and the EU). Brexit and the Swiss rejection of the InstA may then turn out to constitute a watershed moment, since it should require the EU to reflect thoroughly on its approach vis-à-vis some of its neighbours that have turned sovereignty into a fetish that trumps pragmatism and the objective reality of mutual interdependence. Unless a new agreement on a comprehensive approach to EU-Swiss relations is found, the five cases in which Switzerland structurally participates in an EU agency might continue to constitute the only cases for a long time to come.

CHAPTER 7

The *Case-by-Case* Cooperation between the EU and Switzerland in Foreign Policy, Security and Defence

Christophe Hillion

1 Introduction

The relationship between the European Union (EU) and the Swiss Confederation is founded on an intricate patchwork of more than a hundred bilateral agreements.[1] Incrementally assembled as the EU legal order substantively and institutionally expanded, that patchwork covers a wide range of fields relating primarily to the EU Single Market,[2] and the Area of Freedom, Security and Justice (AFSJ). It also governs matters that have traditionally pertained to the EU Common Foreign and Security Policy (CFSP).[3]

1 For the detailed list of agreements, see <https://www.eeas.europa.eu/switzerland/european-union-and-switzerland_en< (accessed 2 May 2022); <https://www.eda.admin.ch/missions/mission-eu-brussels/fr/home/politique-suisse/principaux-accords.html> (accessed 2 May 2022); and their analysis in the various chapters of this volume. See also M. Maresceau, 'EU-Switzerland: Quo vadis?' *Georgia Journal of International & Comparative Law* 39 (2011), p. 727; M. Maresceau, *Bilateral Agreements concluded by the European Community*, Recueil des cours de l'Academie de droit international – Collected Courses of the Hague Academy of International Law (2006), p. 309, M. Vahl, N. Grolimund, *Integration without Membership: Switzerland's Bilateral Agreements with the European Union* (Centre for European Policy Studies, 2006); A. Lazowski, 'Switzerland', in S. Blockmans and A. Lazowski (eds.), *The European Union and Its Neighbours: A Legal Appraisal of the EU's Policies of Stabilisation, Partnership and Integration* (TMC Asser Press, 2006).

2 See in this respect: CJEU, Case C-506/10 *Graf and Engel*, ECLI:EU:C:2011:643; Case C-656/11 *UK v Council*, ECLI:EU:C:2014:97.

3 As confirmed by the CJEU (see, e.g., Case C-244/17, *Commission* v. *Council* (*Kazakhstan*), EU:C:2018:662), the Treaty of Lisbon has blurred the substantive definition of the CFSP, which in turn renders the analysis of the EU cooperation with third States in that field rather approximate. On the consequence of the Lisbon Treaty for the articulation of the CFSP, C. Hillion, 'Cohérence et action extérieure de l'Union', in E. Neframi (ed.), *Objectifs et compétences de l'Union européenne* (Bruylant, 2012), p. 229 ; *cf.* A. Dashwood, 'The Continuing Bipolarity of EU External Action', in I. Govaere, E. Lannon, P. Van Elsuwege and S. Adam (eds.), *The European Union in the World – Essays in honour of Marc Maresceau* (Brill, 2014), p. 1; M. Cremona, 'The position of the CFSP/CSDP in the EU's constitutional structure', in S. Blockmans, P. Koutrakos (eds.) *Research Handbook on EU's Common Foreign and Security Policy* (Edward Elgar, 2018), p. 5.

© KONINKLIJKE BRILL NV, LEIDEN, 2023 | DOI:10.1163/9789004529984_009

The Council of the EU has indeed expressed its appreciation of "the continued cooperation between the EU and Switzerland in the area of [CFSP] [...] and looks forward to enhancing [it]".[4] That cooperation has developed, incrementally, alongside the other bilateral frameworks that structure the EU-Switzerland relationship.[5] It has progressively widened as the EU itself has been more active in matters of foreign policy, security and defence, through the development of its CFSP, including the Common Security and Defence Policy (CSDP), which the Treaty of Lisbon further integrated into the EU constitutional order.[6]

The "continued cooperation", which the Council has commended does not rely on a single arrangement. As in other fields of their relationship, the EU-Switzerland collaboration in CFSP involves a variety of "*bilaterals*" that cover specific sectors of that policy area. The "*sectoral bilateralism*"[7] that has characterised the cooperation between the Confederation and the EU, and which the latter has increasingly criticised,[8] therefore seems to hold true in the specific CFSP terrain too. To add to the complexity, some bilateral CFSP agreements are binding while others are not, and as in other areas of their cooperation and perhaps even more so, the effectiveness of their collaboration greatly relies on Switzerland's voluntary adaptation to EU CFSP measures, which occurs on a case-by-case basis, when in the interest of the country.

Admittedly, the piecemeal and sectoral character of the EU-Switzerland cooperation in CFSP is not exclusive to this relationship. The Union's collaboration with third States in matters of foreign policy, security and defence tends to be qualitatively and quantitatively more limited in scope and effect, and less institutionally structured, than in other areas of its external action. This phenomenon is partly due to the specific nature of the EU CFSP competence.[9]

---

4 EU Council, <https://www.consilium.europa.eu/en/press/press-releases/2017/02/28/conclusions-eu-swiss-confederation/> (accessed 2 May 2022); see also: EU Council, <https://www.consilium.europa.eu/media/24878/146315.pdf> (accessed 2 May 2022) and EU Council <https://www.consilium.europa.eu/en/press/press-releases/2019/02/19/council-conclusions-on-eu-relations-with-the-swiss-confederation/> (accessed 2 May 2022).

5 See other contributions in this volume.

6 In this respect, see, e.g., S. Blockmans and P. Koutrakos (n. 3); and Editorial Comments: 'A stronger Common Foreign and Security Policy for a self-reliant Union?', *Common Market Law Review* 55 (2018), p. 1675.

7 A. Lazowski, 'Enhanced multilateralism and enhanced bilateralism: Integration without membership in the European Union', *Common Market Law Review* 45 (2008), p. 1433.

8 See, e.g., EU Council, <https://www.consilium.europa.eu/uedocs/cms_data/docs/pressdata/en/foraff/118458.pdf> (accessed 2 May 2022); EU Council, <https://www.consilium.europa.eu/en/press/press-releases/2019/02/19/council-conclusions-on-eu-relations-with-the-swiss-confederation/> (accessed 2 May 2022).

9 Article 2(4) TFEU; Article 24(1) TEU. Further, see the literature mentioned above (n. 1).

Except for a few (modest) "strategic partnerships" (e.g., with Canada or Japan),[10] and more recent forms of EU association agreements (e.g., with Ukraine),[11] the EU external cooperation in CFSP matters tends to be sectoral and technical in nature, and dependent on the partner's *ad hoc* voluntary support for its implementation, rather than governed by deep, comprehensive, let alone richly institutionalised arrangements as is otherwise the case in, e.g., trade and economic matters.[12]

Against this background, the present chapter unpacks the specific "CFSP cooperation" between the EU and the Swiss Confederation. It begins by mapping the various areas where the two parties have collaborated (below section 2). Such a discussion does not aim to provide an exhaustive analysis of all the instruments organising that cooperation, but rather to shed light on their variety and specific modalities, compared to some of the arrangements the EU has elaborated with other European States. The chapter also explores (legal) avenues for possible expansion of the CFSP cooperation between the two (difficult) partners (section 3). Recent developments in the EU foreign policy, security and defence may indeed provide new avenues (and incentives) for EU-Swiss collaboration, particularly in the wake of the Russian invasion of Ukraine in February 2022. The discussion will end with some concluding remarks (section 4).

2 A Cooperation in Line with the Traditional EU-Switzerland "Sectoral Bilateralism"

The cooperation between the EU and Switzerland in CFSP matters covers all traditional aspects of the EU action in the field: viz. foreign policy dialogue,

10 Strategic Partnership Agreement between the European Union and its Member States, of the one part, and Canada, of the other part (OJ 2016, L 329/45); Strategic Partnership Agreement between the European Union and its Member States, of the one part, and Japan, of the other part (OJ 2018, L 216/4).

11 Association Agreement between the European Union and its Member States, of the one part, and Ukraine, of the other part (OJ 2014, L 161/3). Further: G. van der Loo, *The EU-Ukraine Association Agreement and Deep and Comprehensive Free Trade Area: New Legal Instrument for EU Integration without Membership* (Brill, 2016).

12 On EU external cooperation in CFSP matters, see, e.g., C. Törő, 'External State Partners in ESDP Missions: Third Country Participation in EU Crisis Management' *European Foreign Affairs Review* 15 (2010), p. 325; T. Tardy, 'CSDP: getting third states on board', EUISS *Brief* (March 2014), C. Hillion, *Norway and the changing Common Foreign and Security Policy of the European Union,* NUPI Report 1, 2019.

restrictive measures, and CSDP activities. Yet, as should become evident, the terms of the Swiss cooperation with the EU in all these terrains depart from the more established channels and methods of EU cooperation, particularly, but not only with other European States – and chiefly with the EEA EFTA States like Norway. In other words, the Helvetic Confederation is a "special case" in the EU external cooperation in CFSP matters too.[13] While the two parties acknowledge the commonality of the principles underpinning their respective foreign policies, concerns for autonomy appear to entail a degree of reticence towards more institutionalised forms of cooperation.

2.1 *No Formal Political Dialogue but Ad Hoc Foreign Policy Cooperation*

The establishment of a political dialogue constitutes an important if not fundamental component of the EU's external cooperation in foreign policy, security and defence matters. Since the establishment of the CFSP in the early 1990s, the EU has deployed political dialogues with several non-Member States, particularly in Europe. These dialogues have generally aimed at increasing the convergence of the parties' positions on international issues, fostering common views on security and stability in Europe, as well as cooperation in the areas covered by the CFSP more generally.

Usually, political dialogues are conducted in the context of EU framework agreements. Europe Agreements,[14] Partnership and Cooperation Agreements,[15] Stabilisation and Association Agreements,[16] and the more recent Association Agreements with, e.g., Ukraine, Georgia and Moldova have all contained, to varying degrees, provisions to that effect, while setting up common institutions within which the dialogue may be held. Even the Agreement on the EEA, whose purpose is primarily to extend the EU Single Market to the three EEA EFTA States (Iceland, Liechtenstein and Norway),[17] includes an institutional

13 S. Gstöhl, Reluctant Europeans: Norway, Sweden, and Switzerland in the Process of Integration (Lynne Rienner Publishers, 2002).

14 See, for example, Articles 1–5 of the Europe Agreement establishing an association between the European Communities and their Member States, of the one part, and the Republic of Poland, of the other part (OJ 1993, L 348/2).

15 See, for example, Articles 6–9 of the Agreement on partnership and cooperation establishing a partnership between the European Communities and their Member States, of one part, and the Russian Federation, of the other part (OJ 1996, L 327/3).

16 See, for example, Articles 10–13 of the Stabilisation and Association Agreement between the European Communities and their Member States, of the one part, and the Republic of Serbia, of the other part (OJ 2013 L278/14).

17 See, e.g., CJEU, Case C-431/11 *UK v Council*, ECLI:EU:C:2013:589; Case C-897/19 PPU, *Ruska Federacija*, ECLI:EU:C:2020:262.

framework within which the parties have developed a regular (and indeed important) political dialogue.[18]

As well established, and lamented on the EU side,[19] the latter's relationship with Switzerland does *not* involve a framework agreement, nor *a fortiori* does it comprise (yet) any horizontal institutional set-up within which the overall relationship, including its CFSP components, could be discussed, managed and developed.[20] That general lacuna has not only circumscribed the development of EU-Switzerland cooperation relating to the Single Market,[21] but it also affects their cooperation in CFSP matters. To be sure, the EU and Switzerland do not have any formal political dialogue, in the sense that there is no established forum for that particular purpose. Instead, such a dialogue takes place informally on an *ad hoc* basis,[22] with the effect that their cooperation in areas of foreign policy, security and defence, has remained (even) more fragmentary and unstructured than in EU relationships with the other European States.[23]

That said, the absence of formal political dialogue has not prevented the development of foreign policy cooperation between the Union and the Confederation altogether. It has indeed been acknowledged that

18 See, e.g., EEA Council, <https://www.efta.int/sites/default/files/documents/eea/eea-news/EEA-Council-28-May-2021-Joint-Statement.pdf> (accessed 2 May 2022); EEA Council, <https://www.efta.int/sites/default/files/documents/eea/eea-institutions/conclusions-of-the-50th-meeting-of-the-eea-council.pdf> (accessed 2 May 2022).

19 See, e.g., EU Council, <https://www.consilium.europa.eu/en/press/press-releases/2019/02/19/council-conclusions-on-eu-relations-with-the-swiss-confederation/> (accessed 2 May 2022).

20 See S. Lavenex, R. Schwok, 'The Swiss Way. The nature of Switzerland's relationship with the EU' in E.O. Eriksen, J.E. Fossum (eds.), *The European Union's Non-Members: Independence under hegemony?* (Routledge, 2015), p. 36. Further on the (negotiated) EU-Switzerland institutional framework, see the contributions by C. Kaddous and R. Schwok in this volume.

21 See, e.g., EU Council, <https://www.consilium.europa.eu/en/press/press-releases/2019/02/19/council-conclusions-on-eu-relations-with-the-swiss-confederation/> (accessed 2 May 2022).

22 The two parties have for long evoked their shared aspiration to establish a more formal/structured dialogue: EU Council, <https://www.consilium.europa.eu/uedocs/cms_data/docs/pressdata/en/foraff/118458.pdf> (accessed 2 May 2022); and more recently at a meeting in Brussels in November 2021: <https://www.eda.admin.ch/europa/fr/home/aktuell/medienmitteilungen.html/content/eda/fr/meta/news/2021/11/15/85874> (accessed 2 May 2022).

23 Note that Switzerland has an annual strategic dialogue with the UK: <https://www.eda.admin.ch/europa/en/home/aktuell/medienmitteilungen.html/content/eda/en/meta/news/2021/11/22/86006> (accessed 2 May 2022).

> Switzerland and the EU pursue very similar foreign policy objectives: both promote the peaceful co-existence of nations, human rights, democracy and the rule of law, the mitigation of poverty and the preservation of the environment. For this reason, Switzerland and the EU foster a close and substantive dialogue, working in partnership to achieve their objectives on important issues within the European neighbourhood, in regions further afield, or in multilateral forums.[24]

Thus, the EU and Switzerland have joined forces, together with other partners, in various multilateral diplomatic endeavours, for instance on Sudan,[25] and Syria.[26] Switzerland has been part of the Asia-Europe Meeting (ASEM) since 2012 and has thereby contributed, including financially, to ASEM projects relating to, e.g., the promotion of human rights and good governance, as well as sustainable development in Asia.[27] The Confederation has also provided support to various EU foreign policy initiatives.[28] For instance, it has contributed to EU election observations throughout the world. A report of 2019 indicates that over the last 30 years, the Swiss authorities have provided 305 observers in the framework of 81 EU missions.[29] Conversely, the EU has given support to Swiss foreign policy/diplomatic engagement, e.g., in relation to Cameroon.[30]

---

24 Official website of the Swiss Mission to the EU: <https://www.eda.admin.ch/missions/mission-eu-brussels/en/home/key-issues/foreign-security-policy.html> (accessed 2 May 2022); see in the same vein: Rapports du Conseil Fédéral sur la politique européenne de la suisse (2010): <https://biblio.parlament.ch/e-docs/353018.pdf> (accessed 2 May 2022).

25 Sudan: Statement by the Troika, the European Union, Switzerland and Canada, Brussels, 22/11/2021, <https://eeas.europa.eu/delegations/switzerland/107644/node/107644_en> (accessed 2 May 2022).

26 EU Council, Brussels III Conference on 'Supporting the future of Syria and the region':co-chairsdeclaration,14March2019,<https://www.consilium.europa.eu/en/press/press-releases/2019/03/14/brussels-iii-conference-on-supporting-the-future-of-syria-and-the-region-co-chairs-declaration/> (accessed 2 May 2022).

27 <https://www.eda.admin.ch/eda/en/fdfa/foreign-policy/international-organizations/the-asia-europe-meeting/switzerland-in-the-asia-europe-meeting.html> (accessed 2 May 2022).

28 <https://www.vtg.admin.ch/content/vtg-internet/en/aktuell/einsaetze-und-operationen/militaerische-friedensfoerderung/_jcr_content/contentPar/tabs/items/downloads/tabPar/downloadlist/downloadItems/247_1639413429090.download/2021_4_Swiss_Peace_Supporter.pdf> (accessed 2 May 2022).

29 <https://www.eda.admin.ch/content/dam/eda/en/documents/publications/MenschenrechtehumanitaerePolitikundMigration/30-Jahre-Teilnahme-der-CH-an-Wahlbeobachtungen_EN.pdf> (accessed 2 May 2022).

30 EU Council, <https://www.consilium.europa.eu/en/press/press-releases/2019/10/14/cameroon-council-adopts-conclusions/> (accessed 2 May 2022).

That the Confederation supports or indeed contributes to EU diplomatic initiatives does not mean however that it formally *aligns* itself with the Union's foreign policy positions. Instead, the Swiss authorities have usually opted for participation in multilateral enterprises *alongside* the EU, thus "working in partnership" as mentioned above. For example, Switzerland *co-signed* a "Joint Statement on the situation of women and girls in Afghanistan", a posture that contrasts with that of the "[t]he Candidate Countries Montenegro and Serbia, the country of the Stabilisation and Association Process and potential candidate Bosnia and Herzegovina, and the EFTA countries Iceland and Liechtenstein, members of the European Economic Area, as well as Ukraine, the Republic of Moldova and Georgia [which] *align*[*ed*] themselves with th[e] declaration".[31]

2.2 *Voluntary Adaptation to EU Restrictive Measures*

Switzerland's *formal non-alignment* with EU foreign policy initiatives is particularly conspicuous in its approach to the Union's "restrictive measures" (also referred to as "sanctions"), which constitute the bulk of EU (legal) initiatives in the CFSP area.[32] Unlike the other three EFTA States that are part of the EEA (Iceland, Liechtenstein and Norway), or indeed other European countries linked to the EU through SAAS or AAS, Switzerland has rarely, if ever, featured in the list of States that explicitly "align" themselves with EU sanctions.[33]

Typically, a "Declaration by the High Representative on behalf of the European Union on the alignment of certain countries concerning restrictive measures in view of the situation in [a particular country]" would mention, e.g., "[t]he Candidate Countries, the Republic of North Macedonia, Montenegro, Serbia and Albania, and the EFTA countries Iceland, Liechtenstein and Norway, members of the European Economic Area, [that] *align themselves with this*

31 EU Council, Joint Statement of 18 August 2021 on the situation of women and girls. The document was "co-signed by Albania, Argentina, Australia, Brazil, Canada, Chile, Colombia, Costa Rica, Dominican Republic, Ecuador, El Salvador, European Union, Honduras, Guatemala, North Macedonia, New Zealand, Norway, Panama, Paraguay, Senegal, Switzerland, United Kingdom and United States of America", <https://www.consilium.europa.eu/en/press/press-releases/2021/08/18/afghanistan-joint-statement-on-the-situation-of-women-and-girls/> (accessed 2 May 2022, emphasis added).

32 Further, see C. Eckes, 'The law and practice of EU sanctions', in S. Blockmans and P. Koutrakos (n. 3) p. 206.

33 Further on third countries' alignment with EU sanctions: V. Szép, P. Van Elsuwege, 'EU Sanctions Policy and the Alignment of Third Countries: Relevant Experiences for the UK?', J.S. Vara, R. Wessel (eds.), *The Routledge Handbook on the International Dimension of Brexit* (Routledge, 2020), p. 226.

Council Decision".[34] The non-alignment of the Confederation with EU restrictive measures holds true also with respect to the thematic sanctions which the Union (recently) established, e.g., against serious human rights violations and abuses,[35] or against cyber-attacks threatening the Union or its Member States.[36] Featuring in any such list presupposes that the aligned third country received and accepted an EU invitation to join the initiative at hand, and in turn made the commitment to "ensure that [its] national policies conform to [the] Council Decision".[37] Conversely, the absence of a country from the list indicates that either it was not invited to join, or it did not accept the Union's invitation.

While it has not *formally* aligned itself with EU restrictive measures, at least not in the same systematic and committing fashion as, e.g., other EFTA States, Switzerland has *in practice* autonomously followed them on a case-by-case basis. The *de facto* alignment is testified by a cursory comparison of various EU restrictive measures with Swiss legislation. For example, the Swiss blacklist of December 2021 concerning Belarus includes an explicit reference to its "EU

34 EU Council, <https://www.consilium.europa.eu/en/press/press-releases/2021/12/22/declaration-by-the-high-representative-on-behalf-of-the-european-union-on-the-alignment-of-certain-countries-concerning-restrictive-measures-in-view-of-the-situation-in-belarus/> (accessed 2 May 2022, emphasis added); see also EU Council, <https://www.consilium.europa.eu/en/press/press-releases/2021/08/20/declaration-by-the-high-representative-on-behalf-of-the-eu-on-the-alignment-of-certain-third-countries-concerning-restrictive-measures-regarding-iran/> (re. sanctions against Iran) (accessed 2 May 2022); EU Council, <https://www.consilium.europa.eu/en/press/press-releases/2021/07/27/declaration-by-the-high-representative-on-behalf-of-the-european-union-on-the-alignment-of-certain-countries-concerning-restrictive-measures-in-view-of-the-situation-in-myanmar-burma/> (re. Sanctions concerning Myanmar) (accessed 2 May 2022); EU Council, <https://www.consilium.europa.eu/en/press/press-releases/2020/11/20/declaration-by-the-high-representative-on-behalf-of-the-eu-on-the-alignment-of-certain-third-countries-concerning-restrictive-measures-against-the-leadership-of-the-transnistrian-region-of-the-republic-of-moldova/> (sanctions concerning Transnistria) (accessed 2 May 2022). Also on Syria, see <https://reliefweb.int/sites/reliefweb.int/files/resources/131757.pdf> (accessed 2 May 2022).

35 EU Council, <https://www.consilium.europa.eu/en/press/press-releases/2020/12/22/declaration-by-the-high-representative-on-behalf-of-the-european-union-on-the-alignment-of-certain-countries-concerning-restrictive-measures-against-serious-human-rights-violations-and-abuses/> (accessed 2 May 2022).

36 EU Council, <https://www.consilium.europa.eu/en/press/press-releases/2020/09/11/declaration-by-the-high-representative-on-behalf-of-the-eu-on-the-alignment-of-certain-third-countries-concerning-restrictive-measures-against-cyber-attacks-threatening-the-union-or-its-member-states/> (accessed 2 May 2022).

37 *Ibid.*

origin".[38] In the same vein, Switzerland followed the EU restrictive measures of 10 January 2022 imposing sanctions on several Nicaraguan nationals and entities. The Swiss authorities have also applied the EU *delisting* of individuals.[39]

According to Goetschel, the "DFA [Department of Foreign Affairs] has indeed developed a political "EU reflex" that is hardly inferior to that within the legislative process".[40] In foreign policy too, the Swiss Confederation, therefore, pursues its traditional policy of "voluntary adaptation" to,[41] and of autonomous implementation of EU measures, with all the issues that this may raise. It is indeed the way the Swiss approach has been understood within the Union. The EU Council thus "note[d] Switzerland's *voluntary alignment* to restrictive measures of the EU *on a case-by-case basis*".[42]

Not appearing in the list of aligned countries epitomises the Swiss eagerness not to be constrained by the EU approach, and conversely to maintain maximum autonomy in its relation to the Union's foreign policy. Even if it may have similar concerns and the same interest as the EU in sanctioning a third State, an organisation or individuals, not being formally aligned arguably allows the Confederation to enjoy full discretion as to *whether* to sanction a State/organisation/individual in a particular case, as to the *terms* of any potential restrictive measure, and as to the degree of their domestic *enforcement*, in line with its national interest.[43] Not formally aligning itself to EU restrictive measures the way the other European States often do, indeed entails that, formally, Switzerland does not commit itself to "ensur[ing] that [its] national policies conform to [a particular] Council Decision".[44] In many ways again,

38 <https://www.seco.admin.ch/dam/seco/de/dokumente/Aussenwirtschaft/Wirtschaftsbeziehungen/Exportkontrollen/Sanktionen/Verordnungen/Belarus/belarus_2021-12-20.pdf.download.pdf/Belarus_2021-12-20.pdf> (accessed 2 May 2022); <https://www.europeansanctions.com/news/jurisdictions/switzerland/> (accessed 2 May 2022).

39 For instance, it delisted Jean-Claude Kazembe Musonda, the former Governor of Haut-Katanga province and leader of the CONAKAT party from its DRC sanctions list, after the EU had done it, <https://www.europeansanctions.com/news/jurisdictions/switzerland/> (accessed 2 May 2022).

40 L. Goetschel, 'Switzerland and European Integration: Change Through Distance', *European Foreign Affairs Review* 8 (2003), p. 327.

41 On the notion of 'voluntary adaptation', see, e.g., S. Lavenex and R. Schwok (n. 20).

42 EU Council, <https://www.consilium.europa.eu/en/press/press-releases/2017/02/28/conclusions-eu-swiss-confederation/> (accessed 2 May 2022, emphases added).

43 Unless the restrictive measures find their origins in a UNSC resolution.

44 E.g., EU Council, <https://www.consilium.europa.eu/en/press/press-releases/2020/09/11/declaration-by-the-high-representative-on-behalf-of-the-eu-on-the-alignment-of-certain-third-countries-concerning-restrictive-measures-against-cyber-attacks-threatening-the-union-or-its-member-states/> (accessed 2 May 2022).

the Confederation's stance on EU restrictive measures amounts to a particular articulation of its traditional approach to EU norms, outside specific agreements.[45]

And yet, the difference between the two approaches – i.e., that of Switzerland *v.* that of formally aligned countries – should not be exaggerated. Its significance might indeed be more symbolic than legally meaningful. Apart from Candidate States for membership, which might consider themselves *politically* compelled to follow the EU CFSP as part of their pre-accession preparation,[46] none of the other States usually included in the list of aligned countries, is in any way bound to take that position. While a case could be made that some sanctions are "EEA relevant", in so far as their implementation relates to the functioning of the Single Market, and thus made compulsory for the EEA EFTA States, this to date is not the official view among EEA parties.[47] On the whole, formal alignment of a third country with EU restrictive measures remains a matter of its own decision, taken on a case-by-case basis. A state, including a Candidate State, is free to accept or not the invitation of the EU. Indeed, the ensuing commitment, flowing from a third state's formal alignment, to ensure that its "national policies conform to [the] Council Decision" can hardly be conceived as a legally enforceable obligation, even in the context of a comprehensive (association) agreement.

To be sure, the piecemeal approach to EU restrictive measures, which the Confederation has adopted, is not without creating challenges notably in terms of their efficacy. In the wake of Russia's annexation of Crimea, the EU Council already expressed its "regrets [...] that Switzerland ha[d] not *fully* aligned itself with the EU's restrictive measures in respect of actions undermining or threatening the territorial integrity, sovereignty and independence of Ukraine and in view of Russia's actions destabilising the situation in Ukraine".[48] More: the Council "encourage[d] Switzerland *to remain close*

45 Further on this point, see the contribution by M. Oesch and M. Brugger in this volume.

46 Although within limits as epitomised by Serbia's reluctance to follow some of the EU restrictive measures against Russia; <https://www.reuters.com/world/europe/serbia-will-not-impose-sanctions-against-moscow-president-says-2022-02-25/> (accessed 2 May 2022). Further on pre-accession adaptation of candidate States in CFSP matters, see C. Hillion, 'Adaptation for autonomy? Candidates for EU membership and the CFSP', *Global Affairs* (2017), p. 265.

47 On the argument that some EU restrictive measures are EEA relevant, and thus constraining on the EEA EFTA States, see C. Hillion, *Norway and the changing Common Foreign and Security Policy of the European Union*, NUPI Report 1/2019.

48 EU Council, <https://www.llv.li/files/sewr/st-16583-2014-init-en.pdf> (accessed 2 May 2022).

and consistent in the application of the restrictive measures including preventing their circumvention [while] invit[ing the Confederation] to *maintain and further improve its alignment with the* EU's *restrictive measures* in respect of actions undermining or threatening the territorial integrity, sovereignty and independence of Ukraine".[49] The "encouragement" and "invitation" to prevent the circumvention of EU sanctions have been reiterated since: while "not[ing] Switzerland's voluntary alignment [the Council] encourage[d] [it] to *pursue a close and consistent application of restrictive measures including preventing their circumvention*".[50]

Concern that the country's *ad hoc* approach to EU restrictive measures could undermine their effectiveness has thus led the EU Council to add pressure on the Confederation. That pressure has seemingly increased in the wake of the Russian invasion of Ukraine in February 2022 and considering the unprecedented arsenal of EU sanctions and initiatives that ensued.[51] At its extraordinary meeting on 25 March, 2022, the European Council "call[ed] on all countries to align with [the specific EU] sanctions [against Russia and Belarus]", adding that "[a]ny attempts to circumvent sanctions or to aid Russia by other means must be stopped".[52]

While sticking to its principled approach of voluntary adaptation,[53] in the sense of not being included in the list of countries that align themselves to EU sanctions, Switzerland appears to have espoused the Union's measures against Russia more closely.[54] Thus, the Federal Council took the decision to follow the successive packages of EU restrictive measures, including against

49 EU Council, <https://www.consilium.europa.eu/en/press/press-releases/2017/02/28/conclusions-eu-swiss-confederation/> (accessed 2 May 2022, emphasis added).

50 EU Council, <https://www.consilium.europa.eu/en/press/press-releases/2019/02/19/council-conclusions-on-eu-relations-with-the-swiss-confederation/> (accessed 2 May 2022, emphasis added).

51 EU Council, <https://www.consilium.europa.eu/en/policies/sanctions/restrictive-measures-ukraine-crisis/> (accessed 2 May 2022).

52 European Council, <https://data.consilium.europa.eu/doc/document/ST-1-2022-INIT/en/pdf> (accessed 2 May 2022), para. 4.

53 EU Council, <https://www.consilium.europa.eu/en/press/press-releases/2022/03/15/declaration-by-the-hr-on-behalf-of-the-eu-on-the-alignment-of-certain-third-countries-concerning-restrictive-measures-in-view-of-russia-s-actions-destabilising-the-situation-in-ukraine/> (accessed 2 May 2022).

54 <https://www.admin.ch/gov/en/start/documentation/media-releases.msg-id-87677.html> (accessed 2 May 2022); see also the op-ed of the Confederation's President in Le Temps, <https://www.eda.admin.ch/dam/eda/fr/documents/aktuell/interviews/2022/20220319-opinion-cassis-letemps.pdf> (accessed 2 May 2022).

the Russian President and his Foreign Minister.[55] Indeed, the President of the Confederation was noticeably outspoken about Switzerland's "adoption" of those EU sanctions,[56] and about the need for a pragmatic interpretation and application of the country's sacrosanct principle of neutrality.[57] That same principle of neutrality has since, however, been invoked to justify the Swiss authorities' refusal to allow Germany's supply of arms to Ukraine, which uses ammunition manufactured in the Confederation.[58] The Swiss stance thus appears to be that of "military neutrality", as opposed to "political neutrality".[59]

2.3 *Swiss Participation in Multiple EU CSDP Missions*

To be sure, Switzerland's neutrality has not prevented it from taking part in various EU initiatives in the context of its Common Security and Defence Policy. Alongside Norway, Switzerland is one of the most active third countries in terms of the number of EU CSDP missions to which it has contributed,[60] even if each contribution remains limited.

---

55 On the those decisions, see <https://www.seco.admin.ch/seco/fr/home/Aussenwirtschaftspolitik_Wirtschaftliche_Zusammenarbeit/Wirtschaftsbeziehungen/exportkontrollen-und-sanktionen/sanktionen-embargos/sanktionsmassnahmen/massnahmen-zur-vermeidung-der-umgehung-internationaler-sanktione.html> (accessed 2 May 2022); <https://www.fedlex.admin.ch/eli/cc/2022/151/fr> (accessed 2 May 2022); <https://www.eda.admin.ch/europa/en/home/aktuell/medienmitteilungen.html/content/eda/en/meta/news/2022/2/28/87386> (accessed 2 May 2022); <https://www.eda.admin.ch/europa/en/home/aktuell/medienmitteilungen.html/content/europa/en/meta/news/2022/3/4/87474> (accessed 2 May 2022).

56 <https://www.fedlex.admin.ch/eli/cc/2022/151/fr> (accessed 2 May 2022).

57 See interview of Swiss President Cassis: <https://www.rts.ch/play/tv/-/video/-?urn=urn:rts:video:12899486> (accessed 2 May 2022).

58 <https://www.reuters.com/world/europe/swiss-veto-german-request-re-export-ammunition-ukraine-paper-2022-04-24/> (accessed 2 May 2022).

59 Some have argued that Switzerland has abandoned its neutrality, with one important Swiss politician considering a popular initiative to prohibit the use of economic sanctions (see, e.g., <https://www.nzz.ch/schweiz/christoph-blocher-prueft-die-lancierung-einer-volksinitiative-fuer-neutralitaet-ld.1674256>, accessed 2 May 2022). The Federal Council does however contest such a contention (see in particular here: <https://www.eda.admin.ch/eda/en/fdfa/fdfa/aktuell/newsuebersicht/2022/03/neutralitaet.html> (accessed 2 May 2022). Thanks to Christa Tobler for this point.

60 See N. Koenig, 'Revamping CSDP Partnerships in the Shadow of Brexit' (March 2019) <https://www.iai.it/sites/default/files/eugs_watch_9.pdf> (accessed 2 May 2022); T. Tardy, 'Getting third states on board', *EUISS Brief*, March 2014; see also House of Lords, EU Committee, Report: Brexit: Common Security and Defence Policy missions and operations (2018) <https://publications.parliament.uk/pa/ld201719/ldselect/ldeucom/132/13207.htm> (accessed 2 May 2022).

For instance, two Swiss civilian experts have participated in the EU "Capacity Building Mission"[61] in order to train local security forces in Mali.[62] Switzerland has also seconded a counsellor to the EU Advisory Mission for Civilian Security Sector Reform in Ukraine (EUAM Ukraine).[63] It has taken part, by way of a civilian border control specialist in the EU integrated border management assistance Mission on Libya (EUBAM Libya),[64] in the EU "Rule of Law" mission (EULEX Kosovo),[65] and has provided monitors to the EU monitoring mission in Aceh (Aceh Monitoring Mission – AMM).[66] About two dozen members of the Swiss Armed Forces have also joined the EU military crisis management operation (EUFOR Althea)[67] and the earlier European Union Police Mission (EUPM)[68] in Bosnia and Herzegovina,[69] while contributing to the EU police mission in the former Yugoslav Republic of Macedonia (EUPOL 'Proxima').[70]

---

61 Participation Agreement between the European Union and the Swiss Confederation on the participation of the Swiss Confederation in the European Union CSDP mission in Mali (EUCAP Sahel Mali) (OJ 2016, L 105/3).

62 <https://www.eda.admin.ch/europa/en/home/weitere-dossiers/friedensfoerderung.html> (accessed 2 May 2022).

63 Participation Agreement between the European Union and the Swiss Confederation on the participation of the Swiss Confederation in the European Union Advisory Mission for Civilian Security Sector Reform in Ukraine (EUAM Ukraine) (OJ 2016, L 104/3).

64 Participation agreement between the European Union and the Swiss Confederation on the participation of the Swiss Confederation in the European Union Integrated Border Management Assistance Mission in Libya (EUBAM Libya) (OJ 2014, L 205/3).

65 Agreement between the European Union and the Swiss Confederation on the participation of the Swiss Confederation in the European Union Rule of Law Mission in Kosovo (EULEX KOSOVO); OJ (2008) L 217/24.

66 Agreement between the European Union and the Swiss Confederation on the participation of the Swiss Confederation in the European Union Monitoring Mission in Aceh (Indonesia) (Aceh Monitoring Mission – AMM) – Declarations (OJ 2005, L 349/31).

67 Agreement between the European Union and the Swiss Confederation on the participation of the Swiss Confederation in the European Union military crisis management operation in Bosnia and Herzegovina (operation ALTHEA) (OJ 2005, L20/42).

68 Agreement between the European Union and the Government of the Swiss Confederation, represented by the Federal Department of Foreign Affairs, on the participation of Switzerland in the European Union Police Mission (EUPM) in Bosnia and Herzegovina (BiH) (OJ 2003, L 239/14).

69 <https://www.eda.admin.ch/europa/en/home/weitere-dossiers/friedensfoerderung.html> (accessed 2 May 2022).

70 Agreement between the European Union and the Swiss Confederation on the participation of the Swiss Confederation in the European Union police mission in the former Yugoslav Republic of Macedonia (EUPOL 'Proxima') (OJ 2004, L 354/78). Switzerland also took part in EU military operation in support of the UN Mission in the Democratic Republic of the Congo: Agreement in the form of an Exchange of Letters between the European Union and the Government of the Swiss Confederation on the participation of the Swiss Confederation in the European Union military operation in support of the

The EU Council has praised the Swiss Federal Council's "firm commitment to preserve and further strengthen its cooperation with the EU and *encourage[d] the development of that cooperation, including on key foreign policy issues*".[71] Indeed, "other options for participation in EU missions are regularly examined".[72]

For each EU mission, the Swiss authorities usually commit themselves, voluntarily, to participate "in accordance with" the Council CFSP Decision that establishes the specific mission.[73] Alignment of the Swiss authorities with the EU legal framework setting out a specific CSDP mission is, therefore, more tangible than in relation to EU sanctions; the earlier agreements on the Swiss participation indeed used the language of *association*.[74] Apart from the commitment to observe the terms of the founding CFSP decision, Switzerland's participation in CSDP missions is also subject to general conditions, and notably the duty to comply with obligations contained in the Agreement on the security procedures for the exchange of classified information which it concluded with the EU.[75]

At an operational level, the Confederation must ensure that its personnel – whose participation it finances – act in conformity with the EU CFSP Decision, the mission plan and the implementing measures: they are expected to "carry

---

United Nations Organisation Mission in the Democratic Republic of the Congo (MONUC) during the election process (Operation EUFOR RD Congo) (OJ 2006, L 276/111).

71 EU Council, <https://www.consilium.europa.eu/en/press/press-releases/2017/02/28/conclusions-eu-swiss-confederation/> (accessed 2 May 2022); <https://www.consilium.europa.eu/en/press/press-releases/2019/02/19/council-conclusions-on-eu-relations-with-the-swiss-confederation/> (accessed 2 May 2022), see also EP resolution: <https://www.europarl.europa.eu/doceo/document/TA-8-2019-0241_EN.pdf> (accessed 2 May 2022, emphasis added).

72 <https://www.eda.admin.ch/missions/mission-eu-brussels/en/home/key-issues/foreign-security-policy.html> (accessed 2 May 2022).

73 See, for instance, Article 1 of the Participation Agreement between the European Union and the Swiss Confederation on the participation of the Swiss Confederation in the European Union Advisory Mission for Civilian Security Sector Reform in Ukraine (EUAM Ukraine) (OJ 2016, L 104/3).

74 Thus in the 2008 Agreement on EULEX Kosovo, Article 1 stipulated that the "Swiss Confederation shall *associate* itself with the Joint Action 2008/124/CFSP (...) on the European Union Rule of Law Mission in Kosovo, EULEX KOSOVO (hereinafter 'EULEX KOSOVO'), and with any Joint Action or Decision by which the Council of the European Union decides to extend EULEX KOSOVO" (emphasis added); Agreement between the European Union and the Swiss Confederation on the participation of the Swiss Confederation in the European Union Rule of Law Mission in Kosovo (EULEX KOSOVO) (OJ 2008, L 217/24).

75 OJ 2008, L 181/58.

out their duties and conduct themselves solely with the interest of the specific mission at hand".[76] Although they remain under the full command of the Swiss authorities, the latter nevertheless transfer the operational and tactical command of their personnel to the EU Civilian Operations Commander. In many respects, therefore, the Swiss experts are assimilated into those coming from the EU Member States.

Unlike most countries with which the EU cooperates in CSDP matters, Switzerland has not (yet) concluded such a Framework Participation Agreement, whose purpose is to set out the basic legal and political infrastructure for the third State's participation in *all* EU CSDP missions.[77] The EU invited Switzerland in 2004 to sign such an agreement, but discussions are still ongoing.[78] In the meantime, the Confederation and the EU have had to define the conditions for the Swiss participation in *each* EU operation to which it contributes, on the basis of *ad hoc* participation agreements. In other words, in CSDP matters too, the EU-Switzerland cooperation remains governed by a case-by-case approach.

The Confederation's compound participation in the EU's CSDP activities also involves a collaboration with the European Defence Agency (EDA), on the basis of a non-binding Framework for cooperation between EDA and the Swiss Federal Department of Defence, Civil Protection and Sports was signed to that effect on 16 March 2012.[79] It allows that department to participate, on an *ad hoc* basis, in EDA projects and programmes, notably as regards armament, but also in the terrain of education and training.

According to the Agency, Switzerland has been involved in six EDA Capability Technology Groups (CapTechs) and has joined research projects including the Protection of Autonomous Systems Against Enemy Interference (PASEI) project in the land domain. It has taken part in several capability development

76 See, e.g., Article 1 of the Participation Agreement between the European Union and the Swiss Confederation on the participation of the Swiss Confederation in the European Union Advisory Mission for Civilian Security Sector Reform in Ukraine (EUAM Ukraine) (OJ 2016, L 104/3).

77 A list of such agreements is available here: <https://eur-lex.europa.eu/legal-content/EN/TXT/HTML/?uri=LEGISSUM:ps0013> (accessed 2 May 2022).

78 <https://www.parlament.ch/fr/ratsbetrieb/suche-curia-vista/geschaeft?AffairId=20073354> (accessed 2 May 2022); <https://www.parlament.ch/en/ratsbetrieb/suche-curia-vista/geschaeft?AffairId=20163671> (accessed 2 May 2022).

79 <https://eda.europa.eu/docs/default-source/documents/aa---ffcooperation-eda---switzerland-16-03-12.pdf> (accessed 2 May 2022); <https://www.eda.admin.ch/missions/mission-eu-brussels/en/home/key-issues/foreign-security-policy.html> (accessed 2 May 2022).

activities, from cyber to Countering Improvised Explosive Devices (C-IED). Indeed, it shares its national defence planning priorities with the Agency to support the identification of possible collaborative opportunities with EDA countries. The Confederation has also taken part in several EDA activities such as the Single European Sky Military Aviation Board (ESMAB) related to the Single European Sky, and in the Consultation Forum on Sustainable Energy in the Defence and Security Sector. It has participated in the Agency's Military Airworthiness Authorities (MAWA) Forum and in several expert groups to build common approaches.[80] In this context too, the participation of Switzerland has been made possible thanks to its horizontal agreement with the EU on the security procedures for the exchange of classified information.[81]

The foregoing (non-exhaustive) account of the EU-Switzerland CFSP cooperation indicates that the latter covers virtually all key areas of the EU foreign policy, security and defence. The multiplicity of arrangements governing this complex cooperation, both in terms of scope and nature, attests to the Confederation's predilection for a case-by-case bilateral approach to the EU CFSP, which is congruent with the tenets of its relationship with the Union more generally. As in most other areas of their cooperation, this posture has permitted Switzerland to preserve its autonomy, while allowing a high degree of flexibility in its interactions with the EU, in line with its interests.

The Confederation indeed displays some reticence further to institutionalise its cooperation in CFSP matters. It typifies its penchant for sectoral arrangements rather than horizontal mechanisms. The protracted discussion to establish a general framework for Switzerland's participation in CSDP missions partly replicates the equally lengthy and hitherto unsuccessful process of setting up an institutional arrangement to oversee the cooperation in selected Single Market related areas. Similarly, the formal non-alignment with EU sanctions echoes the *voluntary adaptation* approach that has been the hallmark of the Confederation's relationship with the EU, and which seems to prevail even as the Union is becoming more concerned and pressing about their effectiveness.

---

80 Switzerland is indeed joining EDA's Helicopter Exercise Programme; <https://eda.europa.eu/news-and-events/news/2022/03/17/eda-switzerland-10-years-of-cooperation> (accessed 2 May 2022); <https://www.eda.admin.ch/europa/fr/home/aktuell/medienmitteilungen.html/content/europa/fr/meta/news/2021/11/24/86049> (accessed 2 May 2022).

81 Agreement between the Swiss Confederation and the European Union on the security procedures for the exchange of classified information (OJ 2008, L 181/58), <https://www.eda.admin.ch/europa/fr/home/aktuell/medienmitteilungen.html/content/europa/fr/meta/news/2021/11/24/86049> (accessed 2 May 2022).

Whether the sacrosanct principle of neutrality explains the reluctance of the Helvetic authorities to forge a closer and more institutionalised CFSP cooperation is not evident.[82] As Goetschel already pointed out in 2003: Swiss foreign policy is "basically compatible with the EU [...] CFSP".[83] The latter's compatibility with the principle of neutrality was indeed discussed in a Federal Council Report of 2010 on the evaluation of the European Policy of the Confederation.[84] The Report even pondered the implications for the country's neutrality of a potential accession of Switzerland to the EU, and the adoption of the CFSP *acquis* it would entail. The study concluded that the CFSP and Switzerland's neutrality could be accommodated, in the sense that the Confederation would not have to abandon its neutrality if it were to accede to the EU.

While admitting that the CFSP and CSDP have significantly expanded since that Report was published, it is arguable that the principle of neutrality is still no obstacle to the deepening of the CFSP cooperation between the Confederation, as a third state, and the EU. In other words, neutrality cannot fully explain the Helvetic reticence to move beyond its traditional case-by-case approach. To be sure, the principle of neutrality may be adapted where necessary and when it is in the interest of the country, as the Swiss authorities made clear in the wake of the war in Ukraine. The position of the Swiss authorities rather appears to be primarily determined by considerations of autonomy of decision-making, and independence.

3 Options and Conditions for Further Cooperation in Foreign Policy, Security and Defence

The EU has expressed a willingness to strengthen its CFSP cooperation with the Confederation, both substantively and institutionally. Judging from a Federal Council Report of 2021,[85] many of Switzerland's interests in, and objectives of

---

82 See discussion on the compatibility of CFSP CSDP and neutrality law in Rapport du Conseil fédéral sur l'évaluation de la politique européenne de la Suisse (en réponse au postulat Markwalder [09.3560] 'Politique européenne. Evaluation, priorités, mesures immédiates et prochaines étapes d'intégration'), 17 septembre 2010 <https://www.newsd.admin.ch/newsd/message/attachments/20609.pdf> (accessed 2 May 2022).

83 L. Goetschel (n. 40).

84 See Rapport du Conseil fédéral sur l'évaluation de la politique européenne de la Suisse (n. 82).

85 See Rapport sur la politique de sécurité analyse l'environnement politico-stratégique de la Suisse en matière de sécurité et l'évolution de la situation: <https://www.vbs.admin.ch/content/vbs-internet/fr/home/meta-suche/suche.download/vbs-internet/fr/documents/politiquedesecurite/rapports-politique-de-securite/2021/Politique-securite-Suisse-Rapport-Conseil-federal-2021.pdf> (accessed 2 May 2022), see also L. Goetschel (n. 40).

foreign affairs and security indeed coincide with those of the EU, and could, therefore, offer grounds for further collaboration.

This section explores the potential elaboration of the EU-Switzerland CFSP cooperation by looking at how, following its hitherto case-by-case approach, and provided it has an interest in doing so, the Confederation could connect to new EU initiatives in the areas of foreign policy, security and defence. Two such EU initiatives stand out for the purpose of this discussion: namely, the establishment of the "Permanent Structured Cooperation" (PESCO) and the European Defence Fund (EDF), which both comprise provisions for external participation, thus potentially opening new avenues for EU-Switzerland cooperation.

The two new enterprises not only illustrate the post-Lisbon development of the EU foreign, security and defence policies, and the potential it offers for further external contributions in those areas, but also typify the increasing substantive and/or institutional interactions between the CFSP and other areas of EU policy-making, including the Single Market. This, in turn, potentially increases the significance of the agreements that the EU has concluded with third States in those areas, for the development of the latter's cooperation with the EU in foreign policy, security, and defence. As will become apparent, the EU's external cooperation in those fields, and the terms thereof, are indeed functions of pre-existing arrangements structuring the relationship between the EU and its partners more generally. This means that the enduring absence of a horizontal institutional agreement between the EU and Switzerland may not only hamper further cooperation in matters associated with the Single Market but may also affect the potential for deeper cooperation in matters of foreign policy, security and defence.

3.1 *Joining PESCO?*

Based on a provision of the TEU introduced by the Treaty of Lisbon,[86] the EU has activated the Permanent Structured Cooperation (PESCO) whereby a large majority of Member States (25) made commitments to one another to fulfil more demanding military missions.[87] Its purpose is to increase the security

86 Article 42(6) TEU, and Protocol 10 to the EU Treaties. Further on these developments, see S. Blockmans, 'The EU's modular approach to defence integration: Inclusive, ambitious and legally binding?', *Common Market Law Review* 55 (2018), p. 1785.

87 Council Decision establishing Permanent Structured Cooperation (PESCO) and determining the list of Participating Member States (hereinafter the "PESCO Decision") (OJ 2017, L 331/17).

spending level in the EU and to build capabilities more efficiently through cross-border cooperation in the context of specific projects.[88]

The initiative includes the possibility for third States to participate in individual PESCO projects,[89] even if such participation should remain *exceptional*, based on the *invitation* of participating Member States, for the purpose of a *particular project only* and therefore on a case-by-case basis.[90] A specific decision "establishing the general conditions under which third States could exceptionally be invited to participate in individual PESCO projects" [hereinafter "PESCO-third States Decision"] was indeed enacted in November 2020.[91]

Article 3 of that Decision requires that the invited third State provide "*substantial added value* to the project, and contributes to achieving its objectives [adding that] the means which it brings into the project must be *complementary* to those offered by PESCO participating Member States, for example by providing technical expertise or additional capabilities including operational or financial support, thus contributing to the success of the project and hence to the advancement of PESCO", and more generally "to strengthening the Common Security and Defence Policy". It is up to the Council, involving representatives of the participating Member States, to decide by unanimity, whether an applicant third State satisfies all those conditions, and then to invite it to take part.[92] Denoting the scalability of, as well as the limits to any external participation in PESCO,[93] the Decision further foresees that, once admitted, the

88 <www.consilium.europa.eu/en/press/press-releases/2017/12/11/defence-cooperation-pesco-25-member-states-participating/> (accessed 2 May 2022).

89 According to Article 9 of the Decision: "(1) The general conditions for the participation of third States in individual projects shall be specified in a Council decision adopted in accordance with Article 4(2), which may include a template for administrative arrangements with third States. (2) The Council shall decide in accordance with Article 46(6) TEU whether a third State, which the participating Member States taking part in a project wish to invite to take part in that project, meets the requirements set out in the decision referred to in paragraph 1. (3) Following a positive decision as referred to in paragraph 2, the participating Member States taking part in a project may enter into administrative arrangements with the third State concerned for the purpose of its taking part in that project. Such arrangements shall respect the procedures and the decision-making autonomy of the Union".

90 See also Articles 4(2)(g) and 9(1) of the PESCO Decision.

91 Council Decision (CFSP) 2020/1639 of 5 November 2020 establishing the general conditions under which third States could exceptionally be invited to participate in individual PESCO projects (OJ 2020, L 371/3).

92 Article 2 of the PESCO-third states Decision; see also Articles 4(2)(g) and 9(2) PESCO Decision.

93 Further on the notion of "scalability" in external participation in CFSP initiatives, see Part III of the Political declaration setting out the framework for the future relationship between the European Union and the United Kingdom (OJ 2019, C 384I/178).

"invited third State *may take part in the decision-making process for the implementation of the project*, taking account of its contribution",[94] having otherwise made clear that "participation must not lead to dependencies on that third State or to restrictions imposed by it against any Member State of the Union".[95]

Indeed, the general conditions for participation, as well as the very title of the Decision, indicate a degree of caution, if not reluctance by the EU, to allow too easy an access to PESCO for any third state.[96] Such conditions, articulated after the United Kingdom of Great Britain and Northern Ireland (UK) had left the Union, recall the basic notion that EU external cooperation in general, and in areas of CFSP in particular, remain determined by various principles underpinning, and aimed at protecting the integrity of the EU. These principles, among which the notion of the autonomy of the EU legal order and decision-making, were made particularly salient in the context of the EU withdrawal and post-membership negotiations with the UK.[97]

Given the Confederation's traditional restrained approach towards EU cooperation, most of the conditions for participation in PESCO projects should not be difficult to meet, should the Swiss authorities have an interest in such cooperation. They would not be required to join PESCO as such, but specific projects only,[98] thus avoiding those which, for instance, may be deemed too sensitive

---

94 Emphasis added. As per Article 4(2) of the PESCO-third States Decision, which also stipulates that "[t]he arrangements (...) shall fully respect the decision-making autonomy of the Union as well as the rights and obligations of the participating Member States, including as regards safeguarding the control of a project and its results within the PESCO framework and decision-making on potential new project members, in accordance with Decision (CFSP) 2017/2315, which establishes PESCO, and with the common set of governance rules for PESCO projects set out in Decision (CFSP) 2018/909". In other words, access to decision-making is limited to the decision-making framework which is specific to the PESCO project. Conversely, participation in a project does not entail broader decision-making rights, i.e., beyond the specific project. The preamble (pt. 8) of the PESCO-third states Decision makes that clear when underlining that "inviting third States will not grant powers of decision to them in the governance of PESCO".

95 Article 3(d) of the PESCO-third States Decision.

96 Further on this: K. Brudzińska, M. Zaborowski and A. Kudzko, *Third country participation in EU Defence Integration Initiatives: How it works and how it is viewed by EU member states* (GLOBSEC Policy Institute, 2020).

97 C. Hillion, *Norway and the changing Common Foreign and Security Policy of the European Union*, NUPI Report 1, 2019.

98 Council Decision (CFSP) 2021/749 of 6 May 2021 on the participation of the Kingdom of Norway in the PESCO project Military Mobility (OJ 2021, L 160/109); Council Decision (CFSP) 2021/748 of 6 May 2021 on the participation of Canada in the PESCO project Military Mobility (OJ 2021, L 160/106); Council Decision (CFSP) 2021/750 of 6 May 2021 on the participation of the United States of America in the PESCO project Military Mobility (OJ 2021, L 160/112).

in view of the principle of neutrality.[99] Joining PESCO on a project basis would also be congruent with Switzerland's case-by-case approach to CSDP missions and programmes of the European Defence Agency. The terms of third states' participation, specifically with respect to decision-making rights, indeed echo those applicable in the context of CSDP missions to which the Confederation has regularly contributed, while some of PESCO's projects appear substantively to dovetail with various EDA programmes that Switzerland has joined.[100] Although limited to the implementation, as opposed to the elaboration of any PESCO projects, such decision-making right could indeed be significant for a partner like Switzerland which has traditionally sought such power in its relationship with the EU.

That said, the lasting character of the commitments that participation in a PESCO project involves, and the ensuing EU monitoring of the participants' performance, are two dimensions of the cooperation that may sit uncomfortably with the Swiss reluctance to institutionalise its engagement in CFSP matters, let alone its aversion to EU scrutiny. It should indeed be recalled that any participation in PESCO generally involves *binding* commitments from all participating States. The High Representative, assisted by the European External Action Service (EEAS), and the Council are empowered to oversee the participants' performance, with a risk of suspension from the project should commitments not be fulfilled.[101] While the potential contribution of a third state is assessed on a case-by-case basis, the continuation of its participation, once allowed, hinges on the enduring fulfilment of its commitments and of the general conditions for joining. Akin to participating Member States, Switzerland's participation in a PESCO project would also be subject to EU *monitoring*,[102] so

99 Although PESCO in itself does not seem to be problematic for neutral Member States like Austria and Ireland, which all take part in the initiative.

100 Cf. <https://eda.europa.eu/news-and-events/news/2021/10/05/EDA-cyber-phalanx-wraps-in-portugal> (accessed 2 May 2022) and <https://pesco.europa.eu/project/eu-cyber-academia-and-innovation-hub-eu-caih/> (accessed 2 May 2022).

101 See Article. 6(3) and (4) of the PESCO Decision.

102 Article 3(h) of the PESCO-third States Decision stipulates that the third state "commit(s) itself, in its request for participation referred to in Article 2(1) of this Decision, to ensuring respect for provisions of Decision (CFSP) 2017/2315 and of Decision (CFSP) 2018/909". Article 5 sets out a review process whereby "information on the individual contribution to the project by that third State and the fulfilment of its commitments to the project, as well as on its continued fulfilment of the general conditions" are to be communicated to the PESCO Secretariat "in accordance with the procedure and timelines set out in Article 2(2) of Decision (CFSP) 2018/909, set out in Article 3 of this Decision".

that based on its performance or lack thereof, the project members could thus agree "that [its] participation in a project should be reassessed".[103]

3.2 *Participating in the Development of a European (Defence) Market?*

A related enterprise in the EU security and defence sphere, which is relevant to this discussion is the establishment of the European Defence Fund (EDF).[104] The initiative aims at supporting joint research and development in the defence industry across the Union, with the ultimate goal of enhancing Europe's strategic autonomy.[105] While it concerns defence matters, the EDF is not a CFSP-based initiative, but an instrument intimately connected to the operation of the Single Market.[106] The Fund was established through a Council Regulation based on Articles 173(3) (industry) 182(4), 183 and 188(2) (research and development) TFEU.[107]

Akin to the PESCO Decision, the EDF Regulation envisages the potential participation of third States, but in more restrictive terms. The preamble of the Regulation thus stipulates that "[a]s the Fund aims to enhance the competitiveness and efficiency of the Union's defence industry, *only legal entities which are established in the Union or in associated countries* and are not subject to control by non-associated third countries or by non-associated third-country entities *should, in principle, be eligible for support*".[108]

While third States' participation in EDF is in principle limited to "Associated Countries", the latter's restrictive definition further reduces the potential for Switzerland's involvement. Article 5 of the Regulation limits the group of Associated Countries to "members of the European Free Trade Association

103 Should Member States decide to suspend the third-State's participation in a specific PESCO project, Article 6(1)(2) of the PESCO-third States Decision foresees that the coordinator or coordinators of the project, with the support of the PESCO Secretariat, inform the Council and the High Representative accordingly. Based on this notification and following an opinion by the Political and Security Committee, the Council may eventually decide in accordance with Article 46(6) TEU and Article 9(2) of Decision (CFSP) 2017/2315 to terminate the participation of the third State in the project.

104 See S. Blockmans (n. 86), p. 1785.

105 See the Commission's proposal for a regulation of the European Parliament and of the Council establishing the European Defence Fund, COM(2018) 476 final. Further on the notion of strategic autonomy: F. Mauro, 'Autonomie Stratégique – le nouveau Graal de la défense européenne', *Les Rapports du GRIP 1/2018.*

106 As further illustrated by the indication that the text has "EEA relevance". See Regulation 2021/697 of the European Parliament and of the Council of 29 April 2021 establishing the European Defence Fund and repealing Regulation (EU) 2018/1092 (OJ L 170/149).

107 As proposed by the Commission, COM(2018) 476 (n. 105).

108 See recital 15 of the Preamble of the Regulation (emphasis added).

which are members of the EEA". For those, the Fund shall be available "in accordance with the conditions laid down in the Agreement on the European Economic Area".[109] The special access to EDF for the EEA EFTA countries is further articulated in Article 9 which, echoing the Preamble, limits the entities eligible for funding to applicants and subcontractors *established in the Union or in an associated country* (as defined in Article 5 above), have their executive management structures *in the Union or in an associated country* and are not controlled by a non-associated third country or by a non-associated third country entity.[110]

The Regulation, therefore, makes clear that while it is a "member of the European Free Trade Association", Switzerland does not benefit from the special treatment the EU grants to the other three EFTA States. Although it might stem from Switzerland's lack of interest in being "associated" to EDF in the first place, such a distinct treatment also appears to find its explanation in the country's non-participation in the EEA, and ultimately in its alternative relationship with the EU Single Market. The specific terms of third States' participation in EDF indicate that cooperation with the EU in this context, and beyond, is a function of existing arrangements governing their cooperation in other domains, and specifically on the degree of their integration into the Single Market.[111]

Indeed importantly, the Commission proposal for the EDF had underlined the "close links between the Fund and projects implemented in the framework of [...] f [PESCO]".[112] In the same vein, the EDF Regulation foresees that "an

109 Emphasis added. Para. 57 of the Preamble mentions that "[t]hird countries which are members of the European Economic Area (EEA) may participate in Union programmes in the framework of the cooperation established under the Agreement on the European Economic Area (...), which provides for the implementation of the programmes on the basis of a decision adopted under that Agreement. A specific provision should be introduced in this Regulation requiring those third countries to grant the necessary rights and access required for the authorising officer responsible, OLAF and the Court of Auditors to comprehensively exercise their respective competences".

110 Article 9(4) of the Regulation contains a derogation to this principle: an applicant established in the Union or in an associated country and controlled by a non-associated third country or a non-associated third country entity could be eligible for funding provided that, among other considerations, its participation "would not contravene the security and defence interests of the Union and its Member States as established in the framework of the CFSP". Indeed, various other guarantees, listed in the same provision, should also be given.

111 Indeed, the same holds true in other contexts; see, e.g., the contribution by C. Tobler in this this volume, on the cooperation during the pandemic.

112 COM(2018) 476 (n. 105).

action developed in the context of a project of PESCO (…) may benefit from a funding rate increased by an additional 10 percentage points". In other words, once assessed as eligible, a "PESCO bonus", in the form of a higher funding rate, may be granted to eligible PESCO projects. While point 11 of the preamble of the PESCO-third States Decision underlines that "[t]he participation of third States in a PESCO project does not imply that third-country entities will necessarily have access to the European Defence Industrial Development Programme (EDIDP) or other relevant Union instruments", EEA EFTA States' broader access to the EDF could facilitate their participation in PESCO, and vice-versa.

In sum, the more integrated a third State is with the EU legal order, and chiefly with the EU Single Market, the more it may enjoy access to EU initiatives in foreign policy, security and defence, e.g., EDF, and in turn PESCO. It is so because being integrated into the Single Market substantively facilitates cooperation in CFSP given the latter's increased interactions with other dimensions of the EU legal order. But this is also the result of the particular type of relationship that integration agreements like the EEA entail with the EU, both in terms of compliance, loyalty, and in turn trustworthiness among the partners,[113] which can then spill over to other areas of cooperation.[114]

3.3 *The Significance of other EU-Switzerland Agreements in Furthering CFSP Cooperation*

Considering the above discussion, a deeper EU-Switzerland cooperation in CFSP could consist of Swiss participation in new CFSP related initiatives, on an *ad hoc* basis. Following its piecemeal approach, the Confederation could add sectoral arrangements to the existing panoply of instruments governing its CFSP cooperation with the EU, for instance, to take part in individual PESCO projects.

113 The CJEU has acknowledged the 'special' character of the relationship; CJEU, Case C-897/19PPU, *Ruska Federacija*, ECLI:EU:C:2020:262, as further discussed by F. Haukeland Fredriksen and C. Hillion, 'The "special relationship" between the EU and the EEA EFTA States – free movement of EEA citizens in an extended area of freedom, security and justice', *Common Market Law Review* 58 (2021), p. 851.

114 In this respect, note the prominent reference to Norway in the recent *Strategic Compass for Security and Defence*, as "the most closely associated partner [of the EU] through the Agreement on the European Economic Area". It is also noteworthy that the associated partner in question did contribute to the elaboration of that Compass, which can be found here: <https://www.eeas.europa.eu/eeas/strategic-compass-security-and-defence-1_en> (accessed 2 May 2022).

As it has become clear, however, its participation could be made more difficult than for its EEA EFTA counterparts, considering the shallower arrangements governing its relationship with the EU in other areas, and in particular, in matters relating to the Single Market. Conversely, the establishment of an EU-Swiss institutional framework, long sought after by the EU[115] but seemingly ruled out by the Swiss Federal Government,[116] could provide the basis for facilitating cooperation in areas relating to the CFSP, at several levels.

While the defunct Institutional Agreement would not have covered CFSP issues at all,[117] the establishment of an equivalent horizontal arrangement could arguably lay the groundwork for further CFSP cooperation the way for instance the EEA has made it possible for EEA EFTA States to obtain privileged access to EU initiatives relating to defence, viz. EDF and in turn PESCO. That is so given that the purpose of the envisaged Institutional Agreement has been to secure and consolidate Switzerland's participation in the Single market.[118] As Single Market rules pervade aspects of the CFSP and CSDP, it could also lead to further interactions between these aspects and the Single Market related agreements governing EU-Switzerland relations, beyond the sole case of the EDF. For example, since EU sanctions are not only CFSP in nature but often imply economic or financial applications, and thus implications for the functioning of the Single Market, one could contemplate regular exchange within the institutional arrangement on the EU sanctions policy, at least in their Single Market dimensions.

At another related level, an institutional arrangement of the kind envisaged in the InstA could arguably provide a framework for the missing formal political dialogue between the EU and the Confederation. Admittedly, the InstA had a limited scope and ambition,[119] and did not explicitly envisage such a political dialogue. However, should the parties so wish, such an institutional framework,

115 See, e.g., EU Council, <https://www.consilium.europa.eu/en/press/press-releases/2019/02/19/council-conclusions-on-eu-relations-with-the-swiss-confederation/> (accessed 2 May 2022).

116 The Swiss Federal Government is favouring a vertical / sector-by-sector rather than a horizontal approach, see <https://www.admin.ch/gov/en/start/documentation/media-releases/media-releases-federal-council.msg-id-87349.html> (accessed 2 May 2022).

117 See Article 2, draft Accord facilitant les relations bilatérales entre l'Union européenne et la Confédération suisse dans les parties du marché intérieur auxquelles la Suisse participe (herein after 'draft InstA'): <https://www.fdfa.admin.ch/content/dam/europa/fr/documents/abkommen/Acccord-inst-Projet-de-texte_fr.pdf> (accessed 2 May 2022).

118 Art. 1 draft InstA. It would *a fortiori* be the case if Switzerland were to join the EEA. See C. Baudenbacher: <https://www.brusselsreport.eu/2022/03/17/is-switzerland-considering-to-join-the-european-economic-area-eea/> (accessed 2 May 2022).

119 See Article 15 draft InstA.

and in particular its mixed committee, could *in practice* operate like any other bodies, viz. association councils or indeed the EEA Council, and provide the forum for such a dialogue. The EEA Council in particular has offered such a forum for EEA parties to discuss political/foreign policy issues,[120] such as Brexit or the EU enlargement policy towards the countries of southeast Europe, despite the narrow terms of its mandate stipulated in the EEA Agreement.[121] Also, officials of the EEA EFTA States are regularly invited to "political dialogues held at the level of the relevant EU Council working parties",[122] which may be further employed as fora for consultation on CFSP matters.[123] These fora could in turn become channels of CFSP dialogue and cooperation for the EU and Switzerland too, should it be of interest to the parties.[124]

4 Concluding Remarks

Unlike most European non-Member States – with the noticeable exception of the UK – Switzerland does not as a matter of principle, *explicitly* align itself with EU foreign policy initiatives. While covering most aspects of EU CFSP, the Swiss cooperation with the Union in that area consists instead of occasional voluntary support, and intermittent association with specific EU CFSP undertakings, through specific sectoral (participation) agreements. Akin to other areas of cooperation with the EU, Switzerland's engagement in CFSP

120 Article 89(1) of the EEA Agreement foresees that the 'EEA Council is responsible for giving the political impetus in the implementation of th[e EEA] Agreement and laying down the general guidelines for the EEA Joint Committee [...] [it shall] assess the overall functioning and the development of the Agreement'. It meets twice a year.

121 See Conclusions of the 49th meeting of the EEA Council, Brussels, 23 May 2018, see also Conclusions of the 52nd meeting of the EEA Council, Brussels, 19 November 2019.

122 As underlined in the Conclusions of the 50th meeting of the EEA Council, Brussels, 20 November 2018, pt. 1, pt. 2 of the Conclusions of the 51st EEA Council meeting, Brussels, 20 May 2019, and at pt. 2 of the Conclusions of the 52th meeting of the EEA Council, Brussels, 19 November 2019.

123 *Ibid.* As indicated on the website of the Norwegian MFA: "policy coordination and consultation take place on a regular basis, primarily with the European External Action Service (EEAS) and the member states. The EU invites Norway and the EFTA partners to consultations with the Council Working Groups and the EEA Agreement facilitates biannual political dialogue on foreign policy", see <https://www.norway.no/en/missions/eu/areas-of-cooperation/foreign-policy/> (accessed on 2 May 2022).

124 Similarly, the Schengen mixed committee may serve as a forum for dialogue and consultations on Schengen-related CFSP developments. Schengen-related decision-shaping rights may thus be used actively in relation to some CFSP aspects. For example, the management of Europe's southern borders has involved a significant CFSP dimension.

matters appears to be motivated by a deep concern for autonomy, considered best preserved by a case-by-case approach. In many ways, therefore, the *sectoral bilateralism* that has generally characterised the relationship between the Confederation and the Union seems to hold true in the specific CFSP terrain, and may thus raise similar dissatisfaction on the side of the EU.

Indeed, the protracted absence of a comprehensive framework covering the whole EU-Swiss relationship and, more acutely, of an institutional arrangement governing the latter's connection with the Single Market, not only hinders the future of their trade and economic cooperation, but it may also have a knock-on effect on the development of CFSP cooperation. The CFSP and other areas of EU external cooperation are increasingly interwoven so that low level of cooperation in the latter areas may hamper cooperation in the former. As the EU relations with the EEA EFTA States epitomise, deeper integration into the ever-evolving Single Market generated by the EEA Agreement also engenders a level of proximity and trustworthiness among parties that makes the EU potentially more disposed towards cooperation in foreign, security and defence policy areas too. In other words, should Switzerland establish an institutional framework of the kind it has negotiated with the EU, it could potentially help deepen its cooperation in the CFSP area. Any such deepening would however likely entail additional constraints and in turn, cause disquiet in the Confederation.[125]

125 G. Kreis, 'Looking back. 1992 as a critical juncture', in P. Dardanelli, O. Mazzoleni (eds.), *Switzerland-EU Relations. Lessons for the UK after Brexit?* (Routledge, 2021), p. 6.

CHAPTER 8

The Road to Tax Transparency in Switzerland

Hans-Joachim Jaeger and Katharina Manz

1 Introduction

If there has been one overarching theme in the world of international taxation in recent years, it is the broad-based transparency debate. The developments and legislative processes that have triggered this discussion primarily concern taxpayers – individuals and legal entities alike – about whom dramatically more information is exchanged between tax authorities at the international level than in previous years. But a wide range of financial institutions, which must collect the data and forward it to the tax authorities, as well as the tax authorities themselves, are also affected. The latter must receive the data, exchange it with other tax authorities and analyse the plausibility of the data they have received from foreign tax authorities. The latest developments in the international tax environment already show that further transparency initiatives also involve the advisory industry (tax advisors, wealth advisors, family offices) in the data exchange system. It is already being discussed that the platform economy, which acts as an intermediary between buyers and sellers (e.g., in the online auction business or in the brokerage of accommodation and hotel services) and the "gig economy" should also be embedded in a system of information and data exchange between the tax authorities. Furthermore, extended information obligations in the area of cryptocurrencies are also at the discussion stage.

The most prominent of these tax transparency systems, which also affects the most taxpayers, is the automatic exchange of information on financial accounts in tax matters (henceforth: AEOI). The present contribution describes the development of the AEOI, its basic functioning and importance for Switzerland. It will focus less on the system's technical functioning, for which extensive literature[1] already exists, and more on the path taken by the various transparency initiatives that ultimately led to the AEOI.

---

1 X. Oberson, *International exchange of information in tax matters: towards global transparency* (Edward Elgar, 2018). Specifically for Switzerland, see for example G. Moloi, L. Schlichting and S. Vorpe (eds.), *Automatischer Informationsaustausch in Steuersachen. Kommentar* (Helbing Lichtenhahn, 2018); S. Emmenegger (ed.), *Automatischer Informationsaustausch,*

© KONINKLIJKE BRILL NV, LEIDEN, 2023 | DOI:10.1163/9789004529984_010

The call for tax transparency is not new. Similarly, the AEOI is not the "keystone" in the arch of tax transparency. Other initiatives will follow that integrate other market participants into a (more sophisticated?) transparency system. However, precisely because the AEOI builds on earlier initiatives, this contribution will present a historical outline of the most important initiatives that have significantly paved the way for the AEOI.

The present contribution will first look at the development of tax transparency in Switzerland (section 2), which is linked to Swiss banking secrecy, offshore markets and Switzerland's role in them as well as the US tax system, followed by an overview of the AEOI (section 3) and its effects before concluding with an outlook on the future of tax transparency initiatives (section 4).

2 Development of Tax Transparency in Switzerland

To place the calls for tax transparency in relation to Switzerland in a historical context, one must consider three issues: Swiss banking secrecy, the importance of Switzerland as an offshore banking location and the US tax system. All of these acted as strong catalysts for international transparency and for transparency systems to come.

2.1 *Swiss Banking Secrecy*

2.1.1 Origin and Sources

The banking law in force in Switzerland today has its historical origins in the banking crisis of 1910 to 1913, during which several local and regional banks suffered heavy losses. Between 1906 and 1915, a total of 85 Swiss banking institutions were deleted from the commercial register. The resulting loss of confidence in Swiss banks ultimately led to calls for increased state supervision.[2] In November 1934, the National Council and the Council of States (which together make up the Federal Parliament) adopted the Banking Act, which is still in force today, if in an amended form.[3] Article 47 of that Act contains a

---

Beiträge zur Schweizerischen Bankrechtstagung 2016 (Helbing Lichtenhahn, 2016); M. Beke, B. Fassl, A. Naderer, Ch. Obermair and Th. Windhager, *Gemeinsamer Meldestandard-Gesetz: Kommentar* (Linde, 2016).

2 R.U. Vogler, *Das Schweizer Bankgeheimnis: Entstehung, Bedeutung, Mythos*, Beiträge zur Finanzgeschichte, Verein für Finanzgeschichte, Heft 7 (Verein für Finanzgeschichte (Schweiz und Fürstentum Liechtenstein), 2005), p. 11 et seq.

3 Federal Law on Banks and Savings Banks of 8 November 1934 (Banking Act), SR 952.0, unless otherwise indicated, status as of 1 January 2020.

provision with regard to protection under criminal law for banking secrecy.[4] Banking secrecy is defined as "the obligation of a bank and its employees, reinforced by criminal and possibly regulatory sanctions, to keep secret from the outside world all information entrusted to them by the client in the course of the business relationship or which comes to their knowledge in this context".[5]

It should be noted that private law already obliged Swiss bankers to maintain secrecy before the Banking Act came into force.[6] Indeed, the banking secrecy doctrine finds its legal basis in the protection of legitimate expectations, which in turn flow directly from the concept of good faith.[7] In this regard, the Federal Council stated, *inter alia*, that banking secrecy is based, on the one hand, on the contractual obligation of the bank towards the client to maintain confidentiality about the client's personal circumstances and, on the other hand, on the fact that the income and assets of each individual belong to the protected sphere of personality.[8] Alongside the contractual duty of loyalty, the protection of personality rights forms an independent basis for the protection of banking secrecy.[9]

Also of importance is the Swiss Data Protection Act (DPA).[10] As private individuals within the meaning of the DPA, banks process their customer data within the meaning of this Act, so that this data falls within the scope of the DPA. According to the provisions contained therein, personal data may only be transferred to third parties if there is a justification, whereby the scope of these standards is narrower than that of Article 47 of the Banking Act. While both laws apply side-by-side in principle as they cover different legal areas, the Banking Act is considered *lex specialis* vis-à-vis the Data Protection Act in case

4 Since only the bank client himself can derive personal rights from banking secrecy, it is perhaps more appropriate to speak of bank client confidentiality (cf. Swiss Federal Supreme Court, decision 74 I 485 (10 December 1948)), p. 492.

5 Swiss Federal Supreme Court, decision 137 II 431 (15 July 2011), cons. 2.1.1 (translated by authors from German).

6 Cf. also the Federal Council in Fed. Gaz. 1970 I 1144, p. 1161: "Banking secrecy is by no means based solely on the Banking Act" (translated by authors from German).

7 M.-A.B. Schauwecker, 'Die Rechtsgrundlagen zum schweizerischen Bankgeheimnis', *Jusletter* 16 April 2018, p. 4, with further references.

8 Federal Council Dispatch of 18 August 1982 on the popular initiative "against the abuse of banking secrecy and banking power" (Banking Initiative), Fed. Gaz. 1982 II 1201, p. 1224; cf. also Swiss Federal Supreme Court, decision 137 II 431 (15 July 2011), cons. 2.1.1. with further references.

9 M.-A.B. Schauwecker (n. 7), p. 3.

10 Federal Data Protection Act (DPA) of 19 June 1992, SR 235.1, unless otherwise indicated, status as of 1 January 2019.

of conflicts. This means that where, for example, definitions in the two acts conflict, the Banking Act provisions would prevail.[11]

2.1.2 Scope of Banking Secrecy under Article 47 of the Swiss Banking Act

Article 47 of the Banking Act merely provides for the protection of banking secrecy under criminal law; this does not give rise to any further fiduciary duties under civil law.[12] Accordingly, the provision prohibits banks, their staff, and certain other persons from disclosing information about bank clients to third parties; banking secrecy may be violated intentionally or negligently.

While France, Austria, Luxembourg and the Netherlands also have criminal law protection of banking secrecy in addition to civil law protection, the possibility of committing an offence through mere negligence and the fact that the offence is structured as an *ex officio* offence are particularly noteworthy in the Swiss regulation. Only the Principality of Liechtenstein has a similar provision.[13]

Banking secrecy is by no means absolute; the bank already has a contractual duty to provide information to clients' authorised representatives, spouses and legal successors.[14] In addition, according to Article 47(5) of the Swiss Banking Act, federal and cantonal provisions on the duty to provide evidence or on the duty to provide information to an authority shall be exempted from banking secrecy.[15]

As described above, the economic circumstances of each individual are part of his or her private sphere. This is protected both by Swiss civil law and, as part of the fundamental right to privacy, by the Swiss Federal Constitution and by the European Convention on Human Rights (ECHR).[16] However, according

---

11 M.-A.B. Schauwecker (n. 7), p. 6 et seq.

12 *Ibid.*, p. 5.

13 M.-A.B. Schauwecker (n. 7), p. 5. For Liechtenstein: Article 14 in connection with Article 63(1)(a) Act on Banks and Securities Firms of 21 October 1992 (Banking Act), LR 952.0, Liechtenstein Gaz. 1992.108.

14 See for instance Articles 170(1) and (2) Swiss Civil Code of 10 December 1907 (CC), SR 210, or Articles 607(3) and 610(2) CC in connection with Article 400(1) Federal Act on the Amendment of the Swiss Civil Code (Part Five: The Code of Obligations) of 30 March 1911 (CO), SR 220.

15 See also Fed. Gaz. 1982 II 1201, p. 1225.

16 Swiss Federal Supreme Court, decision 137 II 431 (15 July 2011), cons. 2.1.2. Refer for instance to European Court for Human Rights Judgment *G.S.B. v. Switzerland* (Application no. 28601/11, (22 December 2015)) concerning the question whether the transmission of an individual's banking data to the authorities of another State under a bilateral agreement infringed upon that individual's rights under Article 8 ECHR.

to relevant case law, banking secrecy is not considered an independent (un) written constitutional right. It therefore does not always take precedence in the event of collisions with other interests, for example with regard to the forwarding of client data abroad.[17] Under the Swiss Federal Constitution and the ECHR, bank client data may be transferred abroad if there is a legal basis, either in Swiss domestic law or a relevant tax treaty, and a public interest in doing so, and if the measure is proportionate. Under Article 8(2) ECHR, justifications for such a measure include the maintenance of order and the economic well-being of a country.[18] According to the relevant Swiss case law, banking secrecy can only be regarded as belonging to the "essential interests of Switzerland" to the extent that the information requested is one "the disclosure of which would virtually undermine banking secrecy or cause damage to the entire economy".[19]

2.1.3 UBS Case

On 16 July 2008 (supplemented on 29 August 2008), the US Internal Revenue Service (IRS) requested administrative assistance from the Swiss Federal Tax Administration (SFTA) based on the double taxation agreement (DTA) between Switzerland and the United States of America.[20] In December of the same year, the US Department of Justice (DoJ) informed the Swiss bank UBS AG that charges would be brought against it immediately if the requested data were not provided. On 17 February 2009, the threat was repeated.[21]

On 18 February 2009, UBS AG transmitted information on 256 client files to the Swiss Financial Market Supervisory Authority (FINMA) on the basis of an order issued by FINMA; which transmitted this data to the US after a Deferred Prosecution Agreement was reached between UBS AG and the DoJ on the same day.[22]

---

17 Swiss Federal Supreme Court, decision 137 II 431 (15 July 2011), cons. 2.1.2, with reference to decision 115 Ib 68 (4 April 1989), cons. 4b.

18 Swiss Federal Supreme Court, decision 137 II 431 (15 July 2011), cons. 2.1.2.

19 *Ibid.*, cons. 2.1.2 (translated by authors from German), with references to Swiss Federal Supreme Court decisions 125 II 83 (29 October 1998), 123 II 153 (8 April 1997), cons. 7, and 115 Ib 68 (4 April 1989), cons. 4b.

20 Convention between the Swiss Confederation and the United States of America for the Avoidance of Double Taxation with Respect to Taxes on Income dated 2 October 1996, SR 0.672.933.61.

21 Swiss Federal Supreme Court, decision 137 II 431 (15 July 2011), cons. B.b and C.a.

22 Federal Council Dispatch of 14 April 2010 on the approval of the Agreement between Switzerland and the United States of America on a request for administrative assistance concerning UBS AG and the Protocol of Amendment, Fed. Gaz. 2010 2965, p. 2972.

An appeal was lodged with the Swiss Federal Administrative Court by three companies against the disclosure of their client information. The Swiss Federal Administrative Court held that (parts of) the order issued by FINMA were unlawful. Specifically, the Court opined that FINMA could not have acted by delegation of the Swiss Federal Council in the context of constitutional emergency law as the Federal Council had not taken emergency measures itself. Therefore, the appealed order was not issued on a sufficient legal basis to justify the restriction of fundamental legal rights; there had been no sufficient legal possibility for FINMA to order the transmission of client data outside the mutual legal or administrative assistance procedures explicitly intended for use in such cases.[23]

FINMA appealed the Federal Administrative Court's decision. The Swiss Federal Supreme Court (FSC) held the following at last instance:[24] FINMA, which had handed over the data in question to the US authorities, is not itself subject to banking secrecy. However, it is subject to official secrecy, within the scope of which it must maintain banking secrecy.[25] While the Banking Act allows FINMA to order protective measures if there is a well-founded concern regarding the over-indebtedness of a bank or the timely fulfilment of capital adequacy requirements, it cannot – according to the wording of the relevant provisions of the Banking Act – breach banking secrecy and provide client data to foreign tax authorities as part of such measures. In particular, the protective measures are intended to enable affected banks to continue to carry out their activities and are thus primarily directed at the banks themselves, with only indirect effects for bank clients.[26]

It should be noted that FINMA remains bound by its other legal obligations and the principle of legality when taking protective measures. Orders must therefore be directed primarily at the bank concerned; bank clients may be affected by them "only selectively and indirectly".[27] Furthermore, administrative assistance procedures under financial market and tax laws, which also

23 Swiss Federal Administrative Court, decision B-1092/2009 (5 January 2010).

24 Swiss Federal Supreme Court, decision 137 II 431 (15 July 2011). For commentary on this decision from the legal community, refer for instance to W. Kälin, J. Künzli, A. Lienhard, P. Tschannen, A. Tschentscher and J. Wyttenbach, 'Die staatsrechtliche Rechtsprechung des Bundesgerichts in den Jahren 2011 und 2012', *Zeitschrift des Bernischen Juristenvereins* 148/2012, p. 673 et seq., specifically pp. 675–679, with additional references.

25 Swiss Federal Supreme Court, decision 137 II 431 (15 July 2011), cons. 2.2.1.

26 *Ibid.*, cons. 2.2.2 et seq.

27 *Ibid.*, cons. 2.2.3 (translated by authors from German), with references to Swiss Federal Supreme Court, decisions 136 I 87 (30 September 2009), cons. 3.1., and 132 I 49 (25 January 2006), cons. 6.2.

serve to protect the economic personality of bank clients, definitively regulate the exchange of information with foreign authorities. It is therefore not possible for FINMA to transfer client data abroad by circumventing the relevant administrative or legal assistance procedures.[28]

The FSC also examined whether FINMA's disclosure of UBS data was permissible in order to protect overriding private or public interests.[29] In the present case, there was a threat of charges being brought against UBS AG, which, due to the bank's systemic relevance, appeared to be capable of impairing both the national and the international financial markets. These impairments of the Swiss and international economic systems would have affected "essential and existential interests of the country [Switzerland]".[30]

According to the Court, the economic stability of a country and the protection of its financial market may, in exceptional cases, constitute a fundamental legal interest worthy of protection; both property and good faith in business transactions constitute classical legal interests worth protecting.[31] Furthermore, the potential consequences for the financial system were severe, as UBS AG is systemically important for the Swiss economy (*"too big to fail"*).[32] An indictment of UBS AG in the US would most likely have threatened the bank's very existence, especially in light of the fact that indictments in the US – regardless of their outcome – generally lead to irreparable losses of reputation and assets; especially in the banking sector, and this can quickly lead to over-indebtedness.[33]

Based on these considerations and the confirmation of the proportionality of the measure taken,[34] the FSC concluded that the FINMA order of 18 February 2009 and the subsequent transfer of data should be confirmed in substance.[35] However, in recent rulings, the FSC has in some cases denied an overriding public interest in the transfer of client data to the United States.[36]

---

28 Swiss Federal Supreme Court, decision 137 II 431 (15 July 2011), cons. 2.3.

29 *Ibid.*, cons. 3.1. No reference is made here to the Swiss division of competencies and the corresponding legal basis; it is assumed that FINMA had the authority to transfer the UBS data to the US on 18 February 2009. Cf. in this regard cons. 3.2.1. et seq.

30 *Ibid.*, cons. 4.1. (translated by authors from German).

31 *Ibid.*, cons. 4.1.

32 *Ibid.*, cons. 4.2; on the quantification of possible losses in the event of the failure of a bank such as UBS, cf. Federal Council Dispatch of 5 November 2008 on a package of measures to strengthen the Swiss financial system, Fed. Gaz. 2008 8943, pp. 8945 and 8958 et seq.

33 Swiss Federal Supreme Court, decision 137 II 431 (15 July 2011), cons. 4.3.2 et seq.

34 *Ibid.*, cons. 4.4.

35 *Ibid.*, cons. 5.4.

36 See, for example, Swiss Federal Supreme Court, decision 4A_73/2017 (26 July 2017).

2.1.4 Findings

It follows from the above that banking secrecy is not absolute; in certain cases, client data may be disclosed. Bank client data may be transferred abroad if there is a legal or treaty basis and a public interest in doing so, and the measure is proportionate. With growing pressure from the international community, Switzerland has brought banking secrecy into line with international standards over the years. While it remains largely unchanged within Switzerland, banking secrecy has been severely restricted vis-à-vis other countries. Banking secrecy has been softened in particular in connection with data on clients domiciled in an AEOI country or in the US (cf. section 3 for a more in-depth discussion).

2.2 *Modern Challenges: Offshore Markets*

Offshore markets in banking are characterised by the fact that an individual client holds an account or custody account with a financial institution that is domiciled outside of the client's country of residence. Consulting firms regularly estimate the size and importance of these offshore markets. Boston Consulting Group (BCG) has published its annual Global Wealth Report for 20 years. The assets under management of the largest offshore markets have remained unchanged over the past few years at just under USD 10 trillion[37] – or just under USD 10,000 billion. Figure 8.1 below is taken from the BCG publication for 2020. The figures for 2021 and 2022 are comparable. What is remarkable about these figures is that the three largest offshore markets are home to almost half of all assets under management. In 2022, of the almost USD 10 trillion, 2.5 trillion are managed in Switzerland, 2.3 trillion in Hong Kong and a further 1.5 trillion in Singapore. This makes Switzerland the largest offshore asset management location in the world today. However, the annual growth rates achieved and forecast for the next few years for these assets under management in the two Asian offshore centres of Hong Kong and Singapore are significantly higher (by a factor of 2.5 in various scenarios) than in Switzerland. This means that, barring any major political uncertainties in Hong Kong, the two largest offshore markets are likely to converge in the coming years. BCG forecasts that Hong Kong could overtake Switzerland in terms of offshore assets under management as early as 2023.[38]

---

37 Notations "trillion" and "billion" are used in their US definitions.

38 Boston Consulting Group, Standing Still Is Not an Option. Global Wealth 2022, <https://web-assets.bcg.com/24/f5/f3776eb4427fa57471dddc921211/bcg-global-wealth-standing-still-is-not-an-option-jun-2022-r-4.pdf> (accessed 2 October 2022), p. 7.

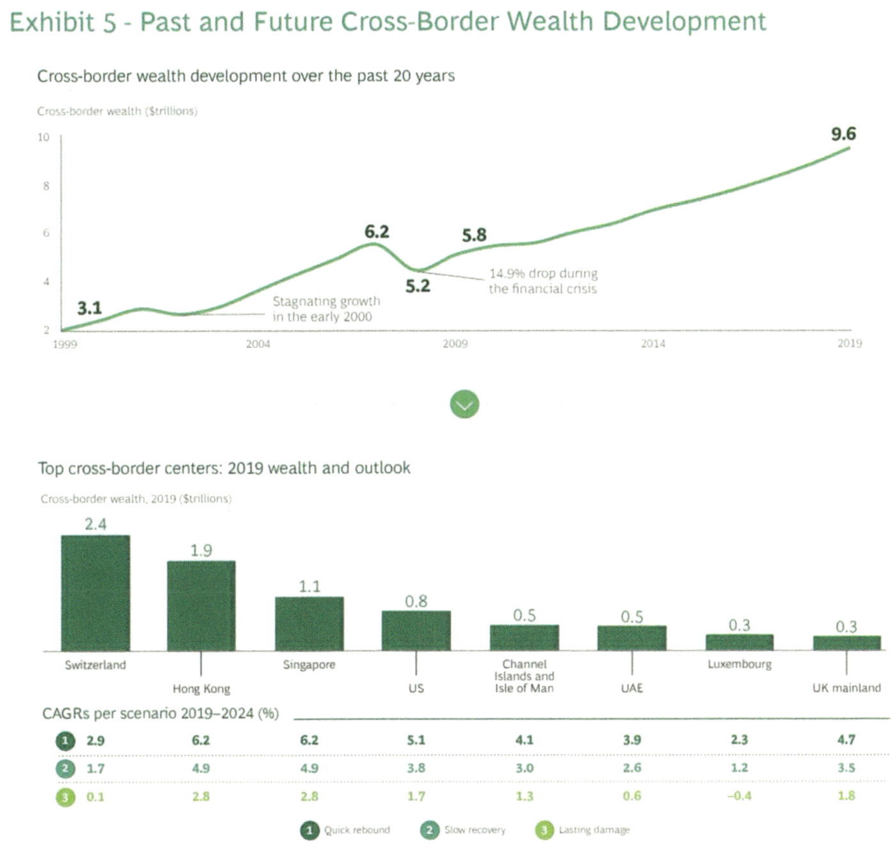

FIGURE 8.1 Size and development of cross-border markets
Note: UK mainland consists of England, Scotland, and Wales.
SOURCE: BCG, GLOBAL WEALTH 2020–20TH EDITION, P. 11

Not too unexpectedly, the largest share of assets under management in Switzerland comes from Western Europe, while Hong Kong and Singapore manage a large majority of assets from Asia. The corresponding numbers are shown in Figure 8.2 below for the year 2022.

The sheer size of these offshore asset management markets immediately suggests that the investors', or account or custody account holders' countries of residence have an inherent interest in information about the size of the assets and the income flows therefrom. Without any information, these States have had little ability to verify whether portions of these assets or income therefrom remained undeclared in the investors' home countries. Moreover, the information has also been protected by rules such as banking secrecy. It is true that, in the past, DTAs already provided the possibility of granting administrative or

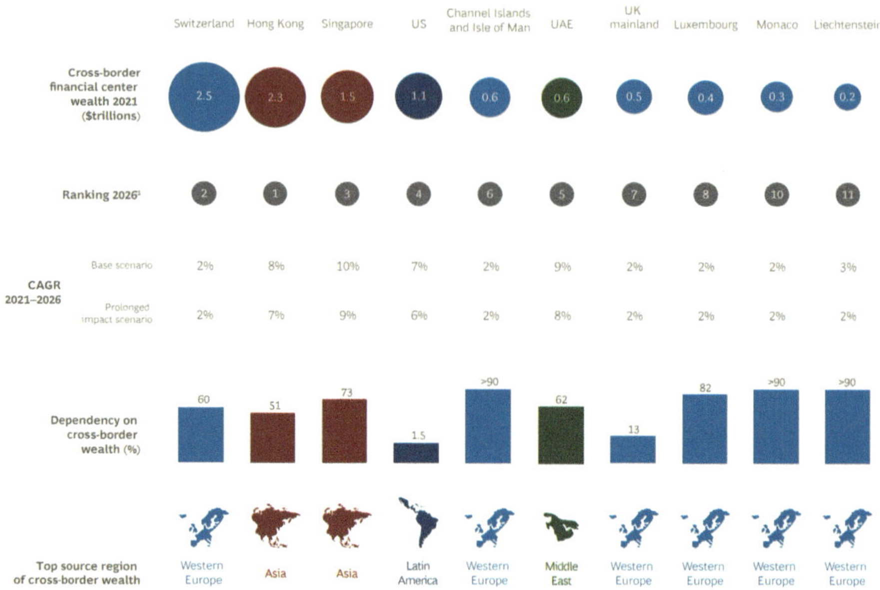

FIGURE 8.2 Absolute size and growth of selected offshore markets
SOURCE: BCG, GLOBAL WEALTH 2022, P. 7

legal assistance to the other partner State upon request. However, the granting of such information was regularly subject to high hurdles. The fact pattern on the basis of which the partner State requested information from Switzerland (e.g., in the case of foreign tax evasion) also had to be punishable in Switzerland (principle of double criminality). This requirement often failed because Switzerland draws a clear distinction between tax evasion (understood as intentionally or negligently causing an incomplete tax declaration) and tax fraud (intentionally or negligently causing an incomplete tax declaration using forged, falsified or substantively untrue documents). Obviously, this case-by-case treatment was not suitable for mass auditing as envisioned by foreign tax authorities.

2.3 *The US Tax System*

To the authors' best knowledge, the US is the only country in the world (apart from Eritrea to a limited extent) that links tax liability to citizenship, in particular, in addition to other criteria. Accordingly, a "United States person" (hereafter: "US person") is an individual who resides in the US for a minimum period of time, has a qualified residence permit ("green card") in the US, or who holds US citizenship.[39] These US persons are subject to income taxation in the US.

39 See 26 USC § 7701(a)(30). US citizenship may also be acquired by birth in the US (see 8 USC § 1401 et seq.).

This means that the US also taxes the income of those US persons who live abroad permanently. All other countries in the world usually link a tax liability to tax residency in that country. Thus, if a US person lives in Switzerland, for example, his or her income is taxed both in Switzerland (due to tax residency) and in the US (due to the fact that he or she is a US person). Whether or not there is an effective double taxation of the income depends on the provisions of a DTA between the US and the state of residence (in this case: Switzerland). As a rule, such DTAs provide that the taxes paid in the country of residence are credited against the tax liability in the US. In other words, the effective tax burden corresponds to the higher of the two tax rates in the country of residence or in the US.

Although taxation on the basis of citizenship had already begun in the United States after the Civil War, this regulation was not enforced internationally, especially since the US tax authorities (Internal Revenue Service, IRS) lacked information about the assets and income flows that US persons held and earned abroad. An apt quote was provided in 1862 by the Republican Senator from the State of Vermont, Jacob Collamer: "If a man draws his income from our public debt, or from property here, and resides in Paris, skulking away from contributing his personal support to the Government in this day of its extremity, he ought to pay a higher income tax".[40]

2.3.1 Qualified Intermediary System

It was not until 2001, with the introduction of the Qualified Intermediary ("QI") system, that the IRS was able to obtain comprehensive information on the assets of US persons abroad for the first time. Simply put, banks in approximately 70 countries initially undertook – under no small amount of political pressure from the US and to the extent permitted by their domestic banking laws – to document their customers and segregate US persons from non-US persons.[41] For the former, account balances and income flows from US sources had to be reported directly to the IRS. Non-US persons, on the other hand, provided they were adequately documented via KYC (know-your-customer) rules, could in turn avail themselves of their countries of residence's DTAs with the US. They then received US dividends and interest without or with deduction of a reduced US withholding tax, without having to engage in further administrative work (e.g., by completing detailed forms).

---

40 Quoted in M.S. Kirsch, 'Taxing Citizens in a Global Economy', 82 *New York University Law Review* 443 (2007), p. 451.

41 So-called Non-Resident Aliens (NRA).

In 2007, the US Government Accountability Office (GAO) published a report on the effectiveness of the QI system.[42] According to the GAO report, the system worked in principle, but had two shortcomings: first, non-US sourced income received by US persons was not reported to the IRS. Second, the QI system could not see through corporations and other fiscally opaque structures. Thus, if the US person was the owner of a non-US corporation or, for example, the settlor or beneficiary of a non-US trust, and the corporation or trust was the account holder (so-called "indirect account relationship"), the banks were not required to look through these legal entities under their interpretation of the QI Agreement.[43] Consequently, the US person who controlled the entity and was then often the ultimate beneficiary ("beneficial owner") was regularly not reported to the IRS.

The interpretation of the QI Agreement by the IRS differed from the banks' view: the US tax authorities also wanted foreign (i.e., non-US sourced) income to be understood as being reportable. Among other issues, this led the DoJ to bring charges against several banks. The most prominent case was the above-mentioned UBS' February 2009 Deferred Prosecution Agreement[44] with the DoJ.[45]

2.3.2 Shortcomings of the QI System and FATCA as a Remedy

Immediately thereafter, the US government introduced new legislation to increase tax transparency and close the loopholes that were evident in the QI Agreement. As part of a larger economic stimulus package,[46] the so-called FATCA legislation (Foreign Account Tax Compliance Act) was also introduced.

At its core, FATCA is exclusively an information system in which banks and financial institutions worldwide undertake to provide the IRS with information on US persons if they maintain accounts or custody accounts for such persons (this can also be a US legal entity). In contrast to the QI system, the

42 United States Government Accountability Office: Report to the Committee on Finance, U.S. Senate. TAX COMPLIANCE Qualified Intermediary Program Provides Some Assurance That Taxes on Foreign Investors Are Withheld and Reported, but Can Be Improved (Washington D.C., December 2007).

43 Further information can be found at <https://www.irs.gov/businesses/corporations/qualified-intermediary-system with the full text of the current agreement at https://www.irs.gov/pub/irs-drop/rp-17-15.pdf> (accessed 12 October 2022).

44 Cf. <https://www.justice.gov/opa/pr/ubs-enters-deferred-prosecution-agreement> (accessed 20 September 2022).

45 See above, 2.1.3.

46 So-called HIRE Act (Hiring Incentives to Restore Employment Act) of 18 March 2010, 26 USC §§ 1471–1474, 26 USC § 6038D.

report also includes income and assets of non-US origin, i.e., also dividends and interest income from non-US securities. Sales proceeds are also reported. In addition to the reporting of account holders, banks are also required to identify and report the so-called "substantial US owner" in the case of indirect account relationships. Thus, FATCA requires financial institutions to look through fiscally opaque corporate and trust structures and report US persons behind these entities to the IRS. The inadequacy of the QI system, which failed to capture US persons behind opaque structures, was thereby addressed. To this end, the institution of the "controlling person" was introduced. These persons are individuals identified under the applicable AML (anti-money laundering)/KYC regulations of the respective country who control companies that are so-called passive "Non-Financial Foreign Entities" (NFFEs).[47] Passive NFFEs are companies that are not financial institutions and that derive the majority of their income from passive sources (in particular dividends, interest and royalty income). The IRS seems to have considered such companies to be vulnerable to being misused for tax evasion purposes.[48] In light of this, the IRS is interested in obtaining information about the US persons who control or otherwise exert influence over such passive NFFEs.

In order for the FATCA system to function globally and comprehensively, the US also devised a penalty mechanism: if a bank or financial institution does not participate in the FATCA system, does not identify its customers and accordingly does not report any US persons to the IRS, the US Central Securities Depository (CSD), where US securities (in particular the US securities pertaining to the bank's customers) are usually located and through which payment of dividends is made, will be forced to withhold a penalty tax of 30% on all US dividends and interest as well as on all sales proceeds resulting from the sale of these shares or bonds and pay this amount to the IRS. The same applies to US interest-bearing securities, which are otherwise exempt from US withholding taxes,[49] but are held in the custody of the CSD. The same withholding obligation applies to any financial institution worldwide that has entered into a FATCA agreement with the IRS. If this bank acts as a (sub-) custodian for another bank, it is obliged to ask this other bank whether it has concluded a FATCA agreement with the IRS. If this is the case, no withholding obligation

47 See 26 CFR §1.1471–1(b)(128).

48 Banks are not required to seek controlling persons in the case of companies engaged in commerce and industry, as well as in the case of listed companies (which are subject to separate disclosure requirements), all of which derive income primarily from "active economic activities".

49 See 26 USC §§ 871(h) and 881(c).

arises. However, if the other bank does not participate in the FATCA system,[50] the upstream bank/custodian must withhold the 30% penalty deduction on US -sourced income and sales proceeds and remit it to the IRS. In this way, the FATCA system ensures that participation in and the resulting obligations from it cascade down to the last member of the custody chain. In addition, any client wishing to hold US securities will carefully consider doing so at a bank that does not participate in the FATCA system. After all, in such a case, the client would risk receiving only 70% of the US dividends and interest and, at best, only 70% of the proceeds from the sales of their US securities.

2.3.3 FATCA Becomes a "National" Set of Rules

Following the enactment of the FATCA regulations in the US in 2010, five European countries[51] negotiated with the IRS at the end of 2012 on how the complex set of regulations – and in particular the 30% penalty tax – could be made more manageable for banks in these countries. This concern suited the IRS just fine and it was indeed able to offer a relief: the 30% penalty tax would not have to be levied. In return, however, the countries would have to attempt to embed the FATCA legislation in their own legal systems, to introduce and transpose American law into their own national laws. This led to unusual situations, such as in the German FATCA Act, in which the German and English versions apply equally.[52] In the latter, the American terminology is present, which leads to a need for interpretation. For the IRS, this development had the not-to-be-underestimated advantage that it no longer needed to check and respectively ensure compliance with the FATCA provisions: with the embedment in the respective national law, it was henceforth incumbent on the national regulatory authorities to ensure compliance. This compromise formed the basis for negotiations between the US and many other countries. The results of these negotiations were set out in intergovernmental agreements (IGAs) between

---

50 In this case, one speaks of a Non-Participating Foreign Financial Institution (NPFFI).

51 Germany, France, Great Britain, Italy and Spain.

52 Cf. Gesetz zu dem Abkommen vom 31. Mai 2013 zwischen der Bundesrepublik Deutschland und den Vereinigten Staaten von Amerika zur Förderung der Steuerehrlichkeit bei internationalen Sachverhalten und hinsichtlich der als Gesetz über die Steuerehrlichkeit bezüglich Auslandskonten bekannten US-amerikanischen Informations- und Meldebestimmungen vom 10. Oktober 2013 (Federal Law Gazette Year 2013 Part II No. 29, issued at Bonn on 15 October 2013), p. 1362 et seq., <https://www.bundesfinanzministerium.de/Content/DE/Standardartikel/Themen/Steuern/Internationales_Steuerrecht/Staatenbezogene_Informationen/Laender_A_Z/Verein_Staaten/2013-10-15-USA-Abkommen-FATCA-Gesetz.pdf?__blob=publicationFile&v=3> (accessed 20 September 2022).

2014 and 2017. Today, the US has concluded IGAs with 113 countries.[53] The vast majority follow the so-called Model 1, which provides for the adoption of the FATCA provisions into national law and requires banks to report to the IRS via their national central tax authorities. A minority of countries – including Switzerland, Austria, Japan and Hong Kong – have opted for the Model 2 IGAs. Under this Model 2, banks have an agreement directly with the IRS, provide their data directly to the IRS (and not via their central national tax authorities), and the FATCA rules are not transferred congruently into national law. By choosing the Model 2 contractual arrangement, Switzerland has decided to allow bank clients who are US persons a right of choice. The financial institutions report the data of the US persons directly to the IRS only if these US persons have consented to the data delivery and only to the extent permitted by local Swiss law. If a US person does not consent to the data transfer, the information will only be relayed to the IRS in an aggregate form without naming the client. The US – or the IRS – can then attempt to obtain information through the usual channels of administrative assistance (laid down in the double taxation agreement). In addition to Article 26 of the double taxation agreement,[54] the IRS also has the possibility of a so-called group request.[55] With this instrument, the US can request information on specific account holders and accounts that had previously only been provided to the IRS in this anonymized and aggregate form, usually due to lack of the client's consent. In general, this will be information on accounts identified as US accounts to which foreign reportable amounts were paid. The bank's clients who would then be subject to a specific reporting can still take a limited appeal route if they think that the report would be made wrongly.

In October 2014, the Federal Council decided on a negotiation mandate that envisaged a change from FATCA Model 2 to the internationally more common Model 1 for Switzerland. To date, however, there are no signs of such a change.

For the US, the introduction of FATCA has been a great success. By the end of July 2021, more than 392,000 financial institutions worldwide had registered with the IRS, committing to report data on US persons for whom they hold

53 As of August 2021. The list of countries and the texts of the respective agreements can be found at <https://home.treasury.gov/policy-issues/tax-policy/foreign-account-tax-compliance-act> (accessed 20 September 2022).

54 Agreement of 2 October 1996 between the Swiss Confederation and the United States of America for the avoidance of double taxation in the field of taxes on income (DTA CH-US; SR 0.672.933.61), as amended by the Protocol of 23 September 2009.

55 Administrative assistance based on Article 5 of the Agreement of 14 February 2013 between Switzerland and the United States of America on Cooperation for Facilitated Implementation of FATCA (FATCA Agreement, SR 0.672.933.63).

accounts or custody accounts.[56] The IRS uses the data on US persons for data matching. This means that information provided by the US taxpayer in their tax return can be matched with the aggregated information that banks provide to the IRS under FATCA.[57] If there are discrepancies, the taxpayer would be asked to explain them. The one-to-one mapping of data to an individual is done using the US Social Security Number (SSN), which doubles as the taxpayer identification number (TIN). While in the US the SSN has served as an identifier for tax purposes for many years, other countries have only introduced the TIN at a later date (in Germany, a uniform federal TIN has existed since 2008) or even only with the introduction of the AEOI (in Switzerland, the OASI [Old Age and Survivors Insurance]/social security number has only been used as a tax identification number as of 2016).

2.4 *Transparency Initiatives of the European Union and of the OECD*

Other countries and organisations – with less political clout than the US – have also had an interest in obtaining data from taxpayers who hold their accounts and custody accounts abroad. However, many of these initiatives did not last long after the introduction of the AEOI in early 2016. The following part of this contribution turns to the European Union (EU), certain European States and to the Organisation for Economic Co-operation and Development (OECD).

2.4.1 The EU Taxation of Savings Income

The first EU transparency initiative was the so-called EU Savings Tax Directive.[58] It required, from 2004 onwards, banks within the EU to report interest income credited to clients (i.e., natural persons) resident in another EU Member State to the clients' home tax authorities. The reports were made within the EU

56 The list can be found at <https://apps.irs.gov/app/fatcaFfiList/flu.jsf> (accessed 20 September 2022).

57 The data is reported electronically by the financial institutions to the IRS in form of an xml file. Alternatively, the report can be made on an official form (IRS Form 8966, <https://www.irs.gov/pub/irs-pdf/f8966.pdf>, accessed 20 September 2022). A reconciliation of the data can then be made by using Form 8938 (IRS Form 8938 "Statement of Specified Foreign Financial Assets", <https://www.irs.gov/pub/irs-pdf/f8938.pdf>, accessed 25 September 2022), by means of which the taxpayer must declare foreign accounts. The taxpayer must also file a "Report of Foreign Bank and Financial Accounts" (FinCEN Form 114, so-called "FBAR") with the Financial Crimes Enforcement Network (FinCEN), an agency of the US Department of the Treasury that is independent of the IRS.

58 Council Directive 2003/48/EC of 3 June 2003 on taxation of savings income in the form of interest payments (OJ 2003, L 157/38) (no longer in force).

Member States, although certain third countries (in particular Switzerland,[59] Liechtenstein and the English Channel Islands and Overseas Territories) were also included in the regulatory framework.[60] However, these reports related only to interest and interest-equivalent income. The arrangement was the first of its kind where Switzerland entered into a type of double taxation agreement with the EU as a whole rather than negotiating bilateral agreements with a number of EU Member States.

In order to maintain its banking secrecy, Switzerland had stipulated that the EU-resident client could opt for an anonymous deduction of 35% of the interest income instead of being named. This amount (less a deduction of a quarter of such amount in favour of Switzerland) was then transferred anonymously via the SFTA to the respective clients' countries of residence.[61] The reporting or optional withholding on interest between Switzerland and the EU took place between 1 July 2005 and 31 December 2014. During this period, Switzerland transferred a total of approximately CHF 3.9 billion in interest withholding to EU countries. On average, approximately 63,000 additional notifications were made to EU countries per year, covering interest income totalling CHF 850 million per year.[62] The fact that the EU taxation of savings income only covered interest income naturally made such a transparency system porous, especially since there were alternative products on the financial markets and investors could also switch to dividend-heavy equity investments or structured products. Most of these structured products consist of a bond part and an option part, both of which are "packaged" into a single product. The bond part (usually a zero bond or similar instrument) results in interest income, while the option embedded in the product (or combination of several options) creates a capital gain in case of a favourable price development. Although the product also contains interest-bearing elements, these products were explicitly exempt from EU interest taxation. Moreover, the EU taxation of savings also

59 Based on the Agreement of 26 October 2004 between the Swiss Confederation and the European Community providing for measures equivalent to those laid down in Council Directive 2003/48/EC of 3 June 2003 on taxation of savings income in the form of interest payments, SR 0.641.926.81.

60 For additional background on the negotiations of the EU Savings Tax Directive as they relate to Switzerland, cf. M. Maresceau, *Bilateral Agreements Concluded by the European Community, Hague Academy of International Law. Collected Courses* (Martinus Nijhoff Pusblishers, 2006), pp. 416–419.

61 Also M. Maresceau (n. 60), p. 418.

62 Data for the years 2005 up to and including 2014 is available at <https://www.estv.admin.ch/estv/de/home/allgemein/steuerstatistiken/fachinformationen/fiskaleinnahmen/eu-zinsbesteuerung.html> (accessed 20 September 2022).

did not require any look-through in case of fiscally opaque structures, as provided for by FATCA. This meant that a natural person with tax residence in an EU Member State could relatively easily set up an (asset-managing) company whose assets consisted only of interest-bearing instruments. Instead of the investor, the company, as a client of a Swiss bank, could have its assets managed in a custody account of this bank. Since the company was not subject to the regulations of the EU taxation of savings income, there was neither a notification or report nor a withholding.

FATCA attempted to counteract this deficiency, that the transparency initiatives did not look through a company (or also through trusts) to the beneficial owner or majority owner behind it, by introducing the so-called passive non-financial entities.[63]

2.4.2 State-to-State Agreements on Final Withholding Taxes

Conscious of the inadequacies of the EU taxation of savings income, Germany, Austria and the United Kingdom attempted to reach an agreement with Switzerland on how a more far-reaching transparency for taxpayers in these countries with offshore banking relationships in Switzerland could be attained. The countries sought a comprehensive reporting system in their negotiations. In the area of tension between the legitimate transparency interests of the countries in which the investors were domiciled and the traditional Swiss interest in protecting the privacy of domestic and foreign investors from state interference, a two-component approach was negotiated: (i) on the one hand, a regularisation of already existing account and custody account balances was to take place in an anonymous manner in the sense of a self-disclosure without penalty.[64] Secondly, (ii) a final tax was to be levied by Swiss banks on future income and, if applicable, capital gains and transferred anonymously to the clients' countries of residence. However, clients were also given the possibility of opting for reporting (instead of the final withholding tax). This negotiation result was concretised in two Federal laws for the procedures with Austria[65] and the United Kingdom.[66] A corresponding agreement with Germany failed

63 Cf. 2.3.2 and 3.2.

64 Cf. Federal Council Dispatch of 18 April 2012 on the approval of the agreements with Germany on tax and financial market cooperation and with the United Kingdom on tax cooperation and on the Federal Act on International Withholding Tax, Fed. Gaz. 2012 4943, p. 4956 et seq.

65 Agreement between the Swiss Confederation and the Republic of Austria on cooperation in the areas of taxation and the financial market of 13 April 2012, SR 0.672.916.33.

66 Agreement between the Swiss Confederation and the United Kingdom of Great Britain and Northern Ireland on cooperation in the field of taxation of 6 October 2011, SR

in the German *Bundesrat*[67] due to resistance from the German opposition parties at the time.

Regularisation was carried out on the basis of a sophisticated formula value that took into account the capital assets at the time of introduction of the final withholding tax and in previous years, the duration of the business relationship as well as the capital assets at the beginning of the business relationship and finally, inflows and outflows during a defined period. The withholding tax levied on this amount (one-off payment), which was forwarded by the SFTA to the Austrian or UK tax authorities, or the alternative voluntary reporting, then ensured that the relevant taxpayers were exempt from penalties.

From 2013 onwards, the Swiss banks effectively assumed the function of an English or Austrian paying agent for clients domiciled in those countries. To this end, all payment flows relating to these clients' accounts and custody accounts needed to be interpreted according to UK or Austrian readings and the English or Austrian tax rates applied to them. These interpretations were regulated in detail in so-called concordance tables[68] for many possible income streams. These included not only ordinary interest and dividend payments, but also corporate actions, securities lending payments, structured products, and even certain compensation payments or payments from the split or merger

---

0.672.936.74. For additional background and information cf. for instance: R. Matteotti, N.E. Krenger, in M. Zweifel, M. Beusch and R. Matteotti (eds.), *Kommentar zum internationalen Steuerrecht* (Helbing Lichtenhahn, 2015), Einleitung N 51–198, N 92, or P.V. Kunz, *Wirtschaftsrecht* (Stämpfli, 2019), pp. 539, 546.

67 <https://www.bundesrat.de/SharedDocs/texte/12/20121123-schweiz.html> (accessed 20 September 2022).

68 For Austria <https://www.estv.admin.ch/dam/estv/de/dokumente/intsteuerrecht/themen/quellensteuerabkommen/wegleitungen/Anhang18.pdf.download.pdf/Anhang18-d.pdf>; for the United Kingdom <https://www.estv.admin.ch/dam/estv/de/dokumente/intsteuerrecht/themen/quellensteuerabkommen/wegleitungen/Anhang6.pdf.download.pdf/Anhang6-d.pdf> (both accessed 20 September 2022). For additional background information on the Swiss-Austrian agreement, cf. Federal Council Dispatch of 20 April 2012 on the approval of the treaty with Austria on tax and financial market cooperation, Fed. Gaz. 2012 5307, and the materials published by the Austrian Parliament on the same agreement, <https://www.parlament.gv.at/PAKT/VHG/XXIV/I/I_01770/fnameorig_250965.html> (accessed 20 September 2022). For additional background and information on the Swiss-UK agreement, cf. Federal Council Dispatch of 18 April 2012 on the approval of the agreements with Germany on tax and financial market cooperation and with the United Kingdom on tax cooperation and on the Federal Act on International Withholding Tax, Fed. Gaz. 2012 4943, and HM Revenue & Customs publication "Tax Agreement Between the United Kingdom and Switzerland", <https://assets.publishing.service.gov.uk/government/uploads/system/uploads/attachment_data/file/192140/uk_switzerland_tax_agreement.pdf> (accessed 20 September 2022).

of investment funds. In simple terms, the banks had to replicate English and Austrian tax law and their interpretations in their IT systems and keep them up to date in the event of changes. The taxes paid were then deemed to be settled, i.e., the anonymous payment of the withholding taxes to the Austrian and English tax authorities settled the tax obligations of the affected clients in their home countries. As proof of the final payment in the event of a possible later audit, clients received a deduction certificate from the Swiss banks.

In the case of the final withholding tax, it is particularly worth mentioning that – like FATCA – it obliged financial institutions to look through fiscally opaque structures and to treat the beneficiaries behind them as the persons concerned. Therefore, the dispatch also states: "Thus, the agreements cannot in principle be circumvented by the interposition of such structures" (meaning trusts, foundations, trust companies and life insurance shells).[69]

The SFTA published that from mid-2013 to the beginning of 2015, assets of more than GBP 10 billion (for the UK) and almost EUR 6 billion (for Austria) were disclosed and taxed in the context of regularisation.[70] In the case of ongoing final taxation, Swiss banks remitted GBP 32 million and EUR 27 million in withholding taxes to the UK and Austria, respectively, between 2013 and 2016.[71] At the same time, an average of 26,000 notifications for a total of GBP 520 million p.a. in investment income were sent to HMRC, and an average of 15,500 notifications with investment income averaging EUR 157 million p.a. were sent to the Austrian tax authorities.

The technical complexity of the final withholding taxes resulted in high costs for both the authorities and the banks involved. The SFTA estimated annual costs of CHF 8.25 million, and the banks estimated implementation costs in the mid-three-digit million range.[72] This complexity was probably one of the reasons why Switzerland did not enter into negotiations with more countries

69 Cf. Federal Council Dispatch of 18 April 2012 on the approval of the agreements with Germany on tax and financial market cooperation and with the United Kingdom on tax cooperation and on the Federal Act on International Withholding Tax, Fed. Gaz. 2012 4943, p. 4965 (translated by authors from German).

70 <https://www.estv.admin.ch/estv/de/home/internationales-steuerrecht/fachinformationen/quellensteuerabkommen/statistiken/regularisierung-unversteuerter-vermoegen.html> (accessed 22 September 2022).

71 <https://www.estv.admin.ch/estv/de/home/internationales-steuerrecht/fachinformationen/quellensteuerabkommen/statistiken/abgeltende-quellensteuer-auf-kapitaleinkuenften.html> (accessed 22 September 2022).

72 Cf. Federal Council Dispatch of 18 April 2012 on the approval of the agreements with Germany on tax and financial market cooperation and with the United Kingdom on tax cooperation and on the Federal Act on International Withholding Tax, Fed. Gaz. 2012 4943, p. 5032 et seq.

to introduce final withholding taxation. The introduction of the AEOI in 2017 consequently meant that the withholding tax agreements between the Swiss Confederation and the UK respectively Austria no longer had a *raison d'être*. Accordingly, repeal agreements were agreed with the two States.[73]

2.4.3 OECD: Base Erosion and Profit Shifting (BEPS) and Multilateralism

In addition to transparency in the tax affairs of individuals, the Organisation for Economic Co-operation and Development (OECD) in particular had set itself the task of coordinating and promoting action by its Member States to increase transparency in the area of legal entities as well.

The emergence of global trading led to an atomisation of the value chain into small parts with players in different countries (original producers, processors and refiners, trading, marketing and commission agent companies as well as licensing and patent exploitation companies). As a result, the tax authorities in a single country no longer had any possibility of checking whether, for instance, transfer pricing payments or royalties had not led to artificial profit reduction or profit shifting ("base erosion and profit shifting") within a group. In other words, in the case of internationally active corporations (such as Google, Apple, Facebook, Amazon, Starbucks), there was obvious suspicion that profits were not being taxed where value was actually created, but that the majority of their profits were artificially being shifted to low-tax countries through tax planning. In this context, a large number of interviews and surveys conducted by tax authorities and politicians led to an increased need for cross-border information. These surveys, in which the corporations were unable to sufficiently explain why large turnovers in some countries were contrasted by comparatively modest profit margins, were taken up by the press and the online media with great publicity.[74]

---

73 Cf. Agreement between the Swiss Confederation and the Republic of Austria on the Repeal of the Agreement of 13 April 2012 between the Swiss Confederation and the Republic of Austria on Cooperation in the Fields of Taxation and the Financial Market, OC 2017 201. As well as: Agreement between the Swiss Confederation and the United Kingdom of Great Britain and Northern Ireland on the Repeal of the Agreement of 6 October 2011 between the Swiss Confederation and the United Kingdom of Great Britain and Northern Ireland concerning Cooperation in the Field of Taxation, as amended by the Protocol of 20 March 2012, OC 2016 5103.

74 E.g., video "MPs condemn Amazon executive over tax payments" on YouTube, 12 November 2012, <https://youtu.be/DxaLrW49awc> (accessed 25 September 2022), in which Andrew Cecil, director of public policy at Amazon, was questioned by an English parliamentary committee about Amazon's structure and its influence on the calculation of profits in various countries.

In October 2015, the OECD then presented a framework of various measures in a final report, which it recommended its member countries implement.[75] This list of so-called Actions comprised a total of 15 recommendations, four of which related to improving the *coherence of tax regimes:*

First, the same set of facts should be assessed equally and coherently for tax purposes in the countries, so that arbitrage based on different interpretations would no longer be possible. It would be conceivable to treat a payment in one country as a (tax-deductible) interest expense and in the receiving country as a dividend, which can generally be received tax-free.

The second group of Actions set minimum requirements for the *substance* that a company would have to maintain in a country: a company within a group would only be considered resident for tax purposes in a country if it had a minimum level of infrastructure and staff with decision-making powers and if decisions of importance to the company were actually and demonstrably taken by this staff.

The third group of Actions concerned *transparency* rules: on the one hand, taxpayers were to be obliged to disclose their aggressive tax planning models. Action 11, the measurement and monitoring of profit reduction and profit shifting, was also intended to directly serve transparency in this package of measures. To this end, a database was set up containing information on statutory and effective tax rates for over 110 countries,[76] as well as on tax concessions (e.g., deductions for research and development activities, regimes for the exploitation of licences and patents (intellectual property), rules for controlled foreign companies and interest limitation rules).

Finally, transfer pricing documentation was to be revised and standardised and certain dispute resolution mechanisms (in case of the tax authorities involved having conflicting views) were to be introduced. This transfer pricing issue is specifically addressed in Action 13. However, in order to get a first overview of the atomised value chains mentioned previously, this item also contained the so-called country-by-country reporting (CbCR). This is a minimum standard that all OECD member countries and the G20 countries have undertaken to introduce. Internationally active companies with a certain minimum consolidated turnover (for Switzerland, the threshold is an annual turnover of more than CHF 900 million; the OECD documentation provides for a threshold

---

75 OECD (2016), BEPS Project Explanatory Note: Final Reports 2015, OECD/G20 Profit Shifting Project, OECD Publishing, Paris.

76 <https://www.oecd.org/tax/tax-policy/corporate-tax-statistics-database.htm> (accessed 20 September 2022).

of EUR 750 million)[77] must provide data to their home tax authorities, which then exchange the data with the other partner States. In Switzerland, the data must be delivered to the SFTA. For the first time, data had to be transmitted for financial years that began on or after 1 January 2018. The first exchange of data then took place in 2020.

What data is now exchanged under CbCR? The OECD has developed a standard grid for this purpose. All participating countries must report the type of principal activity (manufacturing, service provision, financial services, insurance, trading, holding company functions) and information on turnover, taxes paid and accrued, pre-tax and after-tax profits, capital, cash and fixed assets, and the number of employees for the reporting companies.[78] This makes it possible, in a first step, to understand how much turnover per employee is generated at what tax rate. If, in particular, there is a high turnover with very few employees in combination with a very low tax burden, it is at least reasonable to assume that there may have been an artificial shifting of profits to this country. The OECD has drawn up several tax risk indicators for this purpose. In addition to the above-mentioned question, the following indicators are also listed by name: High corporate profits with a low degree of corporate substance; significant activities of the company with low corporate profits; a company has geographically mobile functions in jurisdictions with low tax rates; patents and licenses are held in a different jurisdiction than the related production activities; a group of companies includes companies with dual or multiple tax residency (dual resident companies).[79]

The legal basis for CbCR and the other information exchanged under the BEPS actions in Switzerland was laid with the signing of the Multilateral Agreement on the Exchange of Country-by-Country Reports.[80] The corresponding federal law[81] and ordinance govern domestic implementation. The

77 OECD, Guidance on the Implementation of Country-by-Country Reporting, BEPS Action 13 (OECD Publishing, 2019), pp. 18–22.

78 OECD, Transfer Pricing Documentation and Country-by-Country Reporting, Action 13 – 2015 Final Report, OECD/G20 Base Erosion and Profit Shifting Project (OECD Publishing, 2015), p. 29 et seq.

79 OECD, Country-by-Country Reporting: Handbook on Effective Tax Risk Assessment (OECD Publishing, 2017), p. 64 et seq.

80 Multilateral Competent Authority Agreement on the Exchange of Country-by-Country Reports. Concluded on 27 January 2016, Fed. Gaz. 2017 33. Entered into force on 1 December 2017.

81 Federal Act on the International Automatic Exchange of Country-by-Country Reports of Multinational Corporations of 17 June 2016 (ALBAG), SR 654.1, and the respective Ordinance.

BEPS rules thus follow a pattern that is increasingly seen in intergovernmental information exchanges: because the exchange of information must take place between a large number of countries, many bilateral negotiations between the individual countries would be neither expedient nor temporally efficient. Therefore, a multilateral instrument or treaty was developed, which all interested countries or competent authorities could sign, ratify and transpose into domestic law.[82] In this case, the OECD effectively acted as a clearing house between the individual States. As soon as the treaty was ratified, it was deemed to have entered into force between the signatory state and all other signatories, unless a reservation was made on individual points.

2.4.4 Sixth Directive on Administrative Cooperation of the European Union

With the 6th Directive amending the EU Mutual Assistance Directive,[83] often referred to as "DAC 6", the EU instructed its Member States to introduce a comprehensive information regime in their domestic legal systems by 31 December 2019, which also includes financial intermediaries and advisors in the exchange of information. Classically, these are tax advisors, auditors, lawyers, other consultants and banks established in the EU. With information on the cross-border financial accounts of individuals and legal entities already being reported, the transparency regime was to be extended to include advisors and other financial intermediaries. The obvious aim of this extension was to identify potentially aggressive tax planning schemes involving multiple countries or taxpayers.

As soon as advisors or financial intermediaries provide advice to their clients on cross-border tax structuring, design, market, organise, provide, or manage the implementation of such a structuring, they must submit a standardised notification to their home tax authority. Cross-border tax structuring in this context means that the structure of a transaction involves two or more EU Member States or an EU Member State and a third country. In general, all types of taxes are affected, with the exception of value added tax, customs and

82 Multilateral Competent Authority Agreement on the Exchange of Country-by-Country Reports (CbC MCAA), <https://www.oecd.org/tax/automatic-exchange/about-automatic-exchange/cbc-mcaa.pdf> (accessed 20 September 2022). As of 22 November 2022, 93 countries had signed this multilateral agreement, <https://www.oecd.org/tax/beps/CbC-MCAA-Signatories.pdf> (accessed 28 November 2022).

83 Council Directive (EU) 2018/822 of 25 May 2018 amending Directive 2011/16/EU as regards the mandatory automatic exchange of information in the field of taxation on reportable cross-border arrangements (OJ 2018, L 139/1).

excise duties. Income taxes, profit taxes, property taxes and also inheritance or gift taxes are all affected. In order not to let the definition of a "reportable structure" get out of hand, only structures and arrangements that fulfil certain characteristics (so-called "hallmarks") are to be reported. Some of these characteristics are only fulfilled if they are accompanied by tax saving (e.g., acquisition of a loss-bearing company or conversion of ordinarily taxed income into capital gains that are taxed at a lower rate or not at all). This is also referred to as the main benefit test. Other features do not require actual tax savings. In the area of transparency, these are, for example, structures or instructions that serve to circumvent the AEOI or that make use of a non-transparent or obfuscated chain of beneficial owners.

In each case, the identity of the intermediary and the taxpayer (name, address, TIN) must be reported, as well as a description of the structure or arrangement, its legal basis, the hallmark concerned and the value of the arrangement (presumed tax savings). The information obtained from the respective notifications is exchanged by the Member States on a quarterly basis. This enables all EU Member States to gain insight into those designs and structures which are planned or implemented in another Member State but which at the same time have an impact on taxation in their own country. If it is not possible for the advisor or intermediary to make a report to the tax authorities, e.g., due to professional secrecy enshrined in law or in a code of professional conduct, the reporting obligation applies subsidiarily to the clients themselves. The clients must then disclose themselves, so to speak, to their home tax authorities together with their design or structure.

The notifying parties concerned, whether advisors or, as the case may be, their clients, are faced with a complex situation in terms of timing: on the one hand, notification of an affected structure or design must be made within a very short time window of only 30 days from provision or implementation. In other words, there may be a continuous number of notifications per advisor; on the other, DAC 6 had a retroactive effect. From mid-2020 onwards, in addition to ongoing notifications, all arrangements and transactions that retroactively affected the period from 25 June 2018 (when DAC 6 came into force) were to be reported once. It is self-evident that a retroactive reporting obligation dating more than two years before the actual start of application meant an enormous challenge for the advisors and financial intermediaries concerned. This is all the more so because not only structured data but also descriptive data (description of the structure, value of the structure) had to be reported.

Switzerland is not an EU Member State. On the face of it, financial intermediaries and advisors who have their legal domicile in Switzerland and do not serve their EU-resident clients through permanent establishments and branches in the EU are therefore not affected by DAC 6. However, they are indirectly affected to the extent that providing advice to EU-resident clients may give rise to a reporting obligation on the part of the clients. In this case, Swiss-resident advisors will be expected to inform their clients of the specific reporting obligations being transferred to them.

2.5 *Summary of the Historical Development of Transparency*

Thus, six major transparency initiatives (see Figure 8.3 below) were launched between 2001 and 2013. Four of these initiatives concerned mainly individuals (QI, EU taxation of savings income, FATCA and the final withholding taxes) or their foreign account relationships. In contrast, the BEPS packages of measures (the first being the CbCR package) were dedicated to transparency in the area of legal entities. As the last measure for the time being, the DAC 6 directive for reporting from 1 October 2020 completes the set of rules on transparency and also includes advisors, lawyers, auditors and financial intermediaries in the reporting system.[84]

The following schematic overview illustrates these transparency milestones once again.

3 Automatic Exchange of Information

The fifth transparency initiative on the list – the AEOI – represents the culmination of transparency efforts for the time being, particularly in terms of the amount of information exchanged. Over 100 countries worldwide have agreed to automatically exchange financial account information (see Figure 8.4 below). While the QI and FATCA regimes are effectively a 1:m relationship ("1 to m" meaning that one country (the US) entered into contractual relationships with many countries ("m")), the AEOI is an n:m relationship. That means, many countries ("n") enter into contractual relationships with essentially all other countries ("m"), thus greatly increasing the number of channels that need to be filled with information. Based on a multilateral agreement between tax authorities and because of the reciprocity of information flow provided, over 110 countries mutually exchange information about financial account holders

84 Cf. Taxation: Commission proposes postponement of taxation rules due to Coronavirus crisis, <https://ec.europa.eu/taxation_customs/news/taxation-commission-proposes-postponement-taxation-rules-due-coronavirus-crisis-2020-05-08_en> (accessed 26 September 2022).

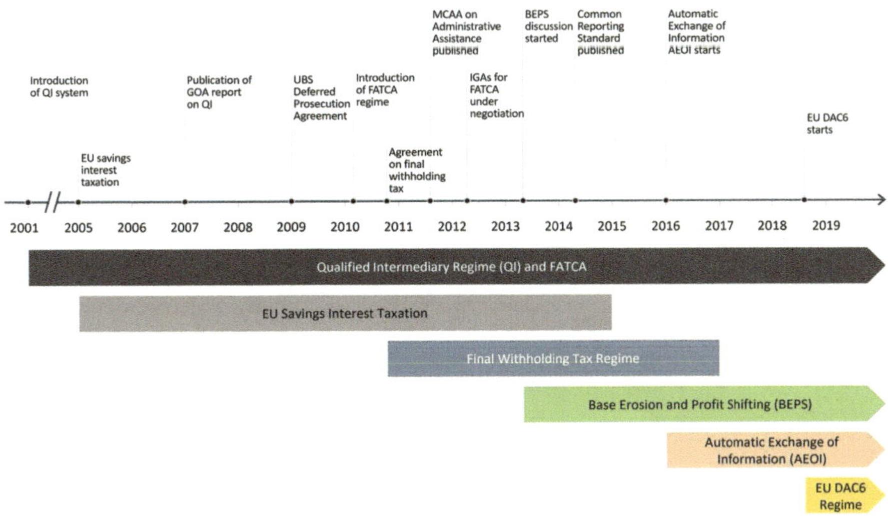

FIGURE 8.3 Milestones of transparency in the tax area (own illustration)

(see Figure 8.4 below).[85] If all 110 countries exchange information with each other, there are a total of 6,100 channels to be filled with information from both sides.[86] This consideration alone gives an idea of the scale of the AEOI and its global significance. The map below shows the countries that participate in the AEOI and have signed a multilateral agreement (as of August 2021).

Of course, it is noticeable from the above map that the US does not participate in the international automatic exchange of information. It already receives information on its own taxpayers via the FATCA regime and passes on – albeit to a very limited extent[87]– information on accounts held by persons resident in partner countries under reciprocal FATCA agreements. In this respect, the US did not and does not consider it necessary to participate in the AEOI regime.

Four years before the AEOI came into force in Switzerland, the Federal Council signalled in June 2013 that it would cooperate in the development of

85 As of 22 November 2022, 119 countries have signed the Multilateral Competent Authority Agreement. The list of signatories is available at <https://www.oecd.org/tax/exchange-of-tax-information/crs-mcaa-signatories.pdf> (accessed 28 November 2022).

86 With a number of countries equal to "n", in this case 110, there would be exactly (n+1) · n / 2 = 111 · 110/2 = 6,105 connections between the countries.

87 For example, the US does not report controlling persons who are beneficial owners behind legal entities or trust and foundation structures.

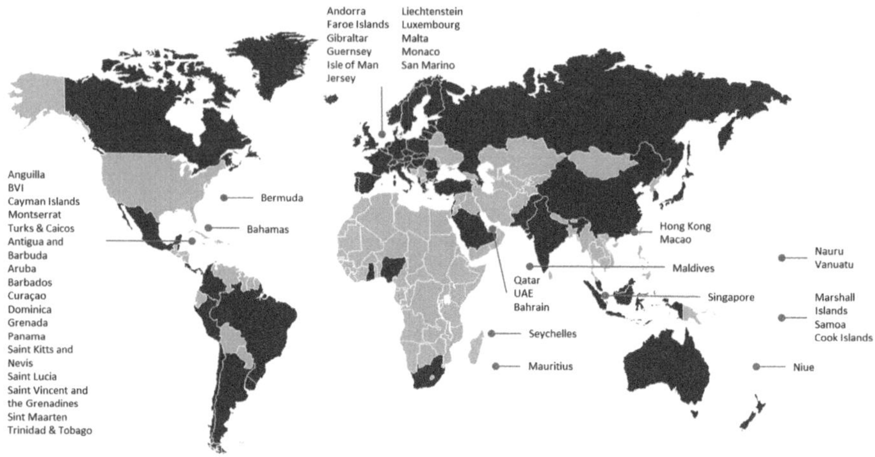

FIGURE 8.4 Countries participating in the AEOI (own illustration)

a common reporting standard under certain conditions. This was generally perceived as the beginning of the end of Swiss banking secrecy.[88] Less than three more years then passed before the "mental shift" took place – a relatively short period of time in political terms: in the 2016 spring session of the Swiss Parliament, Federal Councillor Ueli Maurer declared: "Above all, it is also a mental shift away from the banking secrecy that we have cultivated over the decades towards this exchange. This is a mental shift. Perhaps we originally approached it under pressure – we would cut our teeth on banking secrecy, we once said from the Federal Council – today we are making this change out of conviction, because we think that this AEOI standard must be met".[89] With the first data delivery to the partner States in September 2018, banking secrecy was effectively lifted for bank clients domiciled in many foreign states.[90]

3.1 *FATCA as a Blueprint for the AEOI*

The technical provisions of the AEOI cannot deny their origins. They are modelled on the FATCA model agreement and also use FATCA terminology. The

88 Cf. 'Bankgeheimnis behutsam opfern', *Neue Zürcher Zeitung* 15/16 June 2013; Schauwecker (n. 7), p. 19.

89 Votum Federal Councilor Maurer, AB 2016 p. 161 (translated by authors from German).

90 For additional background and information, refer for instance to C.B. Bühler, 'Vom Bankgeheimnis zum automatischen Informationsaustausch', in: S. Breitenmoser, B. Ehrenzeller (eds.), *Internationale Amts- und Rechtshilfe in Steuer- und Finanzmarktsachen. Aktuelle Fragen und Entwicklungen in der Praxis* (Dike, 2017), 5–23.

OECD has thus designed a set of rules for the common reporting standard (CRS) that uses FATCA as a blueprint. In particular, the AEOI has also adapted the idea of piercing the veil of legal entities or trust and foundation structures, reaching out to the beneficial owners behind them as persons subject to reporting requirements. For example, both regimes speak of "non-reporting financial institutions", "investment entities", "specified insurance companies" or "non-financial (foreign) entities".[91]

3.2 *Introduction of the Automatic Exchange of Information in Switzerland*

Various legal bases had to be adopted for the introduction of the AEOI in Switzerland: firstly, the Federal Assembly approved the *Multilateral Convention on Mutual Administrative Assistance in Tax Matters* in December 2015.[92] Its instrument of ratification was deposited with the OECD in Paris in June 2016.

Prior to this, Switzerland had already signed the Multilateral Competent Authority Agreement on the Automatic Exchange of Information on Financial Accounts (Multilateral Competent Authority Agreement, MCAA) along with 50 other countries at the plenary meeting of the Global Forum, which took place in Berlin in October 2014.[93] Together with its annex,[94] this agreement constitutes the "instruction manual" for the AEOI. It regulates the technical specifications for client identification, classification of legal entities, their underlying controlling persons as well as the granularity of the information to be reported, the form and cadence of the reports and, finally, the confidentiality and data protection requirements with which the exchanging authorities must comply. Switzerland, like other States that had already signed the MCAA in Berlin, had agreed to start collecting data in 2017 and to exchange it for the first time in 2018. This meant that Switzerland did not belong to the group of so-called early adopter countries that intended to exchange data for the first time in 2017. The explicit aim of the MCAA was to "promote tax honesty in

---

91 FATCA speaks (from a US perspective) of "Non-Financial Foreign Entities" (NFFE), while the AEOI uses the term "Non-Financial Entities" (NFE).

92 The MCAA can be found at <https://read.oecd-ilibrary.org/taxation/the-multilateral-convention-on-mutual-administrative-assistance-in-tax-matters_9789264115606-en#page1> (accessed 12 October 2022).

93 The template text in English and French can be found at <https://www.oecd.org/tax/automatic-exchange/international-framework-for-the-crs/multilateral-competent-authority-agreement.pdf> (accessed 12 October 2022).

94 The annex is the common reporting and due diligence standard for financial account information, a translation of the OECD's CRS.

international situations"[95] – the automatic reporting of foreign accounts was intended to increase the risk of detection of tax evasion in a partner country to such an extent that potential tax evasion no longer appeared feasible at all.

At the same time as the Multilateral Convention on Mutual Administrative Assistance in Tax Matters, the Federal Assembly adopted the *Federal Act on the International Automatic Exchange of Information in Tax Matters* (AEOI Act).[96] The AEOI Act and the associated Ordinance govern Switzerland-specific definitions and exceptions (e.g. rental deposit accounts), thresholds, clarifications of due diligence obligations, procedural provisions, the rights of persons subject to the reporting obligations, the treatment and utilisation of data received from abroad, as well as legal remedies and penalty provisions. In doing so, the AEOI Act created the internal legal conditions for the exchange of data with foreign tax authorities.

In contrast to other countries that decide to introduce automatic data exchange with the mutual signing of the MCAA, Switzerland has decided not to begin the exchange with individual countries until Parliament has approved the exchange with the specific country. In doing so, Switzerland wishes to ensure that the respective partner country offers a guarantee that the tax data supplied will be treated appropriately in the other country in terms of data protection, will only be used for tax purposes (principle of speciality) and that the taxpayer has been granted the possibility of regularisation/exempting self-disclosure in advance. Australia was the first country with which Switzerland concluded the AEOI based on the activation of an MCAA.[97]

Switzerland has taken a different path in the form of a bilateral agreement in its relationship with the EU and its now 27 EU Member States. Since 2008, the EU had consistently attempted to expand the scope of the EU Savings Tax Directive. Confining the reporting purely to interest payments was considered to be too restrictive. Structured products with capital protection[98] or

---

95 Preamble to the Multilateral Competent Authority Agreement on the Automatic Exchange of Financial Account Information, SR 0.653.1, OC 2016 4721 (translated by authors from German).

96 Federal Act on the International Automatic Exchange of Information in Tax Matters of 18 December 2015 (AEOI Act), SR 653.1, OC 2016 1297.

97 Cf. on behalf of other partner countries: Federal Council Dispatch of 18 November 2015 on the introduction of the automatic exchange of information on financial accounts with Australia, Fed. Gaz. 2015 8641, and Federal Decree of 31 May 2016 on the introduction of the automatic exchange of information on financial accounts with Australia, OC 2016 4795.

98 Such products usually contain a bond component (zero bond) and an option component (e.g., a call option). The option component can generate a tax-free capital gain. The bond component, on the other hand, assures the investor a guaranteed repayment amount and

capital-forming life insurance policies were not covered by the EU savings tax, despite their interest character.

In order to legally introduce the AEOI with EU Member States, the Swiss legislator used a skilful trick or short cut. The negotiations with the EU on the introduction of a mutual automatic exchange of information were conducted under great time pressure, as the OECD was simultaneously drafting its proposal for the Common Reporting Standard (CRS). In its dispatch, the Federal Council even spoke of a "temporarily precarious" situation[99] and observed that a purely technical update of the savings taxation agreement in view of the imminent introduction of the AEOI would have been incomplete in terms of content as well as disproportionately costly. Instead of running a new agreement between the EU and Switzerland through the parliamentary and editorial processes,[100] the Savings Tax Agreement, which had been signed in 2004,[101] was adapted to the requirements of the AEOI by means of an amending protocol signed on 27 May 2015.[102] In fact, it is no longer possible to speak of an amendment; in terms of content and technical details, the Savings Tax Agreement and the AEOI are so far apart that one must indeed speak of a "gutting" of the agreement. With one exception,[103] the entire content of the original agreement has been deleted and replaced by the AEOI provisions. Accordingly, there were also critical comments during the parliamentary discussions: Councillor of State Hannes Germann asked in the 2016 spring session:

interest over the term. In this respect, this is also interest income, but it was excluded from the scope of interest taxation.

99 Federal Council Dispatch of 25 November 2015 on the approval and implementation of a Protocol amending the Savings Tax Agreement between Switzerland and the EU, Fed. Gaz. 2015 9208.

100 The term "editorial processes" refers to the Swiss process whereby, if the decisions of the National Council and the Council of States on a draft decree do not match, a process to adjust or clear up these differences is launched (German term: *Differenzbereinigungsverfahren*). Such process may generally go through up to three iterations.

101 Agreement between the Swiss Confederation and the European Community providing for measures equivalent to those laid down in Council Directive 2003/48/EC on taxation of savings income in the form of interest payments (OJ 2004, L 385/28).

102 Amending Protocol to the Agreement between the European Community and the Swiss Confederation providing for measures equivalent to those laid down in Council Directive 2003/48/EC on taxation of savings income in the form of interest payments (OJ 2015, L 333/12).

103 This concerns the abolition of withholding tax on cross-border payments of dividends, interest and royalties between associated companies in relation to Switzerland.

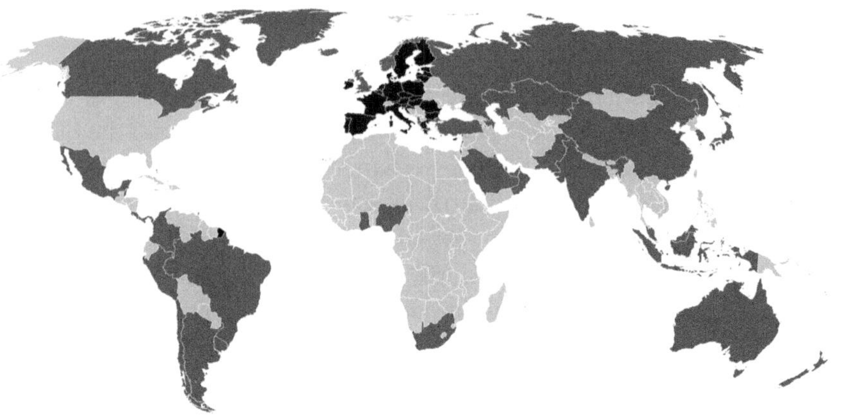

FIGURE 8.5 Switzerland's AEOI partner countries (own representation). Partner countries are shaded in dark; EU Member States to which the Protocol of Amendment applies integrally are shown in black

> One general question specifically concerns the EU, the taxation of savings income. We know we have the Savings Tax Agreement; under this legal mantle we can elegantly implement the automatic exchange of information. [...] Wouldn't the abolition of the taxation of savings currently in force, which is a real safeguard tax, be the logical consequence of the transition from the taxation of savings to the automatic exchange of information?[104]

On the basis of a bilateral treaty or based on the MCAA between the competent authorities, Switzerland currently (as of October 2021) maintains automatic data exchange with a total of 109 States or territories.[105] Their names can be found on the website of the State Secretariat for International Financial Matters (SIF)[106] or on the OECD AEOI Portal.[107] Figure 8.5 above shows these countries in a schematic way:

104 Votum Councillor of State Germann (SH), AB 2016 p. 161 (translated by authors from German).

105 Territories include, for example, the overseas communities of the Netherlands or the British Channel Islands.

106 <https://www.sif.admin.ch/sif/de/home/multilateral/steuer_informationsaust/automatischer-informationsaustausch/automatischer-informationsaustausch1.html> (accessed 25 September 2022).

107 <https://www.oecd.org/tax/automatic-exchange/international-framework-for-the-crs/exchange-relationships/> (accessed 24 September 2022).

Due to the reciprocal nature of the agreements, all of Switzerland's partner countries also send information to the SFTA on offshore accounts held by individuals or legal entities resident or domiciled in Switzerland. In addition, accounts of passive NFEs controlled by persons domiciled in Switzerland (so-called "controlling persons") are reported. However, not all partner countries require reciprocal reporting from Switzerland. In particular, some Caribbean and Middle Eastern States[108] have declared themselves to be so-called "permanent non-reciprocal jurisdictions" and refrain from receiving information on financial accounts held in Switzerland by persons or entities resident and domiciled in these States. This is because some of these countries do not know any income taxation or they do not seem to have any increased interest in obtaining information on the foreign accounts of their residents.

4 Effects of the AEOI and outlook

In contrast to the EU taxation of savings income at the time, for which the SFTA annually published meaningful statistics,[109] there had long been no statistical information published on the AEOI by the SFTA. In June 2019, the OECD released a statement saying that since 2018, more than 90 countries had exchanged information on already more than 47 million offshore accounts with an aggregate value of more than EUR 4.9 trillion (or EUR 4,900 billion) among themselves.[110] In the context of the figures on the size of the international offshore markets (see section 2.2 above), it appears that only half of the offshore funds were covered by the AEOI. This may have been because not all countries that had committed to exchanging information had started to do so in 2018. Another factor could be that US persons and entities are reported under FATCA and not under the AEOI, and that Middle Eastern assets are not reported or underreported because, for example, Qatar and the United Arab Emirates, as permanent non-reciprocal jurisdictions, forgo data submissions altogether. However, this statement was put into perspective in 2020, when the

108 Anguilla, Bahamas, Bahrain, Bermuda, British Virgin Islands, Cayman Islands, Kuwait, Marshall Islands, Nauru, Turks & Caicos Islands, Qatar, United Arab Emirates.

109 Figures are available at <https://www.estv.admin.ch/estv/de/home/allgemein/steuerstatistiken/fachinformationen/fiskaleinnahmen/eu-zinsbesteuerung.html> (accessed 28 September 2022).

110 See notification on the OECD Automatic Exchange of Information Portal, 7 June 2019. Available at <https://www.oecd.org/tax/automatic-exchange/news/implementation-of-tax-transparency-initiative-delivering-concrete-and-impressive-results.htm> (accessed 28 September 2022).

OECD again announced in a press release[111] that 84 million financial accounts had now been reported in 2019, representing a total of EUR 10 trillion in financial assets. In terms of size, this corresponds quite closely to the estimates for the entire offshore market (see again Section 2.2 above).

In October 2021, the SFTA released a statement saying that in 2021, information had been exchanged with 96 countries. Of these, 70 countries also shared information with Switzerland (reciprocal exchange of information). The remaining 26 countries, either failing to meet the international requirements on confidentiality and data security or choosing not to receive information, shared information with Switzerland but did not receive any in exchange. The SFTA further stated that it had provided information on 3.3 million financial accounts to partner States and received information on around 2.1 million accounts; the SFTA declined to quantify the amount of financial assets reported.[112]

Taken on their own, these figures are impressive, and the OECD accordingly chalked this up to the success of its initiative:

> This system of multilateral exchange created by the OECD and managed by the Global Forum is providing countries around the world, including many developing countries, with a wealth of new information, empowering their tax administrations to ensure that offshore accounts are being properly declared. Countries are going to raise much needed revenue, especially critical now in light of the current COVID-19 crisis, while moving closer to a world where there is nowhere left to hide.[113]

However, the true value – from a budgetary perspective of the participating countries – of the AEOI was already demonstrated in the run-up to its enactment and implementation: the deterrent effect of tax evasion detection, combined with quite a few national non-punitive voluntary disclosure programs, had resulted in more than EUR 95 billion in additional tax revenues (taxes, penalties and interest) in OECD and G20 countries from 2009 to 2019.[114] Most

111 See notification on the OECD Automatic Exchange of Information Portal, 30 June 2020, <https://www.oecd.org/newsroom/international-community-continues-making-progress-against-offshore-tax-evasion.htm> (accessed 28 September 2022).

112 Exchange of information with 96 countries on around 3.3 million financial accounts, <https://www.admin.ch/gov/en/start/documentation/media-releases.msg-id-85417.html> (accessed 12 October 2022).

113 *Ibid.*

114 Cf. n. 109.

of this amount is likely to have been generated in the two or three years before the introduction of the AEOI (2015 to 2017), after it became clear that the AEOI would emerge as a near-global standard for information exchange.

For Switzerland, surveys were conducted by the media among the cantonal tax offices. It emerged that between 2010 and 2019, almost 150,000 voluntary declarations were made in Switzerland, in which assets of over CHF 50 billion were disclosed. This led to additional tax revenue totalling CHF 4.4 billion.[115] Impressive as these figures may be, they are "merely" a one-off effect.

With regard to the recurring information that Switzerland receives from abroad, Swiss television reported that 2.4 million accounts were reported for 2018, the first exchange year. Evaluating this volume of data poses major challenges for the cantonal tax authorities, especially as the quality of the data is disappointing, said the head of the Bern cantonal tax office.[116]

Interestingly, reviewing the information provided by the OECD, no data or estimates can be found on how the additional tax revenues relate to the additional compliance costs of financial institutions worldwide. A cost-benefit analysis of the implementation and ongoing costs (plus the costs incurred by tax and regulatory authorities for compliance audits of financial institutions) versus the additional tax revenues is therefore unlikely to be feasible.

What can be said in principle, however, is that if the AEOI initially led to the majority of potential tax evaders disclosing undeclared funds, the additional gain in knowledge for the tax authorities from the annually recurring reports is only marginal. However, the reports generate high annual costs (system maintenance and compliance checks), especially as the AEOI data can only be used for plausibility checks and not for tax assessments. This is because the data is collected and processed according to the tax rules of the donor and not those of the recipient countries. In practice, this even increasingly leads to situations in which taxpayers are asked by their tax offices to explain why the data from AEOI reporting does not match the data in their tax returns.

Both the AEOI and the AEOI Agreement concluded between Switzerland and the EU thereby join the ranks of a series of transparency initiatives that – coming into existence under pressure from either international or supranational organisations – were rolled out globally or on a large scale and whose

---

115 Cf. D. Vonplon, 'Steuersünder legalisieren über 50 Milliarden Franken Schwarzgeld', *NZZ Online Edition* 3 February 2020, <https://www.nzz.ch/schweiz/selbstanzeige-ueber-50-milliarden-franken-schwarzgeld-legalisiert-ld.1537536> (accessed 28 September 2022).

116 Cf. SRF Tagesschau 19:30 h, 6 February 2020, with additional information at <https://www.srf.ch/news/schweiz/austausch-von-informationen-6-milliarden-franken-schwarzgeld-aufgedeckt> (accessed 28 September 2022).

costs are borne by the financial industry (and ultimately, presumably, by the financial industry's clients), whose revenues, however, benefit the participating countries' Governments.

CHAPTER 9

A Comparison between the Swiss Cohesion Payments and the EEA and Norway Grants

Benedikt Pirker

1 Introduction

Both Switzerland and the EEA EFTA States Iceland, Liechtenstein and Norway are non-EU Member States that are, nonetheless, closely linked to the EU and in particular its internal market. The present chapter focuses on a specific element common to the two different models of docking onto the internal market, but not necessarily much discussed in legal scholarship:[1] both Switzerland and the EEA EFTA States have paid contributions typically used to enhance cohesion within the EU, i.e., to further the economic and social development of disadvantaged regions. The term "cohesion payment" will be used from here onwards to describe this phenomenon to avoid any potentially confusing terminology.[2]

The topic of cohesion payments can be tackled in a variety of ways. It is suggested to focus on a comparison between the two cases, setting out first the historical development and certain facts and figures (how much is paid and who receives the funds? see below section 2). Secondly, the chapter assesses the legal framework underlying the contributions to highlight how they operate and what constraints and opportunities this framework creates for the involved States (section 3). Finally, the chapter tackles what is termed "conditionality" for the present purposes, namely the practice of contributing States to make their payments conditional upon certain facts, be they adherence to

1 As an example, in C. Baudenbacher (ed.), *The Handbook of EEA Law* (Springer, 2016), the topic is not dealt with in a specific section or chapter at all.

2 As an example, in the Swiss context, the English websites of the Swiss Confederation tend to use the somewhat generic "Swiss contribution", but also "enlargement contribution" (often in brackets) for Switzerland's first cohesion payment, and subsequently struggle to establish a uniform denomination for the second cohesion payment, see <www.eda.admin.ch/europa/en/home/verhandlungen-offene-themen/offene-themen/beitrag.html> (accessed 1 February 2022).

© KONINKLIJKE BRILL NV, LEIDEN, 2023 | DOI:10.1163/9789004529984_011

common values or the state of relations (and progress of negotiations) with the EU (section 4).

The overall red thread pursued is that cohesion payments are a borderline topic between law and politics. There is a legal framework for cohesion payments that imposes certain constraints; at the same time, significant political room for action remains. How much contributing States pay, to what extent those States at least implicitly accept to be under some sort of obligation to contribute and the way in which conditionality is used, seem to be shaped to a considerable extent by politics, namely the perspective on the relations with the EU of a contributing State. At least Norway as the biggest EEA EFTA State seems to be somewhat more inclined to perceive cohesion payments in the form of the EEA and Norway Grants as part of an overall, durable integration structure. For Switzerland, although some additional differences in the circumstances might be at play, cohesion payments seem to be predominantly a political bargaining chip in the relations with the EU and in a continuous process of negotiating and renegotiating a delicate balance of rights and obligations.

2 Historical Development, Facts and Figures

To understand cohesion payments and to compare the case of the EEA and Norway Grants with the Swiss cohesion payments, a historical and factual primer is needed. The comparison reveals parallels in the objectives and States targeted by cohesion payments, but considerable differences in the amounts paid.

2.1 *The EEA Grants and the Norway Grants*

With the European Union having established a fund for regional development already in the mid-1970s[3] and formalised the creation of structural funds to promote economic and social cohesion in the Single European Act,[4] the topic of a financial contribution of the EFTA States to disadvantaged regions within the EU also came up during the EEA negotiations.[5]

3 To a considerable extent upon the insistence of the United Kingdom; see G. Stephen, *An Awkward Partner: Britain in the European Community* (Oxford University Press, 1990), p. 56 et seq.

4 Article 23 of the Single European Act (OJ 1987, L 169/1), adding a Title V on economic and social cohesion to the then European Economic Community Treaty.

5 S. Norberg, K. Hökborg, M. Johansson and C.-D. Ehlermann, *The European Economic Area – EEA Law – A Commentary on the EEA Agreement* (Fritzes, 1993), p. 673.

From 1994 to 1998, as part of a first "Financial Mechanism", the EEA EFTA States committed to the financing of interest rate rebates on loans[6] provided by the European Investment Bank which amounted to 1.5 billion euros In addition, they provided 500 million EUR[7] in direct project support to Greece, Ireland, Northern Ireland, Portugal and Spain.[8] However, due to delays in the implementation process, only about 109 million euros could be effectively paid during this first phase.[9] The subsequent "Financial Instrument" distributed a similar amount of 119.6 million euros in project support from 1999 to 2003 to projects in the same countries.[10]

With the successive enlargements of the EU in 2004 and 2007, twelve new countries joined the EU and the EEA. Whereas Ireland and Northern Ireland no longer received funding in the phase of 2004 to 2009, the accession of countries with a significantly lower Gross Domestic Product (GDP) brought a need to substantially increase the contributions towards European cohesion. Therefore, with the agreement of the EEA EFTA States, the allocation was raised substantially to an overall 1.3 billion euros in grants supporting more than 1200 projects for this period in all the new Member States as well as in Greece, Portugal and Spain.[11]

Moreover, the Norway Grants were established as a second supplementary mechanism financed entirely by Norway. At this time, Norway and in particular, Iceland disagreed about the basis and necessity of continuous payments, with Iceland wanting to discontinue the Financial Mechanism. Under pressure from the EU side, Norway agreed to fund a separate scheme of similar size to the EEA Grants.[12] About 600 million euros of the mentioned 1.3 billion euros

6 From the 1999 to 2003 period onwards, the relevant instruments only relied on grants and no longer on interest rate rebate schemes, P. Christiansen, 'Article 117', in F. Arnesen, H.H. Fredriksen, H.P. Graver, O. Mestad and C. Vedder (eds.), *Agreement on the European Economic Area – A Commentary* (Nomos, 2018), p. 895, para. 7.

7 At that time European Currency Units (ECU).

8 Financial Mechanism Office, Final Report, Financial Mechanism 1994–1998 (EEA Grants, 2009) <eeagrants.org> (accessed 1 February 2022), p. 2. When Finland, Sweden and Austria left EFTA to join the EU, the European Commission took over responsibilities for the contributions of the three countries to the Financial Mechanism, see <https://eeagrants.org/about-us/history> (accessed 1 February 2022).

9 P. Christiansen (n. 6), p. 894, para. 4, fn. 5.

10 Financial Mechanism Office, Final Report, Financial Instrument 1999–2003 (*EEA Grants*, 2009) <eeagrants.org> (accessed 1 February 2022), p. 1.

11 Nordic Consulting Group, Final Report January 2012, End Review – EEA and Norway Grants 2004–2009 (EEA Grants, 2019), p. 10.

12 Norges offentlige utredninger, Utenfor og innenfor – Norges avtaler med EU, 2012:2 (Regjeringen, 2012) <www.regjeringen.no/contentassets/5d3982d042a2472eb1b20639cd8b2341/no/pdfs/nou201220120002000dddpdfs.pdf> (accessed 1 February 2022), p. 762.

were thus covered by the EEA Financial Mechanism and the remainder by the Norway Grants. In the case of the Norway Grants, these were established at least partly in parallel with negotiations on improved market access for seafood as an area in which the EEA Agreement did not provide for full market access.[13]

For the period of 2009–2014, the funding granted by the EEA Grants and the Norway Grants amounted to 1.8 billion EUR, the former contributing about 993 million euros and the latter about 804 million EUR.[14] After its accession in 2013, Croatia was added as a beneficiary country of the grants in 2014. This funding period was also marked by a move from a project-focused approach to a programme-focused approach in the phase of 2009–2014, with observers noting certain advantages (like possible joint overall objectives and possible synergies), but also disadvantages (decreased focus on specific locations and targeted groups).[15]

During the funding period of 2014 to 2021, the EEA Grants amounted to about 1.55 billion euros and the Norway Grants to 1.25 billion euros.[16] Spain was no longer a beneficiary country, and Greece and Portugal no longer received funding under the Norway Grants.[17] Once again, the negotiations of the EEA and Norway Grants were accompanied by parallel negotiations on improved access for Norwegian and Icelandic seafood to the EU internal market;[18] the example of the 2014–2021 funding period also shows that the share of the EEA Grants funded by Iceland (about 3%) and Liechtenstein (about 1%) is very limited (about 4% of the overall funding).[19] The funding period was prolonged to seven years as negotiations were only finalised after the beginning of the period and as a more sustainable development and execution of programmes was expected because of such a prolonged funding period.[20] The implementation

13 Norwegian Ministry of Foreign Affairs, EEA and Norway Grants – Solidarity and Cooperation in Europe, Meld. St. 20 (2011–2012) Report to the Storting (white paper), p. 5.

14 Ecorys, Final Report, End Review of the EEA and Norway Grants 2009–2014 (EEA Grants, 2019) <eeagrants.org>, p. 10.

15 Nordic Consulting Group (n. 11), p. 7.

16 EEA Grants and Norway Grants, Blue Book Priority Sectors and Programme Areas 2014–2021 (EEA Grants, 2019) <eeagrants.org> (accessed 1 February 2022), 1.

17 P. Christiansen (n. 6), p. 898, para. 19.

18 Liechtenstein's informal "compensation" took the form of regular extensions of its partial exemption from the right of free residence for EU citizens. The author thanks Georges Baur for this comment.

19 Norwegian Government, Agreement between Norway and EU on EEA and Norway Grants and tariff-free quotas for fish, Press release, 20 July 2015.

20 Prop. 119 S (2015–2016), Proposisjon til Stortinget (forslag til stortingsvedtak), Samtykke til ratifikasjon av avtale mellom EØS/EFTA-statene og EU om en EØS-finansieringsordning

period of this phase extends until 2024.[21] Funds are divided between country-specific allocations and a global fund for regional cooperation funded both by the EEA Grants and the Norway Grants, the latter fund is supposed to promote youth employment and to a lesser extent, regional cooperation, including with neighbouring (non-EU) countries.[22] Also, during the funding phase 2014–2021, the programme-based approach is maintained, but there is an increasing focus on fewer, albeit larger programmes.[23]

This overview shows that in particular the enlargement of the EU has been the major influencing factor in the development of the EEA and Norway Grants. Introduced as a rather minor-scale, temporary measure, these financial mechanisms evolved with an increasing number of beneficiary States and a substantial rise in the amounts involved. In this context, clear comparisons are difficult. If one takes, for example, the contributions that the EU Member States pay, the power of comparison is weakened by the complexity that EU Member States provide gross contributions from which one has to deduce transfers from the EU, but also by other contributions EEA EFTA States pay such as in the case of EU research programmes.[24] Grossly simplified, one could calculate that for about twenty-five years of EEA integration Norway as the main contributor has paid roughly 6 billion euros for very comprehensive access to the EU's internal market (the lion's share of this amount after the 2004 and 2007 enlargements).

2.2 *The Swiss Cohesion Payments*

Similar to the case of the EEA EFTA States, a distinction must be made between other contributions paid by Switzerland to the EU to participate in various programmes and agencies and the Cohesion Payments.[25] Only the latter will be covered in this contribution.

2014–2021, avtale med EU om en norsk finansieringsordning 2014–2021 og tilleggsprotokoll til frihandelsavtalen mellom Norge og Det europeiske økonomiske fellesskap om handel med fisk, alle av 3. mai 2016 (*Regjeringen* 2016) <www.regjeringen.no/contentassets/b3d3160646104ccbfb1e4d285d37de8/no/pdfs/prp201520160119000dddpdfs.pdf> (accessed 1 February 2022), p. 9.

21 EEA Grants and Norway Grants (n. 16), p. 5.

22 Prop. 119 S (2015–2016) (n. 20), p. 16.

23 P. Christiansen (n. 6), p. 899, para 24.

24 *Ibid.*, p. 893, para 4.

25 For a comprehensive overview of such "other" payments in comparison, see, e.g., a report by the Swiss Federal Council drafted based on a parliamentary request, Swiss Parliament, Interpellation no. 19.4008, 'Aktualisierte Zusammenstellung aller Zahlungen und Beiträge der Schweiz an die EU' (Parlament, 11 September 2019), <www.parlament.ch/fr/ratsbetrieb/suche-curia-vista/geschaeft?AffairId=20194008> (accessed 1 February 2022).

With the accession of ten new Member States to the EU in 2004, discussions intensified in the relations between Switzerland and the EU on a contribution of Switzerland to these States. Based on a Memorandum of Understanding (MoU) of 2006,[26] the Swiss legislature adopted the Federal Act on Cooperation with the States of Eastern Europe 2016.[27] Although opponents of the law successfully requested a referendum, the latter resulted in a clear yes (53,4% of the votes).[28] In 2007, the Swiss Parliament thus approved the framework credit of 1 billion Swiss Francs.[29] In the same year (and in 2010 and 2015 after the accession of Romania and Bulgaria and Croatia, respectively), bilateral framework agreements were concluded with the new EU Member States. In 2009[30] and in 2014,[31] the Swiss Parliament approved framework credits for Romania and Bulgaria (257 million Swiss Francs) and Croatia (45 million Swiss Francs). The respective commitment periods ended for the first ten new EU Member States in 2012, for Romania and Bulgaria in 2014 and for Croatia in 2017. Project implementation for the EU10 ended in 2017.

Evaluations of the implementation of the first Swiss Cohesion Payment showed an overall positive picture. Many of the 210 projects that had been financed received good marks; criticism was rather focused on the fact that there were too many projects of insufficient size.[32]

The question of a second cohesion payment arose. For this purpose, the Swiss Parliament had to renew the Federal Act on Cooperation with the States

---

26 See more in section 3.2.

27 SR 974.1. This act is based on an earlier federal act dating back already to 1995 which can be seen as part of the Federal Council's strategy of presenting such payments as a 'normal' part of bilateral economic development cooperation with Central and Eastern Europe and to play down a potential perception as paying a price or fee for EU integration. The author thanks Georges Baur for this comment.

28 Bundesratsbeschluss vom 9. Januar 2007 über das Ergebnis der Volksabstimmung vom 26. November 2006, BBl 2007 451.

29 Bundesbeschluss vom 14. Juni 2007 über den Beitrag der Schweiz zur Verringerung der wirtschaftlichen und sozialen Ungleichheiten in der erweiterten Europäischen Union, BBl 2007 4951.

30 Bundesbeschluss vom 7. Dezember 2009 über den Beitrag der Schweiz zugunsten von Bulgarien und Rumänien zur Verringerung der wirtschaftlichen und sozialen Ungleichheiten in der erweiterten Europäischen Union, BBl 2009 9131.

31 Bundesbeschluss vom 11. Dezember 2014 über den Beitrag der Schweiz zugunsten von Kroatien zur Verringerung der wirtschaftlichen und sozialen Ungleichheiten in der erweiterten Europäischen Union, BBl 2014 9719.

32 Association suisse de politique étrangère, 'Fiche téchnique Suisse – UE: La contribution de cohésion à l'Union européenne: chère ou bon marché?' (SGA, January 2018), <www.sga-aspe.ch/wp-content/uploads/2018/01/SGA_FICHE-TECHNIQUE-SUISSE-UE_10.pdf> (accessed 1 February 2022), pp. 2–3.

of Eastern Europe, which it did in 2016[33] with the act entering into force the following year, but for a limited period until 2024. In 2018 the Federal Council published its Dispatch on the second Swiss Contribution to provide reasons for Parliament to adopt the relevant federal decision that would allow for actual payment.[34]

An important element here is that two decisions had to be adopted to tackle separate issues. A first decision was needed with respect to cohesion payments of about 1047 million Swiss Francs for the thirteen EU Member States who acceded since 2004. A second decision had to provide for 190 million Swiss Francs that could be used also in the other EU Member States for measures in the area of migration, notably to improve the operation of the Schengen and Dublin legal regimes in which Switzerland participates via association agreements.[35]

After a long debate, the Swiss Parliament finally adopted the two federal decisions[36] in late 2019, thereby authorising the spending of the funds for the Second Cohesion Payment. The decision on cohesion was, however, limited, first, in that financial engagements had to be undertaken within five years[37] and at the latest with the expiry of the underlying Federal Act at the end of 2024 and, more importantly, subject to the condition that the EU would not take discriminatory measures against Switzerland.[38]

---

33 Bundesgesetz vom 30. September 2016 über die Zusammenarbeit mit den Staaten Osteuropas, AS 2017 3219.

34 Botschaft vom 28. September 2018 zum zweiten Schweizer Beitrag an ausgewählten EU-Mitgliedstaaten zur Verringerung der wirtschaftlichen und sozialen Ungleichheit in der erweiterten EU sowie zur Unterstützung von Massnahmen im Bereich der Migration, BBl 2018 6665.

35 *Ibid.* pp. 6666 and 6693. This decision is based on the Swiss Law on Asylum (AsylG, SR 142.31) and therefore different timeframes can apply.

36 Bundesbeschluss vom 3. Dezember 2019 über den zweiten Schweizer Beitrag an ausgewählte EU-Mitgliedstaaten zur Verringerung der wirtschaftlichen und sozialen Ungleichheiten in der erweiterten EU (Rahmenkredit Kohäsion), BBl 2020 757, and Bundesbeschluss über den zweiten Schweizer Beitrag an ausgewählte EU-Mitgliedstaaten zur Unterstützung von Massnahmen im Bereich der Migration (Rahmenkredit Migration), BBl 2020 759.

37 Under the decision on migration commitments can be undertaken for ten years.

38 BBl 2020 757 (n. 36). See for more information on the parliamentary debate Swiss Parliament, Item No. 18.067 '1. Bundesbeschluss über den zweiten Schweizer Beitrag an ausgewählte EU-Mitgliedstaaten zur Verringerung der wirtschaftlichen und sozialen Ungleichheiten in der erweiterten EU (Rahmenkredit Kohäsion)' (Parlament, 3 December 2019) <www.parlament.ch/en/ratsbetrieb/amtliches-bulletin/amtliches-bulletin-die-verhandlungen?SubjectId=47818> (accessed 1 February 2022).

This condition stems from a dispute between the EU and Switzerland: the EU Commission had not prolonged its (unilateral) recognition of the equivalency of Swiss stock exchange regulation in mid-2019 in an attempt to increase the political pressure on Switzerland to agree to make progress on the Draft Institutional Agreement by this – rather unrelated – measure.[39] The Swiss Federal Council understood "discriminatory measures" in this context as measures falling within the scope of an international law prohibition of discrimination, in this case WTO law. In its view, it was hard to see an adequate legal justification for the different treatment of Switzerland compared to other partner States of the EU.[40] After the Federal Council decided to terminate the negotiations of the Draft Institutional Agreement,[41] relations between Switzerland and the EU quickly deteriorated. As a consequence, the Federal Council proposed to the Swiss Federal Parliament to authorise the spending for the Second Cohesion Payment, thereby abandoning the non-discrimination condition.[42] After some quarrels between the chambers,[43] the Parliament agreed to this proposal end of September 2021,[44] clearing the way for the negotiations of a new Memorandum of Understanding between Switzerland and the EU which

39 See in more detail B. Pirker, L. Matter, 'Europarecht: Schweiz–Europäische Union', (2020) 30 *Swiss Review of International and European Law* 75, p. 82. See also the contribution by M. Oesch and M. Brugger in this volume.

40 See with more details the Swiss Federal Council's reply to a parliamentary inquiry, Swiss Parliament, Interpellation no. 194299, Diskriminierende Massnahmen der Europäischen Union gegenüber der Schweiz, <www.parlament.ch/de/ratsbetrieb/suche-curia-vista/geschaeft?AffairId=20194299> (accessed 1 February 2022). More sceptical on whether there is indeed discrimination are C. Tobler, J. Beglinger, *Tobler/Beglinger-Brevier zum institutionellen Abkommen Schweiz-EU*, edition 2021-05.1 (2 May 2021), <www.eur-charts.eu/wp-content/uploads/2021/05/Tobler-Beglinger-Brevier-Institutionelles-Abkommen_2021-05.1.pdf> (accessed 1 February 2022), p. 62.

41 See Press Release of the Federal Council, Das Institutionelle Abkommen Schweiz-EU wird nicht abgeschlossen (26 May 2021) <https://www.admin.ch/gov/de/start/dokumentation/medienmitteilungen.msg-id-83705.html> (accessed 1 February 2022); see also the accompanying report of the Federal Council 'Bericht betreffend die Verhandlungen über ein institutionelles Abkommen zwischen der Schweiz und der EU' (26 May 2021), <https://www.newsd.admin.ch/newsd/message/attachments/66828.pdf> (accessed 1 February 2022).

42 Press Release of the Federal Council, 'Europapolitik: Bundesrat überweist Botschaft zur Freigabe des zweiten Schweizer Beitrags' (11 August 2021), <https://www.admin.ch/gov/de/start/dokumentation/medienmitteilungen.msg-id-84668.html> (accessed 1 February 2022).

43 F. Schäfer, 'Taktische Winkelzüge im Streit um die Kohäsionsmilliarde', *Neue Zürcher Zeitung* 28 September 2021.

44 F. Schäfer, 'Die Hauruckübung glückt – nach harten Debatten gibt das Parlament die Kohäsionsmilliarde frei', *Neue Zürcher Zeitung* 30 September 2021.

were concluded successfully in late November 2021.[45] The signature of the Memorandum will follow after the procedures of approval on the EU side have been concluded. The next step is the negotiations of the bilateral implementation agreements with the partner States.[46]

At this point, two observations can be made. First, in the Swiss case, like in that of the EEA EFTA States, cohesion payments are inextricably bound to EU enlargement. The more complex second point is that it appears that Switzerland seems to be paying "much less" than, e.g., Norway in terms of its cohesion payments. There are some studies supporting this impression. According to a 2016 study based on the previous years and comparing EU Member States with selected non-Member States, Switzerland pays about 0,02% of its GDP or 12 euros per capita in annual net financial contribution, as opposed to Norway which pays about 0,16% of GDP and 115 euros per capita under this calculation.[47] Another 2018 report notes that if a yearly perspective is adopted, Switzerland has paid about 130 million euros per year since 2006, whereas the EEA EFTA States have paid around 300 million Euro annually from 2009–2014 and Norway is paying around 400 million euros per year for the period 2014–2021, about three times more than Switzerland.[48] There may certainly be difficulties or simplifications with these sorts of calculations that economists may be better placed to identify. Nonetheless, based on the amounts involved, the overall impression is hard to shake that Switzerland is paying significantly less. It should nonetheless be noted that these disparities are not entirely without foundation. Because of the chosen sectoral approach of the bilateral agreements, Switzerland's access to the EU internal market is not as extensive as that of the EEA EFTA States. In this light, the EU seems to accept, as a matter of principle, that Swiss Cohesion Payments are lower than the EEA Grants and Norway Grants.[49] At the same time, a 2019 study suggests

45 See on the approval of the Federal Council Press Release of the Federal Council, Bundesrat genehmigt Memorandum of Understanding mit der EU und will zweiten Schweizer Beitrag rasch umsetzen (24 November 2021), <https://www.admin.ch/gov/de/start/dokumentation/medienmitteilungen.msg-id-86078.html> (accessed 1 February 2022).

46 On these agreements see also section 3.2.

47 Z. Darvas, *Single market access from outside the EU: three key prerequisites* (Bruegel, 19 July 2016), <www.bruegel.org/2016/07/single-market-access-from-outside-the-eu-three-key-prerequisites/> (accessed 1 February 2022).

48 Association suisse de politique étrangère, Fiche téchnique Suisse – UE: La contribution de cohésion à l'Union européenne: chère ou bon marché? (SGA, January 2018), <https://www.sga-aspe.ch/wp-content/uploads/2018/01/SGA_FICHE-TECHNIQUE-SUISSE-UE_10.pdf> (accessed 1 February 2022), 2.

49 C. Tobler, J. Beglinger (n. 40), p. 62.

that Switzerland benefits more than EU Member States from EU integration in economic terms.[50] It appears thus that the amount of cohesion payments depends to a significant extent on situational circumstances and the conduct of negotiations.

3 Legal Framework and Governance

Turning to the law, the present chapter – due mostly to reasons of space and ease of comparison – presently focuses less on national legal frameworks, but rather on the international elements of the legal framework regulating cohesion payments. It becomes visible that although in the case of the EEA and Norway Grants, the EEA legal framework and thus multilateral elements are important, at the end of the day, the content of the regulatory framework seems comparable and is to a significant extent structured in a bilateral way (contributor State – beneficiary State), leaving significant discretion for the contributor State, but also to the beneficiary State called to implement the financed projects and programmes. Payments follow this bilateral structure and never go to "the EU", but are always channelled from the contributor State to the beneficiary State directly. It is notable that – contrary to the EU's wish as examined later – the contributing States tend to insist generally that the legal framework does not impose a continuous obligation of cohesion payments, even if they agree to such payments.

3.1 *The EEA Grants and the Norway Grants*

The EEA Grants and the Norway Grants are regulated through several instruments. In examining this framework, we encounter elements of discretion for the EEA EFTA States, but also elements where the EU side somewhat imposes its will.

Generally, the EEA Agreement regulates the "Financial Mechanism" in its Part VIII. The overall objective is the reduction of economic and social disparities to ensure a harmonious development of the EEA; the relevant Article 115 EEA Agreement explicitly takes note at the same time of "relevant provisions" of the Agreement including "certain of the arrangements regarding agriculture and fisheries". This reference is to be read as relating to Protocol 42,

50 G. Mion, D. Ponattu, *Estimating economic benefits of the Single Market for European countries and regions* (Bertelsmann-Stiftung, 2019), <www.bertelsmann-stiftung.de/fileadmin/files/BSt/Publikationen/GrauePublikationen/EZ_Study_SingleMarket.pdf> (accessed 1 February 2022), p. 11.

which refers to bilateral agreements on trade in agricultural products signed at the same time as the EEA Agreement and which provided certain important advantages to less-developed EU Member States as a tool to counter existing regional disparities.[51] Since the beginning, the Financial Mechanism thus always has had to be understood in light of solutions found in the field of agriculture and fisheries.[52] Cohesion as an idea also appears in the sixth recital of the EEA Agreement which provides that the agreement aims at promoting a harmonious development of the European Economic Area and that there is a need to contribute to the reduction of economic and social regional disparities.

The EEA Agreement itself leaves quite some discretion. Article 116 merely provides that a financial mechanism is to be established that should supplement the EU's efforts already deployed in this regard.[53] Article 117 and its later revised versions refer to the subsequent Protocols 38, 38a, 38b, 38c and the Addendum to Protocol 38b that contain the governing provisions of the EEA Grants.[54]

The first Financial Mechanism was created in the form of Protocol 38 to the EEA Agreement. After the expiry of the previous Financial Mechanism, despite the initial disagreement of the EEA EFTA States, the EU side insisted that financial payments should continue, which resulted in negotiations of the new financial instrument for the period from 1999 to 2003, even though for example, Norway did not concede that there was a clear legal-formal obligation of repeated payments.[55] Legally, this instrument took the form of an EEA Joint Committee Decision amending Protocol 31 to the EEA Agreement

51 S. Norberg (n. 5), p. 4.

52 P. Christiansen (n. 6), p. 892 para. 2.

53 This reference is typically read as referring to the EU's European Structural and Investment Funds.

54 The norm has accordingly been revised over the years to add additional protocols, see Agreements in the form of exchange of letters concerning the provisional application of the Agreement on the participation of the Czech Republic, the Republic of Estonia, the Republic of Cyprus, the Republic of Hungary, the Republic of Latvia, the Republic of Lithuania, the Republic of Malta, the Republic of Poland, the Republic of Slovenia, and the Slovak Republic in the European Economic Area and the provisional application of four related agreements (OJ 2004, L 130/3); Agreement on the participation of the Republic of Bulgaria and Romania in the European Economic Area (OJ 2007, L221/15); Agreement between the European Union, Iceland, the Principality of Liechtenstein and the Kingdom of Norway on an EEA Financial Mechanism 2009–2014 [2010] OJ L 291/4; and Agreement on the participation of the Republic of Croatia in the European Economic Area and three related agreements (OJ 2014, L 170/5).

55 Norges offentlige utredninger (n. 12), p. 764.

on cooperation in specific fields outside the four freedoms.[56] The 2004–2009 phase was again regulated by a new Protocol 38a[57] as far as the EEA Grants are were concerned. The Norway Grants are not formally linked to the EEA Financial Mechanism or even the EEA legal framework *stricto sensu*, but were established as the so-called Norwegian Financial Mechanism in a separate bilateral agreement between the EU and Norway.[58] Both the EU and Norway tried to establish a formal link with EEA law during each relevant negotiation round, but Liechtenstein and Iceland refused as this would have meant to accept and support the additional obligation by Norway in 2004 in the form of the Norway Grants and would have created an unwanted precedent in their view.[59] Nonetheless, the context of and connection to the EEA Financial Mechanism cannot be missed. The agreement, for example, refers in Article 1 to Norway's participation as an EFTA State in the EEA as the basis of the commitments undertaken by Norway. Also, the implementation of the EEA Grants and the Norway Grants has to be "closely coordinated".[60]

This practice continued. In the 2009–2014 phase, Protocol 38 b[61] laid down the rules for the EEA Grants, whereas a new bilateral agreement between the EU and Norway regulated the Norway Grants.[62] It is in this phase that transparency, accountability and cost efficiency were taken into account more than in the past, while increased attention was paid to the monitoring and control of programmes.[63] Finally, for 2014–2021, Protocol 38c lays down the relevant agreement on the EEA Grants,[64] whereas the Norway Grants for

56 Decision of the Joint Committee No 47/2000 of 19 May 2000 amending Protocol 31 to the EEA Agreement on cooperation in specific fields outside the four freedoms (OJ 2000, L 174/59). This Protocol is for example also the basis for the participation of the EEA EFTA states in the EU's research programmes.

57 Protocol inserted in the EEA Agreement by the 2004 EEA Enlargement Agreement (OJ 2004, L 130/3) (n. 48), amended by the 2007 EEA Enlargement Agreement (OJ 2007, L 221/15).

58 Agreement between the Kingdom of Norway and the European Community on a Norwegian Financial Mechanism for the period 2004 – 2009 (EEA Grants, 2004), <eeagrants.org> (accessed 1 February 2022).

59 The author thanks Georges Baur for this comment.

60 Article 7(1) of Protocol 38a and Article 7 of the bilateral agreement (n. 52). This approach has been followed also in later funding phases, see, e.g., Article 9(1) of Protocol 38 c.

61 Agreement between the European Union, Iceland, Liechtenstein and Norway on an EEA Financial Mechanism for the period 2009–2014 (OJ 2010, L 291/4).

62 *Ibid.*, 10ff.

63 P. Christiansen (n. 6), p. 898, para 16.

64 Agreement between the European Union, Iceland, the Principality of Liechtenstein and the Kingdom of Norway on an EEA Financial Mechanism 2014–2021 (OJ 2016, L 141/3).

this period are regulated again in a bilateral agreement between the EU and Norway.[65]

Some elements of continuity and change over the years should be noted. Objectives and priorities of the Financial Mechanisms were always coordinated with the EU Commission, leading to priorities developing over the years.[66] Throughout the lifecycle of the Financial Mechanisms, there are continuous consultations between EEA EFTA States and the EU Commission to ensure complementarity and synergies with the EU cohesion policies.[67]

Moreover, already during the Protocol 38 phase, the EEA EFTA States contributions never entered the EU budget but were paid directly, among others so that the origin of funds could be clearly identified,[68] in order to strengthen bilateral relations between beneficiary States and EEA EFTA States and in order to allow the latter to be clearly identified as the origin of funding.[69] An additional benefit is the potential positive impact on public opinion in the contributing States. Since Protocol 38b, this goal of strengthening the EEA EFTA States' relations with the beneficiary States has been added explicitly.[70] At the same time, the initial political decision on what should be the beneficiary EU Member States is typically made by the EU side without much say of the EEA EFTA States.[71]

As an element of change and as a potential legal basis for conditionality measures, Protocol 38c for the 2014–2021 funding period provides for the first time an explicit requirement that all programmes and activities "shall be based on the common values of respect for human dignity, freedom, democracy, equality, the rule of law and the respect for human rights including the rights of persons belonging to minorities".[72] This clause undoubtedly takes up the common values of the EU enshrined in Article 2 TEU.

---

65 Agreement between the Kingdom of Norway and the European Union on a Norwegian Financial Mechanism for the period 2014–2021 (OJ 2016, L 141/11).

66 See for these priorities, respectively, Financial Mechanism Office, Final Report, Financial Mechanism 1994–1998 (n. 8) 2; Financial Mechanism Office, Final Report, Financial Instrument 1999–2003 (n. 10), p. 1; P. Christiansen (n. 6), p. 897, para 13. See also Nordic Consulting Group (n. 11) 10; Ecorys, Final Report (n. 14), pp. 69–70; EEA Grants and Norway Grants (n. 16), p. 1.

67 Article 4(2) of Protocol 38c.

68 P. Christiansen (n. 6) 895 para 5.

69 See, with examples, Norges offentlige utredninger (n. 12), p. 765.

70 See Article 1(1) of Protocol 38b (and also Protocol 38c).

71 Norges offentlige utredninger (n. 12), p. 764.

72 Article 1(2) of Protocol 38c.

In terms of governance, in the case of the EEA Grants, the Financial Mechanism Committee assembles representatives of the foreign ministries of the EEA EFTA States. It draws up policies and guidelines to implement the financial contributions, decides on grants and ensures their monitoring and evaluation.[73] In the case of the Norway Grants, the Norwegian Foreign Ministry acts alone.[74] While application procedures are similar, under the Norway Grants separate bilateral agreements are drawn up between Norway and the beneficiary State.[75]

Whereas in the early phases the European Investment Bank managed the contributions on behalf of the EEA EFTA States,[76] in 2004, the Financial Mechanism Office was created as an administrative body to assist the management of the EEA Grants and the Norway Grants; it forms part of the EFTA Secretariat in Brussels, but operates independently.[77]

A final important element pertains to the Memoranda of Understanding (MoU) which are signed as bilateral agreements between a beneficiary State and the contributing States and which provide the operational framework of financial contributions.[78] Such an MoU designates a National Focal Point, i.e., the entities responsible for implementation at the national level and their functions, and specifies the programme areas and programmes funded in a beneficiary State.[79] Often these Focal Points are located within ministries. National Focal Points act as representative of the beneficiary State towards the Financial Mechanism Committee, but also as a contact point for the Financial

73 See, e.g., the Regulation on the implementation of the European Economic Area (EEA) Financial Mechanism 2014–2021 adopted by the EEA Financial Mechanism Committee pursuant to Article 10.5 of Protocol 38c to the EEA Agreement on 8 September 2016 and confirmed by the Standing Committee of the EFTA States on 23 September 2016 (EEA Grants, 2019), <eeagrants.org> (accessed 1 February 2022).

74 See, e.g., the Regulation on the implementation of the Norwegian Financial Mechanism 2014–2021 adopted by the Norwegian Ministry of Foreign Affairs pursuant to Article 10.5 of the Agreement between the Kingdom of Norway and the European Union on a Norwegian Financial Mechanism for the period 2014–2021 on 23 September 2016 (EEA Grants, 2019), <eeagrants.org> (accessed 1 February 2022).

75 P. Christiansen (n. 6), p. 901, para. 31.

76 *Ibid.*, p. 895 para. 5.

77 Decision of the Standing Committee of the EFTA States No 1/2004/SC of 5 February 2004; Decision of the Standing Committee of the EFTA States No 6/2010/SC of 9 December 2010 extending the tasks of the Office for the EEA Financial Mechanism and the Norwegian Financial Mechanism.

78 Article 10 (3) of Protocol 38c.

79 P. Christiansen (n. 6), p. 902, para. 35.

Mechanism Office, in particular in cases where there are tensions over how grants are to be spent in light of the MoU.[80]

While a large degree of responsibility is thus given to the beneficiary State, based on Protocol 38c, the beneficiary State must ensure control over the sound implementation and management of projects. The relevant EEA EFTA State is allowed to carry out additional controls. The beneficiary State must provide assistance in such cases. As a worst-case scenario, the EFTA State may suspend financing and require recovery of funds in the case of irregularities.[81]

With regard to dispute settlement, both the EEA Grants and the Norway Grants Regulations are subject to Norwegian law with regard to the cooperation between the Financial Mechanisms and the beneficiary States.[82] This is primarily due to the fact that the Norwegian Financial Supervision Authority is competent for the audits of the Norway Grants.[83] All parties waive their rights to bring "disputes related to the programme agreement" before any "national or international court" and agree to settle disputes in an amicable manner.[84] If a National Focal Point does not comply with a demand for reimbursement of funds to the Financial Mechanism Committee or a dispute related to such a demand arises, the parties can bring the dispute before the Oslo District Court.[85]

The governing framework and legal bases of cooperation in the context of the EEA and Norway Grants thus exhibit both elements of significant constraint and coordination with the EU, but also elements of discretion and bilateralism for the EEA EFTA States in their relations with the beneficiary States. Put somewhat bluntly, the Commission decides at the political level on the beneficiary countries and coordinates with the EEA EFTA States on the priorities to be pursued. At the same time, EEA EFTA States contributions are paid directly to the relevant beneficiary States. The EEA EFTA States can thus openly use them to strengthen bilateral relations with these States. Moreover, the implementation

80 See for examples of such tensions Norges offentlige utredninger (n. 12) 766, P. Christiansen (n. 6), p. 903, para 36.

81 See Article 10(3)b, c and d Protocol 38c.

82 Article 14(1) of the Regulation on the implementation of the European Economic Area (EEA) Financial Mechanism 2014–2021 (n. 67). Article 14 of the Regulation on the implementation of the Norwegian Financial Mechanism 2014–2021 (n. 68) is practically identically phrased.

83 In the case of the EEA Grants, the Norwegian authority cooperates with the authorities of Liechtenstein and Iceland. The author thanks Georges Baur for this comment.

84 Article 14(2) Regulation on the implementation of the European Economic Area (EEA) Financial Mechanism 2014–2021 (n. 67).

85 *Ibid.*, Article 14(3).

and dispute settlement phases are largely bilateral, with no involvement of, e.g., the EFTA Court or the EFTA Surveillance Authority (ESA), which leaves a lot of discretion to the beneficiary State and the contributing State.

3.2 *The Swiss Cohesion Payments*

In contrast to the situation of the EEA Grants, in particular, the international legal basis of the Swiss Cohesion Payments are mere Memoranda of Understanding. The first such Memorandum of Understanding was established in 2006 (hereinafter MoU 2006) between Switzerland and the EU, with the Swiss side emphasising the non-binding nature of the document as a matter of international law.[86] On the EU side, the European Court of Justice similarly classified the MoU 2006 in a legal dispute between EU institutions over questions of competences as an external action measure, but also as a "non-binding agreement".[87] It has nonetheless been published in the section for legislative acts of the *Official Journal of the European Union* (though as a legal act that does not require formal publication).[88]

The preamble of the MoU 2006 emphasises the close links between Switzerland and the EU and the fact that EU enlargement contributes to safeguarding "peace, freedom, stability and prosperity in Europe", for which the Swiss Federal Council is "determined to demonstrate the support" of Switzerland. The MoU 2006 then sets out which countries receive which amounts of funding and the funding guidelines and areas.[89] There are specific provisions on regular communication and coordination in policy matters between the EU Commission and the Federal Council, regarding the compatibility between projects and programs of both sides; cooperation and co-financing of projects and programmes is possible.[90] The concrete selection of projects and programmes is nonetheless decided by the Federal Council, but in agreement with the beneficiary States and taking into account their requests.[91]

86 Interestingly enough, the German, French and Italian language versions of the relevant Department of Foreign Affairs' website state this explicitly, as opposed to the English language version which contains no such text and simply provides a link to the text of the memorandum, see <www.eda.admin.ch/europa/en/home/bilaterale-abkommen/abkommen-umsetzung/abkommenstexte/beitrag.html> (accessed 1 February 2022).

87 CJEU, Case C-660/13, *Council v Commission*, EU:C:2016:616, paras. 35–40. See also for a more extensive analysis coming essentially to the same conclusion, Conclusions of Advocate General Sharpston, Case C-660/13, *Council v Commission*, EU:C:2015:787, paras. 66–68.

88 OJ 2004, L 385/43.

89 Points 2 and 4 MoU 2006.

90 Point 5 MoU 2006.

91 Point 6 MoU 2006.

Depending on the project or programme, implementation is thus bilateral or multilateral;[92] again, however, payments only flow from Switzerland to the beneficiary State(s) and never to the EU itself. As mentioned in the context of the EEA EFTA States, an additional "psychological" benefit is that cohesion payments may be easier to explain and justify with regard to public opinion in Switzerland in this way. An annex to the MoU 2006 describes the content of the bilateral framework agreements that are to be concluded between Switzerland and each individual beneficiary State, containing among others the aims of the cooperation, start and end dates and other important elements. Two "addenda" of 2008[93] and 2014[94] to the MoU 2006 add Romania and Bulgaria as well as Croatia, respectively, to the list of beneficiary States and establish the guidelines for funds they are to receive.

Governance of the cooperation is strictly bilateral and again comes with significant room for discretion for the beneficiary States, as the example of the Swiss-Polish bilateral agreement shows. Apart from the mentioned elements of coordination with the EU Commission, the Swiss authorities decide on submitted project proposals, whereas the Polish authorities, in particular the National Coordination Unit (NCU), are competent for controlling, monitoring, reporting and auditing. The Swiss side can merely ask for an independent evaluation.[95]

The mentioned bilateral framework agreements are highly technical; they do not contain, e.g., clauses on common values like the previously mentioned clause in Protocol 38c in the context of the EEA Grants, but rather focus on procedures, the amount of the contribution and the way in which it can be used and the determination and role of an NCU on the side of the beneficiary State.[96] There is, however, a "common concern" clause on corruption, deeming the latter a problem both parties intend to tackle and sufficient grounds for

---

92 Point 7 (a) MoU 2006.

93 Addendum to the Memorandum of Understanding between the President of the Council of the European Union and the Swiss Federal Council of 27 February 2006 (EDA, 5 May 2008), <www.eda.admin.ch/dam/europa/en/documents/abkommen/MoU-erweiterungs beitrag-2007-addedum-rumaenien-bulgarien_en.pdf> (accessed 1 February 2022).

94 *Ibid.*

95 See Annex 2 of the relevant framework agreement for detailed rules. Annex 3 deals with certain specific types of funding schemes such as block grants or the scholarship fund.

96 See, for example in the case of Poland, Articles 2, 6 and 9 of the Framework Agreement between the Swiss Federal Council and the Government of the Republic of Poland Concerning the Implementation of the Swiss-Polish Cooperation Programme to Reduce Economic and Social Disparities Within the Enlarged European Union, 20 December 2007 (EDA, 2017), <www.eda.admin.ch/dam/erweiterungsbeitrag/en/documents/Laen der/Rahmenabkommen-Polen_en.pdf> (accessed 1 February 2022).

termination of the bilateral agreement or a respective project agreement and the annulment of an award of procurement.[97] Apart from two more technical annexes, Annex 1 to the agreements – as an "integral part" of the various framework agreements – sets out additional "principles" for the cooperation, notably transparency, social inclusion, equal opportunities and rights and environmental sustainability.[98]

On this basis, one might question whether there is thus a significant legal difference between clauses in these agreements and the Protocol 38c clause. At a glance, one may be tempted to argue that the mentioned Annex "principles" cannot have the same legal effect compared to corruption, because only the latter is mentioned explicitly as a ground for termination of project agreements or awards in Article 10 of the relevant bilateral agreement itself. However, there are two arguments against this position. First, the Annex is expressly declared by the parties to be an integral part of the agreement. Second, such an *a contrario* argument must always be nuanced based on context;[99] it is hard to accept that the parties would include these principles expressly as the basis for cooperation in a setting involving one party giving funds to the other and then to argue that a violation of these values could not be invoked by the party providing funding at all, not even for less restrictive measures than a total rupture of relations such as a renegotiation of a project agreement or the temporary withholding of funds.

4 Conditionality Approaches

The term "conditionality" can mean a variety of things in EU law. It is applied as an enforcement tool in areas as different as EU enlargement,[100] financial assistance in the context of the financial crisis[101] or most recently in the

97 Article 10 of the Bilateral Agreement (n. 88).

98 Point 2 of Annex I Conceptual Framework of the Swiss-Polish Cooperation Programme (EDA, 2012), <www.eda.admin.ch/dam/erweiterungsbeitrag/en/documents/Laender/Annex1-Polen_en.pdf> (accessed 1 February 2022).

99 J. Klingler, 'Expressio Unius Est Exclusio Alterius', in J. Klingler, Y. Parkhomenko and C. Salonidis (eds.), *Between the Lines of the Vienna Convention? Canons and Other Principles of Interpretation in Public International Law* (Kluwer Law International, 2019), p. 103.

100 See, e.g., E. De Ridder, 'Democratic Conditionality in the Eastern Enlargement: Ambitious Window Dressing', *European Foreign Affairs Review* 16 (2011), p. 589.

101 See, e.g., A. Poulou, 'Financial assistance conditionality and human rights protection: What is the role of the EU Charter of Fundamental Rights?', *Common Market Law Review* 54 (2017), p. 991; see also more generally R. Bieber, F. Maiani, 'Enhancing

context of the rule of law crisis.[102] For the present chapter, we use this label to look at the way in which Switzerland and the EEA EFTA States have used their funding to achieve political objectives. For this purpose, we first look at the perception of the cohesion payments. Are they a mere part of the political bargain to be struck in concrete negotiations, in the sense of a bargaining chip? Or are they part of a longer-term balance of rights and obligations, which in turn influences how cohesion payments are "used" in terms of conditionality? Of course, the present analysis remains somewhat limited, as there is a diverse group of actors "within" Switzerland, the EEA EFTA States and the EU. For reasons of simplicity, general representative statements thus have to be relied upon. Nonetheless, the practice of conditionality makes it possible to draw at least certain inferences.

4.1 *The EEA Grants and the Norway Grants*

With regard to the question of whether the EEA Grants and the Norway Grants are something like a "fee" that needs to be paid repeatedly, there is no clear legal provision providing an answer. Some authors look at the preamble of the EEA Agreement which mentions cohesion and note that, contrary to the perspective of some observers in the "well-off EFTA States", structural funds are to be seen as part of the deal of the EEA and not as "charitable alms" given to the less fortunate regions of the EEA.[103] Others observe that in the EEA context, the EEA EFTA States' contributions are indeed sometimes described as a "fee" for access to the EU internal market, but warn of perceiving things as being so simple. In their view, market integration has both economic advantages and disadvantages for the participating States and may produce diverse and even contradictory economic effects, depending also on economic sectors, so that each State must weigh in overall terms the positive and negative impacts of EEA integration.[104]

Although the initial idea was that the Financial Mechanism in the EEA context was supposed to be a temporary measure, it has become over the years

---

centralized enforcement of EU law: Pandora's Toolbox?', *Common Market Law Review* 51 (2014), p. 1057.

102 See, e.g., N. Kirst, 'Rule of Law Conditionality: The Long-awaited Step Towards a Solution of the Rule of Law Crisis in the European Union?', *European Papers* 6 (2021), p. 101 ; J.-V. Louis, 'Respect de l'état de droit et protection des finances de l'Union', *Cahiers de Droit Européen* 57 (2021), p. 3.

103 F. Arnesen, H.H. Fredriksen, 'Preamble', in F. Arnesen, H.H. Fredriksen, H.P. Graver, O. Mestad and C. Vedder (eds.), *Agreement on the European Economic Area – A Commentary* (Nomos,2018), p. 162, para. 26.

104 P. Christiansen (n. 6), p. 893, para. 3.

something of an integral part of the EEA and thus moved in the direction of an obligation of continuous payments. The law provides a hint in the form of the "review" clause of Article 11 of Protocol 38c, which states that at the end of the 2041–2021 period the parties shall review the need to address economic and social disparities within the EEA. Independently of the above-noted insistence of, for example, Norway that there is no binding legal obligation for continuous cohesion payments, the power imbalance between the EU and the EEA EFTA States makes it practically inevitable that this clause will form the basis of new negotiations resulting in additional substantial financial support in the coming years.[105] This does not exclude certain reciprocal advantages from being granted by the EU, as the mentioned parallel negotiations on improved market access for Norwegian and Icelandic seafood show. In fact, some suggest that the EEA EFTA States' insistence on the inexistence of a clear obligation can be seen as part of a ritual of recurring negotiations to influence the amount of future payments and the mentioned parallel negotiations of unrelated advantages.[106]

The practice of conditionality seems to strengthen this overall perspective of cohesion payments as part of the EEA integration process rather than a one-time bargaining chip. Namely, contrary to the Swiss case discussed below there is no approach of withholding funding as part of achieving a more acceptable overall political bargain. Rather, the well-known example cases of withholding funding evolve around a classic conditionality controversy in the EU law-sense, namely a disagreement over certain values to be upheld in the process of implementing programmes funded by the EEA and Norway Grants. There are several examples that support this point.

In a 2014/2015 dispute between Norway and Hungary, Norway decided to suspend disbursements of funds from the EEA Grants and the Norway Grants to Hungary. The object of the dispute was a Non-governmental Organisation (NGO) Fund with the objective of developing civil society in Hungary. The Norwegian Financial Mechanism Office selected a Hungarian operator based among others on the latter's independence from national authorities, to ensure that funded NGOs could be critical of government policies. The Hungarian authorities, however, contended that many NGO projects favoured an opposition party, and that the financing mechanism constituted interference in the country's domestic affairs. They, therefore, adopted changes to the control and implementation of the funding, which was rejected by Norway as being not in conformity with the agreement concerning the EEA funds. Norway

105 *Ibid.*, p. 904, para. 41.
106 The author thanks Georges Baur for this comment.

thus decided to suspend most payments to Hungary from May 2014.[107] The situation deteriorated after additional investigations, the filing of criminal complaints and even police raids concerning the fund's operator; in a public statement, the competent Norwegian Minister explicitly invoked the failure of the Hungarian government "to respect common European values relating to democracy and good governance".[108] Only in late 2015 could an agreement be found on the performance of control functions and the implementation of the grants, including the respect for the legal framework for the civil society programme.[109] However, the problem recently re-emerged in a similar form. Based on a Memorandum of Understanding signed at the end of 2020, an independent fund operator for civil society funding in Hungary had to be found. As no agreement on such an operator could be reached between the EEA EFTA States on one side and Hungary on the other, no planned programmes (even not those focused on other topics than civil society) can be implemented, and all in all, near 215 million euros are currently being withheld.[110]

In February 2020, Norway again blocked payments of about 65 million euros aimed at the strengthening of the Polish justice system because of recent reforms and their damaging impact on the independence of the judiciary.[111] Moreover, later that year, another set of grants was blocked by all three EEA EFTA States for Polish cities which had declared themselves "LGBT (Lesbian, Gay, Bi-sexual, Transsexual)-free" zones.[112] Once again, Norway's Foreign

107 Norwegian Ministry of Foreign Affairs, Suspension of EEA and Norway Grants to Hungary, Press release of 9 May 2014 (Regjeringen, 2014), <www.regjeringen.no/en/aktuelt/hungary_suspension/id758873/> (accessed 1 February 2022).

108 Norwegian Ministry of Foreign Affairs, Unacceptable police raid on EEA and Norway Grants fund operator in Hungary, Press release of 9 September 2014 (Regjeringen, 2014), <www.regjeringen.no/en/aktuelt/raid_eea/id2000182/> (accessed 1 February 2022).

109 Norwegian Ministry of Foreign Affairs, Suspension of EEA and Norway Grants payments to Hungary lifted, Press release of 11 December 2015 (Regjeringen, 2015), <www.regjeringen.no/en/aktuelt/suspension-of-eea-and-norway-grants-payments-to-hungary-lifted/id2467020/> (accessed 1 February 2022). See for a more exhaustive discussion P. Christiansen (n. 6), pp. 900–901, paras. 27–28.

110 News release, No agreement reached on funding for Hungary (23 July 2021), <https://eeagrants.org/news/no-agreement-reached-funding-hungary> (accessed 1 February 2022). See in more detail R. Hermann, 'Norwegen streicht Ungarn Gelder aus dem EU-Erweiterungs-Beitrag', *Neue Zürcher Zeitung* 26 July 2021.

111 R. Hess, 'Kohäsionsmilliarde: Norwegen zeigt, wie es geht und streicht Geld für Demokratie-Schleifer in Ungarn und Polen', *Luzerner Zeitung* 6 November 2020.

112 R. Savage, 'Norway, Iceland, Lichtenstein cancel grant to Polish "LGBT-free zone"' (Reuters, 2 February 2021), <www.reuters.com/article/us-poland-lgbt-norway-trfn-idUSKBN2A22MD> (accessed 1 February 2022). See in this context on early effects of similar pressure by the EU on the relevant cities, 'Polnische Gemeinden geben sich jetzt besonders LGBT-freundlich', *Der Standard* 29 September 2021.

Minister referred explicitly to the obligations of receiving States to respect certain core values under the mechanism of the EEA and Norway Grants.[113]

4.2 *The Swiss Cohesion Payments*

As set out before, cohesion payments were always perceived on the Swiss side as a voluntary contribution not based on any kind of obligation and there was consistent hesitance to perceive cohesion payments as some kind of entry prize to be paid for EU internal market access. The text of the Draft Institutional Agreement[114] clearly also points in this direction. It contains a joint declaration on cohesion in which both parties agree on the need for continuous cooperation. The EU "salutes" in this context Switzerland's confirmation to finance projects and programmes "autonomously", but in coordination with EU programmes in the area; the implementing provisions are to form part of a "political agreement" in the form of a Memorandum of Understanding between the parties. Pointing at this language and the similar emphasis on the "autonomous" character of Swiss contributions in the preamble of the draft agreement, the Swiss side sees no basis for a legal obligation.[115]

On the EU side, the Swiss Cohesion Payments were, however, simultaneously perceived – from early on – as part of the overall deal of Swiss-EU relations that was negotiated in the form of the first and second package of the bilateral agreements (*Bilateral Agreements I and II*). The Council stated this somewhat implicitly at the occasion of the establishment of the MoU 2006[116] and repeated this view more explicitly in the 2008

113 R. Hess (n. 102). In this context, the question can be raised about the exact content of the mentioned core values. In the EEA context, EEA EFTA States had previously successfully opposed the incorporation of EU non-discrimination legislation into EEA law, based at least partly on the absence of a parallel provision to Article 19 TFEU in EEA law (although the EEA EFTA States have later adapted autonomously to the legislation at issue). The author thanks Christa Tobler for this comment.

114 The full text of the original French as well as the inofficial German and Italian translations and some supporting documentation (partly in English) is available at <www.eda.admin.ch/europa/de/home/verhandlungen-offene-themen/verhandlungen/institutionelles-abkommen.html> (accessed 1 February 2022).

115 Swiss Confederation, Erläuterungen zum Institutionellen Abkommen Schweiz–EU, 16 January 2019 (*EDA*, 2019), <www.eda.admin.ch/dam/europa/de/documents/abkommen/InstA-Erlaeuterungen_de.pdf> (accessed 1 February 2022), p. 16; see also Matthias Oesch, *Schweiz – Europäische Union – Grundlagen, Bilaterale Abkommen, Autonomer Nachvollzug* (EIZ Publishing 2020), p. 190, para. 330.

116 Council of the EU, Permanent Representatives Committee, 'EU-Switzerland relations', 17 May 2004, Document ST 9544/04 AELE 12 CH 8 ECOFIN 181 FISC 108 JAI 152 MI 165 LIMITE, p. 3.

addendum.[117] Moreover, in its relevant conclusions, the Council continued to call for new negotiations to renew Switzerland's financial contribution to cohesion in 2012, 2014, 2017 and 2019. In its last conclusions, the Council described the cohesion payments as an "integral part" of the relationship between the EU and Switzerland, highlighted that they should be "proportionate to the significant benefits Switzerland draws from its participation in the internal market" and emphasized the importance of coordinating the contribution with the EU multi-annual programming cycle.[118] The European Court of Auditors also understood (both the EEA EFTA States' and Swiss) cohesion payments as a "counterpart" to the participation in the EU's internal market.[119] Advocate General Sharpston described Switzerland's payments as "in exchange for Swiss access to the enlarged internal market" and as "part of an overall compromise resulting in the conclusion of [the Bilateral Agreements]".[120] There seem thus to be two important points implied in the EU side's perspective: cohesion payments should be made regularly and ideally based on a binding commitment, and they should be seen as a price for market access as granted by the framework of the bilateral agreements.

This difference in views between the EU and Switzerland mirror the one that also exists between the EU and the EEA EFTA States as mentioned before. On top of this, however, the Swiss perspective seems to be much more transactional if one focuses on the practice of conditionality. Compared to the mentioned value-based blockades of funds by the EEA EFTA States, no similar conditionality measures have been taken by Switzerland to date, even though as explained a legal basis for such measures would arguably exist. The competent Federal Department of Foreign Affairs emphasized that Switzerland had agreed to the payment of the relevant funds by means of international agreements with Poland and Hungary and that the cooperation had ended in 2017

117 Council of the EU, Conclusions of the Council and of the Representatives of the Governments of the Member States meeting within the Council on an Addendum to the Memorandum of Understanding between the President of the Council of the European Union and the Swiss Federal Council of 27 February 2006, 5 May 2008, Document ST 8681/2008 INIT, p. 1, para. 1.

118 Press release of the Council of the EU, Council conclusions on EU relations with the Swiss Confederation (19 February 2019), <https://www.consilium.europa.eu/en/press/press-releases/2019/02/19/council-conclusions-on-eu-relation-with-the-swiss-confederation/> (accessed 1 February 2022), para 11.

119 European Court of Auditors, Financial contributions from non-EU countries to the EU and Member States, Review 3/2021, <https://www.eca.europa.eu/Lists/ECADocuments/RW21_03/RW_third_countries_contributions_EN.pdf> (accessed 1 February 2022), p. 5.

120 CJEU, Conclusions of Advocate General Sharpston, Case C-660/13, *Council v Commission* (n. 87), para. 1.

according to plan and with good results. According to the Department, during the preparatory works of the second Cohesion Payment the topics of the rule of law, democracy and human rights had been discussed, but the resulting general view was that the Swiss cohesion payments should be seen as principally aimed at people in a particular receiving State and not the Government.[121]

This basis of the Swiss approach has also been set out in the initial Federal Council's Explanatory Memorandum ("dispatch") on the second Swiss Contribution. The dispatch proposed to the parliament that the payment be linked to progress in other areas of Swiss-EU relations,[122] which the Parliament initially did by means of the non-discrimination condition, as explained above. This Swiss approach to the Second Cohesion Payment met – somewhat obviously – opposition from EU Member States in Eastern and Central Europe who were meant to benefit from the contributions and who did not accept the argument about the discriminatory measures taken by the EU Commission in the field of equivalency of stock exchange regulation.[123] It also met opposition from the EU Commission, which argued that Switzerland should not be treated differently from the EEA EFTA States.[124] In the meantime, notably after the Swiss abandonment of the Draft Institutional Agreement, the EU side hardened its stance in a similar manner. First, the Commission requested as two core demands that a formally binding solution for regular future cohesion payments had to be found and that it should be clearly stated that these payments were in exchange for market access.[125] Secondly, the Commission also used linkages to non-internal market related topics to put pressure on Switzerland, for example by not granting the status of associated country to Switzerland in the framework of the new research programme Horizon Europe, even after Switzerland agreed to make the Second Cohesion Payment without conditions.[126] Ultimately, the Commission seems to have renounced its mentioned two core demands in the new Memorandum of Understanding.[127] Still, the

121 R. Hess (n. 102).

122 BBl 2018 6665 (n. 34), p. 6667.

123 R. Hess (n. 102).

124 *Ibid.*

125 S. Israel, C. Walser, 'Die Schweiz und die EU streiten über die Auszahlung der Kohäsionsmilliarde', *Tages-Anzeiger* 25 October 2021.

126 D. Steinvorth, 'Die EU begrüsst die Freigabe der Kohäsionsmilliarde – verspricht aber kein Entgegenkommen bei Horizon Europe', *Neue Zürcher Zeitung* 1 October 2021; C.G. Schmutz, D. Steinvorth, 'Die EU will nicht bis 2024 warten – Brüssel möchte mit der Schweiz bis Januar einen Fahrplan vereinbaren', *Neue Zürcher Zeitung* 15 November 2021.

127 At the time of writing, the text of the Memorandum is not yet available; the author thanks a member of the Swiss administration for this information.

EU side now makes a clear connection between progress on an institutional solution for the relations between Switzerland and the EU and access to the internal market. Cohesion payments are but one – small[128] – bargaining chip that is indispensable for the EU to continue to grant the same level of market access but does not seem to be able on its own to tip the balance in any meaningful way in favour of Switzerland. What is more, the Commission's approach shows an increased willingness to interpret internal market access issues broadly[129] or even use non-market access related issues in its own conditionality approach towards Switzerland. This approach may not exclusively be related to or caused by the Swiss approach to cohesion payments, but still generally shows the dangers of a transactional relationship in which one larger party seems to hold more cards than the smaller one.

5 Conclusion

The law and politics of cohesion payments are a complex amalgam. There is a significant amount of law governing these payments – from the EEA Agreement via Memoranda of Understanding to bilateral agreements. And yet, as shown, politics remain crucial. Although benefitting substantially from its chosen "bilateral" path of EU approximation, Switzerland pays much lower contributions compared to the formally more integrated EEA EFTA States. A comparison with EU Member States' contributions seems even more difficult to undertake. The legal framework of cohesion payments leaves a lot of discretion and freedom in the governance of the mostly bilateral relations between the contributing and the beneficiary States. This discretion is, however, then used by the EU side to repeatedly claim a more binding character of the need for cohesion payments – and the continuity of such payments – than may actually be the case *de lege lata*; as opposed to the claims of Switzerland and the EEA EFTA States that payments are made autonomously and without legal obligation. Most strikingly, this importance of "politics" plays out once questions of conditionality, i.e., of linking the payment of contributions with

---

128 It should be noted that an initiative to double the Second Cohesion Payment in order to buy more goodwill from the EU side was short-lived and rather quickly voted down by the Swiss Parliament beginning of December 2021, see: 'Le National refuse de doubler le milliard de cohésion pour relancer les discussions avec l'UE', RTS *Info* 1 December 2021.

129 See, e.g., in this regard on the debated agreement on health policy between Switzerland and the EU that is not making progress due to this view taken by the Commission C. Tobler, J. Beglinger (n. 40), p. 64.

political issues, come into play. Legal room for manoeuvre exists in both examined cases for value-based conditionality and for conditionality to further one's negotiating position towards the other party in a transactional negotiation setting. However, in the EEA context only the former and in the Swiss context only the latter form of conditionality seems to have been used. This could be simply due to factual circumstances. And yet, public statements of the parties involved allow at least the weak inference that one's perception of cohesion payments matters, i.e., whether they are seen as part of an ongoing integration framework or rather as a bargaining chip in concrete negotiations with the EU.

Should the conclusion from all this be that more law is needed to stem the tide of politics, to the extent that one disagrees with the latter? Arguably, this is not necessarily the case. For example, transforming the currently ambiguous and in their view autonomous decision of EU partners to provide cohesion payments into a clear legal obligation may be counterproductive if the politics of appearance are taken into account. Presently, an important feature of cohesion payments is their often highly bilateral nature that serves to improve relations between the contributing and the beneficiary State. This feature arguably also renders the payments more palatable to the general public of a contributing State. To create a legal obligation may feed into a general political reflex of rejecting EU approximation and thereby destroy what can otherwise serve as a symbol of – expected, but not imposed – solidarity.

CHAPTER 10

The Shelved Institutional Agreement EU-CH from a Political Science Perspective

René Schwok

1 Introduction

The decision of the Swiss Federal Government (Federal Council) of 26 May 2021 to reject the Institutional Agreement (InstA)[1] has given rise, and continues to give rise, to incomprehension. On the side of the European Union, the European Commission has declared that it did not comprehend the unilateral decision of the Swiss Government, in particular in view of the significant concessions that it considers to have made.[2] Stéphanie Riso, the chief negotiator of the European Commission, for her part indicated that she had absolutely not expected Switzerland to dare to unilaterally abandon the talks.[3] It appears that the Commission believed that Switzerland was bluffing and practising a "brinkmanship" approach to try to raise the stakes according to the rational choice theory.

1 Accord facilitant les relations bilatérales entre l'Union européenne et la Confédération suisse dans les parties du marché intérieur auxquelles la Suisse participe, draft text of 23 November 2018, <https://www.eda.admin.ch/dam/europa/fr/documents/abkommen/Acccord-inst-Projet-de-texte_fr.pdf> (accessed 31 May 2022 ; there is no translation of this text in English). For an analysis of the InstA from a legal point of view, see the contribution by C. Kaddous in this volume.

2 P. Mavromichalis, 'Union européenne – Suisse: et maintenant?', *Le Temps* 25 June 2021. Petros Mavromichalis is the EU Ambassador to Switzerland and Liechtenstein. – For more details on the "formulated compromises", which, according to the EU, "go a long way towards the Swiss concerns", see European External Action Service, *Basic Facts on the Framework of EU-Switzerland Relations*, Brussels, 25 May 2021, <https://eeas.europa.eu/sites/default/files/str_ifa_eu-switzerlandrelations_factsheet_final.pdf> (accessed 31 May 2022), p. 4.

3 According to a confidential note written by the Federal Council, and quoted by the journalist Stefan Bühler, Stéphanie Riso and her team apparently could not imagine, "despite clear indications", that "'Switzerland would dare to break off negotiations"; see S. Bühler, 'Verhandlungsabbruch: Was am 26. Mai in Brüssel passiert', *NZZ am Sonntag* 6 June 2021 (translated by author from German). EU Commissioner Maroš Šefčovič confirmed that "it is no secret that we were surprised when Switzerland broke off the negotiations"; S. Israel, 'EU-Kommissions-Vize im Interview', *Der Bund* 17 November 2021 (translated by author from German).

© KONINKLIJKE BRILL NV, LEIDEN, 2023 | DOI:10.1163/9789004529984_012

The few European media that have taken an interest in the InstA have also expressed their total incomprehension. The term "*Unverständnis*" ("incomprehension") is the one that best characterises their reaction, according to a synthesis made by *Swissinfo*.[4] Similarly, inside Switzerland, many circles did not understand why the Federal Council had refused the InstA. Indeed, never before had the Swiss Government, known for its legendary prudence, put an end to international negotiations of such importance, moreover, with its most important economic, political, social and scientific partner. This decision to break up is not easy to explain, especially since most of the employers' organisations, economic sectors, the media and academic circles had spoken out in favour of the InstA. So did many socialist and green leaders, as well as a good part of their electorate, who appeared to support the InstA. There was also strong support for the Agreement among liberal and Christian-democrat politicians, as well as within their electoral base. Opinion polls even suggested that nearly two-thirds of the population was well disposed towards such an agreement.[5]

Consequently, the objective of this contribution is, in the first part, to try to elucidate why the Federal Council adopted such an exceptional decision. To do this, we will review the motivations of the seven federal councillors and the pressures to which they were subjected. We will examine each of their positions, their ideological conceptions and their political tactics (below, sections 2–6). In a next part, we will try to show why the rejection of the InstA caused so much incomprehension in Switzerland and in Europe even though this agreement had been relatively well negotiated by Switzerland, that the EU had made substantial concessions and had not been particularly intransigent, that the last remaining obstacles seemed to have been exaggerated and could be overcome by domestic measures in Switzerland and, finally, that the harmful consequences of a rejection of the InstA were well known (section 7). The contribution ends with some concluding remarks (section 8).

---

4 For an inventory of reactions, see S. Bondolfi, 'Rahmenabkommen: Unverständnis im Ausland über Verhandlungsabbruch', *Swissinfo* 27 May 2021, <https://www.swissinfo.ch/ger/rahmenabkommen--unverstaendnis-im-ausland-ueber-verhandlungsabbruch/46652242> (accessed 31 May 2022).

5 In April 2021, an opinion poll still showed that 65% of the Swiss population would have said "yes" or "rather yes" to the InstA; see GfS, *Institutionnelles Abkommen mehrheitlich akzeptiert, allerdings nicht als Königsweg*, April 2021, <https://www.gfsbern.ch/wp-content/uploads/2021/05/standort-schweiz_europafragen_kurzbericht.pdf> (accessed 31 May 2022).

2 Elements Which Explain the Federal Council's Decision to Reject the InstA

To begin, we try to expound the factors that led to this decision of the Federal Council. Such an approach is indeed necessary from a scientific point of view in order to establish the causal links that led to the Swiss Government's choice. As a reminder, the decision to abandon the InstA was taken solely by the Federal Council, without a prior vote of the two chambers of the Federal Parliament, even though they had been consulted. Officially, in its report of 25 May 2021, the Federal Council justified its decision by arguing that the European Union had not met Switzerland's expectations concerning: (1) the EU Citizens' Rights Directive 2004/38,[6] (2) salary protection for posted workers and (3) State aid[7] (see further section 7).

Beyond the official arguments put forward by the Swiss Government, it is important to establish what were the real motivations of each of the seven Federal Councillors. From an epistemological and methodological point of view, it should be noted that it is difficult to answer this question due to a lack of information. First of all, there was no official communication on the positions of the seven Federal Councillors. Perhaps from a legal point of view, this is not astonishing since votes within the Federal Council are secret. Unfortunately, there were no leaks to the media that would have given a more precise idea of the orientations of each of the members. It is also not known officially whether there was an actual vote by the college and if so, whether the decision was reached by majority or by unanimity. In fact, it seems that the President of the Federal Council did a simple assessment of the opinion of his colleagues, without a formal vote.[8]

6 Directive 2004/38/EC of the European Parliament and of the Council of 29 April 2004 on the right of citizens of the Union and their family members to move and reside freely within the territory of the Member States amending Regulation (EEC) No 1612/68 and repealing Directives 64/221/EEC, 68/360/EEC, 72/194/EEC, 73/148/EEC, 75/34/EEC, 75/35/EEC, 90/364/EEC, 90/365/EEC and 93/96/EEC (OJ 2004, L 158/77).

7 Conseil fédéral, *Rapport relatif aux négociations sur un accord-cadre institutionnel entre la Suisse et l'UE*, Bern, 26 May 2021, <https://www.newsd.admin.ch/newsd/message/attachments/66827.pdf> (accessed 31 May 2022). This report has not been published in English; for a summary in English see: Conseil fédéral, *No signing of Swiss-EU InstA*, 26 May 2021, <https://www.admin.ch/gov/en/start/documentation/media-releases.msg-id-83705.html> (accessed 31 May 2022).

8 This was confirmed to me by a former Federal Councillor, private interview, Geneva, 29 October 2021.

Consequently, at this stage of our knowledge, we can only limit ourselves to conjectures based on indirect sources: speeches by Federal Councillors, statements by political parties and associations, written and audio-visual media, and oral interviews. In order to explain the attitude of the Federal Council, give it meaning and establish causal links, it is necessary to present, for each of the seven Federal Councillors, their political affiliations, their functions, their personalities and their personal convictions. Above all, it is necessary to highlight the political pressure they were under, as well as the political climate that preceded the burial of the InstA in May 2021.

3 Government Members of the Swiss People's Party (SPP)

3.1 *The Attitude of the SPP*

There is little doubt that the two Federal Councillors of the Swiss People's Party (SPP) took a negative stance with regard to the InstA. From the beginning of the negotiations, the SPP has always been a firm opponent of the InstA. In fact, the SPP has been the only Government party that has remained constant in its attitude. The SPP has issued numerous statements on the subject[9] and has unambiguously repeated its rejection during the consultation procedure that was launched by the Federal Council in 2019.[10]

It should be remembered that, in general, the SPP has consistently opposed almost any form of integration of Switzerland into the European Union system. The SPP has thus launched or supported numerous referenda or constitutional initiatives to sabotage the bilateral agreements between Switzerland and the European Union. Its actions have generally failed, except for the vote on the European Economic Area in 1992 and the initiative on "Mass Immigration" in 2014. Its positions have, however, helped to transform this party into the largest political force in Switzerland (about 26% of the vote in the National Council,

9 Schweizerische Volkspartei, *Institutionelles Rahmenabkommen mit der EU*. Opinion of the Swiss People's Party (SPP), <https://www.eda.admin.ch/dam/europa/de/documents/bericht_konsultationen_insta/stellungnahmen/SVP-Stellungnahme-InstA_de.pdf> (accessed 31 May 2022).

10 After the publication in December 2018 of the text of the InstA, the Federal Council, already very hesitant, started a broad consultation with political parties, the Governments of the 26 cantons and pressure groups to find out their position. This resulted in 54 often very detailed reports, <https://www.eda.admin.ch/europa/fr/home/europapolitik/politique-europeenne/institutionelles-abkommen/institutionelles-abkommen-stellungnahmen.html> (accessed 31 May 2022). There were also numerous hearings and debates in committees of both chambers of the federal parliament.

the lower house of the Federal Parliament). Above all, the SPP has paralyzed the other political formations, particularly on the right, which have become more reluctant to promote policies of rapprochement that are too strongly marked with the EU.

With regard more precisely to the InstA, the SPP has always been opposed to the principle of dynamic adoption of the evolution of EU law. According to this party, it is unacceptable for a sovereign State like Switzerland to commit itself *a priori* to adopting legal norms in which it has not participated in their elaboration. The SPP has never been convinced by official explanations that the InstA only entails a *dynamic*, but not *automatic*, adoption of EU law.[11] In SPP rhetoric, a dynamic adoption of the development of EU law is described as submission, subjugation and colonialism.[12]

The SPP has also vehemently opposed the role of the Court of Justice of the European Union (CJEU) in dispute settlement. The party has always contested the official arguments that the CJEU would only be involved in the event of a deadlock in the arbitral tribunal and only on matters that affect EU law. The SPP was also not convinced by the explanation according to which the InstA would have allowed Switzerland to refuse the rulings of the arbitral tribunal, even if it meant incurring "proportionate" sanctions on the part of the EU. For the SPP, this is subjection to "foreign judges". This type of rhetoric is frequently used in nationalist circles in relation to the original myths of Swiss independence. According to this conception of history, the Confederation has resisted "foreign judges" for 700 years.[13] Consequently, accepting foreign judges amounts to denying the deep values on which Switzerland was founded.

For the SPP, there was also no doubt that if Switzerland had accepted the InstA, it would have had to agree to the inclusion of the EU Citizens' Rights Directive 2004/38 into the bilateral law very quickly, even though it was not explicitly mentioned in the draft of the InstA. In the view of the SPP, this would have resulted in an incentive for many EU citizens to move to Switzerland in order to benefit from the "El Dorado" of Swiss social benefits. According to the SPP's argument, tens of thousands of EU citizens would come to Switzerland

---

11 See G. Baur, C. Tobler, '"Automatische" vs. „dynamische" Rechtsübernahme. What's in a name?', in: A. Epiney, M. Kern and L. Hehemann (eds.), *Schweizerisches Jahrbuch für Europarecht 2015/2016* (Stämpfli/Schulthess, 2016), 347–361.

12 Yves Nidegger, 'Politique européenne: les dés pipés du Conseil fédéral', *SVP publications*, September 2015, <https://www.udc.ch/parti/publikationen/edition-speciale/edition-speciale-de-septembre-2015/politique-europeenne-les-des-pipes-du-conseil-federal/> (accessed 31 May 2022).

13 Schweizerische Volkspartei, *Institutionelles Rahmenabkommen mit der EU* (n. 8), point 7.

to pretend to work for a few months in order to thereafter obtain unemployment benefits or other social benefits. This would cost hundreds of millions of Swiss Francs and would jeopardise Switzerland's social security. Moreover, these EU nationals would bring along their families in the broadest sense, not only the children, but all sorts of close or distant relatives. The SPP was also strongly opposed to a clause in the Directive that makes it impossible to send *all* European criminals back to their home countries (Article 27(2) of Directive 2004/38). Indeed, the issue of returning foreign criminals has often been a campaign theme of the SPP, on which it has launched numerous constitutional initiatives, some crowned with success.

Having taken note of the SPP's position on Switzerland's European integration in general and on the InstA in particular, it is therefore not surprising that the two Federal Councillors belonging to this party have expressed their opposition to the latter.

3.2 *The Two SPP Federal Councillors: Functions, Personalities and Personal Convictions*

Federal Councillor Ueli Maurer, who has been in office since 1 January 2009 and has been in charge of the Department of Finance since 2016, belongs to the most nationalistic and anti-European wing of the SPP. When he was president of the SPP between 1996 and 2008, he was always a supporter of the hard line embodied by his mentor, Christoph Blocher.

Federal Councillor Guy Parmelin, who has been in office since 1 January 2016 and is in charge of the Department of Economic Affairs, Education and Research, also belongs to the Eurosceptic current of the SPP. He is, however, a more consensual person than Ueli Maurer and generally moderately expresses himself. Moreover, his ministry has been subject to pressure from integrationist business circles and from academics who are particularly sensitive to the exclusion of Swiss research institutes from European research. In addition, in 2021, Guy Parmelin was President of the Confederation by rotation; which led him to further embody the sense of general interest. Even so, there is a lot of evidence that Guy Parmelin also supported the denunciation of the InstA. It was in fact he who announced the end of the process and justified it by giving the impression of being personally convinced. It was also he who had given the clearest warning signs of failure, during the "last chance" meeting with Commission President Ursula von der Leyen on 23 April 2021.[14]

14 C.G. Schmutz, D. Steinvorth, T. Gafafer, L. Rhyn, F. Schäfer and C. Forster, 'Der Anfang vom Ende? Das Spitzentreffen in Brüssel bringt keine Annäherung beim Rahmenvertrag', *Neue Zürcher Zeitung* 23 April 2021.

While the positioning of Federal Councillors belonging to the SPP is not in doubt, it is much more difficult to carry out an analysis of the positioning of the Federal Councillors belonging to other parties. The difficulty stems from the very hesitant attitude of these political formations throughout the process of evaluating the InstA.

4 Government Members of the Socialist Party (SP)

4.1 *The Attitude of the SP and the Swiss Trade Unions*

The attitude of the two Federal Councillors belonging to the Socialist Party (SP) reflected the very ambiguous attitude of the Socialist Party towards the InstA.[15] On the one hand, this political formation has constantly reaffirmed its support for the InstA, as well as its willingness to deepen the existing links between Switzerland and the EU.[16] This is in line with the policy of a party that has always been the Swiss political movement best predisposed towards European integration, going so far as to include the goal of EU membership in its program. Paradoxically, the SP has even maintained this objective of joining the EU after May 2021,[17] even though it was unable to support a modest InstA. On the other hand, many leaders of the Socialist Party, and mainly of its trade union wing, have not stopped shooting at the InstA. They criticised it for leading to the dismantling of the so-called flanking measures, to massive wage dumping and even to a profound weakening of Swiss social law (which is actually the opposite of the thesis that they had been defending for decades). The trade unions' point of view was very clearly expressed: the InstA is a "threat to wages and jobs". It is moreover with this affirmation in the title that the Swiss Federation of Unions submitted its position paper to the Federal Council.[18]

---

15 Socialist Party position paper, <https://www.eda.admin.ch/dam/europa/de/documents/bericht_konsultationen_insta/stellungnahmen/SP-Stellungnahme-InstA_de.PDF> (accessed 31 May 2022).

16 The Green Party has said little. It has generally followed the Socialist Party, which is why little attention is paid to it in this analysis, especially since it is not represented in the Federal Council. The small Green Liberal Party, on the other hand, is the only political party that has always supported the InstA without any restrictions.

17 Socialist Party, *For a European policy that offers perspectives*, 26 May 26, 2021, <https://www.sp-ps.ch/fr/publications/communiques-de-presse/pour-une-politique-europeenne-qui-offre-des-perspectives> (accessed 31 May 2022).

18 Swiss Federation of Trade Unions, Statement, 13 March 2019, <https://www.eda.admin.ch/dam/europa/fr/documents/bericht_konsultationen_insta/stellungnahmen/SGB-USS-Stellungnahme-InstA_fr.pdf> (accessed 31 May 2022).

As a reminder concerning the *flanking measures,* these were introduced during the referendum on the adoption of *Bilateral Agreements I* (2000), and also during the referendum that accompanied its renewal (2009). The Federal Council, the right-wing parties and the employers had to make concessions to the unions and the left-wing parties. The latter had threatened not to support the *Bilateral Agreements I*. These flanking measures aim to combat social dumping through: (1) measures on posted workers; (2) the possible introduction of minimum wages in border cantons; (3) the partial and facilitated extension of collective labour agreements. In the context of the process of signing the InstA, Swiss trade union circles were particularly critical of the measures imposed by the EU concerning posted workers. The EU has imposed a protocol on the draft InstA that requires Switzerland to adopt the more recent EU directives on the posting of workers.[19]

To avoid risks of "social dumping", Switzerland has adopted legislation that requires EU companies to provide notification at least eight days before posting workers to Switzerland. But the EU wanted to remove this restriction in the InstA, which it considers to be contrary to EU law and discriminatory to its workers. Finally, in the InstA draft, a compromise was reached on a notification period of four days (instead of eight).

Second, Switzerland requires a financial guarantee from companies posting workers to ensure that they pay all social security costs for their posted employees. Again, the EU considered this to be contrary to EU law because it is discriminatory. Indeed, such a measure is not required in the same way from Swiss companies. In the end, an arrangement was reached in the InstA draft. It provided that Switzerland would waive this guarantee, but that a financial guarantee could however be requested from EU economic operators who had already been convicted of failure to meet their financial obligations.

However, the trade unions and the Socialist Party were not reassured by these compromises and considered that these provisions were likely to lead to an influx of posted workers accepting to work under working conditions inferior to those existing in Switzerland.

Specifically, trade union circles[20] have denounced certain judgments of the CJEU such as the one in the *Čepelnik* case of November 2018, which in their view would go against measures aimed at protecting the level of wages and employment in the face of posted labour.[21] Given that the CJEU ruled that the

19 See the contribution on posted workers by K. Pärli in this volume.

20 P. Schmuck, 'La justice européenne nuit à la protection des salaires', *24 Heures* 15 November 2018.

21 CJEU, Case C-33/17 *Čepelnik*, EU:C:2018:896.

Austrian measures were contrary to EU law in this judgment and that they are similar to the Swiss flanking measures (on the obligation to pay a deposit in this specific case), the Swiss unions expressed their fear of giving too much power to the CJEU. They argued that this weakening of wage protection would only be the first step in a vicious circle that would lead to more unfavourable conditions for workers in the Swiss labour market in the future.

More generally, the Swiss Federation of Trade Unions also considered that the adoption of EU standards in social matters would weaken the Swiss model and would potentially run counter to collective labour agreements and national measures to maintain a high level of wages. This is why the Swiss Federation of Trade Unions has stated in its position paper: "Adopting the EU directives on wage protection (implementation directive and posting directive) would seriously dismantle the flanking measures".[22]

In addition to these points, some trade unions and part of the left have made much tougher demands. They demanded that Switzerland should not agree to include in the bilateral law any future changes in EU law and any case law of the CJEU in the field of labour law. It is therefore no longer only the issue of posted workers that poses a problem for them, but also the adoption of a significant part of EU law and its case law on the free movement of persons.

However, it is necessary to underline that the SP was reluctant to support the InstA not only for ideological reasons but also for reasons of political expediency. Indeed, this party was afraid that its second seat in the Federal Council would be in jeopardy in the elections of 2023. In this context, it should be remembered that the Federal Council is composed of seven members. The Federal Councillors are elected for four years by the combined chambers of the Federal Assembly (246 members). The composition of the Federal Council depends on a so-called "magic formula". This distribution of seats in the Federal Council depends on largely unwritten rules which concern the balance between linguistic communities, gender, regions, religions (in the past) and above all political parties. On this last point, which is the only one that concerns our chapter, there have been unwritten rules for more than 60 years according to which the distribution of seats must reflect the approximate weight of the main parties in the Federal Assembly, particularly in the National Council, the lower house elected by proportional representation. Thus, two seats are reserved for the Socialist Party (SP), two for the Radical-Liberal Party (RLP), two for the Swiss People's Party (SPP) and one for the Christian Democratic

22 Statement of the Swiss Trade Unions (n. 19), p. 5 (translated by author from French); <https://www.eda.admin.ch/dam/europa/fr/documents/bericht_konsultationen_insta/stellungnahmen/SGB-USS-Stellungnahme-InstA_fr.pdf> (accessed 31 May 2022).

Party (CDP), now called "The Centre".[23] From an arithmetic point of view, the second socialist seat in the Federal Council is therefore no longer justified, since the party received only 17 per cent of the vote in the October 2019 elections to the National Council. And it could even less legitimately claim to maintain its overrepresentation after the 2023 elections if its level of popularity remained as low or declined. Consequently, the Socialist Party is very careful to prevent its electorate, especially low-income ones, from continuing to leave it, mainly for the SPP.

4.2 *The Two Federal Councillors of the SP: Functions, Personalities and Personal Convictions*

Simonetta Sommaruga and Alain Berset, the socialist Federal Councillors, are known to be pragmatic people. They support a social market economy and are in favour of a Switzerland that is open to the world. They have always been unhesitatingly committed to the bilateral agreements with the European Union.

This is particularly true of Simonetta Sommaruga. As Head of the Federal Department of Justice and Police from 1 November 1, 2010, to 31 December 2018, she has been on the front line to fight with conviction certain constitutional initiatives of the SPP directed against the bilateral agreements between Switzerland and the EU. She was particularly involved in the fight against the SPP's 2014 initiative on "Mass Immigration", adopted by the Swiss citizens in a referendum, which called into question the Agreement on the Free Movement of Persons (AFMP) with the EU which was part of the *Bilateral Agreements I* package. However, since 1 January 2019, Simonetta Sommaruga has been in charge of the Federal Department of the Environment, Transport, Energy and Communications, which has distanced her from the legal and social policy aspects of the InstA.

Alain Berset, since taking office on 1 January 2012, has been in charge of the Federal Department of the Interior. This led him to be directly responsible for dealing with the COVID-19 crisis and, as in other countries in the world, to be overwhelmed by it. As a result, he was not particularly involved in the management of the InstA. However, he is known to be very close to Christian Levrat, also from the canton of Fribourg, a former trade unionist and president of the Socialist Party until October 2020. The latter has often spoken out publicly against the InstA.

---

23 From 1959 to 2003, this distribution was quite similar, with the only difference being that the CDP had two ministers, while the SPP had only one.

In conclusion, the two Federal Councillors belonging to the Socialist Party probably did not show support for the InstA because of the very strong pressure exerted within their party and the left in general, even though they were not *a priori* unfavourable.

5 Government Members of the Radical-Liberal Party (RLP)

5.1 *The Attitude of the RLP and the Business Community*

Like the Socialist Party, the Radical-Liberal Party (RLP) has maintained an ambiguous attitude towards the InstA. Indeed, historically the RLP has always been very supportive of European integration in the form of bilateral agreements[24] and has expressed its support for the InstA in particular. In addition, this party is very close to the economic interests, particularly the export industry and the service sector, which were strongly in favour of the InstA.

Officially, the RLP has issued numerous statements in support of the InstA. In addition, parliamentarians from this party have explicitly taken a position in favour of the InstA.[25] Significantly, the title of its response to the consultation procedure was: *"A reasonable YES"* to the InstA.[26] The RLP recalled that the InstA was a means of consolidating the bilateral agreements on a stable basis and ensuring long-term non-discriminatory access to the European internal market. It emphasised that this access required a dynamic adoption of the evolution of EU law and its interpretation. It also recalled that the legal basis should be homogeneous between the law of the internal market and the sectoral bilateral agreements. Common rules should provide legal certainty for Swiss exporters and allow new sectoral market access agreements to be concluded in the future. The RLP considered that the overall assessment was positive. It noted that the InstA did not constitute a loss of sovereignty. It also pointed out that, unlike the other EFTA States, Switzerland had managed to escape surveillance by a European administration. The RLP considered the InstA draft a diplomatic success. The RLP was also of the opinion that an adequate answer was provided to the issue of dispute settlement by the fact that an arbitration tribunal could independently and definitively review the

---

24 B. Fontanellaz, *Entre Sonderfall et intégration* (Academia/L'Harmattan, 2019), pp. 175–178.

25 Swiss Telegraphic Agency, 'Un oui de raison du PLR à l'accord-cadre avec l'UE', *24 Heures* 3 February 2019.

26 RLP Steering Committee, *Un 'Oui de raison' à l'Accord-cadre*, 4 March 2019, <https://www.eda.admin.ch/dam/europa/fr/documents/bericht_konsultationen_insta/stellungnahmen/d-Stellungnahme-InstA_fr.pdf> (accessed 31 May 2022).

proportionality of the compensation measures. With regard to the flanking measures, the RLP noted that the three most important of these were durably guaranteed. It saw nothing in the InstA that compromised them. It noted that the draft InstA did not contain any new standards (except for aviation). The only reservations of the RLP concerned the EU Citizens' Rights Directive 2004/38. Gently, the RLP recalled that the legal developments concerning the free movement of persons should be limited to the labour market. It only asked the Federal Council to clarify this point.

The main Swiss economic associations, from the export industry, services, banks and tourism, also clearly supported the InstA.[27] Many of them were even prepared to contribute massively to a referendum campaign in favour of the InstA. In general, all these associations emphasised the success of the Swiss negotiators and the concessions made by the EU, as well as the low risks involved in the Agreement. Above all, they insisted on the difficulties for Swiss companies that would arise if the agreements between Switzerland and the EU were not updated. They made it clear that this would have many negative consequences for Swiss companies and, above all, for Switzerland as a business location.

However, it should be noted that not all Swiss business associations and interest groups were in favour of the InstA. This is the case of the Swiss Trade Association, which represents small and medium-sized enterprises. This association is known for regularly expressing its misgivings about Switzerland's European policy.[28] It expressed its fears mainly over the EU Citizens' Rights Directive 2004/38, citing the risk of "social tourism". With regard to the flanking measures, it made it clear that it would not support actions aimed at increasing controls in companies to compensate for the abolition of the deposit on posted workers. Further, the emergence of new economic associations, *Kompass-Europa* and *Autonomie Suisse*, close to ultra-liberal financial circles, which intervened massively in German-speaking Switzerland, was also observed.[29] It is difficult to say whether their influence directly affected the position of the two RLP federal Councillors, but in any case, they contributed to the general climate of Euroscepticism.

---

27 Their positions can be found on the website, <https://www.eda.admin.ch/europa/fr/home/europapolitik/politique-europeenne/institutionelles-abkommen/institutionelles-abkommen-stellungnahmen.html> (accessed 31 May 2022).

28 B. Fontanella, F. Saint-Ouen, *Switzerland-European Union. The debates around the Inst*A (Dusan Sidjanski Competence Center, 2019), pp. 66–69.

29 M. Wieser, *Les milieux économiques suisses face à l'Accord institutionnel* (Master Université de Genève, 2021), pp. 25–35.

5.2 *The Two Federal Councillors of the RLP: Functions, Personalities and Personal Convictions*

The two RLP Federal Councillors are in charge of ministries that are very sensitive to a positive EU policy of Switzerland. And yet, they did not support the InstA. Ignazio Cassis and Karin Keller-Sutter are known as pragmatic and moderate people. They support a liberal and non-protectionist economy. They have always been unhesitatingly committed to the bilateral agreements with the European Union.

This is particularly true of Ignazio Cassis. As Head of the Federal Department of Foreign Affairs since 1 November 2017, he has been in the forefront of promoting Switzerland's international and European openness. Moreover, being from an Italian family and having been binational (Swiss and Italian) until his election to the Federal Council, he is naturally sensitive to European and neighbourhood issues. As soon as he arrived at his ministry, he sought to continue the negotiations on the InstA that had been initiated by Didier Burkhalter, his predecessor, also from the RLP, while pretending to carry out a *reset*. At the end of 2018, it still looked as if he was supporting the InstA[30] that had been negotiated mainly by Roberto Balzaretti, the also Italian-speaking Secretary of State he had appointed in January 2018. This appointment of the former Swiss Ambassador to the European Union gave the impression that Ignazio Cassis supported the steps taken by Roberto Balzaretti.

However, feeling the wind change, Ignazio Cassis let go of his Secretary of State[31] who was sent as ambassador to Paris, and he became very discreet about the InstA, even though he was supposed to have carried the project as Minister of Foreign Affairs in charge of the European file. It is difficult to know why Ignazio Cassis has shown such a lack of leadership on this issue. Perhaps he realised that the opposition was too strong and that it was risky to take on the responsibility of carrying the draft InstA. He was probably trying to avoid facing all the criticism alone, as well as the consequences of a popular rejection in a referendum.

It should be borne in mind that his seat in the Federal Council is fragile. Indeed, Ignazio Cassis had been relatively poorly elected and re-elected, and he was aware that his continuation in government depended on the support of the SPP. In this respect, the analysis we made above about the Socialist Party, therefore, also applies to the Radical-Liberal Party. This party received only

30 Private interview with Federal Councilor Ignazio Cassis, following the conference we gave together at the invitation of Coscienza Svizzera, Lugano, 13 October 2018.

31 Private interview in Geneva with Secretary of State Roberto Balzaretti who already confided to us on 3 April 2019 that he felt let down by the Federal Council.

15% of the votes in the 2019 elections. It would no longer deserve, arithmetically, to keep two seats in the Federal Council. If the results of 2023 continued to be so unfavourable to the RLP, this party could no longer legitimately claim to keep its second seat in the Federal Council and would have to sacrifice that of its Italian-speaking representative. Indeed, this party would not want to give up the seat of its other representative, Karin Keller-Sutter, because it is occupied by a person from the important Swiss-German part of the country, which represents the key to Swiss political life. Moreover, it is politically sensitive to attack the position of a woman, who is also very competent.

In conclusion, Ignazio Cassis was aware that his seat in the Federal Council will be particularly threatened in 2023 and that it was important for him not to suffer a major defeat in a referendum on the InstA. This is also why he has pursued a political line that is further to the right than the majority of his party, not only on the European issue but also on immigration. This was the only way for him to secure the support of the SPP (Switzerland's largest party), which he will need for his re-election.

The other representative of the RLP in the Federal Council is Karin Keller-Sutter. She has been in charge of the Federal Department of Justice and Police since 1 January 2019. She has the reputation of being a particularly hard-working and intelligent person. As head of the Justice Ministry, she had an important say in institutional matters, especially those related to the Court of Arbitration and the role played by the Court of Justice of the European Union. In general, she has always supported the bilateral agreements between Switzerland and the EU and has fought against SPP initiatives that could have challenged them, such as the 2020 initiative on "Mass Immigration". At the same time, she was quick to express her deepest misgivings about the InstA.[32] As soon as she was elected, she communicated that she was skeptical about the very principle of the dynamic adoption of the evolution of EU law and the leading role played by the CJEU in the settlement of disputes. She considered these to be too great a loss of sovereignty for Switzerland.

In this regard, it should be noted that representatives of the European Commission and some observers suspected that the Federal Council had never really accepted the principle of the dynamic adoption of the relevant EU law and that it was in fact these sovereignty considerations which constitute

32 H. Gmür, M. Schönenberger, 'Karin Keller-Sutter: "Wir müssen Schikanen der EU aushalten"', *Neue Zürcher Zeitung* 20 November 2018.

the real reason for the rejection of the InstA.[33] As already mentioned, this is undeniably the case for the two SPP Federal Councillors and likely for Karin Keller-Sutter. For the other four Federal Councillors, however, it is unlikely and impossible to prove.

Regarding the risks of a rejection of the InstA, Karin Keller-Sutter constantly tried to minimise them by emphasising the strengths of the Swiss economy and the framework conditions which the country offers to economic actors. Finally, with regard to the pressure from the trade unions and the Socialist Party, she made it clear that this could lead to too many concessions from the employers and that it could cost the Federal Council too much money if additional controls on companies had to be financed to counterbalance the risks of wage dumping.

In conclusion, Karin Keller-Sutter's scepticism was a major factor in the Federal Council's decision to reject the InstA. Her strong personality, her determination and her position in the Government had a decisive influence.

6 Government Member of the Christian Democratic Party (CDP) / The Centre

We do not deal here in detail with the position of the Christian Democratic Party (CDP)/The Centre[34] and its Federal Councillor Viola Amherd. Broadly speaking, the CDP has followed a fairly similar trajectory to the RLP. It is a centre-right party, traditionally favourable of the bilateral path and moderate in its positions. However, it has been unusually more uncompromising than the RLP in its stance on the InstA, which is already reflected in the title of its position paper of 3 March 2019: "Yes to the continuation of the bilateral path, but not at any price".[35]

The CDP Federal Councillor, Viola Amherd, has been extremely discreet on the subject of the InstA. Moreover, she was in charge of the Department of Defence, which was the one least affected by the Agreement. The CDP's single

33 S. Walter, 'Quo vadis, Swiss-European Union relations', *Bruegel Blog* 7 June 2021,<https://www.bruegel.org/2021/06/quo-vadis-swiss-european-union-relations/> (accessed 31 May 2022).

34 Since 2021, this party has changed its name following the absorption of another center-right party. It is now called the Center.

35 Christian Democratic Party, *Oui au développement des bilatérales, mais pas à n'importe quel prix*, 5 March 2019, <https://www.cvp.ch/fr/news/2019-03-05/oui-au-developpement-des-bilaterales-mais-pas-nimporte-quel-prix> (accessed 31 May 2022, translated by author from French).

seat on the Federal Council is less threatened than that of the RLP, as it reflects the party's arithmetical weight (13% of the votes in the National Council, as well as a relatively stronger representation in the Council of States).

In general, the CDP is losing momentum and feels threatened by the SPP in its traditional and conservative strongholds in the Catholic cantons of the peripheral parts of German-speaking Switzerland. Like the RLP, the CDP also did not want to give the SPP any pretext for surfing on themes related to the country's sovereignty, immigration and "social tourism".

7 InstA: Incomprehension about Its Rejection

The Federal Council's rejection of the InstA has confused many people in Switzerland and Europe. They did not understand the radical nature of this decision which had been taken even though 1. the Swiss negotiators had obtained substantial concessions from the EU, 2. the EU had been less intransigent with Switzerland than with other countries, 3. the risks with regard to wage protection, social tourism and State aid had been exaggerated, 4. the Federal Council could have promoted internal measures to allay fears and 5. the detrimental consequences of a rejection of the InstA were known.

7.1 *Relatively Well-Negotiated Agreement and Substantial Concessions from the EU*

A first incomprehension comes from the fact that there was a broad consensus that Switzerland had negotiated the InstA relatively well and had obtained significant concessions from the EU. These elements were underlined by both the European Commission and the Federal Council. On the part of the Commission, it is indeed unusual to acknowledge that it has given in on many points in relation to the objectives of its negotiating mandate. Thus, according to Petros Mavromichalis, the EU Ambassador to Switzerland: "During the negotiations between 2014 and 2018, and even more recently in the talks to find solutions for the three remaining open issues, the EU has made numerous concessions to address the Swiss concerns".[36] And on the part of the Swiss Government, it is also not trivial to admit that the outcome of the negotiations

36 P. Mavromichalis, 'Union européenne – Suisse: et maintenant?', *Le Temps* 25 June 2021 (translated by author from French).

"corresponds to a large extent to the interests of Switzerland and to the negotiating mandate".[37]

It is therefore necessary to recall these concessions from the EU obtained by the Swiss negotiators. We do so in broad outline, as some of these points are developed in a more substantial way elsewhere in this book.[38]

Firstly, the scope of the planned Agreement was limited to the five existing market access agreements, as well as to future market access agreements. Thus, contrary to the EU's initial request,[39] the InstA did not include the 1972 Free Trade Agreement, nor the ones on certain aspects of government procurement and simplification of inspections and formalities in respect of the carriage of goods and customs security measures.

Secondly, the InstA ruled out the principle of an *automatic* takeover of developments in EU law. Instead, it favoured the principle of a *dynamic* takeover (even if the term is not expressly used). The autonomy of the Swiss legislator could thus have been guaranteed. This means that Switzerland could have had sufficient time to continue to decide independently on the adoption of each development of EU law, in accordance with its internal approval procedures (including the possibility of a referendum).

In addition, Switzerland was granted the right to participate in the elaboration of new EU legislation relevant to the Bilateral Agreements ("decision-shaping"), which has been one of its long-standing demands since its failure to participate in the EEA in 1992.

With regard to the settlement of disputes, the InstA provided for the establishment of an arbitration tribunal as requested by Switzerland. Arbitrators appointed by Switzerland and the EU would have a seat in the tribunal on an equal basis with the EU. Switzerland had to accept the jurisdiction of the CJEU to interpret the EU law contained in the agreements. And if Switzerland had not complied with an arbitration award, the EU would have had the possibility of taking compensatory measures. But these would have had to be proportionate, a condition whose compliance could have been verified by the arbitral tribunal.

---

37 Federal Council, *European Policy – Federal Council decides to launch consultations on the text of the InstA*, 7 December 2018. The Federal Council considers the current outcome of the negotiations to be largely in Switzerland's interests and in line with the negotiating mandate, <https://www.admin.ch/gov/fr/accueil/documentation/communiques.msg-id-73292.html> (accessed 31 May 2022).

38 See notably also the contributions by C. Kaddous and K. Pärli in this volume.

39 Council of the European Union, *Council Decision Authorising the Opening of Negotiations on an Agreement between the European Union and the Swiss Confederation on an Institutional Framework Governing Bilateral Relations*, 6 May 2014, point 2.1 (unpublished).

With regard to the supervision in Switzerland of the agreements covered by the InstA, the Swiss authorities and courts would have remained competent to ensure the correct application and interpretation of market access agreements. In other words, the EU failed to impose its demand that an authority independent from Switzerland, such as the EFTA Surveillance Authority[40] or the European Commission, monitor them. This last requirement is reflected in the unpublished Commission's negotiating mandate guidelines of 6 May 2014. Indeed, it states that "the Commission should supervise the application of the agreements by Switzerland; the Commission should also be granted specific powers if required depending on each sector, such as investigatory and decision-making powers. These powers should reflect those already vested on the Commission in the field of the internal market".[41]

However, following meetings between Yves Rossier and David O'Sullivan in 2014, the EU moved closer to the Swiss position on the issue of supervision and finally abandoned its demand for a role for the European Commission.[42]

Thus, the draft InstA provided a two-pillar model (Articles 6 and 7). Switzerland and the EU would each have been responsible for the correct application of the agreements on their respective territories. The solution found, therefore, did not involve the creation of a supranational supervisory body and did not provide for any competence of the European Commission vis-à-vis Switzerland (except for air transport).[43]

As regards State aid, it would have applied only to the Agreement on Air Transport. As for other areas of State aid, the substantive rules contained in the InstA were limited to defining a legal framework, which would have had to be taken up and possibly supplemented in future market access agreements in order to be able to apply. The Commission had thus refrained from mentioning a contentious reference providing that the State aid rules defined by the

40 Swiss Secretary of State Yves Rossier and European External Action Service (EEAS) Administrative Director General David O'Sullivan discussed different options in a "non-paper". The first option was to redesign the institutional pillar of the European Free Trade Association (EFTA) to allow its Surveillance Authority and Court to rule on the interpretation and application of bilateral agreements. However, this solution was considered difficult to implement. It could also have been interpreted as a form of manipulation to join the European Economic Area, even though the Swiss people did not want it in 1992; Y. Rossier, D. O'Sullivan, *Éléments de discussion sur les questions institutionnelles entre l'Union européenne et la Confédération helvétique*, Non-paper, May 2013 (unpublished).

41 Council of the European Union, *Council Decision Authorising the Opening of Negotiations* (n. 40), Annex, Article 1(5).

42 Conseil fédéral, *Rapport relatif aux négociations* (n. 6), point 2.2.3.1, p. 12.

43 On the issue of surveillance, see also the contribution by C. Kaddous in this volume.

InstA would be relevant for interpreting the State aid provisions of the 1972 Free Trade Agreement.[44]

Whilst Switzerland did not succeed in explicitly excluding the inclusion of the EU Citizens' Rights Directive 2004/38 in the draft Agreement, the fact that the Directive was not mentioned in the draft of the Agreement was a concession on the part of the EU and opened a window of ambiguity that could have been exploited by Switzerland.

With regard to the flanking measures, the EU explicitly recognised for the first time that, given the particularities of its labour market, Switzerland should retain its flanking measures.[45] Specifically, with regard to posted workers, the EU had agreed in Protocol 1 of the InstA draft to guarantee a 90 days limit on the provision of services, a rule that does not exist in the EU. It had also consented to a 4 day pre-notification regime, which does not exist either in the EU. In addition, it had also admitted a system of financial guarantees (in case of past infringement).

Finally, the Commission expressed its agreement in principle to Switzerland establishing additional administrative and control measures, provided that they are justified and proportionate. It also agreed to leave Switzerland free to determine the frequency and organisation of controls; to explicitly recognize the key role of the social partners in determining the remuneration of workers; and to guarantee that Switzerland could participate fully in the work of the new European Labour Authority.

It is not easy to explain why the EU agreed to grant so many concessions to Switzerland. Let us venture into three hypotheses.

Firstly, the economic importance of Switzerland, in terms of trade, finance, transport services and people, is not negligible.

Secondly, Switzerland had a good negotiating position on the InstA in that, even if it failed, the agreements already concluded with the EU would not have been called into question (even if they could be eroded). Thus, unlike the UK, which risked losing everything after its withdrawal from the EU in the absence of a trade agreement, or the Eastern Partnership countries, which were in a geo-strategically weak position, Switzerland was not condemned to give in to most of the EU's demands.

Thirdly, there is the so-called "two-level game" according to Robert Putnam's theory. This is particularly present in Switzerland, perhaps even more so than

44 The Federal Council acknowledges: "the point relating to State aid could be satisfactorily resolved provided that agreement is reached on the other two points"; Conseil fédéral, *Rapport relatif aux négociations* (n. 6), p. 17.

45 See the contribution by K. Pärli in this volume.

elsewhere in the world. The Federal Council must indeed systematically act at the same time at the international and domestic levels. Its negotiators are obliged to obtain concessions from the EU and to consolidate all the details, otherwise, they cannot obtain the approval of the Federal Parliament and, above all, of the Swiss citizens in referenda.

It should be remembered that the Swiss system differs from that of other States. As already explained, the Federal Council is composed of four political parties whose members do not consider themselves bound by the options of the Federal Council, even though they have a large majority in the Federal Parliament.

More fundamentally, there is almost certainly a referendum against any agreement signed with the EU. There have already been 18 popular votes linked, directly or indirectly, to the issue of relations with the EU![46] It is thus the European country where the Government can least control the ratification of an international agreement. The European Union was aware of this very particular situation as recognised by the EU Council in an internal document: "Agreement was possible due to the *Commission's understanding of the political constraints* in Switzerland and a willingness to compromise in the interest of a balanced outcome".[47]

7.2 *The European Union Has Been Less Intransigent Towards Switzerland Than towards Other Third Countries and Ultimately the Brexit Did Not Play a Decisive Role*

A second incomprehension concerns the supposed inflexibility of the European Union.[48] This is the thesis that has been defended by the Federal Council and its supporters to explain the failure of the InstA. Thus, according to Ignazio Cassis, "Brexit has reduced Brussels' flexibility towards Switzerland".[49] This EU

46 R. Schwok, *Suisse-Union européenne. L'adhésion impossible?* (PPUR, 2021), pp. 183–185.

47 Council of the European Union, General Secretariat, *EU-Swiss Relations: Note to College and Letter of Commissioner Hahn to College*, (18 June 2019) WK 7493/2019 INIT, p. 2 (not published, emphasis added). Commissioner Johannes Hahn, in a private letter to the President of the European Commission Jean-Claude Juncker, makes the same point: "the [InstA] goes a long way in addressing Swiss domestic concerns".

48 W. Streeck, 'Swexit', *New Left Review* (17 June 2021), <https://newleftreview.org/sidecar/posts/swexit?pc=1354> (accessed 31 May 2022).

49 'Le Brexit a diminué la flexibilité de Bruxelles envers la Suisse' (translated by author from French); L. Bailat, N. Lamon, 'Interview du nouveau président', *Le Matin Dimanche* 1 January 2022. These are also the opinions of the political scientists Stefanie Bailer and Stefanie Walter, as indicated in J. Wermuth, '"Verzerrte Wahrnehmung auf Schweizer Seite" – 6 Lehren aus dem InstA-Aus', *Watson* 2 June 2021.

intransigence was thus reinforced by the concomitance of negotiations with the United Kingdom of Great Britain and Northern Ireland, which would have radicalised the position of the European Commission. Brussels would have been led not to grant the slightest concession to Switzerland in order to prevent London from seeking to benefit from it. Some observers have pointed out that it was the same person, Stéphanie Riso, who was generally considered to be inflexible, and who had very important responsibilities in the negotiations with both the United Kingdom and Switzerland. She had indeed been the senior strategy officer in the task force led by Michel Barnier during the Brexit negotiations. Then, she had become Deputy Chief of Staff of the president of the European Commission Ursula von der Leyen and the main interlocutor of Switzerland to try to save the draft of the InstA after the Federal Council refused to initial it in December 2018.

These comparisons with the Brexit discussions are relevant for the period 2016–2019, but not beyond. It is certainly true that the negotiations with the United Kingdom interfered for a time with those with Switzerland and that the Commission was afraid of granting concessions to Switzerland that could have been claimed by the United Kingdom, and *vice versa*.

At the same time, the fact remains that circumstances had changed dramatically by the time Boris Johnson came to power and had set his sights on a completely different objective than the one sought by Switzerland. Unlike his predecessor, Theresa May, he no longer sought a solution that would have maintained a certain degree of UK access to the EU's internal market but had mainly limited his ambitions to a simple free trade area based on the abolition of tariffs.[50] In any case, neither Theresa May nor Boris Johnson had sought to maintain the free movement of persons with the EU. In Switzerland, it is, let us recall, around two issues related to the free movement of persons that the InstA failed (namely flanking measures in the context of posted workers and the rights of persons under the EU Citizens' Rights Directive 2004/38). In addition, as of January 2020, the negotiations with the United Kingdom were completed. The European Union was therefore free of any risk of parallelism in its discussions with Switzerland.

In substance, this thesis of EU intransigence does not seem convincing either, because the European Union has made fewer demands on Switzerland in the InstA than it had in the 1990s with the European Economic Area (EEA). In contrast to the EEA, the InstA included many of the concessions that we

---

50 R. Schwok, 'British and Swiss Rejections of the New EU External Governance', in D. Chryssochoou, C.V. Gortson, V.G. Hatzopoulos and A.G. Passis (eds.), *European Governance in Times of Uncertainty* (Nomiki Bibliothiki, 2021), pp. 75–87.

have already mentioned. Above all, it was limited to a restricted number of areas and would not have been managed in a multilateral way as in the EFTA pillar of the EEA.

In conclusion, it is difficult to understand the discourse that the EU has been more intransigent with Switzerland than at other times or with other third countries when everything indicates that it has not been more or even less so.

7.3 *The Risks with Regard to Wage Protection, Social Tourism and State Aid Seemed Exaggerated*

A third incomprehension concerns the catastrophic discourse that was put forward by the opponents of the InstA. They simply claimed that Swiss wages would no longer be protected, that there would be massive immigration attracted by the generous Swiss social system and that State aid would be abolished. It is difficult to comprehend why such exaggerations were put forward and why the Federal Council did not try to put them into perspective.

As far as wage protection is concerned, it should first be recalled that posted work only concerns about 0.7% of the workforce in Switzerland. It mainly affects the construction, agriculture and tourism sectors where Swiss citizens hardly work. In other words, almost 99.3% of Swiss workers are not affected by competition from this category of workers. Therefore, it is difficult to grasp how Swiss wages could have been jeopardised by a slight flexibilisation of the constraints concerning posted workers.

It is also important to remember that, in order to avoid the repetition of wage dumping and to appease the European leftist parties and the rich member States, the EU has recently adopted more modern rules enshrining the principle of "equal pay for equal work in the same workplace". This means that posted workers must be paid the same as local employees, not just the minimum wage.[51]

With regard to the risks of "social tourism" linked to the eventual adoption of the EU Citizens' Rights Directive 2004/38, it should be recalled that European law does not allow an EU national to settle in a country for the sole purpose of taking advantage of its social benefits. In fact, EU case law and practice show that Switzerland could have implemented the Citizens' Rights Directive in a way that avoids abuse of social assistance. In the Swiss public discourse, criticism focused on the right to social assistance for an indefinite period of time for EU citizens who involuntarily lost their jobs after at least twelve months in Switzerland. However, this change from the current situation would have been

51 See again the contribution by K. Pärli in this volume.

much less revolutionary than it seemed: it would have occurred at the earliest 29 months after the arrival of the EU: citizen in Switzerland. Although the adoption of the Directive would have meant additional costs for Switzerland, according to estimations, these would have been modest; between 27 million and 75 million Swiss Francs per year in the worst case.[52] This is a drop in the ocean of Swiss social spending (168 billion Swiss Francs per year).

In the case of State aid, the risks had also been exaggerated and distorted. Many cantons had begun to claim that they would no longer be able to maintain their guarantees to their cantonal banks and their hydropower resources. This is reflected in the particularly critical report on the InstA by the Conference of Cantons, whereas this body had always been previously very supportive of European integration.[53]

In addition, some Swiss leftist circles were spreading the rumour that housing subsidies,[54] as well as other social benefits such as pensions and health care, were to be abolished. They even claimed that the public service would be undermined,[55] without producing any evidence to support this assertion. There is no doubt that this was not true, and that State aid is much more widespread in almost all EU Member States than in Switzerland, a country with a liberal and relatively non-statist tradition. At worst, it would have been necessary to make minor legislative changes, as is already the case for some cantonal banks such as in Geneva.[56]

It was also clear that the European Union not only allowed but encouraged, all State aid aimed at promoting renewable energies, such as hydropower. Finally, it was obvious that State aid for social, housing, social security and investment in special areas is proliferating in the European Union at levels that Switzerland will never experience.

---

52 D. Farman, *Directive citoyenneté: pas d'explosion de l'aide sociale en vue* (Avenir Suisse, 2021), 13 January 2021, <https://www.avenir-suisse.ch/fr/directive-citoyennete%E2%80%AF-pas-dexplosion-de-laide-sociale-en-vue/> (accessed 31 May 2022).

53 See <https://www.eda.admin.ch/dam/europa/fr/documents/bericht_konsultationen_insta/stellungnahmen/KdK-Stellungnahme-InstA_fr.pdf> (accessed 31 May 2022), as well as <https://www.eda.admin.ch/dam/europa/de/documents/bericht_konsultationen_insta/stellungnahmen/Kantonsrat-ZH-Stellungnahme-InstA_de.pdf> (accessed 31 May 2022).

54 See <https://www.eda.admin.ch/dam/europa/de/documents/bericht_konsultationen_insta/stellungnahmen/SMV-Stellungnahme-InstA_fr.pdf> (accessed 31 May 2022).

55 <https://www.eda.admin.ch/dam/europa/fr/documents/bericht_konsultationen_insta/stellungnahmen/SGB-USS-Stellungnahme-InstA_fr.pdf> (accessed 31 May 2022), p. 7. Further, private interview with the President of the Swiss Trade Union, Pierre-Yves Maillard, Geneva, 27 February 2020.

56 Private interview with Former Secretary of State Jacques de Watteville, Geneva/Lausanne, 12 May 2021.

7.4 *The Federal Council Could Have Promoted Measures to Allay the Fears that Had Been Aroused among the Population*

A fourth incomprehension concerns the reasons that led the Federal Council not to promote measures to allay the fears that had been aroused in the population. The Federal Council could have tried to reassure the population and to find solutions to compensate for the possible risks posed to salary protection.

This could have consisted, for example, in taking up the broad lines of the proposals of the think tank *foraus.*[57] These are already applied in the canton of Geneva to the satisfaction of the left and the right. They allow strengthened inspections at workplaces and the involvement of unions as well as employers. This would have made it possible to compensate for the disappearance of the deposit. More severe measures could also have been taken than at present against entrepreneurs who employ posted workers at rates lower than the wages in force in Switzerland.

The federal and cantonal authorities could also have encouraged the extension of the scope of Collective Labour Agreements. Indeed, sectors not covered are more likely to face threats to wages. At a minimum, the effort could have been focused on sectors under pressure, such as retail trade, landscaping, cleaning and information technologies.

Finally, it would have been necessary to explore the possibility of transitional phases for the implementation of the waiver of the deposit on posted workers. The same applies to the EU Citizens' Rights Directive 2004/38. It is difficult to understand why the Federal Council did not, as suggested by the think tank *foraus*,[58] propose to introduce the Directive in stages and to evaluate after a number of years whether it really resulted in "social tourism".

In any case, the Federal Council could have explained that, even if Switzerland had decided not to properly apply the EU Citizens' Rights Directive 2004/38, the risks incurred would not have been very significant. At worst, the Confederation would have been obliged, after a long procedure, by a ruling of the Arbitration Tribunal, to better implement the regulation in this area. And the sanction, in case of non-compliance would have had to be proportionate

---

57 D. Farman, C. Najy and W. Zülch, *Mesures d'accompagnement: 10 propositions pour construire un consensus interne en vue d'un accord institutionnel* (Foraus, 2019), <https://www.foraus.ch/wp-content/uploads/2019/03/FlaM_versionWEB.pdf> (accessed 31 May 2022). foraus is a think tank founded 2009. It is based on a grassroots model of students between 20 and 30 years old who have a common goal: to constructively shape Swiss foreign policy.

58 D. Farman, F. Maurer and C. Najy, *Deux propositions pour finaliser l'accord institutionnel entre la Suisse et l'UE* (foraus, 2020), <https://www.foraus.ch/wp-content/uploads/2020/01/20200117_FlaM-FR.pdf> (accessed 31 May 2022).

and of such a nature as to ensure a balance in the rules (i.e., a corresponding treatment for Swiss nationals in the EU area).

7.5 *The Damaging Consequences of a Rejection of the InstA Were Known*

A fifth incomprehension concerns the negative consequences of a rejection of the InstA. Why did the Federal Council not take these more into account? They were known. Not only the European Commission but also the Federal Council itself had communicated widely on this subject. In its *Explanatory* of the rejection of the InstA in May 2021, the Federal Council itself clearly recognised that without this agreement: "The *situation will deteriorate* as the existing agreements cannot be updated [...] *the competitiveness* and competitive advantages of Swiss players in the internal market may be *reduced*, not only vis-à-vis competitors in the EU but also vis-à-vis third countries with which the EU concludes new agreements. *Legal uncertainty* [...] could be accompanied by a *decline in the attractiveness of Switzerland as a business location and a slowdown in investment* in Switzerland".[59]

The Federal Council was thus fully aware that, without an InstA, the sectoral agreements in force could no longer be updated. At the time of writing, this primarily concerns trade in medical devices, a sector that accounts for as large a share of GDP as tourism. Switzerland is closely integrated into the EU internal market through the Mutual Recognition Agreement, which provides for the recognition of conformity assessment certificates between the EU and Switzerland on the basis of equivalent regulations. The new EU regulatory framework governing medical devices became applicable in May 2021. As a result, new Swiss medium- and high-risk devices must be approved by certification bodies established in the EU. Switzerland exports 46% of its medical devices to the EU and imports 54%. Less fluid trade may result in a loss of business for the medical device industry. The Swiss machine and chemical industries are also threatened by the failure to update agreements with the EU. The same goes for trade in agricultural products.

It was also known that without InstA, no new market access agreement would be concluded with Switzerland. This primarily concerns energy and the risk of losing the privileged connection to the EU electricity system. By not accepting the common rules, Switzerland would be obliged to leave the European electricity exchange platforms and cooperation platforms for grid operators or regulators and would gradually lose its privileged connection

59 Conseil fédéral, *Rapport relatif aux négociations* (n. 6), p. 30 (translated by author from French, emphasis added).

to the EU electricity system. This is all the more damaging as Switzerland is dependent on electricity imports from neighbouring countries for almost half the year (in winter). Moreover, Switzerland has decided to decarbonize its electricity production and, therefore, produce more electricity from renewable energy sources while abolishing nuclear power. Variable energy production requires aggregation across larger regions so that excess production can be sold, and electricity purchased from neighbouring countries as needed.

Finally, the risks of exclusion and marginalisation of the Swiss research sector from European programs had been the subject of a very large information campaign conducted by the universities.[60] This is what happened very quickly with the relegation of Switzerland to a status inferior to that of countries such as the United Kingdom, Turkey and Israel, countries with which the EU has far more litigation than Switzerland.

Thus, it remains very difficult to understand why the Federal Council did not communicate more about the harmful consequences of a rejection of the InstA, even though it had all the data on this subject and had mentioned them itself.

8 Conclusion

This analysis has shown that there are good reasons for not understanding the decision of the Federal Council to reject the InstA. Indeed, this Agreement had been relatively well negotiated and many concessions had been wrested from the EU. Aware of the internal political constraints in Switzerland, the Commission had not, moreover, shown itself to be more intransigent than at other times with Switzerland or with other third countries. As for the concomitance of the Brexit negotiation, it had not exercised a decisive influence.

In addition, the risk posed by accepting the InstA had been greatly exaggerated and there were many solutions to allay the fears that had been raised. Furthermore, the negative economic and political consequences of a rejection of the InstA were well known and even emphasised by the Federal Council itself.

60 swissuniversities, *Accord-cadre avec l'UE: swissuniversities demande la poursuite des discussions pour assurer la participation de la Suisse aux programmes de recherche et de formation de l'UE*, 17 March 2021, <https://www.swissuniversities.ch/fr/actualite/accord-cadre-avec-lue-swissuniversities-demande-la-poursuite-des-discussions-pour-assurer-la-participation-de-la-suisse-aux-programmes-de-recherche-et-de-formation-de-lue> (accessed 31 May 2022).

Nevertheless, to understand the Federal Council's rejection of the InstA, we tried to proceed by empathy. In this way, we were able to observe that its decision was an indicator both of its sense of weakness in domestic politics and of its perception of economic strength internationally,

In domestic politics, this feeling of weakness first affected the Socialist Party (SP). The Federal Councillors belonging to this party did not consider themselves strong enough to oppose the trade unions, which had stormed the InstA with a rare determination. They feared that a possible referendum would turn out very badly if the unions had converged with the far-right Swiss People's Party (SPP), Switzerland's largest party, to oppose the InstA. They also dreaded that the Socialist Party would suffer the consequences of the controversies surrounding this referendum in the 2023 federal elections. Knowing that the socialist party's second seat on the Federal Council is contested, they did not want to risk further weakening the party, when it can already arithmetically no longer claim a second seat.

All in all, the reasoning of the Radical-Liberal Party (RLP), and to a lesser extent, the Christian Democratic Party (CDP), was quite similar to that of the Socialist Party. The RLP feared that a referendum on the InstA would be won by the SPP, which would have raised the spectres of the loss of sovereignty, submission to foreign judges and an increase in "social tourism". Like that of the SP, the second RLP seat in the Federal Council is no longer arithmetically justified either. And *a fortiori*, if its score was even lower in 2023, it could no longer be able to maintain it.

The only seat of the CDP in the Federal Council is less precarious since it reflects more the arithmetic weight of this party. Nevertheless, in general, this political formation also considers itself threatened by the SPP in its traditional strongholds.

This thesis of "weakness" is confirmed by the Federal Council itself. In its Report aiming to explain the rejection of the InstA, it wrote in black and white that if it had signed such an unbalanced agreement for Switzerland, it would never have been able to "obtain the approval of the Federal Parliament and face the referendum that would most likely be launched against the InstA".[61]

61 Conseil fédéral, Rapport relatif aux négociations (n. 6), p. 34: 'Only a globally balanced negotiation result in the interest of Switzerland could guarantee sufficient support from the domestic political actors, which is a prerequisite for obtaining the support from domestic political actors, which is essential to obtain parliamentary approval and parliamentary approval and to face the referendum that would most likely be launched against the institutional agreement. In this respect, the Federal Council believes that the rejection of the agreement by the people would constitute the worst-case scenario (...)' (translated by author from French, emphasis added).

At the same time, the Federal Council's decision reflects its perception of the balance of power vis-à-vis the European Union. The Swiss Government dared to adopt such a decision because it believed that Switzerland was strong enough to withstand any negative consequences.

First of all, there is often a misperception in Switzerland of the supposed weakness of the EU. Indeed, the EU was regularly portrayed as fragile, if not on the verge of collapse (eurozone and migrant crises), undermined by internal divisions (Poland, Hungary) and unable to assert itself in the face of third countries such as the United Kingdom, Turkey or Russia. For example, according to a study commissioned by the Federal Council in January 2021, the EU would have been so discredited, especially the Commission, that it would have been prepared to abandon the InstA and accept many concessions to Switzerland in another treaty in order to regain its image and have a diplomatic success to its credit.[62]

In addition, the Federal Council has produced various analyses which tend to prove that the EU would be as much dependent on Switzerland as Switzerland is on the EU. The Federal Council did not fail to point out that Switzerland is one of the EU's top four economic partners in terms of trade in goods, services and investments. Nor did it fail to point out that the number of EU nationals living in Switzerland reached 1.4 million, to which must be added 340,000 cross-border commuters, as well as EU nationals subject to the obligation to register (approximately 200,000).[63] These statistics are of course exact, but they can never hide the fact that Switzerland is far more dependent on the EU than the other way round. In other words, a few well-targeted measures by the EU against Switzerland would cause a psychodrama in Switzerland, while the opposite would hardly be noticeable in the EU.

Thus, the Federal Council considered that the EU would not risk calling everything into question because it rejected the InstA. It also considered that the political sanctions adopted by the EU would be bearable and that they could be remedied by a few gestures such as a structured political dialogue, interim agreements and the payment of cohesion funds to the countries of Central and Eastern Europe.

With more distance in time, the assessment of the Swiss Government's decision will evolve according to the vicissitudes of the relationship between

62 N. Levrat, *Profiter d'un contexte favorable pour renégocier un nouvel accord-cadre avec l'UE* (Bern, 2021), <https://www.eda.admin.ch/dam/eda/fr/documents/aktuell/news/2021/21211712-gutachten-levrat-alternativen-verhandlungsprozess_FR.pdf> (accessed 31 May 2022), pp. 18–19.

63 Federal Department of Foreign Affairs, *No signing of Swiss–EU InstA* (no. 6).

Switzerland and the EU. In the positive hypothesis that Switzerland would continue to perform better economically than its neighbours and not suffer too much from its more difficult access to the EU's internal market, the Federal Council's decision will likely appear much more understandable than it is the case today. Its decision will be all the better judged if a new InstA ends up being negotiated between the EU and Switzerland and if that new agreement takes more account of the Swiss demands than the draft InstA of 2018.

If, on the other hand, no new agreement is reached with the EU, and if the Swiss economy were to flourish less than that of its European neighbours, further the difficulties of access to the EU market were to lead to significant relocations, the electricity sector were to experience difficulties and the research institutes were to lose their attractiveness, the decision of the Federal Council to reject the InstA would likely give rise to even more misapprehension than it is already the case.

CHAPTER 11

Switzerland and the EU

The Failure of the Institutional Agreement from a Legal Perspective

Christine Kaddous

1 Introduction

The Swiss Confederation, located in the heart of the European continent, is not a member of the European Union (EU), nor indeed of the European Economic Area (EEA). Even so, Switzerland's relations with the EU are dense and intense. They have been developed in an ad hoc way and are founded on specific institutional mechanisms. Some twenty-five agreements of primary importance together with more than one hundred secondary agreements link Switzerland with the EU today.[1] Among these agreements, the two sets of *Bilateral Agreements I* (1999) and *Bilateral Agreements II* (2004)[2] as well as the other agreements like the Free Trade Agreement (1972) are key in the relations between the partners. Some of these agreements provide for partial participation of Switzerland in the EU's internal market. Most of these bilateral agreements include institutional provisions for their adaptation to new legal developments in the EU *acquis*, the surveillance of their application, their interpretation as well as the dispute settlement mechanism to be applied between the contracting parties. These institutional issues were the focus of the Institutional Agreement (InstA) that was foreseen between Switzerland and the EU.[3]

---

1 A list of these agreements is available in French at <https://www.eda.admin.ch/dam/europa/fr/documents/publikationen_dea/accords-liste_fr.pdf> (accessed 25 April 2022).

2 For a commentary on the *Bilateral Agreements I*, see D. Felder, C. Kaddous (eds.), *Accords bilatéraux Suisse-UE (Commentaires). Bilaterale Abkommen Schweiz-EU (Erste Analysen)*, Dossier de droit européen n° 8 (Helbing-LGDJ-Bruylant, 2001), and on the *Bilateral Agreements II*, see C. Kaddous, M. Jametti Greiner (eds.), *Accords bilatéraux II Suisse – UE et autres Accords récents, Dossier de droit européen*, n° 16 (Helbing-LGDJ-Bruylant, 2006); C. Kaddous, *The Relations between the EU and Switzerland*, in A. Dashwood, M. Maresceau (eds.), *Law and Practice of EU External Relations. Salient Features of a Changing Landscape* (Cambridge University Press, 2008), p. 227 et seq.

3 No English version of the agreement is available. The official French version is entitled "Accord facilitant les relations bilatérales entre l'Union européenne et la Confédération suisse dans les parties du marché intérieur auxquelles la Suisse participe» ("Agreement

© KONINKLIJKE BRILL NV, LEIDEN, 2023 | DOI:10.1163/9789004529984_013

Since 2008, the EU has been emphasising, through successive Council conclusions, that the system of the bilateral agreements between Switzerland and the EU is too complex, incomplete and lacks of homogeneous conditions for citizens and businesses in the areas of the extended internal market in which Switzerland participates.[4] The idea of the possibility of a "framework agreement" to consolidate the bilateral approach had gained ground. Exploratory discussions took place between Switzerland and the EU since 2010 and despite major differences, the findings were seen as encouraging on both sides.[5] After having examined the possible options for such an agreement, in May 2014, Switzerland and the EU entered into negotiations on an InstA to consolidate and develop the relationship between the partners. These negotiations have come to a close at the end of 2018. However, the InstA has not been signed and remained a mere draft text.

The Federal Council initiated in January 2019 a wide consultation on the text as it resulted from the last phase of the negotiations. All relevant stakeholders were able to participate and an intense discussion took place in Switzerland on all important aspects of the InstA. At the end of this process, the Federal Council reiterated its support, in principle, for the text negotiated. It did, however, decide in June 2019 to ask the EU for clarifications concerning the scope of the envisaged agreement on three aspects: the protection of wages, the EU

facilitating bilateral relations between the European Union and the Swiss Confederation in parts of the internal market to which Switzerland participates"). On the InstA, see notably S. Breitenmoser, S. Hirsbrunner, 'Der Entwurf für ein Institutionnelles Rahmenabkommen zwischen der Schweiz und der EU: offene Fragen im Schnittpunkt zwischen Europa und Völkerrecht', in A. Epiney, P.E. Zlătescu (eds.), *Schweizerisches Jahrbuch für Europarecht/ Annuaire Suisse de droit* européen 2019/2020 (Schulthess, 2020), p. 511 et seq.; Th. Cottier, 'Die Souveränität und das institutionnelle Rahmenabkommen', *Schweizerische Juristen-Zeitung* 2019, p. 345 et seq.; A. Epiney, 'Der Entwurf des Institutionellen Abkommens Schweiz-EU, Überblick und erste Einschätzung', *Jusletter* 17 December 2018; B. Pirker, 'Zum Schiedsgericht im Institutionellen Abkommen', *Jusletter* 3 June 2019; C. Tobler, 'Wie weiter mit dem Institutionellen Abkommen', *Jusletter* 20 January 2020; C. Kaddous, 'Switzerland and the EU: current issues and new challenges under the Draft Institutional Framework Agreement', in S. Gstöhl, D. Phinnemore (eds.), *The Proliferation of Privileged Partnerships between the European Union and its Neighbours* (Routledge, 2019), p. 68 et seq.

4 Press release 116/19 of 19 February 2019, on Council conclusions on EU relations with the Swiss Confederation, paragraph 8 and the conclusions themselves, available at <https://www.consilium.europa.eu/en/press/press-releases/2019/02/19/council-conclusions-on-eu-relations-with-the-swiss-confederation/> (accessed 25 April 2022).

5 Report on the negotiations on an Institutional Agreement between Switzerland and the EU, 26 May 2021, available at <https://www.eda.admin.ch/dam/europa/en/documents/abkommen/20210526-bericht_verhandlungen_institutionelles-Abkommen_ch-eu_EN.pdf>, p. 2.

Citizens' Rights Directive 2004/38[6] and State aid.[7] For the EU, the negotiations on the InstA were concluded at the end of 2018. However, discussions between the partners took place between January and May 2021. These allowed a better reciprocal understanding of the respective positions but also revealed the remaining material differences on the sensitive issues. In light of these developments, the Federal Council decided, on 26 May 2021, not to sign the text negotiated and consequently to end the negotiation process on the InstA.

The purpose of this contribution is to analyse the failure of the conclusion of the Institutional Agreement from a *legal* perspective.[8] After a brief look at Switzerland's European policy (below section 2),[9] the institutional characteristics of the existing bilateral agreements are outlined in order to allow an analysis of the main issues dealt with in the InstA (section 3). The failure of the InstA has various consequences (section 4). Some of these consequences are simply related to the non-existence of the specific provisions that were foreseen in the agreement, while others depend on the decisions or measures taken by the EU after the refusal of Switzerland to sign the agreement. This range of consequences might be partially mitigated by domestic measures taken by Switzerland (section 5). Finally, this contribution provides some concluding remarks on the challenges Switzerland and the EU are facing to fight against the negative dynamic of the current situation and stabilise their relationship (section 6).

---

6 Directive 2004/38/EC of the European Parliament and of the Council of 29 April 2004 on the right of citizens of the Union and their family members to move and reside freely within the territory of the Member States amending Regulation (EEC) No 1612/68 and repealing Directives 64/221/EEC, 68/360/EEC, 72/194/EEC, 73/148/EEC, 75/34/EEC, 75/35/EEC, 90/364/EEC, 90/365/EEC and 93/96/EEC (OJ 2004, L 158/77).

7 Letter from the Federal Council to the President of the European Commission, Mr Jean-Claude Juncker, dated 7 June 2019, available in an unofficial translation on the following website: <https://www.eda.admin.ch/dam/europa/en/documents/bericht_konsultationen_insta/20190607_Lettre-CF-President-Commission-europeenne_en.pdf> (accessed 25 April 2022).

8 For an analysis from a political science perspective, see the contribution by R. Schwok in this volume.

9 For a historical background and a full overview of the current relationship between Switzerland and the EU, see C. Kaddous, 'Die Zusammenarbeit zwischen der EU und der Schweiz (La coopération entre l'Union européenne et la Suisse)', in A. Hatje, P.C. Müller-Graff (eds.), *Enzyklopädie des Europarechts. Europäisches Organisations- und Verfassungsrecht* (Nomos Verlag, 2022), p. 1391 et seq.

2 Switzerland's European Policy: Bilateral Agreements and Autonomous Adaptation of Swiss Law to EU Law

Switzerland is very close to the EU geographically,[10] culturally[11] and economically.[12] The EU and Switzerland are both founded on common fundamental values such as democracy, human rights, the rule of law and respect for international law. These common features have been recently highlighted in the framework of the war in Ukraine through the adoption by Switzerland of the packages of sanctions imposed by the EU against Russia and Belarus since February 2022.[13]

The EEA Agreement, which had been negotiated by Switzerland with the other EFTA States,[14] was rejected in Switzerland in a popular vote in December 1992. That agreement would have allowed Switzerland full participation in the EU internal market. The specific issue of access to the EU market was at the heart of the institutional discussions between Switzerland and the EU. In that context, it must be recalled that Switzerland applied for EU membership in May 1992, as did the other EFTA Member States at that time. These other EFTA States joined the EU in 1995, whereas Switzerland had to find its "own" way to ensure access to the EU internal market after the negative vote on the EEA Agreement. It initially froze and eventually in July 2016 – just after the UK's referendum on withdrawal from the EU – decided to withdraw its 1992 application for EU membership.

Despite the rejection of the EEA Agreement by the Swiss population, the relations between Switzerland and the EU have intensified through the conclusion of the *Bilateral Agreements I* and *II* of 1999[15] and

10 The neighbouring States of Switzerland are Austria, France, Germany and Italy and they are all members of the EU. Liechtenstein is a contracting party to the EEA Agreement.

11 According to Article 4 of the Switzerland Federal Constitution of 18 December 1998, SR 101, the national languages are: German, French, Italian and Romansh. It is worth noting that three of them are official languages of the EU.

12 In fact, the European Union is by far the most important trading partner of Switzerland.

13 See further below, in section 4.

14 Agreement on the European Economic Area (EEA Agreement) (OJ 1994, L 1/3).

15 The *Bilateral Agreements I* of 1999 are published in the OJ 2002, L 114: Agreement on the Free Movement of Persons between the European Community and its Member States on the one part, and the Swiss Confederation, on the other part, of 21 June 1999 (OJ 2002, L 114/6); Agreement between the European Community and the Swiss Confederation on the Carriage of Goods and Passengers by Rail and Road of 21 June 1999 (OJ 2002, L 114/91); Agreement between the European Community and the Swiss Confederation on Air Transport of 21 June 1999 (OJ 2002, L 114/73); Agreement between the European Community and the Swiss Confederation on Trade in Agricultural Products of 21 June 1999 (OJ 2002, L 114/132); Agreement on Scientific and Technological Cooperation

2004,[16] as well as through various subsequent agreements. Since 2004, the EU and Switzerland have continued to negotiate and conclude agreements and arrangements which cover various fields of common interest, such as Europol, Eurojust, cooperation in the armaments sector with the European Defence Agency (EDA), cooperation in the field of enforcement of competition rules in cross-border matters, cooperation in the field of satellite navigation (Galileo and European Geostationary Navigation Overlay Service, EGNOS), and

---

between the European Community and the Swiss Confederation of 21 June 1999 (OJ 2002, L 114/468); Agreement between the European Community and the Swiss Confederation on Mutual Recognition in relation to Conformity Assessment of 21 June 1999 (OJ 2002, L 114/369); Agreement between the European Community and the Swiss Confederation on Certain Aspects of Government procurement of 21 June 1999 (OJ 2002, L 114/430). – See also the dispatch of the Federal Council, which is the Swiss Federal Government, to the Parliament of 23 June 1999, Fed. Gaz. 1999 6128 et seq., that gives details of explanatory report for each agreement.

16 The *Bilateral Agreements II* were signed on 26 October 2004. Agreement between the European Community and the Swiss Confederation amending the Agreement between the European Economic Community and the Swiss Confederation of 22 July 1972 as regards the provisions applicable to processed agricultural products of 26 October 2004 (OJ 2005, L 23/19); Agreement between the European Community and the Swiss Confederation on cooperation in the field of statistics of 26 October 2004 (OJ 2006, L 90/2); Agreement between the European Community and the Swiss Confederation concerning the participation of Switzerland in the European Environment Agency and the European Environment Information and Observation Network (EIONET) of 26 October 2014 (OJ 2006, L 90/37); Agreement between the European Community and the Swiss Confederation in the audiovisual field, establishing the terms and conditions for the participation of the Swiss Confederation in the Community programme MEDIA 2007 of 11 October 2007 (OJ 2007, L 303/11); Agreement between the European Union, the European Community and the Swiss Confederation on the Swiss Confederation's association with the implementation, application and development of the Schengen *acquis* (OJ 2008, L 53/52); Agreement between the European Community and the Swiss Confederation concerning the criteria and mechanisms for establishing the State responsible for examining a request for asylum lodged in a Member State or in Switzerland (OJ 2008, L 53/5); Cooperation Agreement between the European Community and its Member States, of the one part, and the Swiss Confederation, of the other part, to combat fraud and any other illegal activity to the detriment of their financial interests (OJ 2009, L 49/8); Agreement between the European Community and the Swiss Confederation envisaging measures equivalent to those provided for in Council Directive 2003/48/EC on taxation of the incomes of the saving in the form of payments of interests of 26 October 2004 (OJ 2004, L 385/30); Agreement between the Swiss Federal Council and the Commission of the European Communities with a view to avoiding the double taxation of retired officials of the institutions and agencies of the European Communities resident in Switzerland (not published in the Official Journal of the European Union), available at <https://www.fdfa.admin.ch/dam/europa/en/documents/abkommen/pensionen_en.pdf> (accessed 25 April 2022).

cooperation in the field of asylum (European Asylum Support Office, EASO) and of business taxation.[17]

Apart from these bilateral agreements containing international obligations in relation to EU law, the Federal Council decided *unilaterally* in 1988 to bring Swiss legislation with international implications in line with European standards in order to reduce the differences between the Swiss legal order and that of the EU.[18] This decision was taken at the time of the preparation of the Swiss legal order regarding the potential future participation in the EEA Agreement. Since then, the "autonomous adaptation" of Swiss legislation to EU regulations and standards, without any treaty obligation, is often reverted to and remain important for those matters not covered by the bilateral agreements.[19] The autonomous adaptation mechanism is put today at the heart of the possible measures to be taken by Switzerland to mitigate the negative consequences of the failure of the InstA.

---

17 Agreement between the Swiss Confederation and Europol of 2004, available at <https://www.eda.admin.ch/dea/en/home/bilaterale-abkommen/abkommen-umsetzung/abkommenstexte/europol.html (accessed 25 April 2022); Agreement between Eurojust and Switzerland of 2008, available at <http://www.eurojust.europa.eu/doclibrary/Eurojust-framework/agreements/Agreement%20between%20Eurojust%20and%20Switzerland%20(2008)/Eurojust-Switzerland-2008-11-27-EN.pdf> (accessed 25 April 2022); Framework for Cooperation between the European Defence Agency and the Federal Department of Defence, Civil Protection and Sports of the Swiss Confederation of 2012, available at <https://www.eda.admin.ch/dea/en/home/bilaterale-abkommen/abkommen-umsetzung/abkommenstexte/zusammenarbeit-eva.html> (accessed 25 April 2022); Agreement between the European Union and the Swiss Confederation concerning cooperation on the application of their competition laws of 2013 (OJ 2014, L 347/3); Cooperation Agreement between the European Union and its Member States, of the one part, and the Swiss Confederation, of the other, on the European Satellite Navigation Programmes of 2013, available at <https://www.admin.ch/ch/d/gg/pc/documents/2407/COOPERATION_AGREEMENT.pdf> (accessed 25 April 2022); Arrangement entre la Confédération suisse et l'Union européenne sur les modalités de sa participation au Bureau européen d'appui en matière d'asile de 2014 (only in French or German), available at <https://www.admin.ch/opc/fr/official-compilation/2016/747.pdf> (accessed 25 April 2022); Mutual Understanding on Business Taxation between Switzerland and the EU of 2014.

18 Fed. Gaz. 1988 III 388.

19 On this question, see C. Kaddous, 'L'influence du droit communautaire sur l'ordre juridique suisse', in Yves Bot et al. (eds.), *En l'honneur de Philippe Léger. Le droit à la mesure de l'homme* (Pédone, 2006), p. 407 et seq.; W. Wiegand, M. Brülhart, *Die Auslegung von autonom nachvollzogenem Recht der Europäischen Gemeinschaft*, Swiss Papers on European Integration 23 (1999), p. 29 et seq. See further the contribution by M. Oesch and M. Brugger in this volume.

3 Comparison between the Bilateral Agreements and the Institutional Agreement on Institutional Issues

3.1 *Introductory Remarks*

The current system of the bilateral relationship between Switzerland and the EU is based on classical intergovernmental institutional cooperation, with the exception of some agreements integrating institutional provisions that go beyond this classicism.

In most of the bilateral agreements of primary importance, cooperation takes place through Joint Committees, in charge of the administration and surveillance of the application of the agreements. Decisions are taken by consensus. Each of the parties is responsible for implementing the agreements on its territory, except in the case of certain rules in the Agreement on Air Transport.[20] As a rule, the current institutional framework of the bilateral agreements does not create a judicial body or tribunal to supervise the correct application and uniform interpretation of these agreements.

The InstA between the EU and Switzerland would have largely modified the institutional arrangements provided for in the bilateral agreements, at least for the agreements covered by it. It would have only applied to five of the existing market access agreements of the 1999 *Bilateral Agreements I* in the fields of the free movement of persons, overland transport, air transport, mutual recognition in relation to conformity assessment and agriculture.[21] It was also intended to cover future agreements on market access between the EU and Switzerland. The first new agreement to be covered would have probably been the Agreement on Electricity.

By contrast, the InstA was not meant to apply to either the Agreement on Government Procurement (1999) or the Free Trade Agreement (1972).[22] However, the EU and Switzerland have stated their willingness to enter into negotiations to modernise the Free Trade Agreement and other agreements related to trade,[23] such as the agreements on Government Procurement, Mutual Recognition as well as the one on the exchanges of agricultural

20 See *supra* n. 14.

21 *Ibid.*

22 Article 2(2) of the draft InstA. See also the document entitled «Accord institutionnel Suisse-UE: document explicatif », dated 16 January 2019, under Section B.1. Preamble, objectives (Article 1) and scope of application (Article 2), p. 5.

23 Joint Declaration EU- CH on the agreements related to trade, attached to the draft Institutional Agreement.

products.[24] This declaration had no binding effect and left open the issue of the content of the possible modernisation.[25]

In the following sections, the analysis considers the current arrangements as well as those that were proposed in the draft InstA. The focus is on the mechanisms foreseen with regard to developments in EU law (below 3.2), legal interpretation (3.2), surveillance of the application of the agreements (3.3), surveillance (3.4), dispute settlement between the contracting parties (3.5) and the termination clause (3.6).

3.2 *Developments in EU Law*

Almost none of the existing bilateral agreements are "dynamic" in character. Generally, only the *acquis* prior to the signature of the agreements and to which reference is made, is applied in the relations between Switzerland and the EU.[26] This means that a change in EU legislation does not automatically bring about a change in the bilateral agreements. However, the principle of "equivalence of legislation" acts as an incentive for the parallel evolution of the two legal orders: the EU and the Swiss legal orders, including the bilateral agreements.[27]

Since the bilateral agreements do not entail acceptance of the relevant EU *acquis* post signature, with the exception of the Schengen and Dublin Association Agreements,[28] Switzerland cannot participate in all the EU

---

24 Agreement between the European Community and the Swiss Confederation on Mutual Recognition in relation to Conformity Assessment of 21 June 1999 (OJ 2002, L 114/369); Agreement between the European Community and the Swiss Confederation on Certain Aspects of Government procurement of 21 June 1999 (OJ 2002, L 114/430).

25 See further on this issue the contribution by M. Hahn in this volume.

26 There is an exception with the Schengen and Dublin Association Agreements.

27 The agreements are updated gradually, but evidently with some delay in comparison with the acts adopted within the EU in the same field. To illustrate this gap between the two legal orders, the Joint Committee of the AFMP Agreement adopted to date ten decisions which brought modifications of the Agreement. The last act adopted in this regard is Decision No 1/2020 of the Joint Committee of 15 December 2020 amending Annex II (Coordination of social security schemes) (OJ 2021, L 42/15). This last change is related to the withdrawal of the United Kingdom from the EU. The former act adopted by the Joint Committee within the AFMP was Decision No 1/2015 of 8 June 2015 amending Annex III (Mutual recognition of professional qualifications) (OJ 2015, L 148/38).

28 A difference is to be made between the agreements based on the "equivalence of legislation" and agreements based on the "application of the EU *acquis*" (Schengen and Dublin Association Agreements). On the Schengen and Dublin Association Agreements, see notably the contribution by S. Gutzwiller, 'Komitologie und Gemischte Ausschüsse im Rahmen der Assoziierung der Schweiz an Schengen/Dublin', in C. Kaddous, M. Jametti Greiner (n. 2), pp. 245 et seq.

committees involved in the administration and the development of the *acquis*. However, it has obtained the right for its representatives to participate as active observers in the meetings of important committees in the fields of research, air transport, social security, recognition of diplomas,[29] as well as that of Schengen and Dublin.[30] In all these cases, Swiss representatives have a right to take the floor but not to vote. They take part in the decision-shaping but not in the decision-making process.

The respect for the "equivalence of legislation" principle anchored in the bilateral agreements is key to the proper functioning of the agreements. In order to secure Switzerland's long-term access to the EU's internal market, bilateral market access agreements have to be regularly adapted to relevant EU law developments. If adaptation does not occur regularly, divergences between the two legal orders are likely to emerge and to constitute potential obstacles to trade for the individuals and the economic operators of both contracting parties. Therefore, the draft InstA provided for a system that would have allowed the incorporation of relevant EU law developments into the respective bilateral agreements as soon as possible after their adoption by the EU. However, Switzerland would have been able to decide on each "incorporation" on a case-by-case basis, allowing it to respect its constitutional requirements. There was no automatic adaptation of the bilateral agreements to developments in EU law. Swiss constitutional rules would have been fully safeguarded. The system envisaged would have also preserved Switzerland's legislative autonomy. The country would have been in a position, if needed after having held a referendum, to refuse to adapt a bilateral agreement to specific EU law developments. However, a refusal to adapt would have run the risk of the EU initiating the dispute settlement procedure envisaged in the InstA.

With regard to the incorporation of new EU *acquis* into existing agreements, the InstA envisaged Switzerland being involved early on in the shaping of EU legislation. The European Commission would have consulted Swiss experts in the same way as it consults the experts from the EU Member States or the EEA EFTA States in drafting legislative proposals, including delegated and implementing acts.[31] This would have allowed Switzerland to present its concerns in the EU decision-making process, albeit without a right to vote. The InstA also provided for a formal exchange of views between the EU and Switzerland within the Joint Committee established in the relevant bilateral agreement in the phase preceding a decision taken by the Council during a

29 Council Declaration annexed to the Final Act of signature of the Agreements of 1999.

30 Article 6 Schengen Association Agreement and Article 2 Dublin Association Agreement.

31 Article 12(1), (4), (5) and (6) of the draft InstA.

legislative procedure.[32] In this last instance, Switzerland would have been able to express its point of view through direct contact with the Member States' representatives.

3.3 *Legal Interpretation*

The EU and Switzerland interpret the bilateral agreements independently. As noted above, most of the current agreements that refer to EU rules are based on the principle of equivalence. They require regular adaptation to EU law developments in order to maintain the equivalence of rights and obligations on the territories of the respective contracting parties. In addition, a mechanism is needed to ensure that the provisions of the bilateral agreements involving concepts of EU law are interpreted in accordance with the case-law of the Court of Justice of the European Union (CJEU).[33] In the bilateral Agreement on the Free Movement of Persons (AFMP), for example, only case-law prior to the date of signature of the agreement has to be taken into account by the Swiss courts.[34] This mechanism has worked well and enables a parallel interpretation of the EU law concepts enshrined in that Agreement by the CJEU and the Swiss Federal Supreme Court.

In the negotiations on the InstA, the mechanism provided in the AFMP for taking into consideration the case-law of the CJEU was deemed to be a good starting point for the future InstA. Based on that *acquis*, an additional step had been taken by the contracting parties by introducing the "principle of uniform interpretation".[35] This principle referred to the objectives of the InstA as well as to public international law principles.[36] The general objective of the InstA was to ensure greater legal certainty and equal treatment of the contracting parties, economic operators and individuals in the areas of the internal market in which Switzerland participates. A more specific objective was to ensure homogenous conditions for individuals and businesses.[37]

32 Article 12(2) and (3) of the draft InstA.

33 Article 4(2) of the draft InstA.

34 Article 16(2) AFMP states: "Insofar as the application of this Agreement involves concepts of Community law, account shall be taken of the relevant case-law of the Court of Justice of the European Communities prior to the date of its signature. Case-law after that date shall be brought to Switzerland's attention. To ensure that the Agreement works properly, the Joint Committee shall, at the request of either Contracting Party, determine the implications of such case-law". The Air Transport Agreement also contains such a provision, see Article 1(2).

35 Article 4 of the draft InstA.

36 Article 4(1) of the draft InstA.

37 Article 1(1) of the draft InstA.

The concept of public international law principles was not specified further in the InstA, hence leaving a margin of manoeuvre for the identification of these principles that might have been applied in the context of the internal market.[38] It is worth noting that the mention of these principles may refer to the famous Court of Justice *Polydor* judgment of 1982.[39] This judgment allows for differentiation in the application of the uniform interpretation principle. According to the main statements made in that judgment, EU legal provisions embodied in the bilateral agreements with Switzerland are to be interpreted in light of the particular object and purpose of the agreements in question. This means that EU case-law cannot be transposed automatically to the bilateral agreements, which do not provide for full integration of Switzerland into the EU internal market, as the Court of Justice had the opportunity to state in the *Grimme* and *Zurich Airport* cases.[40]

The uniform interpretation principle was to be applied to the five agreements that fell under the scope of the InstA and to the EU legal acts to which it referred.[41] The principle as it is formulated in the InstA was stronger than the one expressed in the corresponding relevant provision in the AFMP, which "only" refers to the consideration of the CJEU's case-law that came before the date of signature of the agreement and which does not mention the idea of uniform interpretation.

In the InstA, uniformity of interpretation was the principled rule and the reference point was the case-law of the CJEU, irrespective of whether it was rendered prior to or after the signature of the agreement concerned.[42] The term "agreement concerned" should have been understood, as the case might have been, as the InstA itself, the five current bilateral agreements that would have fallen within its scope, or future EU-Switzerland international agreements related to market access.

38 Articles 1(3) and 4(1) of the draft InstA.

39 CJEU, Case 270/80, *Polydor*, EU:C:1982:43.

40 CJEU, Case C-351/08, *Grimme*, EU:C:2009:697, paras. 27–29; Case C-547/10 P, *Switzerland v Commission*, EU:C:2013:139, paras. 78–80. See further the contribution by P. Van Elsuwege in this volume.

41 Article 4(1) of the draft InstA.

42 Article 4(2) of the draft InstA states that: "To the extent that their application involves the concepts of European Union law, the provisions of this Agreement and the relevant agreements and the European Union legal acts to which reference is made are interpreted and applied in accordance with the case-law of the Court of Justice of the European Union, whether prior or subsequent to the signature of the agreement concerned". (Translated by the author from French).

Since the agreements concerned give Switzerland access to the internal market and refer to concepts of EU law, it made sense to refer to relevant CJEU interpretations. It was unusual, however, in the field of international relations to agree on such a commitment, given the unknowns related to the content and implications of future case-law at the time of signing the agreements in question.

The continued participation of Switzerland in the EU internal market – the main Swiss objective in the negotiations of the InstA – shed further light on the country's commitment to respect the principle of uniform interpretation. With the InstA, the Swiss Federal Government intended to consolidate the bilateral approach, which characterises its relations with the EU, in particular, in guaranteeing sustainable access to the internal market while maintaining maximum political autonomy.[43] The InstA would have allowed to keep the bilateral route open for the conclusion of new market access agreements, for example, in the field of electricity. It must also be noted that this pragmatic approach to accept the proposed mechanism of uniform interpretation could have been applied by Switzerland without major difficulties, given the case law of the Swiss Federal Supreme Court, for example, in the field of the AFMP. The Swiss Court, as a matter of principle, does take into consideration the CJEU's judgments issued in that field after 21 June 1999, the date of signature of that Agreement.[44]

3.4 *Surveillance*

Surveillance has always been a sensitive issue in the EU-Switzerland negotiations. From a Swiss perspective, each party should supervise the application of the agreements on its own territory, given that the overall supervision is the responsibility of the Joint Committee in each of the bilateral agreements. For the EU, however, an independent surveillance mechanism has always been preferred and sought. The current bilateral agreements do not provide for such an independent joint surveillance mechanism. In most instances, each

43 See Foreign Policy Report 2018, Fed.Gaz. 2019 1505, p. 1513.

44 In the AFMP, account shall be taken of the case law issued prior to the signature of the Agreement (Article 16), even if the Swiss highest Court usually agrees to take into consideration the case law rendered after that date when it constitutes a development of a prior one. See on this point and on the detailed position of the Swiss Federal Supreme Court, decision 130 II 1 (4 November 2003), confirmed in decision 134 II 10 (30 November 2007). On the application of the FMP Agreement in Switzerland, see C. Kaddous, D. Grisel, *Libre circulation des personnes et des services,* Dossier de droit européen n° 26 (Helbing & Lichtenhahn, 2012), pp. 845–945. On the question of reference to the case law of the Court of Justice, see in the same book, pp. 860–863.

contracting party is responsible for the proper application of the agreements on its own territory. The exception is the Air Transport Agreement where the European Commission and the CJEU play a central role in certain matters.

In the negotiations on the InstA, the question of surveillance was again put on the agenda. This was one of the difficult aspects of the institutional negotiations due to the different positions held by the EU and Switzerland as to the kind of surveillance desired and its scope. It was not possible to reach a common solution. Therefore, the draft InstA did not provide for the establishment of any common supervisory body. There was no institution in the draft InstA comparable to the EFTA Surveillance Authority in the EEA Agreement.

Switzerland and the EU would have cooperated and assisted each other in the surveillance and implementation of the agreements falling under the scope of the InstA. They might have exchanged information and views and discussed issues of mutual interest.[45] Under the bilateral agreements, each of the contracting parties takes appropriate measures to ensure the effective and harmonious application of the agreements on its own territory.[46] This model is referred to as a "two-pillar model", not to be confused with the multilateral "two-pillar" set-up in the EEA.

The surveillance mechanism envisaged in the draft InstA respected fully the sovereignty of Switzerland over its national territory. This outcome of the negotiations had been rightly regarded as one of the successes of Swiss negotiators because the EU had initially rejected any national surveillance model. It is worth noting, however, that specific rules had been put in place regarding State aid. The principle according to which "each is responsible for its own territory" also applied there. However, specific provisions were envisaged as to the exchange of information between the respective contracting parties' supervisory bodies in order to ensure homogenous conditions for the proper functioning of the parts of the internal market in which Switzerland participates.[47]

3.5 *Dispute Settlement*

The current bilateral agreements generally provide for a classical intergovernmental dispute settlement mechanism. Again, a notable exception is the Air Transport Agreement, which for certain issues, grants an important role to the Commission and the CJEU. According to the general system, each contracting party may bring a matter under dispute concerning the interpretation or application of an agreement to the Joint Committee which may, in turn, settle the

45 Article 6 of the draft InstA.
46 Article 7 of the draft InstA.
47 State aid provisions are enshrined in Articles 8A to 8C of the draft InstA.

dispute. The Joint Committee has to be supplied with all relevant information, thus enabling an in-depth examination of the situation with a view to finding an acceptable solution. In doing so, the Joint Committee considers every possible means to maintain the good functioning of the relevant agreement.

The proposed mechanism in the InstA foresaw that the competence to resolve such a dispute remained with the Joint Committee. If, however, the Joint Committee was unable to find a solution acceptable to both parties within three months, either party could request that the dispute be referred to an "arbitral tribunal" composed of members appointed in equal numbers by both Switzerland and the EU.[48] If resolving the dispute required clarification of a question concerning the interpretation or application of concepts of EU law, the arbitral tribunal would in turn refer the matter to the CJEU whose interpretation would then bind the arbitral tribunal.[49]

In turn, the arbitral tribunal's decision would have been binding on the EU and Switzerland.[50] Failure by either party to implement the decision, or non-conformity of a measure by any of the parties with the arbitral decision would have resulted in proportionate compensatory measures up to the suspension of all or part of the agreements concerned in order to remedy the imbalance. Disagreement by the parties regarding the proportionality of the compensatory measure would have been submitted to the Joint Committee for its decision on the proportionality of those measures. If the Joint Committee was unable to reach a decision within six months on that issue, each party would then submit the question of the proportionality of those measures to arbitration.[51]

The proposal for an arbitral tribunal came rather late in the negotiations.[52] In an earlier version of the draft InstA, provision was made in cases where the dispute was not settled before the Joint Committee that questions of interpretation and application of concepts of EU law were to be submitted to the CJEU by either party. In that regard, the latest version of the draft InstA better reflected Swiss concerns that the dispute settlement mechanism should be bilateral. In domestic Swiss politics, the role of the CJEU is regularly disputed as no Swiss judge sits in that court.

It is worth noting that the CJEU was not deemed to resolve the dispute between Switzerland and the EU. Its task would have consisted of indicating how EU law concepts incorporated into the bilateral agreements had to be

48 Article 10 of the draft InstA and Protocol 3 on the Arbitral Tribunal.

49 Article 10(3) of the draft InstA.

50 Article 10(5) of the draft InstA.

51 Article 10(6) and (7) of the draft InstA.

52 The Swiss mandate has been adapted on this issue in March 2018.

interpreted. It would then have been up to the arbitral tribunal to decide while taking into account the interpretation provided by the CJEU. The arbitral tribunal would have endeavoured to make decisions by consensus. If, however, it proved impossible to reach a decision by consensus, the decision was to be reached by majority vote.

The envisaged dispute settlement mechanism did address Swiss concerns for equal participation of the EU and Switzerland in the bodies involved at the different steps of the procedure. The EU was satisfied in having developed a judicial system that would have avoided the difficulties currently resulting from the intergovernmental dispute settlement mechanism and the consensus rule applied for decisions taken by the respective Joint Committees. However, for Switzerland, the role of the CJEU is and remains sensitive, as the Court is considered to be composed of "foreign judges".

3.6 *Termination Clause*

The draft InstA included a termination clause that would have allowed either party to terminate the agreement.[53] The clause also provided for the consequences of such termination. Any market access agreement concluded after the signature of the InstA and expressly referring to it would have ceased to have effect together with the InstA six months after the InstA's termination. In a way, that would have meant a kind of "double guillotine clause": termination of the InstA itself and of potential new market access agreements referring to the former.

However, the five existing market access agreements that would have been covered by the InstA would have not been immediately terminated if the InstA was itself terminated. As to these agreements, the InstA provided for a three-month consultation process during which the parties would have discussed the consequences in relation to the existing agreements and the steps to be taken. A whole procedure was foreseen.[54] If no solution was agreed upon between the Contracting Parties, the agreements would have ceased to have effect after six months. However, the guillotine clause contained in the existing 1999 *Bilateral Agreements I* would have only been applied if, during the three-month consultation no alternative solution was found.

53 Article 22 of the draft InstA. See also the Report on the negotiations on an institutional framework agreement between Switzerland and the EU, 26 May 2021, available at <https://www.eda.admin.ch/dam/europa/en/documents/abkommen/20210526-bericht_verhandlungen_institutionelles-Abkommen_ch-eu_EN.pdf> (accessed 25 April 2022), pp. 21–22.

54 Article 22(2) of the draft InstA.

In practice, this termination clause would have radically reduced the decision-making power of each Contracting Party to terminate or amend the InstA.[55]

4 Consequences of the Non-signature of the Institutional Agreement

The decision by Switzerland not to sign the InstA has various consequences. The first one is that the Swiss-EU relationship remains based on the sectoral and bilateral approach that was developed over the decades. The "*status quo*" situation means that the rules applicable between the Contracting Parties are the ones resulting from the current versions of the bilateral agreements (below 4.1). A second consequence is related to the decisions and measures the EU took, or is going to take, after the non-signing of the agreement. These have already been largely identified (4.2). A third consequence, more general, relates to the deterioration in the relationship between Switzerland and the EU (4.3).[56]

4.1 *The* "status quo", *Current Version of the Bilateral Agreements*

The bilateral agreements continue to cover the relations between Switzerland and the EU with the institutional mechanisms that each of them provides for the adaptation of the agreements to new developments in the EU legal *acquis*, surveillance of the application of the agreements, the interpretation of these agreements as well as dispute settlement. As noted, most of these agreements are based on the "equivalence of legislation" principle[57] and can be adapted, by decisions taken by consensus, by the respective Joint Committees.

As to the legal interpretation of the bilateral agreements, the surveillance of their application and the dispute settlement mechanism between the contracting parties, no changes occur as to what has been noted above under

55 Report on the negotiations on an institutional framework agreement between Switzerland and the EU, 26 May 2021, available at <https://www.eda.admin.ch/dam/europa/en/documents/abkommen/20210526-bericht_verhandlungen_institutionelles-Abkommen_ch-eu_EN.pdf> (accessed 25 April 2022), p. 27.

56 The consequences have been discussed in the Report on the negotiations on a institutional framework agreement between Switzerland and the EU, 26 May 2021, available at <https://www.eda.admin.ch/dam/europa/en/documents/abkommen/20210526-bericht_verhandlungen_institutionelles-Abkommen_ch-eu_EN.pdf> (accessed 25 April 2022), p. 29.

57 Except the Air Transport as well as the Schengen and Dublin Association Agreements that are applying the EU *acquis* and are not based on the "equivalence of legislation".

section 3. The termination clause that was included in the InstA, and strongly debated in Switzerland, was avoided. At the same time, the topics on which Switzerland requested clarifications from the EU as to the scope of the InstA – the protection of wages, the EU Citizens' Rights Directive, and State aid –,[58] which are of fundamental concern to the country (red lines), were not put at risk. However, these topics will probably stay on the table in future negotiations between Switzerland and the EU.

4.2 *Decisions and Measures Taken or To Be Taken by the EU*

Three main types of decisions or measures impact heavily on the relationship between Switzerland and the EU. Firstly, the statement made by the EU not to update the existing market access agreements (4.2.1), secondly, the conclusion of the InstA as a precondition for the EU to conclude future market access agreements with Switzerland (4.2.2), and thirdly, other decisions or measures connecting the InstA with other dossiers (4.2.3).

4.2.1 No Update of Existing Market Access Agreements

In December 2018, the European Commission already announced that it was no longer prepared to update existing market access agreements unless it had an overriding interest in doing so.[59] It wanted to increase the pressure on Switzerland to sign the InstA. For instance, the Agreement on Mutual Recognition in relation to the conformity assessment in Annex I, Chapter 4, on medical devices was not updated. This happened just after the announcement by Switzerland, on 26 May 2021, of the non-signature of the InstA.[60]

---

58 Details on these three issues and the Swiss requests are explained in the Report on the negotiations on an institutional framework agreement between Switzerland and the EU, 26 May 2021, available at <https://www.eda.admin.ch/dam/europa/en/documents/abkommen/20210526-bericht_verhandlungen_institutionelles-Abkommen_ch-eu_EN.pdf> (accessed 25 April 2022), p. 32–33.

59 See notably the Swiss report on the negotiations on an institutional framework agreement between Switzerland and the EU, 26 May 2021, available at <https://www.eda.admin.ch/dam/europa/en/documents/abkommen/20210526-bericht_verhandlungen_institutionelles-Abkommen_ch-eu_EN.pdf> (accessed 25 April 2022), p. 29, but also the Council conclusions on EU relations with the Swiss Confederation, of 19 February 2019, available at <https://www.consilium.europa.eu/en/press/press-releases/2019/02/19/council-conclusions-on-eu-relations-with-the-swiss-confederation/> (accessed 25 April 2022).

60 Regulation (EU) 2017/745 and its modification occurred in 2020, Regulation (EU) 2020/561 of the European Parliament and of the Council, of 23 April 2020 amending Regulation (EU) 2017/745 on medical devices, as regards the dates of application of certain (OJ 2020, L 130/18). See notably J. Beglinger, C. Tobler, 'Gleichwertigkeit, Angemessenheit, Äquivalenz, Adäquanz. Ein Hotspot in den Beziehungen zwischen der Schweiz und der EU im rechtlichen Kontext', in A. Epiney, P.E. Zlatescu (n. 3), p. 549.

The AFMP was not updated either as to the last modifications related to Directive 2005/36 on the recognition of professional qualifications. However, in this last example, the non-adaptation of Annex III of the AFMP is due to the rather "regular" delay in updating the bilateral agreements to EU law developments and not to an "active" refusal by the EU to adapt the content of the agreement.[61]

If the bilateral agreements are not adapted to the relevant EU law developments, the parallelism between the rules applicable within the EU legal order and the Swiss legal order, which is central to the proper functioning of the bilateral agreements, is not guaranteed anymore. As a result, the EU and Switzerland are no longer applying the same rules, whereas this is a *de facto* condition for Switzerland's access and participation in the EU internal market. The main objective of the respective market access agreements, whether it is the AFMP or the Agreement on Mutual Recognition, is jeopardized. Moreover, in the case of the last instance, the principle of mutual recognition, the basis of the system, can no longer work.

4.2.2 No Conclusion of Future Access Market Agreements

In its 2019 Council conclusions, the EU already stated that the conclusion of the InstA was a precondition for the conclusion of future agreements on Swiss participation in the EU's internal market.[62] Clearly, this firstly concerns the market access agreements, including notably the electricity agreement that has been in the pipeline of the negotiations between the partners since 2017. This decision also impacts the negotiations in the areas of agriculture, food safety, product safety and public health, as they aim to provide Switzerland partial access to the EU internal market. The negotiations are currently suspended.

Apart from these consequences, impacts have been recognised in areas of cooperation not directly linked to market access. In the field of research, for instance, Switzerland was partially associated to Horizon 2020 (framework programme 2014–2020) until the end of 2016 and fully associated from

61 See M. Oesch, *Schweiz-Europäische Union. Grundlagen. Bilaterale Abkommen. Autonomer Nachvollzug* (EIZ Publishing, 2020), p. 104 et seq.; J. Günthardt, 'Die Nichtaufdatierung der bilateralen Abkommen Schweiz-EU am Beispiel der Diplomanerkennung', *Schweizerische Juristen-Zeitung* 2022, p. 159 et seq.

62 Council conclusions on EU relations with the Swiss Confederation, 19 February 2019, available at <https://www.consilium.europa.eu/en/press/press-releases/2019/02/19/council-conclusions-on-eu-relations-with-the-swiss-confederation/> (accessed 25 April 2022).

2017 to 2020.[63] Today, Switzerland seeks full participation in the Horizon Europe Programme (period 2021–2027), without success. The participation of Switzerland in other EU framework programmes is also problematic, i.e., in the field of culture, creativity and the audiovisual sector (Creative Europe).

The effect of the EU statement on the non-conclusion of new agreements goes indeed beyond the market access agreements. It concerns the participation of Switzerland in a series of cooperation agreements. In legal terms, these agreements are considered to be new agreements. Even if they are successive, each of them relates to a new framework programme, envisaged for a limited period.

It is worth noting that despite the principled decision taken by the EU of not concluding new (market access) agreements with Switzerland, the EU made exceptions. It concluded an agreement allowing the linkage of its trading systems for CO2-equivalent emission allowances with the Swiss system. The agreement was signed in 2017 and entered into force on 1 January 2020.[64] The agreement was also updated through a decision of the Joint Committee in 2020.[65] The EU does not systematically exclude the possibility of entering into new agreements if it considers that important interests are prevailing to do so. Such decisions of the EU are based on a political assessment. They are related to the discretionary powers that each actor enjoys on the international scene in the conduct of its international relations. Switzerland should not feel offended and the EU cannot be blamed for this.

4.2.3 Decisions Impacting Other Fields of the Bilateral Relationship

These decisions are EU decisions adopted based on unilateral EU legal acts. These are mainly concerned, till now, with the recognition of equivalence of services (financial services).[66] But they are not limited to those. Data

63 The full participation took place after the ratification by Switzerland of Protocol III to the FMP agreement following the implementation of the result of the vote on the popular initiative "Against Mass Migration" on 9 February 2014.

64 Agreement between the European Union and the Swiss Confederation on the linking of their greenhouse gas emissions trading systems, SR 0.814.011.268 (OJ 2017, L 322/3).

65 Decision No 2/2020 of the Joint Committee established by the Agreement between the European Union and the Swiss Confederation on the linking of their greenhouse gas emissions trading systems of 5 November 2020 on amending Annexes I and II to the Agreement and the adoption of Linking Technical Standards (LTS) (2021/1034) (OJ 2021, L 226/16).

66 Article 25(4)(a) of Directive 2014/65/EU of the European Parliament and of the Council of 15 May 2014 on markets in financial instruments and amending Directive 2002/92/EC and Directive 2011/61/EU (OJ 2014, L 173/349). It deals with the notion of "equivalent third

protection and electricity are also two important fields where the same might happen.[67]

The refusal by the EU to recognise the stock market equivalence after the end of June 2019 is a good example of unilateral decisions. In response to this decision, Switzerland activated, on 1 July 2019, a measure to protect the Swiss stock exchange infrastructure.[68] Switzerland remains to consider it meets all the EU requirements for unrestricted recognition of the equivalence of Swiss stock exchange regulation by the EU.[69] However, it is worth noting that these kinds of decisions are unilateral decisions taken most of the time by the European Commission the aim of which is to check whether the EU standards and level of protection of public interest within the EU are also respected by third country economic operators acting on the EU internal market. In doing so, the EU may equally pursue the objective of not allowing potential competitors originating from third countries to benefit from the advantages of offering their products or services at lower prices due to potentially less restrictive legislation to respect in their home countries.[70] In an assessment on equivalence, the European Commission is conducting the process in accordance with the EU priorities and the interests of EU financial markets.[71] The margin of

---

country market". This is to be examined in conjunction of Article 23(2) of Regulation (EU) No 600/2014 of the European Parliament and of the Council of 15 May 2014 on markets in financial instruments and amending Regulation (EU) No 648/2012 (OJ 2014, L 173/84).

67 Report on the negotiations on a institutional framework agreement between Switzerland and the EU, 26 May 2021, available at <https://www.eda.admin.ch/dam/europa/en/documents/abkommen/20210526-bericht_verhandlungen_institutionelles-Abkommen_ch-eu_EN.pdf> (accessed 25 April 2022).

68 The Swiss protective measure vis-à-vis the EU remains in force without change. On the recognition of the stock exchange market, see notably J. Beglinger, C. Tobler (n. 3), p. 549; S. Emmengger, A. Bigler, 'Fortress Europe: Die Äquivalenzverfahren im Bereich der Finanzdienstleistungen', Schweizerische Zeitschrift für Wirtschafts- und Finanzmarktrecht 2019, p. 155 et seq.

69 The Federal Council remains of the opinion that Switzerland meets all the requirements for unrestricted recognition of the equivalence of Swiss stock exchange regulation by the EU. The Federal Council's objective and the best solution for all affected market players in Switzerland and abroad therefore remain an unlimited extension of stock market equivalence. See Swiss position, available at <https:/www.sif.admin.ch/sif/en/home/finanzmarktpolitik/meuasure-protect-swiss-stock-exchange-infrastructure.html> (accessed 25 April 2022).

70 M. Hahn, Je t'aime… Moi non plus : Rechtsfragen des Verhältnisses Schweiz-EU, ZBJV 2021, p. 77 ff.

71 Communication from the Commission to the European Parliament, the Council, the European Central Bank, the European Economic and social Committee and the Committee of the Regions, Equivalence in the area of financial services, COM/2019/349 final, in particular point 4.

manoeuvre of the Commission is therefore very large and goes much beyond the technical criteria that are enshrined in the respective EU legal acts.

This kind of issues will also be raised in the future as to data protection. In 2000, the European Commission adopted a decision considering that Switzerland was providing an adequate level of protection for personal data transferred from the EU. The said decision was taken on the adequacy of protection provided for in Switzerland with a view to meeting the requirements of Directive 95/46 (Article 25), which was then in force.[72] With the adoption of Regulation 2016/679 on the protection of natural persons with regard to the processing of personal data (GDPR),[73] the European Commission will assess, sooner or later, the adequacy of the level of protection in Switzerland in case of the transfer of personal data from the EU.[74] The full revision of the Swiss federal legislation at stake is supposed to enter into force in September 2023.[75]

4.3 *General Deterioration in the Relationship between Switzerland and the EU*

More generally, the decision made by the Swiss Federal Government, on 26 May 2021, not to sign the InstA had a generally negative effect on the whole relationship developed between the EU and Switzerland over decades. The trust at the heart of the relationship was broken. This is particularly serious as Switzerland is considered to be the EU's closest European State after the three EEA EFTA countries.

72 *Commission Decision 2000/518/EC, of 26 July 2000 pursuant to Directive 95/46/EC of the European Parliament and of the Council on the adequate protection of personal data provided in Switzerland (notified under document number C(2000) 2304), OJ L 215, 25.08.2000, p. 1. This Decision has been amended in 2016 (new article 3 and insertion of article 3 a), see* Commission implementing Decision (EU) 2016/2295, of 16 December 2016, amending Decisions 2000/518/EC, 2002/2/EC, 2003/490/EC, 2003/821/EC, 2004/411/EC, 2008/393/EC, 2010/146/EU, 2010/625/EU, 2011/61/EU and Implementing Decisions 2012/484/EU, 2013/65/EU on the adequate protection of personal data by certain countries, pursuant to Article 25(6) of Directive 95/46/EC of the European Parliament and of the Council, (notified under document C(2016) 8353), *OJ L 344, 17.12.2016, p. 83.*

73 Regulation (EU) 2016/679 of the European Parliament and of the Council of 27 April 2016 on the protection of natural persons with regard to the processing of personal data and on the free movement of such data, and repealing Directive 95/46/EC (General Data Protection Regulation), OJ L 119, 4.5.2016, p. 1.

74 Articles 44 and 45 of Regulation (EU) 2016/679.

75 The Federal Council still has to take a decision on the entry into force, see <https://www.ejpd.admin.ch/bj/fr/home/staat/gesetzgebung/datenschutzstaerkung.html> (accessed 25 April 2022).

The concrete impacts of such deterioration are difficult to identify. They are more of a political nature. They are also probably not immediately recognisable. But no doubt they are there. They can take different forms: lack of coordination of EU and Swiss positions on issues of mutual interest in multilateral fora (*i.e.*, economic and financial field, taxation of multinationals), or simply more restrictive EU positions towards Switzerland in the bilateral relations in areas like cybersecurity, climate change, the COVID certificate, data protection, etc.[76]

Some attempts have been made by Switzerland to counter this general deterioration of the EU-Switzerland relationship. On 15 November 2021, Switzerland reiterated its continuous interest and willingness to pursue the bilateral approach and its readiness to set up a political dialogue with the EU at the ministerial level.[77] On 25 February 2022, the Federal Council highlighted, at its European policy retreat, its interest to maintain good, stable and mutually beneficial relations with the EU. It adopted a set of guidelines for its negotiating package with the EU. Regarding the institutional issues, the Federal Council decided on a vertical approach aimed at anchoring the different institutional aspects in each market access agreement. It also explained that the package of measures might include new agreements for electricity and food safety as well as association agreements for research, health and education. The Federal Council also indicated being prepared to consider continuing the Swiss contribution to the EU as part of the negotiating package.[78]

Last but not least, in the context of the war in Ukraine, Switzerland took the decision on 28 February 2022 to adopt the packages of sanctions imposed by the EU against Russia.[79] On 4 March 2022, it adopted a further set of EU sanctions against Russia, while underlining that it decides autonomously on

---

76 On COVID-related measures, see also the contributions by M. Oesch and M. Brugger and by C. Tobler in this volume.

77 On 15 November 2021, Federal Councillor Ignazio Cassis travelled to Brussels to meet with Maroš Šefčovič, Vice-President of the European Commission. Mr. Šefčovič is Switzerland's new point of contact at the European Commission, available at <https://www.eda.admin.ch/europa/en/home/aktuell/medienmitteilungen.html/content/eda/en/meta/news/2021/11/15/85874> (accessed 25 April 2022).

78 Swiss position available at <https://www.eda.admin.ch/europa/en/home/aktuell/medienmitteilungen.html/content/eda/en/meta/news/2022/2/25/87349> (accessed 25 April 2022).

79 Press release available at <https://www.eda.admin.ch/europa/en/home/aktuell/medienmitteilungen.html/content/eda/en/meta/news/2022/2/28/87386> (accessed 25 April 2022).

whether to adopt any further EU sanctions against Russia.[80] Furthermore, on 18 March 2022,[81] and 13 April 2022,[82] Switzerland took the decision to adopt the new EU sanctions against Russia and Belarus. All these decisions to adopt the packages of sanctions imposed by the EU against Russia and Belarus prove the willingness and readiness of Switzerland to act on the same line as the EU in this sad context. By doing so, Switzerland emphasised the fact that it shares common values with the EU, in particular the respect for international law and solidarity in welcoming Ukrainian refugees.[83]

5 Consequences Partially Mitigated by Domestic Measures Taken by Switzerland

Switzerland started to implement, where necessary and feasible, measures to mitigate the negative consequences of not signing the InstA. The very first measure of this type took place before 26 May 2021. In June 2019, Switzerland activated, as previously mentioned, a measure to protect the Swiss stock exchange infrastructure after the EU's decision not to extend Swiss stock exchange equivalence.[84]

In the same line of reasoning, Switzerland decided to make amendments to Swiss legislation in the field of medicinal products in order to compensate as much as possible for the non-update of the Mutual Recognition Agreement and to safeguard supply chains and market surveillance in the country.[85] As to the refusal by the EU to allow the Swiss association to Horizon Europe programme, Switzerland decided to support 24 start-ups whose projects had been selected in the European Innovation Council Accelerator 2021. These start-ups

80 Press release available at <https://www.eda.admin.ch/europa/en/home/aktuell/medienmitteilungen.html/content/europa/en/meta/news/2022/3/4/87474> (accessed 25 April 2022).

81 Press release available at <https://www.eda.admin.ch/europa/en/home/aktuell/medienmitteilungen.html/content/europa/en/meta/news/2022/3/18/87677> (accessed 25 April 2022).

82 Press release available at <https://www.eda.admin.ch/europa/en/home/aktuell/medienmitteilungen.html/content/europa/en/meta/news/2022/4/13/88028> (accessed 25 April 2022).

83 On this issue, see further the contribution by C. Hillion in this volume.

84 Swiss report on the negotiations on an Institutional Agreement between Switzerland and the EU, 26 May 2021, available at <https://www.eda.admin.ch/dam/europa/en/documents/abkommen/20210526-bericht_verhandlungen_institutionelles-Abkommen_ch-eu_EN.pdf> (accessed 25 April 2022), p. 30.

85 *Ibid.*, p. 30.

will receive funding from the Swiss Federal Government, instead of being funded by the European Commission.[86]

On 26 May 2021, at the same time as the information on the non-signature of the InstA, the Federal Council decided to launch an assessment on the potential for autonomous adaptation of Swiss legislation to stabilise Swiss–EU relations. The task was to identify current discrepancies between EU and Swiss law and determine where alignment of the Swiss legislation to the EU's one might be appropriate. This process has been carried out on the federal as well as the cantonal levels. The report of the assessment, issued on 10 January 2022, concludes that there is a wide variety of situations to be tackled differently. It analyses in detail the various areas of free movement of persons, air transport, road transport, agriculture, media and culture, State aid, and mutual recognition in conformity assessments and it assesses the feasibility of the reduction of the differences between the two sets of legislation in the respective fields.[87] The Report is of a technical character and does not bring any political assessment of the results. What is clear is that the autonomous adaptation of Swiss law to EU law is only helpful in specific and limited circumstances. This unilateral mechanism may mitigate the negative effects of the failure to update the existing agreements or to conclude new agreements with the EU up to a certain point. However, the autonomous adaptation is unhelpful where the domestic reduction of the differences between EU and Swiss law does not suffice to achieve the fixed objectives (e.g., mutual recognition). In these circumstances, only the bilateral approach ensures the application of the reciprocity principle.

6 Concluding Remarks

Relations between the EU and Switzerland are complex. This reflects Switzerland's identity and the specificities of a country located in the middle of Europe that although it shares common values and principles with the EU, has chosen to develop its pragmatic bilateral approach. Indeed, since the 1992

86 Transitional measures for Horizon Europe, dated 22 March 2022, available at <https://www.eda.admin.ch/europa/en/home/aktuell/medienmitteilungen.html/content/europa/en/meta/news/2022/3/29/87763> (accessed 25 April 2022).

87 Rapport au Conseil fédéral du 10 janvier 2022, Différences entre les réglementations de la Suisse et de l'Union européenne. Analyse des possibilités d'adaptation du droit suisse afin de réduire ces différences, available at <https://www.newsd.admin.ch/newsd/message/attachments/70430.pdf> (accessed 25 April 2022).

rejection of the EEA Agreement by the Swiss population, the Federal Council has pursued its relations with the EU through bilateral agreements. The 1999 *Bilateral Agreements I* were perceived as a solution in order to bridge the gap between the European and the Swiss markets. The second series of *Bilateral Agreements II* concluded in 2004 went beyond the purely economic aspect of Swiss-EU relations and covered fields like asylum, environment, statistics and culture. The agreements concluded after 2004 allowed to expand the cooperation notably in fields such as police, justice, competition and satellite navigation.[88]

Overall, the bilateral agreements are considered helpful for a country like Switzerland, which for reasons of identity-related factors such as direct democracy, is neither ready nor willing to pursue EU membership. From a Swiss perspective, the bilateral approach is still considered to be, even after the non-signature of the InstA, the most appropriate way to pursue Swiss interests in Europe.

That being said, negotiations on institutional issues have been regarded as overdue by the EU. In 2010, the Council considered in its biannual conclusions on the EU's relations with Switzerland that it was time to move beyond the system of bilateral agreements, which had become complex and unwieldy to manage and had clearly reached its limits.[89] In February 2019, the Council stressed that these limits had been reached "due to the complexity [of the system of bilateral agreements], its incompleteness and the resulting lack of homogeneous conditions for citizens and businesses in the areas of the internal market in which Switzerland participates".[90]

The negotiations on the InstA have been complex. And the outcome of the UK referendum on continued EU membership also had an impact. There are clearly similarities between the Swiss and the UK situations not only in the area of free movement of persons but also regarding institutional issues. Both countries face the same kind of challenges related to their participation in the internal market but in the end, they came out with different final solutions.[91]

---

88 See n. 15.

89 Council conclusions on EU relations with EFTA countries, Brussels, 14 December 2010, para. 48, available at <http://www.consilium.europa.eu/uedocs/cms_data/docs/pressdata/EN/foraff/118458.pdf> (accessed 25 April 2022).

90 Council conclusions on EU relations with the Swiss Confederation, 19 February 2019, available at <https://www.consilium.europa.eu/en/press/press-releases/2019/02/19/council-conclusions-on-eu-relations-with-the-swiss-confederation/> (accessed 25 April 2022).

91 On the Swiss-UK relationship post Brexit, see the contribution by G. Baur in this volume.

The Swiss Federal Government identified as one of its foreign policy priorities for 2016–2019 the consolidation of its relationship with the EU/EFTA States. The strengthening of the relationship with the EU, the securing of the effective implementation of the bilateral agreements as well as their continuation were essential. Access to the EU internal market and the conclusion of further agreements, such as the one envisaged in the field of electricity were at the heart of the negotiations on the institutional issues that came to a close at the end of 2018. However, the Swiss Federal Government did not fully endorse the outcome of the negotiations and decided, in January 2019, to launch a wide consultation. All relevant stakeholders were able to participate and to draw attention to important aspects of the institutional provisions as well as three aspects linked to the scope of the envisaged agreement. The protection of wages, the EU Citizens' Rights Directive and State aid were of important concern. Discussions took place between the EU and Switzerland on these issues, but material differences remained mainly in the protection of wages and in the EU Citizens' Rights Directive that were part of the red lines to be safeguarded on the Swiss side. In light of these developments, the Swiss Federal Government decided on 26 May 2021 not to sign the InstA.

The consequences of the failure of the InstA were immediate. In some cases, the EU took measures even before the decision of the Swiss Federal Government not to sign the agreement, the conclusion of the InstA being a precondition to any future market access agreement since 2019. Negotiations were suspended in a certain number of areas. No updates of specific bilateral agreements were envisaged. The heart of the system has been affected. Trust was lost between the partners. Since then, Switzerland is trying to undertake steps to regain that trust that was developed over decades but lacked during the last twelve months. Switzerland and the EU are close allies. By adopting the EU sanctions against Russia and Belarus, Switzerland demonstrated its willingness and readiness of acting on the same line as the EU in that conflict. Switzerland and the EU are also key economic partners. The economic interdependence between them is considerable in terms of trade in goods, services and direct investment. The areas of cooperation are broad as evidenced by the large number of bilateral agreements.

In the InstA, neither the EU nor Switzerland were able to fully enforce the wishes and interests they asserted ahead of the commencement of the negotiations. The text of the 2018 draft agreement was a compromise. Assessing whether the compromise was fair or not is a political question. What is clear is that the current situation is unsatisfactory for both partners. Lack of legal certainty in the interpretation of the agreements, in the development of their content, in the surveillance as well as in the dispute settlement mechanism are impacting negatively the two legal orders and the respective economic actors and citizens. The institutional issues and the remaining controversial topics in the areas of free movement of persons and State aid will have to be dealt with anyway in the search for a balance of interests to render the bilateral relations between Switzerland and the EU stable again. The global context of the war in Ukraine and the adoption by Switzerland of the EU sanctions against Russia and Belarus has improved the overall framework for Switzerland and favours the path to future negotiations with the EU. Undoubtedly, these future negotiations are a priority for Switzerland. It is, however, uncertain whether they present the same attractiveness to the EU.

CHAPTER 12

The Federal Council's Suggested Sectoral Approach Post-26 May 2021 and the Future of EU-Swiss Trade Relations

Michael Hahn

1 Stocktaking and Line of Inquiry

The current legal fundament of the bilateral relationship between the European Union (EU) and Switzerland has become fragile since the Federal Council decided on 26 May 2021 to formally declare the termination of the negotiations on a new Institutional Agreement.[1] It will be recalled that the reason for the pertinent efforts over the last decade or so had been the EU's conclusion that the *status quo* of the current haphazard regime of Switzerland's participation in the EU Internal Market (in the following Internal or Single Market) was no longer compatible with the Union's interest of not just discriminating against its own Members and their economic operators, but also against the European Economic Area (EEA)-European Free Trade Association (EFTA) States and their economic operators.[2] These ground rules have, not the least due to the influence of the former French Foreign Minister Michel Barnier – now a failed hard-right presidential candidate, but for a long time the skilled nemesis of the UK negotiating partner in the context of the UK's withdrawal from the EU –, become more rigid and more dogmatic. The term "level playing field" now describes an EU concept, pursuant to which the price for privileged market access for close neighbours[3] goes beyond accepting and

1 Accord facilitant les relations bilatérales entre l'Union européenne et la Confédération suisse dans les parties du marché intérieur auxquels la Suisse participe, draft dated 23 November 2018, <https://www.eda.admin.ch/dam/europa/fr/documents/abkommen/Acccord-inst-Projet-de-texte_fr.pdf> (the French version being authoritative, accessed 19 March 2022).

2 Council of the European Union, *Council conclusions on EU relations with EFTA countries*, 14 December 2010, <https://www.consilium.europa.eu/uedocs/cms_data/docs/pressdata/EN/foraff/118458.pdf> (accessed 19 March 2022).

3 See to that effect: Joint report from the negotiators of the European Union and the United Kingdom Government on progress during phase 1 of negotiations under Article 50 TEU on the United Kingdom's orderly withdrawal from the European Union, TF50 (2017) 19, 8 December 2017, para. 49. See also the much-commented presentation slide to that joint report: Slide presented by Michel Barnier, European Commission Chief Negotiator, to the Heads of State

© KONINKLIJKE BRILL NV, LEIDEN, 2023 | DOI:10.1163/9789004529984_014

adapting to the standards prescribed by the Union, a condition for the lawful marketing of a given product. Rather, the Commission has made clear that quasi-fully integrated economies and their operators also need to be subject to (potentially costly) regulatory processes and methods ("regulatory input"), even though they may be irrelevant to the stated regulatory outcome ("regulatory output"). This rather massive projection of EU rules and regulations upon its "close neighbourhood" is intended to protect the EU industry from disadvantages vis-à-vis foreign competitors that would otherwise potentially benefit from "lighter" or "smarter" third-country (read in particular: Swiss and UK) financial, environmental, social and economic regulations. Whether this rather cavalier approach of the regional hegemon is compatible with general international law, and World Trade Organization (WTO) law, in particular, is an issue for another day.[4]

In other chapters in this volume, the history and state of play of the Swiss-EU relationship have been thoroughly examined.[5] Until 26 May 2021, Switzerland could be understood to participate in the Single Market regime, certainly with regard to goods covered by the Mutual Recognition Agreement (MRA):[6] not because it is an EU Member State (it is not),[7] nor because of being fully associated like the EEA EFTA States on the basis of a comprehensive foundational

---

and Government at the European Council (Article 50) on 15 December 2017, TF50 (2017) 21, 19 December 2017, <https://ec.europa.eu/info/sites/default/files/slide_presented_by_barnier_at_euco_15-12-2017.pdf> (accessed 19 March 2022). See also European Council, European Council Guidelines to Art. 50 TEU, EUCO XT 20001/18, 23 March 2018, para. 7.

4 Cf. House of Lords Select Committee on the European Union, Uncorrected oral evidence: The level playing field and State aid, 27 February 2020, <https://committees.parliament.uk/oralevidence/83/pdf> (accessed 19 March 2022), notably the very pointed statements by L. Bartels, pp. 2 and 3: «The point is that the level playing field is essentially about ensuring that the other side raises costs to your level. You can dress it up as values, but really it is hard-nosed economics at its best» (p. 3); see also M. Hahn, 'Je t'aime… Moi non plus: Rechtsfragen des Verhältnisses Schweiz – EU', *Zeitschrift des Bernischen Juristenvereins* 157 (2021), pp. 77–125.

5 See in particular the introduction to this volume as well the contributions by and R. Schwok (Chapter 10) and C. Kaddous (Chapter 11).

6 Agreement between the European Community and the Swiss Confederation on mutual recognition in relation to conformity assessment (OJ 2002, L 114/369; published in the Systematic Compilation of Swiss law SR 0.946.526.81, reprinted at <https://www.seco.admin.ch/seco/en/home/Aussenwirtschaftspolitik_Wirtschaftliche_Zusammenarbeit/Wirtschaftsbeziehungen/Technische_Handelshemmnisse/Mutual_Recognition_Agreement_MRA0/MRA_Schweiz_EU.html>, accessed 19 March 2022).

7 Switzerland has been called, i.a., a «*zugewandter Ort*» (allied country), a *de facto* Member State and a passive Member State of the EU, see M. Oesch, *Schweiz-Europäische Union: Grundlagen, Bilaterale Abkommen, Autonomer Nachvollzug* (EIZ Publishing, 2020), para. 7 for further references.

legal text (it is not), but rather on the basis of a bundle of many sectoral and, as such, mostly rather narrowly defined arrangements that in their totality have created with regard to certain goods a (somewhat limping) substitute for the EEA. It will be recalled that the 1999 "*Bilaterals I*" were the result of the joint Swiss-EU *post mortem* efforts to salvage some of the intended benefits of the EEA[8] that had failed to win the double approval of popular and cantonal support necessary for Switzerland's ratification.[9]

Since 2010, various Commission statements[10] and Council conclusions[11] have defined that for the Union, the *essentialia negotii* for a continuing special relationship with its neighbour would be (1) the dynamic alignment to EU Internal Market legislation by Switzerland; (2) creating a level playing field with regard to State aid;[12] (3) the establishment of a dispute settlement mechanism (DSM) that would ensure that disputes could not be tabled *ad infinitum* without a

8 Switzerland's chief negotiator *Franz Blankart* was the leading negotiator on the EFTA side; cf. C. Longchamp, 'Er war Blochers grosser Gegenspieler in der EWR-Schlacht: Spitzendiplomat Franz Blankart ist tot', *Aargauer Zeitung*, 19 January 2021, <https://www.aargauerzeitung.ch/ld.2086944> (accessed 19 March 2022); see also F. Münger, 'Der Alleingang – Chance oder Irrweg?', *swissinfo.ch* 5 December 2002, <https://www.swissinfo.ch/ger/der-alleingang---chance-oder-irrweg-/3059368> (accessed 19 March 2022).

9 Federal Council, Arrêté du Conseil fédéral constatant le résultat de la votation populaire du 6 décembre 1992 (Espace économique européen [EEE]) du 28 janvier 1993, FF 1993 I 147, <https://www.fedlex.admin.ch/eli/fga/1993/1_168_147_/fr> (accessed 19 March 2022).

10 European Commission, EU-Swiss relations, MEMO/16/3185, 25 September 2016, https://ec.europa.eu/commission/presscorner/detail/en/MEMO_16_3185 (accessed 19 March 2022); European Commission, Press remarks by Vice-President Šefčovič following his meeting with Ignazio Cassis, SPEECH/21/6043, 15 November 2021, <https://ec.europa.eu/commission/presscorner/detail/en/speech_21_6043> (accessed 19 March 2022). See also the statement of President *von der Leyen* in European Commission, Minutes of the 2380th meeting of the Commission (Brussels, 2 June 2021), PV(2021) 2380 final, 6 July 2021, <https://ec.europa.eu/transparency/documents-register/api/files/PV(2021)2380_0/090166e5df69ffff?rendition=false> (accessed 19 March 2022), p. 35: "*Elle réitère que droits et obligations vont de pair et que vouloir bénéficier des premiers sans respecter les secondes n'est pas acceptable.*"

11 Council of the European Union, Council conclusions on EU relations with the Swiss Confederation, 6767/17, 28 February 2017, <https://data.consilium.europa.eu/doc/document/ST-6767-2017-INIT/en/pdf> (accessed 19 March 2022), para. 5; Council of the European Union, Council conclusions on EU relations with the Swiss Confederation, 6578/19, 19 February 2019, <https://data.consilium.europa.eu/doc/document/ST-6578-2019-INIT/en/pdf> (accessed 19 March 2022), para. 9.

12 According to M. Baldi, 'Zu den Auswirkungen des geplanten Rahmenabkommens mit der EU', *Jusletter* 18 May 2019, paras. 18–29, the issue of 'State aid' is suitable for being integrated into a comprehensively modernised FTA.

proper resolution[13] and, lastly (4) a mechanism ensuring that Switzerland would financially contribute to the EU cohesion policy[14] in a manner reflecting the *status quo* pursuant to which Switzerland benefits more than most Member States from its far-reaching, albeit not complete integration into the Single Market and with regard to other Union projects.[15] These fundamental points were repeated by the Commissioner now in the lead for relationships with the close neighbours the United Kingdom (UK) and Switzerland, Vice-President Šefčovič.[16] It is noteworthy that this view was once shared by the Swiss Government, notably, the acceptance of a DSM (that would, however, not replace the Court of Justice of the European Union [CJEU, European Court of Justice] as the final arbiter of all issues of EU law) and the recognition that it was a matter of course that full integration into the EU Single Market required

13 See Y. Fauconnet, 'Streitbeilegungsmechanismus im Institutionellen Abkommen', *Jusletter* 12 April 2021, para. 25.

14 Known in Switzerland as "*Kohäsionsmilliarde/milliard de cohésion*" and in Brussel as "financial contribution to the EU cohesion policy". See D. Steinvorth, 'Genugtuung in Brüssel', *Neue Zürcher Zeitung* 2 October 2021, <https://www.nzz.ch/ld.1648295> (accessed 19 March 2022); European Commission (n. 10); Council of the European Union (n. 11). See also the contribution by B. Pirker (Chapter 9).

15 See, e.g., Bertelsmann Stiftung (ed.), G. Mion, D. Ponattu, Estimating economic benefits of the Single Market for European countries and regions, 2019, <https://www.bertelsmann-stiftung.de/fileadmin/files/BSt/Publikationen/GrauePublikationen/EZ_Study_SingleMarket.pdf> (accessed 19 March 2022). See also H. Schöchli, 'EU-Binnenmarkt verhilft Österreich zu höherem Wachstum', *Neue Zürcher Zeitung* 11 February 2020, <https://www.nzz.ch/ld.1539617> (accessed 19 March 2022); D. Mariani, 'Die Schweiz profitiert am meisten vom EU-Binnenmarkt', *swissinfo.ch*, 10 May 2019 <https://www.swissinfo.ch/ger/wirtschaft_die-schweiz-profitiert-am-meisten-vom-eu-binnenmarkt/44954096> (accessed 19 March 2022).

16 Pertaining to the United Kingdom, see, e.g., European Commission, Press remarks by Vice-President Šefčovič after the meeting of the Joint Committee of the Withdrawal Agreement, 21 February 2022, <https://ec.europa.eu/commission/presscorner/detail/en/speech_22_1261> (accessed 19 March 2022); H. von der Burchard, J. Posaner, 'Maroš Šefčovič: Post-Brexit talks will 'probably' drag into next year', *Politico* 23 November 2021, <https://www.politico.eu/article/post-brexit-talks-sefcovic-northern-ireland/> (accessed 19 March 2022). Pertaining to Switzerland, see, e.g., European Commission, Press remarks by Vice-President Šefčovič following his meeting with Ignazio Cassis, 15 November 2021, <https://ec.europa.eu/commission/presscorner/detail/en/speech_21_6043> (accessed 19 March 2022); and, most recently, the leaked letter by Šefčovič's Chef de Cabinet to the Swiss chief negotiator, Letter from Juraj Nociar to Livia Leu, Ares(2022)3495574, 6 May 2022, <https://twitter.com/remohess/status/1525105318870515712> (accessed 14 May 2022).

full and "dynamic" adherence of (sometimes too) dynamically evolving market rules.[17]

Even though the official "termination" of negotiations has been a case of surprising and shocking diplomatic malpractice,[18] it was almost two years in the making. Contrary to the wording and the spirit of the Federal Constitution,[19] the Federal Council had started consultations with political and societal actors without supporting the result of its negotiations[20] and without forwarding the treaty draft officially to Parliament.[21] The feedback was lukewarm,[22] even by those political parties and actors typically inclined to support pragmatic and mutually beneficial arrangements with the EU. But the infighting between

17 Former chief negotiators, then Swiss State Secretary *Yves Rossier* and then Chief Operating Officer of the European External Action Service *David O'Sullivan*, came to an agreement on the role of the CJEU in the spring of 2013, see T. Gafafer, F. Schäfer, 'Das Rahmenabkommen – eine fast unendliche Geschichte', *Neue Zürcher Zeitung* 26 May 2021, <https://www.nzz.ch/ld.1398081> (accessed 19 March 2022). See also J. Flückiger, 'Den bilateralen Weg erneuern, um ihn zu erhalten', *Neue Zürcher Zeitung* 19 December 2013, <https://www.nzz.ch/ld.1058629> (accessed 19 March 2022).

18 A more positive view is held by the former Swiss chief negotiator State Secretary *Michael Ambühl*. He considers the decision to terminate the negotiations the right choice, with "bad" and "worse" being the available options: M. Ambühl, D.S. Scherrer, *Alternativen im Verhandlungsprozess: Gutachten zuhanden des EDA*, 8 February 2021, <https://www.eda.admin.ch/dam/eda/de/documents/aktuell/news/2021/20211712-gutachten-ambuehl-scherer-alternativen-verhandlungsprozess_DE.pdf> (accessed 19 March 2022), p. 6.

19 Federal Constitution of the Swiss Confederation of 18 April 1999 (FC) (SR 101), <https://www.fedlex.admin.ch/eli/cc/1999/404/en> (accessed 19 March 2022).

20 Which it claimed had only been a proposal. The EU has officially disputed this narrative; Swiss participants in the final negotiating round in Zurich's Savoy Baur au Lac shared the EU's surprise. See to that effect T. Gafafer, C.G. Schmutz and D. Steinvorth, 'Das Missverständnis von Zürich', *Neue Zürcher Zeitung* 22 June 2021, <https://www.nzz.ch/ld.1630710> (accessed 19 March 2022).

21 According to Swiss constitutional law, the Federal Assembly ratifies international treaties after that the Federal Council has submitted a dispatch. See to that effect Article 166(2) FC as well as Article 24(2) and Article 141 of the Federal Act on the Federal Assembly (Parliament Act, ParlA; SR 171.10), <https://www.fedlex.admin.ch/eli/cc/2003/510/en> (accessed 19 March 2022). For an analysis, see M. Graf, C. Theler and M. von Wyss (eds.), *Parlamentsrecht und Parlamentspraxis der Schweizerischen Bundesversammlung – Kommentar zum Parlamentsgesetz (ParlG) vom 13. Dezember 2002* (Helbing Lichtenhahn Verlag, 2014), and its 2021 supplement by M. Graf, A. Caroni (eds.), *Parlamentsrecht und Parlamentspraxis der Schweizerischen Bundesversammlung – Kommentar zum Parlamentsgesetz (ParlG), Aktualisierung 2021* (Verlag parliaments.ch, 2021), <https://www.parlament.ch/centers/documents/de/Erg%c3%a4nzung%20Parlamentskommentar.pdf> (accessed 19 March 2022).

22 See Y. Fauconnet (n. 13), para. 9–11 for an overview of reactions by stakeholders and the media.

certain members of the Federal Council, lack of leadership and the fear of a popular rejection of the treaty and of losses at the 2023 general elections led political parties and the current Swiss executive to "duck and cover", obviously without a proper assessment of the diplomatic consequences.[23]

These consequences have been dire: at the time of this writing, the EU-Swiss MRA[24] trade facilitating potential has been suspended with regard to upcoming regulatory changes concerning the MRA-covered products.[25] Medicinal products[26] and their producers have been the first to be hit, and the upcoming reform of the EU legislation on machinery and construction products[27] will affect the pertinent Swiss industries next.

Unsurprisingly, this has led to significant reactions by trade and industry and to the shedding of crocodile tears by the same political parties and non-governmental organisations that had failed to actively support the updating of Swiss-EU relations when their engagement would have made a difference.[28] As announced at least since December 2018, the Union has reacted to the Swiss refusal to adapt the bilateral framework in kind and refuses now to adapt the existing agreements to new developments and to conclude new

23 See M. Guillaume, 'Après l'abandon de l'accord-cadre avec l'UE, le champ de ruines', *Le Temps* 27 May 2021, <https://www.letemps.ch/suisse/laccordcadre-lue-abandonne-reste-un-champ-ruines> (accessed 19 March 2022), as well as F. Fellmann, M. Häfliger, 'Der Plan B ist nur ein Plänchen', *Tages-Anzeiger*, 27 May 2021, <https://www.tagesanzeiger.ch/874776492370> (accessed 19 March 2022), and more recently P.A. Fischer, 'Economiesuisse warnt vor weiterem Zuwarten', *Neue Zürcher Zeitung* 4 February 2022, <https://www.nzz.ch/ld.1667706> (accessed 19 March 2022). See also *Cottier*'s passionate political indictment, T. Cottier, 'Rahmenabkommen Schweiz–EU: Der Bundesrat hat am 26. Mai 2021 seine Kompetenzen überschritten', *Jusletter* 28 June 2021. See also the contribution by R. Schwok in this volume.

24 See n. 6.

25 See the 20 chapters regarding specific categories of goods, annexed to the MRA, which cover approximately two thirds of Swiss exports, see C.G. Schmutz, 'Die Briten sind dreissig Jahre im Rückstand', *Neue Zürcher Zeitung* 21 January 2021, <https://www.nzz.ch/ld.1597075> (accessed 19 March 2022).

26 As per Chapter 4 of Annex I to the MRA; the EU legislation uses the term «Medical devices»; see the then applicable Council Directive 93/42/EEC of 14 June 1993 concerning medical devices (OJ 1993, L 169/1).

27 See, European Commission, Proposal for a Regulation on Machinery products, 21 April 2021, COM(2021) 202 final, and European Commission, Proposal for a Regulation laying down harmonised conditions for the marketing of construction products, 30 March 2022, COM(2022) 144.

28 Unsurprisingly with the exception of the hard-right People's Party SVP/UDC/SPP (not to be confused with the centre-right European People's Party political family) and (surprisingly) the trade unions and their political representatives.

agreements,[29] even when they are mutually beneficial.[30] As a consequence, despite Switzerland's modification of its laws and regulations to mirror the new EU Medical Devices Regulation (MDR),[31] the EU refuses to participate in (and thus, due to the consensus requirement, blocks) an equivalence-affirming decision of the Joint Committee under the EU-Swiss MRA.[32] Such a formal endorsement of equivalence is a precondition for MRA-covered Swiss products to benefit from the MRA's potential to reduce the regulatory costs for accessing the EU Internal Market.[33]

In light of a political mess, largely created by the lack of political leadership on one side, and, on the other side, a possibly not completely realistic optimism regarding one's own ability to convince the rest of the world of the advantages of EU rules and regulations, both the Union and Switzerland have to decide what course to pursue under the circumstances.

---

29 See C.G. Schmutz, N. Nuspliger, 'Die EU droht mit bilateralem Stillstand', *Neue Zürcher Zeitung* 18 December 2018, <https://www.nzz.ch/ld.1445443> (accessed 19 March 2022). See also the passive-aggressive signals from Brussels a month later, N. Nuspliger, 'EU stoppt Anpassung der Bilateralen', *Neue Zürcher Zeitung* 17 January 2019, <https://www.nzz.ch/ld.1452165> (accessed 19 March 2022).

30 It is said that the internal Commission guidance only exempts treaties that are in the overwhelming interest of the Union from the treaty-freeze. Also, the EU has occasionally recognised adaptations of Swiss laws since 2019, see C.G. Schmutz, 'EU aktualisiert doch noch ein Abkommen', *Neue Zürcher Zeitung*, 6 July 2021, <https://www.nzz.ch/ld.1634049> (accessed 19 March 2022); T. Gafafer, 'Trotz scharfer Rhetorik ist die EU auch pragmatisch', *Neue Zürcher Zeitung*, 7 January 2022, <https://www.nzz.ch/ld.1663090> (accessed 19 March 2022).

31 Regulation (EU) 2017/745 of 5 April 2017 on medical devices (OJ 2017, L 117/1), see also Federal Office of Public Health, Revision of Swiss medical devices legislation, <https://www.bag.admin.ch/bag/en/home/medizin-und-forschung/heilmittel/aktuelle-rechtsetzungsprojekte/revision-med-prod-verord-mepv.html> (accessed 19 March 2022).

32 For the consensus requirement, see Article 5 and 11 MRA. The last actualisation of the MRA dates back to July 2017: Decision No 1/2017 of the Committee established under the Agreement between the European Community and the Swiss Confederation on mutual recognition in relation to conformity assessment of 28 July 2017 on the amendment of Chapter 4 on medical devices, Chapter 6 on pressure vessels, Chapter 7 on radio equipment and telecommunication terminal equipment, Chapter 8 on equipment and protective systems intended for use in potentially explosive atmosphere, Chapter 9 on electrical equipment and electromagnetic compatibility, Chapter 11 on measuring instruments, Chapter 15 on medicinal products, GMP inspection and batch certification, Chapter 17 on lifts, and Chapter 20 on explosives for civil use, and the update of legal references listed in Annex 1 [2017/2118] (OJ 2017, L323/51; Official Compilation of Swiss law AS 2015 2645).

33 Article 1(2) 3rd sentence MRA: "Conformity marks required by the legislation of one of the Parties must be affixed to products placed on the market of that Party."

Although the EU *overall* would not suffer significant economic damage from a downgrading of the special Swiss-EU relationship to a normal WTO Most Favoured Nation (MFN) trade environment – which would be cold comfort indeed for certain border regions of Switzerland's neighbouring States[34] –, the political costs would be high: regional hegemons not getting along with their small neighbour cannot expect much sympathy these days. Also, the chances for the Swiss opponents of Switzerland's integration into the European labour market to finally shoot down the least popular "bilateral" agreement, the Agreement on the Free Movement of Persons (AFMP),[35] would increase if the Union was perceived to retract trade benefits that are viewed by many – rightly or wrongly – to be a *quid pro quo* for the opportunity of more than 1.5 million EU citizens to live and work in Switzerland.[36]

It seems that this calculus is, for the moment, guiding official EU policy: the Commission goes out of its way to present itself as being prepared to continue looking for the next phase of trying to find a mutually acceptable compromise with the EU's small and wealthy neighbour, not without declaring the four points cited above to be non-negotiable.[37] All the while, it is not hiding its frustration with the process so far and applies significant pressure on its Swiss partner, sometimes even at the price of considerable self-harm, be it actual (e.g., ending research cooperation, affecting *inter alia* the cooperation with Europe's highest-ranked engineering schools)[38] or potential

34 But note the interdependence, particularly visible in the context of the pandemic: C. Lecomte, 'La Suisse est dépendante de ses frontaliers', *Le Temps* 8 February 2021, <https://www.letemps.ch/suisse/suisse-dependante-frontaliers> (accessed 19 March 2022); see also *infra*, section 2.2.

35 Agreement between the European Community and its Member States, of the one part, and the Swiss Confederation, of the other, on the free movement of persons (OJ 2002, L 114/6; SR 0.142.112.681).

36 According to the Swiss authorities, a little more than 1.5 million EU/EFTA citizens lived in Switzerland, see State Secretariat for Migration, *Statistiques annuelles sur l'immigration 2021*, <https://www.sem.admin.ch/dam/sem/fr/data/publiservice/statistik/auslaenderstatistik/monitor/2021/statistik-zuwanderung-2021-jahr.pdf.download.pdf> (accessed 19 March 2022), p. 3.

37 See the interview with Vice-President Šefčovič reported by S. Israel, 'Wir brauchen ein politisches Signal', *Tages-Anzeiger* 17 November 2021, <https://www.tagesanzeiger.ch/749949623387> (accessed 19 March 2022).

38 According to the QS World University Rankings 2022, the Swiss Federal Institute of Technology (ETH Zürich) was ranked 8th, and the EPFL 14th, see QS World University Rankings 2022, <https://www.topuniversities.com/university-rankings/world-university-rankings/2022> (accessed 19 March 2022).

(e.g., endangering the safety of the European grid by sabotaging efficient grid management).[39]

Whereas the EU position is thus firm on a limited (but very significant) number of *essentialia negotii*, the Swiss position – after the initial confusion and shocked silence – has been a return to a previously discarded approach. Instead of trying to establish a robust and potentially comprehensive legal fundament for future Swiss-EU relations, it now proposes the very sectoral approach that had been considered a dead-end by both sides in the years 2010–2021.[40] In the opinion of the Federal Council and the majority of Swiss parliamentarians, the approach to first create a framework for the bundle of Swiss-EU agreements that define "*la voie bilatérale*" (the "bilateral path") has proven too complex to communicate to Swiss voters, possibly because of its proximity to a full *de jure* integration of Switzerland into the EU legal order.[41] A majority of political parties currently consider such an approach politically toxic: even the Swiss Social Democratic Party (SP/PS), traditionally supportive of good relationships with the EU, is now catering to its anti-EU trade union wing.[42]

While the rejection of a comprehensive approach may be a missed opportunity for Switzerland, the following contribution will attempt to test the argument whether the sectoral approach[43] proposed by the Swiss Federal Council may be compatible with the EU's stated goals. It would seem that a more limited sectoral architecture would enjoy the genuine advantage of being easier to explain to the Swiss voters: An agreement ensuring quasi-Member State (sectoral) access to the Single Market allows to compare directly the ensuing advantages with the corresponding sovereignty costs. However, such an approach will only be compatible with the EU's interests if (1) the sectors addressed in the prototype agreement negotiations are broad enough to put a significant part (if not a majority) of Swiss-EU trade on a new basis, and (2) the

39 The Commission's attitude led the Swiss national transmission grid operator Swissgrid to submit an action against the EU, see Case T-127/21: Action brought on 26 February 2021 — *Swissgrid v Commission* (OJ 2021, C 189/18).

40 Federal Council, EU relations: Federal Council sets out approach for negotiations, 25 February 2022, <https://www.admin.ch/gov/en/start/documentation/media-releases.msg-id-87349.html> (accessed 19 March 2022).

41 At least in the perception of the voting public that has been exposed to pertinent political rhetoric since 1991; see V. Capodici, 'Köppels Bannon-Show', *Tages-Anzeiger* 7 March 2018, <https://www.tagesanzeiger.ch/17767792> (accessed 19 March 2022).

42 See F. Schäfer, 'Der Europa-Knorz der SP', *Neue Zürcher Zeitung* 8 June 2021, <https://www.nzz.ch/ld.1629122> (accessed 19 March 2022). See also the contribution of R. Schwok (Chapter 10) in this volume.

43 As opposed to a comprehensive framework agreement or "Institutional Agreement."

four "*priorities*" (alignment, also with regard to State aid; DSM; and burden sharing) will be met.

In the following, this chapter will therefore attempt to explore what the constituent elements of a (first) negotiating package could be, so that the negotiating outcome would be an agreement with a realistic chance to receive the approval from the Swiss referendum voters while meeting both the Swiss condition to be "sectoral" (as opposed to "horizontal") and the Union's demand that its four "essentials"[44] are met. It will be submitted (section 2), that an ambitious WTO *plus* trade in goods-centred package has the biggest chance to meet that demanding set of *a priori* deliverables. While obvious reasons would advocate trying a relaunch of negotiations regarding some of the politically most contentious issues concerning the free movement of persons, the paper suggests that this should be postponed until a first sectoral package has allowed resetting the dented relationship. In the next step (section 3), the elements of a possible package will be presented. This includes examining whether it would be possible to create room for the involvement of the EFTA Court. The obvious difficulty to render such an approach compatible with the European Court of Justice's "autonomy of the Union legal order" jurisprudence is subsequently addressed (section 4).

2 Conceptualising a Model Sectoral Agreement

2.1 *Introduction*

This contribution tries to shed some light on the question of whether a window exists for reconciling the interests of the EU and Switzerland on the basis of the new position of the Swiss Government that future negotiation on EU-Swiss relations would best be dealt with on a sectoral basis. In doing so, it does not propose or endorse such an approach; rather, it takes note of the Swiss Government's view that this is the only available option and tests its viability. Whereas the preference for a sectoral approach has now been shared with the EU and the public, it remains to be seen what this paradigm shift entails for the bilateral (negotiating) agenda.

From a Swiss perspective, the three most urgent issues at hand[45] would be (1) to render the MRA operational

44 See the *essentialia negotii* mentioned *supra*, pp. 339–340 of this contribution.

45 See Schweizerische Depeschenagentur (SDA), 'Livia Leu stellt der EU den Schweizer Vorschlag vor', *Tages-Anzeiger* 31 March 2022, <https://www.tagesanzeiger.ch/914831072352> (accessed 31 March 2022).

again;[46] (2) to end Switzerland's being squeezed out of the European electricity grid that it helped create in the 1950s;[47] and lastly, (3) the Swiss participation regarding research.[48] Two of these issues concern goods: this is obviously the case with regard to the MRA, but electricity is also a good, pursuant to the Harmonized System's legal presumption.[49] In the case of the electricity agreement, much of the necessary work would already have been completed, as significant negotiation progress had been achieved prior to the suspension of negotiations in 2018.[50]

However, scepticism as to whether the EU will be open to addressing these three issues before other negotiations seems warranted. By doing so, the EU could almost be perceived as rewarding Switzerland for having brought 10 years of negotiations to an unscheduled halt on 26 May 2021. Maybe due to a lack of imagination, this author would therefore exclude the possibility that any of these dossiers would be suitable for stand-alone negotiations. That does not exclude the possibility if trust is re-established quickly, that these three urgent issues could be fast-tracked. While one would expect the re-establishment of trust to depend heavily on achieving concrete negotiating results, a rather specific roadmap for future negotiating may suffice to render these difficulties provisionally moot.

2.2 *Keeping It Light: AFMP for another Day*

Opting for a sectoral approach does not yet determine what sectors, i.e., what subject-matters – regardless whether they have already been regulated in bilateral agreements or not – should be addressed. One obvious solution would be to address head-on the dossier that provided the Federal Council with most of the publicly stated reasons for ending the decade-long effort to future-proof Switzerland's trade relationship with its by far most important trading partner.

---

46 See to that matter the not necessarily expected German support regarding the med-tech sector, C.G. Schmutz, 'Medtech-Firmen erhalten Support aus Deutschland', *Neue Zürcher Zeitung* 2 February 2022, <https://www.nzz.ch/ld.1667570> (accessed 19 March 2022).

47 Hahn (n. 4), p. 96–101.

48 F. Schoop, '«Das hat gravierende Konsequenzen»', *Neue Zürcher Zeitung* 24 January 2022, <https://www.nzz.ch/ld.1666058> (accessed 19 March 2022).

49 Electricity is classified under HS 2716.0000 in the Harmonized System of tariff nomenclature; cf. the International Convention on the Harmonized Commodity Description and Coding System (OJ 1987, L 198/3; SR 0.632.11), to which Article 2 of the Agreement between the European Economic Community and the Swiss Confederation (OJ 1972, L 300/189 in French; Series I Volume 1972 [31.12], L300/191 in English; SR 0.632.401; FTA 72) refers to.

50 Negotiations started in 2007, see Swiss Directorate for European Affairs, *Electricité*, September 2020, <https://www.eda.admin.ch/dam/europa/fr/documents/fs/02-FS-Strom_fr.pdf> (accessed 19 March 2022).

While the AFMP is overall working exceedingly well,[51] the objectively minor hiccups associated with it and its proximity to politically toxic issues such as EU citizenship and migration[52] have been the single most important reason for breaking up the grand coalition (concerning EU questions) of Swiss political parties left of the hard-right Swiss People's Party (SVP/UDC/SPP) and, maybe even more importantly, the *ad hoc* alliance between Switzerland's employers' associations and the Swiss trade unions, as the latter completely and comprehensively rejected the results of the negotiations, despite the internalisation of so-far unilateral flanking measures ("*flankierende Massnahmen*", FlaMs) into the (draft) agreement.[53]

Still, the reasons why the Commission may want issues regarding the AFMP to be included in the first round of "sectoral" negotiations are not to be dismissed out of hand. After all, some very specific grievances have accumulated over the last decade or so, from certain measures in the Swiss Canton of *Ticino*,[54] to the non-alignment with the EU Citizens' Rights Directive (CRD),[55]

51 Numbers are said to be incapable of lying, see *supra*, n. 36.

52 In particular, the thorny compatibility of Switzerland's flanking measures with the Citizen's Rights Directive (CRD), Directive 2004/38/EC of the European Parliament and of the Council of 29 April 2004 on the right of citizens of the Union and their family members to move and reside freely within the territory of the Member States amending Regulation (EEC) No 1612/68 and repealing Directives 64/221/EEC, 68/360/EEC, 72/194/EEC, 73/148/EEC, 75/34/EEC, 75/35/EEC, 90/364/EEC, 90/365/EEC and 93/96/EEC (OJ 2004, L 158/77).

53 See, for example, para. 2 of Protocol 1 of the draft Institutional Agreement which internalises a "prior warning" (minimum delay) period that requires that service providers alert the competent authorities at least 4 days before for posted workers start to work; so far, Swiss legislation requires 8 days, but is subject to being challenged against the benchmark of the AFMP; see the contribution by K. Pärli (Chapter 4) in this volume.

54 The 2016 "*prima i nostri!*" ("Ours first!") initiative modified the cantonal constitution in such a way that the authorities in Ticino must favour Swiss citizens or lawful residents over non-resident aliens; see Article 14(1)(b) of the Constitution of Ticino, <https://www3.ti.ch/CAN/RLeggi/public/index.php/raccolta-leggi/pdfatto/atto/8021> (accessed 19 March 2022): "*Il Cantone provvede affinché* [...] *sul mercato del lavoro venga privilegiato a pari qualifiche professionali chi vive sul suo territorio per rapporto a chi proviene dall'estero* (*attuazione del principio di preferenza agli Svizzeri*)" (The Canton insures on the labour market that people with equivalent qualifications who live in Switzerland are favoured compared to people living abroad [execution of the principle of Swiss preference]; translation by author from Italian). See U. Geiser, 'Ticino wants to protect residents on labour market', *swissinfo.ch* 25 September 2016, <https://www.swissinfo.ch/eng/september-25-cantonal-vote_ticino-wants-to-protect-residents-on-labour-market/42472732> (accessed 19 March 2022).

55 The incorporation of the CRD (n. 52) into Swiss law is a long-standing unresolved matter, see Federal Department of Police and Justice, Rapport au Conseil fédéral – Différences entre les réglementations de la Suisse et de l'Union européenne, 10 January 2022,

or to administrative measures accompanying the flanking measures that seem disproportionate even to some Swiss courts.[56] For that reason alone, cleaning the dossier of irritations would seem a desirable outcome and a worthwhile negotiating goal.

On balance, such an approach may prove to be counterproductive, though. The first reason for such scepticism is the utter lack of urgency: the AFMP ensures the Swiss industry's smooth access to the EU labour market and has contributed significantly to the sustained growth of the Swiss economy in the last decades. From an EU perspective, Switzerland offers employment to many EU citizens and contributes significantly to the economic well-being of at least two EU border regions which are home to a significant number of commuters who work in Switzerland, but choose to keep their residences in their respective home countries (French: "*frontaliers*", English: frontier workers).

Despite all these benefits for the Swiss population, the issue of migration and in particular the AFMP is the least popular aspect of the bilateral relationship in Switzerland. Combining the AFMP dossier with, e.g., the topics mentioned above as being of immediate interest to Switzerland (electricity, research cooperation, re-establishing the functioning of the MRA) would seem to be hardly consistent with the very reason for the return to a sectoral approach, i.e., Swiss political leaders' belief that a complex agreement, characterised by cross-sectoral trade-offs, renders it all but impossible to make any such arrangement palatable to Swiss voters. Whether that belief is well founded or not is largely irrelevant: its reality made the Federal Council accept long term damage to the Swiss economy as the political costs of the alternative position was considered too steep from a political economy perspective. While the EU is not obliged in the least to accept that premise, the likely price for refusing to engage would increase popular support for those who advocate the "Swexit" approach, whereas current opinion polls[57] reveal that there is overwhelming support for a privileged Swiss-EU relationship, including the rather sovereignty-costly practice of "autonomous alignment" ("*autonomer Nachvollzug*").[58]

<https://www.newsd.admin.ch/newsd/message/attachments/70430.pdf> (accessed 19 March 2022), p. 9.

56 See the judgment of the Administrative Court of the Canton of Zurich (*Verwaltungsgericht des Kantons Zürich*), *Gesellschaft A gegen Amt für Wirtschaft und Arbeit*, VB.2017.00474, <https://entscheidsuche.ch/docs/ZH_Verwaltungsgericht/ZH_VG_001_-VB-2017-00474_2018-07-04.html> (accessed 19 March 2022), paras. 2.2–2.3.

57 S. Bühler, 'EU: Bevölkerung offen für Zugeständnisse', *Schweiz am Wochenende/Aargauer Zeitung* 5 March 2022, <https://www.aargauerzeitung.ch/ld.2257914> (accessed 19 March 2022).

58 See the contribution by M. Oesch and M. Brugger (Chapter 1) in this volume.

Both the Union's and Switzerland's standard *modus operandi* is incremental change. The last effort to ensure a new lease of life for the special Swiss-EU relationship failed because the Federal Council did not even try to communicate its efforts to the general public, fearing rejection so much that the possible voting-down by the voter became the central narrative advanced to explain the radically undiplomatic termination of negotiations. Regardless of whether the real stumbling block was indeed the voter or, rather, the lack of leadership at the top: the definition of "insanity" is doing the same thing over and over again and expecting different results.[59] This would suggest starting the next generation of Swiss-EU treaties with a somewhat more modest and easy-to-communicate coverage and leaving the thorny compatibility of Switzerland's flanking measures with EU law in general and the alignment with the EU.

2.3 *Allowing Success: Focus on the Politically Possible*

If AFMP issues are left for another day (as this contribution humbly suggests), then what would make the EU entertain the return to a sectoral approach going forward? Given the European Commission's interest in "*unité de doctrine*" and reduction of complexity, any acceptance of the Federal Council's new sectoral approach is likely to depend on whether the next agreement (or the package of re-negotiated agreements) could at least serve as a political precedent for later arrangements. Thus, the new agreement would have to either be suitable to serve, *mutatis mutandis*, as a prototype for the next generation of Swiss-EU agreements or be sufficiently weighty to create a critical mass of desirable negotiating outcomes. An obvious choice would be a comprehensively updated Free Trade Agreement of 1972 (FTA 72)[60] that would expand beyond the current scope of application and solidly move into the realm of harmonisation and integration.

The *Joint Declaration on Trade Agreements*[61] (attached to the draft Institutional Agreement) would seem to indicate that there was a genuine interest on the EU side at the time to deepen the integration level of the Swiss-EU Free Trade Zone, thereby making it possibly the most ambitious bilateral trade relationship with a third-country EU partner, other than the EEA EFTA States which have fully joined the Internal Market.

---

59 A quote commonly (and possibly wrongly) attributed to Albert Einstein.

60 See n. 49.

61 Projet de décision du Comité conjoint de l'article 29 de l'Accord entre la Confédération suisse et la Communauté économique européenne, conclu à Bruxelles le 22 juillet 1972, attached to the draft Institutional Agreement (n. 1), p. 31.

Picking the trade-in-goods-relationship as the first sector to be discussed under the new approach, a comprehensive and ambitious Swiss-EU FTA (in the following: Switzerland – European Union FTA, SEUFTA) should go beyond the minimum content that qualifies an international trade agreement as an Article XXIV GATT/Article V GATS free trade agreement. Rather, it should include the harmonisation dimension (i.e., the internalisation of EU rules and regulations into the Swiss legal order) that characterises the Swiss-EU relationship, albeit largely on the basis of *legally* autonomous unilateral Swiss measures.

Thus, in the first place, this agreement would pursue the traditional Free Trade Agreement approach to eliminate border measures concerning – to use the language of Article XXIV GATT – "substantially all the trade" in goods, possibly expanding the scope of application of the current FTA 72 to include (more) agricultural goods, electricity and related trade facilitating arrangements in the broadest sense, including customs procedures. Additionally, though, it would contain the legal obligation to adapt the Swiss legal order to EU law ("harmonisation") and provide the *quid pro quo* for such a sovereignty-costly exercise: the treaty-based recognition of harmonised Swiss regulations, including those in the area of State aid.[62]

Insofar, SEUFTA would stand on the shoulders of the current MRA, but could also draw extensively on the *prior art* of the draft Institutional Agreement, as the pertinent provisions on alignment and on ensuring market integrity[63] create efficient mechanisms to ensure that the non-EU Member State Switzerland would be sufficiently integrated into the Single Market regulatory space to be benefitting from quasi-full participation.

Focusing on goods and to a limited extent on services (see later in this chapter) would consolidate the topics that are the main reason for Switzerland's internalisation of EU law since 1989: not admiration – EU legislation tends to be more often than not, poorly drafted, is often unintelligible and lacks consistency –, nor legal obligation – Switzerland has, so far, never ceded "control"[64] –,

62 State aids are currently addressed more extensively than appreciated by many in Article 23 FTA 72; see R. Höltschi, 'Lichtet die EU den Schweizer Subventionsdschungel?', *Neue Zürcher Zeitung* 27 March 2019, <https://www.nzz.ch/ld.1470372> (accessed 19 March 2022). For a thorough legal analysis see C. Tobler, 'State Aid Under Swiss-EU Bilateral Law: The Example of Company Taxation', in M. Bulterman, L Hancher, A. McDonnell and H.G. Sevenster (eds.), *View of European Law from the Mountain – Liber Amicorum Piet Jan Slot* (Wolters Kluwer, 2009), pp. 195–205.

63 Article 4 (principle of uniform interpretation) and Articles 5 and 12–15 (legislative alignment) of the draft InstA.

64 To paraphrase the Brexiteer slogan «take back control».

but economic incentives have made Switzerland align both "autonomously" and via international agreements. The prize is securing the 450-million-consumer-encompassing EU market as the home market for its competitive producers of goods and services. That means that preserving and expanding the legal basis for trade and services is not just relevant for Swiss economic operators, but directly affects a significant part of the Swiss voters who work for and with those companies. This, in turn, increases the chance of convincing both the total voting population and the cantons ("*Volk und Stände*") to approve an eventual result of any new sectoral agreement. As things stand, there seems to exist widespread popular recognition that the sovereignty costs that come with harmonisation are commensurate with the benefits for Swiss industry and Swiss workers.

3 Some Further Thoughts on Coverage

In light of the current Federal Council's position that only a sectoral approach to the necessary updating and weatherproofing of the EU-Switzerland special relationship is feasible, "something more" is required than just a repetition of an ultimately doomed exercise in order to justify the EU's investment of resources and political capital. An ambitious and comprehensive agreement that would transcend the FTA 72's scope of application and integrate harmonisation and alignment provisions should merit the EU's attention and effort. Such an agreement would modify and replace, *inter alia*, the FTA 72, thus (a) developing the *acquis bilatéral*, but also (b) taking inspiration from the bilateral roadmap elaborated already in the context of the Institutional Agreement.

3.1 *Trade in Goods*

A future Swiss-EU FTA (SEUFTA) firstly ought to replace the current FTA 72 (including all amendments regarding processed agricultural goods). In addition, SEUFTA would need to include (e.g., in chapters) or internalise (e.g., via an Annex) the agreements adding to and supplementing this foundational agreement, such as the MRA, the (bilateral) Government Procurement Agreement (GPA)[65] or the (bilateral) Agreement on Agricultural Goods.[66]

65 Agreement between the European Community and the Swiss Confederation on certain aspects of government procurement (OJ 2002, L 114/430; SR 0.172.052.68).

66 Agreement between the European Community and the Swiss Confederation on trade in agricultural products (OJ 2002, L 114/132; SR 0.916.026.81).

The FTA 72 belongs to the first generation of free trade agreements[67] concluded by the then European Economic Community (EEC) with all EFTA States, then together with Switzerland, i.a., Sweden,[68] Finland,[69] Austria,[70] Portugal,[71] Iceland[72] and Norway.[73] It is one of the oldest trade agreements signed by the EU;[74] in fact, it is the only "surviving" agreement of its kind.[75] The 1972 agreements were at creation not without ambition[76] – but would today be labelled "shallow."[77] Despite its age and limited coverage, the Federal Council deems the FTA 72 to be one of the most important agreements binding Switzerland and the EU.[78] For context, as of 2020, the EU had concluded more than 37

67 In EU parlance, "first generation" FTAs are those concluded before 2006 and "tend to focus on tariff liberalisation", see European Commission, Report from the Commission to the European Parliament, the Council, the European Economic and Social Committee and the Committee of the Regions on Implementation of Free Trade Agreements 1 January 2018–31 December 2018, 14 October 2019, COM(2019) 455 final, p. 5.

68 Agreement between the European Economic Community and the Kingdom of Sweden (OJ 1972, L 300/97 in French; Series I Volume 1972 [31.12], L 300/99 in English).

69 Agreement between the European Economic Community and the Republic of Finland (OJ 1973, L 328/2).

70 Agreement between the European Economic Community and the Republic of Austria (OJ 1972, L 300/2 in French; Series I Volume 1972 [31.12], L 300/2 in English).

71 Agreement between the European Economic Community and the Portuguese Republic (OJ 1972, L 301/165 in French; Series I Volume 1972 [31.12], L 301/167 in English).

72 Agreement between the European Economic Community and the Republic of Iceland (OJ 1972, L 301/2 in French; Series I Volume 1972 [31.12], L 301/4 in English).

73 Agreement between the European Economic Community and the Kingdom of Norway (OJ 1973, L 171/2).

74 European Commission, Commission Staff Working Document – Individual information sheets on implementation of EU Trade Agreements, 27 October 2021, SWD(2021) 297 final, p. 84; see also P. Conconi, C. Herghelegiu, L. Puccio, 'EU Trade Agreements: To Mix or Not to Mix, That Is the Question', *Journal of World Trade* 55 (2021), 231–260, p. 254, table A-2.

75 T. Cottier, N. Diebold, I. Kölliker, R. Liechti-McKee, M. Oesch, T. Payosova and D. Wüger, *Die Rechtsbeziehungen der Schweiz und der Europäischen Union* (Stämpfli, 2014), para. 310.

76 See the expansion clause of Article 32 FTA 72; see C. Zeynep Pirim, 'The EU-Turkey Customs Union: From a Transitional to a Definitive Framework?', *Legal Issues of Economic Integration* 42:1 (2015), 31–56.

77 The *Commission Staff Working document – Individual reports and info sheets on implementation of EU Trade Agreements*, 14 October 2019, SWD(2019) 370 final, rightly points out, p. 231, that while the "EU-Swiss trade relations are among the deepest worldwide outside the context of a customs union/internal market .... [t]he gap is growing between the current legal arrangements of EU and Switzerland and the standards of modern and comprehensive FTAs concluded by the EU and Switzerland/EFTA, respectively."

78 Federal Council, Rapport sur la politique économique extérieure 2020 comprenant des messages concernant des accords économiques internationaux et rapport sur les mesures tarifaires prises en 2020, 20 January 2021, FF 2021 343, p. 37.

preferential trade agreements with 67 countries,[79] whereas Switzerland has concluded 33 FTAs with 43 partners (as well as with the EFTA and EU),[80] with significant differences as to scope and ambition.[81]

The FTA 72 seeks to "eliminate progressively the obstacles to substantially all [the] trade" between the Union and Switzerland.[82] However, the FTA 72 coverage is largely limited to industrial goods,[83] whereas most primary agricultural goods are being excluded pursuant to Article 2 FTA 72;[84] some important processed agricultural goods are now covered, due to the 2002 Agreement on Processed Agricultural Goods.[85] None of the subject-matters that distinguish ambitious WTO *plus* FTAs from more pedestrian "Tariffs and Trade"-focused "first-generation FTAs" can be found in the FTA 72: it does not include chapters on technical barriers to trade (TBT) or sanitary and phytosanitary measures (SPS) and no provisions on dynamic alignment. Services are not included,[86] nor is intellectual property (IP); digital trade and Sustainable Development Goals (SDG) chapters cannot be expected to be addressed in an FTA dating back to pre-*Dassonville*[87] times. An important "modern" feature is the comparatively strong regulation of trade-related competition and State aid that has

79 See European Commission, Report from the Commission to the European Parliament, the Council, the European Economic and Social Committee and the Committee of the Regions on Implementation and Enforcement of EU Trade Agreements, 27 October 2021, COM(2021) 654 final, p. 7.

80 State Secretariat for Economic Affairs SECO, *Free Trade Agreements*, <https://www.seco.admin.ch/seco/en/home/Aussenwirtschaftspolitik_Wirtschaftliche_Zusammenarbeit/Wirtschaftsbeziehungen/Freihandelsabkommen.html>, 29 October 2021 (accessed 19 March 2022).

81 T. Cottier, R. Arpagaus and M. Oesch, 'Grundlagen in Verfassung und Staatsvertragsrecht', in T. Cottier, M. Oesch (eds.), *Allgemeines Aussenwirtschafts- und Binnenmarktrecht*, Schweizerisches Bundesverwaltungsrecht Volume XI, 3rd ed. (Hebling Lichtenhahn Verlag, 2020), para. 35.

82 See the second recital of the FTA 72 preamble.

83 Cottier et al. (n. 75), para. 315.

84 This aspect of bilateral trade between Switzerland and the EU has since been codified the Agreement on Agricultural Goods (n. 66). Protocol 2 to the FTA 72 includes provisions on some agricultural products.

85 The agreement changes a protocol attached to the FTA 72; cf. Agreement between the European Community and the Swiss Confederation amending the Agreement between the European Economic Community and the Swiss Confederation of 22 July 1972 as regards the provisions applicable to processed agricultural products (OJ 2005, L 23/19; SR 0.632.401.23).

86 Negotiations on a trade agreement regarding services stopped in 2003; see Federal Council, Rapport Europe 2006, 28 June 2006, FF 2006 6461, p. 6538; Cottier et al. (n. 75), para. 312.

87 CJEU, Case 8/74, *Dassonville*, EU:C:1974:82.

been the legal starting point for the EU's largely successful fight against the Swiss tax regime for holding corporations.[88]

Because the FTA 72 is but one of many (existing or planned) Swiss-EU agreements that address trade in goods[89] (complemented by a very limited number of agreements addressing trade in services), past discussions about its reform reflected the current *status quo*, i.e., a complex legal regime characterised by the lack of a single comprehensive and foundational treaty, but rather by the existence of a bundle of interconnected treaties. In the eyes of the Federal Council and, so it seems, the population, that "*voie royale*"[90] (the "King's Path") offer(ed) the best of both worlds: the same beneficial economic outcomes as the EEA, but with less sovereignty costs (or so we are being told).[91] This mindset has contributed to leaving the old FTA 72 largely untouched: in its last comprehensive analysis of Switzerland's relationship with the EU in 2006, the Federal Council reflected upon the negotiation of a (new) FTA for the agri-food sector,[92] but did not consider a comprehensive reform as a pressing issue, since the FTA 72 was viewed as being "satisfactory for both Parties."[93] The dispute regarding the cantonal tax regimes privileging holding companies did not lead

88 See Federal Council, Federal Act on Tax Reform and OASI Funding, 19 May 2019, <https://www.admin.ch/gov/en/start/documentation/votes/20190519/Federal-acton-tax-reform-and-oasi-funding.html> (accessed 19 March 2022); Federal Council, TRAF implementation: ordinances enter into force on 1 January 2020, 13 November 2019, <https://www.admin.ch/gov/en/start/documentation/media-releases.msg-id-77046.html> (accessed 19 March 2022).

89 Pursuant to M. Oesch (n. 7), para. 124, approximately 130 protocols and exchanges of letters as of 2020.

90 This term has been used by the Federal Council to entice support for the bilateral agreements after the EEA refusal by the Swiss people and cantons; see S. Jaberg, 'La Suisse profite-t-elle vraiment des accords bilatéraux avec l'UE?', *swissinfo.ch* 12 April 2016, <https://www.swissinfo.ch/fre/querelle-d-%C3%A9conomistes_la-suisse-profite-t-elle-vraiment-des-accords-bilat%C3%A9raux-avec-l-ue/42067056> (accessed 19 March 2022).

91 Federal Council, Accord institutionnel Suisse–UE: document explicatif, 16 January 2019, <https://www.dfae.admin.ch/dam/europa/fr/documents/abkommen/InstA-Erlaeuterungen_fr.pdf> (accessed 19 March 2022), p. 5. See also R. Höltschi, 'Was den Rahmenvertrag vom EWR unterscheidet', *Neue Zürcher Zeitung* 13 December 2018, <https://www.nzz.ch/ld.1444349> (accessed 19 March 2022).

92 Federal Council (n. 86), p. 6481, 6534 and 6537.

93 Federal Council (n. 86), p. 6538: "*Depuis près de trente ans, l'accord fonctionne à la satisfaction des Parties* [...]". This assertion was echoed in later reports (specifically, in 2009 and 2010). The federal government reiterated this analysis in a 2011 report on Switzerland's external commercial policy; the FTA 72 was "generally working fine", Federal Council, Rapport sur la politique économique extérieure 2011, 11 January 2012, FF 2012 675, <https://www.fedlex.admin.ch/eli/fga/2012/196/fr> (accessed 19 March 2022), p. 725: "*L'ALE de 1972 fonctionne dans l'ensemble bien.*"

to a reconsideration, as the Federal Council claimed that this subject-matter had nothing to do with the FTA 72,[94] a position not easily reconcilable with the "real-world-where-people-live-work-and-die"[95] reality of the matter.[96] The preliminary outcome of the negotiations is much closer to the EU's notorious "Decision on the incompatibility of certain Swiss company tax regimes"[97] than to the Federal Council's bland statement that "there was nothing to see here."[98]

The Swiss lack of interest in a total or even partial revision of the FTA 72 is linked to the long-standing practice to conclude new side agreements for new issues, rather than integrating them into the FTA 72: the MRA, concluded after the 25th anniversary of the FTA 72, is technically a stand-alone agreement, but stands on the shoulders of the FTA 72; together, they form the legal basis for Switzerland's considerable integration into the Single Market (for goods). The bilateral Government Procurement Agreement[99] is also a stand-alone agreement that has not been formally integrated; in a similar fashion, the (draft) electricity agreement is supposed to be a stand-alone agreement rather than an annex to the FTA 72, despite electricity being in principle covered by the latter, as it is *de lege lata* defined as a good by the Harmonized System (HS).[100] In addition, several agreements regarding agricultural goods have been added to the *acquis bilatéral*, instead of amending the FTA 72. And, of course, services are not being addressed in an (amended or modified) FTA 72, but rather in specialised stand-alone agreements, such as the Agreement on Non-Life

94 Federal Council, Rapport du Conseil fédéral sur l'évaluation de la politique européenne de la Suisse, 17 September 2010, FF 2010 6615, p. 6650.

95 WTO Appellate Body Report, *EC Measures Concerning Meat and Meat Products-Hormones*, WT/DS26/AB/R and WT/DS48/AB/R, 16 January 1998, para. 187: "It is essential to bear in mind that the risk that is to be evaluated [...] is not only risk ascertainable in a science laboratory operating under strictly controlled conditions, but also effects on human health in the real world where people live and work and die".

96 While Switzerland could present a tenable argument that the matter had not been addressed by the FTA 72, the EU's position (see just below) was not less tenable and diametrically opposed the Swiss position. See, e.g., Tobler (n. 62).

97 European Commission, Commission Decision of 13 February 2007 on the compatibility of certain Swiss company tax regimes with the Agreement between the European Economic Community and the Swiss Confederation of 22 July 1972, C(2007) 411 final, 13 February 2007, <https://eeas.europa.eu/archives/docs/switzerland/docs/c_2007-411_en.pdf> (accessed 19 March 2022).

98 See to that matter D. Felder, K. Siegwart, 'Die sektoriellen Abkommen I und II von 1999/2004 sowie das Freihandelsabkommen von 1972 in ihrer praktischen Anwendung', in A. Epiney, M. Wyssling (eds.), *Schweizerisches Jahrbuch für Europarecht 2006/2007* (Stämpfli/Schulthess 2007), pp. 385–395.

99 See n. 65.

100 See n. 49; Article 2(i) FTA 72.

Insurance[101] (which focuses on the establishment and the regulation of service providers), the AFMP as well as the Agreements on Air Transport (ATA)[102] and Land Transport (LTA).[103]

In contrast, the Commission has been critical of the FTA 72 for some time, due to its "limited scope [...], shallower disciplines and ... [its lack of] effective dispute settlement mechanism when compared to the EU's modern trade agreements, some of which were concluded with more distant partners of lesser economic relevance."[104] The FTA 72 was judged to have outgrown its shelf-life, being "not up to speed for what the EU and Swiss relationship should and could be."[105] Therefore, a "modernisation of the FTA [72] is [...] needed to unlock the potential for further bilateral trade",[106] and thereby enhance "access to the Swiss market for operators from the EU, notably in the agri-food and services sectors."[107]

---

101 Agreement between the European Economic Community and the Swiss Confederation on direct insurance other than life assurance (OJ 1991, L 205/3; SR 0.961.1). The TFEU's distinct fundamental freedoms regarding "services" and "establishment" are both covered by Article I:2 GATS and its four modes of services delivery. See the preamble of the Agreement which underlines the intention of the contracting parties " [...] to avail themselves of the occasion offered by the establishment of a unified Community insurance market to consolidate existing economic relations between the two Parties in this field, and to promote, under fair conditions of competition, the harmonious development of these relations by ensuring protection for insured persons; resolved to that end to remove obstacles to the taking-up and pursuit of the business of direct insurance, other than life assurance, on a reciprocal and non-discriminatory basis safeguarded by the necessary legal conditions in respect of supervision, and thus to introduce between themselves freedom of establishment in this field [...]".

102 Agreement between the European Community and the Swiss Confederation on Air Transport (OJ 2002, L 114/73; SR 0.748.127.192.68).

103 Agreement between the European Community and the Swiss Confederation on the Carriage of Goods and Passengers by Rail and Road (OJ 2002, L 114/91; SR 0.740.72). See also the Agreement on the International Carriage of Passengers by Road by means of Occasional Coach and Bus Services (ASOR) (OJ 1982, L 230/39; SR 0.741.618).

104 European Commission, Report from the Commission to the European Parliament, the Council, the European Economic and Social Committee and the Committee of the Regions on implementation of EU trade agreements, 1 January 2019–31 December 2019, 16 November 2020, <https://op.europa.eu/s/u7nA> (accessed 19 March 2022), p. 21.

105 European Commission, Commission Statement on the decision by the Swiss Federal Council to terminate the negotiations of the EU-Swiss Institutional Framework Agreement, 26 May 2021, STATEMENT/21/2683, <https://ec.europa.eu/commission/presscorner/detail/en/statement_21_2683> (accessed 19 March 2022).

106 European Commission (n. 74), p. 85; see also M. Ambühl, D.S. Scherer, 'Schweiz-EU: Wie weiter?', *Jusletter* 2 August 2021, para. 38.

107 Council conclusions on EU relations with the Swiss Confederation (OJ 2019, C 147/2), para. 12.

A 2015 report by the Swiss Government analysed and compared the legal similarities and differences between a (CETA-inspired) "global FTA" solution and the existing main bilateral agreements (including the 1999 package of Swiss-EU agreements [*Bilaterals I*] and the 2004 package of Swiss-EU agreements [*Bilaterals II*]).[108] While the 2015 report offers an interesting overview of the Swiss-EU relationship (with useful references to FTAs concluded by EFTA countries and the EU with third countries respectively), it sticks to its mandate to explain to a very EU-sceptic parliamentarian[109] that the envisaged comprehensive update of Swiss-EU relations through the conclusion of an Institutional Agreement is superior to an FTA. Because the latter term is used by the Swiss executive branch in the "traditional" sense, i.e., limited to the abolishment or reduction of border measures such as tariffs and contingents, a replacing the *status quo ante* by an FTA was seen as an undesirable downgrading: the Swiss-EU transboundary trade in goods regime is characterised by a multimodal and pluri-sectoral internalisation of EU law by Switzerland. "Traditional" FTAs, even the advanced "Canadian" (CETA)[110] variation, remain less ambitious than the "Swiss option" for which a distinct place had been reserved on the by now famous "Barnier ladder."[111] Thus, the 2015 report by the Swiss Government concluded that in light of the complex and multi-facetted Swiss-EU relationship a new legal fundament such as the Institutional Agreement would be better suited; in particular, the FTA was said to not be the right place for the necessary provisions on legislative alignment (e.g., in technical barriers to trade).[112]

However, it is restating the obvious that the EU and Switzerland are free to use the empty vessel of an FTA as they wish, in particular, to add an ambitious harmonisation and integration chapter, provided tariffs and quotas "with

---

108 Federal Council, Rapport du Conseil fédéral en réponse au Postulat Keller-Sutter [13.4022] « Un accord de libre-échange avec l'UE à la place des accords bilatéraux », June 2015, <https://www.newsd.admin.ch/newsd/message/attachments/39667.pdf> (accessed 19 March 2022).

109 Said parliamentarian (Karin Keller-Sutter) is now Swiss Federal Councillor, head of the Federal Department for Finance (since January 2023). See for current purposes M. Guillaume, 'Cassis-KKS, le duel qui plombe le dossier européen', *Le Temps* 17 December 2021, <https://www.letemps.ch/suisse/cassiskks-duel-plombe-dossier-europeen> (accessed 19 March 2022).

110 Comprehensive Economic and Trade Agreement (CETA) between Canada, of the one part, and the European Union and its Member States, of the other part (OJ 2017, L 11/23).

111 *Supra*, n. 3. There, the Swiss-EU arrangement was positioned between the EEA and the EU-Turkey Customs Union, on one side, and CETA, on the other side. It would seem to be a fair assessment that the Swiss option is much closer to full participation in the EEA than to WTO MFN status, see n. 3.

112 Federal Council (n. 108), p. 29.

regard to substantially all the trade" are abolished. Once a Swiss-EU FTA fulfils the minimum standard of Article XXIV GATT,[113] it may go much further and include whatever the contracting parties consider desirable and opportune, including harmonisation. The Treaty on the Functioning of the European Union (TFEU)[114] itself is an example of this possibility: while establishing a Free Trade Zone pursuant to Articles XXIV GATT and V GATS, it clearly transcends the minimums standards of said WTO provisions. Thus, SEUFTA could not just replace but rather develop the current state of affairs and increase Switzerland's integration into the goods-related part of the Union's Single Market legal regime by integrating subject-matters currently covered by standalone agreements, such as the MRA.

By 2019, the gap between the two different narratives had narrowed down. In the draft *Joint Declaration on Trade Agreements* attached to the draft Institutional Agreement,[115] the parties agree that the FTA 72 requires a thorough[116] modernisation.[117] That statement – read in context with pertinent parts of the draft Institutional Agreement, notably the provisions on harmonisation (incl. the provisions on decision making and interpretation) as well as the dispute settlement provisions – may serve as a starting point for a comprehensive, deep and ambitious new FTA that could address the majority of all issues considered essential by each side. While it would not claim to determine legally how other (non-integrated) agreements would be structured or work, it should, due to its suggested broad and deep coverage *ratione materiae* and its status as a prototype very much shape the next generation of Swiss-EU agreements.

In the EU-Switzerland draft *Joint Declaration on Trade Agreements* the parties expressed the following position:

> 6. The undersigned therefore believe that [their] trade agreements should be modernized. This modernization concerns in particular the following areas:
>   – Improved market access and movement of goods in all areas;

---

113 The sister provision, Article V GATS, demands substantial sector coverage.

114 Consolidated version of the Treaty on the Functioning of the European Union (OJ 2016, C 202/47).

115 *Supra*, n. 61.

116 C. Tobler, 'Wie weiter mit dem Institutionellen Abkommen?', *Jusletter* 20 January 2020, para. 30.

117 Federal Council, Accord institutionnel Suisse–UE: document explicatif (n. 91), p. 15; see also A. Epiney, 'Der Entwurf des Institutionellen Abkommens Schweiz – EU', *Jusletter* 17 December 2018, para. 8. For a deeper analysis of the draft joint decision, see Baldi (n. 12).

- Provisions for the application of trade measures between the parties, particularly in the area of safeguard measures, taking into account the close economic integration of their markets;
- Facilitation of customs exchanges and cooperation, including coordinated border management;
- Origin of goods: simplification of rules, taking into account the very high level of integration of Swiss and EU businesses, their interdependence and the intensive trade based on the results of the discussions on the revision of the Regional Convention on Pan-Euro-Mediterranean Preferential Rules of Origin;
- Rules on the protection of intellectual property, which are not included in the FTA and which are of great importance today in the trade of a wide range of goods and services;
- Taking into account a set of values that the parties share and defend in their respective trade policies, in particular the social and environmental dimensions of sustainable development and efforts to combat climate change;
- Further develop provisions on access to public procurement to promote better transparency regarding access opportunities, for instance taking into account the increasing digitalization of procurement;
- Improve mechanisms for mutual recognition of conformity assessments;
- Rules concerning State aid applicable to industrial products and services traded between the parties in order to ensure a level playing field with a view to the proper functioning of the internal market.[118]

This list of worthwhile issues in trade in goods is a summary of the many topics addressed in recent EU[119] and Swiss[120] FTAs, but also of issues that have been the subject of bilateral discussions, such as EU safeguard measures (triggered by WTO-incompatible measures by the 45th US President) and applied to Switzerland on an MFN-basis or discussions regarding Swiss State aid for financial services providers. The dynamic alignment of Swiss laws and regulations should be based on the pertinent provisions of the Institutional Agreement[121]

118 Translation by the author from the unofficial German version (see n. 1).

119 Such as in the FTA with Mercosur (not yet in force); see also the EU-Japan FTA and CETA.

120 For example, the EFTA-Indonesia FTA, the EFTA-Equador FTA.

121 Articles 5, 7 and 4(2) of the draft Institutional Agreement.

and thus ensure the mutual recognition of pertinent product standards[122] and also the recognition of the EU State aid regime.[123]

3.2 *Trade in Services*

In order to maximise mutual trade benefits stemming from trade, SEUFTA would have to include regulations on services. Indeed, the draft *Joint Declaration* deplores that "services, which today occupy an important place in trade between Switzerland and the European Union, are excluded from the scope of the FTA [72]" and advocates the inclusion of

> provisions for the liberalization of trade in services and investment, while maintaining the relevant general exceptions, including in the area of financial services, and the right of each Party to adopt rules to achieve domestic policy objectives. [...] This would also make it possible to include a digital dimension in the agreement.

The three agreements on trade in services covered by the draft Institutional Agreement were the Agreement on Air Transport, the Agreement on Land Transport (by Road and Rail) and, with regard to the short-term provision of services (90 working days),[124] the AFMP.[125] Recent FTAs concluded by the EU and Switzerland, respectively, contain rather shallow services chapters:[126] given that the draft *Joint Declaration* specifically mentions the shared intention

---

122 The MRA covers 20 product categories, including: machinery; personal protective equipment; toys; medical devices; gas appliances and boilers; pressure vessels; radio equipment and telecommunications terminal equipment; equipment and protective systems intended for use in potentially explosive atmospheres; electrical equipment and electromagnetic compatibility; construction plant and equipment; measuring instruments and prepackages; motor vehicles; agricultural and forestry tractors; good laboratory practice (GLP); medicinal products; GMP inspection and batch certification; construction products; lifts, biocidal products, cableway installations; and explosives for civil use; see Annex I to the MRA.

123 See Article 8A(2) of the draft InstA (n. 1), which is quasi-identical to Article 107 TFEU. This new regime on State aid would have applied to the ATA and represented the default position for subsequent market access agreements between Switzerland and the EU. See Y. Hasani, 'Die Beihilfenkontrolle in der Europäischen Union', *Jusletter* 29 April 2019, paras. 35–45.

124 See n. 53.

125 See Article V*bis* GATS and *supra*, section 2.2.

126 See Chapter 8 of the Agreement between the European Union and Japan for an Economic Partnership (OJ 2018, L 330/3); see in general Y. Nakanishi, 'The Economic Partnership Agreement and the Strategic Partnership Agreement between the European Union and Japan from a Legal Perspective', *Hitotsubashi Journal of Law and Politics* 47 (2019), 1–15.

of the parties to keep exceptions for financial services in place, the ambitious liberalisation of financial services and sufficient further service sector coverage is not a foregone conclusion.[127] However, the mutual trust that exists between regulators of both sides may be a starting point for paradigm-shifting mutual recognition agreements with regard to services or failing that, at least the establishment of institutionalised channels for mutual information and coordination.[128]

While going beyond trade in services, the quick reintegration of Swiss research and education capacities into the European framework would seem to be in the interest of both parties. In contrast to the electricity agreement, that subject-matter may not be a "natural" part of a potential SEUFTA; but its inclusion would still be highly desirable. Firstly, it is a priority for one of the partners. Secondly, from a purely economic perspective, full participation of Switzerland's scientific infrastructure in the EU research network appears to be in the best long-term economic interests of both sides: the manifold challenges associated, e.g., with artificial intelligence (AI), the digital economy generally, energy-dependence, climate change or the rapid disappearance of effective antibiotics, raise economic questions of the highest magnitude. It would seem more than appropriate to have European centres of excellence in those fields work in an integrated fashion.

3.3 *Institutional Set-Up*

It would seem that the absence of involvement of political leaders at the ministerial, let alone the highest, level from the management of the bilateral economic relationship in the last two decades has allowed the respective leadership levels to de-engage with regard to the concerns and issues of the negotiating partners. Drawing on the examples of the architecture provided

127 See Article V:1 GATS («substantial sectoral coverage») and its footnote 1.

128 When signing the TCA, the UK and the EU had preliminarily agreed on a "Joint Declaration on Financial Services Regulatory Cooperation", in which the two sides committed to agreeing on a Memorandum of Understanding to establish structured regulatory cooperation on financial services. While that memorandum has not yet been formally signed or entered into force, it would be a possible model for the Swiss-EU relationship.

Since 2020, the EU has granted two equivalence decisions for UK financial services, both of which have been time limited and one of which has since expired. Conversely, the UK has granted equivalence to EEA member states in 28 of the 32 areas identified for the equivalence process. Cf. Declarations referred to in the Council Decision on the conclusion, on behalf of the Union, of the Trade and Cooperation Agreement and of the Agreement concerning security procedures for exchanging and protecting classified information (OJ 2021, L 149/2549).

by the draft Institutional Agreement which itself is influenced by *prior art* in a multitude of trade agreements,[129] it would seem of the essence to ensure the involvement of the political leadership with regard to the administration and development of the agreement. Depending on whether the final structure of a SEUFTA would integrate (former) stand-alone agreements (e.g., on electricity or agriculture) as chapters or, rather, would annex them, the principals' forum (e.g., a "*comité mixte horizontal*" or an "*Association Council*")[130] would need to be accompanied by specialised fora ("*Councils*") which should allow continuing the practice of having high civil servants taking care of business, as has been the case for decades in the joint committees.[131]

3.4 *Legislative Approximation and Decision-Shaping*

3.4.1 Alignment As a Precondition for Privileged Market Access

The obligation to align Swiss law to the law of the continental hegemon is politically and legally not self-evident for a country whose founding myth is the successful resistance against a regional hegemon (more specifically: the house of Habsburg). However, the EU's demand of close alignment as a precondition for granting to a non-member neighbouring State market access of a depth and breadth that resembles that enjoyed by Member States is not some nasty "*ruse de guerre*" by hard-nosed Commission trade negotiators: it is worthwhile to remember that both in *van Gend en Loos*[132] and in *Costa*,[133] the European Court of Justice justified its embrace of direct effect and supremacy of Union law with the importance to preserve the integrity of the Single Market. It was

---

129 Association Agreement between the European Union and its Member States, of the one part, and Ukraine, of the other part (OJ 2014, L 161/4). See in detail G. Van der Loo, *The EU-Ukraine Association Agreement and Deep and Comprehensive Free Trade Area* (Brill/Nijhoff, 2016), pp. 292–303.

130 See for example the pertinent provisions in the EU-Ukraine Association Agreement (AA); its Article 460 reads: "1. The highest level of political and policy dialogue between the Parties shall be at Summit level. [...]. The Summit shall provide overall guidance for the implementation of this Agreement as well as an opportunity to discuss any bilateral or international issues of mutual interest. 2. At ministerial level, regular political and policy dialogue shall take place within the *Association Council* established by Article 461 of this Agreement and within the framework of regular meetings between representatives of the Parties by mutual agreement." Article 461 reads as follows: "1. An Association Council is hereby established. It shall supervise and monitor the application and implementation of this Agreement and periodically review the functioning of this Agreement in the light of its objectives. 2. The Association Council shall meet at ministerial level [...]."

131 Article 3(b) and 15 of the draft InstA.

132 CJEU, Case 26/62, *van Gend & Loos*, EU:C:1963:1.

133 CJEU, Case 6/64, *Costa*, EU:C:1964:66.

then (and is still today) the opinion of the CJEU that allowing Member States to enact *leges posteriores* to undo (unintended) pain resulting from the EU rules and regulations would open the floodgates for unilateral deviations from the Single Market regime: as a consequence, the economic fundament of the European experiment – the Single Market – would, in the opinion of the Court, be fatally weakened. The Court has been a pitiless enforcer of that doctrine, even with regard to natural treasures such as the Italian and German regulations for pasta and beer.[134] What is sometimes perceived in the Swiss capital of Bern as a dogmatic and inflexible approach to protecting the integrity of the Market is a consequence of that foundational context.

Pursuant to the draft Institutional Agreement, the EU seems prepared to continue to allow deviations from the rules of the Single Market legal regime, thereby taking into consideration that the partners are not Member States. However, the right of the EU to use "rebalancing measures"[135] reminiscent of what the EEA Agreement[136] and Article 8:2 of the WTO Safeguard Measures

134 For Italian pasta, see CJEU, Case 90/86, *Zoni*, EU:C:1988:403; for German beer, Case 178/84, *Commission v Germany* (*Reinheitsgebot*), EU:C:1987:126.

135 Cf. Article 10(6) of the draft InstA.

136 Agreement on the European Economic Area (OJ 1994, L 1/3), in particular Articles 102, 111 and 105. Article 105(3) EEA Agreement reads: "If the EEA Joint Committee within two months after a difference in the case law of the two Courts has been brought before it, has not succeeded to preserve the homogeneous interpretation of the Agreement, the procedures laid down in Article 111 may be applied."

Article 111(3) reads in relevant parts: "If a dispute concerns the interpretation of provisions of this Agreement, which are identical in substance to corresponding rules of the [Founding treaties] and to acts adopted in application of these two Treaties and if the dispute has not been settled within three months after it has been brought before the EEA Joint Committee, the Contracting Parties to the dispute may agree to request the Court of Justice of the European Communities to give a ruling on the interpretation of the relevant rules. If the EEA Joint Committee in such a dispute has not reached an agreement on a solution within six months from the date on which this procedure was initiated or if, by then, the Contracting Parties to the dispute have not decided to ask for a ruling by the Court of Justice of the European Communities, a Contracting Party may, in order to remedy possible imbalances

– either take a safeguard measure in accordance with Article 112(2) and following the procedure of Article 113

– or apply Article 102 mutatis mutandis."

Article 102(5) reads in pertinent parts: "If, at the end of the time limit set out in paragraph 4, the EEA Joint Committee has not taken a decision on an amendment of an Annex to this Agreement, the affected part thereof, as determined in accordance with paragraph 2, is regarded as provisionally suspended, subject to a decision to the contrary by the EEA Joint Committee."

Agreement[137] allow, is supposed to create an incentive to maintain the parallelism that is the essence of alignment.

In order to ensure that SEUFTA would not impose a *legal* obligation similar to that of the EEA – namely to adapt to *all* legislation relevant for the functioning of the Single Market –, the parties would have to determine the relevant EU legislation. Potential examples for pertinent referencing can be found, *inter alia*, in the Swiss Schengen Association Agreement[138] and the Dublin Association Agreement,[139] the MRA,[140] and more broadly in the EEA Agreement,[141] the EU-Ukraine AA,[142] and the Trade and Cooperation Agreement (TCA) with the UK.[143] Another possibility would be to include an obligation to align with Single Market legislation to the extent that it is relevant to the agreement and leave the determination to the Joint Committee (or its progeny) and in case of non-consensus to dispute settlement. Obviously, the finer points of this issue are of the utmost importance and merit further analysis.

137 See to that matter M. Hahn, 'Balancing or Bending? Unilateral Reactions to Safeguard Measures', *Journal of World Trade* 29:2 (2005), 301–326.

138 Agreement between the European Union, the European Community and the Swiss Confederation on the Swiss Confederation's association with the implementation, application and development of the Schengen *acquis* (OJ 2008, L 53/52; SR 0.362.31). Cf. in particular Article 1(2) and Annex A as well as Article 2(2) and Annex B. Pertinent EU legislation developing the Schengen *acquis* enacted after the signature of the SAA is not listed in these annexes, but Switzerland references modifications in SR 0.362.

139 Agreement between the European Community and the Swiss Confederation concerning the criteria and mechanisms for establishing the State responsible for examining a request for asylum lodged in a Member State or in Switzerland (OJ 2008, L 53/5; SR 0.142.392.68), in particular Article 1(1). EU legislation adopted according to Article 1(3) and Article 4 DAA is not added to the DAA proper, but is referenced by Switzerland in SR 0.142.392.680.

140 Although the MRA does not have specific provisions for legislative approximation, its incentive structure set out in Article 1(2) MRA produces similar effects; equivalences are listed in Annex I of the MRA, modifications of this Annex are listed in Federal Department of Foreign Affairs, *Liste des accords Suisse – Union européenne en vigueur le 1er décembre 2021*, 1 December 2021, <https://www.eda.admin.ch/dam/europa/fr/documents/publikationen_dea/accords-liste_fr.pdf> (accessed 19 March 2022), pp. 14–16; see also Federal Council, Recueil de textes juridiques sur les accords sectoriels avec l'UE: 3. Accord du 21 juin 1999 entre la Confédération suisse et la Communauté européenne relatif à la reconnaissance mutuelle en matière d'évaluation de la conformité, <https://www.fedlex.admin.ch/fr/sector-specific-agreements/EU-acts-register/3> (accessed 19 March 2022).

141 Cf. Article 98 EEA Agreement and the Annexes to the EEA.

142 Article 474 EU-Ukraine AA and the Annexes to the EU-Ukraine AA.

143 Agreement between the European Union and the European Atomic Energy Community, of the one part, and the United Kingdom of Great Britain and Northern Ireland, of the other part (OJ 2021, L 149/10), and, e.g., in Good Manufacturing Practices (GMP), Article 8 of Annex 12 to the TCA and Appendix 12-B to the TCA.

3.4.2 Decision-Shaping: Quid pro quo for Legislative Approximation

The necessary flanking measure for Switzerland's dynamic alignment is the participation in the elaboration of the very EU rules it will have to align to ("decision-shaping").[144] Switzerland's experience in the context of its association to the EU's Schengen and Dublin regime has overall been very positive.[145] The decision-shaping possibilities ensure that Swiss officials can fully participate in the preparatory work, the *cuisine interne*, of EU legislative procedures – a process of finding the common denominator of 30+ views and standpoints. In this context, any Swiss input is not introduced (or viewed) as being "against" an EU position; rather it highlights a concern that is more often than not shared by a significant part of the Member States. During that informal phase of the legislative process, the status as a non-EU Member State (and hence, a non-voting third country) is largely irrelevant to the weight attributed to the pertinent input.

As of today, Switzerland is "the" champion of (legally) "autonomous" alignment, i.e., Switzerland enacting "equivalent" (read: most of the time quasi-identical) legislation in order to (1) either reap the benefits of MRA-based equivalence (which is not provided automatically but depends on a consensus-decision to attest equivalence)[146] or (2) to enable Swiss industry to benefit from the increasing number of unilateral EU equivalence provisions.[147] In

144 This feature was included in the draft InstA (see Article 12) but is not included in all EU agreements that include such a dynamic alignment obligation for the partner. However, see Article 463 EU-Ukraine AA, pursuant to which Ukraine may be consulted and invited to express opinions and concerns on draft amendments of relevant legislation. G. Van der Loo, P. Van Elsuwege and R. Petrov, *The EU-Ukraine Association Agreement: Assessment of an Innovative Legal Instrument*, EUI Working Papers 2014/09, <http://ekmair.ukma.edu.ua/bitstream/handle/123456789/7868/The_EU-Ukraine_Association.pdf?sequence=1> (accessed 19 March 2022), p. 19, consider this procedure to be a "a limited form of 'decision-shaping'".

145 This is the case for both SAA and DAA. One notable example where Switzerland managed to bring forward a new disposition in its favour was during the elaboration of Directive (EU) 2017/853 of 17 May 2017 amending Council Directive 91/477/EEC on control of the acquisition and possession of weapons (OJ 2017, L 137/22); see to that matter T. Gafafer, 'Die Übernahme von EU-Recht funktioniert meist reibungslos', *Neue Zürcher Zeitung* 12 April 2019, <https://www.nzz.ch/ld.1474012> (accessed 19 March 2022). See also the contribution by P. Van Elsuwege in this volume.

146 See Article 5 and 11 MRA; currently, none of this is happening, due to the breakdown of negotiations.

147 Examples of these unilateral provisions are the equivalence of Swiss trading venues, clinical trials and equivalence for banking and financial regulations. See State Secretariat for International Finance, Measure to protect Swiss stock exchange infrastructure, 25 November 2021, <https://www.sif.admin.ch/sif/en/home/finanzmarktpolitik/meuasure-protect-swiss-stock-exchange-infrastructure.html> (accessed 19 March 2022); M. Hahn

contrast, only the highly technical Air Transport Agreement provides for real (albeit limited) treaty-based integration into the Single Market legal regime.[148] Obviously, no *bilateral* treaty-based legal right of Swiss (sovereign or private) actors exists with regard to unilateral equivalence clauses in EU legislation. However, EU administrative law (which tends to take a back seat when foreign relations are at stake) and the EU's multilateral treaty obligations offer some legal protection regarding the process of determining whether Swiss legislation or rules are equivalent to EU legislation. It is particularly helpful (from a purely legal perspective!), if the EU has granted equivalence status to foreign legislation that both in terms of content and implementation deviates significantly more from EU rules than Swiss law, as unilateral equivalence clauses must be administered in an MFN-compatible fashion, as they are subject to the rules of WTO law, i.e., Article XVI:4 WTO Agreement.

3.5 *State Aid*

The alignment of Switzerland to the EU's State aid regime has been extensively addressed by the draft Institutional Agreement.[149] For present purposes, two remarks must suffice: in contrast to competition law, where Switzerland has after 1995 largely aligned with the EU's legal regime,[150] the vast majority of Swiss substantive subsidies law can be found in its international treaties, in

et al., *Ressortforschung: Humanforschungsgesetz. Auswirkungen der Verordnung (EU) Nr. 536/2014 über klinische Prüfungen mit Humanarzneimitteln auf die Schweiz*, 20 March 2019, <https://www.bag.admin.ch/dam/bag/de/dokumente/biomed/forschung-am-menschen/klinische-pruefungen/RFA_536_FINAL_20190315_an_BAG.pdf> (accessed 19 March 2022); J. Deslandes, C. Dias, M. Magnus, *Third country equivalence in EU banking and financial regulation*, PE 614.495, August 2019, <https://www.europarl.europa.eu/RegData/etudes/IDAN/2018/614495/IPOL_IDA(2018)614495_EN.pdf> (accessed 19 March 2022). See also Federal Council, Rapport sur la politique économique extérieure 2021 comprenant des messages concernant des accords économiques internationaux et rapport sur les mesures tarifaires prises en 2021, 26 January 2022, FF 2022 655, <https://www.fedlex.admin.ch/eli/fga/2022/655/fr>, pp. 40–41.

148 Article 23 ATA. See to that matter R. Dettling-Ott, '10 Jahre Luftverkehrsabkommen zwischen der EU und der Schweiz – eine Bilanz', *Schweizer Fachzeitschrift für Luft- und Weltraumrecht* 144 (2012), 6–19, pp. 11–12.

149 In particular in Articles 8A and 8B of the draft InstA.

150 For a general overview, M. Sturny, *Der Einfluss des EU-Rechts auf das schweizerische Kartellrecht – Historische Entwicklung und Analyse* (Stämpfli, 2014); V. Martenet, P. Tercier, 'Intro. LCart', in V. Martenet, C. Bovet and P. Tercier (eds.), *Commentaire romand – Droit de la concurrence*, 2nd ed. (Helbing Lichtenhahn Verlag, 2013), para. 22.

particular the WTO Agreement on Subsidies and Countervailing Measures (SCM) and Article 23 FTA 72.[151]

At the time of writing, a discussion on whether Switzerland should align autonomously to the EU's State aid regime has begun, as it has become obvious that the idea of Switzerland as an ultra-liberal economic order relying only on market forces (while leaving inefficient State aid to its less successful neighbours) is not always an accurate description of the reality on the ground.[152] While one would probably find much support for accepting the EU's ground rules, certain State aids for green energy and certain financial service providers (such as guarantees for state-owned cantonal banks) would not belong to the low-hanging fruits in future negotiations.

3.6 *Financial Contribution*

The Union has signalled that it views the special relationship between Switzerland as a substitute for the EEA,[153] and wants to end the discrimination of its EEA partners; the latter have faithfully contributed – indirectly – to the EU budget[154] whereas Switzerland has so far benefitted from very limited

151 Article 23(1)(iii) FTA 72 reads: "The following are incompatible with the proper functioning of the Agreement in so far as they may affect trade between the Community and Switzerland: [...] any public aid which distorts or threatens to distort competition by favouring certain undertakings or the production of certain goods." In the domain of air transport, the Air Transport Agreement provides for rather comprehensive alignment regarding that industry, see Article 13 ATA.

152 See to that matter Avenir Suisse (ed), S. Rutz, *Die Schweiz – das Land der Subventionen*, 17 February 2022, < https://cdn.avenir-suisse.ch/production/uploads/2022/05/die-schweiz-das-land-der-subventionen_avenir-debatte.pdf> (accessed 19 March 2022); C. Eisenring, 'Subventionen haben sich seit 1970 versechsfacht', *Neue Zürcher Zeitung* 17 March 2022, <https://www.nzz.ch/ld.1674806> (accessed 19 March 2022); E. Garessus, 'Les politiques d'aides suisses, un frein à l'accès au marché européen?', *Le Temps* 18 March 2022, <https://www.letemps.ch/economie/politiques-daides-suisses-pourraient-freiner-lacces-marche-europeen> (accessed 19 March 2022), p. 14.

153 Council of the European Union, Council conclusions on a homogeneous extended single market and EU relations with Non-EU Western European countries, 16 December 2014, <https://www.consilium.europa.eu/uedocs/cms_data/docs/pressdata/en/er/146315.pdf> (accessed 19 March 2022), para. 44: "The Council reaffirms that by participating in parts of the EU's internal market and policies, Switzerland is not only engaging in a bilateral relation but becomes a participant in a multilateral project."

154 Pursuant to Article 78 of the EEA Agreement, the EU and the non-member EEA States "shall take the necessary steps to develop, strengthen or broaden cooperation on matters falling outside of the four freedoms, where such cooperation is considered likely to contribute to the attainment of the objectives of [the] Agreement, or is otherwise deemed by the Contracting Parties to be of mutual interest". This obligation is implemented by non-member EEA States' participation in EU programmes (Protocol 31 of the EEA Agreement).

contributions to specific projects in the Members States that joined the Union in 2004.[155]

It seems that this EU demand meets the Swiss preparedness to accept financial contributions as a new normal.[156] Of course, the devil is in the detail: should the contribution surpass that of other EFTA States? Should it be similar? Or should it rather be reflective of a lesser degree of association than the EEA (and ensuing benefits) and therefore be lower?[157] While budgets may be tighter in the future due to new realities, a pertinent solution would seem one of the more doable challenges.

3.7 *Dispute Settlement*

Despite the draft Institutional Agreement's DSM[158] not appearing in the Federal Council's June 2019 list of three issues needing clarification and

---

The modalities for the financial contribution are set down in Article 82 of the EEA Agreement; EEA EFTA States undertake multiannual commitments for payments toward the programmes they have agreed to participate in. The amounts are calibrated according to the relative size of the gross domestic product of the participating EFTA States. See the contribution by B. Pirker (Chapter 9) in this volume.

155 These contributions by Switzerland benefit specific programmes and projects; see to that matter Federal Department of Foreign Affairs, *Second Swiss contribution to selected EU member states*, November 2021, <https://www.eda.admin.ch/dam/europa/en/documents/fs/01-FS-Beitrag_en.pdf> (accessed 29 March 2022), p. 2. For the political and legal basis of the Swiss contribution, see Swiss contribution (enlargement contribution) to selected EU states, Memorandum of Understanding of 27 February 2006, as amended by Addenda of 25 June 2008 (regarding the accession Bulgaria and Romania) and 2 May 2014 (regarding the accession of Croatia), <https://www.eda.admin.ch/europa/en/home/bilaterale-abkommen/abkommen-umsetzung/abkommenstexte/beitrag.html> (accessed 19 March 2022), the bilateral agreements between Switzerland and the new EU Member States and the Arrêté fédéral relatif à la deuxième contribution de la Suisse en faveur de certains États membres de l'UE visant à réduire les disparités économiques et sociales au sein de l'UE élargie (crédit-cadre pour la cohésion), FF 2020 739, <https://www.fedlex.admin.ch/eli/fga/2020/74/fr> (accessed 19 March 2022).

156 In February 2022 (after the beginning of the Russian military attack on Ukraine), the Federal Council declared it is "prepared to consider continuing the Swiss contribution as part of its negotiating package" (the French wording "*disposé à envisager une pérennisation de la contribution de la Suisse*" has another ring to it), see Federal Council, EU relations: Federal Council sets out approach for negotiations, 25 February 2022, <https://www.admin.ch/gov/en/start/documentation/media-releases.msg-id-87349.html> (accessed 19 March 2022). See also C.G. Schmutz, 'Keine Freudenschreie aus Brüssel', *Neue Zürcher Zeitung* 26 February 2022, <https://www.nzz.ch/ld.1671788> (accessed 19 March 2022).

157 See the contribution by B. Pirker (Chapter 9) in this volume.

158 Cf. Article 10(2) and 10(7) and Protocol 3 of the draft InstA.

renegotiation,[159] it seems that one of the most important (and least heralded) reasons for the Federal Council's belief that the Institutional Agreement would not find a majority in Parliament and amongst voters was the complexity of the planned dispute settlement mechanism.[160] For anyone familiar with EU law, this was a well-crafted compromise, empowering an arbitral tribunal with the settlement of inter-party disputes, while ensuring the autonomy of the Union legal order by establishing an obligation (reminiscent of Article 267 TFEU) to refer to the CJEU when the interpretation of bilateral law based on EU law was at stake. Thus, it seems fair to say that the Institutional Agreement's dispute settlement chapter had been conceptualised in a manner that considered the CJEU's increasingly emphatic use of the concept of "autonomy of the Union legal order" to snuff out real and anticipated interferences from treaty-based adjudicate bodies with its position as the sole authoritative interpreter of EU law. The Commission (and no doubt the Swiss negotiators) were aware that they had to ensure the CJEU's last word with regard to the interpretation of EU law.[161] By obliging the (bilateral) arbitral tribunal to ask the European Court of Justice for binding interpretation[162] in cases where an EU law provision was determinative for the outcome of the tribunal's decision,[163] the Court's established requirements for compatibility with the "autonomy of the Union legal order" would have been met.

However, this negotiating result has more likely than not created a significant pushback in Switzerland: while it had been accepted at the outset that the expansion of the Single Market could not diminish in any way the ultimate authority of the Union's High Court for the proper interpretation of Union law, the dispute settlement chapter met open opposition by the trade unions and silent rejection by influential back-benchers from traditionally EU-friendly parties who felt that the occasional *de facto* final word of the CJEU would

159 Federal Council, Institutional agreement Switzerland-EU: Federal Council to demand clarifications, 7 June 2019, <https://www.admin.ch/gov/en/start/documentation/media-releases.msg-id-75346.html> (accessed 19 March 2022).

160 The current system of multiple DSMs in various agreements is contributes to this state of play; see M. Maresceau, 'Les accords d'intégration dans les relations de proximité de l'Union européenne', in C. Blumann (ed.), *Les frontières de l'Union européenne* (Bruylant, 2013), p. 184.

161 In the jurisprudence of the Court that includes in particular provisions of treaties concluded by the EU and third states that restate and internalize EU law: cf. CJEU, Opinion 1/91 (*EEA Agreement I*), EU:C:1991:490.

162 Article 10(4) of the draft InstA.

163 Regarding the exact nature of the obligation to refer to the CJEU for a binding interpretation, see Y. Fauconnet (n. 13), paras. 67–69, and B. Pirker, 'Zum Schiedsgericht im Institutionellen Abkommen', *Jusletter* 3 June 2019, para. 35.

not be compatible with the (impression of) impartial settlement of bilateral disputes.

One way to work around this potential deal-breaker, suggested by the former Swiss chief negotiator *Ambühl*, would be to leave the dispute settlement *stricto sensu* in the hands of the contracting parties and bring in adjudication only with regard to the proportionality of rebalancing measures.[164] Such a structure would aim to keep disputes in the political realm and thus not affect the jurisdiction of the European Court of Justice.

This author would rather suggest sticking with the concept developed in the draft Institutional Agreement, i.e., keeping an (institutionally strengthened)[165] arbitral tribunal (in the following "Tribunal") dealing with the inter-party legal disputes. However, the *jurisprudence constante* of the CJEU does not allow said Tribunal to have the last word regarding the interpretation of EU law (or of provisions that are in essence EU law).[166] This is why the referral procedure to the European Court of Justice found its way into the Institutional Agreement in the first place.

In light of the quiet but nonetheless highly effective resistance in many influential quarters, it may be worth exploring to separate the non-negotiable and necessary position of the European Court of Justice as the exclusive source of authoritative interpretation of EU law concepts from its *regular* involvement in future Swiss-EU treaty disputes that concern the interpretation of EU law. It is submitted that on the basis of the CJEU's "autonomy of the Union legal order"-jurisprudence a small window exists to satisfy pertinent proposals in Switzerland to allow the EFTA Court to become (in a first stage) the addressee of Tribunal requests for advisory opinions on the interpretation of EU law-based provisions of SEUFTA, with an (exceptional) second stage not dissimilar to the existing EEA provisions ensuring that the CJEU settles the

---

164 M. Ambühl, D. Scherer (n. 106), paras. 30 and 33–34.

165 Like the Uruguay-Round negotiators, the drafters of the InstA underestimated the prospective workload. It would seem advantageous to establish a standing tribunal, attached, e.g., to the EFTA Court or to the EFTA Secretariat in Brussels or Geneva, allowing to draw on pre-existing administrative support.

166 Cf. the analysis of the Court's jurisprudence in G. Van der Loo, 'Opinion 1/17 – Legitimising the EU's Investment Court System but Raising the Bar for Compliance with EU Law', in M. Hahn, G. Van der Loo (eds.), *Law and Practice of the Common Commercial Policy – The first 10 years after the Treaty of Lisbon* (Brill, 2021), pp. 98, 101–106; and M. Hahn, 'Never Get High on Your Own Supply – 'Autonomy of the EU Legal Order' and Effective Treaty-Based Dispute Settlement Mechanisms', in M. Hahn, G. Van der Loo (eds.), Law and Practice of the Common Commercial Policy – The first 10 years after the Treaty of Lisbon (Brill, 2021), pp. 128–160, pp. 128, 133–160.

matter authoritatively, if the Commission comes to the conclusion that the EFTA Court's decision was not on line with its obligation to ensure full parallelism (homogeneity) between its holdings and the CJEU jurisprudence; this safety net would ensure the European Court of Justice's ultimate control over the interpretation of EU law.[167]

Of course, the EFTA Court does not currently have the competence to provide advisory opinions to anyone but EEA EFTA domestic courts. However, if the EU and Switzerland would agree that an expansion of the EFTA Court's competences would be a desirable outcome, it is difficult to imagine the EEA EFTA States ultimately standing in the way of such a treaty modification. In any case, arriving at a role for the EFTA Court in Swiss-EU disputes requires significant alterations of treaty law: the EFTA Court would have to be granted the competence to provide (binding)[168] advisory opinions to the Tribunal. As the EFTA Court has received *ex ante* approval by the European Court of Justice (in fairness, for a somewhat different task),[169] and has a track record that has justified the CJEU's leap of faith by faithfully following its jurisprudence (which is reflected in the latter's not infrequent use of EFTA Court jurisprudence as persuasive precedent), this idea merits further exploration.[170]

A modification of the kind discussed above would depart from the institutional light touch the Swiss side had convinced the EU to accept by drawing on the infrastructure of the Hague-based Permanent Court of Arbitration.[171] If it was made legally possible to rely (in the first stage) *directly* on the already established EFTA Court infrastructure, they would also have to address whether the parties would want to have the right to nominate ad-hoc Swiss and EU judges.

Integrating the EFTA Court would satisfy the need of certain parts of the Swiss public to ensure that fairness and even-handedness *are seen* to be practised in the preliminary proceedings, while from the CJEU's perspective the involvement of its "little brother" – distinguished by a track-record of internalising the guidance it receives from the CJEU's jurisprudence – may make

---

167 See below, section 4.3, text after n. 196.

168 Thus, any question as to the binding nature of such opinions would have to put to rest; see EFTA Court, E-3/12, *Staten w/ Arbeidsdepartementet v Stig Arne Jonsson*, para. 60 and E-18/11, *Irish Bank Resolution Corporation Ltd v Kaupthing Bank hf.*, para. 58; see also B. Hammermann, 'Dialog und Kontrolle? – Perspektiven aus dem EFTA-Gerichtshof', *Europarecht* 2020 (Beiheft 1: 25 Jahre Europäischer Wirtschaftsraum), pp. 146–148, and G. Bauer, M. Sánchez Rydelski, C. Zatschler, *European Free Trade Association and the European Economic Area (EEA)*, 2nd ed (Wolters Kluwer, 2018), paras.525–526.

169 See *in extenso* CJEU, Opinion 1/92 (*EEA Agreement II*), EU:C:1992:189.

170 For a first attempt see *infra*, section 4.3.

171 See Article I.2 of Protocol 3 to the draft InstA.

this solution acceptable, given that the Commission would be in a position to trigger direct involvement of the CJEU if necessary.

4 Fault Lines

4.1 *Compatibility with Constitutional Law*

The Swiss Federal Constitution (FC) provides that "[t]he Confederation shall ensure that the independence of Switzerland and its welfare is safeguarded [...]."[172] Those constitutionally mandated goals are also pertinent for Switzerland's relations with the EU: economic well-being is not the only aspect to be considered.[173] In addition, Article 101 FC provides that the "Confederation shall safeguard the interests of the Swiss economy abroad."[174]

Contrary to some concerns voiced by hard-right political quarters,[175] neither the draft Institutional Agreement nor SEUFTA would be incompatible with Swiss constitutional law, never mind the fact that acts of the Federal Assembly and the Federal Council, as such, are not subject to judicial review.[176] The self-imposed treaty obligation to become a "rule-taker" in some sectors is manifestly not incompatible with the constitutional mandate to preserve Switzerland's independence.[177] The Swiss Federal Constitution even allows joining a supranational organisation, which would imply transferring, *pro tempore*, the exercise of certain central manifestations of state sovereignty to another subject of

172 Article 54(2) FC.

173 B. Ehrenzeller, R. Portmann, 'Art. 54', in B. Ehrenzeller, B. Schindler, R.J Schweizer and K.A. Vallender (eds.), *Die schweizerische Bundesverfassung – St. Galler Kommentar*, 3rd edition (Dike/Schulthess, 2014), para. 46.

174 Article 101(1) FC.

175 See, e.g., F. Schäfer, '«Leider ist der Rahmenvertrag noch nicht tot»', *Neue Zürcher Zeitung* 14 October 2020, <https://www.nzz.ch/ld.1581424> (accessed 19 March 2022); R. Wattenhofer, 'Nationalrat arbeitet sich ein weiteres Mal am Rahmenabkommen ab', *Aargauer Zeitung* 16 December 2020, <https://www.aargauerzeitung.ch/ld.2076190> (accessed 19 March 2022).

176 Article 189(4) FC.

177 Article 2(1) FC: "The Swiss Confederation shall protect the liberty and rights of the people and safeguard the independence and security of the country"; Article 54(1) FC: "The Confederation shall ensure that the independence of Switzerland [...]." Note *Marc Maresceau*'s clear-eyed observation that "sovereignty and independence [...] [are] two of the main and almost magic concepts in the Swiss foreign policy discourse," see M. Maresceau, 'EU-Switzerland: Quo Vadis?', *Georgia Journal of International and Comparative Law* 39 (2011), 727–755, p. 755.

law.[178] *A maiore ad minus*, a significantly less far-reaching association with the EU would not be unconstitutional. In any case, the obligation to take certain measures on the basis of an undertaking in an international agreement is a privilege of sovereign states. In fact, one of the manifestations of sovereignty is the ability to enter into binding international agreements.

4.2 *Compatibility with the Law of the WTO*

Of course, concluding and implementing SEUFTA would be in violation of the two parties' WTO obligations, unless the conditions of Article XXIV GATT and its sister provision, Article V GATS, are met. In *Turkey – Textiles*,[179] the WTO Appellate Body considered that Article XXIV GATT 1994 may justify measures that are inconsistent with certain other GATT provisions, provided that two cumulative conditions are fulfilled: (i) the party claiming the benefit of this defence must demonstrate that the measure at issue is introduced upon the formation of a customs union or FTA that fully meets the requirements of Article XXIV; and (ii) that party must demonstrate that the formation of that customs union or FTA would be prevented if it were not allowed to introduce the measure at issue.[180]

In the context of goods, there is little doubt that SEUFTA would meet the two substantive conditions of Article XXIV:8 GATT, i.e., (1) abolish *duties and other restrictive regulations of commerce* on (2) *substantially all the trade between the constituent territories in products originating in such territories*. With regard to the latter two basic approaches have materialised as good practice: a qualitative approach and a quantitative approach.[181] The former would require the elimination of restrictions with respect to *all* major sectors of the economies of FTA participants; that would probably not be the case here, as one would have to assume that non-processed agricultural goods would largely remain exempt from the coverage of SEUFTA. The latter would require a certain threshold of all the trade – say, 90 or 95% – to be liberated from restrictions. As the value of

---

178 Article 140(1)(a) FC: "The following must be put to the vote of the People and the Cantons: accession […] to supranational communities."

179 Appellate Body Report, *Turkey – Restrictions on Imports of Textile and Clothing Products*, WT/DS34/AB/R, 22 October 1999 (adopted on 19 November 1999), <https://www.wto.org/english/tratop_e/dispu_e/cases_e/ds34_e.htm> (accessed 19 March 2022).

180 M. Hahn, 'The Framework of Bilateral Trade Agreements', in M. Bungenberg, A. Mitchell (eds.), *European Yearbook of International Economic Law 2022 Special Issue: The Australia-European Union Free Trade Agreement* (Springer, 2022), pp. 41–57.

181 N.J. Lockhart, A.D. Mitchell, 'Regional Trade Agreements under GATT 1994: An Exception and Its Limits', in A.D. Mitchell (ed.), *Challenges and Prospects for the WTO* (Cameron May, 2005), p. 232.

agricultural trade tends to be comparatively low, even the exclusion of agricultural products from liberalising efforts would still mean that more than 90% of trade between the EU and Switzerland would be covered.[182] In light of the Appellate Body's flexibility[183] that would suffice to eliminate any pertinent legal exposure.[184]

With regard to the services components, WTO law demands "substantial sector coverage."[185] Depending on the content of SEUFTA, that threshold might not be met. A pertinent legal risk can be avoided, if the parties would not establish a Free Trade Zone pursuant to Article V GATS regarding services, but rather include in SEUFTA mutual recognition chapters concerning certain services sectors (such as financial services). While the Non-Life Insurance Agreement[186] is an example of such a recognition-based approach,[187] several much more ambitious efforts are currently underway so that negotiators would be in a position to draw on lessons learned.

4.3 *Dispute Settlement*

As indicated above, SEUFTA's dispute settlement arrangement will have to pass the CJEU's scrutiny: it will only avoid the same fate as the EU's accession treaty to the European Convention on Human Rights (ECHR)[188] if the Court can be convinced that the "autonomy of the Union legal order" would not be infringed. It does not help that the Court in its most recent jurisprudence seems to view *any* international agreement concluded by the Union as subject to its jurisdiction: As agreements of the EU become an integral part of the

182 In addition, pursuant to Article XXIV:7 GATT, concretised by the Understanding on the Interpretation of Article XXIV, both SEUFTA parties would have to notify the WTO. The notification is to be made to the Council for Trade in Goods which adopts the terms of reference and then transfers the agreement to the Committee on Regional Trade Agreements (CRTA) which was set up in 1996; see the pertinent World Trade Organization, Minutes of Meeting of the General Council of 6 February 1996, WT/GC/M/10, 6 March 1996, para. 11.

183 WTO Appellate Body, *Turkey – Restrictions on Imports of Textile and Clothing Products*, WT/DS34/AB/R (n. 179), para. 48.

184 See for the discussion as to the compatibility of the FTA 1972 T. Cottier, M. Panizzon, 'Die sektoriellen Abkommen und Recht der WTO: Grundlagen und Spannungsfelder', in D. Felder, C. Kaddous (eds.), *Bilaterale Abkommen Schweiz-EU* (*Erste Analysen*) (Hebling & Lichtenhahn, 2001), p. 63 (sceptical); H. Weber, 'Verhältnis bilaterale Verträge zu EU-Recht und WTO-Recht', in D. Thürer, R.H. Weber, W. Portmann and A. Kellerhals (eds.), *Bilaterale Verträge I & II Schweiz-EU – Handbuch* (Schulthess, 2007), para. 4.

185 Article V:1 lit. a GATS.

186 See n. 101.

187 See section II of the None-Life Insurance Agreement (n. 101).

188 See to that matter Opinion 2/13 (European Convention on Human Rights), EU:C:2014:2454.

Union legal order, the Court treats them as EU law and fully subjects them to its authoritative interpretation. In its recent decision in *Republic of Moldova v Komstroy*, the Court held "that the ECT [Energy Charter Treaty] is itself an act of EU law",[189] triggering its ultimate authority to review it. This approach sets the CJEU on a potential collision course with any treaty-based DSM, such as an arbitrary tribunal, despite the principled affirmation that there should be room for meaningful international dispute resolution: In the past, the Court has recognised that the Union's

> competence in the field of international relations and its capacity to conclude international agreements necessarily entails the power to submit to the decisions of a court which is created or designated by such an agreement as regards the interpretation and application of its provisions.[190]

and that, hence, "an international agreement providing for [...] a system of courts was in principle compatible with" Union law.[191] But from the CJEU's perspective, the extension of (some of) the rules of the Single Market to Switzerland and Swiss economic operators must not lead to a situation where the European Court of Justice's role as the supreme arbiter of the Union order is endangered.

In fact, it is the realisation of that danger in the context of the first major expansion of the Union legal order to include non-member States into the EU legal order that gave rise to the use of the concept of "autonomy of the EU legal order" vis-à-vis international agreements.[192] Some 30 years after *van Gend en Loos*' foundational claim that the Treaties had established "a new legal order of international law,"[193] the Court used for the first time the "integrity" of that legal regime to curtail *ab initio* the influence of treaty-based adjudicative bodies.

It will be recalled that the EEA Agreement was designed to expand the Single Market (Article 26 TFEU) to non-Member States, not unlike an ambitious SEUFTA, although the latter would be limited to a sectoral expansion. The original draft EEA Agreement had envisaged an adjudicative body (the "EEA Court") with jurisdiction over all disputes arising out of the interpretation of the EEA Agreement and involving the EEA EFTA States. In light of the

189 CJEU, Case C-741/19, *Republic of Moldova v Komstroy LLC*, EU:C:2021:655, para. 49.

190 CJEU, Opinion 1/91 (*EEA Agreement I*), EU:C:1991:490, para. 40.

191 *Ibid.*, para. 40.

192 M. Hahn, 'Never Get High on Your Own Supply' (n. 166), pp. 142–160.

193 CJEU, Case 26/62 (n. 132), para. 12.

semi-identity of EU and EEA rules, the CJEU had two major concerns. Firstly, it perceived the danger of being unduly influenced by earlier jurisprudence of the EEA Court in cases where it had not yet developed its own *jurisprudence constante*. As the EEA was supposed to be (and actually has become) an extension of the EU Single Market,[194] the EEA Court's interpretation of norms which in essence constitute Union law (projected beyond the Union's territory) would have provided the opportunity to interpret and adjudicate based on norms that represent the *inner sanctum* of Union law. Even if the primacy of the CJEU had been established as a matter of principle,[195] the possibility of a *de facto* infringement of the Court's freedom to develop *independently* its own reading of pertinent norms and decide pursuant to its own standards was far from far-fetched. The involvement of judges, intended as an institutional link to avoid such conflicts, was perceived as an aggravating factor: if the "wrong" approach was (even partly) attributable to some of their own, the subjective and systemic impediment to take a different position would be even greater.[196] Secondly, the Court was not prepared to accept that its advisory opinions would have been just that: opinions, unlike the binding decisions pursuant to Article 267 or 218(11) TFEU.[197] Thus, the CJEU concluded that the draft EEA Agreement, and specifically its dispute settlement mechanism was "likely adversely to affect […] the autonomy of the Community legal order,

194 See Council of the European Union, Conclusions of the 50th meeting of the EEA Council, 20 November 2018, <https://www.consilium.europa.eu/en/press/press-releases/2018/11/20/conclusions-of-the-50th-meeting-of-the-eea-council/> (accessed 19 March 2022).

195 The mechanisms in place, even though ultimately deemed problematic by the CJEU, clearly reflected who was supposed to set the standards and who was to apply them. Protocol 34, to which Article 104(2) of the EEA Agreement referred, established a specific preliminary procedure, under which the CJEU could, however, only express its views in a non-binding fashion; Opinion 1/91 (n. 190), para. 62–64.

196 Opinion 1/91 (n. 190), para. 35: "[…] the jurisdiction conferred on the EEA Court under Article 2(c), Article 96(1)(a) and Article 117(1) of the agreement is likely adversely to affect the allocation of responsibilities defined in the Treaties and, hence, the autonomy of the Community legal order, respect for which must be assured by the Court of Justice pursuant to Article 164 of the EEC Treaty. This exclusive jurisdiction of the Court of Justice is confirmed by Article 219 of the EEC Treaty, under which Member States undertake not to submit a dispute concerning the interpretation or application of that treaty to any method of settlement other than those provided for in the Treaty. Article 87 of the ECSC Treaty embodies a provision to the same effect."

197 *Ibid.*, paras. 45 and 61–62.

respect for which must be assured by the European Court of Justice pursuant to Article 164 of the EEC Treaty".[198]

In response to the Court's decision, the EEA contracting parties separated the EEA pillar from the EU realm, replaced the envisaged EEA Court with an EFTA Court and eliminated the involvement of CJEU judges in the latter. A chapter on *Homogeneity* defines the objective as "to arrive at as uniform an interpretation as possible of the provisions of the Agreement and those provisions of Community legislation which are substantially reproduced in the Agreement".[199] The implementation of this goal depends in the first instance on the EFTA Court's commitment to follow the CJEU's lead, a commitment kept in the last two decades. In addition, however, this substantive duty of the EFTA Court is secured by a political "safety net," as Article 105(2) EEA Agreement tasks the EEA Joint Committee to "keep under constant review the development of the case law of the European Court of Justice of the European Communities and the EFTA Court". If a difference in the case law of the two Courts is relevant enough to be brought before the Joint Committee, any contracting party – but for practical purposes, the Commission as guardian of the Union's interests in foreign relations – may propose that the Joint Committee requests a binding CJEU ruling on the interpretation of the relevant rules.[200] If this effort to allow an authoritative resolution by the Court is blocked, the Commission may trigger commensurate rebalancing measures and the suspension of the pertinent parts of the agreement ensue.[201]

Due to the modifications to EEA Agreement and the Agreement on the Establishment of a Surveillance Authority and a Court of Justice,[202] the supremacy of the CJEU's jurisprudence has been established beyond doubt. In addition, without affecting the independence of the EFTA Court, mechanisms have been put in place that give teeth to the principled lead of the CJEU. A "judicial dialogue"[203] creates transparency and the building of mutual trust;

198 *Ibid.*, para. 35; see H.G. Schermers, 'Opinion 1/91 of the Court of Justice, 14 December 1991; Opinion 1/92 of the Court of Justice, 10 April 1992', *Common Market Law Review* 29 (1992), p. 991.

199 Article 105(1) EEA Agreement.

200 See the excerpts of the EEA Agreement above, n. 136.

201 Article 111 and 102 EEA Agreement.

202 Agreement between the EFTA States on the establishment of a surveillance authority and a Court of Justice (OJ 1994, L 344/1).

203 Article 106 EEA Agreement establishes a system of exchange of information concerning judgments by the EFTA Court, the CJEU and the Courts of last instance of the EFTA States "[i]n order to ensure as uniform an interpretation as possible of this Agreement [and] in full deference to the independence of courts".

the political mechanisms described above allow the Commission to enforce, if need be, the necessary homogeneity of the EEA with the Union legal order.

While the jurisprudence of the European Court of Justice with regard to not allowing treaty-based dispute settlement mechanism to tread on the CJEU's competencies has become stricter, a certain optimism seems warranted that a *modified* copy of (or reference to) the EFTA Court model may be acceptable to the CJEU. In *Komstroy*, the Grand Chamber summarised its pertinent jurisprudence and highlighted the crux of the matter, namely ensuring the Court's "exclusive jurisdiction to give the definitive interpretation of … [EU] law. To that end, that system includes, in particular, the preliminary ruling procedure provided for in Article 267 TFEU".[204] By allowing the EFTA Court to authoritatively advise the bilateral tribunal, that control would not be given up. The EFTA Court has a track record as a "little brother" of the CJEU; nothing would indicate that this would change: the explicit *ex ante*-approval to the EFTA Court in *EEA II* has been rewarded with the utmost commitment to the treaty-based obligation of the EFTA Court to ensure homogeneity.[205] In addition, though, the *current* legal regime of the EFTA Court sketched above, would allow the Commission to refer the matter before the Joint Committee to request a binding CJEU ruling on the interpretation of the relevant rules and could enforce this through pertinent suspensions. Opinion 1/17[206] seems to indicate that the Court is even prepared to consider commitments by the Commission and the respective third-country contracting party to react when a divergence between treaty-based dispute settlement mechanism and CJEU jurisprudence would develop. Based on that premise, the EFTA Court-specific safety net allowing the Commission to defend the Court's privilege "to give the definitive interpretation of that law"[207] should *a maiore* suffice to calm pertinent concerns.

To be sure, the architecture reflected upon here would require significant modifications of the current *status quo*. The EFTA Court as it stands plays no role in disputes between the EU and EEA EFTA States. But it enjoys the trust of both sides: as explained above, the CJEU has every reason to trust

---

204 CJEU, Case C-741/19 (n. 189), para. 45.

205 H.H. Fredikson, 'The EFTA Court 15 Years On', *International and Comparative Law Quarterly* 59:3 (2010), pp. 749–750; C. Baudenbacher, 'The Relationship Between the EFTA Court and the Court of Justice of the European Union', in C. Baudenbacher (ed.), *The Handbook of EEA Law* (Springer, 2016), p. 192.

206 CJEU, Opinion 1/17 (*CETA*), EU:C:2019:341; see G. Van der Loo, 'Opinion 1/17 – Legitimising the EU's Investment Court System but Raising the Bar for Compliance with EU Law', in M. Hahn, G. Van der Loo (eds.), *Law and Practice of the Common Commercial Policy – The first 10 years after the Treaty of Lisbon* (Brill, 2021), pp. 98–127.

207 CJEU, Case C-741/19 (n. 189), para. 45.

the EFTA Court's commitment to homogeneity. Similarly, it can also trust the Commission's commitments to use the (adapted) escalation possibilities provided for in the EEA. The Swiss side has similarly no reason to believe that judges appointed by its EFTA partners would be biased: of course, the pertinent mandate *de lege ferenda* of the EFTA Court would be to interpret legal terms and concepts rooted in EU law on the basis of the jurisprudence of the European Court of Justice. That EU law reigns supreme, though, seems to be accepted; what has proven to be a difficult sell in Switzerland is the role of an organ of one party in a bilateral inter-party dispute. The involvement of the EFTA Court would change that.

The proposal submitted as a way out of an unfortunate impasse requires further elaboration and cannot be a model of elegance: it tries to satisfy two schools of thought that share a certain myopic satisfaction with one's perceived status in the world (or in Europe, that is). The CJEU's insistence that all things international have to satisfy the Luxembourg judges is reminiscent of 19th-century German constitutional law scholars that appreciated public international law exclusively as "external constitutional law" ("*Außenstaatsrecht*"). The Swiss rejection of the CJEU's jurisdiction is largely founded on the unwillingness to communicate to voters what interested constituencies know all too well: while the bilateral relationship is genuinely mutually beneficial, Switzerland's relative benefits clearly exceed those of its partner. Being able to use a foreign power's Internal Market as a home market is an important ingredient for Switzerland's economic success. Under these circumstances, structuring the dispute settlement mechanism into two stages may be another of the face-saving drafting compromises ("*Formelkompromisse*") that have served the bilateral relationship so well in the last decades.[208]

It could be argued, of course, that Switzerland would receive preferential treatment compared to reliable EEA EFTA States by enjoying some (initial) distance from the CJEU in cases of disputes between the EU and its contracting party Switzerland, whereas in cases of disputes between the EU and its EEA EFTA partners the CJEU would always be competent to adjudicate, conditional

208 See, e.g., Articles 2(1) and 7(2) SAA (n. 139). They read, respectively: "The provisions of the Schengen *acquis* [...] shall be implemented and applied by Switzerland"; Article 7(2) explains what that implementation means: "The Council shall notify Switzerland [...] of the adoption of [acts referred to in Article 2] [...] to which the procedures set out in this Agreement have been applied. *Switzerland shall decide whether to accept their contents and to implement them in its internal legal order*" (emphasis added). Non-implementation would entail the quasi-automatic unravelling of Switzerland's association with the Schengen and Dublin system. All pertinent acts have been transposed in the decades since ratification; none has not been internalised into the Swiss legal order.

on the parties' agreement. However, this is a function of the mutual trust that all EEA partners show *vis-à-vis* each other and the Union institutions: the EEA EFTA States are truly integrated into the Single Market and this relationship entails all benefits and burdens of membership. In contrast, Switzerland would, even after a revitalisation of its "bilateral'" relationship with the EU, remain apart and thus may legitimately claim a lighter touch when it comes to CJEU jurisdiction.

5 Conclusion

The Federal Council's proposed sectoral negotiating approach may have the advantage of making costs and benefits easier to grasp for voters. Having said this, given the four "priorities" of Vice-President Šefčovič, the substantive problems will remain the same: *Plus ça change, plus c'est la même chose ...*

The premise of this paper is the refusal to entertain the idea that Swiss-EU relations are going to slowly disintegrate to MFN status, with no benefit for anyone but many disadvantages (or at least nuisances) for many EU and Swiss citizens. The alternative trajectory would be an effort to make lemonade out of the lemons, pursue negotiating efforts, e.g., by attempting SEUFTA, with a focus on goods, and financial services: this would address both the urgent request of Switzerland to preserve the *status quo* with regard to the current MRA regulatory environment and would have a chance to implement the Unions four paradigms. It would seem that this route is a real possibility, with some unknowns (will the CJEU subscribe to an expansion of the EFTA Court's jurisdiction? How should a comprehensive mutual recognition agreement regarding financial services be drafted?) that would however seem doable with the expertise available in Brussels and Bern. By postponing addressing a reform of the well-working AFMP, the parties would allow relaunching the pertinent negotiations once the dust of the last failed negotiating exercise has settled: trust is a fragile commodity and difficult to rebuild once it has been destroyed. Focusing on the comparatively low-hanging fruits, with two somewhat challenging subject-matters (State aid and dispute settlement) could rebuild that trust.

All sketched efforts to artificially slice up the subject matter in order to make SEUFTA palatable to decision makers and voters would of course not provide Switzerland with a genuine Member State's market access, as full and automatic (mutual) recognition on the basis of Article 34 TFEU and the *Cassis* jurisprudence of the Court is reserved for Members only. Having a stream-lined MRA integrated, and thus the legally binding commitment to adapt to EU laws and regulations in a specific sector, but without direct effect and primacy of pertinent norms would change that, unless the EU would give up that dogma that full *Cassis*-privileges are open only to those who take part in the Single Market, lock, stock and barrel.

This is of course the dilemma of any *rapprochement* between Switzerland and the EU: due to the burden of needing for domestic consumption, the possibility to plausibly deny that it is more than just a close trading partner, the country internalises EU rules into its legal order "as if" it was a Member, yet will always face a difference between its actual benefits and its potential benefits as a Member state due to its rejection of full integration.

The economically desirable parallelism between Union and Swiss regulatory environment in the vast areas covered by the Single Market legislation not only reduces options for internal regulatory solutions but also in the relations with other trading partners. While the recent reactions to the Russian attack on Ukraine may be an outlier, due to the shocking nature of the event triggering Switzerland's sanctions, it may also be an indication that the laws of economic gravity curtail Switzerland's ability to determine its relations with the rest of the world. It can be safely assumed that Switzerland's joining EU sanctions was not just an ethical choice – exclusively motivated by the strong reaction of the Swiss civil society –, but was also a function of the close economic ties with its neighbour (and the US).[209]

In light of that possible limitation to any sectoral approach, an old acquaintance may be worth a second look after 30 years. The EEA is now a tested tool for three wealthy, successful and independence-conscious States: it is no longer the anteroom, the purgatory for aspiring candidates that prepares for "the next level". While none of the three EEA EFTA States would be particularly happy to see Switzerland assume the role of the biggest EEA EFTA economy, it would seem unlikely that those three countries would refuse joint efforts by the EU and Switzerland to allow Switzerland in. This would – finally! – provide Switzerland with full and certain market access to the Single Market (the famous "*gleich lange Spiesse*" or "level playing field"), yet provide it (at least *de facto*) with as much flexibility with regard to its relations with the rest of the world as it currently enjoys.

209 On the sanctions, see also the contribution by C. Hillion (Chapter 7) in this volume.

CHAPTER 13

Switzerland-UK Trade Relations: A Future Planned by the Past?

An Overview of the Trade Agreement between Switzerland and the United Kingdom and Related Agreements

Georges Baur

1 Current Foreign Policy Positioning of the United Kingdom

On 31 January 2020, the United Kingdom of Great Britan and Northern Ireland (UK) formally left the European Union (EU). Until 31 December 2020, the relationship between the UK and the EU was in a transitional phase during which the UK was still treated as a Member State. This means that EU law still applied, but the UK no longer had any institutional rights, i.e., it could no longer participate in decision-making in the EU institutions, Council formations or committees. Similarly, it no longer sent representatives to the EU Commission, the Council of the EU, the Court of Justice of the European Union (CJEU) or the European Parliament. By the end of this transition period, the UK and the EU had to negotiate an agreement on the future relationship.

These negotiations progressed rather slowly in the first half of 2020 as there remained major differences between the parties' positions until the very end of the transition period. Already during the negotiations on the UK's withdrawal, the EU was quick to assert certain principles and to point to precedents as indicators of constraints on what the outcome of an agreement on future relations between the EU and the UK might be.

Finally, as is well known, the EU and the UK agreed on a Trade and Partnership Agreement (TPA),[1] which basically is a modern Free Trade Agreement (FTA). In addition, certain parts of the Withdrawal Agreement (WA),[2] mainly on citizenship rights, will extend way into the future and with them some ongoing jurisdiction of the CJEU. Northern Ireland will remain in the internal market

1 Trade and Cooperation Agreement between the European Union and the European Atomic Energy Community, of the one part, and the United Kingdom of Great Britain and Northern Ireland, of the other part (OJ 2021, L 149/10).

2 Agreement on the withdrawal of the United Kingdom of Great Britain and Northern Ireland from the European Union and the European Atomic Energy Community (OJ 2020, L 29/7).

© KONINKLIJKE BRILL NV, LEIDEN, 2023 | DOI:10.1163/9789004529984_015

for goods and *de facto* also in the customs union with the EU, drawing the customs border between the EU and the UK in the Irish Sea.[3]

In the meantime, the UK has continued to pursue its "Global Britain"[4] free trade agenda, albeit not with as much success and within the timeframe as the Government had hoped after the 2016 Brexit referendum. Political representatives seem to believe that the UK Government's negotiations on a trade agreement with the United States could give it leverage over the EU.[5] However, it seems that no significant progress has been made in these negotiations so far either.

In fact, at the time of writing, the only trade agreement that the UK has been able to conclude with a relatively important trading partner is the one with Switzerland.[6] In addition, there are other agreements that Switzerland has concluded with the UK as part of its so-called "mind the gap" strategy. The Swiss Government's "mind the gap" strategy aims to ensure legal continuity and safeguard mutual rights and obligations, thus "avoiding a legal vacuum". In addition to ensuring legal continuity, Switzerland also aims at further developing its relations with the UK ("mind the gap+").[7]

On the basis of an additional agreement to the trade agreement, parts of the latter are also applicable to Liechtenstein.[8]

Among the UK's non-EU trading partners, Switzerland is number three after the USA and China in terms of trade volume (2019)[9] and is thus definitely of

3 Martin Kettle, 'What the EU procurement furore tells us about Johnson's real priorities', *The Guardian* 22 April 2020.

4 Select Committee on Foreign Affairs, Global Britain (HC 2017–19, 780), paras. 3–5.

5 M. Landler, A. Swanson, 'About That Much Vaunted U.S.-U.K. Trade Deal? Maybe Not Now', *New York Times* 2 March 2020.

6 Trade Agreement between the United Kingdom of Great Britain and Northern Ireland and the Swiss Confederation, CS Swiss 4.2019, and HM Government, Explanatory Memorandum on the Trade Agreement between the United Kingdom of Great Britain and Northern Ireland and the Swiss Confederation (EM CS Swiss 4.2019, CP 55).

7 See <www.eda.admin.ch/europa/en/home/weitere-dossiers/brexit.html> (accessed 12 January 2022).

8 Additional Agreement between the United Kingdom of Great Britain and Northern Ireland, the Swiss Confederation and the Principality of Liechtenstein extending to the Principality of Liechtenstein certain provisions of the Trade Agreement between the United Kingdom of Great Britain and Northern Ireland and the Swiss Confederation (CS Liechtenstein 1.2019, CP 65).

9 Department for International Trade, UK Trade in Numbers (February 2021) 6, <https://www.gov.uk/government/statistics/uk-trade-in-numbers/uk-trade-in-numbers-web-version> (accessed 1 February 2022).

great economic importance.[10] Total trade in goods and services between the UK and Switzerland amounted to £ 31.4 billion in 2019.[11]

However, it is also interesting to take a look at the Trade Agreement[12] between Switzerland and the United Kingdom (CH-UK TA) from a comparative perspective. On the one hand, the UK has regulated its post-transition period trade relationship with Switzerland in a way that it originally intended to negotiate with the EU.[13] This largely corresponds to a bilateral approach *à la Suisse*. On the other hand, it is also known that the EU would like to avoid bilateral agreements like the one with Switzerland at all costs.[14]

As Edmund Burke – the alledged *spiritus rector* of the current mindset of the UK's Conservative Party[15] – said: "You can never plan the future by the past".[16] However, this "model", in which a package of pre-existing free trade-related agreements and a few new sectoral agreements is put together, takes us back a generation, if not two.[17] It will have to be seen what Burke's warning holds for the future.

---

10 HM Government, Explanatory Memorandum on the Trade Agreement between the United Kingdom of Great Britain and Northern Ireland and the Swiss Confederation (EM CS Swiss 4.2019), p. 3.

11 TheCityUK/economiesuisse, Future-Proofing the UK-Swiss Financial and Related Professional Services Relationship (24 April 2020), <mcusercontent.com/30c46ca80b0b4c21bdca05c7c/files/2299d43f-0ba3-4ded-92c3-06af85992ac3/2020_04_28_joint_position_paper_TCUK_eco_CH_final.pdf> (accessed 15 Mai 2022).

12 Federal Council, Explanatory Memorandum on the approval of the trade agreement between Switzerland and the United Kingdom and the supplementary agreement on the inclusion of Liechtenstein in the trade agreement, Fed. Gaz. 2020 2081.

13 HM Government, The Future Relationship with the EU, The UK's Approach to Negotiations (CP 211, 2020), para. 6, <www.gov.uk/government/publications/our-approach-to-the-future-relationshipwith-the-eu> (accessed 1 April 2022).

14 R. Atkins, A. Barker, 'The Brexit effect: Brussels tries to blunt the Swiss model', *Financial Times* 2 October 2018, <www.ft.com/content/574ce2e6-c49d-11e8-bc21-54264d1c4647> (accessed 1 April 2022).

15 E. Jones, 'Burke to the Future: The Evolution of Conservatism', *History Today* 67 (2017) 7.

16 Edmund Burke (1729–1797): A letter from Mr. Burke, to a member of the National Assembly: in answer to some objections to his book on French affairs (London: Paris, printed, and London re-printed for J. Dodsley, 1791), p. 73, <https://quod.lib.umich.edu/e/ecco/004804929.0001.000/1:3?rgn=div1;view=fulltext> (accessed 23 January 2022).

17 This is apparently also the view of the EU's former chief negotiator, Michel Barnier, following the disappointing outcome of the third round of negotiations with the United Kingdom on a future agreement: European Commission, Remarks by Michel Barnier following Round 3 of negotiations for a new partnership between the European Union and the United Kingdom of 15 May 2020 (Speech 20/895), <ec.europa.eu/commission/presscorner/detail/en/speech_20_895> (accessed 15 May 2022).

For the sake of completeness, it should also be mentioned that the UK has now concluded agreements with all four EFTA States, Iceland, Liechtenstein, Norway and Switzerland. These Agreements are intended to replace the agreements that applied between these States and the UK as an EU Member State. After transitional Agreements with Iceland and Norway,[18] the three EEA EFTA States Iceland, Liechtenstein and Norway and the UK concluded a comprehensive FTA.[19] Regulating their future relationship with the UK took the three EEA EFTA States somewhat longer due to their membership in the European Economic Area (EEA). This fact of course makes these three countries depend to a greater extent on developments in the relations between the EU and the UK. On other issues, namely fisheries, a specific agreement has been concluded between Norway and the UK,[20] while Iceland and the UK have concluded a MoU on that subject.[21] Finally, it is noteworthy to mention the ongoing negotiations between Switzerland and the UK on financial services. The respective aims have been set out in a Joint Declaration.[22]

In the following, the negotiations and the solution of a framework agreement chosen for the trade agreement will be discussed (section 2). Then the trade agreement will be presented (section 3). Further agreements on future relations between Switzerland and the UK will be discussed (section 4). By its nature, this contribution is rather descriptive, as too much is still uncertain for an analytical consideration. Nevertheless, the chosen form of the trade agreement already gives rise to certain questions regarding interpretation, which are briefly addressed (section 5). For the sake of completeness, the agreements between the other three EFTA States Iceland, Liechtenstein and Norway shall

---

18 Agreement on Trade in Goods between the United Kingdom of Great Britain and Northern Ireland, Iceland and the Kingdom of Norway (MS 8.2020, CP 328).

19 Free Trade Agreement between Iceland, the Principality of Liechtenstein and the Kingdom of Norway and the United Kingdom of Great Britain and Northern Ireland (MS No.3/2021, CP 496).

20 Agreed Record of Fisheries Consultations between the United Kingdom and Norway for 2022 [21 December 2021], <assets.publishing.service.gov.uk/government/uploads/system/uploads/attachment_data/file/1043183/uk-norway-bilateral-fisheries-agreed-record-21122021.pdf> (accessed 12 January 2022).

21 Memorandum of Understanding between the Government of the United Kingdom of Great Britain and Northern Ireland and the Government of Iceland on Enhancing Cooperation on Fisheries [11 November 2020], <assets.publishing.service.gov.uk/government/uploads/system/uploads/attachment_data/file/934643/fisheries-mou-uk-iceland-201111.pdf> (accessed 12 January 2022).

22 HM Treasury and Federal Department of Finance, Deepening cooperation in financial services (Joint Statement, 30 June 2020).

also be briefly mentioned (section 6). The present contribution concludes with a tentative look into the future (section 7).

2 Negotiations

2.1 *Course in an Uncertain Environment*

The UK's withdrawal from the EU meant that it had to leave the EU's Common Commercial Policy and the Customs Union. As a consequence, it sought to autonomously continue the foreign trade relations it had formerly maintained through the EU and to establish new ones on its own. With regard to the first point, this means that the UK had and still has to negotiate successor arrangements to the EU's existing agreements with third countries with over 40 trading partners.[23]

Relations between Switzerland and the EU in particular are complex and go far beyond a mere free trade relationship. Some of the bilateral agreements between Switzerland and the EU are also fully or partially based on the harmonisation of the relevant regulations and the mutual recognition of their equivalence. However, this means that there is also a link to EU law with regard to the new bilateral relationship between Switzerland and the UK. This in turn meant that certain regulations governing future relations between Switzerland and the UK could only be decided upon once there was clarity about the future relationship between the EU and the UK and how, if at all, the latter would be bound by EU law.

Switzerland and the UK concluded the necessary agreements at the beginning of 2019 so that no legal vacuum would arise after the end of the transitional period following the UK's withdrawal from the EU. Nevertheless, the two parties already at that point agreed to not only update the agreements themselves, but also to deepen the entire relationship at a later date.[24]

2.2 *Pragmatic Solution for the Trade Agreement*

With regard to the negotiations for the Switzerland-UK Trade Agreement, it must be borne in mind that they took place over a few months in the second half of 2018 under great time pressure, especially since the UK's exit from the EU was originally scheduled to take place on 29 March 2019. The British side

---

23 (Swiss) Explanatory Memorandum on the CH-UK TA (n. 12), p. 2086.
24 *Ibid.*, p. 2087.

had to negotiate not only the agreements with Switzerland, but also with other States and, of course, the Withdrawal Agreement (WA) with the EU.

Consequently, it was primarily a matter of maintaining the existing trade-relevant rights and obligations between Switzerland and the UK as far as possible after the latter's withdrawal from the EU. Otherwise, the WTO rules and tariff concessions would have had to be applied between Switzerland and the UK at the end of the transition period. Compared to the current and now future legal situation, this would have led to considerable tariff and non-tariff barriers to trade and thus to high additional costs for mutual trade.

In contrast to the other agreements, which can certainly exist on their own,[25] such as an air transport agreement, agreements related to trade in the narrower sense (FTAs, Mutual Recognition Agreements – MRAs, agricultural agreements, etc.) should be regulated jointly. This transfer into a bilateral legal relationship had to be accomplished as quickly and effortlessly as possible. In consequence, two main options were considered:

(1) Adoption of the individual agreements existing between Switzerland and the EU by replicating them for Switzerland-UK relations ("copy & paste option"). Under this option, the agreements between Switzerland and the EU would have been replicated largely verbatim in the form of parallel agreements between Switzerland and the UK.

(2) Generally maintaining the rights and obligations arising from these individual agreements by incorporating them into a framework agreement and applying them *mutatis mutandis*.[26] This solution envisaged a simplified adoption of these agreements without replicating them in full, i.e., "short form agreements" listing the necessary technical amendments would have been created.

Since the first alternative did not seem feasible in view of the limited time available and the effort this would have meant due to the exceptions to be worked out in detail, the parties agreed on an "incorporation" of the existing agreements between Switzerland and the EU and their application *mutatis mutandis*.[27]

25 See below 4.

26 (Swiss) Explanatory Memorandum on the CH-UK TA (n. 12), p. 2085.

27 Article 1(1) 1 CH-UK TA.

3 The Switzerland-UK Trade Agreement

According to its preamble, the parties to the Switzerland-UK Trade Agreement desire "that the rights and obligations between them as provided for by trade-related agreements between Switzerland and the European Union should continue to apply between the Parties". The Trade Agreement itself can be seen as a framework (below: "Framework Agreement") for transposing the content of the various Switzerland-EU trade-related agreements (below: the "Incorporated Agreements") to the relationship between Switzerland and the UK.

3.1 *The Framework Agreement*

The Trade Agreement between Switzerland and the United Kingdom (CH-UK TA) establishes a framework for the various trade-related agreements between the two countries. It is supplemented by a joint declaration on rules of origin as well as an additional agreement concerning the adoption of two agreements relating to Liechtenstein.[28]

As far as the institutional structure is concerned, each of the Incorporated Agreements basically retains "its" Joint Committee.[29] This is a committee made up of representatives of the contracting parties, which is responsible, among other things, for amendments to the agreement, monitoring the functioning of the agreement or settling disputes. The committee for the incorporated Free Trade agreement (i.e., the Switzerland-EU FTA 1972)[30] is also responsible for the proper functioning of the (Switzerland-UK) Framework Agreement. No further institutional structures are foreseen. Dispute settlement is carried out in accordance with the provisions in the respective Incorporated Agreements, again *mutatis mutandis*. These provisions already do not go beyond "diplomatic efforts" in most of the relevant Switzerland-EU agreements, i.e., there is no procedure to obtain mutually binding judicial decisions in favour of one or the other party. Accordingly, no adjustments were necessary in this regard in the new intergovernmental relationship between Switzerland and the UK.

As mentioned above, the relevant Switzerland-EU agreements are, so to speak, incorporated into this Framework Agreement. These "Incorporated Agreements" are, on the one hand, dealing with classic free trade matters, e.g., by regulating the dismantling of customs duties on industrial and agricultural

---

28 Additional Agreement (n. 8).

29 Article 6(1) 1 CH-UK TA.

30 Agreement between the European Economic Community and the Swiss Confederation (OJ 1972, L 300/191).

goods as well as processed agricultural products. On the other hand, some of these agreements enable Switzerland to participate in selected areas of the EU's internal market without discrimination through the harmonisation of legal provisions or the mutual recognition of legal provisions. Because the validity of the latter agreements depended on the rules of future relations between the EU and the UK, they were not immediately applicable upon the entry into force of the Switzerland-UK trade agreement. It was left to the respective Joint Committees to eventually decide on their application, depending on the future UK-EU relationship.[31]

3.2 *The "Incorporated Agreements"*

The following agreements are "incorporated into and made a part of the Trade Agreement".[32] As mentioned before, these agreements apply as in their original context between the EU and Switzerland,[33] however subject to adaptations either due to the specific bilateral context between Switzerland and the UK (*"mutatis mutandis"*) or explicit provisions. Dispute settlement remains at a purely political (diplomatic) level as forseen in the respective provisions of the "Incorporated Agreements".[34]

3.2.1 Free Trade Agreement (FTA) 1972

The Free Trade Agreement between the Swiss Confederation and the European Economic Community (Switzerland-EU FTA 1972)[35] is the central element on which essentially all other incorporated agreements are based. The FTA 1972 was negotiated during the accession to the EEC of the two EFTA States: Denmark and the UK, together with Ireland, as one of the agreements concluded by the then EEC with the other, non-acceding EFTA States individually, but on the basis of standardised texts. These agreements were signed by Austria, Iceland,

31 (Swiss) Explanatory Memorandum on the CH-UK TA (n. 12), p. 2088.

32 Article 1(1) CH-UK TA; the Incorporated Agreements are not explained in the order in which they are listed in the agreement.

33 On the EU-Swiss trade agreements, see the contribution by M. Hahn in this volume.

34 See, e.g., Article 14 Agreement between the European Community and the Swiss Confederation on Mutual Recognition in relation to Conformity Assessment (MRA) [1999] OJ L 114/369; Article 7 Agreement between the European Community and the Swiss Confederation on trade in agricultural products (Agricultural Agreement) (OJ 1999, L 114/132) and Article 10 Agreement between the European Community and the Swiss Confederation on certain aspects of government procurement (Government Procurement Agreement) (OJ 1999, L 114/430).

35 See n. 30. The names of the predecessor organisations or Treaties of the EU are only mentioned as such if this is either indicated in the historical context or necessary due to the specific designation of a legal act. Otherwise, "EU" is used throughout.

Portugal, Sweden and Switzerland on 22 July 1972, by Norway on 14 May 1973 and by Finland on 5 October 1973. They entered into force on 1 January 1973, somewhat later for Portugal, Norway and Finland. At this time, agreements were also signed by the European Coal and Steel Community (ECSC) and each of the EFTA countries.

With the accession of Austria, Finland and Sweden to the (then) EC in 1995, the corresponding free trade agreements ceased to exist. Those with Iceland and Norway as well as the 1972 FTA with Switzerland, as far as Liechtenstein is concerned,[36] were largely replaced by the EEA Agreement.

The main objective of these EEC–EFTA Free Trade Agreements was to remove customs barriers, create a free trade area for industrial products and regulate trade in processed agricultural products. Trade in (non-processed) agricultural products was not initially envisaged. Another objective was the abolition of quantitative restrictions (tariffs; quotas). These were abolished in bilateral trade at the time the agreements came into force. Likewise, measures with the same effect (e.g., discriminatory sales modalities) are prohibited.[37]

As the FTA with Switzerland does not provide for a customs union, it was necessary to establish rules concerning the origin of goods in order to clearly define which goods are eligible for duty-free treatment ("rules of origin"). In simple terms, industrial products that originate entirely in the territory of both contracting parties, or that have been manufactured using materials from third countries, can be traded duty-free.[38]

The Switzerland-EU FTA 1972 is to be continued by Switzerland with the UK largely to the same extent as it exists with the EU. Annex 1 to the trade agreement contains only two technical adjustments. These concern Protocol No. 2 on processed agricultural products and Protocol No. 3 on rules of origin.[39]

The latter protocol is of particular interest. Rules of origin are currently regulated in the extended European (free) trade area (including non-European Mediterranean countries) by the so-called PEM (Pan-Euro-Mediterranean)

---

36 Due to the customs union between Switzerland and Liechtenstein, the latter was included in the Swiss-EU FTA. See 3.4 below.

37 (Swiss) Explanatory Memorandum on the CH-UK TA (n. 12), p. 2091.

38 Protocol 3 to the FTA 1972 concerning the definition of the concept of originating products and methods of administrative cooperation (Current version according to Decision No 2/2021 of the EU-Switzerland Joint Committee of 12 August 2021 amending the Agreement between the European Economic Community and the Swiss Confederation by replacing Protocol 3 thereto concerning the definition of the concept of 'originating products' and methods of administrative cooperation) (OJ 2021, L 404/1).

39 Annex 1 Appendix 1 to the CH-UK TA.

Convention.[40] This convention aims to ensure that cumulation[41] and harmonised rules of origin are applied throughout the Euro-Mediterranean area. It establishes a uniform set of rules that can and should be implemented and applied in all bilateral or regional trade agreements between its signatories in the future. However, a simple reference to the PEM Convention in the incorporated FTA was not possible, as it was not clear whether the UK would join the PEM Convention as an independent member after leaving the EU. Cumulation of originating materials, in simple terms, the crediting of tariff preferences of other contracting parties to the PEM Convention, e.g., the EU, requires an existing free trade agreement between the contracting parties involved.[42] Because the EU-UK TCA had not yet been concluded, this question had to remain open when the CH-UK TA was negotiated. After the conclusion of the TCA, a new Protocol No. 3 was inserted. Therein, the rules of origin of the PEM Convention are largely replicated. However, they only unfold their effect bilaterally between the two contracting parties.

3.2.2 Agreement on Public Procurement

The Switzerland-EU Government Procurement Agreement[43] is based on the corresponding WTO Agreement (Government Procurement Agrement, GPA) and expands its scope of application.[44] Swiss and EU companies will thus gain extended access to the respective markets of the contracting parties. For example, the obligation to publish invitations for tendering for procurements or constructions is extended to municipalities and districts as well as to procurements by public or private companies in certain sectors (e.g., rail transport, energy supply).[45]

The Switzerland-EU Agreement on Government Procurement is *a priori* and fully incorporated and applied in the Swiss relation with the UK. However, because the Switzerland-EU Agreement contains explicit references to the WTO GPA and the UK's membership of the WTO was at the time of negotiations still based on its membership of the EU, transitional rules had to be agreed between Switzerland and the UK until the UK would have formally

40 Regional Convention on Pan-Euro-Mediterranean Preferential Rules of Origin (OJ 2013, L 54/4).

41 DG Trade, Preferential Trade (Guidance on the Rules of Origin, 2020), p. 52.

42 (Swiss) Explanatory Memorandum on the CH-UK TA (n. 12), p- 2102.

43 Government Procurement Agreement (n. 34).

44 Agreement on Government Procurement of the World Trade Organization (WTO) (Agreement on Government Procurement, GPA), <www.wto.org/english/tratop_e/gproc_e/gpa_1994_e.htm> (accessed 2 April 2022).

45 (Swiss) Explanatory Memorandum on the CH-UK TA (n. 12), p. 2092.

joined the WTO as an independent member.[46] These transitional rules incorporated the rules of the WTO GPA, as revised in 2012, to cover the following two cases: Either the UK is not yet a WTO member on the date of entry into force of the Switzerland-UK TA or the revision of the WTO GPA enters into force for Switzerland before the UK. These transitional provisions were, however, not needed: The UK is a member of WTO in its own right since 1 January 2021.[47] On the same date, Switzerland deposited its instrument of acceptance and the UK its instrument of accession as an independent member to the revised GPA.[48] Hence, there is no substantial difference to the Switzerland-EU GPA.

3.2.3 Mutual Recognition Agreement on Conformity Assessment (MRA)

The Swiss-EU Mutual Recognition Agreement on Conformity Assessment (MRA)[49] regulates the mutual recognition of conformity assessments for industrial products between the contracting parties. The first step is to check by means of conformity assessment whether a product complies with the applicable regulations and can be placed on the (respective) market. The MRA ensures that the necessary certification and approval procedures only have to be carried out once and are recognised in the other market. This gives Swiss producers in 20 product areas equal access to the European Single Market as their competitors within the EU.

With regard to the incorporation of the Switzerland-EU MRA into the CH-UK TA, not all product areas are yet covered. The reason for this was again the unsecured equivalence recognition of the regulations concerned between the EU and the UK at the time of negotiations. Setting up an independent MRA regime only between Switzerland and the UK[50] would have been burdensome.

46 *Ibid.*, p. 2102.

47 Cabinet Office, Requirements for contracts covered by the WTO Government Procurement Agreement and the UK-EU Trade and Co-operation Agreement (Procurement Policy Note, PPN 02/21), para. 5.

48 WTO, UK and Switzerland confirm participation in revised government procurement pact, <www.wto.org/english/news_e/news20_e/gpro_02dec20_e.htm#:~:text=As%20of%201%20January%202021,accord%20in%20its%20own%20right.&text=The%20same%20day%2C%20the%20UK,right%20from%201%20January%202021> (accessed 28 January 2022).

49 MRA (n. 34).

50 One need only recall the Tampere Convention (Agreement of 15 June 1988 between the EFTA States on the Mutual Recognition of Test Results and Evidence of Conformity; AS 1990 1704), which has since been repealed. This was not without a certain complexity; see Federal Council, Report on Foreign Economic Policy 88/1 + 2, Fed. Gaz. 1989 I 321, p. 341, which gives an indication of the time required to agree such rules.

Thus, at the time of writing, the CH-UK MRA covers only three sectors, namely motor vehicles, "good laboratory practice", and "inspection of good manufacturing practice for medicinal products and batch certification". However, the remaining 17 sectors can be added by the Joint Committee at a later stage, or other sectors can also be added to the incorporated MRA.[51] In addition, a new provision on the exchange of information was introduced.[52] This was necessary because this is a kind of triangular relationship, whereby the reference point for the two parties is not mutually agreed standards, but EU law. A problem might arise if one party deviates from the corresponding EU provisions that are covered by the Switzerland-EU MRA. However, this also addresses the question of equivalence, which is then decided by the Joint Committee. If necessary, the relevant legal and administrative provisions must be adapted.[53]

3.2.4 Agreement on Agriculture and Exchange of Letters

The Switzerland-EU Agreement on Agriculture[54] aims to facilitate trade in agricultural products between the parties. Similar to the 1972 FTA, this is achieved through the dismantling of tariff and non-tariff trade barriers with regard to certain product categories.[55] The dismantling of tariff barriers to trade mainly concerns the complete liberalisation of cheese and reciprocal tariff concessions for other products such as fruit, vegetables and meat. The dismantling of non-tariff barriers to trade leads to the mutual recognition of technical regulations in areas such as plant health, animal feed, seeds, organic farming, etc. In addition, a "common veterinary area" is created between Switzerland and the EU.[56] It allows the abolition of mutual veterinary border controls. Also of some importance is the protection of geographical indications for food and agricultural products from Switzerland and the EU.[57]

The incorporation of the Switzerland-EU Agreement on Agriculture into the CH-UK TA is similar to that of the FTA 1972. Because certain areas (annexes), such as that concerning the "common veterinary area", but also plant protection, animal feed, etc., originate from the harmonised area of EU law, these could not be declared applicable at the time of negotiations. It will be the Joint

51 Annex 3 nr 1 CH-UK TA.
52 Annex 3 nr 2 CH-UK TA.
53 (Swiss) Explanatory Memorandum on the CH-UK TA (n. 12), p. 2103.
54 Agricultural Agreement (n. 34).
55 (Swiss) Explanatory Memorandum on the CH-UK TA (n. 12), p. 2092.
56 Annex 11 to the Agricultural Agreement.
57 *Ibid.*

Committee's responsibility to find an agreement on these issues in one of its next meetings. Therefore, at the time of writing, only the annexes on customs concessions, trade in wine products, designations in the spirits, fruit and vegetables sector and designations of origin are considered applicable.[58]

In 1995, an Exchange of Letters concerning certain agricultural and fishery products was added.[59] This exchange of letters refers to concessions or declarations of intent in connection with agricultural goods that were attached to the 1972 FTA. With one exception, these are no longer relevant in trade between Switzerland and the EU or have been replaced by new provisions in the Switzerland-EU Agricultural Agreement. This exception concerns an EU concession to Switzerland for freshwater fish.[60] Its transfer to the relationship between Switzerland and the UK did not require any adjustments.

3.2.5 Exchange of Letters on the Generalized System of Preferences

Switzerland, Norway (recently also Turkey)[61] and the EU apply similar rules of origin based on common general principles.[62] Based on the exchange of letters on the Generalised System of Preferences (GSP)[63] for the benefit of developing countries, tariff preferences (up to full exemption from customs duties) for the beneficiary countries can be maintained[64] and the rules of origin can (continue to) be recognised after goods have been handled or subsequently

58 (Swiss) Explanatory Memorandum on the CH-UK TA (n. 12), p. 2104 et seq.

59 Agreement in the form of an Exchange of Letters between the Swiss Confederation and the European Community concerning certain agricultural and fishery products (OJ 1995, L 327/29).

60 (Swiss) Explanatory Memorandum on the CH-UK TA (n. 12), p. 2090.

61 Notice from the Commission pursuant to Article 85 of Regulation (EEC) No 2454/93, implementing the provisions of the Community Customs Code – Generalised System of Preferences (GSP) rules of origin – Extension to Turkey of the bilateral cumulation system established by that article (OJ 2016, C 134/1).

62 See above, at 3.2.1.

63 Agreement in the form of an Exchange of Letters between the European Union and the Kingdom of Norway on the cumulation of origin between the European Union, the Swiss Confederation, the Kingdom of Norway and the Republic of Turkey in the framework of the Generalised System of Preferences (OJ 2019, L 24/3).

64 The Generalised Scheme of Preferences (GSP) is an instrument of the European Union's trade policy to promote developing countries. The aim is to grant tariff preferences to developing countries vis-à-vis industrialised countries, thereby facilitating their exports' access to the Community market. The legal basis is Regulation (EU) No 978/2012 of the European Parliament and of the Council of 25 October 2012 applying a scheme of generalised tariff preferences and repealing Council Regulation (EC) No 732/2008 (OJ 2012, L 303/1).

processed. In this context, materials from the three countries are also treated as such from the EU when processed in one of the beneficiary countries.

This practice is to be continued between Switzerland and the UK. In order to ensure its continuity in their relationship, the references to the trilateral context (EU-Norway-Switzerland) in the Incorporated Exchange of Letters (previous version from 2000)[65] had to be amended to include the UK.[66] This is a question of mutual recognition of the respective preferential rules of Switzerland, the UK, the EU and Norway in the specific context of the origin of goods in certain developing countries. It can therefore be assumed that the extension of the exchange of letters between the EU and Switzerland and Norway to include Turkey will lead to the latter also being included in the incorporated exchange of letters between Switzerland and the UK. In the present author's view, however, this is at the discretion of both parties and is not mandatory.

3.2.6 Anti-Fraud Agreement

The Anti-Fraud Agreement[67] improves cooperation between Switzerland and the EU and its Member States in combating offences in the area of indirect taxation. This includes smuggling, customs duty, value added tax and excise duty fraud as well as fraud in the area of subsidies and public procurement. The agreement covers both administrative and mutual assistance.[68]

The Anti-Fraud Agreement will be transferred largely unchanged into the trade agreement between Switzerland and the UK. There is, however, a provision that excludes Article 47 of the Anti-Fraud Agreement which refers to new EU Member States adhering to it. Equally, Ad Article 25(2) (reference to the Schengen *acquis*) and Ad Article 43 (reference to EU territories) of the "Agreed Minute" shall not apply.[69] This makes perfect sense as the *incorporated* Anti-Fraud agreement only applies between the two parties of the CH-UK TA.

65 Agreement in the form of an Exchange of Letters between the Community and each of the EFTA countries that grants tariff preferences under the GSP (Norway and Switzerland), providing that goods originating in Norway or Switzerland shall be treated on their arrival on the customs territory of the Community as goods with content of Community origin (reciprocal agreement) (OJ 2001, L 38/25).

66 Annex 5 nr 2 CH-UK TA.

67 Agreement on cooperation between the European Community and its Member States and the Swiss Confederation to counter fraud and all other illegal activities affecting their financial interests (OJ 2009, L 46/8).

68 (Swiss) Explanatory Memorandum on the CH-UK TA (n. 12), p. 2094.

69 Annex 6 nr 3 to the CH-UK TA referring to the Agreed Minute of the negotiations on the cooperation agreement between the European Community and its member states, of the

3.2.7 Agreement on Customs Facilitation and Customs Security

The Agreement on Customs Facilitation and Customs Security[70] forms the basis for controls and formalities in trade in goods as well as cooperation in the area of customs security between Switzerland and the EU. In the cross-border movement of goods, mutual border controls and formalities are simplified, above all, through the mutual recognition of the equivalence of controls and documents. In matters of customs security, Switzerland is basically treated the same as an EU Member State. The Agreement prevents Switzerland from being treated as a third country in this area if the EU enacts measures concerning third countries, such as the prior notification requirement for imports.[71] In this case, too, there is a problem of applicability due to the lack of contractually regulated harmonisation between the UK and the EU. For this reason, this agreement remains provisionally inapplicable in *toto*. It is again up to the Joint Committee to decide on its entry into force at a later date, if necessary with adjustments.[72]

3.3 *Memorandum of Understanding (MoU) on the Future Relationship*

With a view to the future development and deepening of the relationship between Switzerland and the UK, the Trade Agreement is supplemented by a Memorandum of Understanding (MoU) between the (Swiss) State Secretariat for Economic Affairs (SECO) and the (UK) Department of International Trade (DIT).[73] In this MoU, the parties declare, among other things, to examine how the annexes to the Incorporated Agreements, in particular those of the above-mentioned MRA and the Agriculture Agreement with regard to the

---

one part, and the Swiss Confederation, of the other part, to combat fraud and any other illegal activity to the detriment of their financial interests ("the Agreed Minute").

70 Agreement between the European Community and the Swiss Confederation on the simplification of inspections and formalities in respect of the carriage of goods and on customs security measures (OJ 2009, L 199/24).

71 See Regulation (EU) No 952/2013 of the European Parliament and of the Council laying down the Union Customs Code (OJ 2013, L 269/1), amended by: Regulation (EU) 2016/2339 of the European Parliament and of the Council (OJ 2016, L 354/32); Regulation (EU) 2019/474 of the European Parliament and of the Council (OJ 2019, L 83/38) and Regulation (EU) 2019/632 of the European Parliament and of the Council (OJ 2019, L 111/54).

72 Article 1(2)(c) CH-UK TA.

73 Memorandum of Understanding between the Department for International Trade of the United Kingdom of Great Britain and Northern Ireland and the State Secretariat for Economic Affairs of the Swiss Confederation, [14 December 2018], <assets.publishing.service.gov.uk/government/uploads/system/uploads/attachment_data/file/803719/memorandum-of-understanding-between-the-uk-and-switzerland.pdf> (accessed 12 January 2022).

provisionally inapplicable areas, as well as the Customs Security Agreement, which is, at the time of writing, still inapplicable in its entirety, can be activated. Furthermore, the mutual recognition of certification bodies is to take place with the entry into force of the future agreement between the UK and the EU.

More importantly, the parties also agree to hold exploratory talks with a view to replacing or adapting, as necessary, the UK-Switzerland trade agreement. In addition, the parties are considering expanding their future bilateral relationship by including provisions on additional areas such as *trade facilitation*, trade in services, protection of intellectual property rights, labour, environment, trade *remedies* and dispute settlement.[74]

Of particular interest to both Switzerland and the UK is the area of financial services. This area has not yet been covered by a Switzerland-EU agreement. Here, too, the regulation of the relationship between the UK and the EU had first to be awaited, since there is a high degree of harmonisation under EU law and it was, at the time of the negotiations, not clear how the existing passporting rights of British financial service providers, for example, would be transferred into a regime of equivalence recognition,[75] if at all. However, interest groups in Switzerland and the UK were jointly pushing for corresponding bilateral regulations.[76] Since then, a Joint Statement between Her Majesty's Treasury and the Federal Department of Finance was issued on deepening cooperation in financial services[77] and next steps were discussed between ministers.[78]

3.4 *Additional Agreement Concerning Liechtenstein*

Liechtenstein has been part of the Swiss customs territory since the conclusion of the Customs Treaty between Switzerland and the Principality of Liechtenstein (CT) in 1923.[79] According to Article 8 CT, the Principality of Liechtenstein "shall not independently conclude trade or customs treaties with any third state during the period of validity of this treaty".[80] In addition,

74 MoU, para. 5.

75 S. Emmenegger, A. Bigler, 'Fortress Europe: Die Äquivalenzverfahren der EU im Bereich der Finanzdienstleistungen', *Schweizerische Zeitschrift für Wirtschafts- und Finanzmarktrecht/ Revue suisse de droit des affaires et du marché financier/Swiss Review of Business and Financial Market Law* 2019, p. 155.

76 TheCityUK/economiesuisse (n. 11).

77 See n. 22.

78 Federal Department of Finance, Switzerland and United Kingdom deepen relationship in financial sector (Press release, 27 January 2021).

79 Treaty between Switzerland and Liechtenstein on the annexation of the Principality of Liechtenstein to the Swiss customs territory [1923], SR 0.631.112.514.

80 Article 8(1) CT (translation by author from German).

the Principality of Liechtenstein "authorises the Swiss Confederation to represent it in negotiations with third states on the conclusion of trade and customs treaties, which take place during the period of validity of the present treaty and to conclude these treaties with effect for the Principality".[81] Since doubts had already arisen in the course of the last century as to whether the original scope of application of the CT also covered more recent trade-related agreements that went beyond pure trade in goods, Liechtenstein representatives were included in the Swiss negotiating delegations in each case and Liechtenstein became an independent contracting partner, insofar as such agreements had effect on Liechtenstein.[82] If Switzerland is not also a contracting party or Member State, as in the case of the EEA Agreement, "the membership of the Principality of Liechtenstein requires a special agreement between the Swiss Confederation and the Principality of Liechtenstein".[83]

Although Liechtenstein had only become a Member State of EFTA in its own right in 1990, the country was already part of the EFTA free trade area on the basis of the Customs Treaty by means of a protocol to the EFTA Convention. Subsequently, Liechtenstein became part of the Switzerland-EU free trade area in 1972 on the basis of an additional agreement to the FTA 1972. Liechtenstein also joined the Switzerland-EU Agricultural Agreement by means of an additional agreement. With the trilateral supplementary agreement Switzerland – Liechtenstein – UK, the provisions of the two trilateral supplementary agreements Switzerland-Liechtenstein-EU to the FTA 1972[84] and to the Agricultural Agreement[85] are continued in the relationship with the UK.

It should only be briefly mentioned that on this basis, the provisions of the FTA 1972 and the Agreement on Agriculture, "as incorporated and amended by the Switzerland – UK Trade Agreement",[86] are also applicable

81 Article 8(2) CT (translation by author from German).

82 This was already the case with the Additional Agreement concerning the validity, for the Principality of Liechtenstein, of the Agreement between the European Economic Community and the Swiss Confederation (OJ 1972, L 300/281); Federal Council, Explanatory Memorandum on the approval of the agreements between Switzerland and the European Communities, Fed. Gaz.1972 II 653, p. 712.

83 Article 8bis(2) CT.

84 Additional Agreement 1972 (n. 8).

85 Additional Agreement between the European Community, the Swiss Confederation and the Principality of Liechtenstein extending to the Principality of Liechtenstein the Agreement between the European Community and the Swiss Confederation on trade in agricultural products (OJ 2007, L 270/6).

86 Article 1(1) Additional Agreement between the Swiss Confederation, the United Kingdom of Great Britain and Northern Ireland and the Principality of Liechtenstein (n. 8).

to Liechtenstein.[87] Liechtenstein may participate in any application and further development of the provisions concerning Liechtenstein in the relevant joint committees and in their working groups.[88] An annex to the Agricultural Additional Agreement lists the names and designations specifically protected for Liechtenstein, which are taken over from the Switzerland-Liechtenstein-EU Additional Agreement to the Agricultural Agreement, and are continued in relations with the UK. Furthermore, the territory of Liechtenstein is also covered by the Joint Declaration on Rules of Origin.

4 Other Agreements

For the overall package of agreements between Switzerland and the UK concerning their trade relations after the latter definitely left the EU, further agreements had to be added. On the one hand, these are essentially adapted copies of the bilateral agreements between Switzerland and the EU that were already in force between the two countries when the UK was an EU member state. On the other hand, these are multilateral agreements that existed before Brexit as agreements between the EU, certain candidate countries as well as the EFTA States. The UK is still in the process of joining some of these agreements as a separate party. However, as will be shown, this is not as straightforward as the UK Government may have hoped.

4.1 *"Bilateral Agreements"*

4.1.1 Road Transport Agreement

The Agreement on the International Carriage of Goods and Passengers by Road between Switzerland and the UK, which was signed on 25 January 2019, is based on the existing Land Transport Agreement between Switzerland and the EU.[89] Based on this agreement, the provisions of the land transport agreement between the EU and Switzerland will essentially continue to apply between the two States even after EU law no longer applies to the UK.

The agreement contains provisions on the transport of passengers and goods; taxation and customs formalities; the application of national laws and regulations as well as infringements and special permits for oversized vehicles. As in the Land Transport Agreement between Switzerland and the EU, the

87 Article 1 Additional Agreement.

88 Article 2 Additional Agreement.

89 Agreement between the Swiss Confederation and the European Community on the Carriage of Goods and Passengers by Rail and Road (OJ 2002, L 114/91).

right to cabotage (transport of goods and passengers within the other state) is excluded. However, due to the geographical situation, the practical implementation of this agreement was dependent on the EU granting the corresponding transit rights, as land transport between Switzerland and the UK is only possible via EU countries. The Switzerland-UK Agreement was also extended to Liechtenstein and Gibraltar and may be further extended by exchange of notes to the Crown Dependencies or other territories for whose international relations the UK is responsible.

4.1.2 Air Transport Agreement

The purpose of this agreement is to allow the Air Transport Agreement between Switzerland and the EU to continue seamlessly as well.[90] It ensures the continuity of the rights of the air carriers of both States conferred by the Switzerland-EU Air Transport Agreement after that agreement ceased to apply to the UK. The Switzerland-UK agreement differs only slightly in content from the current agreement between the EU and Switzerland. Instead of a partial reference to EU institutions, a Joint Committee is foreseen for the management of the agreement.[91]

4.1.3 Direct Insurance Agreement

The Direct Insurance Agreement between Switzerland and the UK also serves primarily to maintain the effects of the Direct Insurance Agreement between Switzerland and the EU[92] between the two States. Therefore, only technical amendments have been made to the agreement between the UK and Switzerland to the extent that these are necessary to make the agreement functional in a bilateral context. The only significant change is the conversion of the currency references from Euro to Pound Sterling.

The agreement between the EU and Switzerland grants mutual branching rights and equal freedom of establishment to companies offering direct insurance other than life insurance, based on mutual recognition of equivalent prudential standards for insurance. By mutually recognising the solvency requirements of each of the two jurisdictions, the Switzerland-UK agreement

---

90 Agreement between the Swiss Confederation and the European Community on Air Transport (OJ 2002, L 114/73).

91 Foreign- and Commonwealth Office, Agreement between the United Kingdom of Great Britain and Northern Ireland and The Swiss Confederation relating to scheduled Air Services, Explanatory Memorandum (CP 25, CS Swiss 2.2019), para. 4.

92 Agreement between the Swiss Confederation and the European Economic Community on direct insurance other than life assurance (OJ 1991, L 205/44).

allows companies to establish branches across borders based on the rules of their home state. This improves market access and makes it easier for companies to operate in both States. The agreement is also accompanied by a joint declaration of compatibility, which reflects Article 2 of Decision No. 11/2018 of the EU-Switzerland Joint Committee of 3 July 2018 amending the Annexes and Protocols to the Switzerland-EU Direct Insurance Agreement. This states that the relevant domestic legislation of both Parties is compatible with the UK-Switzerland Agreement.[93]

This agreement thus also attempts to create an internal market-like legal situation on the basis of mutual recognition outside of a harmonised system in the area of financial services.[94]

4.1.4 Citizens' Rights Agreement

With this agreement,[95] the rights acquired by Swiss nationals in the UK and by UK nationals in Switzerland on the basis of the Agreement on the Free Movement of Persons between Switzerland and the EU (AFMP)[96] remain secure even after the end of the applicability of EU law to the UK. This concerns, *inter alia*, entry and exit, residence, equal treatment on the employment market, social security and the recognition of professional qualifications. Furthermore, the provision of cross-border services for 90 days a year remains permissible for a further five years. The prerequisite is that there is a written contract that was concluded before the end of the transitional period and that the work also began before then. Extensions of the above-mentioned period by decision of the Joint Committee are possible.

93 Decision of the Contracting Parties relating to the Agreement between the Swiss Confederation and the United Kingdom of Great Britain and Northern Ireland concerning direct insurance other than life assurance of 25 January 2019, <www.sif.admin.ch/sif/de/home/bilateral/europa/vereinigtes-koenigreich-uk-.html> (accessed 25 May 2022).

94 TheCityUK/economiesuisse (n. 11).

95 Agreement between the Swiss Confederation and the United Kingdom of Great Britain and Northern Ireland on the rights of citizens resulting from the withdrawal of the United Kingdom from the European Union and the termination of the Agreement on the Free Movement of Persons, <https://www.gov.uk/government/publications/cs-switzerland-no52019-ukswitzerland-agreement-on-citizens-rights-following-withdrawal-of-uk-from-the-eu-and-free-movement-of-persons-agreement> (accessed 3 April 2022).

96 Agreement between the Swiss Confederation, of the one part, and the European Community and its Member States, of the other, on the Free Movement of Persons (OJ 2002, L 114/6).

This agreement also contains a reference to the annexes of the Switzerland-EU, which are to apply *mutatis mutandis*. Therefore, any reference to "Member State" in the EU Directives referred to therein only means Switzerland and the UK. This is to ensure that service providers must be established either in Switzerland or in the UK in order to exercise their profession.[97]

Just for the sake of completeness, the transitional agreement on admission to the labour market[98] should be mentioned as well. It is an example of the will of both Switzerland and the UK not to let the problems stemming from the UK's exit from the EU damage the existing rights of their mutual citizens. It was concluded with the aim to enter into force in the event of a *"no deal"* regarding a withdrawal agreement between the UK and the EU. However, since the UK's withdrawal did happen on 31 January 2020 and the respective issues were addressed therein, this transitional agreement never entered into force.[99]

4.1.5 Agreement (Convention) On Social Security

There was another transitional agreement, namely on social security.[100] It was also geared toward the case that the UK would have left the EU without a withdrawal agreement. As is known, this did not happen and this agreement therefore did not enter into force either.

On 9 September 2021, Switzerland and the UK concluded a new social security agreement which is intended to ensure the long-term coordination of the social security systems of the two States after the UK's withdrawal from the

97 Article 23.4 Citizens' Rights Agreement (n. 96).

98 Agreement on admission to the labour market for a temporary transitional period following the UK's withdrawal from the EU and the Agreement on the free movement of persons, <https://www.ejpd.admin.ch/dam/data/ejpd/aktuell/news/2019/2019-07-10/abkommen-d.pdf> (accessed 15 May 2022).

99 Federal Department of Justice and Police/State Secretariat for Migration (SEM), Agreement between the Swiss Confederation and the United Kingdom of Great Britain and Northern Ireland on the Rights of Citizens resulting from the Withdrawal of the United Kingdom from the European Union and the Termination of the Agreement on the Free Movement of Persons (Explanatory Report on the Opening of the Consultation Procedure of 22 March 2019), <www.sem.admin.ch/dam/data/sem/eu/fza/brexit/vn-ber-d.pdf> (accessed 15 May 2022).

100 Agreement on Social Security for a Temporary Period after the United Kingdom's Withdrawal from the EU and the Agreement on the Free Movement of Persons, <www.gov.uk/government/publications/ukswitzerland-transitional-agreement-on-social-security-for-a-temporary-period-following-the-withdrawal-of-the-uk-cs-switzerland-no72019?utm_source=f654fb0e-a675-4108-8a15-75a84fe480f0&utm_medium=email&utm_campaign=govuk-notifications&utm_content=immediate> (accessed 5 May 2022).

EU.[101] The new social security agreement contains the same social security coordination principles as the Switzerland-EU AFMP, such as equal treatment, determination of applicable legislation, aggregation of insurance periods, export of benefits, administrative assistance and cooperation between authorities and institutions. The provisions stemming from the EU social security coordination law (EU Regulations 883/2004[102] and 987/2009)[103] have been slimmed down and tailored to the needs of the two States.

The agreement has been provisionally applicable since 1 November 2021. It will enter into force once ratified by both States' legislators.

4.1.6 Services Mobility Agreement

The Services Mobility Agreement (SMA) between Switzerland and the UK[104] was signed on 14 December 2020 and has been applied provisionally since 1 January 2021. It will apply for two years unless the parties decide to extend it.

The SMA regulates the reciprocal market access and temporary stay of service providers such as architects, management consultants, translators, IT experts and engineers. It ensures mutual facilitated market access for service providers in Switzerland and the UK after the AFMP ceased to apply to the UK. Furthermore, the SMA also contains provisions on the recognition of professional qualifications. The SMA will allow UK professionals to work in Switzerland for up to 90 days without a work permit. In return, Swiss professionals will be able to deliver contracts in the UK in skilled sectors through the Tier 5 International Agreement visa (Government Authorised Exchange), a temporary worker visa category.

The SMA establishes a working group, through which the UK and Switzerland aim to develop a comprehensive agreement on the recognition of professional qualifications for service suppliers working in each other's markets. This will complement the 2019 Switzerland-UK Citizens' Rights Agreement.[105]

101 Convention on Social Security Coordination between the United Kingdom of Great Britain and Northern Ireland and the Swiss Confederation (CS Switzerland No.4/2021, CP 530).

102 Regulation (EC) No 883/2004 of the European Parliament and of the Council of 29 April 2004 on the coordination of social security systems (OJ 2004, L 166/1).

103 Regulation (EC) No 987/2009 of the European Parliament and of the Council of 16 September 2009 laying down the procedure for implementing Regulation (EC) No 883/2004 on the coordination of social security systems (OJ 2009, L 284/1).

104 Temporary Agreement Between the United Kingdom of Great Britain and Northern Ireland and the Swiss Confederation on Services Mobility, <assets.publishing.service.gov.uk/government/uploads/system/uploads/attachment_data/file/947456/uk-swiss-agreement-services-mobility.pdf> (accessed 5 February 2022).

105 See n. 95.

4.1.7 Mutual Recognition Agreement on Authorised Economic Operators

The Switzerland-UK Authorised Economic Operator Mutual Recognition Agreement (AEO MRA)[106] is designed to facilitate trading for businesses from both countries in the other country respectively, and to reduce technical barriers to trade for such companies with AEO status. The purpose of this agreement is to replicate and provide continuity for UK and Swiss AEO businesses that were previously receiving benefits under the EU-Switzerland Customs Security Agreement.[107] The agreement with the UK entered into force on 1 September 2021.

AEO Programmes are based on the Customs-to-Business partnership as set out in the World Custom Organisation's SAFE Framework of Standards,[108] which assists in securing and facilitating global trade. Businesses can apply for AEO safety and security (AEO-S) status. This status is an internationally recognised quality mark with the objective of ensuring the security of the international supply chain. Holding AEO-S status indicates that a business meets internationally recognised security standards, their customs controls and procedures are efficient and compliant, and their role in the international supply chain is secure. Companies with AEO status are considered particularly trustworthy. This is why they enjoy privileges in security-related customs controls and are entitled to simplified customs clearance.

4.1.8 Police Cooperation Agreement

With regard to police cooperation, a Memorandum of Understanding (MoU) was concluded between Switzerland and the UK in 2019. According to this MoU, the two States intend to explore ways to strengthen police cooperation. In particular, threats to public security are to be prevented and all forms of crime, especially serious crime, are to be combated. This is to be achieved by exchanging information at the strategic and operational levels and by maintaining regular contact between the competent authorities. It also signalled

106 Agreement between the United Kingdom of Great Britain and Northern Ireland and the Swiss Confederation on the Mutual Recognition of their Authorised Economic Operator Programmes (CS Switzerland No.3/2021, CP 452).

107 Agreement between the European Community and the Swiss Confederation on the simplification of inspections and formalities in respect of the carriage of goods and on customs security measures (OJ 2009, L 199/24).

108 See <www.wcoomd.org/en/topics/facilitation/instrument-and-tools/frameworks-of-standards/safe_package.aspx#:~:text=WCO%20tools%20to%20secure%20and%20facilitate%20global%20trade,revenue%20collections%20and%20to%20promote%20trade%20facilitation%20worldwide> (accessed 5 February 2022).

the joint intention to explore more formal arrangements to further enhance police cooperation between law enforcement partners in the future, in order to combat shared threats from crime and terrorism.

The Police Cooperation Agreement[109] builds on the MoU by formalising and further intensifying Switzerland-UK arrangements for law enforcement cooperation. It includes rules on cross-border cooperation between the respective police authorities responsible for exchanging information or coordinating operations. Its provisions are primarily aimed at combating serious crime, but apply to all forms of crime, including money laundering and organised crime. This latter aspect is of particular interest given that London, Zurich and Geneva are among the world's largest financial centres that are notoriously affected by these forms of crime.

4.1.9 Further Topics Likely to Lead to Negotiations?

Other topics that are important for cooperation between Switzerland and the UK have not yet been regulated in an agreement, but there is mostly agreement on the mutual attitude. Examples are data protection and financial services.

In the case of data protection, the Swiss Federal Data Protection and Information Commissioner (FDPIC) assumes that the UK will continue to have an adequate level of data protection after its withdrawal from the EU. The UK has also stated that it will continue to recognise the adequacy of the Swiss level of data protection. This means that for the time being, personal data can be exchanged between Switzerland and the UK without any problems.[110]

4.2 *"Multilateral Agreements"*

With its withdrawal from the EU, the UK, as already mentioned, also withdrew from all multilateral agreements to which it had belonged as an EU Member State. Particular mention should be made here of those which had been concluded between the EU and the EFTA States prior to the conclusion of the EEA Agreement within the framework of the European Free Trade Association.[111] In the context of interest here, these include the following areas:

109 Agreement between the United Kingdom of Great Britain and Northern Ireland and the Swiss Confederation on Police Cooperation (CS Switzerland No.1/2021, CP 369).

110 Federal Data Protection and Information Commissioner (FDPIC), What are the consequences of Brexit for cross-border data traffic? (Media release, 31 January 2020), <https://www.edoeb.admin.ch/edoeb/de/home/aktuell/aktuell_news.html#-181656549> (accessed 15 May 2022); FDPIC, *Adequate data protection post-Brexit* (Annual Report 2020/2021), p. 61.

111 See G. Baur, *The European Free Trade Association* (Intersentia, 2020), pp. 123–129.

4.2.1 Formalities in the Movement of Goods

The Convention on Formalities in Trade in Goods[112] establishes measures to simplify formalities in connection with the movement of goods between the EU and the EFTA States, but also between the EFTA States themselves. In particular, a standard form is introduced. In addition to the standard form, additional administrative documents may only be required if the information in the standard form is not sufficient to carry out the procedure, e.g., the declaration for determining the customs value, or if these other documents are provided for in international agreements, e.g., for veterinary and phytosanitary products. The Convention also contains a provision on administrative assistance between the customs administrations of the EFTA States and the EU Member States.

At the end of the transition period following its formal withdrawal from the EU, the UK became a third country again. As such, it may apply to become a Party to this Convention.[113] On 30 January 2019, the UK deposited its instrument of accession. However, accession could only take effect at the end of the transitional period.[114] At the time of writing, the respective Council decision[115] is still pending.

4.2.2 Common Transit Procedure

The Convention on a Common Transit Procedure between the EU and the EFTA States[116] allows the transportation of goods through different States in a simplified form, without having to subject them to successive national customs procedures. Customs supervision is carried out without interruption from the place of departure to the place of destination. This Convention also allows for the accession of third countries.[117] The UK deposited its instrument

---

112 Convention on the simplification of formalities in trade in goods (OJ 1987, L 134/2).

113 Article 11a(1) of the Convention on the Simplification of Formalities in Trade in Goods (n. 112).

114 European Commission – DG Taxud, Note for the attention of the Trade Contact Group on the Accession of the United Kingdom of Great Britain and Northern Ireland to the Convention on a common transit procedure and to the Convention on simplification of formalities in trade in goods (ARES(2019)686599).

115 Proposal for a Council Decision on the position to be taken on behalf of the European Union in the EU-CTC Joint Committee established by the Convention of 20 May 1987 on the simplification of formalities in trade in goods and in the EU-CTC Joint Committee established by the Convention of 20 May 1987 on a common transit procedure as regards an invitation to the United Kingdom to accede to those Conventions, COM(2018) 576 final.

116 Convention between the European Economic Community, the Republic of Austria, the Republic of Finland, the Republic of Iceland, the Kingdom of Norway, the Kingdom of Sweden and the Swiss Confederation, on a common transit procedure (OJ 1987, L 226/2).

117 Article 15a of the Convention on a Common Transit Procedure (n. 116).

of accession at the same time as for the simplified movement formalities. As with the Convention on Formalities in Trade in Goods, the decision on the UK's accession has not been taken at the time of writing.[118]

4.2.3 Standardisation

In order to be able to offer goods across borders and qualify under mutual recognition agreements, these goods must comply with certain norms or standards. The development of such standards is carried out by recognised European standardisation bodies. The most important are CEN (European Committee for Standardisation), CENELEC (European Committee for Electrotechnical Standardisation) and ETSI (European Telecommunications Standards Institute). On 25 November 2021, the CEN and CENELEC General Assemblies confirmed the British Standards Institution's (BSI) continued membership of the two associations from 1 January 2022. BSI will also continue to be a member of ETSI.[119]

4.2.4 Enforcement and Recognition of Judgments

The recognition and enforcement of civil judgments is of great importance in economic life and trade relations. The UK, and London in particular, as a venue for court and arbitration proceedings in international commercial and financial matters, is particularly dependent on a functioning network of agreements that enable the recognition and enforcement of judgments and decisions of arbitral tribunals. In the European legal area, the relevant EU Regulation 1215/2012[120] between the EU Member States and the Lugano Convention (LC)[121] between the EU Member States and the three EFTA States Iceland, Norway and Switzerland are relevant. With its withdrawal from the EU, the Regulation and the Convention will no longer be applicable to the UK.

As a third country, the LC is open to accession by the UK once it is no longer subject to EU law. In this case, accession requires the unanimous consent of all contracting parties. The UK has applied for accession to the LC and has

118 See n. 112.

119 See <www.bsigroup.com/en-GB/about-bsi/uk-national-standards-body/standards-and-eu-exit/#725209> (accessed 5 February 2022).

120 Regulation (EU) No 1215/2012 of the European Parliament and of the Council of 12 December 2012 on jurisdiction and the recognition and enforcement of judgments in civil and commercial matters (OJ 2012, L 351/1).

121 Convention on jurisdiction and the recognition and enforcement of judgments in civil and commercial matters (OJ 2007, L 339/3).

been supported by Iceland, Norway and Switzerland.[122] However, at the time of writing, resistance is emerging on the part of the EU: the EU Commission has informed the EU Member States that a decision in favour of the British application would not be in the EU's interest and has thus communicated to the depositary state (Switzerland) that it "is not in a position to give its consent to invite the UK to accede to the Lugano Convention".[123] The Commission's argument has been that the Lugano Convention was a "flanking measure for the EU's economic relations with the EFTA/EEA countries" and thus linked to participation in the internal market.[124] The Commission's position, particularly the alleged link to the internal market, has been heavily criticised.[125]

4.2.5 Statistics

Another area that falls into the category of "multilateral agreements" is that of statistics. The EFTA States cooperate very closely with Eurostat, the EU statistical authority, and have a service of the EFTA Secretariat[126] in the same offices in Luxembourg. While the three EEA EFTA States have the EEA Agreement as their legal basis, in the case of Switzerland, this is the Statistics Agreement between Switzerland and the EU.[127] At the time of writing, it still seems unclear whether the UK, as a third country, will participate in the European statistical system. The EU-UK TCA contains a declaration of intent in its Article 730, according to which:

> EUROSTAT and the United Kingdom Statistics Authority may establish an arrangement that enables cooperation on relevant statistical matters and includes that EUROSTAT, with the agreement of the United Kingdom

---

122 Ministry of Justice, Support for the UK's intent to accede to the Lugano Convention 2007, <www.gov.uk/government/news/support-for-the-uks-intent-to-accede-to-the-lugano-convention-2007> (accessed 6 February 2022).

123 See <www.eda.admin.ch/dam/eda/fr/documents/aussenpolitik/voelkerrecht/autres-conventions/Lugano2/20210701-LUG-ann-EU.pdf> (accessed 5 February 2022).

124 Communication from the Commission to the European Parliament and the Council. Assessment on the application of the United Kingdom of Great Britain and Northern Ireland to accede to the 2007 Lugano Convention, COM(2021) 222 final, p. 2.

125 See C. Kohler, 'Ein europäischer Justizraum in Zivilsachen ohne das Vereinigte Königreich?', *Zeitschrift für Europäisches Privatrecht* 29 (2021), p. 784, and C. Tobler, 'Finally Brexit – Alternative Modelle der EU-Integration: von Modellen und Bausteinen', in J. Sild (ed.), *Potentiale und Grenzen europäischer Integration. Tagungsband des 20. Österreichischen Europarechtstages 2021 in Liechtenstein* (Jan Sramek Verlag, 2022) p. 135-158; 155-157.

126 EFTA Statistical Office (ESO).

127 Agreement between the Swiss Confederation and the European Community on cooperation in the field of statistics (OJ 2006, L 90/2).

Statistics Authority, provides statistical data on the United Kingdom for the purposes of this Part, including, in particular, data on the GDP of the United Kingdom.

However, at the time of writing this text, such an agreement has not been concluded.

5 Questions of Interpretation

The system of the Switzerland-UK Framework Agreement has the effect that the relevant (bilateral/sectoral) agreements between Switzerland and the EU are "incorporated" into it by reference,[128] i.e., any amendments are either contained in the Trade Agreement itself[129] or will be decided by the Joint Committee.[130]

In addition to that, the incorporated agreements are to be applied "*mutatis mutandis*", "subject to the provisions of this instrument". This is not the place for lengthy methodological discussions and much would naturally have to remain as speculation as there is little practice yet to gain any insight from. Nevertheless, a few remarks are in order. Application *mutatis mutandis* is defined as application "with the technical adjustments necessary to enable the Switzerland-EU Trade Agreements to be applied as if they had been concluded between the Parties, taking into account the object and purpose of this Agreement".[131]

However, it is not just a simple change of parties. It is also the *character* of the agreements that may change. This is particularly evident where the agreements between Switzerland and the EU refer to a harmonised (EU) legal framework, such as the MRA, which in certain cases, such as the Air Transport Agreement, may also involve competences of EU institutions. In contrast, the aim of, for example, the Trade Agreement between Switzerland and the UK is "to maintain the existing trade relations between the contracting parties in accordance

---

128 Article 1(1)(a)-(h) CH-UK TA.

129 Article 1(2) CH-UK TA.

130 Article 1(3) CH-UK TA.

131 Article 2(1)(a) CH-UK TA; see C. Tobler (n. 125) p. 146; on the "as if" form of thinking in law, see G. Baur, 'Kohärente Interpretationsmethode als Instrument europarechtskonformer Rechtsanwendung – eine rechtspolitische Skizze', in Liechtenstein-Institut (ed.), *Festschrift 25 Jahre Liechtenstein-Institut (1986–2011)* (Liechtensteinische Akademische Gesellschaft, 2011), p. 54 with further references.

with the Switzerland-EU trade agreements and to provide a platform for further trade liberalisation and the further development of trade relations between them".[132] In questions of interpretation, it is therefore also a matter of taking into account the different objectives of the agreements, namely partial participation in the EU internal market, in the one case, and a purely intergovernmental relationship, based on a "free trade logic", in the other.

The differences in interpretation that can arise in the case of different objectives, despite the same or similar wording of an agreement provision, are shown by the controversy over the interpretation of the 1972 FTA between the Swiss Federal Supreme Court and the CJEU. After the decision in *Adams*,[133] in which it had rejected the direct effect of provisions of the FTA 1972, the Federal Supreme Court in 1979 held in *OMO*:[134]

> It should be noted from the history of the FTA that it is purely a trade agreement which, unlike the EEC Treaty, does not aim to create a single internal market with a supranational competition regime, but merely a free trade area. Moreover, it is essentially limited to industrial free trade. In its negotiation, not only was an obligation for mutual harmonisation of Community and Swiss legal norms deliberately excluded; the existing legal systems and their unrestricted autonomous enforcement were rather mutually reserved (BGE 104 IV 179 E. c with references to official opinions). The agreement also does not provide for a body which, like the European Court of Justice as an institution of the EEC, could determine the direct applicability of individual norms in a binding manner for the contracting parties. It makes do with a Joint Committee, which is responsible for the proper fulfilment of the agreement, but can only make recommendations (Article 29 FTA). These differences must also be taken into account when interpreting individual provisions (...). These differences must also be taken into account when interpreting individual provisions, which is why, contrary to the objections of the defendant, it is not appropriate to adopt the case law of the European Court of Justice on analogous provisions of the EEC Treaty unseen. (...) Moreover, the provisions of Article 13 [FTA 1972] are addressed to the Swiss legislature and to the administration. It is not to be inferred from them that they

132 Article 3 CH-UK TA.

133 Swiss Federal Supreme Court, decision BGE 104 IV 175 (2 May 1978).

134 Swiss Federal Supreme Court, decision BGE 105 II 49 (25 January 1979), cons. 3.a) (translation by author from German).

> would establish rights and obligations which the Swiss judge would have to observe in a decision on a civil law dispute.

This case law was confirmed by the Federal Supreme Court in *Physiogel* more than 25 years later.[135] The case was about imported products which were advertised as having a healing effect. These products were not registered as medicinal products and were therefore considered as cosmetics. For cosmetics, however, promotions of any kind that would indicate illness-healing, soothing or preventing effects were prohibited. Promotions such as "in collaboration with dermatologists", "for itchy skin prone to allergies" or "for care for neurodermatitis, diabetes, psoriasis" contradicted the provisions of food legislation. Hence, imports were forbidden by the competent administrative body and ultimately confirmed by the Swiss Federal Supreme Court. The latter reverted to the argument that what is today Article 34 TFEU, although essentially identical in wording with Article 13 FTA 1972, could not be interpreted in the same way as the objectives of the two treaties were different. Furthermore, Switzerland had not agreed to directly apply the Cassis de Dijon principle, nor was there (at the time) anything in internal legislation to that effect.

The CJEU picked up the ball after the Federal Supreme Court's decision in *OMO* (and a similar decision by the Austrian Supreme Court)[136] and ruled in *Polydor* concerning the interpretation of the 1972 FTA in the relationship between the then EEC and the then EFTA State Portugal:[137]

> However, such similarity of terms is not a sufficient reason for transposing to the provisions of the Agreement the above-mentioned case-law, which determines in the context of the Community the relationship between the protection of industrial and commercial property rights and the rules on the free movement of goods.. (…) The scope of that case-law must indeed be determined in the light of the Community's objectives and activities as defined by Articles 2 and 3 of the EEC Treaty. As the Court has had occasion to emphasize in various contexts, the Treaty, by establishing a common market and progressively approximating the economic policies of the Member States, seeks to unite national markets into a single market having the characteristics of a domestic market.
>
> [This does] not apply in the context of the relations between the Community and Portugal as defined by the Agreement. It is apparent

135 Swiss Federal Supreme Court, decision 2A.593/2005 *Physiogel* (6 June 2006).

136 Austrian Supreme Court, OGH 4 Ob 340/78, *Austro-Mechana*, ÖBl 1980, 25.

137 CJEU, Case 270/80, *Polydor*, EU:C:1982:43, paras. 15, 16 and 18.

> from an examination of the Agreement that (...) it does not have the same purpose as the EEC Treaty, inasmuch as the latter, as has been stated above, seeks to create a single market reproducing as closely as possible the conditions of a domestic market.

In the *Kupferberg* case[138] the CJEU then ruled that in the EU context, Community agreements, upon their entry into force, are considered to be an "integral part of the Community legal system" and thus directly applicable and take precedence over the legislative measures of the Community institutions and the Member States. This means that individuals in the EU, and in contrast to the EFTA States, can very well directly refer to provisions in agreements concluded by the EU.

The CJEU remained faithful to the above-mentioned *Polydor* decision in its subsequent case law on the bilateral agreements[139] in relation to Switzerland.[140]

Looking at the agreements between Switzerland and the UK, all this, together with the agreed amendments, will have to be taken into account in an interpretation in good faith, whether this is explicitly stated in the agreement[141] or applies implicitly in accordance with Article 31 Vienna Convention on the Law of Treaties (VCLC).

6 Relationship between the UK and the EFTA States other than Switzerland

6.1 *Separation Agreement*

With Brexit accomplished, the UK has not only left the EU, but also the European Economic Area (EEA). For almost 25 years, that agreement was the basis for economic relations between Iceland, Liechtenstein, Norway (EEA EFTA States) and the UK. Based on the EEA Agreement,[142] the EEA EFTA States' citizens have numerous rights that they can invoke equally in all EU States and which they risked to lose once Brexit happened. Conversely, citizens from

138 CJEU, Case 104/81, *Kupferberg*, EU:C:1982:362.

139 E.g., CJEU, Cases C-351/08, *Grimme*, EU:C:2009:697, C-547/10, *Switzerland v Commission*, EU:C:2013:139.

140 See in detail C. Tobler, 'Die EuGH-Entscheidung Grimme: die Wiederkehr von *Polydor* und die Grenze des bilateralen Rechts', in A. Epiney, N. Gammenthaler (eds.), *Schweizerisches Jahrbuch für Europarecht 2009/2010* (Stämpfli/Schulthess, 2010), p. 369. See also the contribution by P. Van Elsuwege in this volume.

141 Article 4(a) Citizens' Rights Agreement (n. 95).

142 Agreement on the European Economic Area (OJ 1994, L 1/3).

the UK had acquired numerous rights when the UK was still part of the EEA. These acquired rights had to be secured so that Brexit would not have a negative impact on life decisions that have already been made. The withdrawal agreement between the EEA EFTA States and the UK (also known as "EEA Separation Agreement")[143] ensures that EEA EFTA nationals already living in the UK or British nationals living in Iceland, Liechtenstein or Norway will keep their acquired rights. In addition to the right of residence, this also includes social security entitlements, market access rights and the recognition of professional qualifications. As Norway, Iceland and Liechtenstein – contrary to Switzerland – are fully part of the internal market, the separation agreement in addition to citizens' rights also deals with other issues arising from the UK's exit from the EU, such as data protection, intellectual property, goods already placed on the market and public procurement. For all of these issues, it is essentially foreseen that rights acquired before the end of the transition period will continue to be protected or that proceedings still ongoing at the end of the transition period will be terminated under the same provisions under which they were commenced. The Separation Agreement only applies to situations that existed before or on 31 December 2020. It does not regulate future relations with the UK.

6.2 *Free Trade Agreement between Iceland, Liechtenstein, Norway and the UK*

The three EEA EFTA States and the UK concluded a Free Trade Agreement (EEA EFTA-UK FTA), which was signed in London on 8 July 2021.[144] It covers cross-border trade in services, including financial services, as well as areas such as investment, intellectual property protection, digital trade, capital movements and public procurement. The EEA EFTA-UK FTA, like the TCA, essentially is a classical FTA,[145] albeit a very comprehensive one. In terms of content and structure, it is modelled on the TCA between the EU and the UK, but it also resembles many FTAs concluded by the EFTA States with third countries. The

143 Agreement on arrangements between Iceland, the Principality of Liechtenstein, the Kingdom of Norway and the United Kingdom of Great Britain and Northern Ireland following the withdrawal of the United Kingdom from the European Union, the EEA Agreement and other agreements applicable between the United Kingdom and the EEA EFTA States by virtue of the United Kingdom's membership of the European Union (4 November 2019), <www.gov.uk/government/publications/eea-efta-separation-agreement-and-explainer> (accessed 15 February 2022).

144 See n. 19.

145 G. Baur (n. 111), p. 2.

agreement is expected to enter into force in the beginning of 2022, depending on ratification procedures in the countries involved.[146]

As a consequence of the conclusion of the Additional Agreement between Switzerland, the UK and Liechtenstein, the goods part of the EEA EFTA-UK FTA is not applicable to Liechtenstein. This also applies to areas such as patents, as there is a joint patents area between Switzerland and Liechtenstein. A precise delimitation may at times be difficult. Therefore, the Agreement(s) by which Liechtenstein participates in the economic relation between Switzerland and the UK shall prevail "in case of any inconsistencies".[147]

It is important to emphasise, that in the EEA EFTA-UK FTA, there is nothing left of an "internal market logic".[148] An example of where the new economic relationship falls short of the legal framework as it exists in the EEA is the chapter on financial services. These are covered in Articles 3.44 to 3.54 of the EEA EFTA-UK FTA. Contrary to the harmonised rules in the EEA, these are rather standard rules as can be found in many FTAs. For example, financial intermediaries do not have general access through "passports" anymore but they depend on equivalence decisions for their market access in either market. Hence, respective EU equivalence decisions are applied in the EEA EFTA States via the EEA Agreement. Conversely, the UK, for its part, has already issued several unilateral equivalence decisions, e.g., according to Article 2a of the European Market Infrastructure Regulation (EMIR).[149]

7 Outlook

It seems that Switzerland and the UK so far managed to transfer most of their agreements which they had under the Switzerland-EU regime into a purely

146 Liechtenstein Government, <www.llv.li/inhalt/118946/amtsstellen/zukunftige-beziehungen-mit-uk> (accessed 15 June 2022).

147 Article 1.4(2) EEA EFTA-UK FTA.

148 On the difference between FTA- and internal market logic see P. Eeckhout, *Future relations between the EU and the UK: options after Brexit* (European Parliament, 2018), p. 6; G. Baur, 'Privileged partnerships: The partner countries' (institutional) perspectives', in S. Gstöhl, D. Phinnemore (eds.), *The European Union, its neighbours, and the proliferation of 'privileged partnerships'* (Routledge, 2020) p. 23.

149 Regulation (EU) No 648/2012 of the European Parliament and of the Council on OTC derivatives, central counterparties and trade repositories (OJ 2012, L 201/1). See HM Treasury, Equivalence decisions for the EEA States (policy paper, 9 November 2020), <www.gov.uk/government/publications/hm-treasury-equivalence-decisions-for-the-eea-states-9-november-2020/hm-treasury-equivalence-decisions-for-the-eea-states-9-november-2020> (accessed 29 January 2022).

bilateral (with the exception of partly including Liechtenstein) relationship. Given the important economic exchange between the two countries, there are of course substantial economic reasons for securing an uninterrupted relationship. Albeit a bit speculative, however, it can also be said that both countries' partially difficult political relations with the EU may have benefitted a swift conclusion of these agreements.

These reasons may also lead to a more strategic approach to counter the EU's aim to shape the global market.[150] As an example, the financial services policy of Switzerland and the UK – which is not yet supported by a respective agreement – in their mutual relation aims at a more ambitious agenda. In that vein, the UK and Switzerland are indeed negotiating a Financial Services Agreement.[151] The solution in the area of the Direct Insurance Agreement[152] in particular seems to be a (hidden) signal to also grant mutual market access in the area of financial services, based on mutual recognition in the intergovernmental relationship rather than harmonisation in a common market. All this is, however, only the early days of a new development altogether.[153]

With regard to another "thorny" issue in both countries, namely free movement of persons, a similarly forward-looking approach can be observed. It seems that in their bilateral relationship, there is more openness to allow free movement of persons. In any case, Switzerland and the UK signed an MoU on free movement.[154] This MoU, firstly, supplements the Citizens' Rights Agreement[155] between the two countries which essentially regulates the rights acquired prior to the UK leaving the EU. Secondly, it prepares for "more formal arrangements"[156] with regard to, inter alia, "labour migration, mobility of persons including to support cultural exchange, joint action regarding developing

150 A. Bradford, *The Brussels Effect – How the European Union Rules the World* (OUP, 2020).

151 B. Triebe, 'Pragmatisch statt dogmatisch: wenn die EU von der Schweiz lernen darf', *Neue Zürcher Zeitung* 2 July 2020; see also above 3.3.

152 See above 4.1.3.

153 G. Baur, 'Square Pegs and Round Holes (Continued): Financial Market Surveillance Authorities and Internal Market Association', *Cambridge Yearbook of European Legal Studies* 22 (2020), p. 57.

154 Memorandum of understanding between The Home Office of the United Kingdom of Great Britain and Northern Ireland and The Federal Department of Justice and Police of the Swiss Confederation concerning mobility and strengthening migration cooperation, <www.gov.uk/government/publications/uk-and-switzerland-mou-mobility-and-strengthening-migration-cooperation/memorandum-of-understanding-between-the-home-office-of-the-united-kingdom-of-great-britain-and-northern-ireland-and-the-federal-department-of-justice> (accessed 13 January 2022).

155 See n. 95.

156 MoU (Mobility and Migration), para. 5(2).

issues relating to migration and asylum, close cooperation and mutual support through facilitation of secondments of staff between the Participants and partnership working and exchanging information in the above fields".[157]

The CH-UK TA also shows that even with the simplest possible structures, a minimum of institutions and overarching regulations are necessary. The extent to which a few changes to the incorporated agreements compared to the respective original from the bilateral relationship between Switzerland and the EU, as well as the reference to an application *mutatis mutandis*, suffice as a guideline for the interpretation of the trade agreement and probably also the other Switzerland-UK agreements, remains to be seen.

It now seems to be clear though, that Switzerland and the UK rather see the current CH-UK TA as a provisional arrangement. On 28 April 2022, the two countries signed a joint statement by which they declared to drive forward the development of their bilateral trading relationship and pursue "a modernised and enhanced trade agreement."[158]

However, the question also arises as to whether such an intergovernmental "alternative model" based on mutual recognition can only function between States that are economically similarly developed and politically similarly oriented, with a largely identical set of values with regard to trade policy interests. In Europe, this might bring us back to the system competition of the early sixties of the twentieth century between EFTA and the EU.[159] In any case it seems that the future relations between the UK and Switzerland have been planned by the past.

---

157 *Ibid.*, para. 3(2).

158 Joint Statement on enhancing bilateral relations between the United Kingdom of Great Britain and Northern Ireland and the Swiss Confederation, <https://www.newsd.admin.ch/newsd/message/attachments/71288.pdf> (accessed 3 Mai 2022), para. 3.

159 G. Baur, 'EFTA: A Free Trade Area with Internal Market Elements', in A. Epiney, L. Hehemann (eds.), *Schweizerisches Jahrbuch für Europarecht 2016/2017* (Stämpfli/Schulthess, 2017), p. 359.

Index